KU-768-237

THE BLUE GUIDES

Albania
Austria
Belgium and Luxembourg
China
Cyprus
Czechoslovakia
Denmark
Egypt

FRANCE
France
Paris and Versailles
Brittany
Burgundy
Loire Valley
Midi-Pyrénées
Normandy
South West France
Corsica

GERMANY
Berlin and Eastern Germany
Western Germany

GREECE
Greece
Athens and environs
Crete

HOLLAND
Holland
Amsterdam

Hungary
Ireland

ITALY
Northern Italy
Southern Italy
Florence
Rome and environs
Venice
Tuscany
Umbria
Sicily

Jerusalem
Malta and Gozo
Mexico
Morocco
Moscow and Leningrad
Portugal

SPAIN
Spain
Barcelona

Sweden
Switzerland

TURKEY
Turkey
Istanbul

UK
England
Scotland
Wales
London
Museums and Galleries
  of London
Oxford and Cambridge
Country Houses of England
Gardens of England
Literary Britain and Ireland
Victorian Architecture in
  Britain
Churches and Chapels
  of Northern England
Churches and Chapels
  of Southern England
Channel Islands

USA
New York
Boston and Cambridge

Piazza Navona with the Fontana dei Quattro Fiumi by Gian Lorenzo Bernini

BLUE GUIDE

Rome
and environs

Alta Macadam

Atlas, maps and plans by John Flower

13

1999: Frescoes discovered
in Quattro Coronati.

A & C Black
London

WW Norton
New York

Fifth edition 1994

Published by A & C Black (Publishers) Limited
35 Bedford Row, London WC1R 4JH

A CIP catalogue record of this book
is available from the British Library.

ISBN 0-7136-3939-3

Published in the United States of America by
WW Norton and Company, Inc
500 Fifth Avenue, New York, NY 10110

Published simultaneously in Canada by
Penguin Books Canada Limited
10 Alcorn Avenue, Toronto, Ontario M4V 3B2

ISBN 0-393-31259-3 USA

The author and the publishers have done their best to ensure the accuracy of all the
information in Blue Guide Rome; however, they can accept no responsibility for any
loss, injury or inconvenience sustained by any traveller as a result of information or
advice contained in the guide.

For permission to reproduce the illustrations in this guide the publishers would like to
thank **Vittorio Guida**.

Alta Macadam has been a writer of Blue Guides since 1970. She lives in Florence with
her family (the painter Francesco Colacicchi, and their son Giovanni). Combined with
work on writing the guides she has also been associated in Florence with the Bargello
Museum and the Alinari photo archive. She is now involved in work for Harvard
University at the Villa I Tatti in Florence. As author of the Blue Guides to Northern
Italy, Rome, Venice, Sicily, Florence, Tuscany, and Umbria she travels extensively in
Italy every year to revise new editions of the books.

The publishers invite readers to write in with their comments, suggestions and
corrections for the next edition of the Blue Guide. Writers of the best letters will
be awarded a free Blue Guide of their choice.

Printed and bound in Great Britain by
Butler & Tanner, Frome and London

PREFACE

The section of the guide devoted to the environs has been greatly expanded for this edition, to include the whole of northern Lazio, adding the provinces of Rieti and Viterbo to that of Rome. This beautiful and fascinating part of Italy includes the important Etruscan sites of southern Etruria (Tarquinia and Vulci), the medieval towns of Viterbo and Tuscania (as well as Tarquinia), the Villa Lante at Bagnaia, with one of the most beautiful and famous gardens in Italy, and Palazzo Farnese at Caprarola, a splendid Mannerist palace, also known for its exquisite garden. These new routes also cover some lovely unspoilt countryside in the province of Rieti and in 'Alto Lazio'.

Particular attention has been given in this edition to the practical information section, with revised lists of hotels and restaurants, and new sections on parks and gardens and on visiting Rome with children.

Travelling is an art, and mass tourism continues to threaten the enjoyment of the individual visitor to Rome, as it does to other great cities of the world: if you are not in a group it is often difficult to hold your own against a swarm of sight-seers and their guide. If you can avoid the most crowded seasons in Rome (Easter, May to September, and Christmas) your visit will be all the more enjoyable. Masterpieces in the Vatican which are not in rooms 'on the way' to the Sistine Chapel (which at the busiest times can be seen by up to 20,000 people a day) remain ignored by the vast majority of people entering that museum, and are usually deserted, anyway before 11 o'clock. It has been my intention in this guide to indicate how best to visit the world famous sites of Rome, as well as to direct you to the lesser known areas of the city where tour groups are unknown.

A number of changes have taken place in Rome since the last edition of this guide. The appearance of the city has been brightened by the cleaning of numerous church and palace façades, which had been blackened over the years by the polluted air of the city. Excellent results have been obtained at Sant'Andrea della Valle, the Gesù, and Palazzo Spada. The Fontana di Trevi has been cleaned for the first time and is once again a splendid spectacle, and the fountains in Piazza Navona, Piazza Farnese, Piazza di Spagna, and Piazza della Rotonda have also been cleaned. However, there has been justified criticism of some of these operations (including the over-bright façades of the Maddalena and San Carlo al Corso) and of the introduction of pastel shades in the intonaco of some palace façades (eliminating the traditional deep russet colour which has always characterized the appearance of the city).

The Museo Barracco, one of the most delightful small museums in the city, has been reopened and beautifully re-arranged. Numerous statues in the Musei Capitolini have been cleaned. The remarkable church of Santo Stefano Rotondo has at last been reopened. Restoration work proceeds in a number of churches, including Santa Maria in Trastevere (where a painting of the Madonna dating from the eighth century has been returned), Santa Maria della Pace, Sant'Ignazio, Santa Maria del Popolo, and Santa Maria in Aracoeli. The famous frescoes by Filippino Lippi in Santa Maria sopra Minerva have been carefully restored. A definitive decision, thanks to the determination of the Minister of 'Beni Culturali', Alberto Ronchey, was at last taken in 1994 to move the offices and club rooms of the armed forces out of Palazzo Barberini so that the space can be used by the Museo Nazionale d'Arte Antica, and the paintings there re-hung.

While this work has been quietly in progress all over the city, much publicity has been given to the restoration of Michelangelo's frescoes in the Sistine chapel in the Vatican. The project, which took some 14 years, was completed in 1994 when the huge Last Judgment on the altar wall was uncovered. Some discussion has arisen about the techniques of restoration, but most people feel that the results here have also been entirely successful.

However, there are still many museums and monuments closed to the public and it is hard to understand why there is not more determination on the part of the State and Comune of Rome to ensure that the great treasures of the city are made regularly accessible. The Museo Nazionale Romano, one of the great museums in the world, has been all but closed since 1976. It is scheduled to reopen in late 1994 in its new seat (acquired by the State some ten years ago) in the ex Collegio Massimo in Piazza dei Cinquecento. Meanwhile, the Collezione Ludovisi has been arranged in the beautifully restored Palazzo Altemps. The upper floor of the Galleria Borghese is still closed, but since 1993 a selection of the paintings has been on exhibition in Trastevere at the ex Istituto San Michele a Ripa. Other museums and monuments still closed after more than a decade include: the Domus Aurea, the Museo Nuovo and Braccio Nuovo in the Musei Capitolini, the Antiquarium Comunale, the house of Cardinal Bessarion, the Museo Torlonia, the Galleria Comunale d'Arte Moderna, Santa Maria Antiqua in the Forum, the Mausoleum of Augustus, and the basilica di Porta Maggiore.

Large sections of both the Museo di Palazzo Venezia and Villa Giulia are inaccessible, and the Museo Nazionale d'Arte Orientale has not been open since 1991. Only four rooms are open of the Antiquarium in the Forum, and the Palatine Antiquarium and the Museo di Roma have been closed since 1988. The Tomb of the Scipios and the Museo Napoleonico are also closed. Only twelve rooms are at present open out of the seventy-three contained in the Galleria Nazionale d'Arte Moderna.

The equestrian statue of Marcus Aurelius is still 'temporarily' exhibited in the Museo Capitolino, and its pedestal remains empty in the centre of Piazza del Campidoglio (although a bronze replica may be installed here). In 1993 two car bombs (which it seems likely were placed by the Mafia) exploded in the city and seriously damaged the ancient church of San Giorgio in Velabro and San Giovanni in Laterano and its baptistery.

Although there was great enthusiasm among the Romans when they had the chance for the first time in 1993 to elect directly the mayor of the city, it is generally recognized that he has inherited enormous administrative problems. The metropolitan area of the city is about ten times greater than it was in the 1950s, and most of the residents now live in the spawling suburbs which have spread into the Roman campagna in an uncontrolled way. The historic centre suffers from depopulation, and many of the buildings here are now used as offices. The drastic solution to move offices and ministries out of the centre to an area of some 600 hectares to the E of the city (the 'SDO'), which would involve the compulsory purchase of the land here, has met with little success.

In 1994 the new mayor, Francesco Rutelli, decided to close Via dei Fori Imperiali to traffic on Sundays which might be the first step in the long-term project to eliminate this road and open an archaeological park here. This would not only ease the serious traffic problems of the city but help solve the problem of the preservation of the city's ancient monuments from pollution. The protected park around the Via Appia remains a pipe-dream.

Another enlightened decision in 1993 taken by the Minister of 'Beni Culturali' enabled museums and monuments throughout Italy to institute longer opening hours and eliminate the standard Monday closing day. This has taken longer than was at first hoped to be put into operation, but it may take effect in the next year or so.

I am particularly indebted to **Maura Medri** for her help during my work on the revision of the guide. She read some of the descriptions of the monuments of ancient Rome and brought them up-to-date in the light of recent excavations and scholarly research. The excellent photographs were taken specially for the guide by **Vittorio Guida** and I am extemely grateful to him for the trouble and care he took over them. **Tim Potter** very kindly agreed to write an introductory article on ancient Rome.

I would also like to thank Dottoressa Maria Giulia Barberini who offered every possible assistance. As in the past, Francesco Casertano of the Rome EPT helped me to check the practical information section. During my travels in the environs I received particularly generous help from the EPT of Rieti (special thanks to Loris Scopigno and Carla Garutti), and the Azienda Autonoma di Tarquinia (Vincenzo Cesarini and Signora Bruna Pieri).

A Note on Blue Guides

The Blue Guide series began in 1915 when Muirhead Guide-Books Limited published 'Blue Guide London and its Environs'. Findlay and James Muirhead already had extensive experience of guidebook publishing: before the First World War they had been the editors of the English editions of the German Baedekers, and by 1915 they had acquired the copyright of most of the famous 'Red' Handbooks from John Murray.

An agreement made with the French publishing house Hachette et Cie in 1917 led to the translation of Muirhead's London guide, which became the first 'Guide Bleu'—Hachette had previously published the blue-covered 'Guides Joannes'. Subsequently, Hachette's 'Guide Bleu Paris et ses Environs' was adapted and published in London by Muirhead. The collaboration between the two publishing houses continued until 1933.

In 1933 Ernest Benn Limited took over the Blue Guides, appointing Russell Muirhead, Findlay Muirhead's son, editor in 1934. The Muirhead's connection with the Blue Guides ended in 1963 when Stuart Rossiter, who had been working on the Guides since 1954, became house editor, revising and compiling several of the books himself.

The Blue Guides are now published by A & C Black, who acquired Ernest Benn in 1984, so continuing the tradition of guidebook publishing which began in 1826 with 'Black's Economical Tourist of Scotland'. The Blue Guide series continues to grow: there are now 50 titles in print with revised editions appearing regularly and many new Blue Guides in preparation.

'Blue Guides' is a registered trade mark.

CONTENTS

MAPS AND PLANS

EXPLANATIONS

References in the text (Pl. 1; 1) are to the 15-page Atlas at the back of the book, the first figure referring to the page, the second to the square. Ground plan references are given in the text as a bracketed single figure or letter.

Hotels listed on p 36 have been keyed on the Atlas at the back of the book by letters.

Restaurants in the environs of Rome have been divided into three categories: 'Luxury-class' (above Lire 60,000 a head); 'First-class' (around Lire 40,000 a head); and 'Simple Trattorie and Pizzerie' (around Lire 25,000 a head).

Asterisks indicate points of special interest or excellence.

Distances in the environs of Rome are given cumulatively from the starting-point of the route or sub-route in kilometres.

Abbreviations. In addition to generally accepted and self-explanatory abbreviations, the following occur in the guide:

'EPT'	Ente Provinciale per il Turismo (the provincial tourist board)
'ATAC'	Azienda Tramvie e Autobus del Comune di Roma
'COTRAL'	Consorzio Trasporti Pubblici Lazio
fest.	festa, or festival (i.e. holiday)
Pl.	plan reference to the atlas at the back of the book
km	kilometre(s)
Adm	admission
C	century
m	metre(s)
Rte	route
FS	ferrovie dello Stato (Italian State Railways)

For Glossary, see p 478

ANCIENT ROME: AN INTRODUCTION

T.W. Potter

Few cities make quite so indelible an impression as Rome. Although in part brought about by the warm golden-brown hue of the soft volcanic *tufo* stone, and the cheerful, bustling *vivante* atmosphere, it is above all the sense of history that is so pervasive. Every street brings a fresh and exciting vista, sometimes graced by a classical building from the days of the Roman Empire, then an elegant Renaissance *palazzo* or a glorious church, next the imposing façade of a structure erected in the wake of Italy's reunification in 1870, when Rome once again became capital. History is writ large upon the streets and piazzas of Rome, and it is impossible for the visitor, however casual, not to engage with it.

Our archaeological and historical appreciation of Rome's ancient and medieval landscape has in fact advanced enormously over the past decade or so. In response to enlightened proposals put forward by the Archaeological Superintendent for Rome, Professor Adriano La Regina, in March 1981, Parliament voted to release substantial funds for the investigation and, above all, conservation of the city's monuments. As inspection following an earth tremor in 1979 had showed, pollution from car emissions and central heating fumes was having a devastating effect upon the marble and stone that face the monuments of the Eternal City. Visitors were to become all too familiar in the 1980s with the green gauze that draped many of Rome's most famous landmarks. But behind those screens were scholars and conservators, seizing the chance to study and preserve the past, in tandem with teams of archaeologists, Italian and foreign, who were opening new windows into earlier layers all over the city. Plans to close down and remove Mussolini's Via dei Fori Imperiali, which cuts across Rome's ancient centre, may not have come to pass, reflecting the modern dilemma between the conservation of the past and the needs of the present; but enormous strides have been made in our understanding of the evolution of one of the world's greatest cities.

Assimilating and interpreting all this new information is one of the challenges of the 1990s. Coupled with it is the fresh scrutiny of documents and artifacts from discoveries by earlier generations of investigators, like the indefatigable Italian engineer and archaeologist Giacomo Boni ('excavation' in museum store-rooms, as it has become known). This is shedding much light on matters long considered settled. To know that the reliefs on Trajan's Column were almost certainly executed at the behest of his successor, Hadrian, is not a matter of dotting i's and crossing t's, but a fundamental advance in knowledge. It shows how Hadrian, by honouring his adoptive father's military achievements, sought to render more secure his own precarious political position: for the emperor Trajan, while bestowing upon Hadrian favours and high political office, had nevertheless not nominated him publicly as his successor. Countless rulers of Rome, whether consul, emperor, Pope or President, have used architecture as symbolic statements of their power and prestige, a point that will not be lost upon those who gaze upon their monuments.

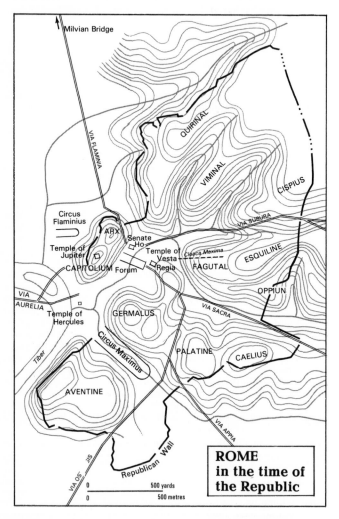

ROME
in the time of
the Republic

Rome was to grow up at the one easy crossing point along the lower reaches of the River Tiber. It is afforded by the Tiber Island, and excavations at nearby S. Omobono show evidence of settlement from as early as about 1500 BC. By the early first millennium BC, villages of oval wooden houses were emerging on the Palatine and Capitoline hills, both natural strongholds, the contours of whose once steep cliffs have been softened over the passage of time. There were also cemeteries on the spurs of the Quirinal, Viminal and Esquiline, which stretch like the fingers of a hand towards the Tiber, as well as on the low-lying ground beneath the Capitol, where later the Roman Forum was to develop. The distinction between the settlements of the living, and the burial grounds of the dead, maintained throughout the ancient history of the city for all but the greatest, was thus established at a very early date.

Traditionally, of course, Rome was founded by Romulus and Remus, perhaps in 753 BC (although the ancients disagreed about the exact date). They are described as descendants of Aeneas who, as a fugitive from the Trojan Wars, settled at Lavinium, near the mouth of the Tiber; Roman historians thus provided their compatriots with a respectable ancestry, firmly locked into Greek mythology. It was one of the marvels of the early 1980s to see emerging from the bottom of the great trench at the foot of the Palatine Hill, a high wall 1.40 m. in width, with a ditch in front. Datable to about 730–720 BC, on good archaeological evidence, it was rather convincingly proclaimed as the wall of Romulus, built to mark the *pomerium*, the sacred zone that surrounded the city. Archaeology and legend for once seem to cohere.

Six kings are supposed to have followed Romulus, and it is clear that some, including the last, Tarquinius Superbus, were Etruscans, from the region to the north of Rome. To Servius Tullius (578–535 BC) is attributed the building of a great wall around the city (as yet unconfirmed by archaeology), and it was the Etruscans who drained the site of the Forum. The first paving stones were laid around 625 BC over a huge deposit of made-up ground (not a village, as was once supposed), and it rapidly developed into the religious, political and commercial centre of what was beginning to be a proper city-state. Nearby was the Regia, the sanctuary of the *Rex Sacrorum*, who was responsible for the official sacrifices of the State; it was constructed on the site of the Temple of Vesta, where the sacred flame of the community had been housed. Of the Agora in Athens, Sir Mortimer Wheeler could write that 'here, in a real sense, is the initial focus of the European mind'; of the Forum Romanum in Rome we might observe that here lie the ground and monuments where the Romans inspired the creation of the first world state. It *does* require imagination to hear Caesar or Cicero speaking from the rostrum; but, by shutting out the noise of modern Rome, we know that it really did happen there.

But we are getting ahead of ourselves. It was therefore in the late 7C and 6C BC that Rome took on characteristics, such as public buildings, squares and fortifications, amongst others, that permit us to describe it as urbanised. To what extent Etruscan rulers were ultimately responsible is a matter of scholarly contention; but there is no doubt that, whilst already a cosmopolitan place, the language and culture were predominantly Latin. Thus in 510 BC the Romans, themselves Latini, expelled their Etruscan tyrant, Tarquinius Superbus and, despite the famous (but perhaps apocryphal) seige of Lars Porsenna of Etruscan Clusium (modern Chiusi, in Tuscany), abolished the monarchy (509 BC). As a Republic, authority now became vested in the hands of two magistrates (later consuls), who were elected annually and chosen only from the aristocratic patrician class. As time went on, however, this exclusive concentration of power caused ever increasing resentment amongst the impoverished *plebs*. An intense class war ensued, which was to linger on for some 250 years. The Twelve Tables (451–50 BC) were an early attempt to introduce some legislative order, and were followed by a succession of new laws. Ultimately the sovereignty of the People was recognised, at least in theory; thus, while a patricio-plebeian élite effectively continued to hold the strings of power, via the magistrates and Senate, democracy ostensibly prevailed. It was a typically Roman, pragmatic solution.

It was also during this period that, through wars and alliances, Rome gradually extended domination over Italy. By 275 BC control had been established all over the peninsula, leaving the way open for intervention overseas. Sicily (241BC), Sardinia (238), Spain (206) and North Africa (146) all were to become provinces, and during the 2C BC and 1C BC, large parts of the East Mediterranean also came under the Roman yoke. From being a parochial, somewhat rustic town in the 6C BC, Rome was now the wealthy mistress of a great Empire.

The effect upon the city was to be profound. New fortifications had been built in the early 4C (still to be seen outside the Stazione Termini), following the sack of Rome in 390 BC by an army of Gauls. Enclosing about 400 ha., they excluded the flattish ground of the Campus Martius, now Vecchia Roma in the bend of the Tiber, where the Roman youth received military training, and popular assemblies met. But the vast area within the walls is eloquent testimony to a fast-expanding population, as well as of a new sense of urban identity and purpose. Development was needed of the riverside dockyards and nearby cattle market (Forum Boarium), to feed the populace and promote commerce; and to Appius Claudius Caecus is due the credit for piping in water by building the city's first aqueduct in 312 BC It must have seemed a miraculous achievement in a chaotic, crowded, and, by Greek standards, still somewhat provincial Italo-Etruscan town.

It was contact through conquest, especially of the Greek world, that was to change this image. Huge profits were realised, not least through the sale of slaves, and Rome became an immediate beneficiary. Victorious generals were accorded triumphal processions into the city and, in return, often paid for the building of a temple, vowed in the midst of battle. This glorified both the city and their own name, and it was Greek deities that were frequently thus honoured. Likewise, Greek statues were brought back to grace the public places of the city, and paintings in the Greek style were commissioned to represent a military success. To the Roman, the Greek world, and its cities, appeared sophisticated and culturally illustrious. From the 2C BC in particular there was a conscious move to Hellenise the city of Rome, not least through literature, architecture and the arts. Whilst moralist Romans like Cato (234–149 BC) denounced such developments, which seemed alien to the noble traditions of the strong farmer-soldier, most accepted them with fervour. The elegant Graeco-Roman temples of Portunus (a god of commerce) and Hercules Victor, both built in the later 2C BC in the Forum Boarium, are still-standing reminders of this.

Rome's population, ultimately to reach a million or more in the first century AD, was by now very substantial. The aristocracy lived in favoured areas like the Palatine, where their mansions were designed with *atria;* here their supporters (*clientes*) might be received. The plebeians inhabited high, multi-storey squalid tenements, ever vulnerable to fire, and often cheek by jowl with great public monuments. Feeding and entertaining these poor classes became an important facet of public life. When the general Gaius Flaminius Nepos built a circus in the Campus Martius in 221 BC, he was to establish the area as a place of popular entertainment. Here Pompey provided the first stone theatre to be built in Rome, in 55 BC, and Caesar planned, and Augustus had constructed, the theatre of Marcellus, Augustus' nephew. Dedicated in 13 BC, it still remains a very imposing and impressive monument.

The great generals of the first century BC, particularly Sulla, Pompey and Gaius Julius Caesar, all sought to increase their prestige by embellishing Rome. Caesar's schemes were the most grandiose. Of lasting significance was his forum, near the old Forum Romanum, and by the Curia (which he rebuilt), where the senate met. The forum was dominated by a high temple of his divine ancestress Venus Genetrix, and the whole complex must have appeared a fitting symbol of the power and pre-eminence of the Julian family. Caesar's murder, in 44 BC, brought his own high personal ambitions to an end; but his adoptive son and heir, Octavian, once he had seized the reins of power by defeating Antony and Cleopatra at Actium in 31 BC, was more than capable of resuscitating them. Bestowed with the title Augustus ('reverend') in 27 BC, he was to rule a largely peaceful empire for a further forty-one years. Rome was particularly to benefit. His famous boast that he 'found a city made of brick and left it made of marble' was far from idle. The white marble quarries at Carrara, in north-western Italy, were greatly developed at this time, and huge quantities were shipped down to Rome. The building programme was on an enormous scale. Immediately initiated was the Augustan forum. It lay close to Caesar's forum, and was crowned, (as it still is), by a temple of Mars Ultor, the Avenger of Caesar's murderers. Filled with statues of Roman heroes, not least those of the Julian clan, it became the monumental focus of Augustan Rome, where proper respect was paid to the city's ancestors, and the great were received. Old buildings of historical and religious significance were restored, amongst them the House of Romulus, close to which, so as to emphasise his illustriousness, Augustus built his own residence; deliberately modest, it was the beginning of a process that was to transform the Palatine into an area of exclusive Imperial palaces.

Augustus was much aided by his devoted ally, the hugely wealthy Marcus Vipsanius Agrippa. Builder of Rome's first major public baths, two aqueducts, and the Pantheon (which still bears his name, although it is a Hadrianic reconstruction), he, like Augustus, was concerned to turn Rome into a well-run and elegant city that was a worthy capital of a great empire. The Ara Pacis, altar of Peace, with its marvellous reliefs depicting legends concerning the foundation of Rome, and of Augustus and his family, symbolised the new stability. A food dole was provided for the needy, and Augustus' own mausoleum in the Campus Martius was a massive architectural statement of the legitimacy and authority of the empire's *princeps*, first citizen.

Many of the ancient standing buildings that one sees in Rome today are of course creations of the post-Augustan age. They are particularly characterised by the use of concrete faced with brick, an invention which seems to have taken place in Campania in the third century BC. It was however not until the days of Augustus' successor, Tiberius (AD 14–37), that the first large-scale building project using concrete was initiated in Rome: the construction of the Castra Praetoria, where the solders of the Praetorian Guard were housed. Set in the north-east part of the city, between the Via Nomentana and the Via Tibertina, it was laid out like a legionary fortress. Troops had never before been based in Rome, for they potentially posed dangers for the unwary ruler. Indeed, when Claudius was proclaimed emperor in AD 41, it was the Praetorian Guard that did so.

Claudius, in AD 43 conqueror of Britain (an event which was commemorated with a triumphal arch), was to provide Rome with two new aqueducts to serve emerging residential areas on the Quirinal, Pincian and Aventine.

He also built an all-weather harbour at Ostia, to facilitate importation of the vast supplies that the city needed: here was responsible civic management. Nero (AD 54–68), by contrast, invested many of his energies into creating a vast palace and pleasure gardens, known as the Domus Aurea, Golden House, between the end of Forum Romanum and the Esquiline. The dark underground rooms that one can sometimes visit today hardly convey the once sumptuous splendour of this extraordinary place, which covered some 50 ha.; but it was architecturally a visionary, if megalomaniac, project. It was later blotted out by the Colosseum (dedicated in AD 80; it may have taken its name from a colossal statue of Nero, set up nearby); the Baths of Titus (AD 79–81); and, in the early second century, by the Baths of Trajan. The heart of the city was once more in the public domain.

Nero did rebuild many streets after the devastating fire of AD 64, including the Sacra Via which was provided with a great colonnade, like cities in the East. They were wider and straighter and, in combination with stringent new fire regulations, must have lent an altogether more organised impression to the city. The Flavian dynasty (AD 69–96), which under Vespasian seized power after a catastrophic civil war, were further to enhance that image. Thus Vespasian was to build a new forum, with as its centrepiece the Temple of Peace, echoing the message of Augustus' Altar of Peace. Although now largely buried, this once elegant architectural creation lay not far from the huge Flavian Colosseum, an amphitheatre where 50,000 people might relish the lavish, if often gruesome, entertainments provided mainly from the Emperor's pocket.

The last Flavian ruler, Domitian (AD 81–96), also built facilities for entertainment; not least was a stadium for athletic competitions, the shape of which is now fossilised by the Piazza Navona. He also started to lay out a new forum, which was completed by his successor, Nerva. However, his most striking achievement was the construction of a vast palace on the Palatine, overlooking the Circus Maximus. Known as the Domus Augustana, it was to become the residence for rulers over the next three hundred years, a symbolic reminder with its innovative architecture, and lavish decoration, of the achievements and power of the Flavian family.

But times were changing. When Trajan became emperor in AD 98, he was to become the first provincial to take the throne. A Spaniard by birth, he nevertheless left his stamp on Rome in a remarkable way. His enormous forum stretched north-eastwards from the Forum of Augustus, and included the Basilica Ulpia, 170 m. in length. His famous column, one of the mightiest monuments in Rome, lay just beyond the basilica, and was flanked by two libraries, one for Latin works, the other for Greek. Also still to be seen are his magnificent purpose-built market halls and shops, constructed beside his forum rather like a modern shopping centre; they underline how the fora had now become places of pomp and ceremony rather than humble commerce. Likewise, he attended to civic needs by building vast public baths, over Nero's Golden House. As much or more places for social concourse as for cleanliness, they further enhanced Rome's image as a truly great city.

Trajan paid for these works largely with booty won in two wars from the Dacians, in the lower Danube region. But he by no means emptied the state coffers, and his successor Hadrian (AD 117–138), also of Spanish origin, had plenty of funds to realise his own projects. Amongst them were the rebuilding of the Pantheon, justly described as one of the masterpieces of Roman architecture; and his mausoleum, now Castel Sant' Angelo, which still dominates part of the skyline of Rome. But it was near Tivoli that he created his main residence, a huge villa whose buildings embodied the architectural ideals of the Greek and Eastern worlds that he so admired. Hadrian was above all a devoted philhellene, who ruled a united and largely harmonious empire. When Aelius Aristides delivered an encomium to Rome in AD 144, only six years after Hadrian's death, he could liken the empire to a single household, enjoying a perpetual holiday.

Yet the pre-eminence of the city of Rome was already beginning to wane. No more were there to be wars of conquest, bringing in fresh funds, and power was gradually slipping away to provinces like those of North Africa, which became ever more wealthy, especially through commerce. Septimius Severus, who ascended the throne in AD 193, was to be the first African emperor. His huge triumphal arch, dedicated in AD 203, is one of the more imposing monuments in the Forum Romanum today, and he also built a great, three-tiered facade to a new wing of the imperial palace. Called the Septizodium, it held statues of seven planetary deities with, at the centre, the Sun, symbolically facing Africa; it was, alas, demolished in 1588.

It was Severus' son, Caracalla, who built the enormous baths that still bear his name; covering some twenty hectares, they remain one of the most impressive sights of ancient Rome. But with the demise of the last Severan, Alexander, in AD 235, much of the empire was to be plunged into nearly fifty years of anarchy, warfare and chaos. It is to this period that the Aurelianic wall circuit belongs. Begun in the early 270s, it extends for 19 km., and was so massively built that it remains as impressive today as in antiquity. Now Rome had become a stronghold in the new world of late antiquity and, when Diocletian (AD 284–305) restored order, the city lost its position as sole capital of the empire. Although he built his great baths (parts of which were converted in the church of S. Maria degli Angeli by Michelangelo), he did not visit Rome until AD 303, and so disliked what he saw that he almost immediately departed. When Constantine founded his New Rome of Constantinople, modern Istanbul, dedicated in AD 330, a page of history was turned: after nearly a thousand years of pre-eminence Rome was no longer mistress of the world.

Constantine did of course endow Rome with many monuments, not least the churches of St. Peter and St. John Lateran, and his triumphal arch by the Colosseum; but we are here looking forward to the shaping of the medieval city, and away from its ancient past. Dark days were to lie ahead, especially in the fifth and sixth centuries as the population dwindled away; but so too was a distinguished and brilliant future as, under Charlemagne and the Popes, a renaissance gradually took place from the early 9C. Rome and the Romans have always shown a remarkable capacity for innovation, and survival, over an immense period of time. There is no other city with so sustained a record of achievements, surely a remarkable tribute to the founding fathers, and their innumerable distinguished successors.

The Walls of Rome

Rome has been a walled city since its formal foundation by Romulus in, according to one tradition, 753 BC. He is said to have laid out this wall around the foot of the Palatine Hill, where the main settlement was, and traces of a tufo-block foundation of this period has indeed now been identified in excavations near the House of the Vestal Virgins. Little by little the inhabitants of Roma obtained the mastery of the neighbouring hills and formed the city of the *Septimontium* by the union of the three summits of

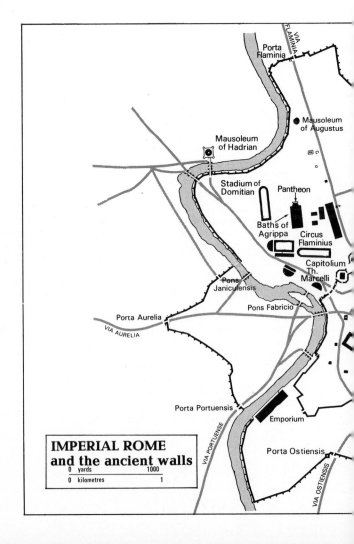

IMPERIAL ROME
and the ancient walls

the Palatine (Palatium, Germalus, and Velia) with the four of the Esquiline (Oppius, Cispius, Fagutalis, and Subura).

After further acquisitions there arose the **City of the Four Regions**. The regions were the Palatine, the Subura (incl. the Celian), the Esquiline, and the Collina (incl. the Quirinal). This area was eventually surrounded by a formidable line of fortifications c 11km long, known as the **Servian Wall**. Its traditional creator was Servius Tullius, sixth king of Rome; it is now thought that the wall dates from about 378 BC, although sections of an earlier earthen bank (*agger*) have been identified, which may be the work

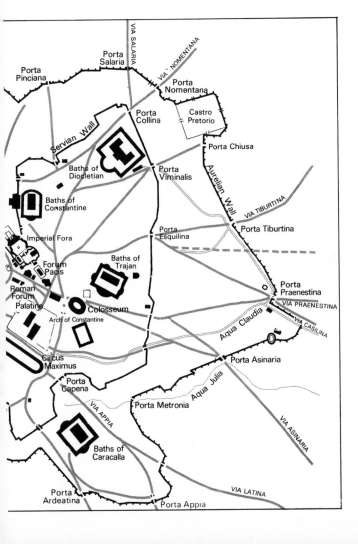

of Servius. There were 12 gates, the sites of some of which are conjectural. The wall ran S from the Porta Collina (N of the Baths of Diocletian) past the Porta Viminale and the Porta Esquilina (W of the Stazione Termini) to the Porta Celimontana, near the present Porta San Giovanni. At this point the wall curved to the W round the base of the Celian to the Porta Capena, below the Palatine, the starting-point of the Appian Way. From there it took an irregular course round the Aventine (several gates) to the Tiber, which it bordered as far as the Pons Aemilius (Ponte Rotto). It then ran N and NE past the W side of the Capitol, and the W and N sides of the Quirinal to the Porta Salutare. From here, after a slight detour, it bore E to the Porta Collina.

After 87 BC, during a period of civil strife between Marius and Sulla, a part of Trastévere was fortified. A new wall ran from the Pons Aemilius to the Porta Aurelia (Porta San Pancrazio), on the Janiculum, and another back to the Tiber, opposite the Aventine.

To Aurelian (emperor 270–75) and Probus (emperor, 276–82) is due the building of the **Aurelian Wall**, most of which survives to this day. Although Aurelian had defeated the invading Alemanni in two decisive battles, he erected his wall immediately afterwards. The enceinte took in all the seven hills, the Campus Martius, and the previously fortified area of Trastévere. It was about 19km round and had 18 main gates and 381 towers. From the Porta Flaminia (now Porta del Popolo) it ran irregularly along the Pincio to the Porta Salaria. From there it turned SE, took in the Castro Pretorio and continued SE to the Porta Tiburtina (Porta San Lorenzo) and the Porta Prenestina (Porta Maggiore). Here describing an acute angle, it bent back past the Porta Asinaria (Porta San Giovanni; near the Porta *Caelimontana*; see above) to the Porta Metronia. It next ran S past the Porta Latina to the Porta Appia (Porta San Sebastiano), thus enclosing part of the Appian Way within the city boundaries. From this point the wall turned W to the Tiber. It now followed the left bank of the river. By the Pons Sublicius (the present Ponte Aventino) it crossed the river. Passing the Porta Portuense (Porta Portese) it ran NW to the Porta Aurelia (see above). Returning NE to the Porta Settimiana, it recrossed the Tiber, and followed the left bank of that river, skirting the Campus Martius, until it turned E to reach the Porta Flaminia. Aurelian made a bridgehead of the Castel Sant'Angelo in his fortifications.

The walls were raised to almost twice their height by Maxentius (306–12), and then restored by Honorius and Arcadius in 403 AD. They continued to be the defence of Rome until 1870 when the army of the Kingdom of Italy breached them with modern artillery, NW of the Porta Pia.

The walls are mostly well preserved and many of the gates are still in use under their modern names. Although the city has spread far beyond Aurelian's wall, most of its famous monuments are within its confines. One important exception is the basilica of San Paolo fuori le Mura; others are San Lorenzo and Sant'Agnese fuori le Mura.

Further Reading

T. Ashby, *The aqueducts of ancient Rome* (Oxford 1935). M.T. Boatwright, *Hadrian and the City of Rome* (Princetown 1987). J. Carcopino, *Daily life in ancient Rome* (Harmondsworth, 1973 reprint). A. Claridge, *Hadrian's Column of Trajan*. Journal of Roman Archaeology volume 6 (1993), 5–22. F.

Coarelli, *Il foro romano* (2 vols, Roma 1983,1985). M. Cristofani (ed.), *La grande Roma dei Tarquinii* (Rome 1990). F. Lepper and S.S. Frere, *Trajan's Column* (Gloucester 1988). R. Krautheimer, *Rome. Profile of a city 312–1308* (Princeton 1980). R. Meiggs, *Roman Ostia* (2nd ed., Oxford 1973). T.W. Potter, *Roman Italy* (2nd ed., London 1992). M. Pallottino, *The Etruscans* (London 1975). L. Richardson, Jnr., *A new topographic dictionary of ancient Rome* (Baltimore and London 1992). J.E. Stambaugh, *The ancient Roman city* (Baltimore and London 1988). M. Todd, *The walls of Rome* (London 1978). J.B. Ward-Perkins, *Roman imperial architecture* (Harmondsworth 1981). P. Zanker, *The power of images in the age of Augustus* (Ann Arbor 1988).

LIST OF ROMAN EMPERORS

27 BC–AD 14 Augustus
14–37 Tiberius
37–41 Caligula
41–54 Claudius
54–68 Nero
68–69 Galba
69 Otho
69 Vitellius

Flavians
69–79 Vespasian
79–81 Titus
81–96 Domitian
96–98 Nerva
98–117 Trajan

Antonines
117–38 Hadrian
138–61 Antoninus Pius
161–80 Marcus Aurelius
161–69 Lucius Verus
180–92 Commodus
193 Pertinax
193 Didius Julianus

Severians
193–211 Septimius Severus
211–17 Caracalla
211–12 Geta
217–18 Macrinus
218–22 Heliogabalus
222–35 Alexander Severus

235–38 Maximinus
238 Gordian I
　　　Gordian II
238 Pupienus
　　　Balbinus
238–44 Gordian III
244–49 Philip I
247–49 Philip II
249–51 Decius
251–53 Trebonianus Gallus
253 Aemilian
253–60 Valerian

253–68 Gallienus
268–70 Claudius II
270 Quintillus
270–75 Aurelian
275–76 Tacitus
276 Florian
276–82 Probus
282–83 Carus
282–85 Carinus
283–84 Numerian
285–305 Diocletian
286–305 Maximian
305–06 Constantius Chlorus
305–10 Galerius
308–24 Licinius
306–07 Flavius Severus
306–12 Maxentius
308–14 Maximinus
306–37 Constantine the Great
337–40 Constantine II
337–50 Constans
337–61 Constantinus II
350–53 Magnentius
361–63 Julian
363–64 Jovian
364–75 Valentinian I
364–78 Valens
367–83 Gratian
375–92 Valentinian II
378–95 Theodosius I

WESTERN EMPIRE
395–423 Honorius
425–55 Valentinian III
455 Petronius Maximus
455–56 Avitus
457–61 Majorian
461–65 Libius Severus
467–72 Anthemius
472 Olybrius
473 Glycerius
474–75 Julius Nepos
475–76 Romulus Augustulus

CHRONOLOGICAL LIST OF POPES

Various points in early papal history are still uncertain: the evidence for Dioscuros as legitimate pope is perhaps stronger than the evidence for Boniface II (No. 55); Leo VIII (No. 132) is an antipope if the deposition of John XII (No. 131) was illegal, and if Leo VIII was a legitimate pope, Benedict V (No. 133) is an antipope; and if the triple deposition of Benedict IX (No. 146) was illegal, Sylvester III, Gregory VI, and Clement II (Nos. 147, 149, 150) must rank as antipopes. Among the popes named John there was never a John XX. The title 'pope' was first assumed by John VIII (d. 882); the triple tiara first appears on the sepulchral effigy of Benedict XII (d. 1342). Adrian IV (d. 1159) was the only English pope, Gregory XI (d. 1378) the last French pope and Adrian VI (d. 1523) the last non-Italian pope, before John Paul II. Anacletus II (d. 1138) was a converted Jew. 'Pope Joan' is placed between John V (d. 686) and Conon.

The names of antipopes and of illegal occupants of the papal chair and particulars as to papal tombs imperfectly identified or no longer in existence are enclosed in square brackets[]. Conjectural dates are followed by a query (?). The title of each pope is given, together with the date of his consecration (for the early popes) or of his election (from Gelasius II onward; No. 162), the date of his death, the duration of his pontificate, and, as far as possible, his birthplace, family name, and place of interment. Martyred popes are indicated by the letter M. Most of the early tombs in the old basilica of St Peter were scattered or lost on the demolition of the church by Julius II; but some of the remains of the popes were collected in two ossuaries in the Grotte Vaticane.

St Peter's remains are preserved beneath the altar of the Confession in St Peter's and the thirteen following popes are believed to be interred close by. Churches mentioned below are in Rome, unless otherwise indicated.

		Began to reign
1.	ST PETER; M.; 42–67	42
2.	ST LINUS of Tuscia (Volterra?); M.; 67–78	67
3.	ST ANACLETUS I, of Rome; M.; 78–90 (?)	78
4.	ST CLEMENT I, of the Roman Flavian gens; M.; 90–99 (?). D. at Cherson (Crimea), relics in San Clemente	90
5.	ST EVARISTUS, of Greece (or of Bethlehem); M.; 99–105 (?)	99
6.	ST ALEXANDER I, of Rome; M.; 105–115 (?)	105
7.	ST SIXTUS I, of Rome, M.; 115–125 (?)	115
8.	ST TELESPHORUS, of Greece; M.; 125–136 (?)	125
9.	ST IGINUS, of Greece; M.; 136–140 (?)	136
10.	ST PIUS I, of Italy; M.; 140–155 (?)	140
11.	ST ANICETUS, of Syria; M.; 155–166 (?)	155
12.	ST SOTER, of Campania (Fundi?); M.; 166–175 (?)	166
13.	ST ELEUTHERUS, of Epirus (Nicopolis?); M.; 175–189	175
14.	ST VICTOR I, of Africa; M.; 189–199	189
15.	ST ZEPHYRINUS, of Rome; M.; 199–217. Int. near the Cimitero di San Callisto	199
16.	ST CALIXTUS I, of Rome; M.; 217–222. Int. in the Cimitero di Calepodio, on the Via Aurelia Vetus; relics in Santa Maria in Trastévere	217
[HIPPOLYTUS, 217–235]		
17.	ST URBAN I, of Rome; M.; 222–230. Int. in the Cimitero di San Callisto; relics in Santa Cecilia in Trastévere	222
18.	ST PONTIANUS, of Rome; M.; 21 July 230–28 Sept. 235. Int. in the Cimitero di San Callisto; relics in Santa Prassede	230
19.	ST ANTERUS, of Greece; M.; 21 Nov. 235–3 Jan. 236. Int. in the Cimitero di San Callisto; relics in San Silvestro in Capite	235
20.	ST FABIAN, of Rome; M.; 10 Jan. 236–20 Jan. 250. Int. in the Cimitero di San Callisto; relics in Santa Prassede (?)	236
21.	ST CORNELIUS, of Rome; M.; March 251–June 253. Int. near the Cimitero di San Callisto; relics in Santa Maria in Trastévere	251
[NOVATIAN, 251–258]		

86.	JOHN VII, of Greece; 1 March 705–18 Oct. 707. [Tomb in St Peter's]	705
87.	SISINNIUS, of Syria; 15 Jan. 708–4 Feb. 708	708
88.	CONSTANTINE, of Syria; 25 March 708–9 April 715. [Tomb in St Peter's]	708
89.	ST GREGORY II, of Rome 19 May 715–11 Feb. 731. [Tomb in St Peter's]	715
90.	ST GREGORY III, of Syria; 18 March 731–10 Dec. 741. [Tomb in St Peter's]	731
91.	ST ZACHARIAS, of Greece; 10 Dec. 741–22 March 752. [Tomb in St Peter's]	741
92.	STEPHEN II, of Rome; 23 March 752–25 March 752. Burial place unknown	752
93.	ST STEPHEN III, of Rome; 26 March 752–26 April 757. [Tomb in St Peter's]	752
94.	ST PAUL I, of Rome; 29 May 757–28 June 767. [Tomb in St Peter's]	757
	[CONSTANTINE II, 5 July 767–murdered 769]	
	[PHILIP, elected 31 July 768–abdicated 768]	
95.	STEPHEN IV, of Sicily; 7 Aug. 768–3 Feb. 772. [Tomb in St Peter's]	768
96.	HADRIAN I, of Rome; 9 Feb. 772–26 Dec. 795 [Tomb in St Peter's]; epitaph, dictated by Charlemagne, under the portico of St Peter's	772
97.	ST LEO III, of Rome; 27 Dec. 795–12 June 816. Tomb and relics in St Peter's (Cappella della Colonna)	795
98.	ST STEPHEN V, of Rome; 22 June 816–14 Jan. 817. [Tomb in St Peter's]	816
99.	ST PASCHAL I, of Rome; 25 Jan. 817–11 Feb. 824. [Tomb in St Peter's]	817
100.	EUGENIUS II, of Rome; 21 Feb. 824–27 Aug. 827.	824
101.	VALENTINE, of Rome; Aug. (?) 827–Sept. (?) 827. Burial place unknown.	827
102	GREGORY IV, of Rome; Oct. 827–25 Jan. 844. [Tomb in St Peter's]	827
103.	SERGIUS II, of Rome; Jan. 844–27 Jan. 847. [Tomb in St Peter's]	844
	[JOHN, 844]	
104.	ST LEO IV, of Rome; 10 April 847–17 July 855. Tomb and relics in St Peter's (Cappella della Colonna)	847
105.	ST BENEDICT III, of Rome; 6 Oct. 855–17 April 858. [Tomb in St Peter's]	855
	[ANASTASIUS, 29 Sept. 855–20 Oct. 855]	855
106.	ST NICHOLAS I, the Great, of Rome; 24 April 858–13 Nov. 867. [Tomb in St Peter's]; epitaph in the Grotte Vaticane	858
107.	HADRIAN II, of Rome; 14 Dec. 867–14 Dec. 872. [Tomb in St Peter's]; epitaph in the Grotte Vaticane	867
108.	JOHN VIII, of Rome, 14 Dec. 872–16 Dec. 882. [Tomb in St Peter's]	872
109.	MARINUS I (MARTIN II) of Gallesium; 16 Dec. 882–15 May 884. [Tomb in St Peter's]	882
110.	ST HADRIAN III, of Rome; 17 May 884–17 Sept. 885. Tomb at Nonantola	884
111.	STEPHEN VI, of Rome; Sept. 885–Sept. 891. [Tomb in St Peter's]	885
112.	FORMOSUS, bishop of Porto; 6 Oct. 891–4 April 896. Thrown into the Tiber	891
113.	BONIFACE VI, of Gallesium; April 896	896
114.	STEPHEN VII, of Rome; May 896–Aug. 897. Strangled in prison	896
115.	ROMANUS, of Gallesium; Aug. 897–end of Nov. 897	897
116.	THEODORE II, of Rome; Dec. 897–Dec. 897	897
117.	JOHN IX, of Tivoli; Jan. 898–Jan. 900. [Tomb in St Peter's]	898
118.	BENEDICT IV, of Rome; Jan. 900–end July 903. [Tomb in St Peter's]	900
119.	LEO V, of Ardea; end of July 903–Sept. 903. Deposed and imprisoned. [Int. in St John Lateran]	903
	[CHRISTOPHER, of Rome; 903, deposed in Jan. 904]	
120.	SERGIUS III, of Rome; 29 Jan. 904–14 April 911. [Tomb in St Peter's]	904
121.	ANASTASIUS III, of Rome; April 911–June 913. [Tomb in St Peter's]	911
122.	LANDO, of Sabina; end of July 913–Feb. 914	913
123.	JOHN X, of Ravenna; March 914–May 928. Strangled in prison. [Int. in St John Lateran]	914
124.	LEO VI, of Rome; May 928–Dec. 928. [Tomb in St Peter's]	928
125.	STEPHEN VIII, of Rome; Jan. 929–Feb. 931	929

126.	JOHN XI, of Rome; Son of Pope Sergius III and Marozia; March 931–Dec. 935. Died in prison	931
127.	LEO VII; 3 (?) Jan. 936–13 (?) July 939	936
128.	STEPHEN IX, of Germany (?); 14 (?) July 939–end of Oct. 942	939
129.	MARINUS II (MARTIN III), of Rome; 30 (?) Oct. 942–May 946	942
130.	AGAPITUS II, of Rome; 10 May 946–Dec. 955. [Int. in St John Lateran]	946
131.	JOHN XII, Ottaviano, of the family of the Counts of Tusculum, aged 19 yr; 16 (?) Dec. 955–deposed 14th May 964. [Int. in St John Lateran]	955
132.	LEO VIII, of Rome, 4 Nov. 963–1 March 965	963
133.	BENEDICT V, Grammatico, of Rome; 22 (?) May 964–expelled from the pontifical see 23 June 964; died at Bremen 4 July 966. Int. first in Bremen, afterwards in Rome (church unknown)	964
134.	JOHN XIII, of Rome; 1 Oct. 965–5 Sept. 972. [Int. in St Paolo fuori le Mura]	965
135.	BENEDICT VI, of Rome; 19 Jan. 973–June 974. Strangled in prison	973
[BONIFACE VII, Francone, of Rome; June–July 974 for the first time]		
136.	BENEDICT VII, of the family of the Counts of Tusculum, of Rome; Oct. 974–10 July 983. Tomb in Santa Croce in Gerusalemme	974
137.	JOHN XIV, of Pavia; Dec. 983–20 Aug. 984; killed by Francone (Boniface VII). [Int. in St John Lateran]	983
[BONIFACE VII, Francone, for the second time, Aug. 984–murdered July 985]		
138.	JOHN XV, of Rome; Aug. 985–March 996	985
139.	GREGORY V, Bruno, of the family of the Counts of Carinthia; 3 May 996–18 Feb. 999. Tomb (an ancient Christian sarcophagus) now in the Grotte Vaticane	996
[JOHN XVI, John Philagathus, of Greece; March 997–Feb. 998]		
140.	SYLVESTER II, Gerbert of Aurillc, Auvergne; 2 April 999–12 May 1003. [Tomb in St John Lateran]; epitaph in the S. aisle	999
141.	JOHN XVII, Sicco, of Rome; June (?) 1003–6 Nov. 1003. [Tomb in St John Lateran]	1003
142.	JOHN XVIII, of Rapagnano; Jan. (?) 1004–July (?) 1009. [Tomb in San Paolo fuori le Mura]; epitaph in the convent	1004
143.	SERGIUS IV, of Rome; 31 July 1009–12 May 1012. [Tomb in St John Lateran]; epitaph in the S. aisle	1009
144.	BENEDICT VIII, John, of the family of the Counts of Tusculum, of Rome; 18 May 1012–9 April 1024	1012
[Gregory, 1012]		
145.	JOHN XIX, of Rome, brother of Benedict VIII; April 1024–1032	1024
146.	BENEDICT IX, Theophylact, of the family of the Counts of Tusculum; elected (at 15 yr of age) for the 1st time in 1032–deposed in Dec. 1044; elected for the 2nd time 10 March 1045–deposed 1 May 1045; elected for the 3rd time 8 Nov. 1047–deposed 17 July 1048. Tomb in the monastery of St Nilus at Grottaferrata	1032
147.	SYLVESTER III, John, bishop of Sabina; 20 Jan. 1045–deposed 10 March 1045	1045
148.	GREGORY VI, Gratian, of Rome; 5 May 1045–banished 20 Dec. 1046; died 1047	1045
149.	CLEMENT II, Suidger, bishop of Bamberg; 25 Dec. 1046–died at Pesaro 9 Oct. 1047. Tomb in Bamberg Cathedral	1046
150.	DAMASUS II, Poppo, bishop of Bressanone, of Bavaria; 17 July 1048–9 Aug. 1048. Died at Palestrina. [Tomb in St John Lateran]	1048
151.	ST LEO IX, Bruno, of Germany, bishop of Toul; 12 Feb. 1049–19 April 1054. Int. in St Peter's and transferred to the new basilica	1049
152.	VICTOR II, Gebhard, of Germany, bishop of Eichstätt; 16 April 1055–28 July 1057. Died at Arezzo; tomb at Florence	1055
153.	STEPHEN X, Frédéric, of the family of the Dukes of Lorraine; 3 Aug. 1057–29 March 1058. Died and int. in Florence [in the church of Santa Reparata, afterwards in the crypt of Santa Maria del Fiore]	1055

[Benedict X, of Rome; 5 April 1058–deposed 24 Jan. 1059. Tomb in Santa Maria Maggiore]

154. NICHOLAS II, Gérard de Bourgogne; 24 Jan. 1059–27 (?) July 1061   1059

155. ALEXANDER II, Anselmo of Milan; 30 Sept. 1061–21 April 1073. [Tomb in St John Lateran]   1061

[Honorius II, appointed by Imperial Diet of Basle 1061–1072]

156. ST GREGORY VII, Hildebrand, di Bonizio Aldobrandeschi, of Sovana; 22 April 1073–25 May 1085. Tomb in Salerno Cathedral   1073

[Clement III, Ghiberto; 25 Jan. 1080–Sept. 1100]

157. B. VICTOR III, Desiderio Epifani, of Benevento; elected 24 May 1086, consecrated 9 May 1087–16 Sept. 1087. Tomb at Monte Cassino   1086

158. B. URBAN II, of Reims; 12 March 1088–29 July 1099. [Tomb at St Peter's]   1088

159. PASCHAL II, Rainiero, of Breda; 14 Aug. 1099–21 Jan. 1118. [Tomb in St John Lateran]   1099

[THEODORIC, Sept.–Dec. 1100; epigraph in the cemetery of La Cava]

[ALBERT, Feb.–March 1102]

[SYLVESTER IV, 18 Nov. 1105–12 April 1111]

160. GELASIUS II, Giov. Caetani, of Gaeta; 24 Jan. 1118–28 Jan. 1119 [Tomb at Cluny]   1118

[GREGORY VIII, Maurice Bourdain, of Limoges, 8 March 1118–deposed April 1121]

161. CALIXTUS II, Gui de Bourgogne, of Quingey; 2 Feb. 1119–13 Dec. 1124. [Tomb in St John Lateran]   1119

162. HONORIUS II Lamberto Scannabecchi, of Fanano (Modena); 15 Dec. 1124–13 Feb. 1130. Died [and buried] in the monastery Sant'Andrea   1124

163. INNOCENT II, Gregorio Papareschi, of Trastevere; 14 Feb. 1130–24 Sept. 1143. Int. in St John Lateran; transferred in 1617 to Santa Maria in Trastévere (monument of 1849) where the original epitaph is under the portico   1130

[ANACLETUS II, Pierleone, a converted Jew; 14 Feb. 1130–25 Jan. 1138]

[VICTOR IV, Gregorio da Monticelli, elected 15 March 1138, abdicated 29 May 1138]

164. CELESTINE II, Guido, of Città di Castello; 26 Sept. 1143–8 March 1144. [Tomb in St John Lateran]   1143

165. LUCIUS II, Gerardo Caccianemici dell'Orso, of Bologna; 12 March 1144–15 Feb. 1145. [Tomb in St John Lateran]   1144

166. B. EUGENIUS III, Bernardo Paganelli, of Montemagno (Pisa); 15 Feb. 1145–8 July 1153. [Tomb in St John Lateran]   1145

167. ANASTASIUS IV, Corrado, of the Suburra, Rome; 12 July 1153–3 Dec. 1154. Int. in St John Lateran, in the porphyry sarcophagus of St Helena (now in the Vatican)   1153

168. HADRIAN IV, Nicholas Breakspeare, of Bedmond (Hertfordshire, England); 4 Dec. 1154–1 Sept. 1159. Died at Anagni; tomb in St Peter's; sarcophagus in the Grotte Vaticane (tablet, 1925)   1154

169. ALEXANDER III, Rolando Bandinelli, of Siena; 7 Sept. 1159–30 Aug. 1181. Died at Civita Castellana; tomb in St John Lateran; epitaph in the S. aisle, on a monument commissioned by Alexander VII   1159

[VICTOR IV (V), Ottaviano; 7 Oct. 1159–20 April 1164]

[PASCHAL III, Guido da Crema; 22 April 1164–20 Sept. 1168]

[CALIXTUS III, John of Strumio, a Hungarian, Sept. 1168, abdicated 29 Aug. 1178]

[INNOCENT III, Lando Frangipane of Sezze, elected 29 Sept. 1179, deposed in Jan. 1180]

170. LUCIUS III, Ubaldo Allucingoli, of Lucca; 1 Sept. 1181–25 Nov. 1185. Died in exile at Verona, int. in the cathedral of Verona (tomb of 1383)   1181

171. URBAN III, Uberto Crivelli, of Milan; 25 Nov. 1185–20 Oct. 1187. Died at Ferrara; int. in the cathedral of Ferrara (sarcophagus of 1305)   1185

172. GREGORY VIII, Alberto di Morra, of Benevento; 21 Oct. 1187–17 Dec. 1187. Int. in the cathedral of Pisa (sarcophagus destroyed in 1595)   1187

173. CLEMENT III, Paolino Scolare, of Rome; 19 Dec. 1187–Mar 1191
[Tomb in St John Lateran]   1187
174. CELESTINE III, Giacinto Bobone Orsini, of Rome; 30 March 1191–8
Jan. 1198. [Tomb in St John Lateran]   1191
175. INNOCENT III, Lotario dei Conti di Segni, of Anagni; 8 Jan. 1198–16
July 1216. Died at Perugia; remains transferred from Perugia Cathedral
to St John Lateran in 1891 (tomb by Giuseppe Luchetti)   1198
176. HONORIUS III, Cencio Savelli, of Rome; elected in Perugia, 18 July
1216–died at Rome, 18 March 1227. Tomb in Santa Maria Maggiore   1216
177. GREGORY IX, Ugolino dei Conti di Segni, of Anagni; elected at the age
of 86; 19 March 1227–22 Aug. 1241. [Tomb in St Peter's]   1227
178. CELESTINE IV, Castiglione, of Milan; 25 Oct. 1241–10 Nov. 1241.
[Tomb in St Peter's]   1241
179. INNOCENT IV, Sinibaldo Fieschi, of Genoa; 25 June 1243–7 Dec. 1254.
Died and int. at Naples (monument in San Gennaro, Naples)   1243
180. ALEXANDER IV, Orlando dei Conti di Segni, of Anagni; 12 Dec.
1254–25 May 1261. Died at Viterbo [and int. in Viterbo Cathedral]   1254
181. URBAN IV, Hyacinthe Pantaléon, of Troyes; elected at Viterbo 29 Aug.
1261; died at Perugia 2 Oct. 1264. Tomb in the cathedral of Perugia 1261
182. CLEMENT IV, Gui Foulques Le Gros, of St-Gilles; elected at Viterbo 5 Feb.
1265–died at Viterbo 29 Nov. 1268. Int. at Viterbo in Santa Maria in Gradi,
afterwards in San Francesco (mon. by Pietro Oderisio)   1265
183. GREGORY X, Teobaldo Visconti of Piacenza; elected at Viterbo 1 Sept.
1271–died at Arezzo 10 Jan. 1276. Tomb in the cathedral of Arezzo
(monument ascribed to Agost. di Giovanni and Angelo di Ventura)   1271
184. INNOCENT V, Pierre de Champagny, of the Tarentaise; 21 Jan. 1276–22
June 1276. [Tomb in St John Lateran]   1276
185. HADRIAN V, Ottobono de' Fieschi, of Genoa; elected at Rome 11 July
1276–18 Aug. 1276. Tomb at Viterbo in San Francesco (mon. by Arnolfo
di Cambio)   1276
186. JOHN XXI, Pedro Juliao, of Lisbon; elected at Viterbo 8 Sept. 1276–20
May 1277. Tomb in the cathedral of Viterbo (mon. of 1884)   1276
187. NICHOLAS III, Giov. Gaetano Orsini, of Rome; elected at Viterbo 25
Nov. 1277–died at Soriano nel Cimino 22 Aug. 1280. Tomb in St Peter's
(sarcophagus in the Grotte Vaticane)   1277
188. MARTIN IV, Simon de Brion, of Montpincé in Brie; elected at Viterbo
22 Feb. 1281–died at Perugia 28 March 1285. Tomb in Perugia cathedral 1281
189. HONORIUS IV, Iacopo Savelli, of Rome; elected at Perugia 2 April 1285–3
April 1287. [Tomb in St Peter's]; sarcophagus with recumbent statue, in
Santa Maria Aracoeli   1285
190. NICHOLAS IV, Girolamo Masci, of Lisciano di Ascoli; 15 Feb. 1288–4 April
1292. Tomb in Santa Maria Maggiore (mon. designed by Dom. Fontana) 1288
191. ST CELESTINE V, Pietro Angeleri da Morrone; of Isérnia, 5 July
1294–abdicated 13 Dec. 1294. Died in the Castello di Fumone near
Alatri 19 May 1296. Int. at Sulmona, afterwards in Santa Maria
Collemaggio, at Aquila (mon. by Girol. da Vicenza, 1571)   1294
192. BONIFACE VIII, Benedetto Gaetani, of Anagni; 24 Dec. 1294–11 or 12
Oct. 1303. [Tomb in St Peter's]; sarcophagus, with recumbent figure, in
the Grotte Vaticane   1294
193. B. BENEDICT XI, Niccolò Boccasini, of Treviso; 22 Oct. 1303–died at
Perugia 7 July 1304. Mon. in San Domenico, Perugia (mon. by Lorenzo
Maitani or Nic. di Nuzzo)   1303
194. CLEMENT V, Bertrand de Got, of Villandraut, near Bordeaux; elected at
Perugia 5 June 1305, died at Roquemaure 14 April 1314. Int. at Uzeste,
Gascony (tomb of 1359)   1305
195. JOHN XXII, Jacques d'Euse, of Cahors; elected at Avignon 7 Aug.
1316–died at Avignon 4 Dec. 1334. Tomb in the cathedral of Avignon 1316
[NICHOLAS V, Pietro da Corvara, 12 May 1328–30 Aug. 1330]

196. BENEDICT XII, Jacques Fournier, of Saverdun, near Toulouse; 20 Dec. 1334–25 April 1342. Tomb in the cathedral of Avignon (mon. by Jean Lavenier; destroyed)   1334

197. CLEMENT VI, Pierre Roger de Beaufort, of Château Maumont, near Limoges; 7 May 1342–6 Dec. 1352. Tomb at La Chaise-Dieu, Auvergne (mon. destroyed, only the sarcophagus remains)   1342

198. INNOCENT VI, Etienne d'Aubert, of Mont, near Limoges; 18 Dec. 1352–12 Sept. 1362. Tomb in the Chartreuse of Villeneuve-lés-Avignon (mon. partly destroyed)   1352

199. URBAN V, Guillaume de Grimoard, of Grisac, near Mende in Languedoc; 16 Oct. 1362–19 Dec. 1370. Tomb in the Abbey of St Victor, Marseille (mon. partly destroyed; only the recumbent figure now remains)   1362

200. GREGORY XI, Pierre Roger de Beaufort, nephew of Clement VI, of Château Maumont, near Limoges; elected at Avignon 30 Dec. 1370–died at Rome 27 March 1378. Mon. in Santa Francesca Romana   1370

201. URBAN VI, Bart. Prigano, of Naples; 9 April 1378–15 Oct. 1389. Tomb in St Peter's (mon. transferred to the Grotte Vaticane)   1378

202. BONIFACE IX, Pietro Tomacelli, of Naples; 2 Nov. 1389–1 Oct. 1404. [Tomb in St Peter's]   1389

203. INNOCENT VII, Cosimo de' Migliorati, of Sulmona; 17 Oct. 1404–6 Nov. 1406. [Tomb in St Peter's]; sarcophagus in the Grotte Vaticane   1404

204. GREGORY XII, Angelo Correr, of Venice; 30 Nov. 1406–abdicated 4 June 1415–died at Recanati 17 Oct. 1417. Tomb in the cathedral at Recanati   1406

Popes at Avignon:

[CLEMENT VII, Robert of Savoy, of Geneva; elected at Fondi 20 Sept. 1378–16 Sept. 1394]

[BENEDICT XIII, Pedro de Luna, of Aragon; 28 Sept. 1394–23 May 1423]

Antipopes at Avignon:

[CLEMENT VIII, Gil Sanchez Muñoz, of Barcelona; 10 June 1423–16 July 1429]

[BENEDICT XIV, Bernard Garnier; 12 Nov. 1425–1430 (?)]

Popes at Pisa:

[ALEXANDER V, Pietro Filargis, of Candia; 26 June 1409–3 May 1410. Tomb in San Francesco, Bologna; mon. by Sperandio]

[JOHN XXIII, Baldassarre Cossa, of Naples; 17 May 1410, deposed 29 May 1415–died at Florence 23 Dec. 1419. Tomb in the Baptistery, Florence; mon. by Donatello and Michelozzo]

205. MARTIN V, Oddone Colonna, of Genazzano; elected (aged 50) at Constance, 11 Nov. 1417–20 Feb. 1431. Tomb in St John Lateran (by Simone Ghini)   1417

206. EUGENIUS IV, Gabriele Condulmero of Venice; elected (aged 48) 3 March 1431–23 Feb. 1447. Int. in St Peter's; whence the mon. (by Isaia de Pisa) has been transferred to the refectory of the Congregation of San Giorgio in Alga, an ancient convent adjoining San Salvatore in Lauro   1431

[FELIX V, Amadeus, duke of Savoy; 5 Nov. 1439–7 April 1449; died 1451 at the Château de Ripaille on the Lake of Geneva]   1447

207. NICHOLAS V, Tommaso Parentucelli, of Sarzana; elected (aged 49) 6 March 1447–24 March 1455. Tomb tin St Peter's (sarcophagus with recumbent figure and fragments of the monument in the Grotte Vaticane)   1447

208. CALIXTUS III, Alfonso Borgia, of Xativa, in Spain; elected (aged 78) 8 April 1455–6 Aug. 1458. Int. in Sant'Andrea near St Peter's (destroyed). The body was removed to Santa Maria di Monserrato (mon. by F. Moratilla, 1881); cenotaph in the Grotte Vaticane   1455

209. PIUS II, Aeneas Silvius Piccolomini, of Corsignano (Pienza); elected (aged 53) 19 Aug. 1458–15 Aug. 1464. Int. in St Peter's, in 1623 the mon. (by Niccolò della Guardia and Pietro da Todi) was reconstructed in Sant'Andrea della Valle   1458

210. PAUL II, Pietro Barbo, of Venice; elected (aged 48) 30 Aug 1464–26 July 1471. Tomb in St Peter's; the mon. by Mino da Fiesole has been reconstructed in the Grotte Vaticane   1464

211. SIXTUS IV, Fr. della Rovere, of Savona; elected (aged 57) 9 Aug 1471–12 Aug 1484. Int. in St Peter's. The tomb was violated during the sack of Rome, 1527; the bronze sarcophagus by Ant. Pollaiolo now in the Museo Storico Artistico in St Peter's   1471

212. INNOCENT VIII, G. B. Cibo, of Genoa; elected (aged 52) 29 Aug 1484–25 July 1492. Int. in St Peter's; the monument, by Ant. and Pietro del Pollaiolo, is in the present basilica   1484

213. ALEXANDER VI, Roderigo Lenzuoli-Borgia, Valencia, Spain; elected (aged 62) 11 Aug 1492–18 Aug 1503. Int. in St Peter's, afterwards removed to the chapel of San Diego in Santa Maria di Monserrato (mon. by F. Moratilla, 1881)   1492

214. PIUS III, Fr. Todeschini-Piccolomini, of Siena; elected (aged 64) 22 Sept. 1503–18 Oct 1503. Tomb in St Peter's; mon. by Pasquino da Montepulciano, reconstructed in Sant'Andrea della Valle   1503

215. JULIUS II, Giuliano della Rovere, of Savona; elected (aged 60) 31 Oct 1503–21 Feb 1513. Int. in St Peter's, afterwards in the sarcophagus of Sixtus IV (?); his remains were scattered in 1527. Parts of a projected mausoleum by Michelangelo are now in San Pietro in Vincoli   1503

216. LEO X, Giov. de' Medici, of Florence; elected (aged 38) 9 March 1513–1 Dec 1521. Tomb in Santa Maria sopra Minerva   1513

217. ADRIAN VI, Adrian Florisz Dedel, of Utrecht; elected (aged 63) 9 Jan 1522–14 Sept 1523. Tomb in Santa Maria dell'Anima   1522

218. CLEMENT VII. Giulio de' Medici, of Florence; elected (aged 45) 19 Nov 1523–25 Sept 1534. Tomb in Santa Maria sopra Minerva, by Ant. da Sangallo.   1523

219. PAUL III, Aless. Farnese, of Camino (Rome) or of Viterbo (?), elected (aged 66) 13 Oct 1534–10 Nov 1549. Tomb in St Peter's (mon. by Gugl. della Porta)   1534

220. JULIUS III, Giov. Maria Ciocchi del Monte, of Monte San Savino, near Arezzo; elected (aged 63) 7 Feb 1550–23 March 1555. Tomb in the Grotte Vaticane (sarcophagus)   1550

221. MARCELLUS II, Marcello Cervini, of Montefano (Macerata); elected (aged 54) 9 April 1555–30 April 1555. Tomb in the Grotte Vaticane (sarcophagus)   1555

222. PAUL IV, Giov. Pietro Caraffa, of Capriglio, Avellino; elected (aged 79) 23 May 1555–18 Aug 1559. Tomb in Santa Maria sopra Minerva (mon. by Tom. da Cerignola from designs by Pirro Ligorio)   1555

223. PIUS IV, Giov. Angelo de' Medici, of Milan; elected (aged 60) 26 Dec 1559–9 Dec 1565. Int. in Santa Maria degli Angeli   1559

224. ST PIUS V, Ant. Ghislieri, of Bosco Marengo, near Tortona; elected (aged 62) 7 Jan 1566–1 May 1572. Tomb in Santa Maria Maggiore   1566

225. GREGORY XIII, Ugo Boncompagni, of Bologna; elected (aged 70) 13 May 1572–10 April 1585. Tomb in St Peter's by Camillo Rusconi   1572

226. SIXTUS V, Felice Peretti, of Grottammare; elected (aged 64) 24 April 1585–27 Aug 1590. Tomb in Santa Maria Maggiore   1585

227. URBAN VII, G. B. Castagna, of Rome; elected (aged 69) 15 Sept 1590–27 Sept 1590. Tomb in Santa Maria sopra Minerva   1590

228. GREGORY XIV, Niccolò Sfondrati, of Cremona; elected (aged 55) 5 Dec 1590–15 Oct 1591. Tomb in St Peter's (sarcophagus without mon.)   1590

229. INNOCENT IX, Giov. Ant. Facchinetti, of Bologna; elected (aged 72) 29 Oct 1591–30 Dec 1591. Tomb in the Grotte Vaticane (sarcophagus)   1591

230. CLEMENT VIII, Ippolito Aldobrandini, of Fano; elected (aged 56) 30 Jan 1592–3 March 1605. Tomb in Santa Maria Maggiore   1592

231. LEO XI, Aless. de' Medici, of Florence; elected (aged 70) 1 April 1605–27 April 1605. Tomb in St Peter's   1605

232.	PAUL V, Camillo Borghese, of Rome; elected (aged 53) 16 May 1605–28 Jan 1621. Tomb in Santa Maria Maggiore	1605
233.	GREGORY XV, Aless. Ludovisi, of Bologna; elected (aged 67) 9 Feb 1621–8 July 1623. Tomb in Sant'Ignazio (mon. by Pierre Le Gros)	1621
234.	URBAN VIII, Maffeo Barberini, of Florence; elected (aged 55) 6 Aug 1623–29 July 1644. Tomb in St Peter's (mon. by Bernini)	1623
235.	INNOCENT X, G. B. Pamphilj, of Rome; elected (aged 72) 15 Sept 1644–7 Jan 1655. Tomb in Sant'Agnese in Agone (mon. by Maini)	1644
236.	ALEXANDER VII, Fabio Chigi, of Siena; elected (aged 56) 7 April 1655–22 May 1667. Tomb in St Peter's (mon. by Bernini)	1655
237.	CLEMENT IX, Giulio Rospigliosi, of Pistoia; elected (aged 67) 20 June 1667–9 Dec 1669. Tomb in Santa Maria Maggiore, under the pavement (mon. in the nave by Guidi, Fancelli and Ercole Ferrata from designs by Carlo Rainaldi)	1667
238.	CLEMENT X, Emilio Altieri, of Rome; elected (aged 80) 29 April 1670–22 July 1676. Tomb and mon. in St Peter's	1670
239.	INNOCENT XI, Bened. Odescalchi, of Como; elected (aged 65) 21 Sept. 1676–11 Aug 1689. Tomb in St Peter's (by Etienne Monnot from designs by Carlo Maratta)	1676
240.	ALEXANDER VIII, Pietro Ottoboni, of Venice; elected (aged 79) 6 Oct 1689–1 Feb 1691. Tomb in St Peter's (mon. by Arrigo di San Martino from designs by Angelo de Rossi)	1689
241.	INNOCENT XII, Ant. Pignatelli, of Spinazzola (Bari); elected (aged 76) 12 July 1691–27 Sept 1700. Tomb and mon. in St Peter's	1691
242.	CLEMENT XI, Giov. Fr. Albani, of Urbino; elected (aged 51) 23 Nov 1700–19 March 1721. Tomb in St Peter's (beneath the pavement of the choir)	1700
243.	INNOCENT XIII, Michelangelo Conti, of Rome; elected (aged 66) 8 May 1721–7 March 1724. Tomb in the Grotte Vaticane (no monument)	1721
244.	BENEDICT XIII, Vinc. Maria Orsini, of Gravina (Bari); elected (aged 75) 29 May 1724–21 Feb 1730. Tomb in Santa Maria sopra Minerva	1724
245.	CLEMENT XII, Lor. Corsini, of Florence; elected (aged 79) 12 July 1730–6 Feb 1740. Tomb in St John Lateran	1730
246.	BENEDICT XIV, Prospero Lambertini, of Bologna; elected (aged 65) 17 Aug 1740–3 May 1758. Tomb in St Peter's (mon. by Pietro Bracci)	1740
247.	CLEMENT XIII, Carlo Rezzonico, of Venice; elected (aged 65) 6 July 1758–2 Feb 1769. Tomb in St Peter's (mon. by Canova)	1758
248.	CLEMENT XIV, Giov. Vincenzo Ganganelli, of Sant'Arcangelo di Romagna (Forlì); elected (aged 64) 19 May 1769–22 Sept 1774. Tomb in Santi Apostoli	1769
249.	PIUS VI, Angelo Braschi, of Cesena; elected (aged 58) 15 Feb 1775–29 Aug 1799. Died at Valence, France; int. in the Grotte Vaticane; mon. by Ant. Canova in the Confessio, St Peter's; the heart of Pius VI is preserved at Valence	1775
250.	PIUS VII, Giorgio Barnaba Chiaramonti, of Cesena; elected (aged 58) at Venice; 14 March 1800–died at Rome, 20 Aug 1823. Tomb in St Peter's	1800
251.	LEO XII, Annibale della Genga, born at La Genga, near Foligno; elected (aged 63) 28 Sept 1823–10 Feb 1829. Tomb in St Peter's, beneath the pavement of the chapel of St Leo the Great; mon. by Gius. Fabris, in the nave	1823
252.	PIUS VIII, Francesco Saverio Castiglioni, of Cingoli; elected (aged 69) 31 March 1829–30 Nov 1830. Tomb in St Peter's (mon. by Pietro Tenerani)	1829
253.	GREGORY XVI, Bart. Cappellari, of Belluno, elected (aged 66) 2 Feb 1831–1 June 1846. Tomb in St Peter's (mon. by Amici)	1831
254.	PIUS IX, Giov. Maria Mastai Ferretti, of Senigallia; elected (aged 54) 16 June 1846–7 Feb 1878. Tomb in the crypt of San Lorenzo. Fuori le Mura	1846
255.	LEO XIII, Gioacchino Pecci, of Carpineto Romano, elected (aged 68) 20 Feb 1878–20 July 1903. Int. in St John Lateran (mon. by Giulio Tadolini)	1878

256. ST PIUS X, Giuseppe Sarto, of Riese (Treviso); elected (aged 68) 4
      Aug 1903–20 Aug 1914. Tomb in the Cappella della Presentazione
      (St Peter's); mon. in St Peter's by Pietro Astorri and Florestano di Fausto 1903
257. BENEDICT XV, Giacomo della Chiesa, of Genoa; elected (aged 60)
      3 Sept 1914–22 Jan 1922. Tomb in the Grotte Vaticane; sarcophagus
      with recumbent effigy by Giul. Barberi (1924). Mon. in St Peter's by
      Pietro Canonica 1914
258. PIUS XI, Achille Ratti, of Desio (Milan); elected (aged 65) 6 Feb
      1922–10 Feb 1939. Tomb in the Grotte Vaticane; mon. in St Peter's
      by Fr. Nagni 1922
259. PIUS XII, Eugenio Pacelli, of Rome; elected (aged 63) 2 March
      1939–9 Oct 1958. Tomb in the Grotte Vaticane; mon. in St Peter's
      by Fr. Messina 1939
260. JOHN XXIII, Angelo Roncalli, of Sotto il Monte, Bergamo; elected
      (aged 77) 28 Oct 1958–3 June 1963. Tomb in the Grotte Vaticane;
      mon. by Emilio Greco in St Peter's 1958
261. PAUL VI, Giov. Battista Montini, of Brescia; elected (aged 65) 21 June
      1963–6 August 1978. Tomb in the Grotte Vaticane 1963
262. JOHN PAUL I, Albino Luciani, of Forno di Canale, Belluno;
      elected (aged 65) 26 August 1978–29 September 1978.
      Tomb in the Grotte Vaticane 1978
263. JOHN PAUL II, Karol Wojtyla, of Wadowice (Krakow), Poland;
      elected (aged 58) 16 October 1978 1978

PRACTICAL INFORMATION

Getting to Rome

Information Offices. General information is available in London from the Italian State Tourist Office ('ENIT', *Ente Nazionale Italiano per il Turismo*), 1 Princes Street, W1R 8AY (Tel. 071/408 1254), who distribute free an invaluable 'Traveller's Handbook' (revised c every year), an annual list of hotels in Rome, etc. In New York the office is at 630 Fifth Avenue, (Suite 1565), NY 10111 (Tel. 2454822/23/24). Their office in Rome is at 2 Via Marghera. The headquarters of the official tourist office for Rome and its province (*Ente Provinciale per il Turismo di Roma*), known as the 'EPT' is at 11 Via Parigi (Tel. 06/4881851); 'EPT' information offices at 5 Via Parigi (Tel. 06/4883748), the main station (Termini; with hotel booking service), and Fiumicino Airport (temporarily closed). These offices supply (free) a list of hotels in Rome, a map, a brief guide to the city, the 'Carnet di Roma', a monthly publication giving details of concerts, exhibitions, etc., up-to-date opening times, etc.

Among the numerous **tour operators** who sell tickets and book accommodation, and also organise inclusive tours and charter trips to Rome are: Martin Randall Travel (Tel. 0572/821330); Prospect Music and Art (Tel. 081/995 2151); Special Tours (Tel. 071/722 2297); Citalia (Tel. 081/686 0677); Italian Escapades (Tel. 081/748 4999); Thomson (Tel. 071/387 9321).

Air services between London and Rome are operated by British Airways (Tel. 081/897 4000) and Alitalia (Tel. 071/602 7111), with discount fares for those under 25. Details of charter flights can be obtained through travel agents and in newspapers, especially the Sunday newspapers, and, in London, the 'Evening Standard' and in 'Time Out'.

By **train** Rome can be reached by through train from Calais in summer, otherwise via Paris.

A **European Bus Service** operates from London to Italy (information from the National Express Office at Victoria Coach Station).

Passports or **Visitors Cards** are necessary for all British travellers entering Italy. American travellers must carry passports. You are strongly advised to carry some means of identity with you at all times while in Italy.

Money. In Italy the monetary unit is the Italian lira (pl. lire). Notes are issued for 1000, 2000, 5000, 10,000, 50,000, and 100,000 lire. Coins are of 10, 20, 50, 100, 200 and 500 lire. The rate of exchange in 1994 is approximately 2400 lire to the £ sterling (1600 lire to the US dollar). Travellers' cheques and Eurocheques are the safest way of carrying money when travelling, and most credit cards are now generally accepted in shops and restaurants. The commission on cashing travellers' cheques can be quite high.

Arriving in Rome

Airports. Fiumicino (*Leonardo da Vinci*; Tel. 06/65951), 26km SW of Rome, served by a motorway, is the airport for both international and internal air services. Trains (FS) from the Stazione Tiburtina via the stations of Ostiense and Trastevere every 30 minutes to Fiumicino Airport in 30 minutes. The service runs from 5.30 am to midnight. There is not at present a direct train or bus service from Termini Station to the airport.

Ciampino (Tel. 06/794921), 13km SE of Rome, a subsidiary airport (used mainly for internal flights and international charter flights), is reached by underground (line A) from Termini Station to 'Anagnina' station; then from Osteria del Curato, the airport bus ('COTRAL') leaves every hour, at half past the hour.

Railway Stations. Stazione Termini (Pl. 5; 4), Piazza dei Cinquecento, the main station for all services of the State railways and for the underground railway. Tel. 06/4775, or 06/47301 (Lost Property, 06/4730 or 06/6682). **Stazione Roma Tiburtina** is used by some fast trains which do not stop at Stazione Termini, and by the train for Fiumicino Airport. Less central than the main station, it is well served by buses, and is on Line B of the underground ('metropolitana'), four stops from Termini underground station. The stations of **Ostiense** and **Trastevere** are on the line to Fiumicino Airport. Subsidiary stations (of little interest to the tourist) include *Roma Tuscolana, San Pietro,* and *Prenestina.*

Banks are usually open Monday–Friday 8.30–13.30, 14.45–15.45 (or 14.30–15.30); closed Saturday, Sunday and holidays. They close early (about 11.00) on days preceding national holidays. Money can also be changed at exchange offices ('cambio') at Fiumicino Airport and Termini Station (open all day, and sometimes until late at night). Hotels, restaurants, etc. normally give a lower rate of exchange.

Police Registration. Police Registration is required within three days of entering Italy. If you are staying at a hotel the management takes care of this. The permit lasts three months, but can be extended on application.

Driving in Rome

Most of the centre of the city is closed to private cars (without special permits) from 7.00–11.00, 15.00–19.00. Access to hotels is allowed. Many hotels have garages. Car parking is extremely difficult anywhere in the city. It is never advisable to leave luggage, etc. in parked cars. You are strongly advised not to use a car in Rome; public transport has become much more efficient since the partial closure of the centre of the city to cars.

Motoring organisations. Italian Automobile Club ('ACI') head office, 8 Via Marsala; Automobile Club of Rome, 261 Via Cristoforo Colombo. For 'ACI' breakdown service, Tel. 116.

Accommodation

The **hotels** in Rome are all listed with their charges in the annual (free) publication of the 'EPT' of Rome: *Alberghi di Roma e provincia* (available from their offices). It is essential to book well in advance at Easter and in summer; you are usually asked to send a deposit to confirm the booking. Information about hotels in Rome can be obtained in London from the 'ENIT' office, and on arrival at the 'EPT' information office at the railway station (which also has booking facilities), or at the other information offices of the 'EPT'.

Most of the hotels in the centre of the city are near the Termini Station and on Via Veneto; a much more attractive area to stay, also with hotels of all categories, is around Piazza di Spagna. Another lovely area of the city near some of its most important monuments is the district around the Pantheon. There are also a few hotels on the Aventine Hill, which is particularly quiet.

Every hotel has to declare its prices annually (and these are published in the 'EPT' hotel list). The total charge for the room should be exhibited on the back of the door of the hotel room. Breakfast (usually disappointing and costly) is by law an optional extra charge, although a lot of hotels try to include it in the price of the room. When booking a room, always specify if you want breakfast or not. It is usually well worthwhile going round the corner to the nearest bar for breakfast. Hotels are obliged by law (for tax purposes) to issue an official receipt to customers; you should not leave the premises without this document (*ricevuta fiscale*).

There are five official categories of hotels in Italy from the luxury 5-star hotels, to the most simple 1-star hotels. Rome has some 750 hotels and only a small selection has been given below; omission does not imply any derogatory judgement. The hotels have been listed according to category and location. The keys refer to the atlas section at the back of the book. Hotels with restaurants have been indicated.

Hotels in Rome

Near Piazza di Spagna. 5-STAR: 'Hassler-Villa Medici' (s; Pl. 4; 1), 6 Piazza Trinità dei Monti (with restaurant). 4-STAR: 'D'Inghilterra' (ii; Pl. 3; 4), 14 Bocca di Leone (with restaurant); 'De la Ville' (t; Pl. 4; 3), 69 Via Sistina (with restaurant); 'Plaza' (u; Pl. 3; 4), 126 Via del Corso; 'Valadier' (e; Pl. 3; 2), 15 Via della Fontanella (with restaurant).

3-STAR: 'Gregoriana', 18 Via Gregoriana (g; Pl. 4; 3); 'Scalinata di Spagna' (bb; Pl. 4; 3), Piazza Trinità dei Monti; 'Mozart' (cc; Pl. 3; 2), 23 Via dei Greci; 'Internazionale' (nn; Pl. 4; 3), 79 Via Sistina; 'Concordia' (ff; Pl. 4; 3), 14 Via Capo le Case.

2-STAR: 'Homs' (gg; Pl. 4; 3), 71 Via della Vite; 'Ausonia' (hh; Pl. 3; 2), 35 Piazza di Spagna; 'Suisse' (k; Pl. 4; 3), 56 Via Gregoriana; 'City Nova' (p; Pl. 4; 3), 97 Via due Macelli; 'Elite' (r; Pl. 4; 3), 49 Via Francesco Crispi.

Near the Pantheon. 4-STAR: 'Sole al Pantheon' (jj; Pl. 3; 6), 63 Piazza della Rotonda; 'Nazionale' (x; Pl. 3; 4), 131 Piazza Montecitorio (with restaurant).

3-STAR: 'Del Senato' (v; Pl. 3; 6), 73 Piazza della Rotonda; 'Santa Chiara' (y; Pl. 3; 6), 21 Via di Santa Chiara; 'Portoghesi' (z; Pl. 3; 4), 1 Via dei Portoghesi; 'Cesari' (tt; Pl. 3; 4), Via della Pietra; 'Genio' (rr; Pl. 3; 3), Via Zanardelli.

2-STAR: 'Abruzzi' (h; Pl. 3; 6), 69 Piazza della Rotonda.

Near Campo dei Fiori. 3-STAR: 'Tiziano' (qq; Pl. 3; 6), 110 Corso Vittorio Emanuele II (with restaurant). 2-STAR: 'Sole' (m; Pl. 3; 5), 76 Via del Biscione; 'Piccolo' (dd; Pl. 3; 6), 32 Via dei Chiavari.

On the Aventine Hill. 3-STAR: 'Domus Aventina' (m; Pl. 8; 5), 11b Via di Santa Prisca; 'Sant'Anselmo' (dd; Pl. 8; 5), Piazza Sant'Anselmo; 'Villa San Pio' (ee; Pl. 8; 5), 19 Via Sant'Anselmo.

Near Via Veneto. 5-STAR: 'Excelsior' (j; Pl. 4; 1), 125 Via Veneto (with restaurant); 'Bernini-Bristol' (l; Pl. 4; 3), 23 Piazza Barberini (with restaurant).

4-STAR: 'Imperiale' (d; Pl. 4; 3), 24 Via Veneto (with restaurant); 'Regina Baglioni' (n; Pl. 4; 1), 72 Via Veneto (with restaurant); 'Eliseo' (o; Pl. 4; 1), 30 Via di Porta Pinciana; 'Victoria' (q; Pl. 4; 1), 41 Via Campania (with restaurant); 'Ambasciatori Palace' (i; Pl. 4; 1), 70 Via Veneto (with restaurant).

3-STAR: 'La Residenza' (kk; Pl. 4; 1), 22 Via Emilia. 2-STAR: 'Merano' (ll; Pl. 4; 1), 155 Via Veneto.

Near Termini Station. 5-STAR: 'Le Grand Hotel et de Rome' (a; Pl. 4; 4), 3 Via Vittorio Emanuele Orlando (with restaurant). 4-STAR: 'Mediterraneo' (c; Pl. 5; 4), 15 Via Cavour (with restaurant); 'Massimo d'Azeglio' (f; Pl. 5; 6), 18 Via Cavour (with restaurant); 'Quirinale' (b; Pl. 4; 4), 7 Via Nazionale (with restaurant); 'Genova' (aa; Pl. 5; 6), 33 Via Cavour (with restaurant).

3-STAR: 'Villa delle Rose' (pp; Pl. 5; 4), 5 Via Vicenza; 'Patrizia' (uu; Pl. 5; 3), 36 Via Torino; 'Diana' (mm; Pl. 5; 6), 4 Via Principe Amedeo (with restaurant); 'Impero' (yy; Pl. 5; 3), 19 Via Viminale; 'Ariston' (oo; Pl. 5; 6), 16 Via Turati; 'Aberdeen' (ww; Pl. 5; 3), 48 Via Firenze; 'Augustea' (xx; Pl. 5; 3), 251 Via Nazionale.

2-STAR: 'Igea' (vv; Pl. 5; 6), 97 Via Principe Amedeo.

Near the Vatican. 4-STAR: 'Atlante Star' (ab; Pl. 2; 3), 34 Via Vitelleschi (with restaurant). 3-STAR: 'Columbus' (ss; Pl. 1; 6), 37 Via della Conciliazione (with restaurant); 'Delle Conciliazione' (zz; Pl. 1; 4), 164 Borgo Pio; 'Sant'Anna' (ac; Pl. 1; 4), 143 Borgo Pio.

Near the Colosseum. 4-STAR: 'Forum' (ah; Pl. 4; 5), 25 Via Tor dei Conti (with restaurant). 3-STAR: 'Edera' (aj; Pl. 9; 2), 75 Via Poliziano; 'Richmond' (ak; Pl. 4; 7), 36 Largo Corrado Ricci. 2-STAR: 'Lancelot' (ai; Pl. 9; 1), 47 Via Capo d'Africa (with restaurant).

In Trastevere. 2-STAR: 'Cisterna' (ad; Pl. 7; 4), 8 Via della Cisterna.

Near Villa Borghese. 5-STAR: 'Lord Byron' (ae; Pl. 11; 5), 5 Via de Notaris (with restaurant). 2-STAR: 'Paisiello Parioli' (af; Pl. 12; 5), 47 Via Paisiello.

N of the centre. 3-STAR: 'Villa del Parco' (ag; Pl. 12; 6), 110 Via Nomentana. 2-STAR: 'Laura', 110 Viale XXI Aprile.

For **hotels in the environs of Rome**, see Rtes 28–40.

Youth Hostels and Students' Hostels

Associazione Italiana Alberghi per la Gioventù (Italian Youth Hostels Association), national headquarters at 44 Via Cavour (Tel. 06/4741256). The

Rome Youth Hostel (and regional headquarters) is at the 'Ostello del Foro Italico', 61 Viale delle Olimpiadi. Enrolled university students can sometimes find accommodation at the 'Civis' International Students' House, 5 Viale Ministero degli Affari Esteri. Girls' hostels include: 'YWCA', 4 Via Balbo, and 'Protezione della Giovane', 158 Via Urbana. The Salvation Army has a hostel at 39/42 Via degi Apuli. Religious organisations run some hostels for students and visitors (list available from the 'EPT').

Camping

The sites are listed in the annual 'EPT' hotel list, divided into official categories by stars, from the most expensive 4-star sites, to the simplest and cheapest 1-star sites. Their classification and rates charged must be displayed at the camp site office. Full details of the sites in Italy are published annually by the Touring Club Italiano and Federcampeggio in 'Campeggi e Villaggi turistici in Italia'. The *Federazione Italiana del Campeggio* have an information office and booking service at 11 Via Vittorio Emanuele, Calenzano, 50041 Florence (Tel. 055/882391). Among the sites on the outskirts of Rome are: 'Roma Camping', Via Aurelia; 'Capitol', 45 Via Castelfusano, Ostia Antica; 'Flaminio', Via Flaminia Nuova; 'Seven Hills', 1216 Via Cassia, and 'Nomentano', Via della Cesarina (corner of Via Nomentana). In the environs there are sites at Anzio, Nettuno, Bracciano, and Subiaco.

Restaurants

Restaurants (*Ristoranti, Trattorie*) of all kinds and categories abound in Rome. The least pretentious restaurant usually provides the best value. Most restaurants display a menu outside which gives you an idea of the prices. However, many simpler restaurants do not provide a menu, and here, although the choice is usually limited, the standard of the cuisine is often very high. Lunch is normally around 1 o'clock, and is the main meal of the day, while dinner is around 8 or 9 o'clock. Prices on the menu generally do not include a cover charge (*coperto*, shown separately on the menu) which is added to the bill. The service charge is now almost always automatically added at the end of the bill. Tipping is therefore not strictly necessary, but a few thousand lire are appreciated. Restaurants are now obliged by law (for tax purposes) to issue an official receipt to customers; you should not leave the premises without this document (*ricevuta fiscale*).

It has become extremely difficult to recommend restaurants in Rome since they change hands frequently and the standard often deteriorates once they become well known. In the simplest trattorie the food is usually good, and considerably cheaper than in the well-known restaurants. However they are less comfortable, and do not often have tables outside.

The best guide (but only in Italian) to eating in Rome is published by **Gambero Rosso Editore** (latest edition 1993). A selection of a few restaurants grouped according to district and price range (in 1994) is given below.

Luxury-class restaurants (above Lire 60,000 a head). TRASTEVERE. 'Fabrizio a Santa Dorotea', 15 Via di Santa Dorotea; 'Paris', 7 Piazza San Callisto; 'Peccati di Gola', 7 Piazza dei Ponziani; 'Alberto Ciarla', 40 Piazza

San Cosimato; 'Checco er Carrettiere', 13 Via Benedetta; 'Hostaria Cornucopia', 18 Piazza in Piscinula; 'Cul de Sac 2', 21 Vicolo dell'Atleta; 'Al Moro', 13 Vicolo delle Bollette; 'Sabatini', 13 Piazza Santa Maria in Trastevere.

NEAR VIA VENETO AND VIA DEL TRITONE. 'Colline Emiliane', 22 Via degli Avignonesi; 'Papà Baccus', 36 Via Toscana; 'Sans Souci', 20 Via Sicilia.

NEAR THE COLOSSEUM. 'Charly's Sauciere', 270 Via San Giovanni in Laterano.

THE GHETTO AND CAMPO DEI FIORI. 'Alberto al Portico d'Ottavia', 16 Via del Portico d'Ottavia; 'Piperno', 9 Monte de' Cenci; 'Sora Lella', 16 Via di Ponte Quattro Capi, Isola Tiberina; 'Girone VI', 2 Vicolo Sinibaldi, Largo Argentina; 'Camponeschi', 50 Piazza Farnese.

PIAZZA NAVONA AND THE PANTHEON. 'Il Convivio', 44 Via dell'Orso; 'Osteria dell'Antiquario', 26 Piazzetta San Simeone; 'Papà Giovanni', 4 Via dei Sediari; 'La Rosetta', 8 Via della Rosetta; 'El Toulà', 29 Via della Lupa.

NEAR THE VATICAN. 'Les Etoiles', 34 Via Vitelleschi.

PARIOLI. 'Relais La Piscine', 6 Via Mangili; 'Relais Le Jardin', 5 Via Giovanni de Notaris; 'Al Ceppo', 2 Via Panama.

TESTACCIO. 'Consolini all'Arco di San Lazzaro', 28 Via Marmorata; 'Checchino', 30 Via di Monte Testaccio.

PIAZZA DEL POPOLO. 'Dal Bolognese', 1 Piazza del Popolo.

NEAR S. GIOVANNI IN LATERANO. 'Dai Toscani (Mario)', 41 Via Forlì.

First-class restaurants (around Lire 40,000 a head). TRASTEVERE. 'Il Ciak', 21 Vicolo del Cinque; 'Da Lucia', 2 Vicolo del Mattonato.

NEAR THE CORSO. 'Al 34', 34 Via Mario de'Fiori; 'Porto di Ripetta', 250 Via di Ripetta.

PIAZZA NAVONA AND THE PANTHEON. 'Il Bacaro', 27 Via degli Spagnoli; 'Le Tre Streghe', Via Montegiordano; 'L'Eau Vive', 85 Via Monterone.

THE GHETTO AND CAMPO DEI FIORI. 'Settimio al Pellegrino', 117 Via del Pellegrino; 'Al Pompiere', 38 Via Santa Maria dei Calderari; 'Pierluigi', 144 Piazza de Ricci.

NEAR PIAZZA DI SPAGNA. 'Le Rampe', Piazza Mignanelli; 'Golden Crown', 85 Via in Arcione.

NEAR SANTA MARIA MAGGIORE. 'La Cicala e la Formica', 17 Via Leonina; 'Osteria Picchioni', 16 Via del Boschetto.

NEAR S. GIOVANNI IN LATERANO. 'Cannavota', 20 Piazza S. Giovanni in Laterano.

Simple trattorie and pizzerie (around Lire 25,000 a head). TRASTEVERE. 'Augusto', 15 Piazza de' Renzi; 'Da Gildo', 31a Via della Scala; 'Panattoni', 53 Viale Trastevere; 'Da Vittorio', 14 Via di San Cosimato.

THE GHETTO AND CAMPO DEI FIORI. 'Grappolo d'Oro', 138 Via dei Baullari; 'Da Francesco', Via del Corallo; 'Da Sergio', 27 Vicolo delle Grotte; 'La Scaletta', Via dell'Anima; 'Le Montecarlo', 12 Vicolo Savelli; 'Sora Margherita', 30 Piazza delle Cinque Scole.

NEAR PIAZZA NAVONA. 'Cul de sac', 73 Piazza Pasquino.

NEAR PIAZZA DI SPAGNA. 'Edy', 4 Vicolo del Babuino; 'Fiaschetteria Beltrammi', Via della Croce.

NEAR THE COLOSSEUM. 'Alle Carrette', 14 Vicolo delle Carrette; 'Cavour 313', 313 Via Cavour.

TESTACCIO. 'Remo' and 'Augustarello', Piazza Santa Maria Liberatrice.

NEAR SAN GIOVANNI IN LATERANO. 'Da Severino il Pugliese', 52 Viale Manzoni.

NEAR VILLA BORGHESE. 'Sorrento', Largo Benedetto Marcello.

Eating in Rome

Food in Rome, as in the rest of Italy, is generally extremely good, despite the fact many Romans lament the disappearance in the last few decades of many typical Roman trattorie with their traditional food. There are still a great number of good restaurants although there tend to be less and less cheaper ones. Excellent pizzas are still made in numerous pizzerie. Some of the best items of traditional Roman cuisine often served in Roman restaurants are listed below.

FIRST COURSES. Pasta dishes include *fettuccine*, ribbon noodles, often served with a meat sauce, or with butter, or *alla matriciana*, with a salt pork and tomato sauce. Spaghetti *alla carbonara*, has a sauce of bacon, beaten egg, and black pepper. *Penne all'arrabbiata* is short pasta with a rich spicy sauce. Other types of pasta include *rigatoni*, *tonnarelli*, *bucatini*, and *bigoli*, served with numerous different sauces. *Pasta con broccoli* is short pasta with broccoli, pine nuts, and garlic. *Timballo* is a rich pasta dish cooked in the oven, usually with peas and ham and a cheese sauce. *Gnocchi alla Romana* is another typical first course, a pasta made with potato, flour, and eggs. A soup often served in Rome is *stracciatella*, broth with beaten egg and cheese. *Polenta*, yellow maize flour, is usually served with a meat or tomato sauce. A summer hors d'oeuvre is *fichi* or *melone* with *prosciutto*, green figs, or melon, with Parma ham. Instead, in winter, a rich warming dish is *pasta e fagioli* or *pasta e ceci* (short pasta with white beans or with chick peas).

MAIN COURSES. *Abbacchio*, roast suckling lamb is usually served roasted. *Saltimbocca alla Romana* is veal escalope with ham and sage. *Involtini* are thin rolled slices of meat in a sauce, and *stracotto* is beef cooked in a tomato sauce, or in red wine. *Pollo* or *Coniglio alla cacciatora* is chicken or rabbit cooked in a tomato sauce, with herbs and onions and usually also pimentos. Unusual traditional dishes served in numerous restaurants in Rome include *coda alla vaccinara*, oxtail cooked with herbs and wine; *pajata* or *pagliata*, a dish made with the intestines of oxen and sheep (also sometimes used as a sauce for pasta); and *coratella d'abbacchio*, a stew of young lamb's liver, heart, etc. Other dishes of this type are: *cotechino e zampone* (pig's trotter stuffed with pork and sausages); *cervello* (brains); *rognoncini trifolati* (sliced kidneys in a sauce); *animelle* (sweetbreads); and *trippa* (tripe).

FISH is always the most expensive item on the menu, but can be extremely good in restaurants specialising in fish. *Zuppa di pesce* is a rich fish stew, usually made with a wide variety of fish, and *anguilla (con piselli in umido)* is eel (stewed with peas). *Filetti di baccalà fritti* are filets of salt cod fried in batter.

Another expensive delicacy (only served in season) is *porcini*, large wild mushrooms (best grilled), also often used as a sauce for pasta. *Scarmorza al forno* is cheese baked in the oven. Another vegetarian main dish is *melanzane alla parmigiana*, aubergine cooked in the oven with a cheese and tomato sauce. Numerous delicious fresh VEGETABLES are served in season. Artichokes (*carciofi*) are an important part of Roman cuisine, and are cooked in a great variety of ways. They are always young and small (and usually eaten whole). They are called *alla giudìa* when fried, or *alla Romana* when stuffed with breadcrumbs, parsley, anchovies, salt, and pepper. They are also delicious when cooked in water, oil, and parsley. Courgettes (*zucchini*) are sometimes served *ripieni* (stuffed) or fried. *Fritto di fiori di zucca* are fried zucchini flowers (sometimes with anchovies). *Insalata di puntarelle* is a typical rich Roman salad served with garlic and anchovies. Particularly good cooked green vegetables found in Rome and Lazio include *cicoria* and *broccoletti*.

CHEESE specialities include *ricotta*, made from ewe milk; *pecorino*, a stronger cheese made from ewe milk; *mozzarella*, made from buffalo milk, the cheese used in pizzas (also 'affumicato', smoked).

Italians usually prefer fresh fruit for DESSERT and sweets are considered the least important part of the meal. In many simple restaurants and trattorie often only fruit is served at the end of the meal. The fruit available varies according to what is in season: strawberries (*fragole*) are good served with fresh lemon juice or red wine (rather than with cream). In summer, water melon (*popone*) is particularly refreshing. Fruit salad (*macedonia*) is often good. If the menu includes *crostata* (tart) this is usually made with fresh fruit. *Zuppa inglese* is a rich trifle sometimes offered in smarter restaurants. Ice-cream (*gelato*) is also widely available (but it is not usually home-made).

Wines. Lazio used to be famous for its *Vini dei Castelli*, with their clear amber tint, but these wines have deteriorated drastically in quality and it is now very difficult to find a good bottled wine from this region. However, some restaurants still buy their wine in demijohns directly from vineyards in the Alban Hills and it is often a good idea to try this 'vino della casa' before ordering a more expensive bottle. The house wine served in Rome is almost always white. The few wines of Lazio still worth looking out for include the white from Capena, Colli Lanuvini, and Montefiascone; the red 'Cesanese' from Piglio; the strong red wine of Marino; and 'L'Aleatico', a red desert wine from Gradoli near the Lago di Bolsena. It is no longer easy to find a good wine from Frascati or Velletri, but, as in other parts of Italy, the wine bottled by the local 'Cantina Sociale' is usually of an acceptable standard. Bottled wines of good quality (but not cheap) are available in most Roman restaurants: those from the Veneto, Puglia, Sardinia, Sicily, and Tuscany are often the best.

Snacks. There are a number of self-service restaurants in the centre of the city (including 'Il Delfino', 67 Corso Vittorio Emanuele, Largo Argentina), and pizzas and other good hot snacks are served in a *Pizzeria*, *Rosticceria*, and *Tavola Calda*. Some of these have no seating accommodation and sell food to take away or eat on the spot. They often sell sliced *porchetta*, roast suckling pig. Other hot snacks include *supplì* (fried rice balls with mozzarella), *arancini* (fried rice balls with tomato), *calzoni*, a pizza 'roll' usually filled with ham and mozzarella, and *crocchette*, minced meat or potato croquettes.

Picnics. Excellent food for picnics can be bought at *Pizzicherie* and *Alimentari* (grocery shops), and bakeries (*fornai*). Sandwiches ('panini') are made up on request, with ham, cheese, etc., and bakeries usually sell numerous excellent individual pizze, cakes, etc. Some of the most pleasant spots in the city to have a picnic include: the Palatine Hill, the Parco Savelli on the Aventine, the Borghese gardens, the Pincio, the Belvedere di Monte Tarpeo on the Capitol Hill, the Circus Maximus, the park of the Villa Doria Pamphilj, the public gardens off Via del Quirinale, the Parco Oppio, the Villa Celimontana on the Celian Hill, the Janiculum Hill, the Park of the Tomb of the Scipios (between Via di Porta Latina and Via di Porta San Sebastiano), and on the Appian Way (in the Circus Maxentius or beyond the tomb of Cecilia Metella).

Cafés. Cafés (*Bar*) are open all day. Most customers eat the numerous excellent refreshments they serve standing up. You pay the cashier first, and show the receipt to the barman in order to get served. In almost all bars, if you sit at a table you are charged considerably more (at least double) and are given waiter service (you should not pay first).

Well-known cafés in the city, all of which have tables (some outside), include: 'Caffè Greco', 86 Via Condotti (a famous café, see Rte 8); 'Babington' (English tea rooms), Piazza di Spagna; 'Rosati', 4 Piazza del Popolo; 'Tre Scalini', 31 Piazza Navona, noted for its *tartufi* (truffles) and ices; 'Giolitti', 40 Uffici dei Vicario (famous for its ice-creams); 'Camilloni a Sant'Eustachio', Piazza Sant'Eustachio; and 'Doney' and 'Caffè de Paris', 90 and 145 Via Veneto. 'Pascucci', Via di Torre Argentina, is justly famous for its fresh fruit milk-shakes. 'La Casa del Caffè', Via degli Orfani (near the Pantheon), serves particularly good coffee.

Transport

Buses provide a good means of transport in Rome where most of the centre of the city has been closed to private traffic. The service is run by 'ATAC' (Information offices, Piazza dei Cinquecento, outside the station, and 65 Via Volturno; Tel. 06/46954444). Tickets (Lire 1200 in 1994 valid for 90 minutes on any number of lines) are sold at tobacconists, bars, and newspaper kiosks, as well as the 'ATAC' information offices; they have to be stamped at automatic machines on board. It is usually well worth while purchasing a ticket valid for 24 hours on any line (Lire 4000 in 1994; this has to be stamped once on board). A 7-day ticket (Lire 18,000 in 1994) can be purchased at the Information Office, Piazza dei Cinquecento. Because of one-way streets, return journeys do not always follow the same route as the outward journey. A selection of the more important routes is given below. An excellent map can usually be purchased at the Information Office, Piazza dei Cinquecento.

Town Buses

119 An electric mini-bus which serves the centre of the city on a circular route. Piazza Augusto Imperatore—Via della Ripetta—Via Monte Brianzo—Via della Dogana Vecchia—Pantheon—Via del Seminario—Piazza Colonna—Via del Tritone—Via Due Macelli—Piazza di Spagna—Via del Babuino—Piazza del Popolo—Via della Ripetta—Piazza Augusto Imperatore.

53 (weekdays only) Piazza San Silvestro—Largo Tritone—Piazza Barberini—Via Po (for the Galleria Borghese)

56 Largo Argentina—Piazza Venezia—Via del Corso—Largo Tritone—Piazza Barberini—Via Veneto—Via Po (for Galleria Borghese)

60 Piazza Sonnino—Largo Argentina—Piazza Venezia—Via del Corso—Largo del Tritone—Piazza Barberini—Via XX Settembre—Porta Pia—Via Nomentana—Piazza Sempione.

64 Stazione Termini—Via Nazionale—Piazza Venezia—Corso Vittorio Emanuele—San Pietro.

70 Via Giolitti—Santa Maria Maggiore—Via Nazionale—Piazza Venezia—Largo Argentina—Corso Rinascimento—Ponte Cavour—Piazza Cavour—Viale Giulio Cesare—Piazzale Clodio.

71 Via Giolitti—Traforo Umberto I—Piazza San Silvestro.

85 Piazza San Silvestro—Piazza Venezia—Colosseum—San Giovanni in Laterano.

87 Corso Rinascimento—Largo Argentina—Piazza Venezia—Via dei Fori Imperiali—Colosseum—San Giovanni in Laterano.

90 Piazza Venezia—Via del Teatro di Marcello—Terme di Caracalla—Porta Metronia—Piazza Zama.

94 Largo Argentina—Piazza Venezia—The Aventine—Via G.A. Sartorio.

95 Piazzale Ostiense—Lungotevere Aventino—Piazza Bocca della Verità—Via del Teatro di Marcello—Piazza Venezia —Via del Corso—Via del Tritone—Via Vittorio Veneto—Villa Borghese—Piazzale Flaminio.

118 (every 20–40 minutes) San Giovanni in Laterano—Colosseum—Terme di Caracalla—Porta San Sebastiano (return by Via di Porta Latina)—Via Appia Antica—Catacombs of San Calisto—Catacombs of San Sebastiano—Tomb of Cecilia Metella—Via Appia Pignatelli—Largo dei Claudiani (Via Appia Nuova).

218 San Giovanni in Laterano—Piazza Epiro—Piazza Galeria—Via Appia Antica—Fosse Ardeatine.

Trams

13 Porta Maggiore—Piazza Santa Croce—San Giovanni in Laterano—Colosseum—Piazza di Porta Capena—Piazzale Ostiense—Ponte Sublicio—Viale di Trastevere.

19 Porta Maggiore—Piazzale Verano (San Lorenzo)—Viale Regina Elena—Viale Regina Margherita—Viale delle Belle Arti—Via Flaminia—Ponte Matteotti—Viale delle Milizie—Piazza Risorgimento.

30b Piazzale Ostiense—Viale Aventino—Colosseum—Porta San Giovanni—Porta Maggiore—Viale Regina Margherita—Viale delle Belle Arti—Piazza Thorwaldsen.

Night Service

60 Piazza Sonnino—Piazza Venezia—Piazza Barberini—Via Nomentana—Tufello.

75 Largo Argentina—Viale Trastevere—Monteverde.

78 Piazzale Clodio—Piazzale Flaminio—Piazza Cavour—Corso Rinascimento—Piazza Venezia—Stazione Termini.

Underground Railway

Line A, opened in 1980, runs from near the Vatican (Via Ottaviano) via Piazzale Flaminio, Piazza di Spagna, and Piazza Barberini, to Termini Station. From there it continues to San Giovanni in Laterano and traverses the S suburbs of Rome along the Via Appia Nuova and Via Tuscolana to terminate beyond Cincecittà. It runs underground for the whole of its length (14km) except for the bridge across the Tiber. The intermediate stops are: Ottaviano, Lepanto, Flaminio, Spagna, Barberini, Repubblica, Termini, Vittorio, Manzoni, San Giovanni, Re di Roma, Ponte Lungo, Furio Camillo, Colli Albani, Arco di Travertino, Porta Furba, Numidio Quadrato, Lucio Sestio, Guilio Agricola, Subaugusta, Cinecittà, and Anagnina.

Line B (the first part was opened in 1952). It runs SW from Stazione Termini to Porta San Paolo, in Piazzale Ostiense, where it comes to the surface just beyond Ostiense Station, running from there alongside the Rome–Lido railway as far as Magliana, beyond the Basilica of San Paolo fuori le Mura. It then runs underground (NE) to terminate at Tre Fontane (Laurentina). It has recently been extended NE from Termini Station as far as Rebibbia. Intermediate stations at: Rebibbia, Ponte Mammolo, Santa Maria del Soccorso, Pietralata, Monti Tibertini, Quintiliani, Tiburtina, Bologna, Policlinico, Castro Pretorio, Termini, Via Cavour, Colosseo, Circo Massimo, Piramide (Porta San Paolo), Garbatella, San Paolo, Magliana, and EUR. A service also runs from Porta San Paolo to Ostia Antica and Ostia Lido.

Taxis (white or yellow in colour) are provided with taximeters; you should always make sure these are operational before hiring a taxi. It is not advisable to accept rides from non-authorised taxis at the airports or train stations. Licensed taxis are hired from ranks; there are no cruising taxis. For Radio taxis dial 3570, 3875, 4994, or 88177. There is an additional night charge (22.00–7.00); and for each piece of luggage. Modest tipping is expected. Horse cabs are used exclusively by tourists, and you should agree the fare before starting the journey.

Bicycle Hire. Stands in Piazza del Popolo, Via del Pellegrino, etc.

Car Hire. The principle car-hire firms have offices at Fiumicino Airport and at Termini Station as well as in the centre of Rome.

Sight-seeing tours of Rome are run by 'ATAC' (see above). Bus No. 110 departs from Piazza dei Cinquecento daily in summer at 15.30, and in winter at 14.30. The tour lasts c 3hrs. Booking and information at the 'ATAC' information office in Piazza dei Cinquecento.

Coach and train services in the environs. There is no central coach station in Rome; the coaches start from and return to various squares or streets. In some instances there is a booking office; in others, tickets are bought on board. The services are run by 'CO.TRA.L' (Azienda Consortile Trasporti Lazio), 25 Via Portonaccio (Tel. 06/5915551). For further details about transport in the environs, see the beginning of Rtes 28–40. CASTRO PRETORIO for buses to Tivoli; PIAZZA DEI CINQUECENTO for Palestrina; VIALE CASTRO PRETORIO for Subiaco; VIA LEPANTO for Cerveteri; EUR underground station ('Fermi') for Anzio and Nettuno; 'ANAGNINA' underground station for the Alban Hills.

STAZIONE TERMINI for trains to Anzio and Nettuno, Cerveteri, and Velletri. PORTA SAN PAOLO (Pl. 8; 7), Piazzale Ostiense, for trains (of the Ferrovia Roma-Lido) to Ostia Antica and Lido di Ostia.

Museums, Collections, and Monuments

The table below gives the hours of admission to the various museums, galleries, and monuments in Rome, in force in 1994. *Opening times vary and often change without warning*; those given below should therefore be accepted with reserve. All museums, etc. are usually closed on the main public holidays: 1 January, Easter Day, 25 April, 1 May, 15 August, and Christmas Day (although this rule is often relaxed; ask at the 'EPT'). On other holidays (see below) they open only in the morning (9.00–13.00). More and more museums are introducing longer opening hours, and staying open also on Mondays (which used to be the standard closing day for all State-owned museums). Most admission charges were doubled in 1990: the major museums and monuments now charge between Lire 6000 and Lire 10,000. British citizens under the age of 18 and over the age of 60 are entitled to free admission to State-owned museums and monuments.

Lecture tours of museums, villas, etc. (sometimes otherwise closed to the public) are organised by the '*Amici dei Musei di Roma*'. These are advertised in the local press and on a duplicated sheet obtainable at most museums. Museum Week (*Settimana dei Musei Italiani*) has now become established as an annual event (usually in November). Entrance to most museums is free during the week, and some have longer opening hours, and private collections may be specially opened.

The museums owned by the Comune of Rome have been marked 'C' in the Museum table below. The opening hours for Sundays usually apply also to holidays.

Hours of Admission to the Museums, Collections, and Monuments in Rome

Name	Open	Page
Accademia di San Luca	Mon, Wed, Fri and last Sun of the month, 10–13	168
Antiquarium Comunale	(C) closed indefinitely	70
Antiquarium Forense	(C) partially closed; adm as for the Forum	92
Ara Pacis	(C) 9–13.30; closed Mon (in summer usually also 16–19 on Tue, Thur, and Sat)	157
Auditorium of Maecenas	(C) 9–13.30 except Mon	204
Basilica of Porta Maggiore	closed indefinitely, *see* Note b	219
Baths of Caracalla	9–15; summer 9–18; Mon, Sun 9–13	231
Baths of Diocletian	*see* Museo Nazionale Romano	
Calcografia Nazionale	9–13 except Sun	168
Casino Pallavicini	1st day of every month 10–12, 15–17	187
Castel Sant'Angelo	9–13 (sometimes open also in the afternoon and closed one day a week)	281
Catacombs (*see* Note c)	normally 8.30–12 and 14.30 (or 15) to dusk	248
Priscilla	closed Mon	264
Sant'Agnese	9–12, 16–18; Sun 16–18	262
San Callisto	closed Wed	249
San Domitilla	closed Tue	254
San Sebastiano	closed Thur	252
Circus of Maxentius	(C) 9–13.30; Sun 9–12.30; closed Mon	254
Colosseum	9–one hour before sunset; Sun, Wed 9–13	114
Domus Aurea	closed indefinitely, *see* Note b	220

Forum (Roman) and Palatine	9–one hr before sunset; Sun, Tue 9–13	76
Forum of Augustus, Forum of Nerva, and Antiquarium	(C) closed indefinitely	109
Forum of Caesar	(C) closed indefinitely	108
Forum of Trajan	*see* Markets of Trajan	
Gabinetto Nazionale delle Stampe	9–13 except Sun, Mon	275
Galleria Barberini (Galleria Nazionale d'Arte Antica)	9–14, Sun 9–13; closed Mon	190
Galleria Borghese: Villa Borghese (sculpture collection)	9–14; Sun 9–13; closed Mon	176
ex Istituto di San Michele (painting collection)	9–19; Sun 9–13; closed Mon	269
Galleria Colonna	Sat 9–13	163
Galleria Comunale d'Arte Moderna	closed	169
Galleria Corsini (Galleria Nazionale d'Arte Antica)	9–14 except Mon	273
Galleria Doria-Pamphilj	Tue, Fri, Sat, Sun 10–13 (the apartments are usually shown at 11, 12)	150
Galleria Nazionale d'Arte Antica	*see* Galleria Barberini and Galleria Corsini	
Galleria Nazionale d'Arte Moderna	9–17 or 19; Sun 9–13; closed Mon	178
Galleria Spada	9–14 or 19 except Mon; fest. 9–13	143
House of Cardinal Bessarion	(C) closed indefinitely	233
Keats–Shelley Memorial House	9–13, 14.30 or 15–17.30 or 18; closed Sat, Sun	171
Mamertine Prison	9–12, 14.30–17 or 18	109
Markets and Forum of Trajan	9–13.30; Apr–Sept 9–13.30, and Thur, Sat 9–18; Sun 9–13; closed Mon	107
Mausoleum of Augustus	*see* Note a	156
Museo dell'Alto Medioevo	9–14; fest. 9–13	299
Museo dell'Arma del Genio	by appointment	288
Museo delle Arte e Tradizioni Popolari	9–14; Sun 9–13	298
Museo Astronomico Copernicano	Wed 9.30–12	290
Museo Barracco	(C) 9–13.30; Tue, Thur also 17–20; closed Mon; Sun 9–13	136
Museo Canonica	(C) Tue–Sat 9–13.30; Tue, Thur also 15–18.30; Sun 9–13; closed Mon, and in Aug	176
Musei Capitolini	(C) Tue–Sat 9–13.30; Sun 9–13; closed Mon; Tue, Thur, Sat also 17–20. In summer as above except on Sat the evening opening hours are 20–23.	58
Museo della Civiltà Romana	9–13.30; Tue, Thur also 15–18; closed Mon; Sun 9–13	299
Museo della Comunità Ebraica di Roma	Mon–Thur 9.30–14, 15–17; Fri 9.30–14.30; Sun 9.30–12.30; closed Sat	238
Museo del Folklore	(C) 9–13.30; Tue, Thur also 17–19.30; closed Mon; Sun 9–12.30	271

Museo delle Mura	9–13.30 except Mon; Tue, Thur, Sat also 16–19	235
Museo Napoleonico	(C) closed	149
Museo Nazionale d'Arte Orientale	closed	204
Museo Nazionale di Castel Sant'Angelo	*see* Castel Sant'Angelo	
Museo Nazionale Preistorico Etnografico 'Luigi Pigorini'	9–14 or 19; Sun 9–13	298
Museo Nazionale Romano:		
Terme di Diocleziano	9–14; Sun 9–13; closed Mon	195
Aula Ottagonale	10–13, 15–18	195
ex Collegio Massimo	being arranged	197
Palazzo Altemps	being arranged	148
Museo Nazionale di Strumenti Musicali	9–13.30 except Sun	218
Museo Nazionale di Villa Giulia	9–14 or 19.30; Sun 9–13; closed Mon	180
Museo Numismatico della Zecca	9–11 except Sun	194
Museo delle Origini	by appointment	259
Museo di Palazzo Venezia	9–14; Sun 9–13; closed Mon	73
Museo di Roma	closed	127
Museo Storico Nazionale dell'Arte Sanitaria	Mon, Wed, Fri 10–12	289
Museo Storico delle Poste e Telecomunicazioni	9–13; closed Sun	300
Museo Storico del Vaticano (Palazzo del Laterano)	1st Sun of the month, 8.45–13	216
Museo Teatrale del Burcardo	closed	126
Museo Torlonia	closed indefinitely	272
Museo della Via Ostiense	9–13 except Sun	292
Orto Botanico	9–15; Sat 9–11: closed Sun	272
Palatine	9–1hr before sunset; Sun, Tue 9–13	94
Palazzo Farnese	adm only by appointment after written application to the French Embassy	144
Palazzo Spada	*see* Galleria Spada	
Pantheon	9–16.30; Sun 9–13	117
Pinacoteca Capitolino	*see* Musei Capitolini	
Quadreria di Villa Borghese	9–19; closed Mon; Sun 9–13	269
Roman Forum	*see* Forum	
Teatro di Marcello	*see* note a	237
Tomba di Cecilia Metella	9–13.30 except Mon	255
Tomba dei Scipioni	closed	234
Vatican Museums	*see* p 318	
Villa Farnesina	9–13 except Sun	274
Villa Giulia	*see* Museo Nazionale di Villa Giulia	
Villa Medici	for adm to the gardens, apply to the French Academy	172
Zoo	8–17 or 18	178

Notes

a can be visited by written request to the Ripartizione X del Comune di Rome, 7 Piazza Campitelli or 29 Via Portico d'Ottavia (Tel. 06/67103819)

b for admission apply to the Soprintendenza Archeologica di Roma, 1 Piazza delle Finanze (Tel. 06/4824181)

c the other catacombs may be visited by special permission only; apply to the Pontificia Commissione di Archeologia Sacra, 1 Via Napoleone III

Parks and gardens in Rome and Northern Lazio

Rome has numerous fine parks and gardens, most of which are kept well. Those described in the text (see the Index) include the following. The largest public park in the centre of the city is the Villa Borghese (particularly attractive around the 'Giardino del Lago'), with the adjoining Pincio. Another huge public park, S of the centre, is the Villa Doria Pamphilj. Part of the Janiculum and Oppian Hills are occupied by gardens. Smaller parks, beautifully kept, include the Villa Celimontana, the Parco Savello (on the Aventine), the park by the Tomb of the Scipios (Via di Porta Latina and Via di Porta San Sebastiano), and two parks off Via del Quirinale. The Palatine Hill is covered with luxuriant vegetation and fine trees, and here are the delightful Farnese gardens laid out in the 16C and still beautifully maintained.

To the N of the centre are the large public parks of Villa Glori, with fine trees, and Villa Ada. The gardens of Villa Torlonia, with neo-classical and neo-Gothic buildings, and of the Villa Blanc, both on the Via Nomentana, are in an abandoned state. The park of the Villa Torlonia (formerly Albani), on the Via Salaria, with its umbrella pines, is still privately owned by the Torlonia. The Villa Sciarra, on the Janiculum, is a public park (fine wistaria). The Orto Botanico is one of the most important botanical gardens in Italy. There is a rose and iris garden (May and June) in Via di Valle Murcia at the foot of the Aventine Hill (above the Circus Maximus). The Spanish Steps are covered with a magnificent display of azaleas at the beginning of May. On the borders of the lake in EUR are a thousand Japanese cherry trees. A flower market is open on Tuesday mornings in Via Trionfale.

Villas and palaces in the city which preserve their gardens (which can be visited only with special permission) include: the 17C formal garden around the Casino del Bel Respiro, in the Villa Doria Pamphilj; the Priorato di Malta on the Aventine; and the House of Cardinal Bessarion. Other gardens which can normally be seen during the opening hours of the palaces include those of the Villa Farnesina (Trastevere), Palazzo Pallavicini Rospigliosi, Palazzo Colonna (the garden can only be seen from the windows of the gallery), and the Villa Giulia. There is a formal garden behind the Palazzina Borghese in Villa Borghese. Perhaps the most beautiful villa garden which survives from the 16C is that of the Villa Medici (normally open one or two days a week; for admission apply to the French Academy). Tours can be taken of the (rather disappointing) Vatican gardens. The beautiful gardens behind the Quirinal palace are only open on rare occasions, and it is also difficult to see the hanging garden of the Villa Madama (used by the Foreign Office).

Some of the most beautiful gardens in Italy are to be found in northern Lazio, described in the text on the environs. These include the Villa Aldobrandini at Frascati, the Villa d'Este at Tivoli, the Villa Lante at Bagnaia, the Villa Farnese at Caprarola, and the Sacro Bosco at Bomarzo.

Visiting Rome with Children

The Roman remains in the centre of the city cannot fail to fire the imagination of children of all ages: the Colosseum and Roman Forum and Palatine hill provide an immediate picture of the splendour of the Empire. The first place to begin a visit to Rome is the Capitol Hill with its views of the Forum. The Capitoline Museum here contains some of the masterpieces of Roman sculpture and is a particularly pleasant museum to visit (it is also open at night and if possible should be visited then). Another Roman monument which gives a clear idea of the scale of ancient Rome is the Baths of Caracalla. The Via Appia, in the stretch around the Tomb of Cecilia Metella and the Circus of Maxentius leaves an indelible impression. For children particularly interested in ancient Rome, the Museo della Civiltà Romana in EUR has a didactic chronological display (using casts) and a splendid scale model of the city in the fourth century. You can walk along a stretch of the Aurelian walls in the Museo delle Mura. At least one of the vast underground catacombs on the Via Appia should be seen.

The fountains of Rome are particularly delightful; the element of surprise provided by the Trevi fountain, as well as its noise, are unforgettable. It is fascinating to discover how many different sculptural motifs were used in the decoration of the fountains all over the city: the boats in Piazza di Spagna and Piazza Santa Maria in Domnica; the grotesque masks in Via Giulia and Piazza Pietro d'Illiria on the Aventine; the tortoises in Piazza Mattei; the bees in Piazza Barberini; the tritons in Piazza Barberini and Piazza Navona, etc.

Piazza Navona and Piazza di Spagna (with the Spanish steps) are perhaps the two most animated places in the city, always fun to visit. The best place to see the Tiber, and some of its oldest bridges, is from the Isola Tiberina. A visit to the Galleria Doria Pamphilj gives a clear picture of how one of the great Roman patrician families lived, and the Keats-Shelley Memorial house preserves the atmosphere of a 'pensione' in the last century, overlooking the Spanish steps. Castel Sant'Angelo is one of the most exciting museums to visit for children: numerous parts of the castle can be explored, from the ramparts to the dungeons.

One of the most curious sights in the city is the policeman who directs the traffic with great aplomb in Piazza Venezia at the head of the Corso. The exceptionally tall Presidents' guards at the Quirinal can usually be seen outside the palace, and the Swiss guards with their splendid uniforms stand at the entrance to the Vatican beside St Peter's. When choosing a means of public transport, try to take a tram (more interesting than a bus); numbers 13 and 30B take an unusual route near the Colosseum.

The Aventine hill is a particularly peaceful place to visit, with several little gardens and a delightful view of the dome of St Peter's through the keyhole of the Priorato di Malta. In Trastevere the small Folklore Museum has charming life-size tableaux showing scenes of life in Rome in the past. A visit to the Vatican is exhausting for grown-ups and children alike, especially when it is crowded. Although a brief visit is obligatory, never attempt to stay too long or see too much. In St Peter's the dome is well worth climbing.

There are a number of 'didactic' museums grouped near each other in EUR; an ethnographical museum related to Italy (Museo Nazionale di Arti e Tradizioni Popolari) and an ethnographical collection from the Americas,

Africa, and Oceania (Museo Etnografico Luigi Pigorini), as well as the Museo della Civiltà Romana, described above. Also here is a museum illustrating postal history, and the development of the telegraph and telephone.

Rome has numerous splendid parks, among the largest are the Villa Borghese (which also has a zoo) and the adjoining Pincio (where a band plays on Sunday morning in May and June). Open-air puppet shows are sometimes held in summer on the Janiculum hill. The largest park of all is the Villa Doria Pamphilj. For all the other parks, see the paragraph above on 'Parks and Gardens'. Breaks during a hard day's sightseeing should always be made at a *gelateria* which sell the best ice-creams; for details about cafés, see above ('Eating in Rome'). Pizzas are generally excellent in Rome. For annual festivals, see below. Post cards and colourful interesting literature are now on sale in most museums.

In the environs the Roman remains of Ostia Antica and Hadrian's Villa are splendid places to spend a whole day with a picnic. The fountains of Villa d'Este in Tivoli are another memorable sight (especially pleasant on a hot day). Further away, in northern Lazio, is the park of Bomarzo with its statues of monsters. The tombs at Cerveteri and Tarquinia provide a remarkable picture of Etruscan civilization, and the remote Etruscan site of Vulci on the border with Tuscany is particularly evocative.

Churches and Church Ceremonies

St Peter's and the other three great basilicas are open all day (7.00–19.00). Other churches are closed between 12.00 and 15.30, 16.00 or 17.00, but almost all of them open at 7 a.m. Some churches, including several of importance, are open only for a short time in the morning and evening (opening times have been given where possible in the text below, but may vary). Most churches now ask that sightseers do not visit the church during a service. If you are wearing shorts or have bare shoulders you can be stopped from entering some churches (including St Peter's and the other main basilicas). Closed chapels, crypts, etc. are sometimes unlocked on request by the sacristan. Many pictures and frescoes are difficult to see without lights which are often coin operated (100 lire or 500 lire coins). When visiting churches it is always useful to carry a torch and a pair of binoculars. Churches in Rome are very often not orientated. In the text the terms N and S refer to the liturgical N (left) and S (right), taking the high altar as at the E end.

The **Basilicas of Rome**. The four great patriarchal basilicas are San Giovanni in Laterano (St John Lateran; the cathedral and mother church of the world), San Pietro in Vaticano (St Peter's), San Paolo fuori le Mura, and Santa Maria Maggiore. These, with the three basilicas of San Lorenzo fuori le Mura, Santa Croce in Gerusalemme, and San Sebastiano, comprise the 'Seven Churches of Rome'. Among minor basilicas rank Sant'Agnese fuori le Mura, Santi Apostoli, Santa Cecilia, San Clemente, and Santa Maria in Trastevere.

Roman Catholic Services. The ringing of the evening Ave Maria or Angelus bell at sunset is an important event in Rome, where it signifies the end of the day and the beginning of night. The hour varies according to the season. On Sunday and, in the principal churches, often on weekdays, Mass is celebrated up to 13.00 and from 17.00 until 20.00. High Mass, with music, is celebrated in the basilicas (see above) on Sunday at 9.30 or 10.30 (10.30 in St Peter's). The choir of St Peter's sings on Sunday at Mass at 10.30, and vespers at 17.00. The Sistine Chapel choir sings in St Peter's on 29 June and whenever the Pope celebrates Mass.

ROMAN CATHOLIC SERVICES IN ENGLISH take place in San Silvestro in Capite, St Thomas of Canterbury, and Santa Susanna; in Irish at St Patrick's, Sant'Isidoro, San Clemente, and Sant' Agata dei Goti. Confessions are heard in English in the four main basilicas and in the Gesù, Santa Maria sopra Minerva, Sant'Anselmo, Sant'Ignazio, and Santa Sabina.

Church Festivals. On saints' days mass and vespers with music are celebrated in the churches dedicated to the saints concerned. The Octave of the Epiphany is held at Sant'Andrea della Valle. The Blessing of the lambs takes place at Sant'Agnese Fuori le Mura, on 21 January c 10.30. In the evening of 6 January there is a procession with the Santo Bambino at Santa Maria in Aracoeli (although the statue was stolen in 1994). The singing of the Te Deum annually on 31 December in the church of the Gesù is a magnificent traditional ceremony. In San Giovanni in Laterano a choral mass is held on 24 June, in commemoration of the service held here on 24 June 1929 by Pius XI, and the Pope attends the Maundy Thursday celebrations in the basilica when he gives his benediction from the loggia on the façade. On the 5 August the legend of the miraculous fall of snow is commemorated at Santa Maria Maggiore in a pontifical Mass in the Borghese Chapel. On Christmas morning in this basilica a procession is held in honour of the sacred relic of the Holy Crib. The church of Sant'Anselmo on the Aventine Hill is noted for its Gregorian chant at 9.30 on Sunday. Holy Week liturgy takes place on Wednesday, Thursday, and Friday in Holy Week, at St Peter's, St John Lateran, Santa Croce, and other churches.

Audience of the Pope, see Rte 27.

British and American Churches. All Saints (Anglican), 153 Via del Babuino; St Paul's (American Episcopal), Via Nazionale; St Andrew's (Scottish Presbyterian), 7 Via Venti Settembre; Methodist, 38 Via Firenze; Christian Science Society, 42 Via dei Giardini.

Jewish Synagogue. Lungotevere dei Cenci. **Mosque and Islamic Centre**, Via della Moschea, Monte Antenne.

Concerts, Plays, and Festivals

Concerts, theatre performances, and exhibitions are advertised on wall posters throughout the city. Free up-to-date information (also in English) on events in Rome is also available in the 'Carnet di Roma' published every month by the 'EPT', and in 'Un Ospite a Roma', issued every two weeks and available at hotels and information offices. Details are also given in the Thursday supplement of 'La Repubblica' newspaper (called 'Trovaroma') and in the fortnightly English magazine 'Wanted in Rome'. Booking facilities at 'Box Office', 88 Viale Giulio Cesare, but you can often buy tickets directly at the theatre on the evening of the performance.

Theatres in Rome include: ARGENTINA (Pl. 3; 6), Largo di Torre Argentina; VALLE (Pl. 2; 8), Via del Teatro Valle; ELISEO, 183 Via Nazionale; DELLE ARTI, 59 Via Sicilia; DELLE MUSE, 43 Via Forli; PARIOLI, 20 Via G. Borsi; QUIRINO, 1 Via Marco Minghetti; and GOLDONI, 3 Vicolo di Soldati.

Concert Halls. ACCADEMIA NAZIONALE DI SANTA CECILIA, 7 Via dei Greci; AUDITORIUM DEL FORO ITALICO, 26 Lungotevere Diaz; ORATORIO DEL GONFALONE, 32 Via del Gonfalone; SAN LEONE MAGNO, 38 Via Bolzano; TEATRO OLIMPICO, 17 Piazza Gentile da Fabriano. **Opera** is held at the TEATRO DELL'OPERA (Pl. 4; 4), Via del Viminale (December to May).

Exhibitions are held at Palazzo delle Esposizioni, Palazzo Venezia, the French Academy (Villa Medici), Galleria Nazionale d'Arte Moderna, Palazzo dei Conservatori, Palazzo Braschi, etc.

Annual Festivals. EPIPHANY (BEFANA), on the night of 5–6 January, cele-brated in Piazza Navona; CARNIVAL is celebrated in the streets and piazze on Shrove Tuesday; FESTA DI SAN GIOVANNI, on the night of 23–24 June, near the Porta San Giovanni; FESTA DI SAN GIUSEPPE, 19 March, celebrated in the Trionfale district; FESTA DELLA REPUBBLICA, first Sunday in June, military parade in the Via dei Fori Imperiali; ANNIVERSARY OF THE BIRTH OF ROME, 21 April celebrated on the Campidoglio; FESTA DI NOANTRI, celebrations in Trastevere for several weeks in July.

General Information

Plan of Visit. The itineraries in the Guide can be accomplished on foot in a day (with the help of public transport only for those routes outside the historical centre of the city). If you have only a short time at your disposal, you should not miss the following areas and monuments:
1. The Capitol Hill (Rte 1)
2. The Forum and Palatine (Rtes 2 and 3)
3. The Pantheon and Piazza Navona (Rtes 5 and 6)
4. The Corso (and Galleria Doria Pamphilj), Piazza del Popolo, and Piazza di Spagna (Rtes 7 and 8)
5. The Colosseum and Esquiline Hill (Rtes 4 and 11)
6. The Baths of Caracalla and the Via Appia (Rtes 14 and 17)
7. St Peter's and the Vatican Museums (Rte 27)
8. Trastevere (Rte 21)
9. Villa Borghese (Rte 9)
10. The Quirinal Hill and (when it reopens) the Museo Nazionale Romano (Rte 10)
In the immediate environs, at least Hadrian's Villa at Tivoli (Rte 33) and the excavations at Ostia (Rte 28) should be seen.

Season. The climate of Rome is exceptionally good except in the height of summer and periodically in the winter. The best months to visit the city are

October and November or March (the most crowded periods to be avoided if at all possible are at Easter, May and June, September, and at Christmas).

Rome for the disabled. Italy is at last catching up with the rest of Europe in the provision of facilities for the disabled. All new public buildings are now obliged by law to provide access for the disabled, and specially designed facilities. In the annual list of hotels in Rome published by the 'EPT', hotels which are able to provide hospitality for the disabled are indicated. Airports and railway stations in Italy provide assistance, and certain trains are equipped to transport wheelchairs. In the list of current opening times of the Museums and Galleries in Rome available from the 'EPT', those which are accessible to wheelchairs are indicated.

Public Holidays. The main holidays in Rome, when offices and shops are closed, are as follows: New Year's Day, 25 April (Liberation Day), Easter Monday, 1 May (Labour Day), 15 August (Assumption), 1 November (All Saints' Day), 8 December (Immaculate Conception), Christmas Day, and 26 December (St Stephen). In addition, the festival of the patron Saints of Rome, Peter and Paul, is celebrated on 29 June as a local holiday in the city.

Telephones and Postal Information. Stamps are sold at tobacconists (displaying a blue 'T' sign) and post offices. There are numerous public telephones all over Rome in kiosks, bars, restaurants, etc. These are operated by coins or telephone cards. A few telephones are still operated by a metal disc known as a 'gettone', which can be bought (200 lire each) from tobacconists, bars, some newspaper stands, and post offices (and are considered valid currency). Most cities in Europe can now be dialled direct from Rome. **Head Post Office** (Pl. 3; 4), Piazza San Silvestro, open weekdays 8.30–21.00; Sat 8.30–12.00 (open until 21.00 for the issue of mail addressed 'fermo posta' and for the acceptance of special delivery registered mail only). Telephone exchange open 24 hours.

Working Hours. Government offices usually work Monday–Saturday from 8.00–13.30 or 14.00. Shops (clothes, hardware, books, hairdressers, etc.) are generally open from 9.00–13.00, 16.00–19.30, including Saturday, and for most of the year are closed on Monday morning. Food shops usually open from 7.30 or 8.00–13.00, 16.30 or 17.00–19.30 or 20.00, and for most of the year are closed on Wednesday afternoon. From mid-June to mid-September all shops are closed instead on Saturday afternoon. In 1994 a new regulation was introduced by the town council of Rome which allowed shops to remain open on Sundays (but many chose not to do so).

Banks are usually open from 8.30–13.30, and for one hour in the afternoon (usually 14.45–15.45), every day except Saturday and Sunday. They close early (about 11.00) on days preceding national holidays. The larger banks in the centre of the city now have machines outside (always open) for changing foreign bank notes.

Embassies. British Embassy (and Consulate) to Italy, 80 Via XX Settembre (Tel. 06/4825441); British Embassy to the Holy See, 91 Via Condotti. American Embassy (and Consulate) to Italy, 119 Via Veneto (Tel. 06/46741).

Cultural Institutions. British School at Rome, 61 Via Antonio Gramsci (Valle Giulia); British Council, Palazzo del Drago, 20 Via delle Quattro Fontane; American Academy, 5 Via Angelo Masina; French Academy, Villa Medici, 1 Viale Trinità dei Monti; Goethe Institut, 267 Via del Corso; German

Archaeological Institute, 79 Via Sardegna; Università degli Studi, Viale dell'Università (Città Universitaria); Istituto Nazionale di Archeologia e Storia dell'Arte, 3 Piazza Venezia; Accademia dei Lincei, 10 Via della Lungara; Società Italiana Dante Alighieri (with Italian language courses), 27 Piazza Firenze; Istituto Centrale del Restauro, Istituto di San Michele, Ripa Grande, and 9 Piazza San Francesco di Paola; Società Geografica Italiana, 12 Via della Navicella (Villa Celimontana); Accademia Filarmonica Romana, 116 Via Flaminia; Accademia Nazionale di Santa Cecilia, 6 Via Vittoria; Associazione Italia Nostra, 287 Corso Vittorio Emanuele; Amici dei Musei di Roma, Palazzo Braschi (Piazza San Pantaleo).

Libraries. Biblioteca Nazionale Centrale, Viale Castro Pretorio; Istituto Nazionale di Archeologia e Storia dell'Arte, 3 Piazza Venezia; Archivio di Stato, 40 Corso Rinascimento; Biblioteca Alessandrina Universitaria, Città Universitaria; Biblioteca Hertziana, 28 Via Gregoriana; Biblioteca Angelica, 8 Piazza Sant' Agostino; Gabinetto Fotografico Nazionale, 1 Piazza di Porta Portese; British Council Library, 20 Via delle Quattro Fontane; American Library, 62 Via Veneto.

Shops. The smartest shops are in Via Frattina and Via Condotti (the Bond Street of Rome), which lead out of Piazza di Spagna. A good shopping area (less expensive) is near the Pantheon. Italy has notably few department stores: the best known are 'La Rinascente', Piazza Colonna, 'Standa', and 'Upim'. English books are stocked at 'The Lion Bookshop', 181 Via del Babuino; 'The Anglo-American Bookshop', 27 Via delle Vite, 'The Corner Bookshop', 48 Via del Moro, etc. Via del Babuino and Via dei Coronari are known for their antique shops.

Open-air markets: Porta Portese (general 'flea market'; open Sunday morning only); Via Sannio (Porta San Giovanni), new and second-hand clothes. Old prints and books are sold at the Mercato delle Stampe, Largo della Fontanella di Borghese. Excellent food markets are open every morning (except Sunday) at Campo dei Fiori, Piazza Vittorio Emanuele II, Via Andrea Doria, and Testaccio.

Public Toilets. There is a notable shortage of public toilets in Italy. All bars (cafés) should have toilets available to the public (generally speaking the larger the bar, the better the facilities). Nearly all museums now have toilets. There are also toilets at the railway stations, and in Piazza di Spagna.

Medical Services. British citizens, as members of the EU, have the right to claim health services in Italy if they have the E111 form (issued by the Department of Health). There are also a number of private holiday health insurance policies. First Aid services ('Pronto Soccorso') are available at all hospitals, railways stations and airports.

   Chemists or Pharmacies (*farmacie*) are usually open Monday–Friday 9.00–13.00, 16.00–19.30 or 20.00. Some are open 24 hours a day. A few are open on Saturdays, Sundays (and holidays), and at night (listed on the door of every chemist, and in the daily newspapers). For chemists open at night, dial 1921.

   For **emergencies**, dial 113. Ambulance service run by the Red Cross, Tel. 5100. 24-hour service run by the Municipality of Rome, 20 Via del Colosseo (Tel. 4826741). *San Giovanni* is the central hospital for road accidents and other emergencies (Tel. 77051).

Crime. For all emergencies, dial 113. As in large towns all over the world, pick-pocketing is a widespread problem in Rome; it is always advisable not to carry valuables in handbags, and be particularly careful on public transport. Cash and documents, etc. can be left in hotel safes on request. It is a good idea to make photocopies of all important documents in case of loss. Help is given to British and American travellers who are in difficulty by the British and American embassies in Rome (see above). They will replace lost or stolen passports, and will give advice in emergencies.

Crime should be reported at once. There are three categories of **policemen** in Italy: 'Vigili Urbani' (municipal police who wear blue uniform in winter and white during the summer and hats similar to London policemen); 'Carabinieri' (military police who wear black uniform with a red stripe down the side of their trousers); and the 'Polizia di Stato' (state police who wear dark blue jackets and light blue trousers). The central police station of the 'Polizia di Stato' is at 15 Via San Vitale (Tel. 4686). Office for Foreigners, 2 Via Genova (Tel. 4686/2987). In emergencies the municipal police can be called on 67691, and the 'carabinieri' on 112. Railway police, Tel. 4819561. A detailed statement has to be given in order to get an official document confirming loss or damage (essential for insurance claims). Interpreters are provided.

Newspapers and magazines. The most widely read Italian newspapers in Rome are *La Repubblica* (with a Thursday supplement on events in the city), *Corriere della Sera, Messaggero*, and *Il Tempo*. The 'Carnet di Roma', a monthly publication of the Rome 'EPT' (available from their offices) and the 'Ospite a Roma', published every fortnight (available at kiosks and in hotels), give up-to-date information on events in the city. 'Wanted in Rome' is a useful English magazine published every fortnight (17 Via dei Delfini).

ROME

ROME (2,777,000 inhab.), in Italian **Roma**, is the capital of Italy and the metropolis of the Roman Catholic Church. The Eternal City, the 'Urbs' par excellence, to which all roads lead, was the Alma Mater of Mediterranean civilisation, and the Caput Mundi, from which law and the liberal arts and sciences radiated to the confines of its vast empire, which covered the whole of the known Western World. Its superb ancient monuments survive all over the centre of the modern city, and blend with its great Renaissance and Baroque buildings. The yellow Tiber, here some 35km from its mouth, divides the city into two unequal parts; but the Rome of the Republic and the early Empire was confined to the left bank, with the famous seven hills; the Palatine and Capitoline in the centre, the Aventine, Celian, Esquiline, Viminal, and Quirinal (from S to N) in an arc to the E.

1

The Capitol and Piazza Venezia

PIAZZA VENEZIA (Pl. 4; 5), a huge and busy square, is the focus of the main traffic arteries of the city. Towards it converge Via del Corso from the N, Via del Plebiscito (the continuation of Corso Vittorio Emanuele) from the W (and St Peter's), Via Battisti (the continuation of Via Quattro Novembre) from the E (and the Station), and, from the SE and SW respectively, Via dei Fori Imperiali and Via del Teatro di Marcello. The piazza was transformed at the end of the 19C when parts of the Renaissance city were demolished and the Capitol Hill itself encroached upon to make way for the colossal Victor Emmanuel Monument (see below) which is an unforgivable intrusion into the centre of the city. A policeman regulates the traffic at the head of the Corso which from the N side of the piazza runs straight for over a mile to Piazza del Popolo with its obelisk.

From here can be seen (left) the Palazzo delle Assicurazioni Generali di Venezia (1907), with a fine winged lion from Padua, and (right) Palazzo di Venezia (see below). Dwarfed by the Monument, and to the right of it is the Capitol Hill. It is separated from Piazza d'Aracoeli (with a fountain of 1589 designed by Jacopo della Porta) by a wide, modern, traffic-ridden road (Via del Teatro di Marcello), one of the most difficult in the city to cross on foot, which runs S to the Tiber past the foot of the hill. Beside the Victor Emmanuel Monument here are the interesting ruins discovered this century of a Roman tenement house or 'insulae' built in the 2C AD and over four storeys high.

The **CAPITOLINE HILL** (in Italian, *Campidoglio*; 50m) is the smallest but most famous of the Seven Hills of Rome. It was the political and religious centre of Ancient Rome, and since the end of the 11C has been the seat of the civic government of the city.

Archaeological finds have confirmed that the hill was already inhabited in the Bronze Age. Its two summits are separated by a depression, occupied by Piazza del Campidoglio. On the S summit (*Capitolium*) stood the Capitol proper, with the **Temple of Jupiter Optimus Maximus Capitolinus**. This was the most venerated temple in Rome, since Jupiter was regarded as the city's special protector. The investiture of consuls took place here, and the triumphant procession awarded to victorious generals ended at the temple (see Rte 2). According to tradition, it was founded by Tarquinius Priscus, completed by Tarquinius Superbus, and dedicated in 509 BC. It is the largest temple known of this period. It was destroyed by fire in 83 BC during the civil wars, rebuilt by Sulla, destroyed again in AD 69, rebuilt by Vespasian and again by Domitian, and was still standing in the 6C. Remains of the earliest temple still exist (see below).

The N summit (altered by the construction of the Victor Emmanuel Monument) was occupied by the *Arx*, or citadel of Rome. During a siege by the Gauls in 390 BC the Capitol was saved from a night attack by the honking of the sacred geese of Juno kept here, who alerted the Romans to the danger. In 343 BC a temple was erected to Juno Moneta; the name came to be connected with the Mint later established here. The site of this temple is now covered by the church of Santa Maria in Aracoeli.

Formerly the Capitoline Hill was accessible only from the Forum but since the 16C the main buildings have been made to face the north, in conformity with the direction of the modern development of the city.

There are three approaches to the hill from Piazza d'Aracoeli. On the left a long steep flight of 124 steps (dating from 1348) mounts to the church of Santa Maria in Aracoeli, more easily reached from Piazza del Campidoglio (see below). On the right, Via delle Tre Pile (a carriage road of 1873 now used by cars), winds up to the Capitol, passing fragments of temples and a stretch of archaic wall. In the middle the stepped ramp known as the *Cordonata* designed by Michelangelo (and modified c 1578 by Giacomo della Porta) provides the easiest way up the hill. It is guarded by two Egyptian lions in black granite (veined with red) of the Ptolemaic period, from the Isaeum. In the garden on the left (traversed by another flight of steps shaded by a pergola) a 19C statue of Cola di Rienzo marks the spot

Piazza del Campidoglio

where he was killed in 1354. Higher up is a cage which, until recently, contained a she-wolf, a symbol of Rome.

At the top is ***PIAZZA DEL CAMPIDOGLIO** (Pl. 4; 7), beautifully designed by Michelangelo to give grandeur to the historical centre of Rome (it was completed to his design in the 17C). It is surrounded on three sides by stately palaces and a balustrade defines its open end. At the back is Palazzo Senatorio; on the left is Palazzo del Museo Capitolino; facing it, on the right Palazzo dei Conservatori. The latter has a very unusual design with Ionic columns supporting a flat open loggia below, and handsome windows with coupled columns on the piano nobile, below a prominent entablature with a balcony. The two storeys are united by the use of the giant order, the first time this solution was used in secular architecture. The similar palace opposite, also designed by Michelangelo, was not built until the mid 17C.

The handsome pavement with an oval star design gave prominence to the famous gilded bronze statue of Marcus Aurelius, removed in 1981 for restoration and 'temporarily' displayed in the Capitoline Museum (see below). In 1538 Michelangelo, having just been made a citizen of Rome, provided its small and elegant base, and its theatrical setting. Discussions continue about making a bronze copy to replace the original here.

On the balustrade are colossal figures of the Dioscuri (much restored), late Roman works, found in the Ghetto in the 16C, two trophies of barbarian arms (Flavian period), known as the 'Trophies of Marius', statues of Constantine and his son Constans (from the Baths of Constantine), and two milestones, the first and seventh of the Appian Way.

The collections housed in the Palazzi del Museo Capitolino, dei Conservatori, and Caffarelli are grouped under the comprehensive title of the ***MUSEI CAPITOLINI**. The title is rather confusing, since one of the museums is called the Museo Capitolino (see below). They are famous for their magnificent Roman sculptures, and constitute the oldest public collection in the world, dating from 1471, when Sixtus IV made over to the people of Rome a valuable group of bronzes (including the 'Spinario' and the she-wolf), which were deposited in Palazzo dei Conservatori. This nucleus was later enriched with finds made in Rome and by various acquisitions, notably the collection of Cardinal Alessandro Albani. A second museum was opened in 1876.

Admission, see p 46. There is one ticket for all the museums which can be bought at the entrance to the Museo Capitolino, on the left of the piazza, or at the entrance to Palazzo dei Conservatori, on the right of the piazza.

Museo Capitolino

Palazzo del Museo Capitolino (Pl. 4; 5), built in the reign of Innocent X (1644–55), contains the ***MUSEO CAPITOLINO**, an extremely interesting collection of ancient sculpture, begun by Clement XII and added to by later popes. It was opened to the public in 1734, during the pontificate of Clement XII.

Ground Floor. Inner Court. Fountain, by Giacomo della Porta, with a colossal figure of a river-god, known as 'Marforio', probably of the 2C AD found at the foot of the Capitol (one of Rome's 'talking' statues). In the side niches are two figures of Pan (telamones), from the Theatre of Pompey.

Portico. The equestrian ***statue of Marcus Aurelius**, formerly in Piazza del Campidoglio, has been displayed here since its restoration. This magnificent colossal gilded bronze is a masterpiece of Roman sculpture. It was beautifully restored in 1981–90 when the gilding was returned to its surface. It is now thought to date from the latter part of the Emperor's reign (AD 161–80), or possibly from the year of his death; it is the only Roman equestrian statue of this period to survive. This popular statue appears time and again in medieval representations of the city, and it is first documented in the 10C when it was believed to represent the Christian emperor Constantine the Great. It is thought to have been on the Lateran hill as early as 782, and was brought from there by order of Paul III in 1538 to the Capitol Hill. In 1873 Henry James commented 'I doubt if any statue of King or

Room V on the first floor of the Museo Capitolino

captain in the public places of the world has more to commend it to the general heart'.

The sculpture in the **atrium** has recently been cleaned: it includes a colossal statue of Minerva, from a 5C original, two statues of women after Kalamides' Aphrodite Sosandra, with portrait heads of the 2–3C AD, and a colossal statue of Mars, dating from the Domitian period. At the left end is the entrance to three rooms (often closed; enquire at the ticket office), containing monuments of Oriental cults.

Room IV: Three representations of Mithras; base dedicated to the Magna Mater, with reliefs representing the Miracle of the Vestal Claudia, who brought the ship bearing the image of the goddess to Rome (205 BC); and statue of a Gaul (early 3C AD), formerly in Wilton House near Salisbury. In the centre is an altar to Sol Sanctissimus, the God of the Sun. **Room V**. 12. Bust of a young boy, follower of the cult of Isis (3C AD); 14. Bust of Serapis. **Room VI**. Sculptures relating to the cult of Zeus Dolichenos.

At the right end of the atrium is the entrance to three more rooms: **Room VII**. Heads, busts, and fragments of calendars from the Palatine and Ostia, including a finely preserved Order of Precedence of the citizens of Ostia (from the time of the Emperor Pertinax). **Room VIII**. 1. Roman head from the period of Trajan; *4. Amendola sarcophagus, with reliefs representing a battle between Gauls and Romans, showing a remarkable affinity with the Pergamene school; 10. Cippus of the master-mason Titus Statilius Aper, with his tools. **Room IX**. Colossal double *sarcophagus, formerly supposed to be that of Alexander Severus, a splendid work of the 3C AD, with portraits of the deceased and reliefs representing the story of Achilles; cippus of Vettius Agorius Praetextatus, pro-consul of Achaia.

A staircase leads up past fragments of sarcophagi with reliefs of animals to the **First Floor**. Beyond the gallery (described below) is **Room I** which exhibits the *Dying Gaul, an exquisitely modelled figure of a Celtic warrior who lies mortally wounded on the ground. It was discovered in the gardens of Sallust and is a copy of the Roman period of one of the bronze statues dedicated at Pergamon by Attalos I in commemoration of his victories over the Gauls (239 BC). The statue was formerly called the 'Dying Gladiator', 'butcher'd to make a Roman holiday', in Byron's phrase. It was found in

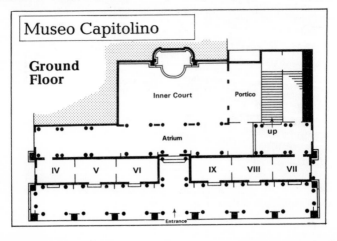

1622 near the Villa Ludovisi, and was beautifully restored in 1986 when the position of the right arm was changed, having been altered in a 17C restoration.

Nearly all the other statues in this room were found at Hadrian's Villa, near Tivoli: 1. Amazon, a Roman work after an original attributed to Pheidias (wrongly restored); 2. Colossal head of Alexander the Great; 3. Hermes, Hadrianic version of a 4C original; 4. Lycian Apollo, copy of a work by Praxiteles; 6. Head of a youth; *7. Satyr Resting, a good replica of an original by Praxiteles (the 'Marble Faun' of Hawthorne's novel; other replicas in the Vatican); *8. Head of Dionysos; 9. Greek cynic philosopher, Roman copy in marble of a bronze original; 10. Head of a general, a Pheidian type; 11. Priestess of Isis, period of Hadrian; 12. Eros and Psyche, Hellenistic work.

Room II. In the centre, *1. Laughing Silenus, in red marble, of the Imperial period from a Hellenistic bronze; 2. Alabaster bust of an unknown Roman, period of Gallienus; 5. Sarcophagus depicting the Hunt of the Calydonian Boar; 8. Child with mask, a Hellenistic work; 11. Sarcophagus with figures of Endymion and Selene (early 3C AD); 16. Herm of Hercules (2C AD); 17. Boy with a goose, copy of a bronze by Boethos of Chalcedon (2C BC); Sarcophagus (2C AD) with the life of Dionysos including his birth, a graceful work. On the wall above is a bronze plaque on which is inscribed the *Lex Regia* of Vespasian, the historic decree conferring sovereign power on the emperor; the text was used by Cola di Rienzo to demonstrate the greatness and the rights of Rome.

Room III (SALONE). In the centre are five statues in dark marble or bronze: 1, 5. Statues of Zeus and Asklepios, both from originals of the 4C BC; 2, 4. Young or laughing centaur, Old or weeping centaur, two remarkable works from Hadrian's Villa, signed by his contemporaries Aristeas and Papias of Aphrodisias in Caria; 3. Infant Hercules, a colossal ugly figure in green basalt, of the late Imperial epoch, on a base decorated with scenes from the myth of Zeus.

The marbles exhibited around the walls include: (on the entrance wall) 27. Huntsman, head of the period of Gallienus on a body of the late-Archaic type; 28. Statue of Harpocrates, period of Hadrian. On the wall opposite the

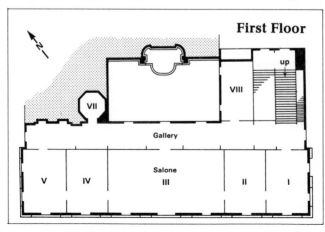

First Floor

N

up

VIII

VII

Gallery

Salone

V | IV | III | II | I

windows: 13. Hadrian as Mars; 20. Archaic statue of Apollo, copy of the so-called Omphalos Apollo in Athens; 21. Statue of a young Roman of the time of Hadrian as Hermes; *22. Old woman in terror, a striking example of the Hellenistic period; 23. Muse, once probably representing Hera, from a 4C original; 24. Colossal statue of Demeter, restored as Hera, from an Attic original of the 4C BC. On the far wall: 7. Colossal statue of Apollo (the head does not belong); 11. Hera, from an original attributed to Agorakritos (5C BC), badly restored with a portrait head. On the window wall: *30. Apollo, from a work of the first half of the 5C; 31. Pothos, from an original by Skopas; 33. Wounded Amazon, signed by the copyist Sosicles, from a 5C original; 34. Roman couple as Mars and Venus, period of Septimius Severus; 36. Athena Promachos, a 4C type from the Villa d'Este.

Room IV. The identifications of the busts (recently cleaned) of philosophers, poets, and others in this room are not all certain. Those whose identity is most probable are Socrates (various types), Theon (17), Sophocles (22–23), Chrysippos (27), Euripides (30–31), Homer (39–41), Demosthenes (43), Aeschines (50), Metrodorus (51), double *portrait of Epicuros and Metrodorus (52), Epicuros (53), Antisthenes (55), Cicero (56), Theophrastus (74). In the centre, 75. Seated figure ('Marcellus') from an original of the 4C BC (head modern). On the walls are fragments of a frieze, perhaps from the Porticus of Octavia, with sacrificial instruments and parts of ships, and Greek votive reliefs.

Room V contains a rich collection of Roman Imperial busts, interesting as portraits and also in some cases because of the precious materials used. On columns: *Augustus, wearing a wreath of myrtle; *15. Woman of the late Flavian period; Commodus. Around the walls: 20. Domitia; 21. Plotina, wife of Trajan, considered her best portrait; 24. Matidia; 32. Faustina the Younger; 39. Julia Domna; *55. Heliogabalus. Above are reliefs, two of which are works of great delicacy, executed in the first centuries of the Empire and following Hellenistic types: F. Perseus rescuing Andromeda; H. Sleeping Endymion. In the centre: *59. Helena, mother of Constantine, a beautiful seated figure inspired by the Aphrodite of Pheidias.

Gallery. 35. Colossal head of an Emperor, 4C AD; 36. Portrait of Marcus Aurelius as a boy; 53. Colossal head of Aphrodite, perhaps an original of the Hellenistic period; 57. Sarcophagus of the 3C AD with reliefs of the rape of Persephone; 61. Roman matron of the Flavian period in the guise of Venus; 65. Torso of the Discobolos of Myron, badly restored by Monnot as a fighting gladiator; 67. Cupid as archer, a good copy of the celebrated work by Lysippos; 68. Hercules slaying the Hydra (so restored by Algardi: and the antique model he used can be seen beside it. It was more probably intended to represent Hercules capturing the hind). 4a. Relief of a man and wife, probably reading a will; 7. Leda and the Swan, replica of a work attributed to Timotheos (4C BC); 8. Head of Marsyas, probably a Hellenistic original; 10. Drunken old woman, perhaps after Myron the Younger, a Pergamene sculptor of the end of the 3C BC; 22. Psyche winged, from a Hellenistic original; 24. Head of Dionysos, a good copy from a 4C BC original; 31. Minerva, copy of a bronze of c 400 BC; 34. Decorative vase (krater) of the 1C AD, resting on a *well-head from Hadrian's Villa, with archaistic decoration representing the procession of the twelve gods (Dii Consentes).

Room VII (CABINET OF VENUS), contains the celebrated *Capitoline Venus, found in the 17C in a house near San Vitale, a superbly modelled statue of Parian marble. It is a Roman replica of a Hellenistic original, thought to be derived from the Cnidian Aphrodite of Praxiteles, and was beautifully cleaned in 1992.

Room VIII (HALL OF THE DOVES) is named from a delicate *mosaic (9) from Hadrian's Villa, after a work by Sosias of Pergamon; 8. Sarcophagus with the story of Prometheus (3C AD); 23. Herm of Hermes Propylaios; 37. Diana of Ephesus; 52. Front panel of a sarcophagus, with the Triumph of Bacchus. In glass cases: 53. Tabula Iliaca or Trojan Tablet, a plaque with small reliefs representing the Trojan cycle, by Theodorus (1C AD); 76. Piece of a shield of Achilles by the same sculptor. In the centre of the room is a charming little statue of a child protecting a dove, a Roman copy of a Greek work of the 2C BC (wrongly restored with a snake).

Palazzo dei Conservatori

The **PALAZZO DEI CONSERVATORI** (Pl. 4; 7) was rebuilt by Nicholas V about 1450 and remodelled after 1564 by Giacomo della Porta and Guidetto Guidetti from a design by Michelangelo. It contains the **Sale dei Conservatori**, the **Museo del Palazzo dei Conservatori**, and the **Pinacoteca**. The first two occupy the first floor, and the Pinacoteca is arranged on the second floor. Adjoining the building, and reached from the Museo del Palazzo dei Conservatori, is the **Museo Nuovo**, which is at ground level, but has been closed since 1984.

Ground Floor. Inner Court. On the right are fragments of a colossal statue (c 12m high) of Constantine the Great, including the head, hand, and foot, which were brought from the Basilica of Constantine in 1486. The body of the statue was made in wood. Near the head is an inscription from the time of Boniface VIII. On the left are bases and transennae with sculptured representations of provinces and nations subject to Rome, which once decorated the Temple of Hadrian in the Piazza di Pietra. Above is an inscription from the arch erected in AD 51 on Via Lata to celebrate the conquest of Britain by Claudius. Beneath the portico at the farther end, a figure of Roma from the time of Trajan or Hadrian, and statues of Barbarians.

Beyond the ticket office a **staircase** leads up to the **First Landing**. Here have been displayed since the 16C four reliefs from triumphal arches, three of them celebrating Marcus Aurelius and his military victories and triumph in 176, including a scene of the emperor sacrificing before the Temple of Jupiter Capitolinus. The fourth panel comes from an arch in Via di Pietra. **Second Landing**: Hadrian, relief from the demolished Arco di Portogallo. The *statue of Charles of Anjou, by Arnolfo di Cambio or his workshop, was made for Santa Maria in Aracoeli c 1270. From this landing at the top of the stairs open the Sale dei Conservatori.

Sale dei Conservatori

Room I, Sala degli Orazi e Curiazi. Frescoes by Cavalier d'Arpino, representing episodes from the reigns of the early kings. *Urban VIII, marble statue, a studio work begun by Bernini; *Innocent X, bronze by Algardi. Here in 1957 the Treaty of Rome, the foundation of the European Economic Community, was signed by Italy, Belgium, France, West Germany, Luxembourg, and Holland.

Room II, Sala dei Capitani. Handsome doors in carved wood (17C); more frescoes from Roman history, by Tommaso Laureti, and 16–17C statues, including one of Alessandro Farnese and of Marcantonio Colonna.

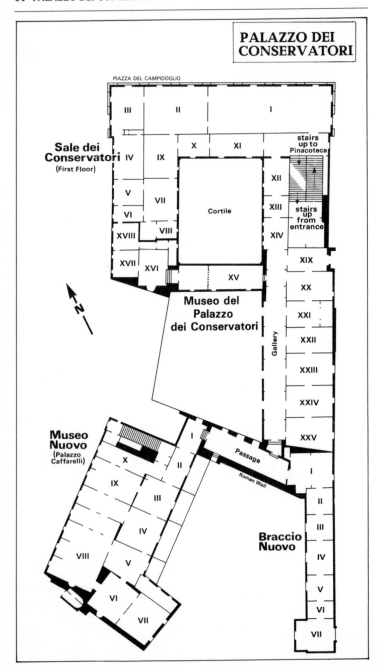

Room III, Sala dei Trionfi di Mario. Frieze by Michelangelo Alberti and Giacomo Rocchetti representing the triumph of Emilius Paulus over Perseus of Macedon. The most famous of the bronzes presented to the Conservatori by Sixtus IV are exhibited here. In the middle is the celebrated *Spinario, or Boy plucking a thorn from his foot. This was formerly known as the 'Fedele Capitolino', because it was thought to be the portrait of Marcius, a Roman messenger who would not delay his mission though tortured by a thorn in his foot. It is a delicate Hellenistic composition in the eclectic style of the 1C BC. Also displayed here: bronze *head, known as L. Junius Brutus, of Etruscan or Italic workmanship of the 3C BC; Camillus, or acolyte (1C AD); bronze krater with an inscription, the gift of King Mithridates to a gymnastic association, part of the booty from a Mithridatic war, found at Anzio; fine sarcophagus front (3C AD).

Room IV, Sala della Lupa, with more frescoes from Roman history. On the wall opposite the windows are fragments of the Fasti Consulares et Trium-phales, from the inner walls of the Arch of Augustus in the Forum, in a frame designed by Michelangelo. These are records of Roman magistrates and of triumphs of the great captains of Rome in 13 BC–AD 12. The famous *She-wolf of Rome is thought to be an Etruscan bronze of the late 6C or early 5C BC, probably belonging to the school of Vulca, an Etruscan sculptor of Veio. It originally stood on the Capitol and may be the wolf which was struck by lightning in 65 BC, when the hind feet are said to have been damaged. It was taken to the Lateran Palace sometime in the Middle Ages. The twins were added by Antonio del Pollaiolo c 1509.

Room V, Sala delle Oche, an interesting example of a 17C apartment, contains a figure of Isis and two 'geese', or more probably ducks (antique bronzes); a bronze bust of Michelangelo; and a marble head of Medusa, by Bernini. In the centre is a mastiff in rare green marble.

Room VI, Sala delle Aquile. From here there is access to Rooms XVI–XVIII of the Museo del Palazzo dei Conservatori (see below). **Room VII, Sala degli Arazzi**. Tapestries executed for the municipality; one shows the goddess Roma, the others represent the Birth of Romulus and Remus (from the painting by Rubens in the Capitoline Gallery), the Vestal Tutia, and the 'defeatist' schoolmaster of Falerii punished by Camillus.

Room VIII, Cappella Nuova. On the altar, Madonna in glory with Saints Peter and Paul, by Avanzino Nucci. **Room IX, Sala delle Guerre Puniche**, is decorated with frescoes by Giacomo Ripanda. In the middle, two girls playing, Hellenistic works (removed for restoration). **Room X, Cappella Vecchia**. On the ceiling, frescoes and stuccoes, by Alberti and Rocchetti; on the walls, Madonna and angels, by Antonio da Viterbo. **Room XI, corridor**. 16C Flemish tapestry; Roman scenes by Gaspare Vanvitelli. The corridor leads back to the landing, where, to the right, is the entrance to the Museo del Palazzo dei Conservatori.

Museo del Palazzo dei Conservatori

Rooms XII, XIII, XIV, Sale dei Fasti Moderni. These rooms contain lists of the chief magistrates of Rome since 1640, and a collection of busts and herms. **Room XII**. 8. Fragment of a group of a giant fighting with two satyrs, derived from the Gigantomachia of Pergamon. **Room XIII**. 2. Cow, Roman copy, thought to be derived from the Cow of Myron; 4. Bust of Faustina, wife of Antoninus Pius; 5. Sarcophagus, depicting a Dionysiac ceremony; 6. Bust of Sabina, wife of Hadrian. **Room XIV**. 4. Panther and wild boar in combat; Roman Imperial busts. From the gallery (see below) is the entrance (right) into Room XV.

Room XV, Sala degli Orti Lamiani, containing sculptures found in the Lamiani Gardens, on the Esquiline. 3. Old fisherman; 5. Old woman with a lamb, two Hellenistic statues of great realism; 4. Seated *girl, a remarkably graceful figure, recently restored. It is probably a Roman copy of a Greek original of the 3C BC. 7. Centaur's head, probably an original of Pergamene art; (in the second part of the gallery) 12. Bust of Commodus as Hercules, a work of considerable refinement; 13, 14. Tritons, perhaps its supporters; 15. Female statue, after an original of the 4C BC. In the centre, *29. Esquiline Venus, a young girl probably connected with the cult of Isis, an eclectic work dating from the 1C BC. The pavement in marble and alabaster is from the Esquiline.

Room XVI, Sala dei Magistrati (admission from Room VI of the Sale dei Conservatori, see above). The sculptures here are being cleaned and restored in situ. 2, 5. Roman umpires starting a race in the time of Constantine; column of rare green breccia from Egypt; inscriptions recording the conferment of Roman citizenship on Petrarch, Michelangelo, Titian, and Bernini; 4. Artemis, from a 4C original, restored to represent Christian Rome; 6. The emperor Decius as Mars.

The *Sale dei Monumenti Arcaici** (Rooms XVII–XVIII). **Room XVII**. In the centre, *10. Torso of an Amazon (late 6C BC), designed for the angle of the temple pediment of Apollo Daphnephoros at Eretria. 2. Headless female statue from a bronze original c 460 BC; 4. Fragment of a stele (5 or 4C BC); 5. Latona, from a 5C original; 7, 9. Two young initiates of the Eleusinian mysteries. **Room XVIII**. 6, 7. Korai in the Archaizing style of the early Imperial era; 8. Nike, probably from a 5C original; 10. Fragment of a stele of Attic workmanship; 11 Head of a lion (5C); 12. Stele representing a girl with a dove (late 6C).

Gallery. 14. Colossal foot, probably of the Rhodian school; 35. Copy of the 'Grande Ercolanese' (original formerly at Dresden); 41. Relief of a 'Scaenae frons' (1–2C AD); 44. Aedicula, or shrine, dedicated to the Earth Mother; 53, 54. Athletes, from 4C types; 56. Fragment of a relief from the Auditorium of Maecenas; 58. Claudia Justa as Fortune (2C AD); 68. Youth, perhaps from an original of the Polykleitan school. **Room XIX** has a fine display of Egyptian *works (well labelled), many from the Serapeum in Campo Marzio. They include: statuette of Ramesses II; sphinx of Pharaoh Arnasis II (568–526 BC); two apes from the tomb of Nectanebes II (358–341 BC); and a Roman crocodile. **Room XX**. Sarcophagi with the Good Shepherd; inscriptions; 13. Head of a Roman matron (5–6C AD). **Room XXI, Sala del Camino**, with remains of a chimneypiece (camino) of the Conservatori. 1. Sarcophagus, with the Calydonian boar hunt. In glass cases: Greek red- and black-figure vases, and antefixes from Capua (6–5C); in a case towards the gallery, Tragliatella oinochoe (7C BC) with paintings and graffiti, and below, Attic kylix of 470 BC from Cerveteri.

Room XXII, Prima Sala Castellani, contains part of the collection presented by Augusto Castellani, the fruit of excavations between 1860 and 1866 in southern Etruria and Lazio. In glass cases along the walls: Etruscan, Italic, and Faliscan vases. In the centre of the room: *Capitoline Tensa, reconstruction of a triumphal chariot overlaid with bronze, which carried the images of the gods at the opening of the Circensian games; Etruscan statuette in terracotta from Cerveteri (end of 7C BC).

Room XXIII, Seconda Sala Castellani. In glass cases along the walls: Corinthian and Attic vases, with red and black figures (6C BC) including (No. 64) the Amphora of Nikosthenes. In the middle of the room: *krater of Aristonothos, with Odysseus and the Cyclops (7C); (No. 132) hydria from Ceretani; three sides of an Etruscan funerary bed, with animal reliefs.

Room XXIV, Sala dei Bronzi. 2, 3, 8. Head, hand, and globe from a colossal statue of Constans II; 5. Rear half of a colossal bull, of very fine workmanship; 6. Globe which originally adorned the Vatican Obelisk, damaged by a musket shot during the Sack of Rome in 1527; *10. Horse, since its restoration thought to be a Greek original dating from the early 4C BC (removed). *11. Bed with exquisite decoration, of the 1C AD; *12. Litter, composed of bronze, found on the Esquiline by Castellani. In a glass case, to the right of the door to Room XXV, statuette of a Lar, with rhyton and patera; statuette of Hecate.

Room XXV, Sala degli Orti Mecenaziani, containing sculptures found in the Gardens of Maecenas on the Esquiline. In the centre, *13. So-called 'Auriga', or charioteer mounting (copy of a 5C original). Since its recent restoration this statue is thought to represent a hero, possibly Theseus, driving his chariot (it was formerly attached to a horse, also displayed here). 2. Statue of Hercules, from an original by Lysippos; 3. Eros(?), from an early 4C BC original; 6. Punishment of Marsyas, in Phrygian marble, probably of the Rhodian school; 7. Head of Augustus; 8. Hygieia, Roman copy of a Hellenistic original; *9. Dancing Maenad, in relief, from an original by Kallimachos; 10. Headless statue of Aphrodite, a fine copy of an Ionic Greek original; *11. Head of an Amazon, from an original by Polykleitos; 18. Rhyton, part of a fountain, by Pontios of Athens, in the neo-Attic style of the 1C AD.

At the end of the gallery is (left) a tufa wall belonging to the Temple of Jupiter Capitolinus (6C BC; see above). Here is the entrance to the **Braccio Nuovo**, or New Wing, seven rooms arranged in 1950–52 and devoted to finds from more recent excavations. This has been closed since 1984. In the first three rooms are remains of the foundations of the Temple of Jupiter Capitolinus. The collection of sculpture includes the frieze from the pediment of the Temple of Apollo Sosianus (or Apollo Medico), three columns of which remain in front of the Theatre of Marcellus. Representing a battle between Greeks and Amazons, with Athena in the centre, this is now thought to be a Greek work of the 5C BC. From the same temple is a Greek statue of Apollo shooting an arrow, perhaps by Pythagoras of Rhegion.

Another important work here is Aristogeiton, the best replica of one of the two statues of the tyrannicides by Kritios and Nesiotes (477–476 BC), which stood in the Agora at Athens. Also preserved here is a fragment of a fresco from a tomb of the early 3C BC possibly showing Q. Fabius Rullianus, consul in 322, the earliest known example of Roman painting.

The **Museo Nuovo** in the **Palazzo Caffarelli**, at the SW end of the Palazzo dei Conservatori, on the other side of the garden, has also been closed for many years. This palazzo was built for Giovanni Pietro Caffarelli in 1580 by Gregorio Canonico. Formerly the German Embassy, it was taken over by the Italian Government in 1918, and, after restoration, was opened as a museum in 1925. For some time it was known as the Museo Mussolini. Some of the ten rooms are now used as a restoration laboratory. The most notable pieces in the collection include: the Muse Polyhymnia; satyrs, maenads, and hermaphrodites after a work at Pergamon by Kephisodotos the

Younger; group of a lion attacking a horse; and a colossal statue of Athena, a fine reproduction of an original by Kresilas.

Pinacoteca Capitolina

This gallery of paintings, founded in 1749 by Benedict XIV, was based on the Pio and Sacchetti collections, formed respectively by Prince Gilberto Pio of Savoy and Cardinal Sacchetti. In the 19C it lost some of its treasures to the Vatican Picture Gallery and to the Accademia di San Luca. It was later enriched by the Cini bequest, which included some interesting 14–15C paintings from the Sterbini collection, as well as ceramics. The Pinacoteca is particularly important for its 16–18C Italian and foreign works.

The gallery is on the second floor of Palazzo dei Conservatori. On the **stair landing**: Apotheosis of Sabina, relief from the Arco di Portogallo (see Rte 7); head of a priest of Isis(?); bull attacked by a tigress, two examples of marble intarsia work from the basilica of Junius Bassus on the Esquiline (4C AD).

Room I. Domenico Panetti, Portrait of a girl; Dosso Dossi, Holy Family; Mazzolino, Christ and the Doctors; Emilian School (1513), *Madonna and Child with Saints; Garofalo, *Annunciation, Madonna in Glory, Holy Family; Francesco Francia(?), Presentation in the Temple; Scarsellino, Adoration of the Magi.

Room II. Paolo Veronese, Strength, Temperance, Rape of Europa; Girolamo Savoldo, *Portrait of a Lady as St Margaret; Gentile Bellini (attrib.), Portrait of a man; Giovanni Bellini, *Portrait of a young man; Palma Vecchio, *Woman taken in adultery; Titian, *Baptism of Christ; Lorenzo Lotto, Man with crossbow; Domenico Tintoretto, Scourging of Christ, Crown of Thorns, Baptism of Christ, *St Mary Magdalene.

Room III. Bartolomeo Passarotti, two portraits of unknown men; Portrait of a man with dog; Van Dyck, the engravers Pieter de Jode, father and son, the painters Luke and Cornelius de Wael; copy of a painting by Jacopino del Conte of Michelangelo; Guido Reni, self-portrait; Rubens, Romulus and Remus fed by the wolf (finished by pupils); Federico Zuccari, self-portrait; 17C Roman school, *Portrait of a man; Salvator Rosa, soldier, witch; Jean Leclerc (attrib.), *Christ with the doctors; Carlo Maratta, Holy Family; Il Borgognone, two battle scenes; Simon Vouet, allegory; Luca Cambiaso, Madonna and Child; Metsù, Crucifixion; Guercino, Holy Family; Denis Calvaert, Marriage of St Catherine.

Room IV. Mainly 14C and 15C works. Cola dell'Amatrice, *Death and Assumption of the Virgin; Macrino d'Alba, *Madonna and saints; Barnaba da Modena, *Ascension; Giovanni Antonio Sogliani, Madonna and Child; School of central Italy (1376), Annunciation, Nativity, Presentation in the Temple, Flight into Egypt, Massacre of the Innocents; Follower of Pietro Lorenzetti, St Mary Magdalene and St Bartholomew; Niccolò di Pietro Gerini, Trinity.

To the right is **Room V** (the CINI GALLERY), containing part of the bequest of Count Giuseppe Cini (1881), and including a fine collection of bronzes and *ceramics from various sources, including excellent Saxon porcelain, clocks, and tobacco boxes. At the end, *St John the Baptist by Caravaggio (there is a replica of this painting in the Galleria Doria). The MEDAGLIERE (adm by special permission), contains a rich collection of Roman, medieval, and modern coins and medals.

Room VI. Pier Francesco Mola, Diana and Endymion, Esther and Ahasuerus; Pietro da Cortona, Rape of the Sabines, Sacrifice of Polyxena, Triumph of Bacchus; Pietro Testa, Joseph sold into bondage; Crescenzio Onofri, landscapes. (Above the window), bust of Benedict XIV; inlaid 17C cabinets. The statue of Hercules in gilded bronze was found in the time of Sixtus IV in the demolition of the Ara Maxima, near the Forum Boarium.

Room VII (to right of Room IV). Domenichino, Sibyl; Guercino, St John Baptist; Giovanni Lanfranco, Herminia among the shepherds; Guido Reni, Magdalen, Anima Beata; Guercino, St Petronilla, a vast canvas, formerly in St Peter's, Antony and Cleopatra, St Matthew and the angel, Persian Sibyl; Elisabetta Sirani, Ulysses and Circe; Francesco Albani, Nativity of the Virgin; Caravaggio, *Gipsy fortune-teller.

Room VIII (left). Pietro da Cortona, Madonna and Child; Veronese, Mary Magdalene; School of Tintoretto, Pentecost; Guido Reni, Christ Child and St John; Agostino Tassi(?), two landscapes; Poussin, Triumph of Flora (replica of a painting in the Louvre).

Room IX. Garofalo, Holy Family, Marriage of Catherine; Guido Reni, Madonna and Child with Saints Alberto and Cecilia; Francesco Albani, Madonna and Child; Annibale Carracci, Madonna and Child; Lodovico Carracci, Head of a boy, a very fine early work; Annibale Carracci, St Francis adoring the Crucifix.

PALAZZO SENATORIO (Pl. 4; 7), the central palace in Piazza del Campidoglio, is the official seat of the Mayor of Rome. An 11C fortress was built by the Corsi on the remains of the ancient Tabularium (see below), and the Senate was probably installed here c 1150. The medieval castle with four towers was renewed in the 13C and redesigned by Michelangelo in the 16C. The present façade (1592), by Giacomo della Porta and Girolamo Rainaldi, is a modification of Michelangelo's design. In front of the double staircase, with converging flights, is a fountain with two colossal statues (2C AD) of the Tiber (right) and the Nile (left); in the recess is a porphyry statue of Minerva, found at Cori and transformed into the Dea Roma. The palace is crowned by a bell-tower (1582), with a clock, a statue of Minerva, and a gilded cross; two bells (1803–04) replace the famous *Patarina*, which had been installed in 1200 to summon the people to 'Parlamento'.

The INTERIOR may only be visited by special permission and previous appointment (entrance in Via San Pietro in Carcere). On the first floor in the COUNCIL CHAMBER is a colossal marble statue of Julius Caesar (the only statue of him which survives), of the period of Trajan, and in the antechamber, L'Aurora by Pietro da Cortona. The ROOM OF THE FLAG contains a fragment of the 14C flag of St George, from the church of San Giorgio in Velabro. In the PROTOMOTECA is a large collection of busts of famous people, mostly dating from the 18C and 19C. The GREAT HALL has a Canova monument, and from here there is access to a terrace with a remarkable view of the Forum.

The **Tabularium** or depository of the State archives survives beneath Palazzo Senatorio, and its great blocks of porous tufa built into the unhewn rock dominate the view of the hill from the Forum. It was erected in 78 BC by Q. Lutatius Catulus: the inscription stone can still be seen by one entrance on the left flank of Palazzo Senatorio. Beyond this, in Via San Pietro in Carcere, is the arcaded gallery of the Tabularium (no adm) with a splendid view of the Forum. Here, also, is part of the frieze from the Temple of Concord (see Rte 2), and in the adjoining gallery (seen through a closed iron gate) is a cast of part of the frieze from the Temple of Vespasian, another section of which can be seen through the arch, still in position above three columns at the foot of the Capitol.

For admission to the Tabularium special permission is required (apply at Palazzo Caffarelli). There are several entrances, as a gallery (which now contains numerous inscriptions, some in Greek) was constructed in 1938 under the Piazza and Palazzo Senatorio, connecting it with Palazzo dei Conservatori and Palazzo del Museo Capitolino. The Tabularium had a rectangular plan, with a central court and two storeys. The first storey is the most interesting; the lower floor was used as a medieval prison and is now a store. Here are considerable remains of the **Temple of Veiovis**, erected first in 196 BC, and rebuilt after fire in the 1C BC. The pronaos is orientated towards Via del Campidoglio, and the podium and cella are well preserved. The external wall of the Tabularium may be seen on two sides; a small gap was left between it and the Temple. Behind the Temple is a colossal marble statue of Veiovis (1C AD, after a 5C BC type), found in the cella. To the right is a perfectly preserved staircase of the Republican period, leading steeply down to the Forum. It was blocked at the bottom by a tufa wall (still in place) when the Temple of Vespasian was built.

From Piazza del Campidoglio the short Via del Campidoglio skirting the right side of Palazzo Senatorio runs downhill, past a stretch of Roman road, to a terrace with an excellent •view of the Forum backed by the Colosseum. The rest of the Capitol Hill can be seen by taking Via di Monte Tarpeo and then Via del Tempio di Giove back uphill from the terrace (or by the staircase which ascends from Piazza del Campidoglio to a portico named after Vignola, the arches of which have been closed in with glass). At the top of Via del Tempio di Giove, enclosed by a modern wall and very much below the level of the road, are the remains of the E angle of the façade of the Temple of Jupiter (see above).

From the peaceful gardens on the terrace known as the BELVEDERE DI MONTE TARPEO there is another extensive •view of Rome to the S and SE, taking in the Forum, the Palatine, the Baths of Caracalla, the Aventine, and the Tiber. The precipice below is thought to be the notorious Tarpeian Rock of ancient Rome, from which condemned criminals were flung, although it has also been connected with the N side of the hill. The road continues past a little 19C temple to the edge of the hill (where steps lead down to Via di Teatro di Marcello), and then turns right under an arch to skirt the side of the hill above gardens and paths which descend to its foot.

In front of the 16C **Palazzo Caffarelli**, built on the site of the Temple of Jupiter, there is another splendid panorama of Rome, this time towards St Peter's. The palace houses the offices of the Capitoline museums and a selection of exhibits from the **Antiquarium Comunale** (admission only with special permission). This extremely important archaeological collection, with some 60,000 works, has been all but closed to the public for decades: part of it has remained on the Celian hill, where it was first exhibited in 1894. The Antiquarium was founded in 1885 for objects found during excavations in Rome and illustrates the everyday life of the city from earliest times to the end of the Empire (including material dating from the 9–6C BC from the Esquiline necropolis, and finds from excavations near Sant'Omobono and on the Capitol). As well as frescoes, mosaics and bronzes, the collection includes fragments of the *Forma Urbis* a marble 'map' of ancient Rome in 193–211 AD found in the Forum of Peace in 1562, and one of the most important documents for our knowledge of the topography of the Roman city.

*SANTA MARIA IN ARACOELI (Pl. 4; 5), an austere brick-built church, dating from before the 7C, when it was already considered ancient, stands on the highest point of the Capitoline Hill. It is approached by a very steep monumental flight of steps, but from the top of the hill it is more easily reached by steps to the E of the Capitoline Museum. The church occupies the site of the Roman citadel, where, according to medieval tradition, the Tiburtine Sibyl foretold to Augustus the imminent coming of Christ in the words, 'Ecce ara primogeniti Dei': hence the name Aracoeli, Church of the Altar of Heaven. In the 10C the church belonged to the Benedictines; in 1250 Innocent IV handed it over to the Franciscans, who rebuilt it in the Romanesque style. The façade, overlooking the great staircase from Piazza d'Aracoeli, was never completed. The staircase was built in 1348 as a thank-offering for deliverance from a plague.

In the Middle Ages the church was the meeting-place of the Roman Council. Here Rienzo addressed the assembly after the events of Whitsun 1347; Charles of Anjou held his parliament of the Romans; and Marcantonio Colonna celebrated his triumph after the battle of Lepanto. It was also in this church, as Gibbon 'sat musing amidst the ruins of the Capitol, while the friars were singing vespers, that the idea of writing the Decline and Fall of the City first started to his mind' (5 October 1764). In the tympanum of the S door is a mosaic of the Madonna and two angels by the school of Pietro Cavallini.

The INTERIOR (open 7.00–12.00, 15.30–dusk), hung with chandeliers, although freely restored has retained its grandeur and severity. The ceiling of the NAVE, with naval emblems and much gold ornamentation, dates from 1575 and commemorates the victory of Lepanto (1571). The 22 antique columns in the nave, of varying sizes and styles, were taken from pagan buildings; the third on the left bears the inscription 'a cubiculo Augustorum', and the fourth on the left has a 15C Sienese fresco of the Madonna and Child. Many tombs are set in the Cosmatesque pavement. To the right of the central door is the *tomb of Cardinal d'Albret, by Andrea Bregno (1465), and the *tomb slab of the archdeacon Giovanni Crivelli (1432; very worn), signed by Donatello; on the left is the tomb of the astronomer Lodovico Grato Margani (1531), by the school of Andrea Sansovino, who himself executed the figure of Christ.

There are notices on each chapel describing their contents (and coin-operated lights). SOUTH AISLE. First chapel (Bufalini): *frescoes from the life of St Bernardino, considered among the finest works of Pinturicchio (c 1486; restored by Camuccini); between the second and third chapels, colossal statue of Gregory XIII, by Pier Paolo Olivieri. Fifth chapel, 16C paintings by Girolamo Muziano; the sixth chapel is a pretty 17C work designed by Giovanni Battista Contini. By the south door (right), monument of Pietro da Vicenza by Andrea Sansovino, and (left) tomb of Cecchino Bracci (d 1545) by Pietro Urbano on a design of Michelangelo. In the last chapel are two Caravaggesque paintings by Daniele Seiter.

In the crossing, on the pilasters facing the high altar, are two *ambones, by Lorenzo and Giacomo di Cosma (c 1200). SOUTH TRANSEPT. The Savelli Chapel contains two fine *tombs: on the left is that of Luca Savelli attributed to Arnolfo di Cambio, with a 3C Roman sarcophagus beneath, and on the right, the 14C tomb of Vana Aldobrandi, wife of Luca, with a statue of her son Honorius III. The Cappella di Santa Rosa (seen through the Cappella del Santissimo Sacramento, to the right) has a fine mosaic of the Madonna enthroned between Saints John the Baptist and Francis dating from the 13C.

CHOIR (being restored). Over the high altar is a small *Madonna, known as the 'Madonna d'Aracoeli', usually attributed to a 10C master. Here from 1512 to 1565 was hung Raphael's 'Madonna of Foligno' (now in the Vatican Pinacoteca), commissioned by Sigismondo Conti, whose tomb is in the pavement near the stalls on the S side. In the APSE, on the left, is the fine monument of Giovanni Battista Savelli (school of Andrea Bregno, 1498).

In the centre of the NORTH TRANSEPT is the little Temple of St Helena, or Santa Cappella, a 17C shrine (reconstructed in the 19C) with eight columns. Beneath it (light) remains of an altar (12C or 13C) showing the apparition of the Virgin to Augustus. Excavations also revealed remains of a Roman wall here. At the end of the transept is the beautiful Cosmati *tomb of Cardinal Matteo di Acquasparta (d 1302), mentioned by Dante ('Paradiso', xii, 124), with a fresco by Pietro Cavallini. To the right is the entrance to the Cappella del Santissimo Bambino, which contained a figure of the Infant Christ, reputed to have been carved from the wood of an olive tree in the Garden of Gethsemane and an object of immense veneration (see below). This was stolen in 1994.

NORTH AISLE, fifth chapel, St Paul, by Girolamo Muziano, and the fine tomb of Filippo Della Valle (1494; left), by Michele Marini or the school of Andrea Riccio; third chapel, St Antony, by Benozzo Gozzoli, and the Renaissance tomb of Antonio Albertoni (1509; right); between the third and second chapels, a statue of Paul III. The second chapel (Cappella del Presepio) is open only during the Christmas festival, when the Christ Child is exhibited (from the Cappella del Santissimo Bambino; see above) and children recite little poems and speeches in front of its crib.

The overwhelming **MONUMENT OF VICTOR EMMANUEL II** (Pl. 4; 5) was inaugurated in 1911 to symbolise the achievement of Italian unity. Some 80m high, it changed irrevocably the aspect of the city, throwing out of scale the Capitol Hill itself, and causing indiscriminate demolition in the area. Familiarly known as 'the wedding cake' or 'Mussolini's typewriter', it can only be described as a colossal monstrosity. It was begun in 1885 by Giuseppe Sacconi, winner of an international competition in which there were 98 entries. He used an incongruous dazzling white 'botticino' marble from Brescia to further alienate it from its surroundings. It has been closed to the public for many years, although there are now plans to reopen it and use it for exhibitions and conferences.

At the sides of the monument are fountains representing the Tyrrhenian Sea, by Pietro Canonica, and the Adriatic, as well as the remains of the tomb of Gaius Publicius Bibulus, dating from the early 1C BC. Above the stylobate are sculptures by Ettore Ximenes, Leonardo Bistolfi, Ludovico Poliaghi, and Augusto Rivalta. The grave of Italy's Unknown Soldier from the First World War, guarded by two sentinels, lies at the foot of the Altare della Patria by Angelo Zanelli. The equestrian statue of Victor Emmanuel II is by Enrico Chiaradia. The two Quadrigae are by Paolo Bartolini and Carlo Fontana.

The **Museo Centrale del Risorgimento**, entered from Via di San Pietro in Carcere, has been closed for many years. It contains exhibits illustrating the story of Italy's struggle for independence, important archives, and a section devoted to the First World War.

Across Piazza Venezia (left) is the battlemented *Palazzo di Venezia, the first great Renaissance palace in Rome. Giuliano da Maiano, Bernardo Rossellino, and Leon Battista Alberti have all been suggested as its architect, but it has recently been attributed to Francesco del Borgo. It was begun in 1455, enlarged in 1464, and finally finished in the 16C. It was built, partly of stone from the Colosseum, for the Venetian Cardinal Pietro Barbo, afterwards Paul II (1464–71), the first of the great Renaissance popes. Barbo is said to have built the palace in order to view the horse-races in the Corso. It later became a papal residence, and was often occupied as such even after it had been given by Pius IV (1559–65) to the Venetian Republic for its embassy. Charles VIII of France stayed here after entering Rome with 20,000 soldiers in 1494. From the Treaty of Campoformio in 1797 until 1915 it was the seat of the Austrian ambassador to the Vatican.

In 1917 Italy resumed possession and the palace was restored. During the Fascist régime it was occupied by Mussolini, who had his office in the Sala del Mappamondo. Some of his most famous speeches were made from the balcony overlooking Piazza di Venezia. The door in the piazza is finely carved and attributed to Giuliano da Maiano. The picturesque inner court (reached from 49 Piazza di San Marco), with its tall palm trees, has a large unfinished 15C loggia on two sides, of beautiful proportions. In the centre is a fountain by Carlo Monaldi (1730).

Adjoining the palace and facing the Via and Piazza di San Marco, to the S and E, is the **Palazzetto di Venezia**. This was originally (c 1467) in Piazza di Venezia, but was moved to its present position in 1911 because it obstructed the view of the Victor Emmanuel Monument. To see the beautiful court and garden, special permission is needed (apply at 49 Piazza di San Marco).

The *MUSEO DEL PALAZZO DI VENEZIA (admission see p 47) occupies several of the papal apartments and many rooms in the Palazzetto di Venezia. The entrance is in Via del Plebiscito. The museum was finally reopened in 1988 after years of closure and the collections are now displayed in modern show-cases designed by Franco Minissi. However the museum has a shortage of staff and some of the thirty rooms often have to be kept closed as a result. In addition to interesting paintings, there is a good collection of wood sculptures, bronzes, Romanesque and 14C ivories, majolica, church silver, and terracottas. It is the only museum of the decorative arts in the city. Up to now the State rooms have been open only for temporary exhibitions, but these may one day be integrated into the Museum and no longer used for exhibitions. These include the Sala Regia, the Sala del Concistoro, the Sala del Mappamondo (so called from a large map mentioned in 1534), and the Sala delle Fatiche d'Ercole ('Labours of Hercules'), named from a painted frieze by the school of Mantegna. The important collection of arms and armour (some of them left to the city by the Odescalchi in 1976) and the 15–17C tapestries (German, Flemish, and Italian), formerly exhibited in these rooms, are not yet on display. The deposits also include the Enrichetta Wurts collection of silver (presented to Mussolini in 1930), mostly German, English, and American ware dating from the 17C to the late 19C, and Oriental porcelain and ceramics.

From Via del Plebiscito a monumental staircase by Luigi Marangoni (1930) leads up to the first floor and the ticket office. To the left is the Appartamento Cibo, the apartments of the Cardinals of San Marco, with some good ceilings and colourful floors, where the first part of the collection is arranged. The rooms are un-numbered but the works are all labelled.

Room 1. Architectural fragments (early 8C–end of 9C) including a well-head; bronzes, ivories, including a 10C *triptych of the 'Deesis' and Saints. **Room 2**. Sculptural fragments; the marble transenna with donors is attributed to Giovanni di Stefano (fl. 1366–91). **Room 3** (to the left). Seated statue of a Pope, sometimes identified as Nicholas IV or as Boniface VIII, a Roman work of the late 13C. The *Madonna of Acuto, an early 13C wood polychrome seated statue, the earliest known work of its kind; *Crucifix, probably painted by a follower of Giotto in the last decade of the 13C. It comes from the church of San Tommaso dei Cenci (and was originally in Santa Maria in Aracoeli).

Room 4 (beyond Room 2). *Head of a woman by Nicola Pisano; 13C relief of an Angel in gilded bronze and cloisonné enamel; 13C Byzantine *crosses, and a *relief of the Crucifixion; Christ Pantocrator, an unusual work in metal and enamel (13C, Byzantine); gilded bronze incised *lunette from the Santuario della Mentorella near Palestrina (thought to be an early 13C German work). It may have been the back of an episcopal seat. To the left, **Room 5** has a ceiling with signs of the zodiac. Here are 14C ceramics from Orvieto, and early medieval ceramics from Rome and Lazio, and a valuable series of dower chests.

In **Room 6** (beyond Room 4) is exhibited the Sterbini collection of paintings, mostly Tuscan 'fondi oro', all of them in good condition. Three exquisite small works: *triptych by the early 15C Florentine school, *reliquary by the 'Master of Santa Chiara of Montefalco' and *diptych by the early 14C Sienese school. Other works include: Bicci di Lorenzo, Imprisonment and Martyrdom of St Catherine of Alexandria; Nanni di Jacopo, triptych with the Madonna and Child and angel musicians, and four saints; Cristoforo da Bologna, Madonna of Humility; 15C Spanish school, *Madonna enthroned. In the little chapel: Francesco Zaganelli da Cotignola, Christ carrying the Cross; Sassoferrato, *St Francis; Girolamo da Santacroce, Rape of Europa, Head of St Michael Archangel; Bachiacca, Vision of St Bernardino.

Room 7, the Salone Altoviti, has grotteschi on the ceiling attributed to Vasari. Here are a reliquary by Jacopo Tondi; and a 14C Venetian *triptych in wood, silver, and enamel with miniatures of the Madonna and Child, Evangelists, prophets, and stories from the Life of Christ. **Room 8**. Fine wood statues, including two of the *Magi (14C works from the Marches). To the left beyond Room 9, **Room 10** displays 12–13C seals. **Room 11** (beyond Room 8) has a view of the E end of the church of the Gesù.

The long **corridor (12)** which connects these apartments to the Palazzetto di Venezia has a splendid view of the delightful courtyard, with palms and a fountain. Here is displayed a representative collection of Italian ceramics with examples from all the main workshops (Faenza, Urbino, Montelupo, Deruta, Pesaro, Casteldurante, etc.). The second half of the corridor displays porcelain (Meissen, Sèvres, Staffordshire, etc.). The first rooms (13–15) of the Palazzetto contain some furniture. **Room 16** displays a 15C marble bust of the Venetian Cardinal Pietro Barbo (afterwards Paul II) who built Palazzo Venezia.

In **Room 17** begins the splendid display of small *bronzes, continued in **Room 18**. Here are works by Il Riccio, Nicolò Roccatagliata, Girolamo Campagna, Giovanni Francesco Susini, Pietro Tacca, Pietro Bracci, Il Moderno, Tiziano Aspetti, Giambologna, François Duquesnoy, Alessandro Algardi, Antonio Susini, and Gian Lorenzo Bernini. **Room 19**. Sculptures by Baccio da Montelupo (Head of the Redeemer), and Francesco Segala, and two *reliefs of the Miracle of St Mark by Jacopo Sansovino (models for

the bronze reliefs in the chancel of the basilica of San Marco in Venice).
Beyond Room 20, **Room 21** has small sculptures, including two models for
sculptures on the Trevi fountain.

Room 22 displays numerous busts, statuettes, and terracotta *bozzetti by
Bernini (model for an angel on Ponte Sant'Angelo and for details of his
Roman fountains), and Alessandro Algardi (bust of Giacinta Sanvitali Conti,
and St Agnes appearing to St Constance). **Room 23**. Relief of the Deposition
by Ignazio Marabitti; two 18C portraits by Vincenzo Pacetti. **Room 24**
contains a relief by Ercole Ferrata. **Room 25**. Bozzetti attributed to
Francesco Mochi and the early 17C Lombard school. Beyond the little room
(**26**) with a pretty barrel vault is the last room (**27**) of sculpture, with a head
('Seneca') attributed to Guido Reni, and a bust of Benedict XIII by Pietro
Bracci (1724).

Room 28 has been closed for conservation reasons. It contains paintings:
Giorgione(?), double Portrait; Lelio Orsi, Pietà; Giuseppe Maria Crespi,
Finding of the infant Moses, David and Abigail; Ciro Ferri, Marriage of St
Catherine; Donato Creti, Nymphs dancing; Jacob Cuyp, two portraits;
Carlo Maratta, Cleopatra; Francesco Solimena, Marriage at Cana.

Other paintings not on display include: Giovanni Bellini, *portrait of a
young man; Nicolò de' Barberi, Woman taken in adultery; Giovanni Cariani, Lovers in a landscape, portrait of a devotee; Rocco Marconi, Woman
taken in adultery; Bachiacca, Lady as St Mary Magdalene; Federico Zuccari, scenes in the life of Taddeo Zuccari; Benozzo Gozzoli, The Redeemer
(part of a fresco); Domenico Puligo, Madonna; Girolamo da Cremona,
Nativity and Annunciation (triptych); School of Giovanni Bellini, Moses
rescued from the water, Meeting of the Madonna and St Anne; Giovanni
da Modena, Crucifixion; Ottaviano Nelli, Madonna; Segna di Tura,
Madonna and Child; Paolo Veneziano, Angelic choir; Benedetto Diana,
Redeemer; Garofalo, St Jerome; Guercino, St Peter; Cornelius Johnson,
Child with a puppy; and Simone Cantarini, Madonna.

The palace is also the seat of the **Istituto Nazionale di Archeologia e
Storia dell'Arte** (entered at 49 Piazza San Marco), founded in 1922. The
library, the most important of its kind in Italy, with c 350,000 vols, was
partially reopened here in 1993, but is in urgent need of new premises (part
of it has been moved to the Collegio Romano).

At the corner of Piazza San Marco is a colossal mutilated bust of Isis, known
as 'MADAMA LUCREZIA'. It has been here since the 15C and was once used
for the display of satirical comments and epigrams (like Pasquino and
Marforio). In the garden in front (right) is a fountain (1927) with a pine-cone,
the emblem of this district, the Rione della Pigna.

In Piazza San Marco is the church of **SAN MARCO** (Pl. 3; 6), which forms
part of Palazzo di Venezia. It was founded in 336 by St Mark the Pope,
restored in 833, rebuilt in the 15C by Paul II, and again restored in the 17C
and 1744. The campanile is Romanesque, and the façade an elegant
Renaissance work with a portico and a loggia which was once used by the
pope in the benediction ceremony. Under the portico are sculptural fragments and inscriptions, and over the beautiful central door, a relief of St
Mark enthroned attributed to Isaia da Pisa (1464).

Steps lead down to the fine INTERIOR which retains its ancient basilican
form with a raised sanctuary. There is a good Renaissance ceiling and
remains of a Cosmatesque pavement (E end). The bright columns of Sicilian

jasper and the stucco reliefs in the nave (between 17C frescoes) date from the Baroque restoration in the 18C.

SOUTH SIDE: first altar, Palma Giovane, Resurrection; third chapel, Carlo Maratta, *Adoration of the Magi. Beyond a niche with a monument to Cardinal Vidman (died 1660) by Cosimo Fancelli, the fourth chapel contains 17C works by Bernardino Gagliardi. By the steps up to the presbytery is the funerary monument of Leonardo Pesaro by Antonio Canova. The chapel to the right of the high altar, by Pietro da Cortona, contains a painting of St Mark the Pope by Melozzo da Forlì and frescoes (very ruined) by Borgognone. In the APSE (coin-operated light) a *MOSAIC (c 829–30) represents Christ with saints and Gregory IV offering a model of the church. Beneath are the Lamb of God with twelve sheep representing the Apostles, and, on the arch, Christ between saints Peter and Paul. In the sacristy (if closed, ring on the left in the church porch), is a recomposed tabernacle by Mino da Fiesole and Giovanni Dalmata, and St Mark the Evangelist (much darkened) by Melozzo da Forlì.

The niches on the NORTH SIDE contain notable Baroque monuments, and here the fourth chapel has works by Francesco Mola and Borgognone. The second chapel was decorated by Emidio Sintes (1764). Remains of the earlier churches have been found beneath the pavement (not at present accessible).

2

The Roman Forum

Admission, see p 46. The admission ticket includes the Palatine (Rte 3). The main entrance is in Via dei Fori Imperiali, opposite the end of Via Cavour. There is another entrance (more convenient for the Palatine) on Via San Gregorio. There is an exit at the Arch of Titus near the Colosseum, and another exit is usually open on Via del Foro Romano, above the Basilica Julia (closed on Sundays). You need more than a single day for a complete visit to the Forum and the Palatine.

The **ROMAN FORUM (Pl. 4; 7) is the heart of ancient Rome. Here is reflected almost every event of importance in the city's development from the time of the kings through the Republican and Imperial eras to the Middle Ages. The ruins stand in the centre of modern Rome as a romantic testament to her past greatness. The site is beautifully kept and planted with trees flowers and shrubs. The visible remains are difficult to under- stand in detail without constant reference to the plans provided in the text. Important excavations are being carried out in various parts of the Forum (see below), and some areas are inaccessible because of this. At the foot of the Capitol Hill, a road which formerly cut off the monuments at the extreme W end of the Forum has been eliminated. There are plans to connect the Forum with the Capitol again via the Clivus Capitolinus.

The best comprehensive view of the Forum is from the Capitol Hill, from the terrace at the bottom of Via del Campidoglio or from the Belvedere di Monte Tarpeo (see Rte 1). The Palatine also provides a good view.

The Roman Forum from the Capitol Hill

The Forum runs WNW and ESE, following the direction of the Capitoline end of the Sacra Via and that of the Nova Via. In the following description it is taken as running W and E, the left side, looking towards the Colosseum, being N and the right side S. The plans in the text have been given this orientation.

History. The site of the Forum was originally a marshy valley lying between the Capitoline and Palatine Hills. It was bounded on the N and E by the foothills of the Quirinal and Esquiline and by the low ridge of the Velia, which connected the Palatine with the Esquiline. In the Iron Age it was used as a necropolis. Buildings appeared here after the union of the Latin villages of the Palatine with the Sabines of the Quirinal, which is traditionally said to have followed the battle of Romans and Sabines on the Palatine slopes. The first monuments of the Forum, such as the Lapis Niger, the Vulcanal, the Temple of Janus, the Regia, the Temple of Vesta, and the Curia date from the period of the kings. Tarquinius the Elder and Servius Tullius (c 616–535 BC) made the area habitable by canalising its stagnant waters into the Cloaca Maxima and it became the market-place (Forum) of Rome.

The original Forum was a rectangle bounded at the W by the Lapis Niger and the Rostra, on the E by a line through the site of the Temple of Julius Caesar, and on the N and S by two rows of shops (*tabernae*) approximately on the line of the Basilica Emilia (N) and the Basilica Julia (S). This area was about 115m by 57m. Adjacent, on the NW, was a second rectangle including the Comitium, reserved for political assemblies, or *Comitia Curiata*, the Curia, or senate-house, and the Rostra, or orators' tribune. Beyond the limits of this second square, to the E, were the Regia, seat of the Pontifex Maximus, the Temple of Vesta, and the House of the Vestals. In this direction ran the *Sacra Via*. Other streets were the *Argiletum* to the N, the *Vicus Jugarius* and the *Vicus Tuscus* to the Velabrum, the *Clivus Argentarius*, which ran between the Capitol and the Quirinal to the Via Flaminia and the Campus Martius, and the *Nova Via*, on the S side, which ran along the side of the Palatine Hill.

The Forum was therefore divided into three distinct areas: the Comitium, or political centre, the religious centre of the Regia, and the Forum proper. The area of the Forum gradually lost its character as market-place and became a centre of civic importance and the scene of public functions and ceremonies. The greengrocers and other shopkeepers were moved to the Velabrum and replaced by money-changers (*argentarii*).

In the 2C BC a new type of building, the basilica, was introduced. This large covered space was used for judicial hearings and public meetings when these could not be held outside. The new construction involved the demolition of private houses behind the tabernae. The first basilica was the Basilica Porcia, built by the censor Cato in 185 BC and destroyed in 52 BC. Others were the Basilica Emilia (179 BC), and the Basilica Sempronia (170 BC), built by T. Sempronius Gracchus, father of the tribunes, and later replaced by the Basilica Julia. The last to be built was the Basilica of Constantine (4C AD).

In 133 Tiberius Gracchus was killed in the Forum. After Julius Caesar's assassination on the Ides of March, 44 BC, his body was cremated in the Forum. He had begun the enlargement of the Forum which Sulla had planned some years before, and which was completed by Augustus. Between 44 and 27 BC the Basilica Julia, the Curia, and the Rostra were completed, the Temple of Saturn and the Regia restored, the Temple of Julius Caesar dedicated, and the Arch of Augustus erected. According to Suetonius, Augustus found the city brick and left it marble.

By this time the area of the Forum had become inadequate for the growing population and the emperors were obliged to build their own Fora (see Rte 4). A fire in the old Forum in the 3C AD caused much damage, which was repaired by Diocletian, but the area reflected the general decline of the city. Temples and sanctuaries were neglected under Christian rule and robbed of most of their treasures. The few that remained were finally despoiled in the barbarian invasions and the abandoned buildings were further damaged by earthquakes.

The medieval Roman barons, notably the Frangipani family, used the tallest of the ruined buildings as foundations for their fortress-towers, and a few churches were constructed. But most of the Forum became the *Campo Vaccino*, or cattle-pasture. Its monuments were used as quarries and its precious marbles were burned in lime-kilns. In the Renaissance the Forum provided inspiration to numerous artists. Many buildings erected from the 15C to 18C took their plans from monuments here, and often parts of the Roman edifices were reused in these buildings.

At the end of the 18C systematic excavations began of the site, which continued with little interruption through the 19C, especially after 1870. The distinguished archaeologist, Giacomo Boni, conducted the excavations from 1898–25, and found archaic monuments of great interest, and his work was continued by Alfonso Bartoli. Since 1980 excavations have been in progress at the W end of the Forum at the foot of the Capitol Hill, in the area of Santa Maria Antiqua and the Temple of Castor, behind the Basilica Emilia and the Curia, and on the northern slopes of the Palatine, between the Sacra Via and the House of the Vestals.

From the main entrance on Via dei Fori Imperiali (Pl. 4; 7) a broad path descends between the Temple of Antoninus and Faustina (left; described below) and the Basilica Emilia on the level of the ancient Forum. The **Basilica Emilia** was built by the censors M. Aemilius Lepidus and M. Fulvius Nobilior in 179 BC, restored by members of the Aemilia gens in 78 BC and rebuilt in the time of Julius Caesar. It was rebuilt in AD 22 after a fire and nearly destroyed by another fire during Alaric's sack of Rome in 410. On the side towards the Forum it faces the Sacra Via; on its W side is the Argiletum, once one of the Forum's busiest streets, which led N to the quarter of the Subura through the Forum of Nerva.

Much of this ancient building was demolished during the Renaissance in order to reuse its marble. It comprised a vast rectangular hall 70m by 29m, divided by columns into a central nave and aisles, single on the S side and double on the N. In the fine pavement of the hall, in coloured marble, are embedded some coins that fused with the bronze roof-decorations during the fire of 410. Casts of fragments of a frieze of the Republican era have been assembled below the terrace at the NE corner. On the S side, facing the Forum, was a two-storeyed portico covering a row of shops, the TABER-NAE NOVAE, still well preserved. The portico was restored during the late empire; the three granite columns which have been set up in front of the Basilica date from this time. On the W side are remains (covered) of the earliest basilica. The MACELLUM, a market building paved in peperino and

The Arch of Septimius Severus and the Column of Phocas in the Roman Forum

surrounded by columns, built in the late 3C or early 2C BC, has recently been unearthed towards the modern road.

The open space in front of the Basilica Emilia is the original **Forum**, through it runs the Sacra Via (see below). As the meeting-place of the whole population, and a market-place, the Forum was kept free of obstructions in Republican days. Here all important ceremonies and public meetings took place. Orators spoke from the Rostra, where magistrates' edicts, legal decisions, and official communications were published. The Forum was where all the main religious festivals were held, and where political offenders were executed, and the funerals of important people took place. The body of Julius Caesar was cremated here. During the Empire the

Forum lost its original character, and new buildings encroached on the area. It remained merely an official centre, and was to a great extent replaced by the new Imperial Fora.

The **Sacra Via**, the oldest street in Rome, traverses the length of the Forum. It was lined with important sanctuaries, and a tradition relates that it was the scene of the peace treaty between Romulus and the Sabine king Titus Tatius. Its oldest section is that between the Temple of Castor and the Velia. The winding road now visible, at a lower level than the later monuments on either side, dates from the late Republican era; the later Imperial road took a slightly different course between the Forum and the Arch of Titus. On the W side it was continued as the CLIVUS CAPITOLINUS, which climbed round the Portico of the Dei Consentes to the Temple of Jupiter on the Capitol. On the E side the Republican road left the Forum to the S of the Velia. In late Imperial times it was continued by another road beyond the Arch of Titus to the Arch of Constantine, near the Colosseum.

It was along the Sacra Via that a victorious general awarded a triumph passed in procession to the Capitol to offer sacrifice in the Temple of Jupiter. He rode in a chariot drawn by four horses, preceded by his captives and spoils of war, and followed by his soldiers. In the Sacra Via, by the SE corner of the Basilica Emilia, is a dedicatory inscription to Lucius Caesar, grandson and adopted son of Augustus, set up in 2 BC; there was probably an arch here dedicated to him and his brother Gaius.

On the S side of the Sacra Via is the **Temple of Julius Caesar**, the site of which marks the E limit of the original Forum. The body of Julius Caesar was brought to the Forum after the Ides of March in 44 BC, and here his body was probably cremated, and his will was read by Mark Antony. The temple was dedicated by Augustus in 29 BC in honour of the 'Divine' Julius Caesar ('Divus Julius'). Tiberius gave a funeral oration here over the body of Augustus before it was buried in his mausoleum in AD 14.

This temple (probably Corinthian prostyle hexastyle) was preceded by a terrace which was an extension of the podium. This was called the ROSTRA AD DIVI JULII, from the beaks of the Egyptian ships of Antony and Cleopatra captured at Actium with which it was decorated. Nothing remains except for the central block of the podium and the round altar (under cover), probably marking the spot where Caesar was cremated. Fragments, thought to belong to the frieze, are in the Antiquarium of the Forum. Remains of foundations on the N and S sides of the temple are thought to be those of the arcaded PORTICUS JULIA, which surrounded the temple on three sides.

About 50m farther W, near the steps of the Basilica Emilia, are the foundations of the circular SHRINE OF VENUS CLOACINA, which stood on the point where the Cloaca Maxima entered the Forum. This great drain, installed by the Tarquins, crossed the Forum from N to S on its way to the Tiber (see Rte 15). It was beside the shrine that Virginia is said to have been killed by her father to save her from the advances of the decemvir Appius Claudius Crassinus. At the W end of the Basilica Emilia is the presumed site of the SHRINE OF JANUS. its bronze doors were closed only in peace-time, which is said to have occurred only three times in the history of Rome.

To the W, in front of the Curia building (described below) lies the area of the COMITIUM, the place where the *Comitia Curiata*, representing the 30 Curiae into which the city was politically divided, met to record their votes. The earliest political activity of the Republic took place here and this was the original site of the Rostra. During the Empire the Comitium was restricted to the space between the Curia, and the Lapis Niger; under the Republic the area was much more extensive.

Here is the **Lapis Niger** with the oldest relics of the Forum. The Lapis Niger was a pavement of black marble laid to indicate a sacred spot. This was traditionally taken to be the site of the tomb of Romulus, or the shepherd Faustulus, or of Hostus Hostilius, father of the third king of Rome, but is now identified as the ancient sanctuary of Vulcan, known as the **Volcanal**. The pavement and the monuments below it were discovered in 1899, now reached by a flight of iron steps (usually closed). They comprise the base of a truncated column (possibly the base for a statue), an altar, and a square stele with inscriptions on all four sides. These provide the most ancient example of the Latin language (6C or early 5C BC) and seem to refer to a lex sacra, i.e. a warning against profaning a holy place. In the space between the pavement and the monuments, bronze and terracotta statuettes and fragments of 6C vases were found, mixed with profuse ashes (indicating a great sacrifice). These are in the Antiquarium of the Forum. Excavations to the E of the Lapis Niger have revealed some remains of the Republican ROSTRA, dating partly from 338 BC, and partly (the curved front and steps) from Sulla's time.

At the N end of the Comitium rises the *Curia Senatus, or Curia Julia. Replacing the original *Curia Hostilia* said to have been built by Tullus Hostilius and several times rebuilt, the senate house was begun by Sulla in 80 BC, and rebuilt after a fire by Julius Caesar in 44 BC. Fifteen years after Caesar's death it was completed by Augustus, who dedicated a statue of Victory in the interior. The present building dates from the time of Domitian (restored by Diocletian after a fire in 283). In 638 it was converted into the church of Sant' Adriano. In 1935–38 Alfonso Bartoli restored to it the form it had under Diocletian. The lower part of the brick façade was originally covered with marble; the upper courses were covered with stucco. It was preceded by a portico. The existing doors are copies of the originals, removed by Alexander VII to St John Lateran. A simple pediment with travertine corbels crowns the building.

The remarkable interior, 27m long, 18m wide and 21m high, has a beautiful green and maroon *pavement in opus sectile, which had been preserved beneath the floor of the church. The three broad marble-faced steps on the two long sides provided seats for c 300 senators. At the end, by the president's tribune, is a brick base which may have supported the golden statue of Victory presented by Augustus. The side walls, with niches, were partly faced with marble. The porphyry statue of Hadrian or Trajan dating from the 1–2C AD was found in recent excavations behind the building.

Also exhibited here are the *PLUTEI OF TRAJAN, or *Anaglypha Trajani,* two finely sculptured balustrades or parapets, found in the Forum between the Comitium and the Column of Phocas. On the inner faces are depicted the animals offered up at public sacrifices (suovetaurilia), a pig, a sheep, and a bull; on the outer faces are famous deeds of the emperor. The first represents the emperor burning the registers of outstanding death duties, an event which took place in 118, during Hadrian's reign; in the second an emperor standing on a Rostra with a statue of Trajan, is receiving the thanks of a mother for the founding of an orphanage. The architectural backgrounds show the buildings on the W, S, and E sides of the Forum systematically depicted. From the right of the first panel to the left of the second: Temple of Vespasian, an arch without decoration, Temple of Saturn, the

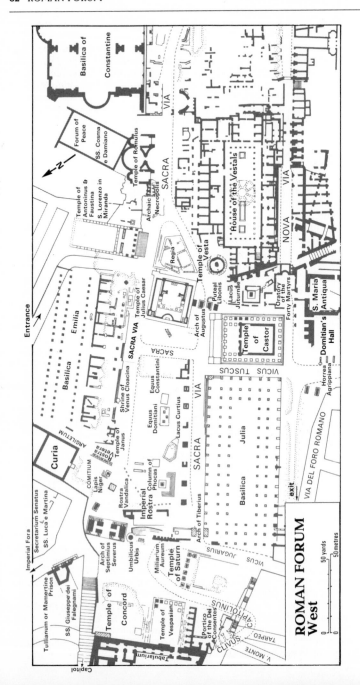

**ROMAN FORUM
West**

0   50 yards
0   50 metres

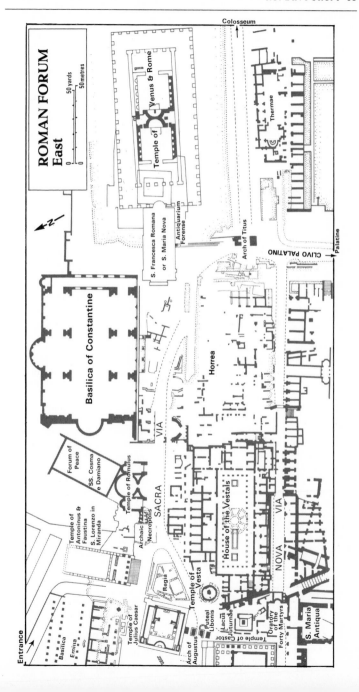

ROMAN FORUM
East

0   50 yards
0   50 metres

Entrance

Basilica of Constantine

Temple of Venus & Rome

S. Francesca Romana or S. Maria Nova

Antiquarium Forense

Arch of Titus

Colosseum

Thermae

CLIVO PALATINO

Palatine

Horrea

VIA

SACRA

Forum of Peace

SS. Cosma e Damiano

Temple of Romulus

Temple of Antoninus & Faustina

S. Lorenzo in Miranda

Archaic Necropolis

House of the Vestals

VIA

NOVA

Basilica Emilia

Temple of Julius Caesar

Temple of Augustus

Regia

Temple of Vesta

Puteal Libonis

Lacus Juturnae

Oratory of the Forty Martyrs

Temple of Castor

S. Maria Antiqua

Vicus Iugarius, and the arcades of the Basilica Julia. The arches are continued on the second panel, followed by an interval for the Vicus Tuscus(?), Temple of Castor, Rostra of the Temple of Julius Caesar (on which the emperor is standing); his attendants mount the ramp of the Rostra through the Arch of Augustus. On both sides is shown the statue of Marsyas beside the sacred fig-tree (see below).

In recent excavations behind the Curia remains of the Augustan building have come to light. Two doors at the rear end opened into a columned portico of the Forum of Caesar (see Rte 4), providing an entrance from the old forum to the new. Connected to the Senate House was the *Secretarium Senatus* used by a tribunal set up in the late Empire to judge senators.

Between the Lapis Niger and the Imperial Rostra (see below) is a large marble COLUMN BASE (recently restored) bearing an inscription of Diocletian to commemorate the decennial games of AD 303; the reliefs on the other sides depict scenes of sacrifice. Close by is the marble base of an equestrian statue with a dedicatory inscription celebrating the victory of Arcadius and Honorius over the Goths in 403.

The remaining part of the NW side of the Forum has been fenced off since 1980 while excavations are in progress and the monuments are being restored. A deposit of ex votoes from the Archaic period has been found, probably connected with an ancient cult of Saturn. The dig has not progressed yet below the medieval level which has revealed an interesting 12C district of the city here. The huge building of the Tabularium on the edge of the Capitol Hill which dominates this area has been restored.

The triple **Arch of Septimius Severus**, nearly 21m high and over 23m wide, entirely faced with marble, was erected in AD 203 in honour of the tenth anniversary of the emperor's accession, and dedicated by the senate and the people to Severus and his sons Caracalla and Geta in memory of their victories over the Parthians, Arabs, and Adiabenians of Assyria. One half of the monument was restored in 1988. The name of Geta, elder son of Severus, who was murdered by Caracalla in 212, was replaced by an inscription in praise of Caracalla and his father, but the holes made for the original letters are still visible. On the well-proportioned arch the four large reliefs depict scenes from the two Parthian campaigns: in the small friezes are symbolic Oriental figures paying homage to Rome, and at the bases of the columns are captive barbarians. There is a small interior staircase (no adm) which leads up to the four chambers of the attic.

To the S of the Arch of Severus are the ruins of the **Imperial Rostra**, or orator's tribune brought from its original site in front of the Curia during Caesar's restoration. It is 3m high, 24m long and 12m deep. The original structure (see above), of very early date, was decorated with the 'rostra' or iron beaks of the ships captured at the battle of Antium (338 BC). On the platform rose columns surmounted by commemorative statues, and its parapet was probably decorated with the sculptured plutei of Trajan. In front, on the right, are the ROSTRA VANDALICA, an extension of the 5C AD; the modern name is taken from an inscription commemorating a naval victory over the Vandals in 470.

At the back of the Rostra is a semicircular wall (*Hemicyclium*), formed by alterations during the building of the Arch of Septimius Severus. At its N end, by the Arch, is a cylindrical construction, the UMBILICUS URBIS (?2C BC), supposed to mark the centre of the city. Opposite the other end of the wall is the site of the MILIARIUM AUREUM, the 'golden milestone', a bronze-covered column set up by Augustus as the symbolic starting-point of all the roads of the Empire, with the distance from Rome to the chief cities engraved in gold letters on its base.

Immediately behind the Umbilicus, protected by a roof, is a quadrangular area once identified as the *Volcanal*, or Altar of Vulcan, but now considered to be an Altar of Saturn, dating from before the 6C BC. Here in Republican times grew two trees, a lotus and a cypress, said to be older than the city itself.

From the SW corner of the original Forum, the VICUS JUGARIUS runs S to the Velabrum between the Basilica Julia on the left (see below) and the Temple of Saturn on the right. The **Temple of Saturn**, one of the most ancient sanctuaries in the Forum, may have been inaugurated in 498 BC in honour of the mythical god-king of Italy, whose reign was the fabled Golden Age. The temple was rebuilt, after several previous reconstructions, by L. Munatius Plancus in the year of his consulship, 42 BC. It was again restored after fires in 283 and c 400 AD. The high podium and eight columns of the pronaos with part of the entablature survive, all dating from Plancus. The pavement and podium are to be entirely reconstructed after excavations have been completed. The columns are nearly 11m high. Six of them, in grey granite, are in front; the other two, in red granite, are at the sides. The Ionic capitals were added in the 5C restoration. The temple was the State treasury, where gold and silver ingots and coined metal were kept. The room (*Aerarium*) E of the narrow stairway of the temple could be locked (the holes for the lock can still be seen). The 'Saturnalia' was held here every year on 17 December.

Near the Temple of Saturn stood the ARCH OF TIBERIUS, erected in AD 16 in honour of the emperor and of his nephew Germanicus, who avenged the defeat of Varus in the Teutoburg Forest (AD 9) by his victory over the German tribes at Idisiavisus (on the Weser). Behind the temple excavations are in progress in an area formerly covered by houses; it is possible another temple may be found beneath the medieval constructions.

The last monuments on the W side of the Forum at the foot of the Capitol Hill lie beyond the **Clivus Capitolinus**, the whole of which has been uncovered since 1980 beneath the modern Via del Foro Romano (which has been eliminated). This is the ancient road with a flint pavement built in the 2C BC which was the W continuation of the Sacra Via (see above) in the Forum, and the only way up to the Capitol in ancient times. It was used for triumphal and other processions to the Temple of Jupiter. There are long-term plans to reopen it to pedestrians when excavations and restorations in this area have been completed.

The **Portico of the Dei Consentes** preserves twelve white columns forming an angle; the original seven columns are in marble, the restorations in limestone. Rebuilt by the prefect Vettius Praetextatus in AD 367, on the pattern of a Flavian structure, and dedicated to twelve Roman deities whose statues were here, it is the last pagan religious monument in the Forum. The portico was reconstructed in 1858 and is being restored.

Beyond are three high columns, all that remains of the hexastyle pronaos of the rich and elegant **Temple of Vespasian** erected in honour of that emperor at the foot of the Tabularium staircase by his sons Titus and Domitian after his death in AD 79. The front part of the basement has recently been excavated. To the N are the remains of the **Temple of Concord**. This was a reconstruction by Tiberius (7 BC–AD 10) of a sanctuary which traditionally was thought to have been built by Camillus in 366 BC to commemorate the concordat between the patricians and the plebeians. The temple may instead have been built for the first time in 218 BC and then rebuilt in 121 BC with the consent of Opimius after the murder of Gracchus. It became a museum and gallery of paintings and sculptures by famous Greek artists. Only the pavement remains in situ; part of the frieze is in the Tabularium. Excavations are also in progress here.

On the other side of the Temple of Saturn (see above) are the scanty but extensive ruins of the **Basilica Julia**, which occupies the area between the Vicus Jugarius and Vicus Tuscus (see below). The basilica, built on the site of the Basilica Sempronia (170 BC), was begun by Julius Caesar in 54 BC, and finished by Augustus. After a fire, it had to be reconstructed and re-dedicated by Augustus in AD 12. It was again damaged by fire in AD 283 and reconstructed by Diocletian in 305. It was damaged yet again in Alaric's sack of 410 and was restored for the last time by Gabinius Vettius Probianus six years later. The Basilica Julia was the meeting-place of the four tribunals of the *Centumviri*, who dealt with civil cases. In the Middle Ages the church of Santa Maria in Cannapara was built on its W side. The surviving remains mostly date from 305; the brick piers of the central hall are 19C reconstructions.

It was even larger than the Basilica Emilia, and measured 101m by 49m. It had a central hall 82m long and 18m wide, bordered all round by a double row of columns which formed aisles. On the long side, facing W, was a colonnade of arches and piers with engaged columns; this contained a row of shops. On the steps here can be seen graffiti in the marble used as 'gaming boards'.

In front of the Basilica Julia is a row of seven brick bases, dating from the 4C. These mark the S limit of the original FORUM which was first paved in the Etruscan period. The surviving pavement was laid by L. Surdinus in the Augustan era (as the restored inscription records). On the bases stood columns bearing statues of illustrious citizens. Two of the columns have been re-erected. In front, towards the W rises the **Column of Phocas** (recently restored), not only a conspicuous feature of the Forum but the last of its monuments. It was set up in 608 by Smaragdus, exarch of Italy, in honour of the centurion Phocas who had seized the throne of Byzantium; its erection may have been a mark of gratitude for the emperor's gift of the Pantheon to Boniface IV. The fluted Corinthian column, probably taken from some building of the best Imperial era, is 13.5m high. It stands on a high base, formerly faced with marble and surrounded by steps. On the top was originally a statue of the usurper.

To the N of the column of Phocas were placed the Plutei of Trajan (now in the Curia; see above). In the intervening pavement is a small square unpaved space, where the statue of Marsyas once stood next to the sacred fig-tree, the olive, and the vine (all recently re-planted here), mentioned by the Elder Pliny. In one of the pavement slabs is incised the name of L. Naevius Surdinus, praetor peregrinus in the time of Augustus, who may have had his tribunal here. This legal dignitary had to deal with cases involving *peregrini*, i.e. individuals who were not Roman citizens.

To the E is the paved area of the LACUS CURTIUS, with the substructure of a puteal (covered), surrounded by a twelve-sided structure of peperino blocks. The lake must have been a relic of the marsh drained by the Cloaca Maxima. According to one tradition a great chasm opened here in 362 BC which the soothsayers said could be closed only by throwing into it Rome's greatest treasure. Marcus Curtius, announcing that Rome possessed no greater treasure than a brave citizen, rode his horse into the abyss which promptly closed (the relief found here illustrating this legend is now in the Palazzo dei Conservatori; a cast is shown in situ). Livy, instead, suggests the name comes from the consul C. Curtius who fenced off this area in 445 after it had been struck by lightning.

In the SE corner of the Forum (surrounded by iron railings, and below ground level) are three travertine blocks formerly taken to be the base of the EQUUS DOMITIANI (AD 91) but now considered by some scholars to be the base of the equestrian statue of Constantine (EQUUS CONSTANTINI), probably dedicated in AD 334 (Domitian's statue is now thought to have been in the centre of the Forum).

At the E end of the original Forum is the Temple of Julius Caesar, described above. To the S are the foundations of the ARCH OF AUGUSTUS, which had a central arch flanked by lower and narrower side passages surmounted by pediments. After recent excavations here this is thought to date from 20 BC, after the standards captured by the Parthians had been returned. The 'Fasti Capitolini' (consular and triumphal registers; see Room IV of the Sale dei Conservatori, Rte 1) which date from this period, may have belonged to this arch. Another triumphal arch (with a single arch) was erected in another part of the Forum by Augustus in 30 BC to commemorate the victory over Antony and Cleopatra at Actium two years earlier. Near the S pier foundation of the arch is a rectangular monument in the shape of a well-head, which is a remnant of the PUTEAL LIBONIS, a monument which stood beside the tribunal of the Praetor Urbanus, who dealt with cases involving Roman citizens.

The monuments to the S of the Arch, including the Temple of Castor and the Lacus Juturnae have been fenced off since excavations began in this part of the Forum in 1983. Beyond the Arch and facing the E end of the Basilica Julia across the Vicus Tuscus is the *Temple of Castor, or Temple of the Dioscuri. It was almost certainly built in 484 BC by the dictator Aulus Postumius in honour of the twin heroes Castor and Pollux, whose miraculous appearance at the battle of Lake Regillus (496 BC) resulted in victory for the Romans over the Tarquins and their Latin allies. This temple, which had three cellae and a deep pronaos, built on a high podium, was restored after 200 BC. It was reconstructed by Metellus Dalmaticus in 117 BC, when a tribune for orators was installed, and it seems to have been used by money-changers (as recorded by Cicero).

This temple was destroyed by fire in 14 or 9 BC, and the present building was inaugurated by Tiberius during the reign of Augustus (AD 6). Peripteral in plan, and c 26 x c 40 metres in area, it had eight Corinthian columns at either end and eleven at the sides. The wide pronaos, excavated in 1982–85, was approached by a flight of steps. Three of the columns, which are 12.5m high, survive from the temple of Tiberius, with their beautifully proportioned entablature. Roman knights regarded the Dioscuri as their patrons; every year, on 15 July, they staged an impressive parade in front of the temple. Fragments of statues of the Dioscuri found here, are now in the Antiquarium. Excavations and restoration work were carried out on the Temple in 1983–87.

On the E side of the temple is the LACUS JUTURNAE, or Basin of Juturna, closely connected to the story of the Dioscuri: a legend related how they were seen watering their horses here immediately after their appearance at the battle of Lake Regillus (see above). Juturna, the nymph of healing waters, was venerated in connection with the springs here. The fountain has a square basin of opus reticulatum lined with marble; a statue probably stood on the rectangular base in the centre. On the parapet is a small marble altar (replaced by a copy; the original is in the Antiquarium), with reliefs of the Dioscuri and their sister Helena on two of its sides, and of their parents Jupiter and Leda, on the other two. In the 4C the Lacus Juturnae was the seat of the city's water administration. In the late Empire a series of rooms was built here presumably for the accommodation of invalids who came to take the waters. These rooms contain fragments of statues of gods and other sculptures. To the S is the shrine itself, an aedicula, restored in 1953–55, with the front built into the brick walls, and with two columns. In front is a marble puteal, with a dedicatory inscription to Juturna by the curule aedile M. Barbatius Pollio. The marble altar has a relief of Juturna and her brother Turnus.

Adjoining the shrine, on the S, is an apsidal building of the late Empire, converted into the ORATORY OF THE FORTY MARTYRS and preserving remains of 8–9C frescoes. The forty martyrs were soldiers frozen to death in an icy pool at Sebaste, in Armenia. The building closes the W end of the Nova Via.

To the S of the Oratory are the considerable remains of the church of *Santa Maria Antiqua** (closed indefinitely; enquire at the Antiquarium in the Forum), the oldest and most important Christian building in the Forum. The 7–8C wall-paintings here are of the highest importance in the history of early Christian art. Excavations were carried out here in 1983–87.

It is on the site of a Roman building which by the 6C is thought to have been used as a guardroom at the foot of the covered ramp which led up to the Palatine where the Byzantine governors were living. The first murals may date from this time during its gradual transformation into a church. Pope John VII (705–07) restored the church, repainted the presbytery, and installed the stone pulpit. The paintings were renovated in the 8C under Pope Zacharias and Pope Paul I. The building was damaged by earthquakes and landslides, and perhaps also by the Saracens. Leo IV (847–55) transferred the diaconate to Santa Maria Nova and rebuilt the church completely. In the 12C the church was rebuilt again and renamed *Santa Maria Liberatrice*. In 1702 a restoration brought to light the remains of the original church, and in 1901–02 Santa Maria Liberatrice, by that time entirely modernised, was pulled down.

The church comprises a quadrangular atrium, a quadriporticus, nearly square, and a presbytery, with three chapels, the central chapel being apsidal. On the left is a ramp leading up to the Palatine. The ATRIUM preserves its impluvium, and has frescoes painted at the time of Hadrian I (772–95), and fragments of ancient and medieval sculptures. In the QUADRIPORTICUS are four Corinthian columns with traces of painting which divide it into a nave and two aisles. In the nave are the low brick walls of the 8C schola cantorum. The 7–8C *wall-paintings are extremely interesting, although they are very ruined. In the apse and on the wall to the right are the remarkable *palimpsests, superimposed layers of painting from the 6C to the 8C.

On the W side of the church is **Domitian's Hall**, a large rectangular brick building (21 x 28m), originally vaulted. With an entrance on the ancient VICUS TUSCUS, it was intended as a monumental entrance to Domitian's palace on the Palatine. The hall was never completed and was transformed into a warehouse. Excavations here in 1983–87 clarified that this was on the site of a large atrium built by Caligula in front of the Temple of Castor which also provided an extension to the Imperial palace on the Palatine. Traces were found of the perimeter wall (26.5 x 22.3m) built of blocks of travertine. On a lower level were Republican buildings facing the Vicus Tuscus, demolished to make way for Caligula's atrium.

Also on the Vicus Tuscus is a vast brick building known as the HORREA AGRIPPIANA. This was a grain warehouse built around three courtyards, each provided with three storeys of rooms, built by Agrippa. The church of San Teodoro (see Rte 15) stands in the second courtyard.

The Vicus Tuscus returns N between the Basilica Julia and the Temple of Castor, and then E, past the bases of the Arch of Augustus (see above), to reach the religious centre of the Forum. Here are the Temple of Vesta, the House of the Vestals, and the Regia.

The *Temple of Vesta**, where the vestals guarded the sacred fire, is a circular edifice of 20 Corinthian columns. It was partially reconstructed in 1930 by Alfonso Bartoli. The circular form recalls the form of the Latin huts and the first temple on this site was possibly made, like these, of straw and wood. Vesta, goddess of the hearth, protected the fire, which symbolised the perpetuity of the State. The task of the vestals was to keep the fire always alight. Its extinction was the most fearful of all prodigies, as it implied the end of Rome. The origin of the cult is supposed to go back to Numa Pompilius, second king of Rome, or even to Aeneas, who brought the eternal fire of Vesta from Troy, together with the images of the penates.

The temple was burned down several times, notably during Nero's fire of AD 64 and in 191. It was rebuilt as often, the last time by Septimius Severus and his wife Julia Domna. It was closed by Theodosius and was in ruins by the 8C. Up until 1930 all that remained of it was the circular basement surmounted by tufa blocks and a few architectural fragments. In the interior was an adytum, or secret place containing the unknown pledges of the duration of Rome (*pignora imperii*). These included the *Palladium*, or statue of Pallas Athena, supposedly taken from Troy by Aeneas. No one was allowed inside the adytum except the vestals and the Pontifex Maximus and its contents were never shown. The Palladium was an object of the highest veneration, as the safety of the city depended on its preservation. When the emperor Heliogabalus tried to steal it, the vestals are supposed to have substituted it by another statue (see Rte 3). The cult statue of Vesta was kept, instead, in a small shrine near the entrance to the House of the Vestals.

Immediately E of the Temple of Vesta is the ***House of the Vestals**, a large rectangular atrium arranged round a spacious courtyard. It dates from Republican times, but was rebuilt after the fire of Nero in AD 64, and was last restored by Septimius Severus; remains of both structures can still be seen.

There were six Vestals, the virgin priestesses of Vesta, who were chosen by the king, and later, during the Republic and Empire, by the Pontifex Maximus. Candidates, between six and ten years of age, had to be from a Patrician family. After her election a vestal lived in the House of the Vestals for thirty years; ten learning her duties, ten performing them, and ten teaching novices. During this period she was bound by the vow of chastity. At the end of the thirty years she was free to return to the world and even to marry. The senior Vestal was called *Vestalis Maxima* or *Virgo Maxima*. If a vestal let out the sacred fire, she was whipped by the Pontifex Maximus, and he then had to rekindle the fire by the friction of two pieces of wood from a *felix arbor*.

The vestals' other duties included offerings to Vesta, sprinkling her shrine daily with water from the Egerian fountain, assisting at the consecration of temples and other public ceremonies, and guarding the Palladium. Maintained at the public expense, they had many privileges, such as an exalted order of precedence, and the right of intercession. Wills (including the emperor's) and treaties were entrusted to their keeping. If a vestal broke her vow of chastity she was immured alive in the Campus Sceleratus and the man was publicly flogged to death in the Forum.

The House of the Vestals seems too large for just six vestals, and part of it may have been reserved for the Pontifex Maximus, whose official seat was in the Regia (see below). It has a delightful courtyard, 61m long and 20m wide, in the middle of which are three ponds irregularly spaced and unequal in size. The central pond was formerly partly covered by an octagonal structure of unknown purpose. A charming rose-garden has been planted among the ruins. Along the sides of the courtyard are statues and statue-bases of vestals which date from the 3C AD onwards. Near the entrance is a base from which the name of the vestal has been removed, possibly because she became a Christian.

There was a two-storeyed portico surrounding the courtyard. In the middle of the short E side is a large hall paved with coloured marbles and flanked on either side by three small rooms, thought to be the sacristy of the priestesses. Behind this hall, towards the Palatine, are an open court-yard with a fountain, and other rooms. Along the S side, which abuts on the Nova Via, is another series of rooms (no adm) opening out of a corridor. In the first of these are the remains of a mill; the second is probably a bakery. On this side staircases lead to the upper floor and to the Nova Via. Near the last staircase is a small shrine. In the middle of the W side is a large room, perhaps the dining-room, leading to the kitchen and other rooms. The N side of the building is less well preserved; stairways on the second floor show that it had more than two storeys.

The **Nova Via** (not accessible; excavations in progress) runs parallel with the Sacra Via along the S slope of the Palatine Hill. It provided a means of communication with the buildings on the Palatine. The visible remains of this road probably date from the Flavian period, but recent excavations at the point where it crosses the *Clivo Palatino* have revealed paving which seems to date from the Republican era.

To the N of the Temple of Vesta and E of the Temple of Julius Caesar are the remains of the **Regia**, traditionally supposed to be the palace of Numa Pompilius, the second king of Rome, and the official headquarters of the Pontifex Maximus. Primitive huts, similar to those on the Palatine (see Rte 3) were found here, and the earliest permanent construction excavated dates from the 7C BC. The edifice, rebuilt by Domitius Calvinus after a fire in 36 BC retains its 6C form. The elegance of its architecture can be seen from scattered fragments. Other parts of the building date from a recon-struction of the time of Septimius Severus.

The Regia may have been the depository of State archives and of the *Annales Maximi*, written by the Pontifex Maximus. It also included the Sacrarium of Mars, with the *ancilia*, or sacred shields, and the chapel of Ops, goddess of plenty. At the SE corner of the Regia have been discovered the foundations of the arch, erected in 121 BC by Q. Fabius Maximus Allobrogicus to span the Sacra Via.

To the N of the Regia rises the **Temple of Antoninus and Faustina** (no adm), near the main entrance to the Forum. One of the most notable buildings of Imperial Rome, it was dedicated by the Senate in AD 141 to the memory of the Empress Faustina and, after his death in 161, to Anton-inus Pius also. The temple was converted into the church of SAN LORENZO IN MIRANDA before the 12C, and given a Baroque façade in 1602. A reconstructed flight of steps leads up to the pronaos, of Corinthian cipollino monolithic columns (17m high), six in front and two on either side. The architrave and frieze of vases and candelabra between griffins, and the side walls of the cella, of peperino blocks, originally faced with marble, also survive. In the pronaos have been placed sculptures, including a female torso. The dedication of the church commemorates the trial of St Laurence, which may have taken place in this temple.

To the E of the temple is an ARCHAIC NECROPOLIS, discovered in 1902. This was the cemetery of the ancient inhabitants of the Esquiline or of the original settlement on the Palatine, and dates back to the Early Iron Age, before the date of the traditional foundation of Rome. Tombs were found for both cremations and burials. Cremated ashes were discovered in urns surrounded by tomb-furniture, in small circular pits. The burials here were either in tufa sarcophagi, hollowed-out tree-trunks, or trenches lined with tufa slabs. The finds are in the Antiquarium.

Here the Sacra Via begins to ascend the Velia to the Arch of Titus. The Velia was a low ridge which connected the Palatine Hill with the Esquiline and which was levelled by Mussolini. On either side of the road are the ruins of private houses and shops (some under cover), including one dating from the Republican era, once wrongly called the Carcer, or prison.

On the left is the so-called **Temple of Romulus** (never open; being restored), a well-preserved 4C structure formerly thought to have been dedicated to Romulus, son of Maxentius who died in AD 309. It has recently been suggested that it could have been the audience hall of the city prefect, or identified with a Temple of Jupiter. It is a circular building built of brick and covered by a cupola flanked by two rectangular rooms with apses, each originally preceded by two cipollino columns (only those on the right survive). The curved pronaos has two porphyry columns and an architrave taken from some other building; the splendid antique bronze *doors are a remarkable survival.

Behind is a rectangular hall, probably the library of the FORUM OF PEACE built by Vespasian in AD 70 (see Rte 4). This hall was converted in the 6C into the church of Santis Cosma e Damiano (described in Rte 4), the temple serving as a vestibule. In the Forum of Peace were probably kept the city plans, cadastral registers, and other documents. On the wall towards the modern Via dei Fori Imperiali was placed the *Forma Urbis*, a famous plan of Rome, fragments of which are kept in the Antiquarium Comunale.

Beyond tower the remains of the *Basilica of Constantine, or Basilica of Maxentius**, also called the '*Basilica Nova*', the largest monument in the Forum and one of the most impressive examples of Roman architecture in existence. The skill and audacity of its design inspired many Renaissance builders, and it is said that Michelangelo studied it closely when he was planning the dome of St Peter's. The three huge barrel-vaulted niches on the N side still dominate the Forum. It was begun by Maxentius (306–10) and completed by Constantine, who considerably modified the original plan.

The huge building is a rectangle 100m long and 65m wide, divided into a nave and two aisles by massive piers supported by buttresses. As first planned, it has a single apse, on the W side. Against the central piers were eight Corinthian columns 14.5m high; the only survivor was moved by Paul V to Piazza Santa Maria Maggiore. The original entrance was from a side road on the E; Constantine added a portico on the S side which opened onto the Sacra Via. The portico had four porphyry columns, which survive in part. In the middle of the N wall Constantine built a second apse, which was shut off from the rest of the building by a colonnaded balustrade; here the tribunal probably held its sittings. The interior walls, decorated with niches, were faced with marble below and with stucco above.

The three arches of the N aisle are 20.5m wide, 17.5m deep, and 24.5m high: the arches of the groin- vaulted nave, whose huge blocks have fallen to the ground, were 35m high and had a radius of nearly 20m. Parts of a spiral staircase leading to the roof can be seen on the ground, having collapsed in an earthquake. A tunnel was built under the NW corner of the basilica, for a thoroughfare which had been blocked by its construction. The entrance to the tunnel (walled up since 1566) can still be seen. In 1487 a colossal statue of Constantine was found in the W apse, fragments of which are now in the courtyard of the Palazzo dei Conservatori. The bronze plaques from the roof were removed in 626 by Pope Honorius I to cover Old St Peter's.

On the opposite side of the Sacra Via is a mass of ruins, among which is a large PORTICO, the vestibule to the Domus Aurea of Nero. Domitian used this to build the HORREA PIPERATARIA, a bazaar for Eastern goods, pepper and spices, to the N of the Sacra Via. Later, the S part became commercialised. Domitian's building was finally destroyed in 284. A small circular base with a relief of a Maenad and an inscription recording its restoration by Antoninus Pius (originals in the Antiquarium) in front, on the Sacra Via, may be the remains of a SANCTUARY OF BACCHUS.

On the ascent to the Arch of Titus is the church of Santa Francesca Romana, or Santa Maria Nova (entered from Via dei Fori Imperiali and described in Rte 4). The former convent of this church is now the seat of the Forum and Palatine excavation offices and contains the **Antiquarium of the Forum** (or *Antiquarium Forense*). Most of it has been closed for a number of years; it is to be rearranged on two floors of the cloister. In 1994 only four rooms were open (adm as for the Forum), displayed in old-fashioned show cases. In the first room is tomb-furniture from the Archaic Necropolis, and a model. Rooms II and III contain objects found near the House of the Vestals; yields from wells, Italo-geometric and Etrusco-Campanian vases, votive objects, glass ware, and lamps. Room IV (beyond Room II) looks into the impressive *cella of the Temple of Venus and Rome (see Rte 4), which cannot otherwise be seen. Here are displayed objects from the area of the Lapis Niger, Comitium, Cloaca Maxima, Regia, and Basilica Emilia.

The rest of the collection, not at present on view, includes: a large capital from the Temple of Concord; a marble basin reconstructed from original fragments found near the Lacus Juturnae, and sculptures from the fountain, including a headless statue of Apollo from a Greek original of the 5C BC; fragments of the frieze of the Basilica Emilia, and part of its architectural decoration; and part of a *fresco removed from the chapel of Saints Cyriac and Julitta in Santa Maria Antiqua.

Dominating the summit of the Sacra Via is the *Arch of Titus**, erected by Domitian (AD 81) in honour of the victories of Titus and Vespasian in the Judaean War, which ended with the sack of Jerusalem (AD 70). In the Middle Ages the Frangipani incorporated the arch in one of their castles, but the encroaching buildings were partly removed by Sixtus IV (1471–84) and finally demolished in 1821. Restoration of the arch was then undertaken by Giuseppe Valadier, who used travertine instead of marble to repair the damaged parts.

The beautiful, perfectly proportioned, single archway, with Composite columns, is covered with Pentelic marble. The two splendid reliefs inside the arch are very worn. One of them shows Rome guiding the Imperial quadriga with Titus and Victory; and the other shows the triumphal procession bringing the spoils from Jerusalem, which include the altar of Solomon's temple decorated with trumpets, and the seven-branched golden candlestick. In the centre of the panelled vault is the Apotheosis of Titus, who is mounted on an eagle. On the exterior frieze is another procession in which the symbolic figure of the vanquished Jordan is carried on a stretcher.

The large area on the northern slopes of the Palatine, to the W of the Arch of Titus as far as the House of the Vestals (between the Via Nova and the Sacra Via), has been fenced off since 1985 while excavations are in progress beneath the visible remains of the **Horrea**, large warehouses on several

The Arch of Titus in the Roman Forum

floors. The building nearest the House of the Vestals probably dates in its present form from the time of Hadrian. The larger building to the E may be the HORREUM VESPASIANI, a market which fronted the Horrea Piperataria (see above), destroyed when the Basilica of Constantine was built. A row of shops against the Palatine Hill is prominent: almost in the centre can be seen a well-preserved vaulted edifice, beside which steps led up to the Via Nova and the upper floors.

The most important result so far of the excavations in this area has been the discovery of **Archaic walls** on three levels: the oldest traces date from 730–675 BC when Romulus is supposed to have founded Rome; above these was a wall in red tufa defended by a ditch (675–600 BC). The latest wall, which seems to be part of the *Roma Quadrata* of Servius Tullius (530–520 BC), was constructed with large block of red tufa. Subsequent levels have shown interesting remains of at least four Archaic *domus*, and at least four Republican houses, one of which, facing the Clivo Palatino, may eventually be opened to the public (see Rte 3). Evidence was also discovered here of the destruction of numerous buildings by Nero for his huge Domus Aurea, which extending from the Oppian and Celian Hills across the Velia to the Palatine, invaded the centre of the Roman city. The horrea (see above) were part of a general plan of the Flavians to reinstall public edifices in this area after the death of Nero.

The Forum can be left by the gate beyond the Arch of Titus. The path descends along an extension of the Sacra Via with the Temple of Venus and Rome (see Rte 4) on the left to the Colosseum. Otherwise the Palatine is reached directly from the Arch of Titus by the Clivo Palatino.

3

The Palatine

Admission, see p 47, and Rte 2. The Palatine can be reached from the Roman Forum near the Arch of Titus (see above; and see the Plan on pp 96-97), where the Clivo Capitolino begins, or by a separate entrance on Via San Gregorio (through a portal by Vignola and Rainaldi). Other ways up from the Forum (by the ramp on the side of the church of Santa Maria Antiqua and from a stairway at the SW corner of the House of the Vestals) have been closed indefinitely.

The topography of the Palatine is intricate, one level after another of multi-storey buildings having been erected on and through the previous levels. Several of the more interesting sites are apt to be fenced off, because of fresh excavations or damage of some kind. The custodians are informed and helpful. The House of Livia is usually open to the public; other enclosed monuments, including the House of Augustus, the House of the Griffins, and the Aula of Isis can usually only be visited with permission from the excavation office in the Forum (see Rte 2). The Palatine Antiquarium, closed for restoration in 1994, is normally open only in the morning.

The ****PALATINE** (Pl. 4; 7) is a four-sided plateau S of the Forum rising to a height of 40m above it and 51m above sea-level. It is about 1750m in circumference. It was here that the primitive city was founded, and splendid Imperial palaces were later built over its slopes, so that the word Palatine came to be synonymous with the 'palace of the emperor' (hence 'palace'). A park, with a profusion of wild flowers and fine trees, inhabited by birds and beautifully kept, now surrounds the ruins. It is one of the most romantic and charming spots in the centre of the city, remarkably isolated from the traffic-ridden streets at the foot of the hill.

History and Topography. The Palatine now has the appearance of a plateau, since the intervening hollows were filled in by the successive constructions in the Imperial era. In ancient times the central summit was called the *Palatium*. It sloped down towards the Forum Boarium and the Tiber, with a declivity called the *Germalus* on the W and N (now occupied by the Farnese gardens) looking towards the Capitol. The *Velia*, a second lower summit, was connected by a saddle through the Roman Forum with the Esquiline. The name of Palatium is said to be derived from Pales, the divinity of flocks and shepherds, whose festival was celebrated on 21 April, the day on which (in 754 or 753 BC) the city of Rome is supposed to have been founded. Long before that date, however, the hill was settled, according to legend, from Greece. Sixty years before the Trojan War (traditional date 1184 BC), Evander, son of Hermes by an Arcadian nymph, led a colony from Pallantion, in Arcadia, and built at the foot of the Palatine Hill near the Tiber a town which he named after his native village. Traces of occupation going back to the 9C BC have been discovered during excavations.

When the twins Romulus and Remus decided to found a new city, the honour of naming it was accorded to Romulus by the omen of twelve vultures which he saw on the Palatine. Some time after its foundation on the hill, the city was surrounded by a strong wall forming an approximate rectangle: hence the name *Roma Quadrata*. Three gates were provided in the walls: the Porta Mugonia on the NE, the Porta Romanula on the NW, and the Scalae Caci at the SW corner overlooking the valley of the Circus Maximus. Excavations begun in 1985 on the lower N slopes of the hill (see Rte 2) would appear to have identified a stretch of this wall, as well as traces of even earlier fortifications.

The northern slopes of the Palatine, in the area nearest to the Forum, was for centuries considered one of the most prestigious residential districts. During the Republic many prominent citizens lived here, including Cicero, Q. Lutatius Catulus, the orator Crassus, the demagogue Publius Clodius, the orator Hortensius, and the triumvir Antony. Remains of these residences have recently been unearthed. Augustus was born on the Palatine, and he acquired the house of Hortensius and enlarged it. His new buildings included the renowned Temple of Apollo, with Greek and Latin libraries attached. Part of his palace has been excavated. The example of Augustus was followed by later emperors, whose residences became more and more magnificent, and the Palatine tended to become an Imperial reserve.

Recent excavations have revealed that the first place on the Germalus summit, still called the 'Domus Tiberiana', was in fact part of Nero's huge Domus Aurea. This was reconstructed by Domitian who seems to have called it the 'Domus Tiberiana'. Caligula extended it and provided a monumental atrium to connect it with the Forum. Hadrian added buildings towards the Via Nova and on the NW side of the hill, but preferred to live on his estate near Tivoli.

The whole of the Palatium was reserved for the constructions of the Palace of the Flavian emperors, which comprised the official palace, the emperor's residence, and the stadium. To provide a water supply, Domitian extended the Acqua Claudia from the Celian hill to the Palatine. Septimius Severus increased the area of the hill to the S by means of a series of arcades. Other remarkable edifices were the emperor's box overlooking the Circus Maximus and the monumental Septizonium. Heliogabalus built a new temple in the Adonaea, in which he placed the most venerated treasures of Rome.

Odoacer, first king of Italy after the extinction in 476 of the Western Empire, lived on the Palatine; so for a time did Theodoric, king of the Ostrogoths, who ruled Italy from 493 to 526. The hill later became a residence of the representatives of the Eastern Empire. From time to time it was favoured by the popes, and some Christian churches were built here. In the 12C there was an important Greek monastery on the hill.

In the course of time, after a period of devastation, the Frangipani and other noble families erected their castles over the ruins. In the 16C most of the Germalus was laid out as a villa for the Farnese (the Orti Farnesiani). Systematic excavations were begun about 1724 by Francesco Bianchini, shortly after Duke Francis I of Bourbon Parma had inherited the Farnese Gardens. They were mainly concentrated in the area of the Domus Flavia. Little more was done till 1860; in that year the gardens were bought by Napoleon III, who entrusted the direction of the excavations to Pietro Rosa. He continued his work after 1870 when the Palatine was acquired by the Italian Government.

In 1907 D. Vaglieri began to explore the Germalus; he was succeeded by Giacomo Boni, who worked on the buildings below the Domus Flavia. Alfonso Bartoli later carried out research under the Domus Augustana and elsewhere and brought to light much information about the earliest inhabitants. Excavations have been in progress since 1985 on the lower northern slopes of the hill, beneath the Domus Tiberiana, on the SW corner of the hill in the area of the Temple of Cybele, and near the Vigna Barberini.

The Clivo Palatino ascends from the Forum passing the Nova Via on the right. A Republican house excavated in 1985, facing the Clivo Palatino, may eventually be restored and opened to the public. With some fifty bedrooms,

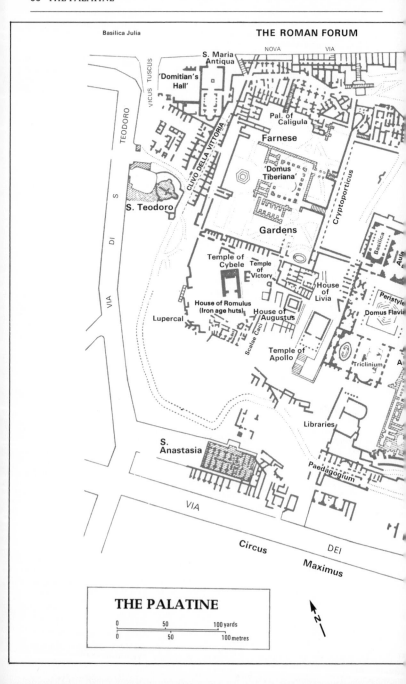

Basilica Julia

THE ROMAN FORUM

VIA NOVA

S. Maria Antiqua

'Domitian's Hall'

VICUS TUSCUS

TEODORO

S DI VIA

CLIVO DELLA VITTORIA

Pal. of Caligula

Farnese

'Domus Tiberiana'

Cryptoporticus

S. Teodoro

Gardens

Basilica

Aula

Temple of Cybele

Temple of Victory

House of Livia

Peristyle

House of Romulus (Iron age huts)

House of Augustus

Domus Flavi

Lupercal

Scalae Caci

Temple of Apollo

Triclinium

A

Libraries

S. Anastasia

Paedagogium

VIA

Circus Maximus

DEI

THE PALATINE

| 0 | 50 | 100 yards |
| 0 | 50 | 100 metres |

N

it is thought that it may have been the servants' quarters attached to the residence of Emilio Scauro (58 BC).

On the right paths and steps lead up to the ***Farnese Gardens**, laid out by Vignola in the middle of the 16C for Cardinal Alessandro Farnese, grandson of Paul III. They extended from the level of the Forum, then much higher, to the Germalus; the various terraced levels were united by flights of steps. Vignola's work was completed by Girolamo Rainaldi at the beginning of the 17C. The modern stairs lead up to the first terrace (formerly approached by a monumental ramp from the Nova Via in the Forum) with a nymphaeum. Above another terrace with a fountain stand the twin pavilions of the aviary on the highest level of the gardens, overlooking the Forum. The classical *Viridarium* instituted by Alessandro Farnese was replanted here by the archaeologist Giacomo Boni (1859–1925). The gardens are still very beautiful. Boni's tomb stands beneath a palm-tree in the part of the gardens overlooking the Forum. Delightful paths continue through the gardens to the W side of the hill. To the S is an ancient palm-tree beneath which is a box-hedge maze reproducing that in the peristyle of the Domus Flavia.

The gardens cover the site of the so called **Domus Tiberiana**, very little of which is visible. Recent excavations here have revealed that the first palace on this site (formerly occupied by Republican houses) was part of Nero's Domus Aurea. This was reconstructed by Domitian, and extended to the NW (towards the Clivo della Vittoria) by Hadrian. A criptoporticus (with entrances, not open to the public, on Via di San Teodoro) dates from the period of Nero. Under Domitian a ramp on four levels was constructed to connect the Domus Tiberiana with the Forum. There is an oval fishpond in the SE corner near the stairs leading down to the cryptoporticus and a series of rooms with brick vaults on the S slope overlooking the Temple of Cybele. These rooms (no adm) were built by the Antonines for the accommodation of the Praetorian Guard; graffiti in them indicate their occupation by soldiers.

Excavations have been in progress since 1978 in the SW part of the hill around the Temple of Cybele, and the top of the Scalae Caci, so that some of the ruins are sometimes fenced off. From the S side of the gardens a modern flight of steps descends past (left) considerable remains of the Domus Tiberiana (see above). On the right are the ruins of the **Temple of Cybele** (or **Magna Mater**) covered by a thicket of ilex. It was built in 204 BC and consecrated in 191 BC. Thirteen years earlier, during a critical period of the second Punic War, an oracle had foretold that the battle could only be won if the Romans obtained from Phrygia the black stone which was the attribute of the goddess Cybele. This proved correct, and the temple was built to house the sacred cult image.

Cybele, the Magna Mater, mother of the gods, was the great Asiatic goddess of fertility. She was worshipped in the town of Pessinus in Phrygia (Asia Minor). She, and her young lover Attis, were served by eunuch priests. The festival of Cybele and Attis was celebrated annually (22–24 March) with primitive orgies.

The temple, raised on a high podium, had six Corinthian columns in antis. It was burned down in 111 BC and rebuilt by Q. Caecilius Metellus, consul in 109. It was restored again in the reign of Augustus (AD 3). It is depicted on a Roman relief set into the garden façade of the Villa Medici. Recent excavations have clarified the various dates of the building. The podium and the walls of the cella date from after the fire of 111 BC. At this time a large platform was built in front of the temple for athletic games and theatrical performances in honour of the goddess, beneath which was a district with an underground road, shops, and a thermal building. Pavements and external architectural decorations survive from the Augustan period. The statue of Cybele and fragments of a marble lion found here have been placed under an arch of the Domus Tiberiana.

To the E of the temple are remains of the TEMPLE OF VICTORY built in 294 BC by the consul Lucio Postumio Megello. Between the two temples is a much smaller one, recently identified as the TEMPLE OF VICTORY VIRGO dedicated by Marco Porcio Cato in 193 BC.

Further E are two ARCHAIC CISTERNS (under cover) dating from the 6C BC, one of which is particularly well preserved. It is circular in form, with a beehive vault of cappellaccio blocks laid in gradually diminishing courses; the top was closed with a single slab. The construction recalls the Mycenean *tholos*.

The area to the S is the most ancient part of the hill. Here are traces of a wall of tufa and the site of the SCALAE CACI, one of the three gates of *Roma Quadrata*. Cacus was the giant who stole the oxen from Hercules, and according to legend had his den in the Forum Boarium, at the foot of the hill, and was killed there by Hercules. Up until the 4C AD it was believed that the house of Romulus, or the hut which belonged to Faustulus where the twins were brought up after they were found by the shepherd, was located in this area. Excavations in 1907–49 revealed the traces of a HUT VILLAGE of the Early Iron Age (9C BC). On the rocky level of the hill are numerous holes and channels indicating the plan of three huts. In the holes were placed poles supporting the roofs. The channels were used to carry away the rain-water from the roofs.

Also in this part of the hill was the LUPERCAL, although traces of it have not yet been found. This was the cave sanctuary of the she-wolf, an animal sacred to Rome. It contained an altar and was surrounded by a grove sacred to the god Lupercus. Here the annual festival of the *lupercalia* was held on 15 February, when the priests of the god, the *luperci*, dressed in goatskins, and processed around the hill, whipping whoever they met. It was believed that the castigation of women symbolised fertility. The name February means purification and expiation. These rites were later connected with the mythical legend of Romulus and Remus suckled by the she-wolf.

The part of the hill between the Temple of Cybele and the Temple of Apollo (see below) has been fenced off while excavations (begun in 1961) of the **House of Augustus** (not the Domus Augustana, which is described below) have been carried out. This may be opened to the public; meanwhile admission is only granted with special permission from the excavation office in the Forum Antiquarium.

In the W wing of the house, thought to be the private quarters of the Emperor, have been found rooms with paintings of the highest interest: one has a charming frieze of pine cones, and another architectural and theatrical motifs. A series of larger rooms were probably used for public ceremonies and included two libraries, and a little nymphaeum decorated with shells. The wall-paintings, dating from 25 BC–AD 25, are remarkable for their vivid colour and intricate design (and refined figure studies). Considerable fragments of the stuccoed vaults and pavements of marble inlay have also come to light.

To the SE of the House of Augustus are some ruins once thought to belong to the Temple of Jupiter Victor, built by Q. Fabius Rullianus in 295 BC after his victory over the Samnites at Sentinum. After a building of the late

Republican era was found beneath it, it was identified instead as the famous **Temple of Apollo** vowed by Augustus in 36 BC and dedicated eight years later. A corridor which is thought to have connected the Temple to the House of Augustus has been excavated here, and more wall-paintings have been discovered near the podium of the temple. Fragments of a colossal statue of Apollo were found near the site of the temple, although they do not belong to the famous statue of Apollo by Skopas known to have been placed here. All that survives is the basement of the temple (44m by 24m) reached on the S side by a long flight of steps (no adm; the existing flight is a modern reproduction).

The Temple of Apollo was surrounded by the PORTICO OF THE DANAIDS, on which were statues of the fifty daughters of Danaus. Some magnificent painted terracotta panels (now in the Palatine Antiquarium) were found here. Near by were the renowned Greek and Latin libraries, rebuilt by Domitian.

To the N of the House of Augustus is the so-called *House of Livia, famous for its wall-paintings. When it was discovered by Pietro Rosa in 1869, it was identified as the house of the wife of Augustus from some lead pipes bearing the inscription *Iulia Augusta*. It is now considered to be part of the house of Augustus himself (see above). The masonry dates from the 1C BC; the mural paintings are Augustan. The house is usually open to the public.

An original staircase descends into the rectangular COURTYARD, in which there are two pillar bases and architectural paintings. The most important rooms open onto it. In front are the three rooms thought to belong to the Tablinum, or reception suite; on the right is a room which was probably the Triclinium, or dining-room. The decorations of the TABLINUM are in the second Pompeian style (1C BC), which imitates in painting the marble of Greek and Roman domestic architecture and introduces figures.

The paintings have been detached but are exhibited in situ. The paintings in the central room are the best preserved, especially that on the right wall of this room. It has panels separated by columns of fantastic design in a free interpretation of the Corinthian style. In the central panel Hermes is seen coming to the rescue of Io, the lover of Zeus, who is guarded by Argus of the hundred eyes; in the left panel is a street scene; the right panel is lost. In the intercolumniations are small panels with scenes of mysterious rites. The central painting on the rear wall of this room, now almost obliterated, shows Polyphemus pursuing Galatea into the sea; on the left wall, which lost its paintings in ancient times, are exhibited the lead pipes which gave the house its name (see above).

The room on the left has architectural decorations (very ruined), with panels of griffins and other fantastic creatures. The room on the right is also architectural in its decorative scheme. The delicate yellow frieze depicts small landscapes and genre scenes. Below is the representation of a Corinthian portico; between the columns are rich festoons of fruit and foliage. In the TRICLINIUM (usually closed) the decorations are also mainly architectural. On the wall opposite the entrance is a portico with an exedra; in front is a trophy with spoils of the chase, and below is a pond with ducks. Above are branches of trees.

To the N of the House of Livia is one of the most interesting features of the Palatine. This is the *Cryptoporticus, a vaulted passage 128m long, skirting the Farnese Gardens and the Domus Tiberiana. Decorated in the vault with fine stuccoes (replaced by casts; originals in the Antiquarium) for part of its length, it receives light and air from windows set high on the E side. This was part of the Domus Tiberiana, and a branch corridor was later added to link it with the Domus Flavia. The Cryptoporticus can be reached also by stairs leading down from the Farnese Gardens.

To the E extends the vast area of the **Palace of Domitian**, which occupies nearly the whole of the Palatium and the former depression between it and the Germalus. This vast collection of buildings was brilliantly planned for Domitian by the architect C. Rabirius, who levelled the central part of the hill to fill up the depression on the W. In the process he demolished or buried numerous earlier constructions, from private houses to Imperial palaces; some of these have been revealed by excavations. The complex includes the Domus Flavia, or official palace, the Domus Augustana, or Imperial residence, and the Stadium. Originally it was reached from the N by a monumental staircase of three flights.

The splendour of the *Domus Flavia, northernmost of the constructions, was praised by numerous Roman poets. On the N side it has a portico of cipollino columns which may have served as a loggia. In the centre of the palace is the spacious PERISTYLE with an impluvium in the form of an octagonal maze surrounding a fountain. A box-hedge reproduction of this maze is in the Farnese Gardens. Because of Domitian's constant dread of assassination he is supposed to have had the walls covered with slabs of Cappadocian marble whose mirror-like surface enabled him to see anyone approaching. On the W side is a series of small rooms with apses, statue-bases, and baths; on the E side are traces of three more rooms.

To the N of the peristyle are three large halls (fenced off) facing N onto an open space identified with the Area Palatina. The central hall is the so-called AULA REGIA, or throne room, originally decorated with 16 columns of pavonazzetto and with 12 black basalt statues: two of the statues were found in 1724 and are now in Parma. In the apse was the Imperial throne where the emperor sat when he presided over meetings of his council and received foreign ambassadors. To the E is the so-called LARARIUM (under cover), in fact thought to be another room used for public ceremonies, or a guardroom protecting the main entrance to the palace. To the W is the BASILICA JOVIS, divided by two rows of columns of giallo antico; it has an apse at the further end, closed by a marble screen. This may have been used as an auditorium. A flight of steps leads down from the Basilica to the Cryptoporticus (see above).

To the S of the peristyle is the TRICLINIUM, or banqueting hall. This is almost certainly the *Coenatio Jovis*. It has an apse reached by a high step; in this was placed the table where the emperor took his meals apart. The hall was paved with coloured marbles, which are well preserved in the apse. Leading out of the hall on either side was a court with an oval fountain. Around the fountain on the W side, which is well preserved, is a magnificent pavement in opus sectile belonging to the Domus Transitoria of Nero. Here, too, is a pavilion constructed by the Farnese as part of their gardens with a double loggia looking NW and decorations attributed to the Zuccari.

Behind the triclinium is a row of columns (partly restored) belonging to the Domus Flavia. Further S are two rooms with apses, once thought to be Domitian's reconstruction of the Greek and Latin Libraries of the Temple of Apollo, but now considered to be reception rooms used by Augustus for legates.

The Domus Flavia covers several earlier constructions of considerable interest. These underground areas are sometimes shown by custodians; for permission to visit them, apply at the Forum Antiquarium (9.00–13.00).

Beneath the Lararium is the *House of the Griffins, named after the two griffins in stucco which decorate a lunette in one of the rooms. It is the oldest Republican building preserved on the Palatine (2C or 1C BC). Its wall-paintings, like those in the House of Livia, are in the second Pompeian style. The house is on two levels; the decorations are on the lower level. Of the several rooms reached by the staircase, the large hall is the best preserved. The pavement is in opus sectile. The mural paintings simulate three planes of different depth; the columns imitate various marbles. Round the top of the room runs a cornice and the ceiling is stuccoed. Paintings from two of the rooms have been detached and are now in the Palatine Antiquarium. Beneath the Basilica is the **Aula of Isis**, a large rectangular hall, with an apse at one end. The mural paintings have been detached and are now exhibited in a room of the Domus Augustana (see below).

Steps lead down from the triclinium to part of the DOMUS TRANSITORIA OF NERO (formerly called the Baths of Tiberius). At the foot of the steps is a court with a partly restored nymphaeum, decorated with rare marbles. Other rooms have traces of pavements with fine marble inlay. Small paintings of Homeric subjects found in a room leading off the court have been removed to the Antiquarium. Beneath the peristyle is the so-called *Palatine Mundus* (no adm; a grate now covers the entrance to the stairs), a pit with a well at one end. This was thought by Boni, when it was discovered, to be the Mundus of Roma Quadrata, but it was more probably a silo. In 1952, on the wall of a building, one of the many destroyed when the Domus Flavia was built, was found a Christian inscription, believed to refer to the celebration of the Eucharist in AD 78 and, if so, the earliest yet discovered.

Overlapping the Domus Flavia on the E are the vast remains of the **Domus Augustana**. This was the private residence of the emperor, 'the Augustus', not that of the Emperor Augustus. It was built on two levels. There are two peristyles on the upper and one on the lower level. Only the bases of the columns survive. The first peristyle, towards Via di San Bonaventura, was open. In the middle of the second peristyle is a large basin with a quadrangular shrine, possibly dedicated to Vesta. Around the court are remains of rooms, one of which has been identified as the 4C ORATORY OF ST CAESARIUS. Close by is the Palatine Antiquarium (see below). In another of the rooms is a graceful 16C loggia decorated with grotesques, formerly part of the Villa Mattei. Here are exhibited *paintings detached from the Aula of Isis (see above).

Dating from the Republican period these were painted before the edict of 21 BC banning the worship of Isis. The fantastic architectural paintings have panels with scenes of the cult of Isis and the fragments of the ceiling decoration are especially interesting. When the hall, with the House of the Griffins, was discovered in 1720–22, the paintings, which were in much better condition than they are now, were copied by Gaetano Piccini and by Francesco Bartoli. Bartoli's water-colours are now in the Topham Collection at Eton.

Another peristyle of the Domus Augustana is on a much lower level (no adm but well seen from above). In the middle is the basin of a fountain. Beyond are rooms with pavements of coloured marbles. A doorway in the bottom wall leads to the exedra of the palace overlooking the Circus Maximus; this was originally decorated with a colonnade.

The **Palatine Antiquarium** occupies the former Convent of the Visitation betwen the Domus Flavia and the Domus Augustana. It was formed with the material collected in 1860–70 from the excavations begun by Napoleon III in the Farnese Gardens and amplified by Pietro Rosa. It lost its most important sculptures when the Museo Nazionale Romano was opened. It has been closed for restoration for a number of years, and when it reopens the arrangement described below may have changed, and new material will be on exhibition. It may only be open in the mornings.

In the room to the left are wall decorations from a Republican house, near the House of Livia, and from the Domus Transitoria; a fresco of Apollo, found near the Scalae Caci; paintings, including a charming frieze from a house dated 130 BC found beneath the Baths of Caracalla; paintings from the Schola of the Praecones, dating from the 3C AD, and graffiti from the Paedagogium, including the notorious *Graffito of Alexamenos*, discovered in 1855. This is a caricature of the Crucifixion and shows a youth standing before a cross on which hangs a figure with the head of an ass; the legend says in Greek 'Alexamenos worships his god'. In the small room opposite are fragments of the stuccoed vault of the Cryptoporticus. In the vestibule, two fragments of marble intarsia from the pavement of the Domus Tiberiana (early 1C AD) and an archaic altar of an unknown god. The second room on the left contains torsos of Mercury (copy of a Greek 5C original) and Diana (Roman copy of a Greek original), and two heads of Attis. Also, *painted terracotta panels from near the Temple of Apollo. The rooms to the right contain objects found beneath the Domus Flavia, and from the Temple of Cybele, and finds (with a model) from the area of the Hut Village.

To the E of the Domus Augustana lies the *Stadium. This is an enclosure 146m long, with a series of rooms at the N end and a curved wall at the S. The interior had a two-storeyed portico with engaged columns covering a wide ambulatory or cloister. The arena has a semicircular construction at either end, presumably once supporting a turning-post (*meta*). In the centre are two rows of piers of a portico of the late Empire. Towards the S end are the remains of an oval enclosure of the early Middle Ages which blocked the curved end of the Stadium. Columns of granite and cipollino, Tuscan, Corinthian, and Composite capitals, and fragments of a marble altar with figures of divinities lie on the surface of the arena. In the middle of the E wall is a wide exedra shaped like an apse, of two storeys, and approached from the outside by a curved corridor. This structure is usually identified as an Imperial box, used by the emperor when he commanded the races and athletic contests here. Some scholars, however, suggest the 'stadium' was in fact a garden, used occasionally as a hippodrome.

Behind the Stadium was the so-called **Domus Severiana**, which was built over a foundation formed by enlarging the S corner of the hill by means of enormous substructures that extended almost as far as the Circus Maximus. The scant remains include part of the BATHS. To the N is the AQUEDUCT built by Domitian to provide water for his palace; it was an extension of the Acqua Claudia which ran from the Celian to the Palatine. The aqueduct was restored by Septimius Severus.

To the S is the site of the Imperial box built by Septimius Severus, from which he watched the contests in the Circus Maximus. In the SE corner of the Palatine is the probable site of the SEPTIZONIUM or SEPTIZODIUM, built by Septimius Severus in AD 203 to impress visitors to Rome arriving by the Appian Way. Here in 1241 Matteo Orsini imprisoned cardinals and forced them to elect Celestine IV; the new pope and three of the cardinals died as a result of the conditions. It was demolished by Sixtus V at the end of the 16C. Renaissance drawings of this building show that it had three floors, each decorated with columns. The façade was divided vertically into seven zones, the number corresponding either to that of the planets or to the days of the week; hence the uncertainty about the name. The columns and blocks of marble and travertine from this ornate structure were reused in various buildings in the city.

Beyond the Severian arches, the S end of the Stadium, and the exedra of the Domus Augustana, lies the **Paedagogium** (no adm), halfway down the hill and facing the Circus. The Paedagogium is so called because it is supposed to have been a training school for the court pages. The name often recurs in the numerous graffiti scratched on the walls; the best-known one is the graffito of Alexamenos, now in the Antiquarium. The building dates from the 1C or 2C AD; the graffiti are later. Other rooms (inaccessible) are situated on the edge of the hill above Via dei Cerchi, including the so-called SCHOLA OF THE PRAECONES (the paintings and mosaics are in the Antiquarium).

The Palatine can be left either by descending the hillside to the E of the Domus Augustana to the exit on Via San Gregorio or by returning across the Domus Augustana and descending the Clivo Palatino (see the Plan) to the exit at the Arch of Titus in the Forum.

Outside the arch (and not included in the Palatine enclosure) Via di San Bonaventura ascends to the NE summit of the Palatine. Here, approached by a 17C portal in the wall of the VIGNA BARBERINI, the former Barberini vineyard, is the small medieval church of SAN SEBASTIANO AL PALATINO; its apse has interesting murals (c 970). Excavations in the churchyard have unearthed the probable site of the ADONAEA, or gardens of Adonis, where this god was worshipped. Later, Heliogabalus built a TEMPLE OF THE SUN in the centre of the gardens. Here he placed numerous treasures from the most ancient cults of the city, including the sacred stone from the Temple of Cybele, and what he took to be the Palladium (see Rte 2). The district acquired the name *Palladii* or *in Pallara* in the Middle Ages, which was given also to the church of San Sebastiano. Recent excavations here have revealed a semicircular exedra which has the same dimensions as the S exedra of the Domus Augustana (see above) overlooking the Circus Maximus, and is therefore probably part of the same palace. The last section of Via di San Bonaventura (which ends at the church) is flanked by 18C terracotta Stations of the Cross.

4

The Imperial Fora and the Colosseum

The five **IMPERIAL FORA**, of Caesar, of Augustus, of Vespasian, of Nerva, and of Trajan, occupy the huge area between the Roman Forum and the lower slopes of the Quirinal and Viminal. They are traversed by the wide **Via dei Fori Imperiali** (Pl. 4; 5, 7) opened in 1933 by Mussolini as the Via dell'Impero and lined with gardens. From Piazza Venezia it runs in a straight line to the Colosseum past the Fora of Trajan and Augustus on the left and the Forum of Caesar on the right. It then crosses over the Fora of Nerva and of Vespasian. During the construction of this thoroughfare, built to add dignity to Fascist military parades, numerous 16C buildings were demolished, the Velia hill levelled, and the Imperial Fora hastily and inconclusively excavated.

In 1980 a project was mooted to eliminate the stretch of road between Piazza Venezia and Via Cavour and to carry out systematic excavations of the Fora at a considerably lower level. After much discussion the Minister declared in 1983 that funds were insufficient to put such a scheme into operation. However in 1988 the local government decided to fence off a large area of gardens beside the Forum of Nerva and excavations were begun here, seen as a positive step towards the eventual closure of the road (which in 1994 was made a pedestrian precinct on Sundays). Meanwhile only one fifth of the Fora are visible and the traffic along this unfortunate road continues to damage the ancient monuments. The Imperial Fora are all visible from outside (with the exception of the Forum of Vespasian) but for many years only the Markets and Forum of Trajan have been open regularly to the public.

With the ever-increasing population of the city, by the end of the Republican era the Roman Forum had become too small for its purpose. It was congested with buildings and overcrowded by citizens and by visitors from abroad. The only direction in which expansion was possible was to the N, even though numerous buildings had to be demolished here. The purpose of any new forum was to be the same as that of the Roman Forum, namely to serve, with its basilicas, temples, and porticoes, as a judicial, religious, and commercial centre.

The first step was taken by Julius Caesar, who built his Forum during the decade before his death in 44 BC. In it he placed the Temple of Venus Genetrix in commemoration of the victory of Pharsalus (48 BC). His example was followed by his successors, most of whom erected temples in memory of some outstanding event in Roman history for which they took the credit. The Forum of Augustus, with the Temple of Mars Ultor, commemorated the battle of Philippi (42 BC); the Forum of Vespasian had its Temple of Peace erected with the spoils of the campaign in Judaea (AD 70); and the Forum of Trajan, completed by Hadrian, had a temple to the deified Trajan in honour of his conquest of Dacia (AD 106). The Forum of Nerva had a Temple of Minerva. All the Fora were connected and the whole area was arranged in conformity with a definite plan.

During the Middle Ages and the Renaissance the Fora were pillaged for their building material and robbed of their marbles and bronzes, and the area was later built over. Until the 20C only parts of the Fora of Trajan and Augustus and the so-called 'Colonnacce' were visible; the clearance of the area was begun in 1924 to make way for Via dei Fori Imperiali.

At the W end of Via dei Fori Imperiali, opposite the corner of the Victor Emmanuel Monument stands Trajan's Column (see below) beside two domed churches of similar design (usually closed). The first, *Santa Maria di Loreto, by Antonio da Sangallo the Younger, with a lantern by Giacomo del Duca (1582), is a fine 16C building. It contains an altarpiece attributed to Marco Palmezzano, and a statue of St Susanna by François Duquesnoy (1630). The second church, dedicated to the NOME DI MARIA is by Antonio Dérizet (1738).

In front of the churches extends the *Forum of Trajan (entered through the Markets of Trajan; see below), built between 107 and 113 and the last and most splendid of the Imperial fora. It was designed by Apollodorus of Damascus in a site excavated in the saddle between the Capitol and Quirinal Hills. The forum itself is in the form of a rectangle 118m by 89m, with a portico and exedra on each of the long sides. In the centre was an equestrian statue of Trajan. At the W end, occupying the whole of its width, was the Basilica Ulpia. Adjoining, on the W, were the Greek and Latin libraries, with Trajan's Column between them, and, still farther W, beneath the area of the two churches, the Temple of Trajan. The entrance was from the E, adjoining the Forum of Augustus, through a monumental arch. To the N of the forum and virtually adjoining it is the semicircle of the Markets of Trajan. In the opinion of ancient writers these constructions made up a monumental group unequalled in the world. Further excavations are to be carried out here.

*TRAJAN'S COLUMN is generally considered to be the masterpiece of Roman sculptural art, still almost intact, and carefully restored in 1980–88. It was dedicated to Trajan by Hadrian in memory of his conquest of the Dacians, the inhabitants of what is now Romania. Around the column shaft winds a spiral frieze 200m long and between 0.89m and 1.25m high, with some 2500 figures in relief illustrating in detail the various phases of the Dacian campaigns (101–102 and 105–106). The carving was carried out in less than four years by an unknown Roman master and his workshop. It is known that the column could originally be seen from buildings which surrounded it on various levels in the Forum of Trajan: it is now more difficult to appreciate the beautiful details of the carving with the naked eye. Casts (made before restoration) of each panel are kept in the Museo della Civiltà Romana.

The column is 100 Roman feet (29.7m) high, or with the statue, 39.8m; it is constructed of a series of marble drums. A spiral stair of 185 steps (no adm) carved in the marble ascends to the top of the Doric capital on which once stood the statue of Trajan (replaced by the statue of St Peter in 1588). The ashes of the emperor, who died in Cilicia in 117, and of his wife Plotina, were enclosed in a golden urn and placed in a vault below the column. An inscription at the base has been interpreted to indicate that the top of the column reached to the original ground-level, thus giving an idea of the colossal excavations necessary for the construction of the forum.

The entrance to the *MARKETS AND FORUM OF TRAJAN (admission, see p 46) in Via IV Novembre is reached from here by steps (Via Magnanapoli). The Markets of Trajan were built before the Forum of Trajan, at the beginning of the 2C AD, and consisted of 150 individual shops, used for general trading. The entrance is through a rectangular HALL of two storeys, with six shops on each floor; on the upper storey is a large covered hall which may have served as a bazaar. Beyond is the large semicircle of three superimposed rows of shops with arcaded fronts, built on the slopes of the Quirinal. The semicircle ends on either side in a well-preserved apsidal hall (only the one on the left can be visited). The portico of the fourth shop on the left of the bottom row has been reconstructed. The apsidal buildings on the second floor are particularly well preserved. An ancient paved road, the VIA BIBERATICA, passes in front of the markets but is now blocked by Via IV Novembre.

The **Torre delle Milizie** (no admission), behind the markets is a massive brick-built tower, a conspicuous feature in the skyline of Rome, and one of the most important civic medieval buildings to have survived in the city. It is thought to have been rebuilt in the 13C by the Caetani. In 1312 the emperor Henry VII stayed here. It acquired its lean after an earthquake in 1348. It later belonged to the Conti family, and was restored and isolated from the convent of St Catherine by Antonio Muñoz in 1914. It originally had three storeys: two of these survive.

Steps descend from the markets to the level of the **Forum of Trajan**. The NORTH PORTICO conforms to the semicircular shape of the markets. In the

Studies of Trajan's Column made in 1927

Middle Ages the portico was stripped of its precious marbles: all that survives are the remains of three steps of giallo antico, a column base, traces of the polychrome marble pavement, and a column of the apse. Behind the apse was the wall of the enceinte; part of this is visible on the left. The site of the SOUTH PORTICO is under Via dei Fori Imperiali. On the E side of the forum little has been discovered.

A passageway (at present closed to the public) leads towards Trajan's Column, in front of which are the extensive remains of the **Basilica Ulpia**, dedicated to the administration of justice, and the largest in Rome. Though not as spacious as the Basilica of Constantine, it was longer (120m; not counting the apses at either end); its width was 60m. It was divided by rows of columns into a nave and four aisles. On each short side was an extensive apse; the N apse was found under Palazzo Roccagiovine beside Via Magnanapoli. The front of the basilica, towards the interior of the forum, had three doors; at the back, towards Trajan's Column, there were two doors. Part of the pavement in coloured marbles has survived; also a fragment of the entablature, with reliefs depicting scenes of sacrifice and candelabra.

On the left of the column is the LATIN LIBRARY and on the right the GREEK LIBRARY, both of them rectangular, with wall niches surmounted by marble cornices to hold the manuscripts. Behind the column is a fragment of a colossal granite column (with its marble capital), virtually all that remains of the huge TEMPLE OF TRAJAN erected after his death in 117 by Hadrian.

At the beginning of Via dei Fori Imperiali, beyond the Victor Emmanuel Monument, the steep Via di San Pietro in Carcere (open only to cars with special permits) diverges right to climb above the Mamertine Prison (see below) to the Capitol. Here, well beneath the level of the road, are the remains of the **FORUM OF CAESAR** (no adm), first of the Imperial fora, and said by Dio Cassius to have been more beautiful than the Roman Forum. Recent excavations behind the Curia building in the Roman Forum (see Rte 2) have shown that Caesar created an entrance to his forum from the Curia. The focal point of this new forum was the Temple of Venus Genetrix, from whom Julius Caesar claimed descent. In the temple, dedicated in 46 BC, two years after the battle of Pharsalus, were exhibited a statue of the goddess by Arcesilaus, a statue of Julius Caesar, a gilded bronze statue of Cleopatra, and two pictures by Timomachus of Byzantium (1C BC) of Ajax and of Medea. In front of the temple stood an equestrian statue of Caesar. Trajan rebuilt the temple and forum and added the Basilica Argentaria, or exchange building, and five large shops over which was an extensive (heated) public lavatory (*forica*).

The entrance to the ruins (which has been locked for many years) is by a staircase near the church of Santi Luca e Martina (see below). Beyond (right) the remains of the FORICA, the level of the Forum is reached. On the left are the shops; at the end is the BASILICA ARGENTARIA. In the middle is the high base of the **Temple of Venus Genetrix**, which has lost its marble facing; three of its Corinthian columns have been re-erected. In front of the basilica are the remains of a large arch which may have been used in a later restoration to reinforce the temple.

From Via di San Pietro in Carcere (see above) a well-preserved stretch of the *Clivus Argentarium*, the Roman road which ran between the Capitol and the Quirinal Hills, is open to pedestrians. Lined with remains of shops and a nymphaeum dating from the time of Trajan, it descends to the little church of SAN GIUSEPPE DEI FALEGNAMI (often closed). This was built in

1598 perhaps by Giovanni Battista Montano, above the TULLIANUM, called the **Mamertine Prison** (adm see p 46) in the Middle Ages, and later consecrated as SAN PIETRO IN CARCERE. This is thought originally to have been a cistern, like those at Tusculum and other Etruscan cities. On the lower level, the form can be seen of a round building which may have had a tholos (which could date it as early as the 6C BC). A spring still exists in the floor. The building was used as a dungeon in Roman times for criminals and captives awaiting execution. Jugurtha, Vercingetorix, the accomplices of Catiline, and, according to Christian tradition, St Peter and St Paul were imprisoned here.

Beside the church steps lead up to the Capitol. There is a good view from here of the monuments at the W end of the Roman Forum. Opposite is the handsome church of *Santi Luca e Martina (Pl. 8; 2; often closed), probably founded in the 7C by Honorius I on the site of the Secretarium Senatus. It was rebuilt in 1640 by Pietro da Cortona, and is considered one of his masterpieces. The two storeys, the upper dedicated to St Luke and the lower to St Martina, have an original and complex design. The façade, built of travertine, and the dome are particularly fine. The church of St Luke has a centralised Greek cross plan. The lower church of Santa Martina is reached by a staircase to the left of the high altar.

In a well-designed chapel (left) are the tombs of Saints Martina, Epifanio, and Concordio, and a tabernacle by Pietro da Cortona. The side chapel with a pretty scallop motif has a fine terracotta group of the three saints by Alessandro Algardi. In the corridor is the tomb of Pietro da Cortona, and in the vestibule, statuettes by Cosimo Fancelli, and a bas-relief of the Deposition by Algardi.

On the other side of Via dei Fori Imperiali, in front of their respective fora, are modern bronze statues of Trajan, Augustus, and Nerva. Adjoining the Forum of Trajan is the *FORUM OF AUGUSTUS (closed since 1984), built to commemorate the victory of Philippi (42 BC) and dedicated to Mars Ultor (the Avenger). It is seen from the railings along Via dei Fori Imperiali (which, however, covers half its area), but the entrance (when it reopens) is at the back, in Piazza del Grillo. This can usually be reached by the raised walk-way (Via di Campo Carleo) which leads out of Via dei Fori Imperiali, and passes between the Markets of Trajan and the Forum of Augustus; if this is closed it must be approached by Via Tor de' Conti (see the plan).

From Piazza del Grillo a modern stairway descends to an arcaded entrance to the forum, beside a huge wall built to isolate the forum from the Subura district. From there a wide antique staircase leads on to the podium of the octastyle *Temple of Mars Ultor, dedicated in 2 BC, with columns on three sides. It had a large pronaos and an apsidal cella. A centre of solemn ceremonies and the Imperial sanctuary, it became a museum of art and miscellaneous relics; among these were the sword of Julius Caesar and the Roman standards surrendered by the Parthians in 20 BC. Three columns at the end of the right flank are still standing. Of the eight Corinthian columns in front four (the two middle and the two end ones) have been partly reconstructed from antique fragments. A broad flight of steps ascends to the capacious pronaos. In the cella, where the effect of undue width is lessened by a colonnade on either side, are the stepped bases of the statues of Mars, Venus, and perhaps Divus Julius. Behind is the curve of the large apse. A stairway on the left descends to an underground chamber once thought to be the temple treasury.

On either side of the temple, marble steps lead up to the site of a BASILICA. These twin basilicas were almost completely destroyed during the Renaissance for their marble; each had a great apse, which Augustus decorated with statues of famous Romans, from Aeneas onwards (some of the niches can still be seen). On the ground between the surviving columns of the temple and the right-hand basilica are architectural fragments of great interest. Behind these is the ARCH OF PANTANUS, formerly an entrance to the forum. The left-hand basilica had an extension at the N end known as the HALL OF THE COLOSSUS, a square room which held a colossal statue of Augustus or of Mars, the base of which remains. Two ancient columns have been re-erected at the entrance.

At the E end of the Forum of Augustus is the **FORUM OF NERVA**, or FORUM TRANSITORIUM (excavations in progress), so called because it led into the Forum of Vespasian. Nerva's Forum, which was begun by Domitian and completed in AD 97, was, in effect, a development of the ARGILETUM, the street that led from the Roman Forum to the Subura. In the middle rose the TEMPLE OF MINERVA, the ponderous basement of which remains in place. The temple was still standing at the beginning of the 17C, when it was pulled down by Paul V to provide marble for the Fontana Paolina on the Janiculum. Beyond the temple and close to the enceinte wall are two enormous Corinthian columns (recently restored), the so-called *COLONNACCE. In the attic between the columns is a high-relief of Minerva, after an original of the school of Skopas. In the rich frieze of the entablature Minerva (Athena) is seen teaching the arts of sewing and weaving and punishing Arachne, the Lydian girl who excelled in the art of weaving and had dared to challenge the goddess. In front of the Colonnacce is a section of the Argiletum.

To the E of the Forum of Nerva extended the **FORUM OF VESPASIAN** or **Forum of Peace**, built in AD 69–79, with the spoils of the Jewish War. Excavations revealed and identified a shrine under the Torre dei Conti, some prone columns, and remains of a pavement in opus sectile; a large hall was converted in the 6C into the church of Santi Cosma e Damiano (see below).

From Piazza del Grillo (see above) is the entrance to the **Casa dei Cavalieri di Rodi**, ancient seat of the Roman priorate of the Order of the Knights of St John of Jerusalem (Hospitallers, Knights of Rhodes, or Knights of Malta). The house was built over a Roman edifice at the end of the 12C, and restored in 1467–70 by Cardinal Marco Balbo, nephew of Paul II. It has a well-preserved colonnaded atrium, dating from the time of Augustus; the roof is a Renaissance addition. It is now used as a chapel by the Knights of St John.

The atrium leads into the ANTIQUARIUM OF THE FORUM OF AUGUSTUS (closed indefinitely), arranged in three Roman shops. The exhibits include fragments of Roman and medieval sculptures (*head of Jupiter from the frieze of one of the basilicas), and a model of the forum. At the top of a flight of Roman stairs (restored) is a fine Renaissance hall (adm sometimes on request), off which are several contemporary rooms; one of these, the Sala del Balconcino contains part of the attic storey of the portico of the Forum of Augustus, with caryatids. Stairs lead up to a loggia with restored frescoes and fine views over the fora.

Via di Campo Carleo or Via Tor de' Conti lead back to Via dei Fori Imperiali which continues towards the Colosseum, passing the entrance to

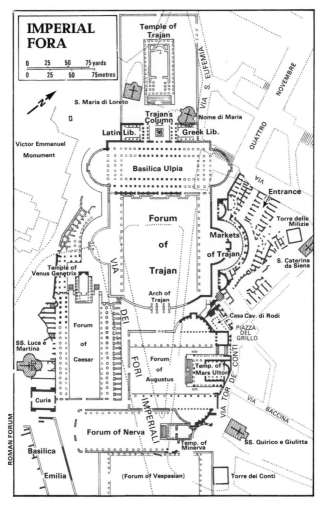

IMPERIAL FORA

0 25 50 75 yards
0 25 50 75 metres

the Roman Forum. Here a large area of gardens has been fenced off adjoining the Forum of Nerva and excavations have been in progress since 1988. So far only the medieval and 16C levels have been explored.

A stairway on the left of the entrance to the Roman Forum leads to the church of San Lorenzo in Miranda, which encloses the Temple of Antoninus and Faustina (no admission; see Rte 2). Farther on is the church of **SANTI COSMA E DAMIANO**, dedicated to two brothers who were miraculous healers from Cilicia. This church occupies a large rectangular hall (probably a library) of the Forum of Vespasian, which St Felix IV adapted in 527, adding mosaics to the apse. The so-called Temple of Romulus in the Roman Forum served as a vestibule to the church. It was rebuilt in 1632, when the pavement was added to make it a two-storeyed building. The church is reached through the early 17C cloisters of the adjoining convent with contemporary frescoes by Francesco Allegrini.

The INTERIOR (lights in each chapel) is celebrated for its 6C *mosaics (coin-operated light near the entrance), copied in several Roman churches (especially in the 9C). On the triumphal arch is the Lamb enthroned, surrounded by seven candlesticks, four angels, and the symbols of the Evangelists. In the apse (restored in 1989), Saints Cosmas and Damian presented to Christ at his Second Coming by St Peter and St Paul; on the right, St Theodore; on the left St Felix IV (restored) presenting a model of the church. Also palms and the phoenix, symbol of the Resurrection. Below is the Lamb on a mount from which four rivers (the Gospels) flow; twelve other lambs (the Apostles) are shown with Bethlehem and Jerusalem on either side.

The ceiling of 1632 has a fresco by Marco Montagna, who also painted frescoes in the nave. The Baroque altar by Domenico Castelli (1637) is adorned with a 13C Madonna and Child. In the first chapel in the right aisle, is a striking fresco of Christ encrowned on the Cross, derived from the Volto Santo in Lucca. It dates perhaps from the 13C, but more probably from a repainting in the 17C by an unknown Lucchese artist. In the vault are frescoes by Giovanni Battista Speranza. In the second chapel are paintings by Giovanni Baglione. The third chapel has an altarpiece of St Anthony of Padua by Spadarino, and frescoes by Allegrini (who also painted the frescoes in the first and second chapels in the left aisle). In a domed Roman vestibule off the cloister is part of an 18C Neapolitan presepio. The models and figures in wood, terracotta, and porcelain are of exceptionally fine workmanship.

Via dei Fori Imperiali next passes on the right the colossal ruins of the Basilica of Constantine (described in Rte 2). The four interesting relief MAPS on a modern brick wall facing the street were set up here in 1932. They show the extent of Roman power at four stages in its history: in the 8C BC; in 146 BC, after the Punic Wars; in AD 14, after the death of Augustus; and in the time of Trajan, AD 98–117.

Adjoining the Basilica of Constantine (and reached by a flight of steps from Via dei Fori Imperiali, or by a short road from Piazzale del Colosseo) is the church of **SANTA MARIA NOVA** or **SANTA FRANCESCA ROMANA** (Pl. 8; 2; open 9.30–12.30, 15.30–19.00, or 15.00–17.00 in winter). It is on the summit of the Velia and encroaches on the Temple of Venus and Rome (see below); a fine stretch of ancient Roman road is conspicuous on the approach to the W door.

The church incorporates an Oratory of Saints Peter and Paul built by Paul I (757–67) in the W portico of the Temple of Venus and Rome. In 847, after grave structural damage to the church of Santa Maria Antiqua in the Forum, that church was abandoned and the diaconate was transferred to the oratory, which became *Santa Maria Nova*. The church was enlarged, and the apse mosaic and *campanile added before it was consecrated anew in 1161. The façade, designed by Carlo Lombardi, was added during his reconstruction in 1615.

Santa Francesca Romana (Francesca Buzzi; 1384–1440), wife of Lorenzo Ponziani, founded the Congregation of Oblates here in 1421, which she herself joined after her husband's death in 1436. Canonised in 1608, she is the patron saint of motorists and on her festival (9 March) the street between the church and the Colosseum is congested with cars. The painter Gentile da Fabriano was buried in the church in 1428. The former conventual buildings now contain the excavation offices and Antiquarium of the Roman Forum (see Rte 2).

INTERIOR. The Cosmatesque pavement in the raised E end was restored in 1952. In the vestibule of the side entrance (right), tombs of Cardinal Marino Bulcani (died 1394) and of Antonio da Rio (or Rido), castellan of Castel Sant' Angelo (c 1450). S transept, tomb of Gregory XI, by Pietro Paolo Olivieri, set up in 1585 by the Roman people in honour of the pope who restored the seat of the papacy from Avignon to Rome (1377). Let into the S wall (behind grilles) are two flagstones from the Sacra Via which are supposed to show the imprint of the knees of St Peter, made as the saint knelt to pray for the punishment of Simon Magus, who was demonstrating his wizardry by flying. The legendary site of Simon's consequent fall is in the neighbourhood. From here stairs lead down to the crypt with the body of St Francesca Romana, and a 17C bas-relief of her with an angel (17C). The confessio, an early work by Bernini, has a marble group of the same subject, by Giosuè Meli (1866).

In the apse are *mosaics of the Madonna and saints (probably completed in 1161), and on either side, statues of angels of the school of Bernini. Above the altar, a 12C Madonna and Child, revealed in 1950 and detached from another painting found beneath it. The earlier painting, a colossal *Virgin and Child, which may have come from Santa Maria Antiqua, is now kept in the SACRISTY. Probably dating from the end of the 6C, it is one of the most ancient Christian paintings in existence. Also in the sacristy, Paul III and Cardinal Reginald Pole (left wall) attributed to Perino del Vaga; fragments of medieval frescoes; Miracle of St Benedict, by Subleyras. On the entrance wall, Madonna enthroned between St Benedict and Santa Francesca Romana, by Girolamo da Cremona, and Madonna enthroned with Saints, by Sinibaldo Ibi of Perugia (1545).

Beyond the church is the summit of the Velia, transformed into a terrace with gardens (no admission), the area of which (145m by 100m) virtually coincides with that of the enormous **Temple of Venus and Rome**. The temple was built by Hadrian on the site of the vestibule of the Domus Aurea, where Nero had placed a colossal bronze statue of himself as the Sun. The statue had therefore to be moved (see below). The temple was built in honour of Venus, the mother of Aeneas and the ancestor of the gens Julia, and of Roma Aeterna, whose cult appears to have been localised on the Velia. It was dedicated in 135, damaged by fire in 283, and restored by Maxentius (307). It is said to have been the last pagan temple which remained in use in Rome, as it was not closed until 391 (by Theodosius). It remained virtually entire until 625, when Honorius I stole the bronze tiles of its roof for the old basilica of St Peter's.

To counteract the unevenness of the ground, it was necessary to build a high basement; this was of rubble, with slabs of peperino and marble-faced travertine. The temple was dipteral, with ten granite Corinthian columns at the front and back and twenty-two on each of the sides. It had two cellae placed back to back; that facing the Forum was the shrine of Rome and the other that of Venus. The visible remains date from the time of Maxentius. The two cellae (the apses and diamond-shaped coffers were added by Maxentius) are still standing. That facing the Forum has been partly restored, and is visible from a room of the Antiquarium in the Forum (see Rte 2). The brick walls were formerly faced with marble and provided with niches framed with small porphyry columns. The apse contains the base of the statue of the goddess. The floor is of coloured marbles. The temple was surrounded by a colonnaded courtyard, with propylae on the N and S sides; in 1935 some of the columns and column-fragments on the S were re-erected, and can be seen from the extension of the Via Sacra which leads from the Arch of Titus down to the Colosseum.

Piazzale del Colosseo (partially closed to traffic), lies in a valley between the Velia on the W, the Esquiline on the N and the Celian on the S.

The **COLOSSEUM** (Pl. 5; 7) is the most famous monument of ancient Rome and the emblem of her eternity. Its original name, *Flavian Amphitheatre*, commemorated the family name of Vespasian, who began the building, and of his son Titus, who completed it. The popular name of the amphitheatre first occurs in the writings of the Venerable Bede (c 673–735), who quotes a prophecy of Anglo-Saxon pilgrims: 'While the Coliseum stands, Rome shall stand; when the Coliseum falls, Rome shall fall; when Rome falls, the world shall fall.' This name is thought to be derived from the proximity of Nero's colossal statue (see below), rather than from the size of the building itself. There is free access to the ground floor from the S, W, and N sides (adm times, see p 45). The first floor (adm from the main entrance on the side facing the Roman Forum; fee) is also open, although the upper storeys have been closed for many years. An antiquarium arranged in underground rooms has also been closed indefinitely.

The amphitheatre, begun by Vespasian between AD 70 and 76 on the site of the lake in the gardens of Nero's Domus Aurea, was completed by Titus in 80. The inaugural festival lasted 100 days, during which many gladiators and 5000 wild beasts were killed. The amphitheatre was restored c 230 under Alexander Severus and in 248 the thousandth anniversary of the foundation of Rome was celebrated here. There is no historical basis for the tradition that Christians were martyred in the arena. Gladiatorial combats were suppressed in 407 and fights with wild beasts in 523. The damage from the earthquake of 422 was probably repaired by Theodosius II and Valentinian III. The building was again shaken by earthquakes in 1231 and 1349. It was later converted into a castle by the Frangipani, and the Annibaldi.

In 1312 the Colosseum was presented to the senate and people of Rome by the Emperor Henry VII. By the 15C it had become a recognised quarry for building material. Its travertine was used during the construction of Palazzo di Venezia and Palazzo della Cancelleria. Other parts of the building were reused in St Peter's and Palazzo Barberini. In 1749, however, Benedict XIV dedicated the Colosseum to the Passion of Jesus and pronounced it sanctified by the blood of martyrs. Pius VII, Leo XII, Gregory XVI, and Pius IX carried out restorations, erecting buttresses and other supports. In 1893–96 it was freed from obstructive buildings by Guido Baccelli, and the interior structures revealed. Further clearances were carried out after the construction in 1933 of Via dei Fori Imperiali. Restoration work was resumed in 1973.

It was particularly admired by 19C travellers to Rome because of its romantic ruined state. Dickens in 1846 declared: 'It is the most impressive, the most stately, the most solemn, grand, majestic, mournful sight, conceivable. Never, in its bloodiest prime, can the sight of the gigantic Coliseum, full and running over with the lustiest life, have moved one heart, as it must move all who look upon it now, a ruin. God be thanked: a ruin!'

Exterior. The elliptical amphitheatre is built of travertine outside and of brick and tufa in the interior. The travertine blocks were originally fastened together with iron tenons; these were torn out in the Middle Ages and their sockets are conspicuous. Despite being pillaged for centuries, the Colosseum preserves its remarkable grandeur and the NE side appears almost undamaged. The mighty exterior wall, which supports the complicated interior, has four storeys. The lower three have rows of arches decorated with engaged columns of the three orders superimposed: Doric on the lowest storey, Ionic on the middle, and Corinthian on the top. The fourth storey, dating from the restoration of Alexander Severus, has no arches but is articulated by slender Corinthian pilasters. Statues originally occupied the arches of the second and third storeys. The exterior dimensions are: length 188m, breadth 15m, circumference 527m, height 50m.

There were 80 entrance arches. All were numbered except the four main entrances at the ends of the diameters of the ellipse, situated NE, SE, SW, and NW. That on the NE (between arches XXXVIII and XXXIX), which was without a cornice and was wider than the others, opened into a hall decorated with stuccoes; it was reserved for the emperor. The numbered arches led to the concentric vaulted corridors giving access to the staircases. Each spectator entered by the arch corresponding to the number of his ticket, ascended the appropriate staircase and found his seat in the cavea by means of one of the numerous passages.

Interior. This was divided into three parts, the arena, the podium, and the cavea. Though more than two-thirds of the original building has been removed, and the rows of the seats in the cavea are missing, the magnificence of the amphitheatre, which could probably hold some 50,000 spectators, can still be appreciated (although the best view is from the top storey, at present closed). The effect of the scene is reduced by the fact that the underground passages of the arena are exposed: they were formerly covered by a wood floor.

The ARENA measures 76m by 46m. Its name comes from the sand which covered the floor in order to prevent combatants from slipping and to absorb the blood. It was also sometimes flooded for mock sea-battles (or 'naumachiae'). The subterranean passages which can now be seen were used for the arrangement of the spectacles, and provided space for the mechanism by which scenery and other apparatus were hoisted into the arena. There were also cages for animals here.

The Cross replaces an earlier one which was set up to commemorate the martyrs who were supposed to have died in the Colosseum. The Chapel of Santa Maria della Pietà was reopened here in 1982. The arena was surrounded by a wall c 5m high to protect the spectators from the animals. At the top of this wall was the PODIUM. This was a broad parapeted terrace in front of the tiers of seats, on which was the imperial couch, or pulvinar. The rest of the terrace was reserved for senators, pontiffs, vestals, foreign ambassadors, etc.

The CAVEA was divided into three tiers, or *Moeniana*. The lowest tier was reserved for knights, the middle one for wealthier citizens, and the top one for the populace. The tiers were separated by landings (*Proecinctiones*), reached by several staircases. Each tier was intersected at intervals by *Vomitoria*, 160 in all, passages left between the seats. The section between two passages was called a *Cuneus*, or wedge, from its shape. Above the topmost tier was a colonnade, to which women were admitted. At the very top was the narrow platform for the men who were responsible for the *Velarium*, or awning, which kept off the sun; the holes for the supporting poles are still visible.

A modern staircase leads up from the second arch on the left of the main entrance to the **first storey** (for adm, see above). The view of the interior is spectacular. A model of the Colosseum and a few architectural fragments can be seen in a hall (behind glass). Above the entrance on the side towards the Palatine another staircase (closed since 1973) leads up to the second and (left) the third floors. From the latter a flight of steps continues to a gallery with a magnificent *view of the amphitheatre, and of the city, in which the salient features are the Forum backed by the green slopes of the Palatine.

The **Antiquarium** (opened in 1984 but since closed) is reached by a steep flight of stairs. It is arranged in part of the interesting sub-vaults built by Vespasian and used for all the trappings necessary for the spectacles in the arena above. Here are exhibited architectural elements (notably capitals) from the highest part of the building, and sculptural fragments from the terminals of the balustrades of the cavea.

Between the Colosseum and the end of Via dei Fori Imperiali is the site (marked by a raised lawn planted with ilexes) of the huge brick base, 7m square, of the COLOSSUS OF NERO, the remains of which were demolished in 1936. This huge gilt bronze statue of Nero as god of the Sun, by Zenodorus, was 35m high and the largest bronze statue ever made, even larger than its model, the Colossus of Rhodes. The statue was provided with a new base and moved here from the vestibule of the Domus Aurea by Hadrian when he built the Temple of Venus and Rome. Decrianus, the architect assigned to the task of removal, used 24 elephants to shift the statue.

The Colosseum in the 19C

Nearby a little garden has been planted with three cypresses. On the other side of a square lawn is an area of recent excavations surrounded by a fence and planted with olive trees. The visible ruins belong to the vestibule of the Domus Aurea. Beneath these were found extremely interesting remains of a temple and a Roman road. A circular fence surrounds the base of the **Meta Sudans**, which was demolished in 1936 by order of Mussolini, and re-excavated in 1982. This marble-faced fountain erected by Domitian marked the boundary of four regions of the Augustan city (II, III, IV, and X). It was restored by Constantine, and received its name from its resemblance to the conical turning-post (meta) for chariot races in circuses, and from the fact that it 'sweated' water through numerous small orifices. It was surrounded by a circular basin.

The triple ***ARCH OF CONSTANTINE** (Pl. 4; 7, 8) was erected in AD 315 in honour of Constantine's victory over Maxentius at Saxa Rubra. This triumphal arch was decorated with sculptural fragments from older Roman monuments, a sad testimony to the decline of the arts in the late Imperial period. However, the proportions of the arch are good, and many of the individual reliefs are of the highest quality. These were severely damaged by the polluted air, but they were beautifully restored in 1989.

The splendid large *reliefs on the inside of the central archway and the two above on the sides of the arch come from the frieze of a monument commemorating Trajan's victories over the Dacians and are probably by the sculptor who carved Trajan's Column. The eight medallions on the two façades, depicting hunting-scenes and pastoral sacrifices, belonged to a monument of Hadrian. The eight high reliefs let into the attic were taken (like the three in Palazzo dei Conservatori) from a monument to Marcus Aurelius, and represent a sacrifice, orations to the army and to the people, and a triumphal entry into Rome. The small bas-reliefs of the frieze and the victories and captives at the base of the columns are of the period of Constantine.

5

The Pantheon and Piazza Navona

The **PANTHEON** (Pl. 2; 6), the best-preserved monument of ancient Rome, remains the most magnificent symbol of the Empire. As the Pantheon, dedicated to all the gods, it was conceived as much as a secular Imperial monument as a shrine. In 609 it was converted into a church, the first temple in Rome to be Christianised. A pedimented pronaos precedes a gigantic domed rotunda, and a rectangular feature as wide as the pronaos and as high as the cylindrical wall is inserted between the two. This combination of a pronaos and rotunda gives it a special place in the history of architecture. Originally the pronaos was raised by several steps and preceded by a much larger piazza. Admission see p 47.

The original temple was built apparently of travertine, during the third consulate of Agrippa (27 BC), son-in-law of Augustus, to commemorate the victory of Actium over Antony and Cleopatra. It was damaged by fire in AD 80 and was restored by Domitian. In spite of the dedicatory inscription on the pediment of the pronaos (*M. Agrippa, L.F. Cos. tertium fecit*), it has been conclusively proved (by examination of the brick stamps) that the existing temple, including the pronaos, is not that of Agrippa, but a new one built and probably also designed by Hadrian of brick, on a larger scale and on different lines. This second building, begun in AD 118 or 119 and finished between AD 125 and 128, received and retained the name of Pantheon.

It was restored by Septimius Severus and Caracalla. Closed and abandoned under the first Christian emperors and pillaged by the Goths, the Pantheon was given to

Boniface IV by the Byzantine emperor Phocas (whose column is in the Forum). Boniface IV consecrated it as a Christian church in 609. It was dedicated to Santa Maria ad Martyres; there was a legend that some twenty-eight wagon-loads of martyrs' bones had been transferred here from the catacombs. In 667 Constans II, emperor of Byzantium, on a twelve-day visit to Rome, robbed the temple of what the Goths had left, and, in particular, stripped off the gilded roof-tiles (probably of bronze). Benedict II (684) restored it, Gregory III (735) roofed it with lead; in 1153 Anastasius IV built a palace beside it.

When the popes took up residence in Avignon the Pantheon served as a fortress in the struggles between the Colonna and the Orsini. In 1435 Eugenius IV isolated the

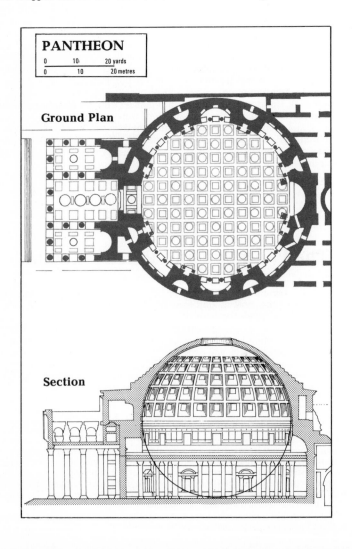

PANTHEON

| 0 | 10 | 20 yards |
| 0 | 10 | 20 metres |

Ground Plan

Section

building, and from then on it was the object of such veneration that the Roman Senator on taking office swore to preserve 'Maria Rotonda' intact for the pontiff, together with the relics and sacred treasures of the City. The monument was greatly admired during the Renaissance; Pius IV repaired the bronze door, and had it practically re-cast (1563). Urban VIII (Barberini), however, employed Bernini to add two clumsy turrets in front, which became popularly known as the 'ass-ears of Bernini'. Urban VIII also melted down the bronze ceiling of the portico to make the baldacchino at St Peter's and 80 cannon for Castel Sant' Angelo, an act of vandalism that prompted Pasquino's stinging gibe, 'Quod non fecerunt barbari fecerunt Barberini'.

The dome of the Pantheon

Alexander VII had the portico restored by Giuseppe Paglia (1662) and the level of the piazza lowered, to provide a better view of the façade; Clement IX surrounded the portico with an iron railing (1668); Benedict XIV employed Paolo Posi (1747) to restore the interior and the atrium. The first two kings and the first queen of Italy are buried here. The incongruous turrets added by Bernini were removed in 1883.

The PORTICO is nearly 34m wide and 15.5m deep, and has 16 monolithic Corinthian columns of red or grey granite, without flutings, each 12.5m high and 4.5m in circumference. The superb capitals and the bases are of white marble. The three columns on the E side are replacements, one by Urban VIII (1625), the others by Alexander VII (1655–67); the arms of these popes may be seen in the decoration of the capitals. Eight of the columns stand in front, and the others are disposed in four rows, so as to form three aisles, the central one leading to the bronze door, which dates from the time of Pius IV, and the others to the two great niches which may formerly have contained colossal statues of Augustus and Agrippa.

The visual impact of the *INTERIOR is unforgettable. The use of light from the opening in the dome displays the genius of the architect. The height and diameter of the interior are the same—43.3m. The great dome has five rows of coffers diminishing in size towards the circular opening in the centre, which measures almost 9m across. The intricate design of the coffers is mainly responsible for the effect of space and light in the interior. They were probably ornamented with gilded bronze rosettes. The diameter of the dome, the largest of its kind ever built, exceeds by more than 1m that of the dome of St Peter's. Its span, which contains no brick arches or vaults, begins at the level of the highest cornice seen on the outside of the building, rather than, as it appears in the interior, at the top of the attic stage.

The cylindrical wall is 6m thick; it contains seven great niches, or recesses, each, except the central apse, preceded by two Corinthian columns of giallo antico, and flanked by pilasters. The apse instead has two free-standing columns. Between the recesses, which originally contained statues, are eight shrines (aediculae), those flanking the apse and entrance with triangular pediments, and the others with segmented pediments. They are supported by two Corinthian columns in giallo antico, porphyry, or granite. Above the recesses is the entablature with a beautiful cornice, and still higher is an attic, unfortunately restored in 1747, making this stage more pronounced than was intended. Part of the original decoration can be seen over the recess to the right of the apse: between the rectangular openings (fitted with grilles) were shallow pilasters of reddish marble alternating with three marble panels. More than half of the original coloured marble sheets on the walls are still in place. The floor, though restored, retains its original design.

RIGHT SIDE. In the first chapel, *Annunciation, a fresco attributed to Melozzo da Forlì or Antoniazzo Romano, and two 17C marble angels. In the aedicule, 14C fresco of the Coronation of the Virgin. Second chapel, tomb of Victor Emmanuel II, first king of Italy (died 9 January 1878), designed by Manfredo Manfredi; third chapel, 15C Madonna and Saints. In the main APSE, above the high altar, 7C icon of the Virgin and Child.

LEFT SIDE. In the third chapel, 16C Crucifix and (right) a monument by Thorvaldsen to Cardinal Consalvi (died 1824), secretary of Pius VII, who represented the Holy See at the Congress of Vienna. Third aedicule, TOMB OF RAPHAEL, inscribed with the famous distich of Bembo, translated by Pope in his Epitaph on Sir Godfrey Kneller ('Living, great Nature feared he might outvie Her works, and dying, fears herself may die'). On the altar is the statue of the Madonna del Sasso, by Lorenzetto, probably with the help of Raffaello da Montelupo, from Raphael's original design. The bronze bust is by De Fabris. Below the empty niche on the right is the short epitaph of Maria Bibbiena, niece of Cardinal Dovizi da Bibbiena, who was to have married Raphael but died before him.

Second chapel: tomb of Humbert I (who was assassinated at Monza on 29 July 1900), designed by Giuseppe Sacconi. Below Humbert's tomb is that of Margherita di Savoia, first queen of Italy (died 5 January 1926). Among other artists buried in the Pantheon are Giovanni da Udine, Perino del Vaga, Taddeo Zuccari, Annibale Carracci, and Baldassarre Peruzzi.

A door on the left of the pronaos leads to a staircase to the cupola (extensive views; adm only with special permission).

Detail of the elephant by Gian Lorenzo Bernini in Piazza Minerva

In **Piazza della Rotonda** is a fountain (1575; restored in 1991), on a model of Giacomo della Porta, surmounted by an obelisk of Ramesses the Great, formerly belonging to the Isaeum and erected here in 1711. In Via della Palombella, at the back of the Pantheon, are remains of Agrippa's BASILICA OF NEPTUNE, reconstructed by Hadrian.

In **Piazza Minerva** is a bizarre but delightful work by Bernini (1667), a marble elephant supporting a small obelisk which belonged to the ISAEUM CAMPENSE, or TEMPLE OF ISIS, that formerly stood nearby. Other relics from the temple are in the Museo Capitolino, in Piazza dei Cinquecento, and in the Egyptian Museum in the Vatican. The hieroglyphic inscription on the obelisk relates to Apries, the last of the independent Pharaohs of Egypt (the Hophrah of the Bible), who was the ally of Zedekiah, king of Judah, against Nebuchadnezzar (6C BC).

*SANTA MARIA SOPRA MINERVA** (Pl. 2; 6; closed 12.00–16.00) stands on the site of a small oratory probably built here before AD 800 on the ruins of a Temple of Minerva. It was rebuilt in 1280 by the Dominicans who modelled it on their church (Santa Maria Novella) in Florence (according to Vasari it was by the same architects, Fra Sisto and Ristoro). It was altered and over-restored in the Gothic style in 1848–55. On the right side of the simple façade (1453; recently cleaned) small marble plaques register the heights reached by floods on the Tiber before it was canalised.

In the INTERIOR (coin-operated lights in every chapel) the vault, the rose-windows, and the excessively colourful decorations date from the 19C restoration. On the right of the central door is the tomb of Nerone Diotisalvi, a Florentine exile (died 1482), and, on the right of the S door, that of Virginia Pucci Ridolfi (1567), the latter with a fine bust by an unknown Florentine.

SOUTH AISLE. By the first chapel, with an altarpiece by Baciccia, tomb of the archivist Castalio, with a fine portrait. The second chapel was decorated by Lazzaro Baldi in the late 17C. The third chapel has vault frescoes by Girolamo Muziano. The fourth chapel was designed by Carlo Maderno. The altarpiece of the Annunciation is by Antoniazzo Romano (1500; restored in 1989), with Cardinal Juan de Torquemada (uncle of Tomás de Torquemada, the inquisitor) presenting three poor girls to the Virgin, commemorating the Confraternity of the Annunziata, founded in 1460 to provide dowries for penniless girls. On the left, tomb of Urban VII, by Ambrogio Buonvicino.

The fifth chapel has a frescoed ceiling by Cherubino Alberti, and an altarpiece of the Institution of the Eucharist, by Barocci. At the sides are the tombs of the parents of Clement VIII, by Giacomo della Porta, and (in a niche to the left) a statue of Clement VIII. Some scholars have recently attributed the statue of St Sebastian in a niche on the right wall of the chapel to Michelangelo as a model for his Christ (see below); it seems to have been finished by Nicolas Cordier. Sixth chapel. On the right, tomb of Bishop Juan Diaz de Coca (1477), by Andrea Bregno, with a fresco attributed to Melozzo da Forlì; on the left, tomb of Benedetto Sopranzi, Bishop of Nicosia (died 1495), by the school of Bregno.

SOUTH TRANSEPT. First chapel, wooden crucifix (early 15C). The *CAPPELLA CARAFA is preceded by a fine marble arch (attributed to Giuliano da Maiano), with a beautiful balustrade. It contains celebrated *frescoes by Filippino Lippi (1489; beautifully restored in 1993). On the right wall, below, St Thomas confounding the heretics, the central figures being Arius and Sabellius (the two youths in the right-hand group are probably the future Medici popes, Leo X and Clement VII, both buried in this church). In the lunette above, St Thomas Aquinas in prayer, and in the vault, the Sibyls. On the altar wall, Assumption (with a splendid group of angels) and altarpiece of the Annunciation, with St Thomas Aquinas presenting Cardinal Olivieri Carafa to the Virgin, also by Filippino. On the left wall, monument of Paul IV (died 1559) by Giacomo and Tommaso Cassignola, from a design by Pirro Ligorio.

To the left of this chapel, *tomb of Guillaume Durand (died 1296), bishop of Mende, by Giovanni di Cosma, with a beautiful 13C mosaic of the Madonna and Child. Third chapel, Carlo Maratta, Madonna and saints. Fourth chapel, frescoed ceiling by Marcello Venusti; on the right, tomb of Cardinal Capranica (1458).

CHOIR. At the foot of the steps, on the left, is *Christ bearing the Cross by Michelangelo (1514–21), commissioned at a cost of 200 ducats by Metello Vari and Pietro Castellani. The bronze drapery is a later addition. Under the 19C high altar lies the body of St Catherine of Siena (see below). In the apse are the tombs of Leo X (left) and Clement VII, designed by Antonio

Sangallo the Younger, with statues by Raffaello da Montelupo and Nanni di Baccio Bigio respectively. In the pavement is the slab-tomb of Cardinal Pietro Bembo (1547), secretary to Pope Leo X from 1512–20, and friend of Michelangelo, Raphael, and Ariosto.

NORTH TRANSEPT. To the left of the choir, in a passageway which serves as an exit, are several large monuments, including those of Cardinal Michele Bonelli (Alexandrinus), by Giacamo della Porta, and of Cardinal Domenico Pimentel, designed by Bernini. Surrounded by a bronze fence (1975) is the *tomb-slab of Fra Angelico, attributed to Isaia da Pisa. The painter died in the convent here in 1455, and the charming epitaph was composed by Pope Nicholas V. In the second chapel to the left of the choir, is a 15C altarpiece (a standard) of the Madonna and Child, attributed to Fra Angelico. The tomb of Giovanni Arberini (died c 1470) is by a Tuscan sculptor (Agostino di Duccio?), who incorporated a splendid *bas-relief of Hercules and the lion, probably a Roman copy of an original Greek work of the 5C BC. To the left is the entrance to the 17C sacristy, behind which is the room (temporarily closed) in which St Catherine of Siena died in 1380; it was brought here from Via di Santa Chiara by Cardinal Barberini. The frescoes, poorly preserved, are by Antoniazzo Romano and his school (1482).

At the end of this transept is the Cappella di San Domenico, with the monument of Benedict XIII (died 1730), with sculptures by Pietro Bracci. At the corner of the nave and transept is the charming small tomb of Andrea Bregno (1421–1506). On the second nave pillar is the tomb of Maria Raggi, a colourful early work by Bernini.

NORTH AISLE. Between the fourth and third chapels, tomb of Giovanni Vigevano (died 1630) with a bust by Bernini (c 1617). Third chapel. Tiny altarpiece (the Redeemer), attributed to Perugino or to Pinturicchio; on the right, statue of St Sebastian, attributed to Michele Marini; on the left, St John the Baptist, by Ambrogio Buonvicino; against the side-walls, tombs of Benedetto and Agostino Maffei, attributed to Luigi Capponi (15C). Second chapel. The tomb of Gregorio Naro, showing the cardinal kneeling at a prieu-dieu, has recently been attributed to Bernini. In the first chapel is a bust of Girolamo Bottigella, perhaps by Iacopo Sansovino. Near the door is the tomb of Francesco Tornabuoni (1480), by Mino da Fiesole, and above is that of Cardinal Tebaldi (1466), by Andrea Bregno and Giovanni Dalmata.

From the piazza a door on the left of the façade leads into the monastery, once the headquarters of the Dominicans, in which Fra Angelico died (1455) and Galileo was tried (1633). It now serves as offices for the Chamber of Deputies. The CLOISTER has late 16C vault frescoes. In the far walk are two funerary monuments attributed to Andrea Bregno and the SALA DEI PAPI (seen through a glass door) with a colossal statue of the Madonna and Child, an unfinished work attributed to Bernini. A small MUSEUM (closed indefinitely) contains icons from Yugoslavia (17–19C), ecclesiastical vestments, and a detached fresco of the Madonna and Child (late 13C or early 14C), etc.

From the piazza the narrow Via dei Cestari (with a number of shops selling liturgical articles) runs S towards the busy Corso Vittorio Emanuele. On the right in Via dell'Arco della Ciambella, part of the circular wall of the central hall of the BATHS OF AGRIPPA is charmingly incorporated into the street architecture. These were the first public baths in the city, begun by Agrippa in 25 BC. Opposite, Via della Pigna leads past the 16C Palazzo Maffei Marescotti to a little piazza in front of the Baroque church of SAN GIOVANNI DELLA PIGNA (usually closed; with interesting tomb slabs inside the entrance wall). At a house here (No. 6) Mussolini met Cardinal Gasparri in

1923 to initiate discussions on the Concordat. Via del Gesù (with a beautiful Renaissance doorway at No. 85) leads down to Palazzo Altieri (1650–60; interesting courtyards) on the traffic-ridden Piazza del Gesù.

Here rises the *GESÙ (Pl. 3; 6; closed 12.30–16.30), or the church of the *Santissimo Nome di Gesù*, the principal Jesuit church in Rome and the prototype of the sumptuous style to which the Order has given its name. It was built between 1568 and 1575 at the expense of Alessandro Farnese. Both the façade (by Giacomo della Porta), cleaned in 1993, and the interior (by Vignola) are important to the subsequent development of the design of Baroque churches in Rome. The cupola planned by Vignola was completed by Della Porta.

The heavily decorated INTERIOR has a longitudinal plan, with an aisleless nave and lateral chapels (coin-operated lights in each chapel, and at the W end, for the vault). On the vault is a *fresco (recently restored) of the Triumph of the Name of Jesus, a remarkably original work, with marvellous effects of foreshortening, by Baciccia. The frescoes of the cupola and the tribune are by the same artist. He also designed the stucco decoration, executed by Antonio Raggi and Leonardo Retti. The marble decoration of the nave dates from 1858–61.

SOUTH SIDE. The first chapel has an altarpiece and frescoes by Agostino Ciampelli. The altarpiece in the third chapel, as well as the vault and walls were painted by Federico Zuccari (the lunettes and pendentives are by Ventura Salimbeni). The four marble festoons incorporated in the decoration are supposed to have come from the Baths of Titus. The elegant SACRISTY is by Girolamo Rainaldi.

SOUTH TRANSEPT. Altarpiece from a sketch by Pietro da Cortona with the Death of St Francis Xavier, by Carlo Maratta. The HIGH ALTAR and presbytery were redesigned in 1840 by Antonio Sarti. Over the high altar, sumptuously decorated with coloured marbles, is the Circumcision, by Alessandro Capalti (1842). On the left, a bust of Cardinal Roberto Bellarmine, by Bernini, was placed in a neo-classical setting after the tomb was destroyed during the rebuilding in the 19C. The two pretty little circular domed chapels on either side of the main apse were decorated by Giuseppe Valeriani (1584–88).

NORTH TRANSEPT (light on left). *Altar-tomb of St Ignatius, by Andrea del Pozzo and others (1695–1700), resplendent with marble and bronze; the columns are encrusted with lapis lazuli and their bronze decorations are by Andrea Bertoni. The statue of St Ignatius is a copy by Adamo Tadolini of the original by Legros (melted down during the French Revolution). Above is a group of the Trinity by Leonardo Retti with a terrestrial globe formed of a splendid block of lapis lazuli, the largest known. In front of the altar is a magnificent balustrade, and at the sides are marble groups: Religion triumphing over Heresy, by Legros (right), and Barbarians adoring the Faith, by Jean Baptiste Théodon (left).

NORTH SIDE. Third chapel, altarpiece of the Holy Trinity by Francesco Bassano, and Baptism of Christ (right wall) by Ventura Salimbeni. The second chapel (being restored) has vault frescoes by Pomarancio, 17C paintings by Giovanni Francesco Romanelli, and interesting sculptures. The first chapel also has its vault frescoed by Pomarancio and two paintings by Francesco Mola. The singing of a Te Deum in this church annually on 31 December is a magnificent traditional ceremony. The room where St Ignatius lived from 1544 to his death in 1556, on the left of the façade, can sometimes be seen on request.

Via d'Aracoeli leads from Piazza del Gesù to Piazza d'Aracoeli and the Capitol. On the right, in Via delle Botteghe Oscure (with the headquarters of the ex Italian Communist Party, now called the 'Partito Democratico della Sinistra') are the remains of a temple (seen from the railings), probably a TEMPLE OF NYMPHS, dating from the 1C BC. On the S side of this road Palazzo Paganica was purchased in 1983 by the Italian State and excavations are in progress beneath it and the adjoining site (entrance at 6C Via Caetani). Remains of the small THEATRE OF BALBUS inaugurated in 13 BC have been uncovered, adjoined to the W by a cryptoporticus known as the CRYPTA BALBI. Later buildings also excavated here include the medieval church of Santa Maria, and a Renaissance monastery. The interesting remains may one day be opened to the public. In Via Caetani a plaque marks the place where the body of the statesman Aldo Moro was abandoned by his murderers in 1978.

The Piazza Navona

Corso Vittorio Emanuele (Pl. 3; 5, 6), now one of the main traffic arteries of Rome running from Piazza Venezia to the Tiber, dates from 1876. It leads from Piazza Gesù to the **Largo Argentina**, a traffic-ridden square with an impressive group of **four Republican temples**, known as the *Area Sacra di Largo Argentina*. The site was demolished in 1926–29 for a new building which, after the temples had been discovered and excavated, was never built. The ruins, now inhabited by cats, are well seen from the railings outside (the entrance on Via di San Nicola dei Cesarini is kept locked).

All the temples face a courtyard to the E paved with travertine. It is not yet known with certainty to whom they were dedicated. The FIRST TEMPLE ('A') is peripteral and hexastyle; most of the tufa columns and stylobate are preserved. In the Middle Ages the church of St Nicholas was built over it; the apses of the church (otherwise demolished) may still be seen. The SECOND TEMPLE ('B'), the most recent, is circular, and six columns survive, as well as the original flight of steps and the altar. A podium behind this temple near Via di Torre Argentina, almost certainly belongs to the Curia Pompei where Caesar was murdered. The THIRD TEMPLE ('C'), oldest of the four, was built at a lower level; it dates from the end of the 4C or the beginning of the 3C BC. In the Imperial era the cella was rebuilt and the columns and podium covered with stucco. In 1935 the altar, with an inscription relating to c 180 BC, was discovered; even this was a replacement of an older altar. The FOURTH TEMPLE ('D'), in travertine, is the largest; it has not been completely excavated as part of it is under Via Florida, to the S. During the excavations the medieval TORRE DEL PAPITO here was restored and isolated.

To the N of the square, on Via dei Cestari, is the church of the STIMMATE, rebuilt at the beginning of the 18C by Giovanni Battista Contini. It contains paintings by Francesco Trevisani, including the high altarpiece of St Francis receiving the Stigmata (1714). On the W side of Largo Argentina is the TEATRO ARGENTINA dating from 1730, and the most important theatre in Rome during the 18C. The façade is by Pietro Holl (1826; cleaned in 1993). Here in 1816 was held the first performance of Rossini's 'Barber of Seville', and in 1851 that of Verdi's 'Rigoletto'. It is now noted for prose productions and the 'Teatro di Roma' is the resident company. It has a small museum (admission by appointment).

On the right of the theatre, Via del Sudario leads out of the square past the handsome S façade of Palazzo Caffarelli Vidoni, attributed to Lorenzo Lotti (c 1515). The CHIESA DEL SUDARIO (1604), opposite, was the court church of the House of Savoy from 1871 to 1946. The façade is by Carlo Rainaldi, and inside are late 19C works by Cesare Maccari. Adjoining is the delightful **Casa del Burcardo**, built in 1503 for Bishop Hans Burchard or Burckhardt. He was author of a remarkable account of the papal court under Innocent VIII and Alexander VI, and called the house the Torre Argentina, which in turn became the name of the piazza. The back doors of the Teatro Argentina (see above) open on to the court. It now houses a theatrical museum (closed a number of years ago) and a library.

Via del Sudario ends in the little Piazza Vidoni where a Roman statue (now decapitated) called '*Abate Luigi*' (one of Rome's 'talking' statues) has been placed against the side wall of the church of ***SANT'ANDREA DELLA VALLE** (Pl. 3; 6; entrance to right). It was begun in 1591 by Fra Francesco Grimaldi, and continued by Carlo Maderno who crowned it with a fine dome, the largest in Rome after that of St Peter's. The façade (1665; beautifully cleaned and restored in 1991) is by Carlo Rainaldi. The aisleless INTERIOR (open 7.30–12.00, 16.30–19.30) has a high barrel-vault and spacious apse. Inspired by the Gesù, it gives the impression of a sumptuous reception hall rather than a house of prayer.

SOUTH SIDE. The first chapel, by Carlo Fontana, has green marble columns and fine sculptures by Ercole Antonio Raggi. The design of the second chapel (Cappella Strozzi) shows the influence of Michelangelo and contains reproductions in bronze of his Pietà and of his statues of Leah and Rachel from the tomb of Julius II. The third chapel has a neo-classical Robilant monument attributed to Giuseppe de Fabris and Rinaldo Rinaldi. At the E end of the nave, high up, are similar monuments of two popes of the Piccolomini family: on the right, Pius III (died 1503) attributed to Francesco Ferrucci and his son Sebastiano; on the left Pius II (died 1464) attributed to Paolo Taccone and a follower of Andrea Bregno. In the little chapel on the right of the presbytery is a 17C Crucifix.

In the DOME high up above the crossing is the Glory of Paradise, by Lanfranco; in the pendentives, the Evangelists by Domenichino (1623). He also designed the splendid PRESBYTERY AND APSE (restored in 1994) and painted the Six Virtues and the scenes from the life of St Andrew; the gigantic frescoes in the tribune are by Mattia Preti. The sacristy has 17C decorations. In the NORTH TRANSEPT is an altar by Cesare Bazzani (1912) in the Baroque style. NORTH SIDE. Third chapel, altarpiece of St Sebastian by Giovanni de' Vecchi; second chapel, altarpiece by Francesco Manno (early 19C). The first chapel, frescoed by Passignano, has four good sculptures: on the left, Mary Magdalene by Cristoforo Stati, and St John the Baptist by Pietro Bernini, and on the right, St John the Evangelist by Ambrogio Bonvicino and Santa Marta by Francesco Mochi.

Opposite the church façade, at the beginning of Corso del Rinascimento, is a fountain by Carlo Maderno decorated with an eagle and a dragon. Corso Vittorio Emanuele continues past **Palazzo Massimo alle Colonne**, skilfully set in a narrow, irregular site, by Baldassarre Peruzzi (1532–36). The convex façade, much blackened by the polluted air, follows the line of the cavea of the Odeon of Domitian which stood here. The beautiful portico (recently restored) is decorated with stuccoes. The palace has two courtyards: one a charming Renaissance work with a frescoed loggia, and a Baroque fountain, and the second (in very poor repair) with 17C decorations. The interior is being slowly restored, and a fresco has been uncovered which may be the work of Giulio Romano. In Piazza dei Massimi, behind the palace (reached from Corso Rinascimento) is the so-called 'Palazzo Istoriato', or PALAZZETTO MASSIMI with remains of its painted façade (1523; by the school of Daniele da Volterra). Here Pannartz and Sweynheim transferred their press (from Subiaco; see Rte 32) in 1467 and issued the first books printed in Rome. The marble cipollino column set up in the piazza belonged to the Odeon of Domitian (see above).

The Corso widens at a little piazza in front of the church of SAN PANTALEO (open only early in the morning) dating from 1216. It was rebuilt in 1681 by Antonio De Rossi and preserves its 17C interior with a vault fresco by Filippo Gherardi. The façade was added by Giuseppe Valadier in 1806. The huge **Palazzo Braschi** by Cosimo Morelli (after 1792) houses the **MUSEO DI ROMA** (Pl. 2; 8) on four floors. This has been closed for restoration since 1988, although important exhibitions are held on the ground floor.

The museum was founded in 1930 to illustrate the history and life of Rome from the Middle Ages to the present day. Many of the works of art come from demolished buildings. At the foot of the magnificent staircase attributed to Valadier (1802–04) and decorated by Luigi Acquisti, is a colossal statue of Christ and St John by Francesco Mochi. The collection includes detached frescoes by Cigoli and Lo Spagna, portraits of illustrious members (including Isaac Newton) of the Accademia dell'Arcadia (see Rte 22), paintings by Pompeo Batoni, Baciccia, Andrea Sacchi, Pietro da Cortona, Guido Reni, Giovanni Paolo Pannini, and Gavin Hamilton. It also has sculptures by Francesco Mochi, Canova and Pietro Tenerani, and mosaics from the old façade of St Peter's. The second floor rooms have ceilings decorated in the early 19C by Liborio Coccetti.

Via di San Pantaleo, which skirts the left side of Palazzo Braschi, ends in Piazza Pasquino. Here is a fragment of a marble group representing Menaleus with the body of Patroclus, the copy of a Hellenistic work of the Pergamene school which may once have decorated the Stadium of Domitian (see below). This famous statue has been known as PASQUINO since it was placed here in 1501. It became the custom to attach witty or caustic comments on topical subjects to the pedestal of the statue. The credit for originating this method of public satire was ascribed to a certain Pasquino, a tailor in the vicinity, hence the origin of the term 'pasquinade'. There were other 'talking statues' in the city; as Stendhal noted on his visit to Rome in 1816 'what the people of Rome desire above all else is a chance to show their strong contempt for the powers that control their destiny, and to laugh at their expense: hence the dialogues between 'Pasquino' and 'Marforio''. Many printing houses and bookshops were opened in the vicinity of the piazza.

From Piazza Pasquino the narrow VIA DEL GOVERNO VECCHIO, an ancient papal thoroughfare with many traces of the early Renaissance, leads W. On the right (No. 39) is PALAZZO NARDINI (or Palazzo del Governo Vecchio), built in 1473 by Cardinal Stefano Nardini, created Governor of Rome by Paul II. It has a splendid Renaissance portal. Opposite is the remarkable PALAZZO TURCI (1500), once attributed to Bramante.

From Piazza Pasquino Via di Pasquino leads into *PIAZZA NAVONA* (Pl. 2; 6) which occupies the site of the Stadium of Domitian. Its form, preserving the dimensions of the Roman building which could probably hold some 30,000 spectators, represents a remarkable survival within the modern city. The name, too, is derived from the athletic games, the 'Agoni Capitolini' held here after the stadium was inaugurated in AD 86. In the Middle Ages the piazza was called the 'Campus Agonis'; hence 'agone', 'n'agona', and 'navona'. Historic festivals, jousts, and open-air sports took place here, and it was also used as a market place from 1477 until 1869. From the 17C to the late 19C the piazza was flooded every week-end in August, for the entertainment of the Romans (the nobles enjoyed the spectacle from their carriages). During the Christmas festival, statuettes for the Christmas crib are sold here, and the fair and toy-market of the Befana, or Epiphany is held. In the total absence of wheeled traffic it remains the most animated piazza in Rome. It has several famous cafés.

Three splendid fountains decorate the piazza. At the S end, the FONTANA DEL MORO was designed by Giacomo della Porta in 1576, with sculptures by Taddeo Landini, Simone Moschino, Silla Longhi, and Egidio della Riviera. In 1874 these were substituted by copies made by Luigi Amici, and in 1909 the originals were moved to the Giardino del Lago in Villa Borghese (see Rte 9). The fountain was altered by Bernini in 1653 when he designed the central figure, known as 'Il Moro' (executed by Antonio Mari).

The central *Fontana dei Quattro Fiumi* is one of the most famous works by Bernini. In the mass of rockwork and grottoes are colossal allegorical figures of the rivers Danube, Ganges, Nile, and Plate, representing Europe, Asia, Africa, and America, carved by Bernini's pupils, Antonio Raggi, Giacomo Antonio Fancelli, Claude Poussin, and Francesco Baratta. The tall obelisk was cut in Egypt and brought to Rome by order of Domitian. It was moved here by Innocent X from the Circus of Maxentius and bears the names of Vespasian, Titus, and Domitian in hieroglyphics. The popular story told to illustrate the rivalry between Bernini and Borromini that the Nile is holding up an arm to block out the sight of Sant'Agnese is apocryphal since the fountain was finished in 1651 before Borromini started work on the church.

The fountain at the N end, representing Neptune struggling with a marine monster, Nereids, and sea-horses, is by Antonio della Bitta and Gregorio Zappalà (1878). Remains of the N curve of the stadium, with the entrance gate, may be seen beneath the modern buildings N of the piazza, in Piazza di Tor Sanguigna.

On the W side of the piazza is **SANT'AGNESE IN AGONE** (open only 17.00–19.00; and fest. 10.00–13.00), an ancient church built on the ruins of the stadium which Christian tradition marks as the spot where St Agnes was exposed (see Rte 19). It was reconstructed by Girolamo and Carlo Rainaldi in 1652. The splendid concave *FAÇADE which adds emphasis to the dome was begun by Borromini (1653–57). The lantern of the dome is by Carlo Rainaldi, and the twin bell-towers are by Giovanni Baratta and Antonio del Grande.

The small Baroque *INTERIOR has an intricate Greek-cross plan in which a remarkable effect of spaciousness is provided by the cupola. The fresco on the dome is by Ciro Ferri and Sebastiano Corbellini; the pendentives are by Baciccia. Above the seven altars 17C bas-reliefs or statues (including an antique statue of St Sebastian altered by Paolo Campi) take the place of paintings. The high altarpiece is a Holy Family by Domenico Guidi. Above the entrance is the monument by Giovanni Battista Maini of Innocent X, who is buried here. Beneath the church the Oratory of St Agnes (usually closed), built before AD 800, survives (although poorly restored) in a vault of the Stadium of Domitian. It contains badly damaged 13C frescoes, and the last work of Alessandro Algardi, a bas-relief of the miracle of St Agnes.

To the S of the church is **Palazzo Pamphilj** (sometimes called PALAZZO DORIA) started by Girolamo Rainaldi, and completed by Borromini for Innocent X, in the mid 17C. It was later occupied by the sister-in-law of Innocent, the notorious Olimpia Maidalchini. It is now the Brazilian Embassy (adm only by written permission).

INTERIOR. At the top of the stairs is the SALA PALESTRINA. This is a magnificent example of Borromini's secular architecture, using the minimum of surface decoration. The busts are by Alessandro Algardi. It has had an interesting history as a music room, since the first performance of the Concerti Grossi of Corelli took place here in the 17C. To the right are the State rooms overlooking Piazza Navona, decorated with delightful friezes, all painted between 1634 and 1671. In the first room, Bacchic scenes, by Andrea Camassei. Room II (to the right), seascapes by Agostino Tassi. Room III, landscapes by Gaspard Dughet. Room IV. Scenes from Roman history by Giacinto Gemignani. Room V. Episodes in Ovid's Metamorphoses by Giacinto Brandi. The long *GALLERY (designed by Borromini), has a magnificent fresco of the story of Aeneas by Pietro da Cortona. His organisation of the long vault is masterly. The charming papal bedroom also has a ceiling fresco by Cortona.

On the opposite side of the piazza, is the church of the MADONNA DEL SACRO CUORE, formerly SAN GIACOMO DEGLI SPAGNOLI, which was rebuilt in 1450 and restored in 1879. The entrance from the piazza is by a side door at the E end. On the S side the choir-gallery is almost certainly by Pietro Torrigiani; the *chapel off the N side is by Antonio da Sangallo the Younger.

Just out of the NW corner of the piazza, in the street of the same name, is the German church of **SANTA MARIA DELL'ANIMA** (Pl. 2; 6), rebuilt in 1500–23. The façade was possibly designed by Giuliano da Sangallo. Above the door is a cast of the Virgin attributed to Andrea Sansovino, a copy of a highly venerated Madonna between two souls in Purgatory, which was formerly in the church and was the origin of its name. The original is kept in the sacristy.

The INTERIOR (entrance through a pretty little courtyard behind the church at 20 Vicolo della Pace, 8.00–19.00; fest. 8.30–12.30, 15.00–19.00) has an unusual plan, derived from late Gothic German churches. The paintings in the vault and on the walls are by Ludovico Seitz (1875–82), who also designed the window over the central door. SOUTH SIDE. First chapel, San Benno by Carlo Saraceni; second chapel, Holy Family, by Giacinto Gimignani, and two funerary monuments by Ercole Ferrata; third chapel, Crucifix by Giovanni Battista Montano and 16C frescoes by Girolamo Siciolante da Sermoneta; fourth chapel, Pietà, by Lorenzetto and Nanni di Baccio Bigio, in imitation of Michelangelo.

In the SANCTUARY, Holy Family with saints, by Giulio Romano, over the high altar; on the right, the magnificent tomb of Hadrian VI (died 1523; of Utrecht), designed by Baldassarre Peruzzi, with sculptures by Michelangelo Senese and Niccolò Tribolo; on the left, Tomb of Karl Friedrich of Clèves (died 1575), by Gilles de Rivière and Nicolas d'Arras (a bas-relief from this tomb is in the corridor leading to the sacristy). NORTH SIDE. Fourth chapel, Descent from the Cross and frescoes, by Francesco Salviati; third chapel, Life of St Barbara, frescoes by Michiel Coxie; first chapel, Martyrdom of St Lambert, by Carlo Saraceni.

In the peaceful little piazza here, in a delightful part of the city, is the beautiful church of *SANTA MARIA DELLA PACE** (Pl. 2; 6; open 10.00–12.00, 16.00–18.00 except Monday; fest. 9.00–11.00). The church was rebuilt by Sixtus IV (1480–84) to celebrate the successful outcome of the Pazzi conspiracy and victory over the Turks. There was also a popular legend that a miraculous image of the Virgin in the portico of the old church bled on being struck by a stone. The architect is believed to have been Baccio Pontelli. The church was partly rebuilt in 1611 and again by Alexander VII, under whose auspices the façade and beautiful semi-circular porch with Tuscan columns were erected by Pietro da Cortona; his design of the delightful little piazza and the surrounding area was never completed.

The entrance is beyond the arch to the left of the façade, at 5 Via Arco della Pace. The *CLOISTERS are among Bramante's finest works in Rome (1504). They have two rows of arcades one above the other; columns of the upper row rise from the centres of the arches in the lower row. The tomb of Bishop Bocciaccio (1497) on the right is by the school of Luigi Capponi.

The INTERIOR of the church is covered for restoration in 1994. It consists of a domed octagon preceded by a simple rectangular nave. Above the arch of the first chapel on the SOUTH SIDE are frescoes of *SIBYLS by Raphael (c 1514), painted for Agostino Chigi, founder of the chapel. They represent (beginning on the left) the Cumaean, Persian, Phrygian, and Tiburtine Sibyls, to whom the future is being revealed by angels, and their varying shades of awe and wonder are beautifully conveyed in look and gesture. The paintings were restored in 1816 by Palmaroli. Above them are four

Santa Maria della Pace

prophets, by Timoteo Viti (Raphael's pupil): on the right, Daniel and David, on the left, Jonah and Hosea. On the altar, Deposition, a fine bronze by Cosimo Fancelli. The second chapel (Cesi) was designed by Antonio da Sangallo the Younger, and has remarkable marble decoration by Simone Mosca (1540–42). The ruined frescoes in the window lunette are by Rosso Fiorentino. The Cesi tombs and sculptures are by Vincenzo de' Rossi.

NORTH SIDE. First chapel. In the niche is a *fresco of the Virgin, Saints Bridget and Catherine, and the donor Ferdinando Ponzetti, by Baldassarre Peruzzi, who also painted the small frescoes of Old Testament subjects on the vaulting of the niche. At the sides of the chapel are the little *tombs of the Ponzetti family (1505 and 1509), with delicately carved decoration and four busts. Second chapel. Altarpiece (much darkened), Madonna and saints, by Marcello Venusti, perhaps from a design by Michelangelo. OCTAGON. Above the high altar, by Carlo Maderno, is the highly venerated 15C image of the Madonna della Pace. The beautiful marble tabernacle in the chapel of the Crucifix (left) is attributed to Pasquale da Caravaggio. On the octagon, to the right of the high altar, Baldassarre Peruzzi, Presentation in the Temple.

Off the other side of Piazza Navona (see above) Via di Sant'Agostino leads to the church of **SANT'AGOSTINO** (Pl. 2; 6), which was built for Cardinal d'Estouteville by Giacomo da Pietrasanta (1479–83). It is dedicated to St Augustine, author of the Confessions. The severely plain façade is one of the earliest of the Renaissance. The INTERIOR (open 7.30–12.00, 16.30–19.30), renovated by Luigi Vanvitelli (1750) contains good frescoes on the vault and nave by Pietro Gagliardi (1855), including five prophets on the nave pilasters which accompany the *PROPHET ISAIAH frescoed on the third pillar on the N side by Raphael. This was commissioned by the Humanist scholar Giovanni Goritz in 1512 for his funerary monument, and shows how much the painter was influenced by Michelangelo's frescoes in the Sistine Chapel. It was restored by Daniele da Volterra. Beneath it is a *Madonna and Child with St Anne, sculpted from a single block of marble by Andrea Sansovino.

At the W end is the so-called *Madonna del Parto, by Iacopo Sansovino (1521), a greatly venerated statue and the object of innumerable votive offerings. The two angels holding stoups at the W end are by Antonio Raggi. SOUTH AISLE. First chapel, paintings by Marcello Venusti; second chapel, Madonna della Rosa, a copy by Avanzino Nucci of the original painting by Raphael which was stolen from Loreto and subsequently disappeared. Third chapel, altarpiece by Giacinto Brandi, and two paintings by Pietro Locatelli. Fourth chapel, Christ giving the keys to St Peter, sculpted by Giovanni Battista Cotignola. Fifth chapel, 16C Crucifix.

SOUTH TRANSEPT. Chapel of Sant'Agostino, altarpiece by Guercino and side panels by his school; 18C stuccoes, and Baroque tomb of Cardinal Renato Imperiali, by Paolo Posi. On the HIGH ALTAR (1628), with two angels designed by Bernini, is a Byzantine Madonna brought from Constantinople. In the chapel to the left of the choir is the tomb of St Monica (mother of St Augustine), by Isaia da Pisa, and vault frescoes attributed to Giovanni Battista Ricci. The next little chapel (seen through a gate) was decorated by Giovanni Lanfranco (1616–19). The chapel in the NORTH TRANSEPT (covered for restoration) has a marble group on the altar finished by Ercole Ferrata.

NORTH AISLE. Fifth chapel, altarpiece by Giacinto Brandi; fourth chapel, St Apollonia, by Girolamo Muziano; third chapel, altarpiece by Sebastiano Conca; second chapel, designed by Bernini, has a Crucifix by Ventura Salimbeni. In the first chapel, *Madonna di Loreto, commissioned for this altar by Ermete Cavalletti from Caravaggio (light on left). This is one of the most beautiful paintings by Caravaggio in the city. In the little vestibule at the N door are Four Doctors by Isaia da Pisa, statues belonging to the tomb of St Monica, and a Crucifix by Luigi Capponi (15C).

In Via delle Coppelle, to the right off Via della Scrofa, is (No. 35) PALAZZO BALDASSINI, a smaller version of Palazzo Farnese, by Antonio Sangallo the Younger (1514–23), with a handsome courtyard and loggia. Garibaldi lived here in 1875.

Via dei Pianellari skirts the left side of Sant'Agostino as far as Via dei Portoghesi. Here are a delightful 15C doorway and tower and, behind a pretty balustrade, the ornate façade of the 17C church of **Sant'Antonio dei Portoghesi**. The good Baroque interior (usually closed) has a painting (first left altar) of the Madonna and Child with Saints Anthony and Francis by Antoniazzo Romano. Across Via della Scrofa Via della Stelletta continues E to the piazza and church of **Santa Maria in Campo Marzio** (Pl. 2; 6). The church, of ancient foundation, was rebuilt in 1685 by Giovanni Antonio de' Rossi on a Greek-cross plan, with a good portico and court. Over the high altar is a Madonna, part of a triptych probably of the 12–13C. Since 1920 the church has belonged to the Roman Catholic Patriarchate of Antioch of the Syrians (services on fest.).

To the S, reached by a street of the same name is the little church of **Santa Maria Maddalena** with a Rococo façade (1735; over-restored in 1991) by Giuseppe Sardi. The pretty *INTERIOR (1695–99), on an original plan, was designed by Giovanni Antonio de'Rossi and Giulio Carlo Quadrio. The statues of Virtues in the nave are attributed to Paolo Morelli, except for the first and third on the left which are by Carlo Monaldi, and by Giuseppe Raffaelli. The vault is frescoed by Michelangelo Cerruti (1732) and the cupola by Stefano Parrocel (1739). The confessionals are by Giuseppe Palma (1762).

South side: second chapel, 16C painting of the Madonna and Child; third chapel, elaborate marble altar with a vault fresco by Sebastiano Conca. By the side door is a fine wood statue of Mary Magdalene (15C). Over the high altar, Mary Magdalene in Prayer by Michele Rocca, and, above, a fresco by Aureliano Milani. North side: third chapel, St Nicholas of Bari by Baciccio; second chapel, St Lawrence Giustiniani in adoration of the Child by Luca Giordano (1704). The elaborate cantoria and organ date from the early 18C. The sacristy (1741) of unique design is entered from the left aisle.

Via delle Colonnelle (which passes the right side of the church dating from the late 17C) leads to Piazza Capranica, which is dominated by PALAZZO CAPRANICA, partly Gothic and partly Renaissance in style. The tower has a delightful loggia. From the Maddalena Via del Pantheon (with a hotel at No. 63 on the left where Ariosto stayed in 1513; plaque) returns to the Pantheon (see above).

From Sant'Agostino Via della Scrofa continues S past the church of **SAN LUIGI DEI FRANCESI** (Pl. 2; 6; closed 12.30–16.00 and Thursday afternoon), the French national church (1518–89). The façade, attributed to Giacomo della Porta, with two superimposed orders of equal height, was over-restored in 1977. The INTERIOR was heavily encrusted with marble and decorated with white and gilded stucco on a design by Antonio Dérizet (1756–64). SOUTH AISLE. By the first pillar is the monument to the French who fell in the siege of Rome in 1849. Second chapel, *frescoes (damaged by restoration) by Domenichino; to the right, St Cecilia distributing garments to the poor, and St Cecilia and her betrothed crowned by angels; to the left, St Cecilia refusing to sacrifice to idols, and her martyrdom; on the ceiling, St Cecilia in Paradise. The altarpiece is a copy by Guido Reni of Raphael's St Cecilia at Bologna. Fourth chapel, altarpiece by Iacopino del Conte, Oath of Clovis; to the right, Army of Clovis, by Pellegrino Tibaldi; to the left, Baptism of Clovis, by Girolamo Sermoneta.

The HIGH ALTARPIECE is an Assumption of the Virgin by Francesco Bassaño. NORTH AISLE. The fifth chapel (coin-operated light on right) contains three famous and very well preserved *paintings by Caravaggio (1597–1602): (left) Calling of St Matthew, (right) his Martyrdom, and (altarpiece) St Matthew and the Angel. On the first pillar is a monument to Claude Lorrain (1600–82) by Lemoyne.

Nearly opposite the church is PALAZZO GIUSTINIANI, by Girolamo Fontana; the main doorway is by Borromini. The huge **Palazzo Madama** (Pl. 2; 6; no adm) has its main façade on the modern Corso del Rinascimento. It has been the seat of the Italian Senate since 1871.

Originally this was a house belonging to the Crescenzi, which passed to the Medici in the 16C as part of the dowry of Alfonsina Orsini. In the 17C the building was enlarged and decorated by Lodovico Cardi and Paolo Marucelli, who are responsible for the interesting Baroque façade. It owes its name to the residence here of 'Madama' Margaret of Parma, illegitimate daughter of Charles V, who married first Alessandro de' Medici and afterwards Ottavio Farnese, and was Regent of the Netherlands from 1559 to 1567. Benedict XIV bought the palace in 1740, and it became successively the residence of the Governor of Rome and the seat of the Ministry of Finance (1852–70), before it became the Palazzo del Senato. The right wing was added in 1931.

Sant'Ivo

Across Via degli Staderari (with a tiny wall fountain) is **Palazzo della Sapienza** (Pl. 2; 6) with a fine Renaissance façade, also on Corso del Rinascimento, by Giacomo della Porta. It was the seat until 1935 of the University of Rome, founded by Boniface VIII in 1303. It now houses the ARCHIVIO DI STATO, and exhibitions are held in a library designed by Borromini. The beautiful *COURT, also designed by Borromini, has porticoes on three sides, and the church of *Sant'Ivo is at the far end (recently cleaned). Begun for the Barberini pope, Urban VIII, both the courtyard and the church incorporate his device (the bee) into their design, as well as the Chigi 'monti' of Alexander VII. The church (open on Sunday at 10.00; or shown by the porter) is a masterpiece of Baroque architecture, with a remarkable light interior. The dome is crowned by an ingenious spiral campanile (copied many times, especially in Germany).

In Piazza Sant'Eustachio (with two well-known cafés) there is a good view of the campanile of St Ivo, and a charming palace with fine windows, a pretty cornice, and remains of its painted façade. Here also is a house (No. 83) built by Giulio Romano for the Maccarani. The church of SANT'EUSTACHIO, of ancient foundation, preserves its campanile of 1196. The pretty interior (usually closed) was designed by Antonio Canevari after 1724 (the two large 18C altarpieces in the transepts are by Giacomo Zoboli). Via della Palombella returns to the Pantheon.

6

Piazza Navona and Campo dei Fiori to the Tiber bend

This route covers part of the ancient **Campus Martius**, or Plain of Mars, which at first included the whole area between the Capitol Hill, the Tiber, and the Quirinal and Pincio Hills, but more precisely came to refer to the low-lying ground enclosed in the Tiber bend. It was said originally to have been the property of the Tarquins, and to have become public land after the expulsion of the kings. It took its name from an ancient Altar of Mars here, which gave a predominantly military nature to the area. After the 2C BC many temples and edifices for public entertainments were built, and on other parts of the land military exercises and athletic competitions were held. The S part of the Campus Martius was the Prata Flaminia, with the Circus of Flaminius. The area was not included in the walls of Rome until Aurelian built his famous wall round the city (272–79).

Between Piazza Navona (described in Rte 5) and Campo dei Fiori, opposite Palazzo Braschi (see Rte 5), on the noisy Corso Vittorio Emanuele, is the elegant little Renaissance palace called the *Piccola Farnesina (Pl. 2; 8), which now houses the Museo Barracco. It was built in 1523 to the order of the French prelate Thomas Le Roy; the architect was almost certainly Antonio da Sangallo the Younger. The palace is also called the *Farnesina ai Baullari* and *Palazzo Le Roy* or *Regis*.

Le Roy, who held important posts at the pontifical court, played an important part in the concordat of 1516 between Leo X and Francis I of France. For his services he was ennobled and permitted to augment his coat of arms with the lilies of France. This heraldic privilege is recorded in the architectural details of the palace: the three floors are divided horizontally by projecting bands displaying the Le Roy ermines and the Farnese lilies, which were substituted for the lilies of France and gave the palace the name of Piccola Farnesina by which it is best known. It has no connection with the Villa Farnesina in Trastevere.

The Piccola Farnesina was built to face Vicolo dell'Aquila, to the S. The construction of the Corso Vittorio Emanuele left exposed the N side of the palace, which backed on houses that had to be pulled down to make room for the new street. A fine new façade on the Corso was therefore built in 1898–1901; the architect was Enrico Guj, who also modified the side of the palace facing Piazza dei Baullari (and added the steps and balustrade).

Since 1948 the palace has contained the ***MUSEO BARRACCO** (admission, see p 46), a museum of ancient sculpture, beautifully re-arranged and reopened to the public in 1991. The collection, not large but choice, was formed by Senator Giovanni Barracco (1829–1914), and presented by him to the city of Rome in 1902. The entrance to the museum is in Piazza dei Baullari della Farnesina. In the **courtyard** is a bust of the founder, Giovanni Barracco, by Giuseppe Mangionello (1914) and the foundation inscription of the palace (found during rebuilding). Beneath the portico is a Hellenistic statue (100.) of Apollo seated on a rock. The room beyond displays (245.) a Christian sarcophagus (4C), and (120.) a headless funerary statue of a woman, a 4C BC Attic work. On the **staircase** are two female statues (175, 166.) of young girls.

First Floor. Room I (straight ahead). Egyptian sculpture from the beginning of the 3rd millennium to the end of the Roman era. First case: 1. Fragment of a relief of Nofer, a court official (4th dynasty). Second case: 2. Bas-relief of a cow being milked and other scenes (5th Dynasty). Third case: 6. Statuette of a woman kneading dough; 7. Wooden statuette of a man; and (17.) a polychrome fragment with the head of a pharaoh (perhaps Amenophis IV). Fourth case: 12. Basalt statuette of a scribe (12th Dynasty). Fifth case: 15. Head of a prince (19th Dynasty); 14. head of a lion in wood (18th Dynasty); 19. head of Ramesses II as a young man; amulets, seals and scarabs. In the middle of the room: 13. Sphinx of queen Hatshepsut, with the seal of Thutmosis III (1504–1450 BC), and a basalt lion (20). On the wall: 24. Statue of Osiride; 35, 309. two canopic vases; 23. bust of a warrior; *21. Head of Ramesses II, as a young man, with a blue chaplet (1299–1233 BC); *31. Head of a priest wearing a diadem, once thought to be a portrait of Julius Caesar, an interesting example from Roman Egypt.

Room II. Egyptian, Sumerian, and Assyrian works. First case: 30. Ptolomaic male head; second case: 22. Gilded funerary mask; 33. Painted stucco head of a mummy (Roman era). In front of the second case: 26, 246. Sarcophagi; *27. Vase, used as a water-clock, with fine reliefs. The third case displays Sumerian and Assyrian works in bronze, terracotta, and alabaster. On the end wall are displayed Assyrian reliefs: 47. Winged deity, from the NW palace of Assurbanipal at Nimrud (883–859 BC); 48. Five women prisoners in a palm grove (period of Sennacherib, 705–681, or Assurbanipal, 669–626 BC); and (58.) Huntsman with a horse.

Room III exhibits Etruscan works. 202, 201. Funerary cippi of the 5C BC from Chianciano and Chiusi; three representations of the Egyptian and Phoenician god Bes, including a statue (60.) from a villa in the Alban hills; and three antefixes in the form of female heads, including one (205.) from Bolsena, probably dating from the 2C BC. The other section of this room (**Room IV**) contains works dating from the 6–5C BC from Cyprus: in the first case, statuettes (61, 62.) of players of musical instruments, and (68.) an unusual little model of a polychrome quadriga ridden by a woman and child. In the second case, 64. Head of a bearded priest wearing a chaplet, showing traces of colour (end of 5C), well preserved. The **loggia**, with a vault frescoed in the 17C, displays (59.) an alabaster lion mask, a Phoenician work found in Sardinia. In the small meeting room at the top of the stairs have been hung four 4C frescoes detached from the Roman edifice below the building (see below), including one with a duck with a snake in its mouth, and another with boats.

A pretty staircase continues up to the **Second Floor** with a frescoed vault and tiled floor. In the **loggia** are Roman sculptures, copies of Greek originals. **Room V** displays Greek originals of the 5C BC. On the wall opposite the entrance: 73. Fragment of an Attic sepulchral stele with a horseman; 80. Archaic head of a youth; 81. Head of Athena, from Greece or Southern Italy; 88. Head of an athlete; *97. Head of Marsyas, replica of the head of the famous statue by Myron; *92. Head of Apollo, after an original by Pheidias, possibly the bronze statue seen by Pausanias near the Parthenon (Athens, before 450 BC); 113. Head of an ephebus (Argive–Sikyonian school).

On the opposite wall are copies of works by Polykleitos: 108. Head of the Doryphoros, good copy of the original bronze; 107. Head of the Diadumenos, after the original bronze; *109. Statuette of Hercules; 110. Head of a young man; 160. Bust of Hermes; *102. Upper part of a statue of an Amazon, after the original in the Temple of Diana at Ephesos, and (103.) part of a leg of this statue. In the centre of the room, *99. Replica of the Westmacott athlete in the British Museum, also after an original by Polykleitos, possibly a portrait of Kyniskos, victor at Mantinea.

Room VI continues the display of Greek works. On the right, first case: (upper shelf) early works from the Cyclades and Mycenae, and on the lower shelf, ceramics, including (223, 231.) two amphorae of the 5C BC, the second attributed to the Berlin Painter. In the second case: 101. head of a girl (5C), and statuettes: (115, 116.) in rosso antico of girls carrying watervessels, (77.) a woman in a peplos (c 470 BC), and (76.) a woman wearing a chiton (early 5C). On the left of the entrance are displayed 4C Attic works including: (127,128.) funeral lekythoi, (143.) head of an old man, possibly Demosthenes, (135.) fragment of a sepulchral relief, (*129.) votive relief to Apollo, (132.) head of a veiled woman, part of a sepulchral relief; and (*131.) Head of Apollo Kitharoidos, the best existing replica of the statue by Praxiteles.

Rooms VII and VIII. Hellenistic art. *139. Bitch licking her wounds, perhaps a replica of the masterpiece by Lysippos, formerly in the Temple of Jupiter on the Capitol; 157. Head of Alexander the Great or Mithras (2C BC); portraits, including (140.) Demosthenes, from an original attributed to Polieuctes, and (155.) Epicurus, after an Ionian original of 270 BC. In two cases are displayed ceramics from Magna Grecia, and sculptures from Taranto. On the wall: 176. Archaistic relief (3C BC), depicting the cave of Pan; 134. Fragment of a relief of a horseman stroking the mane of his horse, from a representation of the Dioscuri (4C, Greco-Italian). At the end of the loggia, with a frescoed vault (1904) is **Room IX** which displays Roman and medieval art. On the wall opposite the entrance: 173. Funerary urn in the form of an Ionic temple; *151. Statuette of Neptune, Roman work of the 1C BC from a 4C Greek original; *194. Head of a Roman boy, perhaps Nero; 190. Bust of a young Roman (probably period of Tiberius). By the door, (195.)

Head of Mars (period of Trajan). On the last wall: 206, 249, 250. Sepulchral reliefs (Palmyra, 3C AD); 208, 207. Two charming marble reliefs from the Duomo of Sorrento (10–11C); 209. Fragment of a mosaic from old St Peter's with the representation of the *Ecclesia Romana*.

In the basement of the palace (usually shown to small groups on request at the ticket office) are remains of a Roman building of the late Imperial period, discovered in 1899. Here can be seen part of a portico, with fine columns and opus sectile paving.

On the right of the Museo Barracco, opening onto Corso Vittorio Emanuele, is Piazza della Cancelleria, along one whole side of which is the graceful façade of the ***PALAZZO DELLA CANCELLERIA** (Pl. 3; 5), a masterpiece of the Renaissance. It was built for Cardinal Raffaello Riario by an unknown architect, probably in 1486, with a double order of pilasters. Showing Florentine influence, it is thought that Bramante may have helped at a late stage, possibly designing the beautiful courtyard; it is also probable that Andrea Bregno was involved in the building. The magnificent ***COURT-YARD** has double loggie with antique columns.

Excavations beneath the courtyard in 1988–91 revealed 4C and 5C remains of the huge palaeochristian basilica of San Lorenzo in Damaso, founded by Pope St Damaso I, and one of the most important early Christian churches in Rome. A cemetery in use from the 8C to the 15C was also discovered here, as well as numerous shards of 15C ceramics.

The palace is now the seat of the three Tribunals of the Vatican, including the Sacra Rota, and of the Pontificia Accademia Romana di Archeologia. Special permission is needed to see the interior, which includes the Sala Grande, decorated under Clement XI in 1718, with twelve paintings by Marcantonio Franceschini and frescoes by Giuseppe Nicola Nasini and Baciccia, and the Salone, decorated by Vasari and his pupils (including Raffaellino dal Colle) in a hundred days in 1546. The chapel has decorations by Francesco Salviati.

Incorporated into the palace is the basilica of **San Lorenzo in Damaso** (entered by a doorway at the right end of the main façade). The ancient basilica (see above) founded in the 4C was finally demolished in the 15C when the present church (built on part of the site), contemporary with the palace, had been completed. It was entirely restored in 1868–82, and again in this century after fire. It has a double atrium, and over the fine doorway in the right aisle is a lunette fresco of angel musicians by Cavalier d'Arpino (detached; formerly in the nave). The adjoining chapel has a 14C Crucifix in wood. In the main apse, Coronation of the Virgin, with Saints, by Federico Zuccari. At the end of the left aisle is the tomb of Cardinal Ludovico Trevisan, called Mezzarota Scarampi (1505), and in the chapel of the Sacrament, a 12C icon of the Virgin brought here from Santa Maria di Grottapinto in 1465.

At the S end of Piazza della Cancelleria, beyond the interesting old Via del Pellegrino which skirts the side of the Cancelleria, with shops set into the façade on street level, opens **CAMPO DEI FIORI** (Pl. 3; 5), once a meadow, which became one of the most important piazze in Rome in the 15C. Executions were occasionally held here; the fine monument (by Ettore Ferrari; 1889) to Giordano Bruno, in the centre, stands on the spot where he was burned alive in 1600. It has been a market-place since 1869, with attractive old stalls and canvas shades. It is the centre of a distinctive district of the city, with numerous artisans' workshops. The beautiful old Via dei

Campo dei Fiori with the monument to Giordano Bruno

Cappellari which leads out of the NW side of the piazza, and the parallel Via del Pellegrino are worth exploring.

The huge 15C PALAZZO PIO (Righetti), at the E end of the piazza, was built over the ruins of Pompey's Theatre (see below), which was surmounted, on the highest part of the cavea, by a Temple of Venus. The late 16C façade of the palace by Camillo Arcucci faces Piazza del Biscione, where at No. 89 is a small house with a painted façade. Impressive remains of the theatre can be seen on request at the restaurant in the piazza. From here a frescoed archway leads into a dark passageway by the old (deconsecrated) chapel of Santa Maria di Grottapinta to Via di Grotta Pinta. If this is closed it is necessary to reach Via di Grotta Pinta via Via del Biscione (where the Albergo Sole is thought to be the oldest hotel in the city), Piazza del Paradiso and Via dei Chiavari (with a good view of the dome of Sant'Andrea della Valle). The semi-circular Via di Grotta Pinta follows the line of the auditorium of the THEATRE OF POMPEY (55 BC; Rome's first stone-built theatre); to the E of it formerly stood the great rectangular Porticus of Pompey, off which opened the 'Curia' (remains of which have been identified in Largo Argentina, see Rte 5) where Julius Caesar was murdered (15 March, 44 BC) at the foot of a statue of Pompey (perhaps the one now in Palazzo Spada). The modern Teatro dei Satiri is here.

Detail of the Palazzo della Cancelleria

The animated Via de' Giubbonari, a busy local shopping street (closed to cars), leads out of the Campo dei Fiori, skirting the side of Palazzo Pio. It ends at Piazza Cairoli, with the domed church of **SAN CARLO AI CATINARI** (Pl. 3; 6), by Rosato Rosati (1612–20), many times restored. The façade was erected in 1636 by Giovanni Battista Soria.

The spacious INTERIOR (open 7.30–12.15, 16.30–19.00) is interesting for its 17C works. SOUTH SIDE. The first chapel, decorated in 1698–1702 by Simone Costanzi, has an altarpiece of the Annunciation by Giovanni Lanfranco. Second chapel, Martyrdom of San Biagio by Giacinto Brandi. Between the second and third chapels is the Hamerani monument, with exquisite classical carved decoration by Luca Carimini (1830–90). The third chapel, the *CAPPELLA DI SANTA CECILIA, beautifully lit from its little oval dome, was designed by Antonio Gherardi. In the SANCTUARY the high altarpiece of San Carlo carrying the sacred Nail to the plague-stricken is a good late work by Pietro da Cortona. In the apse is a fresco of San Carlo received in heaven by Giovanni Lanfranco. In the pendentives of the dome over the crossing are the Cardinal Virtues by Domenichino.

In the SACRISTY is a little bronze Crucifix attributed to Alessandro Algardi, and in an adjoining room (shown by the sacristan) a tondo of St Charles in prayer (a fresco detached from the façade) attributed to Guido Reni, and a painting of St Charles by Andrea Commodi. NORTH SIDE. The third chapel, decorated in the 17C, has frescoed lunettes attributed to Giacinto Gimignani, and a painting of martyrs by Francesco Romanelli. The altarpiece in the second chapel of the Death of St Anna is by Andrea Sacchi.

Opposite the church is Palazzo Santacroce, by Carlo Maderno (1602). On the other side of Via de' Giubbonari several short streets lead into the piazza in front of the MONTE DI PIETÀ (now a bank), with a long history as a pawn-shop. The façade by Ottaviano Nonni (Il Mascherino) was enlarged by Carlo Maderno, with a clock and small marble bell tower attributed to Borromini. A fine domed chapel (admission on request) by Carlo Maderno (1641; restored 1725) contains high reliefs by Domenico Guidi, Pierre Le Gros, and Giovanni Théodon.

Via dell'Arco del Monte di Pietà skirts the right flank of the building into the little piazza in front of the church of SANTISSIMA TRINITÀ DEI PELLE-GRINI (open only for services on Sunday), by Paolo Maggi (1603–16). The façade was added in 1723 by Francesco De Sanctis. The interior contains 17C works by Guido Reni (the Trinity), Borgognone, and Cavalier d'Arpino. In the neighbouring hospice (1625; being restored) the poet Goffredo Mameli, author of the national hymn which bears his name, died in 1849 at the age of 22 from wounds received fighting for the Roman Republic.

From the piazza Via dei Pettinari leads to the Tiber, here crossed by Ponte Sisto (described in Rte 21). The little church of SAN SALVATORE IN ONDA (usually closed) was built at the end of the 11C but transformed in the 17C. The interesting crypt was built over a Roman building of the 2C AD.

Via San Paolo alla Regola leads out of Piazza dei Pellegrini beyond the church of San Paolo alla Regola to the CASE DI SAN PAOLO, a group of over-restored 13C houses now used as offices. Other medieval buildings were demolished to make way for the huge MINISTRY OF JUSTICE built here in 1920 by Pio Piacentini. To the left is the ancient church of SANTA MARIA IN MONTICELLI (closed indefinitely), with a 12C campanile, radically restored in 1860. In the apse is a mosaic head of Christ, and fragments of mosaic decoration dating from the 12C. In the second chapel to the right is a Flagellation (detached fresco) by Antonio Carracci; opposite is a 14C wooden Crucifix.

The narrow Via Capodiferro (where an ancient house has columns set in to the façade) leads out of Piazza dei Pellegrini into Piazza Capodiferro with the huge *PALAZZO SPADA** (Pl. 3; 5), built for Cardinal Girolomo Capodiferro in 1540, probably by Giulio Mazzoni. The palace was acquired in the 17C by Cardinal Bernardino Spada, and has been the seat of the Council of State since 1889. The court and façade are by Giulio Mazzoni or Girolamo da Carpi and are outstanding examples of stucco decoration (beautifully cleaned and restored in 1992).

Courtyard of Palazzo Spada

Borromini restored the palace for his friend Cardinal Spada, and designed a painted niche with a statue on a wall in Piazza Capodiferro to close the view from the garden entrance on Via Giulia. The design of the niche has recently been found beneath the intonaco, and reconstructed here above an ancient sarcophagus which serves as a fountain in the piazza. Borromini also added an ingenious trompe l'oeil perspective on the S side (being restored, but usually reached through a door into the garden, right of the stairs leading up to the gallery). This makes use of the waste space between the Spada garden and the adjoining Palazzo Massari. The dimension of the tunnel is perspectively multiplied more than four times through the use of light and spacing of the columns.

Reached by a staircase from a corridor at the back of the palace is the ***GALLERIA SPADA** (adm, see p 46), a collection of paintings formed by Cardinal Spada and augmented by successive generations of his family. Arranged in four rooms which preserve their 17C decoration and furnishings, the important collection of 17C and 18C paintings (and 2C and 3C Roman sculpture) is a very interesting example of a 17C Roman Patrician family's private collection, which survives almost intact. It was acquired by the State in 1926. The works are numbered as described below, and handlists are available in each room.

Room 1. Two portaits of Cardinal Bernardino Spada by Guido Reni (*32.) and Guercino (35.). 29. Guido Reni, St Jerome. **Room II**. 60. School of Titian, Musician (unfinished); *56. Andrea del Sarto, Visitation; 94. 15C Umbrian school, Madonna and Child; 92. Sigismondo Foschi, Madonna and St John the Baptist; 90. Lavinia Fontana, Cleopatra; 89. Parmigianino (attributed), three heads (a fresco); 86. Titian, Paul III (a copy); 81. Giovanni Battista Bertucci, Madonna and Child with St John; 80. Marco Palmezzano, Way to Calvary, Eternal Father; 76. Fiorenzo di Lorenzo, St Sebastian; *77. Jan van Scorel, Young Man; 78. Hans Dürer, Young Man. 16C Tabernacle in carved and gilded walnut, with a bas-relief of the Annunciation. On the two long walls, fragments of a larger painted frieze by Perino del Vaga, designs for tapestries originally intended for the wall below Michelangelo's 'Last Judgment' in the Sistine Chapel.

Room III. 100. Nicolò dell'Abate, Landscape; 101. Ciro Ferri, Vestals; 146. 17C Flemish school, Winter Scene; Pietro Testa, 145. Iphigenia, 144. Massacre of the Innocents; 141. Antonio Carracci, Young Man; 139. Francesco Trevisani, Antony and Cleopatra; 136. Circle of Scipione Pulzone, Young Girl; 133. Baciccia, *sketch for the vaulting of the Gesù; 132. Guercino, Death of Dido; 126. Baciccia, Christ and the woman of Samaria; 123. Francesco Furini, St Lucy; *120. School of Rubens, Portrait of a Cardinal; 117. Circle of Annibale Carracci, Portrait of a young boy; J.F. Voet, 119. Gentlewoman, 110, 105. Portrait of Urbano and Pompeo Rocci; 113. Nicolò Tornioli, Cain and Abel; 103. P. Snayers, Sack of a village; 106. Giacinto Campana and Guido Reni, Abduction of Helena; 102. Jan Breughel the Elder, Landscape with windmills. Among the Roman sculpture are a Seated Philosopher, a bust of a woman of the 2C AD, and two Roman statuettes of a boy, one dressed in the lion-skin of Hercules, and another in the philosophic pallium.

Room IV. 148. School of Gherardo delle Notti, Betrayal of Christ; 149. Artemisia Gentileschi, St Cecilia; 150. Mattia Preti, Christ tempted; 152. Michelangelo Cerquozzi, At the water trough; 155. Orazio Gentileschi, David; 158. Cerquozzi, Death of the donkey; 159. Anon 17C, Boy with a plumed hat; *161. Cerquozzi, Masaniello's revolt in Naples; 165. Willem

Reuter (formerly attributed to Sweerts), Market; 168. Lubin Baugin, Still-life; 171. Bartolomeo Cavarozzi, Madonna; 172. Orazio Borgianni, Pietà (a replica); 175. 17C Roman school, Madonna and St Anne; 176. Nicolò Renieri (also attributed to Bartolomeo Manfredi), David; 178. School of Carlo Saraceni (also attributed to Francesco Albani), Christ scourged; 182. Cerquozzi, Traveller and shepherds; 184. Le Valentin, Holy Family. The Roman bust of a boy dates from the Julio-Claudian period.

The *State Rooms on the first floor can be seen either with special permission, when not in use, or sometimes on Sunday morning if the porter is available. The GENERAL COUNCIL CHAMBER has magnificent trompe l'oeil frescoes by the 17C Bolognese artists, Agostino Mitelli and Michelangelo Colonna, with birds and figures peering into the room from around columns and window ledges. The colossal statue of Pompey is traditionally thought to be the one at the foot of which Caesar was murdered. The decoration in the next room is extremely fine, with frescoes and stucco in high relief. The last room on this side of the palazzo has another fine ceiling. From here is the entrance to the CORRIDOR OF STUCCOES, a delightful work by Giulio Mazzoni (1559), complemented by his ornamentation of the façade of the court seen through the windows. Further rooms lead to the MERIDIANA, a corridor decorated by Giovanni Battista Ruggeri, mapping the times at various places in the world. The eight Hellenistic reliefs of mythological subjects of the 2C AD are very fine, and in a good state of preservation.

Fountain in Piazza Farnese

Vicolo de' Venti continues to **PIAZZA FARNESE**, created by the Farnese in front of their splendid palace. Here are two huge baths of Egyptian granite brought from the Baths of Caracalla in the 16C and used by the Farnese as a type of 'royal box' for the spectacles which were held in the square. They were adapted as fountains (using the Farnese lilies) in 1626.

PALAZZO FARNESE (Pl. 3; 5) is the most magnificent Renaissance palace in Rome. It is now the French Embassy; it was first used as such in 1635. It was designed by Antonio da Sangallo the Younger for Cardinal Alessandro Farnese, afterwards Paul III. He began the piazza façade and the two sides, and after his death in 1546, Michelangelo finished the upper storeys and added the superb entablature. The work on the back of the palace was continued by Vignola and Giacomo della Porta. In the 18C the palace became the property of the Bourbons of Naples.

The INTERIOR can only be visited by previous written appointment. The entrance is through Sangallo's *VESTIBULE, with a beautiful colonnade and stuccoed ceiling. The *COURTYARD was also designed by Sangallo on the first two storeys; the upper storey is by Michelangelo. At the top of the stairs, to the right, is the huge SALON d'HERCULE, named after the gigantic statue (copy to right of the entrance to the room) of the Farnese Hercules. On his visit to Rome in 1787 Goethe records the loss of the statue together with the magnificent Farnese collection of sculpture to Naples (transferred there by the Bourbons), lamenting 'If they could detach the Gallery with the Carracci from Palazzo Farnese and transport it, they would.' The Salon has a fine wood ceiling by Sangallo. The two statues on either side of the fireplace of Piety and Abundance, by Guglielmo della Porta, were designed (but never used) for the tomb of Paul III in St Peter's.

At the end of the loggia is the GALLERIA, with *frescoes of mythological scenes, the masterpiece of Annibale Carracci (1597–1603). The ingenious treatment of the angles, and the magnificent over-all scheme centring on the Triumph of Bacchus, demonstrate the great imagination of the artist, who here created the model for subsequent Baroque ceiling paintings. Carracci was assisted by his brother Agostino, and (in the frescoes above the doors and niches) by Domenichino.

Just out of the square, on Via di Monserrato, is the exterior in Romanesque style (including an elaborate portal by Luigi Poletti) of the church of **St Thomas of Canterbury**, attached to the **Venerable English College** (entrance at No. 45). The ground on which they stand has been the property of English Catholics since 1362, when it was founded as a hospice for pilgrims, and the record of visitors shows the names of Thomas Cromwell (1514), Thomas Hobbes (1635), Harvey (1636), Milton (1638), Evelyn, and Manning. The church was rebuilt on a design by Virginio Vespignani in 1866–88, a free adaptation of a Romanesque basilica, with elaborate gilded decorations, and frescoes of English martyrs in the matroneum. It contains the beautiful tomb *effigy of Cardinal Christopher Bainbridge, Bishop of York (died 1514), attributed to Nicola Marini, borne on two Romanesque lions, and a monument to Thomas Dereham (died 1739) by Ferdinando Fuga, with sculptures by Filippo Della Valle. The high altarpiece is by Durante Alberti. In the college, of which Cardinal Howard and Cardinal Wiseman were rectors, are portraits of English cardinals.

In Piazza Santa Caterina della Rota is the church of **San Girolamo della Carità** (usually closed; ring at 63 Via San Girolamo), rebuilt in the 17C by Domenico Castelli, with a façade by Carlo Rainaldi. The first chapel on the right has long been attributed to Borromini but recently discovered documents now suggest Cosimo Fanzago as its author. The architect's adaptation of a cramped space into a beautiful funerary house for the Spada is masterly. The next chapel has a wood crucifix of 15C. To the left of the high altar is a decorative chapel (1710) dedicated to San Filippo Neri, by Filippo Juvarra (light to left). The church of SANTA CATERINA DELLA ROTA (also usually closed) has a fine ceiling from a demolished church and 18C works.

Via dei Farnese (with a charming small palace at No. 83) skirts the right flank of Palazzo Farnese, whose rear façade, adapted from Michelangelo's designs by Giacomo della Porta, can be glimpsed above the wall. The design of Michelangelo to connect the palace with the Villa Farnesina by a bridge across the Tiber was never carried out, but a single arch (hung with vines) of the viaduct to the bridge spans Via Giulia at this point. The fountain in the wall on the left, the *Mascherone*, was erected by the Farnese; both the colossal mask and the porphyry basin are Roman.

The straight **•VIA GIULIA** (Pl. 3; 5) runs parallel to the Tiber for over one kilometre. It was laid out by Julius II (1503–13) and was for long the most beautiful of the 16C streets of the city. The church opposite the end of Via dei Farnese, SANTA MARIA DELL'ORAZIONE E MORTE (open only on Sunday and fest. at 18.00) was rebuilt in 1733–37 by Ferdinando Fuga. PALAZZO FALCONIERI, enlarged by Borromini, is distinguished by the giant falcons' heads at either end of its façade (it has been the seat of the Hungarian Academy since 1928). Several rooms inside have fine ceilings (restored in 1979) decorated in stucco by Borromini.

Further on, the church of SANTA CATERINA DA SIENA (closed for restoration), rebuilt by Paolo Posi in 1766, stands opposite Palazzo Varese by Carlo Maderno (c 1617). A street on the left leads to **•Sant'Eligio degli Orefici** (open 10.00–12.00, except Saturday and Wednesday; ring at 9 Via di Sant'Eligio). This beautiful small 16C church surmounted by a cupola, and Greek-cross in plan, is by Raphael (clearly influenced by Bramante). After his death Baldassarre Peruzzi continued the building and added the cupola. The façade, following Raphael's designs, was rebuilt by Flaminio Ponzio.

From the Lungotevere here there is a fine view of the Janiculum, the dome of St Peter's, and the Villa Farnesina. Via della Barchetta, on the other side of Via Giulia, leads to Via di Monserrato on which (right) is the church of **Santa Maria di Monserrato** (Pl. 2; 7; open only on Sunday; for adm apply at 151 Via Giulia), the Spanish national church. It was begun by Antonio da Sangallo the Younger (1518) but altered later, with a façade by Francesco da Volterra.

In the INTERIOR, the first S chapel contains an altarpiece of San Diego, by Annibale Carracci, and the 19C tombs of the two Borgia popes, Calixtus III (died 1458) and Alexander VI (died 1503), and of Alfonso XIII (died 1941). In the third N chapel is a statue of St James, by Iacopo Sansovino, and two fine wall tombs attributed to Andrea Bregno. The first N chapel contains a group of the Madonna and Child with St Anne, by Tommaso Boscoli (1544), and a ciborium (behind wooden doors) attributed to Luigi Capponi. In the court, reached through the sacristy at the end of the nave on the right (or at 151 Via Giulia), are several fine tombs, notably that attributed to Andrea Bregno of Cardinal Giovanni de Mella. In a room off the courtyard is the monument to Pedro de Foix Montoya; this incorporates a remarkable portrait bust, an early work (c 1621) by Gian Lorenzo Bernini.

Via Giulia continues past (left) the church of the SPIRITO SANTO DEI NAPOLETANI, begun by Ottaviano Mascherino in 1619, and restored by Carlo Fontana, and again in the 19C, when the façade was built by Antonio Cipolla. It contains paintings by Pietro Gagliardi and a martyrdom of San Gennaro by Luca Giordano. The street opposite leads to the 16C PALAZZO RICCI with a painted façade by Polidoro da Caravaggio, heavily restored, and now badly faded. Via Giulia next traverses an area demolished before 1940 for a new road, never built; the 18C façade by Filippo Raguzzini of San Filippo Neri survives here.

It is now necessary to make a detour from Via dei Banchi Vecchi (right; see Pl. 3; 5). Opposite the church of Santa Lucia del Gonfalone, Vicolo Cellini (the sculptor had his workshop in the area) leads back to Corso Vittorio Emanuele across which is the **CHIESA NUOVA** or Santa Maria in Vallicella (Pl. 3; 5), built under the inspiration of St Philip Neri and with the patronage of Cardinal Angelo Cesi. Among the architects were Matteo

Bartolini da Città di Castello and Martino Longhi the Elder (1575–1605), but the façade is by Fausto Rughesi. Born in Florence in 1515 St Philip Neri came to Rome c 1530. He was an outstanding figure of the Counter Reformation and founded an 'Oratorio' here. In recognition of his Order Gregory XIII gave him Santa Maria in Vallicella in 1575 which he proceeded to rebuild.

In the INTERIOR, the vault, apse, and dome were decorated by Pietro da Cortona (1664), and the whole church is brilliantly gilded. In the SANCTUARY are three *paintings by Rubens (1608), with splendid colours: over the high altar, Madonna and angels; to the right, Saints Domitilla, Nereus, and Achilleus; to the left, Saints Gregory, Maurus, and Papias. On the right of the apse, under the fine 18C cantoria, is the CAPPELLA SPADA, designed by Carlo Rainaldi, with an altarpiece by Carlo Maratta (Madonna between Saints Charles and Ignatius). St Philip Neri is buried beneath the altar of the sumptuous CAPPELLA DI SAN FILIPPO (1600–04; being restored), on the left of the apse; his portrait in mosaic is copied from a painting by Guido Reni. In the N transept, *Presentation of the Virgin in the Temple, by Federico Barocci. In the fine 17C sacristy, with a fresco by Pietro da Cortona, is a statue of St Philip Neri and an angel, by Alessandro Algardi. From here there is access to another chapel and the rooms of St Philip Neri (works by Guercino, Pietro da Cortona, Guido Reni, Garofalo, etc.) with mementoes of the saint.

In the neighbouring **Oratorio dei Filippini,** rebuilt largely by Borromini (1637–52), St Philip instituted the musical gatherings which became known as oratorios, and have given their name to a form of musical composition. The *façade, between that of a church and a palace, has a remarkably subtle design. The delightful clock-tower can be seen from Via dei Banchi Nuovi, on the right. The extensive convent buildings, also by Borromini, are now occupied by the Vallicelliana Library (history of Rome), the Municipal Archives, and various learned societies. On Corso Vittorio Emanuele at No. 217 (left) is the 16C Palazzo Sora, and (right), in a little piazza, Palazzo Sforza Cesarini (with a 15C courtyard).

Vicolo Cellini (see above) and Via delle Carceri return to Via Giulia. The CARCERI NUOVE here, built in 1655 by Antonio Del Grande, were long considered a model prison. The MUSEO CRIMINALE (closed many years ago for restoration) is arranged in an adjacent prison building designed in 1827 by Giuseppe Valadier (entrance on Via del Gonfalone).

The 16C **Oratorio di Santa Lucia del Gonfalone** (entrance on Vicolo della Scimmia) has a façade by Domenico Castelli. It is usually closed, but concerts are given here regularly by the Coro Polifonico Romano. The interior has a fine pavement, and a carved and gilded ceiling by Ambrogio Bonazzini. But it is particularly interesting for its frescoes by painters of the late 16C Tuscan-Emilian school, including Jacopo Bertoia, Raffaellino da Reggio, Federico Zuccari, Livio Agresti, Cesare Nebbia, and Marco Pino. On Via del Gonfalone and beyond the church of SANTA MARIA DEL SUFFRAGIO (by Carlo Rainaldi), several large rough blocks of masonry protruding into the street are all that remains of a great court of justice designed for Julius II by Bramante but never finished. Here is yet another church, the small San Biagio della Pagnotta. At No. 66 rises Palazzo Sacchetti, by Antonio Sangallo the Younger (1543).

At the end of Via Giulia is **SAN GIOVANNI DEI FIORENTINI** (Pl. 2; 5), the church of the Florentines. Leo X ordered a competition for its erection.

Raphael and Peruzzi were among the contestants; but Iacopo Sansovino was successful and began the work. It was continued by Antonio da Sangallo the Younger and completed by Giacomo della Porta; Carlo Maderno added the transept and cupola. The façade is by Alessandro Galilei (1734; cleaned in 1992).

INTERIOR (open 7.00–11.00, 17.00–19.30). In the SOUTH AISLE, above the door into the sacristy, is a 16C Tuscan statuette of St John the Baptist. On either side of the arch here is a portrait bust; that on the left by Pietro Bernini (1614), and that on the right by his son Gian Lorenzo (1622). Third chapel: Santi di Tito, *St Jerome; (right wall) Ludovico Cigoli, St Jerome, and (left wall) Passignano, Construction of the church. In the SOUTH TRANSEPT, Saints Cosmas and Damian at the stake, by Salvator Rosa. NORTH AISLE. First chapel, altarpiece by Giovanni Battista Vanni; fourth chapel, putti on the wall tombs of the Bacelli, carved by François Duquesnoy. Behind the high altar is a crypt sepulchre of the Falconieri family, a fine late work by Borromini (closed for restoration, but normally shown on request by the sacristan).

It is now necessary to return across Corso Vittorio Emanuele and take Via Banco Santo Spirito out of Largo Tassoni. From here Vicolo del Curato leads to the piazza at the beginning of *Via dei Coronari** (Pl. 2; 5), a beautiful Renaissance street on the line of the Roman Via Recta. It is now famous for its antique shops.

From Piazza dei Coronari Via di Panico leads right into Via di Monte Giordano. Here the 18C PALAZZO TAVERNA (Pl. 2; 5), formerly Gabrielli, has a beautiful fountain by Antonio Casoni (1618) in the court. The palace stands on **Monte Giordano**, a small, apparently artificial, hill already inhabited in the 12C. It takes its name from Giordano Orsini (13C) whose legendary fortress stood here. Dante mentions the 'Monte' ('Inferno', XXVIII, 12) in the description of the pilgrims crossing the Ponte Sant'Angelo on the occasion of the jubilee of 1300. The Orsini continued to own the castle until 1688, and the buildings, here still crowded together, betray their medieval origins.

At the beginning of Via dei Coronari, on the right (Nos 122–3) stands the so-called House of Raphael. In the piazza on the left is SAN SALVATORE IN LAURO a church with a Palladian interior by Mascherino (1594). To the left of the church (No. 15) is the entrance to the fine Renaissance cloister (in poor repair). A small courtyard beyond has two Renaissance portals. The refectory contains the *tomb of Eugenius IV (died 1447) by Isaia da Pisa, one of the earliest sepulchral monuments to exhibit the characteristic forms of the Renaissance.

Farther on in Via dei Coronari is the Piazzetta di San Simeone with PALAZZO LANCELLOTTI (no adm), begun by Francesco da Volterra and finished by Carlo Maderno. From the piazzetta the interesting Via della Maschera d'Oro leads to PALAZZO SACRIPANTE RUIZ (a fine building attributed to Bartolomeo Ammannati), while to the S, also parallel to Via dei Coronari, is the medieval Vicolo dei Tre Archi. Via dei Coronari ends in Piazza di Tor Sanguigna at the N end of Piazza Navona (see Rte 5).

The busy Via Giuseppe Zanardelli leads N from here to Ponte Umberto I past (right) **Palazzo Altemps**, begun c 1480 for Girolamo Riario and completed by Martino Longhi the Elder, with a charming belvedere in the form of a turret. The palace was acquired by the State in 1982 and has been carefully restored. The chapel on the first floor was frescoed by Pomarancio and Ottavio Leoni (1604–17). The Ludovisi collection from the Museo Nazionale Romano (see Rte 10) has been arranged here (but is not yet open to the public). The TEATRO GOLDONI, which adjoins the palace, preserves its 17C decoration.

In Piazza Ponte Umberto I is **Palazzo Primoli**, seat of the Fondazione Primoli. On the ground floor is the **Napoleonic Museum** (closed since 1992 for restoration), presented to the city of Rome in 1927 by Count Joseph Primoli. The collection belonged to Count Joseph and his brother Louis, who were sons of Carlotta Bonaparte. In the fourteen period rooms of the museum are paintings, statues, and relics of the Bonaparte family, with special reference to the Roman branch. The more important works include paintings by Jacques-Louis David of Zenaide and Carlotta, daughters of Joseph, king of Naples; by Gérard of Elisa Baciocchi; by Jean-Baptiste Wicar of Louis, king of Holland; and by Winterhalter of Napoleon III and the Empress Eugénie. The collection also includes sculptures by Antonio Canova, Lorenzo Bartolini, J.B. Carpeaux, and Thorvaldsen; miniatures by Jean-Baptiste Isabey; prints illustrating the contest between Napoleon and Pius VII; State robes; and autographs, including the marriage contract of Napoleon and Marie Louise.

The top floor of Palazzo Primoli was the residence of the art historian and man of letters Mario Praz from 1969 until his death in 1982. His remarkable collection of decorative arts, paintings, sculpture, furniture, etc., particularly representative of the neo-classical period, has been acquired by the State. It is hoped that it will be exhibited in his apartment here.

Nearby, on the corner of Via di Monte Brianzo, is the OSTERIA DELL' ORSO. The medieval building was altered c 1460, and it first became a hotel in the 16C. Rabelais, Montaigne, and Goethe were among its patrons.

7

The Corso and Piazza del Popolo

VIA DEL CORSO (Pl. 3; 6, 4, 2), now called simply *Il Corso*, has been one of the most important thoroughfares in the city since Roman times. It is a straight and fairly narrow street nearly a mile long connecting Piazza Venezia with Piazza del Popolo. It is closed to private traffic, but remains one of the busiest streets in Rome, with many fashionable shops, particularly between Piazza Venezia and Via Condotti. The pavements are hardly wide enough to accommodate the almost incessant stream of pedestrians in either direction during working hours.

The Corso represents the urban section of the Via Flaminia (221 BC), the main road to northern Italy. It was called the *Via Lata* because of its width, exceptional in ancient Rome. Its present name is derived from the celebrated races inaugurated here by Paul II in 1466. Many palaces were built along the street from the 16C to the 18C, and the straightness of its line between Piazza Venezia and Piazza Colonna was perfected by Alexander VII, when he demolished two triumphal arches that formerly spanned it. The Carnival celebrations here from the 17C onwards became famous spectacles; John Evelyn, Goethe, Dickens, and Henry James have left vivid descriptions of the festivities. The street has given its name to the principal street in numerous other Italian cities.

The Corso runs N from Piazza Venezia. At its left corner is PALAZZO D'ASTE RINUCCINI BONAPARTE by Giovanni Antonio dei Rossi (17C), where Letizia Ramolino, mother of Napoleon I, died in 1836. On the right beyond Vicolo del Piombo, are PALAZZO SALVIATI, by Carlo Rainaldi (1662), and PALAZZO ODESCALCHI, of the 17–18C, but with a façade (1887–88) in the Florentine 15C style.

On the opposite side of the Corso is the huge **Palazzo Doria Pamphilj** (Pl. 3; 6), which dates from 1435, but has suffered many vicissitudes. It has been the residence of this important Roman noble family since the 17C. The façade towards the Corso, by Gabriele Valvassori (1731–34), is perhaps the finest and most balanced Rococo work in Rome. The S façade is by Paolo Ameli (1743); that on the N in Piazza del Collegio Romano is by Antonio Del Grande (1659–63), with two very fine wings.

At No. 1A in the piazza is the entrance to the *GALLERIA DORIA PAMPHILJ** (admission, see p 46), the most important of the Roman patrician art collections to have survived in the city. The collection was initiated by Olimpia Maidalchini, the acquisitive sister-in-law of Innocent X, in her palace on Piazza Navona; it was increased by the Aldobrandini and Doria bequests and has been entailed by the State since 1816. The entrance is on the first floor. The period rooms, richly decorated in white and gold, and beautifully maintained, provide a sumptuous setting for the fine paintings. Only a small selection of the works (identified by their number) has been given below.

First Gallery (right). 10. Titian (copy?), Spain succouring Religion; 11. Titian, Angel (fragment); 15. Jacopo Tintoretto, Portrait of a Man; 17. Ferrara School (16C), Portrait of a Man; *20. Correggio, Triumph of Virtue (unfinished sketch for the painting now in the Louvre); *23. Raphael, Navagero and Beazzano(?), Venetian savants; 26. Lorenzo Lotto, St Jerome; 28. Paris Bordone, Venus, Mars, and Cupid; *29. Titian, Salome with the head of St John the Baptist; and, to the left of the door, 38. Carlo Saraceni, St Roch and the angel; Caravaggio, *40. Mary Magdalene, *42. Rest on the flight into Egypt (one of his best works), 44. Young St John the Baptist (a replica of the painting in the Pinacoteca Capitolina); 46. Lo Spagnoletto, St Jerome; 48. Mattia Preti, The Tribute money; I. Alessandro Algardi, Bust of Olimpia Maidalchini; and, to the right of the door, 53. Sassoferrato, Virgin.

Steps lead down into the **Salone Aldobrandini** which displays Antique sculptures (not yet fully catalogued) inlcuding three large sarcophagi, busts and statues (in the centre, young Bacchus in red basalt and a centaur in red and black marble). The four Brussels tapestries illustrate the battle of Lepanto, and on the far wall are marble reliefs by François Duquesnoy. The paintings include: 77. Guercino, Herminia and Tancred; and 103. Mattia Preti, Concert.

Second Gallery. 120. Annibale Carracci (attributed), St Jerome; 122. Sassoferrato, Holy Family; and on the wall behind, 131. Domenico Fetti, Mary Magdalene; behind, IV. Algardi, Bust of Innocent X; 135. Lodovico Carracci, St Sebastian; 136. Guido Reni, Madonna; 137. Annibale Carracci (copy from), Pietà. **Room II**. 172. Giovanni Bellini (possibly with the help of his workshop), Madonna and Child with St John; Giovanni di Paolo, 174. Marriage of the Virgin; *176. Birth of the Virgin; Niccolò Rondinelli, 178, 182. Madonnas; 180. Ortolano, Nativity; 183. Bicci di Lorenzo, St Christopher and St John the Baptist; 185. Vincenzo Catena (attributed; a copy from

Giovanni Bellini), Circumcision; *186. Boccaccino, Madonna and Child; 187. Marco Basaiti, St Sebastian; 191. Niccolò Frangipani, Christ and St Veronica; 194. Jacopo Bassano, Adam and Eve in Earthly Paradise.

Room III. 195. Andrea del Sarto (copy from), Madonna and Child with St John; 207. Parmigianino, Madonna and Child; 208. Garofalo, Visitation; Dosso Dossi, 209. Portrait of Girolamo Beltramoto, 211. Dido; 212. Andrea del Sarto (follower of), Holy Family with St John; Ludovico Mazzolino, 216. Jesus in the Temple, 217. Massacre of the Innocents, 219. Pietà; 231. Garofalo, Holy Family adored by saints.

In the next two rooms are exhibited Dutch and Flemish works. **Room IV**. *237. Thomas de Keyser (attributed), Portrait of a lady; 252. Wybrand de Geest (attributed), Portrait of a man; 244. Jan Lievens, Sacrifice of Abraham; 258. Adriaen Isenbrant, Mary Magdalene; 266. David Ryckaert III, Rural feast; 277. David Teniers the Younger, Fête Champêtre; 278. Jan Brueghel the Elder, Creation of Man; 279. Jan van Scorel, Agatha van Schoonhoven; 280. Jan Brueghel the Elder, Vision of St John in Patmos. **Room V**. Jan Frans van Bloemen, 281, 283, 286, 298, 299, 301, 310. Landscapes; 287. Paul Bril, Landscape with huntsmen; Nicolas Juvenel (attributed), 288, 294. Portraits; 290. Quinten Massys, Usurers; *291. Rubens (or his school), Franciscan; 295. Jan Brueghel the Elder, Earthly Paradise; 306. Herri met de Bles, Ascent to Calvary; 316. Pieter Brueghel the Elder (copy from), Snow scene; 317. Pieter Brueghel the Elder, Battle in the Bay of Naples. In the CABINET, 17C Dutch and Flemish schools.

The delightful **Galleria degli Specchi (Third Gallery)** was created in the 18C by Valvassori (the vault is decorated by Aureliano Milani). 337. School of Raphael, Joan of Aragon, princess Colonna. In the CABINET, *339. Velazquez, Innocent X (1650), the gem of the collection. VII. Bernini, Bust of Innocent X.

Fourth Gallery. Claude Lorrain, *343. The Mill, 346. Rest on the flight into Egypt, 348. Sacrifice at Delphi, 351. Meeting with Diana, 352. Mercury runs away with the oxen of Apollo; 357. Francesco Albani, Assumption; Annibale Carracci, *359. Flight into Egypt, 362. Christ carried to the sepulchre; 365. Jan Joost van Cossiau, River estuary; 381. Alessandro Allori, Christ on the road to Golgotha; Gaspare Vanvitelli, 384, 385. Two views of Venice.

In the *Private Apartments** red dominates the decorations (guided visits of groups of about fifteen people are arranged on request at the ticket office usually at 11 and 12 o'clock). The WINTER GARDEN (or conservatory) is decorated with antique busts, a 16C Brussels tapestry, and an 18C sedan chair. The FUMOIR (or smoking room) was created by Mary Talbot in the 19C (whose portrait hangs here). In the adjoining room is a large polyptych of the Madonna and Child with saints and angels, of the early 15C Tuscan school (attributed to the 'Maestro di Borgo alla Collina') and St Bernardine by Sano di Pietro. The 16C Brussels tapestry depicts the month of February. In the ROOM OF ANDREA DORIA, with a 16C ceiling, a glass case contains some of his possessions, and there are two more Brussels tapestries with scenes of Lepanto. The portrait of Christopher Columbus is by Mabuse.

The SMALL DINING ROOM contains a bust of Princess Emily Doria by Canonica, a collection of Trapani corals, ambers, and ivories, and a 19C frieze showing the fiefs of the Doria-Pamphilj family. The GREEN SALON, contains a Madonna by Beccafumi; a Deposition by Hans Memling; a large mid-15C Tournai tapestry with the medieval legend of Alexander the Great; a bronze bust of Innocent X, by Algardi; and a *portrait (perhaps of himself), by Lorenzo Lotto. In the centre is a rare 18C cradle in carved and gilded wood. In the recess to the left: portraits of Andrea Doria, by Sebastiano del Piombo, and of Gianetto Doria, attributed to Bronzino, and a beautiful *Annunciation, by Filippo Lippi.

It is now necessary to return through the Gallery to the ticket office, off which is the entrance to the APPARTAMENTO DI RAPPRESENTANZA. The ceiling of the first room is decorated with an 18C fresco of Venus and Aeneas by Antonio Nessi. A 17C Florentine marble table here has a carved and gilded wooden base in the shape of four dolphins. In the charming BALL ROOM is a Gobelins tapestry woven for Louis XIV from a 16C Flemish design, representing the month of May. The altar of rare marbles in the large family CHAPEL is 17C work. The ivory Crucifix here is by Ercole Ferrata. The twelve tapestries of the signs of the Zodiac by Claude Audran in the YELLOW ROOM were executed to Louis XV's order, and two exquisite Ming vases are displayed here. The ceiling fresco is by Tommaso Maria Conca. The SMALL GREEN DRAWING ROOM is in the elegant 18C Venetian style, with three Venetian scenes attributed to Longhi. In the SMALL RED DRAWING ROOM are a 17C Gobelins tapestry, four allegorical paintings of the Elements and Seasons by Jan Brueghel the Elder, and a portrait of James Stuart, the Old Pretender, by A.S. Belle.

On the N side of Piazza del Collegio Romano (Pl. 3; 6) is the **Collegio Romano**, a large building erected in 1585 by order of Gregory XIII for the Jesuits. The architect was thought to have been Bartolomeo Ammannati, but was more probably the Jesuit Giuseppe Valeriani. It is now partly used by the Ministry of 'Beni Culturali'.

The founder of the Jesuit College was St Francis Borgia, duke of Gandia, third in succession after Ignatius Loyola as General of the Jesuits. Its pupils included eight popes: Urban VIII, Innocent X, Clement IX, Clement X, Innocent XII, Clement XI, Innocent XIII, and Clement XII. The Jesuit library founded here formed the nucleus of the Biblioteca Nazionale Centrale Vittorio Emanuele which was moved to new premises near the Castro Pretorio in 1975. The Salone della Crociera, with its original bookcases, has been used to house part of the library of the Istituto Nazionale di Archeologia e Storia dell'Arte in Palazzo di Venezia (see Rte 1).

On the S side of the piazza is the former church of SANTA MARTA (restored as an exhibition centre), by Carlo Fontana, with a good doorway. Inside (closed when not in use) is a pretty vault decoration designed by Baciccia, with paintings by him and Paolo Albertoni. Just beyond, on the left of Via del Piè di Marmo, in Via di Santo Stefano del Cacco, is a colossal marble foot (perhaps from an ancient Roman statue of Isis).

In the Corso, beyond Palazzo Doria, rises **SANTA MARIA IN VIA LATA**, a small church of ancient foundation, rebuilt in the 15C. The graceful *FAÇADE (much blackened by the polluted air) and vestibule are by Pietro da Cortona (1660). The pretty little INTERIOR is usually open only in the evening. At the end of the left aisle is the tomb (1776) of the poet Antonio Tebaldeo (1463–1537), tutor of Isabella d'Este, secretary of Lucrezia Borgia, courtier of Leo X, and friend of Raphael (who painted his portrait in the Vatican, a copy of which is placed here). The church also contains tombs of the families of Joseph and Lucien Bonaparte. The high altar and apse, decorated with coloured marbles, have been attributed as an early work to Bernini, but they are now instead thought to be by Santi Ghetti.

The lower level (ring on the left of the façade at No. 306; but usually closed) has remains of a large Roman building which probably served as a warehouse (and which extended along the Via Lata also beneath Palazzo Doria). In the 3C AD the portion beneath the church was divided into six storerooms and two of these in the 5C were converted into a Christian chapel and welfare centre, rebuilt and enlarged as a church in the 7C and 11C. Interesting murals (7–9C) discovered here have been detached because of the humidity and removed for restoration. A tradition that St Paul was guarded here on his second visit to Rome, led to excavations as early as the 17C. The high relief over the main altar of the saints Peter, Paul, Luke, and Matthew by Cosimo Fancelli dates from this period. Also to be seen here; an ancient well, a column inscribed with words of St Paul, and an altar (derived from a pagan cult altar) in a chapel to the right.

Here the Corso was spanned by the *Arcus Novus* erected by Diocletian in 303–04, and demolished in 1491 when the church was rebuilt.

In the Corso, beyond Via Lata, the Banco di Roma now occupies PALAZZO SIMONETTI (No. 307), once the property of the Boncompagni-Ludovisi and for years the residence of Cardinal de Bernis, ambassador of Louis XV at the papal court. Low down on the corner of the palace, in Via Lata, is the FONTANELLA DEL FACCHINO with a sturdy porter holding a barrel; water issues from the bung-hole. Water-sellers are supposed to have resold Tiber or Trevi water from their barrels.

'*Il Facchino*' was one of Rome's 'talking' statues; and, with his flat beret, was once thought to be a caricature portrait of Martin Luther, though it more probably represents Abbondio Rizio, a heavy drinker. In 1751, Vanvitelli attributed the sculpture to Michelangelo.

Opposite Palazzo Simonetti is **SAN MARCELLO** (Pl. 3; 6), a very old church, rebuilt on a design by Jacopo Sansovino after a fire in 1519, with a FAÇADE by Carlo Fontana (1683). The INTERIOR (open 7.00–12.00, 16.00–19.00) was frescoed in the 17C by Giovanni Battista Ricci da Novara (including the Crucifixion on the W wall, the scenes of the Passion between the windows, and the apse). On the W wall is the tomb of Cardinal Giovanni Michiel (died 1503) and his nephew Bishop Antonio Orso (died 1511), by Jacopo Sansovino. SOUTH SIDE. Third chapel, 15C fresco of the Madonna and Child in a marble frame, and, on the altar wall, frescoes by Francesco Salviati. On the ceiling of the fourth chapel are frescoes begun by Perino del Vaga (Creation of Eve, St Mark, and St John the Evangelist), completed after the sack of Rome by Daniele da Volterra and Pellegrino Tibaldi. Beneath the altar, which has a fine 14C Crucifix, is an interesting Roman cippus. The fifth chapel has paintings by Aureliano Milani (c 1725). The fourth chapel on the N side has frescoes by Taddeo Zuccari and busts (on the right wall) of three members of the Frangipane family by Alessandro Algardi. Excavations of the medieval church may one day be opened to the public.

Via del Caravita diverges to the left for the delightful Rococo *•**Piazza di Sant'Ignazio**, a 'theatrical' masterpiece by Filippo Raguzzini (1728). The Jesuit church of *•**SANT'IGNAZIO** (Pl. 3; 6) rivals the Gesù in magnificence. It was begun in 1626 by Cardinal Ludovisi as the church of the Collegio Romano (see above), to celebrate the canonisation of St Ignatius de Loyola by the cardinal's uncle Gregory XV. The design by Carlo Maderno and others was carried out by Orazio Grassi, a Jesuit mathematician from the College, who is also responsible for the fine FAÇADE (covered for restoration).

The spacious aisled INTERIOR (open 7.30–12.30, 16.00–19.15) is sumptuously decorated. In the vaulting of the nave and apse are remarkable *•paintings representing the missionary activity of the Jesuits and the Triumph of St Ignatius, the masterpiece of Andrea Pozzo. The amazing trompe l'oeil perspective projects the walls of the church beyond their architectural limits, and Pozzo even provided a cupola, never built because of lack of funds, in a canvas 17 metres in diameter. The vaulting and 'dome' are best seen from a small yellow disc let into the pavement about the middle of the nave (coin-operated light in the nave). The second chapel on the S side, lavishly decorated with rare marbles, has an altarpiece of the Death of St Joseph by Francesco Trevisani.

In the ornate chapels of the transepts, designed by Andrea Pozzo, with marble solomonic columns, are large marble high reliefs: on the S side, the Glory of St Louis Gonzaga, by Pierre Le Gros, with a lapis-lazuli urn containing the remains of the saint, and two angels, 18C works by Bernardo Ludovisi; on the N side, the Annunciation by Filippo Della Valle, and another lapis-lazuli urn with the relics of St John Berchmans (died 1621), and two 18C angels by Pietro Bracci. In the chapel to the right of the high altar, funerary monument to Gregory XV and his nephew Cardinal Ludovico Ludovisi, the founders of the church, by Pierre Le Gros. From the sacristy there is a lift to a chapel frescoed by Borgognone.

Farther on in the Corso is (No. 239, on the right) PALAZZO SCIARRACOL-ONNA, built in the late 16C by Flaminio Ponzio, under which, in 1887, was found part of the Acqua Virgo. Opposite is a bank building by Cipolla (1874). The street here was once spanned by the triumphal ARCH OF CLAUDIUS (fragments in Palazzo dei Conservatori). Via delle Muratte diverges (right) for the Fontana di Trevi (see Rte 8).

In Piazza di Pietra, a few metres to the left of the Corso by Via di Pietra, are the remains of the **Temple of Hadrian**, built by Antoninus Pius in 145 and dedicated to his father. The wall of the cella and the peristyle of the right side with eleven disengaged fluted Corinthian *columns (15m high) remain. They are incorporated in the façade of the stock exchange building.

The Corso next reaches **PIAZZA COLONNA** (Pl. 3; 4), which for centuries was the centre of the city, and is still one of its busiest squares. On the N side rises the great flank of **Palazzo Chigi**, begun in the 16C by Matteo di Castello (and also possibly Giacomo Della Porta and Carlo Maderno) and finished in the 17C by Felice Della Greca. It is now the official residence of the Prime Minister (no adm; but the interesting 17C courtyard can be seen through the entrance). The famous Chigi library founded by Alexander VII, was presented by the State to the Vatican in 1923. The main façade of the palace faces the Corso and Largo Chigi from which the busy Via del Tritone leads towards Piazza Barberini.

The E side of the piazza is closed across the Corso, by the GALLERIA COLONNA (1914), with shops and cafés in an interior arcade in the form of a Y. On the opposite side of the piazza is the façade of PALAZZO WEDEKIND (1838), incorporating on the ground floor a handsome portico, with twelve Ionic marble columns, brought from a Roman building at Veio. The little church on the S side is SAN BARTOLOMEO DEI BERGAMASCHI (1561). At the beginning of Via del Tritone (see above) is SANTA MARIA IN VIA rebuilt in 1594, with a good Baroque front, completed in 1670.

In the centre of the piazza, beside a graceful fountain, designed by Giacomo della Porta (the dolphins, etc., are a 19C addition by Achille Stocchi), rises the monument from which it derives its name, the majestic *COLUMN OF MARCUS AURELIUS (*Colonna Antonina*; restored in 1984–88). It was erected between AD 180 and 196 in honour of the emperor's victories over the Germans and Sarmatians (169–76), and dedicated to him and his wife, Faustina. The column is made entirely of marble from Luni, and is formed of 27 blocks. The ancient level of the ground was nearly 4m lower than at present. The shaft measures 100 Roman feet (29.6m), and the total height of the column, including the base and the statue, is nearly 42 metres.

The ancient base was decorated with Victories, festoons, and reliefs. It was originally crowned with figures of Marcus Aurelius and Faustina, but in 1589 Domenico Fontana restored it, and a statue of St Paul was placed on the summit. Around the shaft a bas-relief ascends in a spiral of 20 turns, interrupted half-way by a Victory; the lower part of the relief commemorates the war against the Germanic tribes (169–73), the upper that against the Sarmatians (174–76). The philospher-emperor led his troops in all these important battles, which delayed the barbaric invasions for several centuries. On the third spiral (E side) the Roman soldiers are represented as being saved by a rain storm, which in the 4C was regarded as a miracle brought about by the prayers of the Christians in their ranks.

The column was inspired by Trajan's Column, but un-like it was not the focal point of a forum, but instead in the centre of an important group of monuments of the Antonine period. In the vicinity were the *Ustrina Antinorum* (that of Marcus Aurelius under Palazzo del Parlamento, and that of Antoninus Pius S of the column of Antoninus Pius), the *Temple of Hadrian* in Piazza di Pietra (see above), and the *Porticus Vipsanioe* (on the other side of the Corso, in the area of Palazzo della Rinascente). The summit is reached by 203 steps (no adm) lit by 56 tiny windows, in the interior of the column. Casts of the reliefs are kept in the Museo della Civiltà Romana (see Rte 26), but they are not at present on view.

A little farther W is Piazza di Montecitorio, with the old façade of **PALAZZO DI MONTECITORIO**, which, since 1871, has been the seat of the Italian Chamber of Deputies. The original palace was begun for the Ludovisi family in 1650 by Bernini, who was responsible for the general plan of the building and for the idea of enhancing the effect of the façade by giving it a convex, slightly polygonal form. The N façade of the palazzo is in Piazza del Parlamento. In 1918 it was enlarged and given its new façade by Ernesto Basile; the principal entrance is now on this side. The Art Nouveau red-brick front is in contrast to the prevailing style of architecture. In the interior, the Chamber, also of this period, is panelled in oak and brightly illuminated from above by a row of windows pierced in the cornice. Below the cornice is an encaustic frieze by Aristide Sartorio, begun in 1908, representing the development of Italian civilisation. The fine bas-relief in bronze in honour of the House of Savoy is by Davide Calandra.

The **obelisk** (22m high) in the centre of the piazza was originally erected at Heliopolis by Psammetichus II (c 590 BC). It was brought to Rome by Augustus to celebrate his victory over Cleopatra, and set up in the Campus Martius, where it served as the gnomon of an immense sundial. In 1748 it was discovered underground in the Largo dell' Impresa (an open space N of the palace) and in 1792 it was erected on its present site.

In the Corso, beyond Largo Chigi, stands Palazzo della Rinascente, and Palazzo Marignoli (1889), and (left) Palazzo Verospi where Shelley lived in 1819 (plaque). Via delle Convertite leads (right) to Piazza San Silvestro, an important bus terminus, with the **Central Post Office** (Pl. 3; 4). The church of **San Silvestro in Capite** was originally erected here by Pope Stephen III (752–57) on the site of a Roman building, possibly Aurelian's Temple of the Sun. It was bestowed on the English Roman Catholics by Leo XIII in 1890. The 12–13C campanile is surmounted by a 12C bronze cock. It contains interesting 17C works, including the organ, and paintings by Giacinto Brandi, Orazio Gentileschi, Francesco Trevisani, Lodovico Gimignani, and Pomarancio.

Farther along the Corso (now less busy), beyond Piazza del Parlamento (see above), is Palazzo Fiano (left), built over the remains of the Ara Pacis (see below). This was the site of the Roman Arco di Portogallo, demolished in 1662 by order of Alexander VII. A small square opens out just beyond, opposite the pretty Via Frattina, the first of several long straight pedestrian streets which open off this side of the Corso and end in Piazza di Spagna (see Rte 8). In the square, on the left, is **SAN LORENZO IN LUCINA** (Pl. 3; 4), a church probably dating from the time of Sixtus III (432–40), or even earlier, rebuilt in the 12C, and again in 1650. Of the 12C church there remain the campanile (restored) which has several rows of small loggie with colonnettes, the PORTICO with six Ionic columns, and the doorway.

INTERIOR. SOUTH SIDE: in the first chapel a reliquary contains part of the gridiron on which St Lawrence was supposed to have been martyred; second chapel, on the left pillar is the tomb of Nicolas Poussin (1594–1665) by Lemoyne, erected by Chateaubriand in 1830; and the fourth chapel, designed by Bernini for Innocent X's doctor Gabriele Fonseca, decorated with pretty stuccoes, has a fine portrait bust (left of the altar) by Bernini. The Crucifixion on the HIGH ALTAR is by Guido Reni. In the N transept is a monument to Cardinal Genga who died in 1861. NORTH SIDE. The decorative fifth chapel was designed by Simon Vouet, and contains two good paintings of San Francesco by him (on the left and right walls). In the second chapel the altarpiece is by Carlo Saraceni. Pompilia (in Browning's 'The Ring and the Book') was married in this church. Excavations (not at present open to the public) have revealed interesting remains of the palaeochristian basilica, and Roman material, including a black-and-white mosaic.

Beyond is PALAZZO RUSPOLI (No. 418A; left), by Ammannati, with a great marble staircase by Martino Longhi the Younger, and frescoes by Jacopo Zucchi. Since 1990 it has been the seat of the Fondazione Roberto Memmo which holds exhibitions here. At Largo Carlo Goldoni three streets converge on the Corso: Via Condotti, with its fine shops, leading past the church of the SANTISSIMA TRINITÀ DEI SPAGNOLI, with an 18C eliptical interior, to Piazza di Spagna (see Rte 8), Via Fontanella di Borghese, ending in Piazza Borghese (see below), and Via Tomacelli, which leads to Ponte Cavour, an important bridge over the Tiber leading to the Prati district.

Farther on, where the street widens, stands **SANTI AMBROGIO E CARLO AL CORSO** (Pl. 3; 4; usually open only on fest.) built in 1612 by Onorio Longhi, completed by his son Martino. The fine cupola (being restored) is by Pietro da Cortona. The façade (recently heavily restored) is by Giovanni Battista Menicucci and Fra Mario da Canepina (1690). The altarpiece (poorly lit; the Madonna presenting San Carlo to Christ) is one of Carlo Maratta's best works, and on an altar behind it is a rich urn containing the heart of St Charles Borromeo. In the neighbouring ORATORY OF SANT'AMBROGIO (at No. 437, to the left of the church; ring for the porter), on the site of the old church built by the Lombards in 1513 on a piece of land granted them by Sixtus IV, is a marble group of the Deposition, by Tommaso della Porta (1618).

Behind the apse of San Carlo is the ugly Piazza Augusto Imperatore (Pl. 3; 2; now used by tourist buses) laid out by the Fascist regime in 1936–38 around the *MAUSOLEUM OF AUGUSTUS (Pl. 3; 2), or *Tumulus Caesarum* (admission only with special permission, see p 156; part of the interior can be seen through the main S entrance). This was the tomb of Augustus and of the principal members of his family, the gens Julia-Claudia, and was one of the most sacred monuments of Ancient Rome. The last Roman emperor to be buried here was Nerva in AD 98. Erected in 28 BC, it is a circular structure 87m in diameter. It was originally surmounted by a tumulus of earth some 44m high, planted with cypresses and probably crowned with a statue of the emperor.

Excavations carried out in 1926–30 freed the crypt of the mausoleum from the debris that surrounded and partly buried it, and restored as far as possible its original appearance. The circular base, of opus reticulatum, has a series of large niches on the outside. From the entrance a passageway leads into the interior past a series of twelve compartments arranged in a circle to an outer circular passage, at the entrance to which are fragments of statues; beyond is an inner ring and finally the sepulchral cella, with walls of travertine blocks, a central pillar, and three niches. In the central niche were found the cinerary urns of Augustus and of his wife Livia; on either side were those of his nephews Gaius and Lucius Caesar and of his sister Octavia, with an inscription to his beloved nephew Marcellus. On either side of the entrance were two obelisks, one of which is now in Piazza del Quirinale, and the other in Piazza dell'Esquilino, as well as bronze inscriptions with the official will of Augustus, a copy of which was found at Ankara (it is reproduced on the outside wall of the pavilion protecting the Ara Pacis, see below).

In the Middle Ages the tomb became a fortress of the Colonna. Later it was pillaged to provide travertine for other buildings and a wooden amphitheatre was built inside it, where Goethe watched beast-baiting in 1787. Later still it was converted into a concert hall and was used as such until 1936.

To the W of the Mausoleum, between Via di Ripetta and the Tiber, is a platform approached by a flight of steps at either end. Here a building with glass walls was built in 1938 to protect the monumental altar called the *ARA PACIS, reconstructed in 1937–38 from scattered fragments and from reproductions of other dispersed fragments. The carved decoration is a splendid example of Roman sculpture, influenced by Greek Classical and Hellenistic art. Adm, see p 45.

The Ara Pacis Augustae was consecrated in the Campus Martius on 4 July 13 BC, and dedicated four years later after the victorious return of Augustus from Spain and Gaul, in celebration of the peace that he had established within the Empire. This much is known from the document (*Res gestae Divi Augusti*) which the emperor had engraved on bronze tablets (see above) in Rome a year before his death in AD 14. This has been copied on the wall of the modern pavilion.

In 1568, during excavations for the foundations of Palazzo Fiano (on the Corso), nine blocks belonging to the frieze of the altar were found and bought by Cardinal Ricci da Montepulciano for the Grand Duke of Tuscany. To facilitate transport, each block was sawn into three. These went to the Uffizi Gallery in Florence. The cardinal overlooked two other blocks unearthed at the same time. One of these eventually passed to the Louvre in Paris; the other to the Vatican Museum.

In 1859, during a reconstruction of Palazzo Fiano, the contractors found the base of the altar, with the left half of the relief panel of the sacrifice of Aeneas and other architectonic and decorative elements. These were acquired in 1898 by the Italian Government for the Museo Nazionale Romano. In 1903 excavations brought to light further fragments: these included most of the basement of marble blocks supporting the altar, portions of the acanthus frieze (see below) and the right half of the relief of the sacrifice of Aeneas, in which Augustus himself appeared. There was also found a panel with two *Flamines* (priests), but this could not then be dislodged.

In 1937 further excavations were carried out at a depth of 10.5m (by freezing the subsoil water). The fragments from the Museo Nazionale and the Uffizi Gallery were recovered; those in the Louvre, the Vatican, and the Villa Medici were copied, and the altar was reconstructed, as far as possible, in its original form and appearance.

The monument, built throughout of Luni marble, has a simple base with two horizontal bands. On the base is an almost square-walled enclosure, with two open and two closed sides. The open sides are 11.5m and the closed sides 10.5m long. The two openings are each 3.5m square; one of them is approached by a flight of steps. The EXTERNAL DECORATION of the enclosure is in two zones divided by a horizontal Greek key-pattern border. The lower zone is covered with an intricate and beautiful composition of acanthus leaves on which are swans with outstretched wings. In the upper zone is the frieze of reliefs, with a decorated cornice above it. Between the jambs of the main or W entrance are scenes illustrating the origins of Rome. The left panel (almost entirely lost) represented the *Lupercalia*; the right panel shows *Aeneas sacrificing the white sow. The panels of the E entrance depict *Tellus, the earth goddess, possibly an allegory of Peace (left), and Rome (right), much damaged. These were beautifully restored in 1983. Mythology and allegory give way to realism in the subjects of the side panels, which represent the ceremony of the consecration of the altar. In procession are seen Augustus, members of his family including children, State officials, and priests.

Detail of the Ara Pacis

The INTERIOR OF THE ENCLOSURE is also in two zones; because sacrifices took place here, the lower part has no decoration other than simple fluting. The upper zone, however, is decorated with beautifully carved bucrania. The ALTAR is an exact reconstruction of all recovered fragments. Approached by a flight of steps, it has a back and two side walls; a further flight of narrow steps leads up past the walls to the altar proper. The cornice and the anta of the left side wall have been the best preserved; the reliefs indicate the *Suovetaurilia*, or sacrifice of a pig, a sheep, and an ox. Little else of the decoration survives.

To the S, on Via di Ripetta, in a district once inhabited by the Serbs (Schiavoni) who came here as refugees after the battle of Kossovo (15 June 1389) are two churches, SAN GIROLAMO DEGLI SCHIAVONI, rebuilt in 1587, and SAN ROCCO with a neo-classical façade by Valadier (1834), and an early altarpiece by Baciccia in the sacristy. Farther S, Via Borghese diverges left from Via di Ripetta (the name of which is a reminder of the old river bank and port) to **Palazzo Borghese** (Pl. 2; 6, 4; no adm), called from its shape the 'harpsichord of Rome'. It was begun perhaps by Vignola (c 1560) and completed by Flaminio Ponzio, who designed the beautiful terrace on the Tiber front. The palace was acquired by Cardinal Camillo Borghese, who became Pope Paul V in 1605, and was renowned for its splendour. For nearly two centuries it contained the paintings from the Galleria Borghese; they were restored to their former residence in 1891. It is now the seat of the 'Circolo della Caccia', an exclusive club founded in 1869. The pretty courtyard has long lines of twin columns in two storeys, and colossal statues representing Ceres and the empresses Sabina and Julia; a garden beyond contains fountains and Roman sculpture.

It is now necessary to return across Piazza Augusto to the Corso. In Via Vittoria (right) is the renowned Accademia Musicale di Santa Cecilia. Farther N the Corso passes (left) the church of SAN GIACOMO IN AUGUSTA (so called from its proximity to the Mausoleum), with a façade by Maderno; it is known also as SAN GIACOMO DEGLI INCURABILI from the adjoining hospital. Opposite is the small church of GESÙ E MARIA with a façade by Girolamo Rainaldi who was also responsible for the interior decoration completed c 1675. On the left (Nos 518–19) is the former PALAZZO SAN-SEVERINO, now RONDANINI, the seat of a bank, with an imposing double porch.

Opposite (No. 18; plaque) is the house where Goethe lived in 1786–88. The GOETHE MUSEUM here, which contains interesting material relating to the poet's travels in Italy, has been closed for many years. It was acquired by the German government in 1987, and may one day be reopened.

*PIAZZA DEL POPOLO** (Pl. 3; 2), at the end of the Corso, provides a scenographic entrance to the city from Via Flaminia and the north. Numerous famous travellers in the 19C recorded their first arrival in Rome through the Porta del Popolo. The piazza was created by Latino Giovenale Manetti in 1538 for Paul III in strict relationship to the three long straight roads which here penetrate the city as a trident, between the two twin-domed churches added in the 17C. The piazza was given its present symmetry by Giuseppe Valadier after the return of Pius VII from France in 1814. Between four fountains with lions by Valadier (1823; to a 16C design by Domenico Fontana) rises an OBELISK (24m; restored in 1984), on which hieroglyphs which celebrate the glories of the pharaohs Ramesses II and Merenptah (13–12C BC); Augustus brought it from Heliopolis, after the conquest of Egypt, and it was dedicated to the sun in the Circus Maximus. Domenico Fontana removed it to its present site in 1589, as part of the urban plan of Sixtus V.

The three streets which converge on the piazza from the S are Via di Ripetta (see above) on the left, the Corso in the middle, and Via del Babuino (from Piazza di Spagna; see Rte 8) on the right. The ends of the streets are separated by a pair of decorative Baroque churches (not always open), **Santa Maria dei Miracoli** (left) and **Santa Maria in Montesanto** (right); the façades were modified by Bernini and Carlo Fontana (1671–78), after Carlo Rainaldi. In the centre of each hemicycle is a fountain with marble groups (on the left, Neptune with two Tritons, on the right, Rome between the Tiber and the Anio, both by Giovanni Ceccarini; 1824) and at the ends are more neo-classical statues of the Four Seasons. On the W Via Ferdinando di Savoia comes in from Ponte Margherita, and on the E a winding road

Piazza del Popolo

designed by Valadier, Viale Gabriele d'Annunzio, descends from the Pincio (see Rte 8). In the piazza is a fashionable café.

Across the piazza (to the right of the gate) rises the flank of *SANTA MARIA DEL POPOLO (Pl. 3; 2; open 7.00–12.00, 16.00–19.00; fest. 8.00–13.30, 16.30–19.00), on the site of a chapel erected by Paschal II in 1099 over the tombs of the Domitia family, which were believed to be the haunt of demons, because Nero was buried there. The Pope solemnly cut down a walnut tree that was supposed to shelter them. The church was rebuilt in 1227 and again under Sixtus IV (1472–77). The early Renaissance façade is attributed to Andrea Bregno.

The **interior** (lights in each chapel and the apse) was renovated by Bernini and has many important works of art. SOUTH AISLE. First chapel (Della Rovere), *frescoes by Pinturicchio (1485–89); over the altar, the Adoration of the Child; in the lunettes (very worn and restored), scenes from the life of St Jerome; on the right, tomb of Cardinal De Castro (1506), perhaps by Antonio da Sangallo the Younger; on the left, the tomb of Cardinals Cristoforo and Domenico Della Rovere (1477) by Mino da Fiesole and Andrea Bregno. The second chapel (Cybo) is well designed; the architecture is by Carlo Fontana and its marbles are especially rich and varied. The huge altarpiece (Assumption and Four Doctors of the Church) is by Carlo Maratta; at the sides are the tombs of the Cybo family, and of Bishop Girolamo Foscari (died 1463).

The third chapel (being restored), with a worn majolica pavement, was frescoed by the school of Pinturicchio (1504–07); over the altar, the Virgin, four saints, and the Eternal Father; in the lunettes, scenes from the life of the Virgin; on the left, the Assumption. To the right is the tomb of Giovanni Della Rovere (1483; school of Andrea Bregno). Fourth chapel (Costa), altarpiece, Saints Catherine, Vincent, and Anthony of Padua (1489), by the school of Andrea Bregno. On the right, tomb of Marcantonio Albertoni (1485); on the left, tomb of the founder, Cardinal Giorgio Costa (1508). In the lunettes, frescoes by the school of Pinturicchio, the Fathers of the Church (1489). Here has been placed the bronze *effigy of Cardinal Pietro Foscari, for long thought to be the work of Vecchietta, but now attributed to Giovanni di Stefano (c 1485).

SOUTH TRANSEPT. The altarpiece of the Visitation by Giovan Maria Morandi is in a frame supported by two angels by Ercole Ferrata and Arrigo Giardè. On the right, tomb of Cardinal Lodovico Podocataro of Cyprus (1508). In the dome over the crossing are frescoes by Raffaele Vanni. A corridor, passing an altar from the studio of Andrea Bregno, leads to the SACRISTY which contains a *tabernacle by Bregno, with a painted Madonna of the early Sienese school, and the monuments of Bishop Rocca (died 1482) and Archbishop Ortega Gomiel of Burgos (died 1514).

The triumphal arch is decorated with fine 17C gilded stuccoed reliefs, and over the HIGH ALTAR is the venerated 'Madonna del Popolo', a 14C painting. The APSE of the church, behind, with a shell design, is one of Bramante's earliest works in Rome, commissioned by Julius II (light on left). Here are the two splendid *tombs of Cardinal Girolamo Basso della Rovere (1507) and Cardinal Ascanio Sforza (1505), signed by Andrea Sansovino. The *frescoes high up in the vault, of the Coronation of the Virgin, Evangelists, Sibyls, and Four Fathers of the Church, are by Pinturicchio (1508–09). The stained glass, commissioned by Julius II, is by Giullaume de Marcillat.

NORTH TRANSEPT. In the first chapel to the left of the choir, with a pretty vault, (right wall) are two dramatic paintings by Caravaggio: *Crucifixion of St Peter, and (left wall) *Conversion of St Paul. These famous masterpieces were executed in 1600–01. The altarpiece of the *Assumption of the Virgin is by Annibale Carracci, who also designed the frescoes in the barrel-vault above, with pretty stuccoes. In the second chapel to the left of the choir, with another pretty vault, is a marble statue of St Catherine of Alexandria by Giulio Mazzoni and two paintings of the Annunciation by Giacomo Triga (early 18C). The altarpiece in the N transept of the Holy Family by Bernardino Mei is in another frame supported by two angels, by Antonio Raggi and Giovanni Antonio Mari, and (on the left wall), tomb of Cardinal Bernardo Lonati (late 15C).

NORTH AISLE. Fourth chapel, frescoes by Pieter van Lint. The third chapel has fine monuments to the Mellini family: the earliest ones are low down on the right wall, and to the right of the altar (exquisite small tomb of Cardinal Pietro Mellini, 1483). The *tomb of Giovanni Garzia Mellini (with a half figure of the cardinal) on the left wall, is by Alessandro Algardi. The bust of Urbano Mellini is also by Algardi. The second chapel is the octagonal well-lit *Chigi Chapel, founded by the great banker Agostino Chigi (1465–1520). It was designed in a fusion of architecture, sculpture, and painting by Raphael (1513–16). Work on the chapel was interrupted in 1520 with the death of Agostino and Raphael, and it was only completed after 1652 for Cardinal Fabio Chigi (Alexander VII) by Bernini. Raphael prepared the cartoons for the *mosaics in the dome, executed by Luigi De Pace, a Venetian, in 1516. These represent God the Father as creator of the firmament, surrounded by symbols of the seven planets, each of which is guided by an angel as in Dante's conception. The frescoes depicting the Creation and the Fall, between the windows, and the medallions of the

Seasons, are by Francesco Salviati (1552–54). The altarpiece (Nativity of the Virgin) is by Sebastiano del Piombo (1530–34); the bronze bas-relief in front of Christ and the Woman of Samaria, by Lorenzetto, was intended for the base of the pyramidal tomb of Agostino, but was removed here by Bernini. Statues of Prophets: by the altar, *Jonah (left), designed by Raphael, executed by Lorenzetto, and Habakkuk (right) by Bernini; by the entrance, Daniel and the lion, by Bernini and Elijah, by Lorenzetto.

The remarkable pyramidal form of the tombs of Agostino Chigi and of his brother Sigismondo (died 1526), executed by Lorenzetto, were dictated by Raphael's architectural scheme and derived from ancient Roman models. They were altered by Bernini. An unfinished burial crypt has been discovered below the chapel with another pyramid, which in Raphael's original design would have been visible and illuminated from the chapel above. The lunettes above the tombs were painted by Raffaele Vanni in 1653. The marble intarsia figure of Death, with the Chigi stemma, in the centre of the pavement was added by Bernini.

On the left of the chapel is a colourful funerary monument, erected in 1771 in memory of Princess Odescalchi. In the BAPTISTERY are two ciboria by Andrea Bregno, and the tombs of Cardinals Francesco Castiglione (right; 1568) and Antonio Pallavicini (1507). The former Augustinian convent adjoining the church was the residence in Rome of Martin Luther during his mission here in 1511.

Beside the church stands the monumental and historic **Porta del Popolo** (Pl. 3; 2; restored in 1984), which occupies almost the same site as the ancient *Porta Flaminia*. The inner face of the gate was designed by Bernini in 1655, on the occasion of the entry into Rome of Queen Christina of Sweden; the outer face (1561) is by Nanni di Baccio Bigio, who followed a design by Michelangelo. The two colossal statues of Saints Peter and Paul in the outer niches, late works by Francesco Mochi, have been removed for restoration since 1979. The two side arches were opened in 1879. Outside the gate, in the busy PIAZZALE FLAMINIO, is an entrance to the huge park of the Villa Borghese (see Rte 9).

8

Piazza Venezia to Piazza di Spagna and the Pincio

From Piazza Venezia Via Cesare Battisti leads past (right) Palazzo delle Assicurazioni Generali, and Palazzo Valentini (1585), now the seat of the Prefecture, to (left) the long thin Piazza dei Santi Apostoli, the scene in recent years of political demonstrations. On the W side of the piazza is PALAZZO ODESCALCHI, which extends to the Corso; the façade on the piazza is by Bernini, with additions by Niccolò Salvi and Luigi Vanvitelli (1750). At No. 67 is a Museum of Waxworks, opened in 1953. The E side of the piazza is occupied by the huge building of **Palazzo Colonna** (Pl. 4; 5) which is bounded on the S by Via Quattro Novembre, on the E by Via della

Pilotta, and on the N by Via del Vaccaro and Piazza della Pilotta. On the side facing Piazza dei Santi Apostoli the palace embraces the church of the Santi Apostoli.

The palace was built by Martin V (Oddone Colonna), who lived here as pope from 1424 until his death in 1431, and rebuilt in 1730. Here, on 4 June 1802, after the cession of Piedmont to France, Charles Emmanuel IV of Savoy, king of Sardinia, became a Jesuit and abdicated in favour of his brother Victor Emmanuel I. Four arches spanning Via della Pilotta connect the palace with the Villa Colonna (no adm) which has a beautiful garden with tall cypresses (part of which can be seen from the Galleria Colonna; see below). In the garden are the remains of the huge Temple of Serapis, built in the time of Caracalla.

The palace contains the magnificent *GALLERIA COLONNA, begun in 1654 by Cardinal Girolamo I Colonna, who employed the architect Antonio Del Grande, but it was not completed until nearly fifty years later. On Del Grande's death in 1671, Girolamo Fontana took over direction. In 1703 the gallery was opened by Filippo II Colonna. One of the most important of the Patrician collections in Rome, it is arranged in magnificent Baroque galleries, and is beautifully maintained. The entrance is at 17 Via della Pilotta (open to the public only on Saturday; see p 46). The paintings, most of them not labelled, are all numbered according to the description given below. The collection was recatalogued (and some of the attributions revised) in 1981.

From the entrance, stairs mount to the VESTIBULE, in which is displayed a painting of St Julian, attributed to Perino del Vaga. **Hall of the Colonna Bellica**. A 16C column of rosso antico, surmounted by a statue of Pallas Athena, gives the room its name. The ceiling frescoes of the Reception into heaven of Marcantonio II Colonna, are by Giuseppe Chiari.

The paintings include: 132. Pietro Novelli, Isabella Colonna with her son Lorenzo Onofrio; 139. Palma Vecchio, Madonna and Child, with St Peter and donor; 66. Van Dyck (attributed), Lucrezia Tomacelli Colonna; *25. Bonifacio Veronese, Holy Family, with Saints Jerome and Lucy; 28. Hieronymus Bosch (copy from), Temptation of St Anthony; *32. Bronzino, Venus with Cupid and a satyr; 156. 16C Roman school (formerly attributed to Agostino Carracci), Cardinal Pompeo Colonna; 134. Gian Paolo Olmo or Moretto, Portrait of a man with a dog; 186. Domenico Tintoretto, Adoration of the Sacrament; *147. Scipione Pulzone, Pius V; 53. School of Dosso Dossi, Giacomo Sciarra Colonna(?); *106. Lorenzo Lotto (attributed), Cardinal Pompeo Colonna; 37. Bartolomeo Cancellieri (attributed), so-called portrait of Vittoria Colonna; 189. Jacopo Tintoretto, Narcissus; Michele di Ridolfo del Ghirlandaio, 117, 115, 116. Venus and Cupid, Dawn, and Night.

Sculpture: Hercules, Bacchus, and Head of Antinous. On the steps leading down to the Great Hall is preserved a cannon ball which fell here on 24 June 1849, during the siege of Rome.

The **Great Hall** is superbly decorated. The ceiling paintings, by Giovanni Coli and Filippo Gherardi, depict incidents in the life of Marcantonio II Colonna, who commanded the papal contingent at Lepanto (1571); the central panel illustrates the battle. On the walls are four Venetian mirrors with flower paintings by Mario de' Fiori and Giovanni Stanchi, and putti painted by Carlo Maratta.

The paintings include: Salvator Rosa, *162. St John the Baptist, once thought to be a self-portrait, 163. Preaching of St John the Baptist; 14. Francesco Bassano the Younger, Christ in the house of the Levite; 46.

Giovanni Domenico Cerrini, St Irene taking the arrows from St Sebastian; 192. Follower of Jacopo Tintoretto, Portrait of a man with his secretary; Pier Francesco Mola, 123. Hagar and Ishmael, 124. Rebecca at the well; 104. Lombard school (formerly attributed to Scipione Pulzone), family portrait of Alfonso III Gonzaga, Count of Novellara; 165. Copy from Rubens (formerly attributed to Van Dyck), Equestrian portrait of Carlo Colonna, duke of Marsi. Giovanni Lanfranco, 98. Magdalen in glory, 99. St Peter delivered from prison by the angel (perhaps a copy); 7. Nicolò Alunno, Madonna del Soccorso (the Virgin rescuing a child from a demon); 164. Matteo Rosselli (attributed), Allegory of The Fine Arts; 151. Guido Reni, St Francis of Assisi with two angels; 168. Enea Salmeggia, Martyrdom of St Catherine; 82. Guercino, St Paul the Hermit; 6. Alessandro Allori, Descent into hell; 180. Sustermans (attributed), Federico Colonna, viceroy of Valencia; 40. 17C Roman school (formerly attributed to Ribera), St Jerome; 141. Bartolomeo Passarotti, family of Lodovico Peracchini; 167. Rubens (follower of), Assumption of the Virgin. The Roman sculpture includes: Dancing faun; Marcus Aurelius; Gladiator. Fine bas-reliefs and sarcophagi fragments are set into the walls beneath the windows, and into statue pedestals.

The **Room of the Desks** (or 'of the Landscapes') derives its name from two valuable *desks displayed here. The first, in ebony, has 28 ivory bas-reliefs by Francis and Dominic Steinhard after drawings by Carlo Fontana; the central relief is a copy of Michelangelo's Last Judgment, the other 27 are copies of works by Raphael. The second desk, in sandalwood, is adorned with lapis lazuli, amethysts, and other semi-precious stones; in front are 12 small amethyst columns and at the top gilt bronze statuettes representing the Muses and Apollo seated under a laurel tree. The ceiling frescoes, by Sebastiano Ricci, are of the battle of Lepanto.

In this room is a fine series of *landscapes by Gaspard Dughet (54–65), and a further series by J.F. van Bloemen, with figures probably by Placido Costanzi (21–24). Borgognone, 49. Stag hunt, 50. Battle scene; 182. Herman van Swanevelt (formerly attributed to Claude Lorraine), Landscape with ruins of the Palatine Hill; 146. Nicolas Poussin (follower of), Apollo and Daphne; 126. Jan Brueghel the Elder (and Josse de Momper?), Landscape with figures; 31. Paul Brill (attributed), Antigone recovering the bodies of her brothers; 121. 16C Flemish school, Landscape with Noli me tangere; 89. Jacob de Heusch (formerly attributed to Salvator Rosa), Seascape; 181. Herman van Swanevelt, Landscape with the Good Samaritan; 113. Circle of Michele Marieschi (formerly attributed to Canaletto), View of the Campo and Scuola di San Rocco in Venice. Sculpture, Susini, copy in bronze of the Farnese bull; two Roman fire irons in polished bronze; bronze group of a centaur and a female figure.

Room of the Apotheosis of Martin V. This room takes its name from the subject of the ceiling painting by Benedetto Luti. Above the windows, Pietro Bianchi, Fame crowning victory. Above the end wall, Pompeo Batoni, Time discovering truth. 159. Roman school(?), Cain and Abel; Domenico Tintoretto, 187, 188. Portraits; 152. Workshop of Guido Reni, St Agnese; Guercino, 85, 86. Annunciation; 183. German School, 1524 (formerly attributed to Mabuse), Man with clasped hands; 33. Bronzino, Madonna and Child with Saints John and Elizabeth; 190. Jacopo Tintoretto (formerly attributed to Titian), Onofrio Panvinio, the Augustinian; Francesco Salviati, *170. Portrait of a Man, 169. Raising of Lazarus; 1. Francesco Albani, Rape of Europa; 83. Guercino, Guardian Angel; 178. Giovanni di Pietro Spagna, St Jerome; 191. Follower of Jacopo Tintoretto, Spinet player; 8. Andrea del

Sarto (formerly attributed to Puligo), Madonna and Child; 43. Annibale Carracci (also attributed to Bartolomeo Passarotti), Peasant eating beans; 26. Paris Bordone, Holy Family with Saints Jerome, Sebastian, and Mary Magdalene; *197. Paolo Veronese, Man in Venetian costume. Sculpture: Orfeo Buselli, bust of Cardinal Jerome I Colonna; two Roman marble busts.

The **Throne Room** is reserved, as in other princely houses, for the Pope; the chair is turned to the wall so that no one else can sit in it. 144. Pisanello (copy from), Portrait of Martin V, Oddone Colonna; Scipione Pulzone, 149. Portrait of Marcantonio II Colonna; 150. (attributed), Portrait of Felice Colonna Orsini. In this room are (198) a nautical chart presented by the Roman people to Marcantonio II and a parchment diploma given him by the Roman senate after the battle of Lépanto. French clock by I. Godet of Paris. Statuettes in bronze of a Satyr and Aphrodite; and marble busts of Zeus and a Woman.

Room of Maria Mancini, or 'of the Primitives'. 51. Francesco Cozza, Birth of the Virgin; 143. Pietro da Cortona, Resurrection of Christ, with members of the Colonna family; 92. Jacob van Amsterdam, Christ appearing to the Madonna and St John after the Resurrection; *198. Bartolomeo Vivarini, Madonna enthroned; 105. Luca Longhi, Madonna with the young St John and a monk; Francesco Albani, 3, 4. Herminia among the shepherds; *35. Giuliano Bugiardini, Madonna; *154. Rocco Zoppo (attributed; formerly attributed to Melozzo da Forlì), Portrait of a young man in profile, traditionally identified as Guidobaldo della Rovere, duke of Urbino; 10. Iacopo degli Avanzi, Crucifixion; 102. Copy from Leonardo da Vinci, Madonna and Child; 175. Girolamo Sicciolante da Sermoneta, Madonna with the infant St John; *179. Stefano da Zevio, Madonna and Child enthroned with angels; 30. School of Botticelli, Madonna and Child; 130. Gaspar Netscher (attributed), Maria Colonna Mancini, the niece of Cardinal Mazarin; 38. Simone Cantarini, Holy Family; 166. Rubens (copy from), Reconciliation of Esau and Jacob; 29. Workshop of Botticelli (formerly attributed to Jacopo del Sellaio), Apostle St James; 137, 138. Bernart van Orley, The seven joys and seven sorrows of Mary; 90. Innocenzo da Imola, Holy Family with St Francis; 84. Guercino, Moses with the tables of law.

The church of the **SANTI APOSTOLI** (Pl. 4; 5) was built by Pelagius I c 560 to commemorate the defeat and expulsion of the Goths by the Byzantine viceroy Narses, and dedicated to the Apostles James and Philip. It was restored and enlarged in the 15C and 16C and almost completely rebuilt by Carlo and Francesco Fontana in 1702–14. The unusual FAÇADE, which has the appearance of a palace rather than a church, consists of a stately Renaissance double LOGGIA (restored in 1990) of nine arches. This is attributed to Baccio Pontelli, and was built at the cost of Cardinal della Rovere, afterwards Pope Julius II. The upper storey was filled in with Baroque windows by Carlo Rainaldi c 1665 (who also added the balustrade with statues of the Apostles). Behind this and above it can be seen the neo-classical façade of the church added by Valadier in 1827. In the PORTICO (closed by an iron grille), is (left), the tomb of the engraver Giovanni Volpato, by Canova (1807). On the right, *bas-relief of the 2C AD, representing an eagle holding an oak-wreath in his claws; and a lion, signed by Vassalletto. Two 12C red marble lions flank the entrance portal.

The Baroque INTERIOR (open 7.00–12.00, 16.00–19.00) is on a vast scale, with a nave 18m broad. The effect of immensity is enhanced by the manner in which the lines of the vaulting continue those of the massive pillars, and the lines of the apse those of the nave. From the end near the entrance can be seen the surprising effect of relief attained by Giovanni Odazzi in his contorted group of Fallen Angels, on the vault above the high altar. On the ceiling are the Triumph of the Order of St Francis, by Baciccia, and the Evangelists, by Luigi Fontana.

SOUTH AISLE. The first chapel contains a 15C Madonna donated to the church by Cardinal Bessarion (see below). Against the second pillar is a monument to Clementina Sobieska, queen of James III (see below), by Filippo Della Valle. In the Baroque third chapel remains of 15C frescoes were discovered behind the apse (difficult to see) in 1959. The chapel at the end of the aisle has eight columns from the 6C church. In the SANCTU-ARY the high altarpiece, supposed to be the largest in Rome, of the Martyr-dom of Saints Philip and James, is by Domenico Muratori. On the right, tombs of Count Giraud de Caprières (1505) and Cardinal Raffaele Riario, perhaps to a design of Michelangelo; on the left, the beautiful monument of Cardinal Pietro Riario, by the school of Andrea Bregno, with a Madonna by Mino da Fiesole. Fragments of the exquisite frescoes by Melozzo da Forlì which formerly covered the 15C apse are preserved in the Quirinal and in the Pinacoteca of the Vatican.

Steps in front of the sanctuary lead down to the CONFESSIO. Here are preserved the relics of the Apostles Philip and James, and in the chapel to the left, the beautiful *tomb by Andrea Bregno, of Raffaele della Rovere (died 1477), brother of Sixtus IV and father of Julius II. The other chapels were charmingly decorated in 1876–77 in the style of the catacombs, and foundations of the earlier church can be seen here. NORTH AISLE. At the E end, around the door into the sacristy, is the first important work in Rome by Canova, the *mausoleum of Clement XIV. On the second pillar is an epitaph of 1682 dedicated to Cardinal Bessarion (1389–1472), the illustrious Greek scholar, with a 16C portrait of him (his remains were translated here in 1957). In the second chapel, altarpiece of St Joseph of Copertino (the 'flying monk'), by Giuseppe Cades (1777), between two columns of verde antico, which are the largest known.

The two Renaissance CLOISTERS, approached from the left of the façade (at No. 51 in the Piazza) contain a bas-relief of the Nativity by the school of Arnolfo di Cambio, a palaeochristian sarcophagus, and, in the second cloister, a memorial to Michelangelo, whose body was temporarily placed here in 1564 before his burial in Santa Croce in Florence. Also here, is a double inscription in Latin and Greek which was dictated by Cardinal Bessarion for his own tomb.

At the end of Piazza dei Santi Apostoli, is the little Baroque PALAZZO BALESTRA (formerly Muti), which was presented by Clement XI to James Stuart, the Old Pretender, on his marriage in 1719. Here were born his sons Charles, the Young Pretender (1720), and Henry, Cardinal York (1725); and here died James, in 1766, and Charles, in 1788. Via del Vaccaro leads right into Piazza della Pilotta. At the E end of the square is the large UNIVERSITÀ GREGORIANA PONTIFICIA (1930). From here Via dei Lucchesi runs N past (right) Via della Dataria, leading up to Piazza del Quirinale, and (left) Via dell' Umiltà, leading to the Corso.

Beyond the cross-roads the street, now called Via di San Vincenzo, continues to the huge *FONTANA DI TREVI (Pl. 4; 3), one of the most famous sights of Rome, and one of the city's most exuberant and successful 18C monuments. The abundant water, which forms an essential part of the design of the monumental fountain, fills the little piazza with its sound. There is still a rooted tradition that travellers who throw a coin into the fountain before leaving the city will return to Rome (the money is collected periodically and donated to the Italian Red Cross). It was restored for the first time in 1989–91. Its waters are those of the 'Acqua Vergine', which Agrippa brought to Rome for his baths in 19 BC, and which feed also the fountains of Piazza di Spagna, Piazza Navona, and Piazza Farnese. The aqueduct, which is nearly 20km long, runs through the Villa Giulia.

Detail of the Fontana di Trevi

The original fountain was a simple and beautiful basin by Leon Battista Alberti; it was restored by Urban VIII, who is said to have obtained the necessary funds by a tax on wine. Many famous architects, including Bernini, Ferdinando Fuga, and Gaspare Vanvitelli presented projects for a new fountain. In 1732 Clement XII held a competition and Nicola Salvi was given the commission. His theatrical design incorporates, as a background, the entire façade of Palazzo Poli, which had been completed in 1730. Two giant Tritons, one blowing a conch, conduct the winged chariot of Neptune. In the side niches are figures of Health (right) and Abundance (left); the bas-reliefs above represent the virgin of the legend from which the water took its name pointing out the spring to the Roman soldiers, and Agrippa approving the plans for the aqueduct. The four statues above these represent the Seasons with their gifts. At the summit are the arms of the Corsini family, with two allegorical figures. The fountain was completed in 1762, after Salvi's death.

Opposite is the church of **Santi Vincenzo ed Anastasio**, rebuilt in 1630, with a Baroque façade by Martino Longhi the Younger. In the crypt of this church, the parish church of the neighbouring pontifical palace of the Quirinal, are preserved the hearts and lungs of almost all the popes from Sixtus V (1590) to Leo XIII (1903).

From Piazza di Trevi Via delle Muratte leads W to the Corso. In Via della Stamperia, which runs N to the right of the fountain, is the garden of the Accademia di San Luca (see below), opposite the **Calcografia Nazionale** or *Calcografia di Roma*, the most important collection of copper-plate engravings in the world; adm, see p 45. The collection was formed in 1738 by Clement XII and moved in 1837 to its present site; the building is by Luigi Valadier. It contains almost all the engravings of Giovanni Battista Piranesi (1432 plates) and examples of the work of Marcantonio Raimondi, Rossini, Pinelli, and many others. It has a total of more than 19,600 plates. Exhibitions are often held, and any items not on display can be seen on request, and copies purchased. The institute was merged with the Gabinetto Nazionale delle Stampe in 1975 as the ISTITUTO NAZIONALE PER LA GRAFICA, and there are long-term plans to move it next door to Palazzo Poli.

The street opens out into Piazza dell'Accademia di San Luca. Here is Palazzo Carpegna, seat of the **Accademia di San Luca**, moved from the neighbourhood of the Roman Forum when Via dei Fori Imperiali was built. The academy, founded in 1577 by the painter Girolamo Muziano of Brescia, incorporated the 15C Università dei Pittori whose members used to meet in the little church of San Luca. Muziano's successor, Federico Zuccari, gave the academy its first statutes, and it soon became famous for its teaching and for its prize competitions. The eclectic •**GALLERIA DELL' ACCADEMIA DI SAN LUCA** contains gifts and bequests from its members, together with donations from other sources. Adm, see p 45. The collection is arranged on the third floor (lift).

Room I (ahead, beyond the gallery). Baciccia, •**Portrait of Clement IX**; Girolamo and Giovanni Battista Bassano, Shepherds and sheep; Pier Francesco Mola, Spinster; Titian (attributed), St Jerome; Raphael, •**Putto**, fragment of a fresco (1512); Jacopo Bassano, Annunciation to the shepherds; Marcello Venusti, Deposition; presumed mask of Michelangelo; Carletto Caliari, Venus with a mirror; Sebastiano Conca, La Vigilanza; Carlo Maratta, Death of Sisera; Poussin (copy of Titian), Triumph of Bacchus; Titian (attributed), Portrait of Marino Cornaro.

Room II. Donation of Baron Michele Lazzaroni. Paris Bordone, Seduction; Titian (attributed), •**Portrait of Ippolito Rimanaldo**; Giovanni Battista Piazzetta, Judith and Holofernes; Cavalier d'Arpino, Perseus and Andromeda, Taking of Christ; Francesco di Giorgio Martini, Madonna and Child; Federico Barocci, Rest during the flight into Egypt; school of Lorenzo di Credi, Annunciation; Baciccia, Madonna and Child; Florentine school of 15C, Madonna and Child; Flemish school of 17C, Portrait of a woman; Federico Zuccari, •**Self-portrait**; Alessandro Allori, Portrait of a woman.

Room III. Works of the 18C and 19C. Domenico Pellegrini, Augustus Frederick, duke of Sussex, Self-portrait, Hebe; Giuseppe Grassi, portraits of the architect Henry Wood and of Vincenzo Camuccini; Mme Brossard de Beaulieu, Niobe; Angelica Kauffmann, Hope; Anton Wiertz, Portrait of the architect Angelo Uggeri; Mme Vigée le Brun, •**Self-portrait**; Alessandro d'Este(?), Bust of Canova; Joseph Nollekens, Bust of Piranesi.

Room IV. Aniello Falcone, Jacob's Dream; Nicholas Berchem, Cattle and shepherds in the Roman Campagna; P. van Bloemen, Cattle scene, Horses; Sweerts, Genre scene; Giovanni van Bloemen, Pastoral scene; Sweerts, Interior scene, Drinker, Genre scene, Woman combing her hair; Giovanni van Bloemen, Pastoral scene; Master of the St Lucy Legend, Virgin; 16C German school, Deposition.

Room V. Giovanni Bilivert, Tarquin and Lucretia; Canaletto, Architectural perspective; Giovanni Paolo Pannini, landscapes with Roman ruins; Van Dyck, *Madonna and Child with angels; Rubens, Nymphs crowning Abundance; John Parker, landscape; Jan Asselijn, Roman Campagna; Palma Giovane, Susanna; Philip Wouwermans, white horse; Jan van Mytens, Admiral Neewszom Kostenaer; Salvator Rosa(?), study of cats' heads; Philip Peter Roos (Rosa da Tivoli), shepherd and animals; Van Dyck, Madonna and Angels (drawing for the painting above).

Room VI. (**Gallery**). Francesco Trevisani, Scourging of Christ, St Francis; Benedetto Luti, Mary Magdalene at the feet of Christ, *Self-portrait; Anton von Maron, portraits of academicians Raphael Mengs, Teresa Mengs von Maron, Vincenzo Pacetti, Caterina Cherubini Preciado, Thomas Jenkins; Giovanni Battista Canevari, James II as a child, partial copy of Van Dyck's portrait of the children of Charles I in the Galleria Sabauda in Turin; Andrea Locatelli, two genre scenes, two landscapes; Guercino, Venus and Cupid (detached fresco); Claude Joseph Vernet, *Seascape; Gaspare Vanvitelli, view of Tivoli, Porto di Ripa Grande. Sculpture: Clodion (?; formerly attributed to Bernini), *Bust of a young girl; Tribolo, Allegorical figure of a river (terracotta).

Room VII. Sebastiano Conca, Marriage of St Catherine; Baciccia, Sketch for the Birth of St John Baptist in Santa Maria in Campitelli; Sassoferrato, Madonna and Child; Michele Rocca, St Cecilia; Angelo Massarotti, Madonna and sleeping Child; Henrick van Somer, *St Jerome and the Sadducees; J.F. de Troy, Faustulus finding Romulus and Remus; Guido Reni, L'Addolorata; Ciro Ferri, Martyrdom of St Luke.

Room VIII. Terracotta reliefs from prize competitions held in the 18C. Pierre Legros the Younger, The arts paying homage to Clement XI; Michele Slodtz, St Theresa transfixed by an angel; Alessandro Algardi, Leo XI and Henry IV. **Staircase**. Aristide Sartorio, Monte Circeo; Francesco Hayez, Il Vincitore; Canova, Self-portrait and Bust of Napoleon; Pietro da Cortona, Copy of Raphael's Galatea; Guido Reni, Fortune, Bacchus and Ariadne; Pietro Bracci, Sketch in terracotta.

Paintings and sculpture by 20C academicians, donated by the artist or his family, including works by Giorgio Morandi, Fausto Pirandello, Felice Casorati, and Emilio Greco, are no longer on view, and the **Sale Accademiche** have also been closed to the public, except on St Luke's Day (18 October). They contain more important works from the 15C to the present day, including St Luke painting the Virgin, begun by Raphael and finished by assistants.

Just N of the Accademia is the busy **Via del Tritone**. This street ascends gradually from Largo Chigi in the Corso, to Piazza Barberini. Half-way up is LARGO DEL TRITONE, entered from the N by Via Francesco Crispi and Via Due Macelli. On the S side Via del Traforo leads to the *Traforo Umberto I* (Pl. 4; 3), a road tunnel under the Quirinal Gardens, 347m long, built in 1902–05. In Via Crispi, in the ex Carmelite convent of San Giuseppe, the **Galleria Comunale d'Arte Moderna** (formerly in Palazzo delle Esposizioni) is being arranged and may be opened in 1994. Italian and foreign 20C artists represented include: Rodin, Guglielmo de Sanctis, Michele Cammarano, Scipione, Vincenzo Cabianca, Norberto Pazzini, Aristide Sartorio, Giacomo Balla, Arturo Noci, Amerigo Bertoli, Antonio Donghi, Fausto Pirandello, Roberto Melli, Renato Guttuso, Carlo Levi, Giacomo Manzù, Giorgio Morandi, and Pietro Annigoni.

On the N side of Largo del Tritone, is Via Due Macelli, which runs NW. In the first street to the left, Via Capo le Case, is the church of **Sant' Andrea delle Fratte**, which belonged to the Scots before the Reformation. Here in 1678 Alessandro Scarlatti was married. The TOWER (unfinished), and refined fantastical CAMPANILE (recently cleaned), both by Borromini, were designed to make their greatest impression when seen from Via Capo le Case.

INTERIOR. In the second chapel on the right is the tomb of Miss Falconet (1856), with a recumbent figure by the American artist Harriet Hossmer. To the left of the side door is the epigraph of Angelica Kauffmann (1741–1807). The cupola and apse were decorated in the 17C by Pasquale Marini, and the three huge paintings of the Crucifixion, Death and Burial of St Andrew are by Giovanni Battista Lenardi, Lazzaro Baldi, and Francesco Trevisani. By the high altar are two beautiful *angels by Bernini, sculpted for Ponte Sant'Angelo but replaced on the bridge by copies. The Cloister has a garden with four cypresses.

Via Due Macelli leads into the long and irregular ***PIAZZA DI SPAGNA** (Pl. 4; 1), for centuries the centre of the artistic and literary life of the city. Foreign travellers usually chose their lodgings in the pensions and hotels in the vicinity of the square, and here the English colony congregated. John Evelyn, on his first visit to Rome in 1644, stayed near the piazza. Keats died in a house on the square, the British Consul formerly had his office here, and there is still a well-known English tea-room. In the neighbouring Via del Babuino is the English church. The piazza retains a cosmopolitan atmosphere, always crowded with Romans and visitors. The elegant streets leading out of the W side of the piazza to the Corso are famous for their fashionable shops: Via Condotti, Via Frattina, and Via Borgognone are also now pedestrian precincts.

At the S end of the piazza, between Via Due Macelli and Via di Propaganda is the COLLEGIO DI PROPAGANDA FIDE, with a façade (on Via di Propaganda) by Borromini (1622). The detailed friezes are particularly fine. The college, which has the privilege of extraterritoriality, was founded for the training of missionaries (including young foreigners) by Urban VIII as an annex to the Congregazione di Propaganda Fide established by Gregory XV in 1622. The COLUMN OF THE IMMACULATE CONCEPTION (1857) commemorates the establishment by Pius IX in 1854 of the dogma of the Immaculate Conception of the Virgin Mary. On the W side, opposite the small Piazzetta Mignanelli, is PALAZZO DI SPAGNA, which gave the piazza its name, the residence since 1622 of the Spanish ambassador to the Vatican. It is a good building with a fine courtyard by Antonio Del Grande (1647).

In the narrow centre of the piazza is the ***Fontana della Barcaccia** (being restored), the masterpiece of Pietro Bernini, father of Gian Lorenzo. The design (a leaking boat) is well adapted to the low water pressure of the fountain. The scenographic ***Scalinata** or **SPANISH STEPS** were built in 1723–26 by Francesco De Sanctis to connect the piazza with the church of the Trinità dei Monti and the Pincio. The famous monumental flight of 137 well worn steps, which rises between picturesque houses, some with garden terraces, has always been a well loved haunt of Romans and foreigners. It is a masterpiece of 18C town planning. Every day there is a display of flowers for sale at the foot, and the steps are covered with tubs of magnificent azaleas at the beginning of May.

In the elegant 18C house (recently restored and given a bright new colour), on the right looking up, is the apartment (with a little terrace covered with a vine) where the poet John Keats spent the last three months of his life (plaque), now the **Keats-Shelley Memorial House** (on the second floor, entrance at No. 26 in the Piazza; admission times see p 46). This was a small pensione in 1820 when Keats booked rooms for himself and his friend Joseph Severn when he came to spend the winter in Rome on his doctor's advice. Keats lead a 'posthumous life' here until his death from tuberculosis on 23 February 1821, aged 25.

The house was purchased in 1906 by the Keats-Shelley Memorial Association and first opened to the public in 1909 as a delightful little museum and library dedicated to Keats, Shelley, Byron, and Leigh Hunt, all of whom spent much time in Italy. The library contains over 8000 volumes, and numerous autograph letters and manuscripts are preserved here. In the Salone is displayed material relating to Shelley and Byron, including a painting of Shelley at the Baths of Caracalla by Joseph Severn. The kitchen was in the small room opening onto a terrace on the Spanish Steps, and Severn's room now contains mementos of Severn, Leigh Hunt, Coleridge, and Wordsworth. Severn came back to Rome as British Consul in 1860–72. Here is displayed a reliquary of Pius V which was later used as a locket for the hair of Milton and Elizabeth Barrett Browning and was owned by Leigh Hunt (see Keats' poem 'Lines on Seeing a Lock of Milton's Hair'). The death mask of Keats, and a sketch of the poet on his death bed by Severn, are preserved in the little room where he died.

In the house opposite (which retains its fine deep russet colour), at the foot of the Spanish Steps, built by De Sanctis to form a pair with the house where Keats lived, 'Babington's English tea-rooms' survive. The piazza is particularly attractive at its N end with a row of 18C houses and four tall palm trees.

In the fashionable **Via Condotti**, named after the conduits of the Acqua Vergine, is the renowned CAFFÉ GRECO founded in 1760, and a national monument since 1953. Its famous patrons included Goethe, Gogol, Berlioz, Stendhal, Taine, Baudelaire, Thorvaldsen, and Wagner, and it is decorated with personal mementos, self-portraits, etc. Farther down is the 17C palace of the Grand Master of the order of the Knights of St John of Jerusalem. At the NW end of the piazza Via della Croce leads to Via Bocca di Leone in which (right) at the corner of Vicolo del Lupo, was the Brownings' Roman residence.

Via del Babuino, opened in 1525, connects Piazza di Spagna with Piazza del Popolo. Rubens lived here in 1606–08, and Poussin in 1624. In the neighbouring streets many artists still have their studios and it is the centre of the Bohemian artistic life of the city. It is also famous for its antique shops. It takes its name from a 16C fountain statue which has been placed beside the church of SANT'ATANASIO DEI GRECI (by Giacomo della Porta). The neo-Gothic English church of ALL SAINTS (Pl. 3; 2) was built in 1882 by G.E. Street. On the right, near Vicolo Alibert, was the studio in which Thorvaldsen succeeded Flaxman as occupant; and parallel on this side is the 16C **Via Margutta**, the residence of Dutch and Flemish painters in the 17C. Here at No. 53 Sir Thomas Lawrence founded the British Academy of Arts in 1821. It is still a street of artists with art galleries and studios (with interesting courtyards and gardens towards the Pincio), and in Spring and Autumn a street fair is held with paintings for sale. More recently Via Margutta has also become Rome's 'Carnaby Street'.

On the terrace at the top of the Spanish Steps is **Piazza della Trinità dei Monti** with its church. From the balustrade there is a fine view of Rome, with the dome of St Peter's in the distance (beyond the dome of Santi Ambrogio e Carlo al Corso), and to the left the top of the Column of Marcus Aurelius. On the near right can be seen the Villa Medici (described below). The OBELISK here, probably brought to Rome in the 2C or 3C AD, when the hieroglyphs were incised (copied from those on the obelisk in Piazza del Popolo) formerly stood in the Gardens of Sallust. It was set up here in 1788 by Pius VI.

The church of the **TRINITÀ DEI MONTI** (Pl. 4; 1), attached to the French Convent of the Minims, was begun in 1493 by Louis XII. It was restored after damage caused by Napoleon's occupation by F. Mazois in 1816 at the expense of Louis XVIII. The unusual 16C FAÇADE has a double staircase (by Domenico Fontana). The INTERIOR (when closed, ring at the door of the small side staircase on the left, but usually only open 9.30–12.30, 16.00–18.00) is divided by a grille into two parts, only one of which may ordinarily be visited. SOUTH SIDE. First chapel, altarpiece and frescoes by Giovanni Battista Naldini; third chapel, *Assumption, by Daniele da Volterra, the best pupil of Michelangelo, whose likeness is seen in the last figure on the right of the picture. The painting has a remarkable design, but is in very poor condition. The whole chapel is decorated on a plan by Daniele da Volterra, by his pupils. In the second N chapel, *Descent from the Cross, an especially fine work (although very damaged, since it was transferred to canvas in 1811) by the same painter, possibly executed from a design by his master.

The other part of the church contains *frescoes by Perino del Vaga, Giulio Romano and others, in finely decorated chapels. The fourth chapel on the left (N transept) has the Assumption and Death of the Virgin by Taddeo Zuccari, finished by his brother Federico. The vault is painted by Perino del Vaga. Recent excavations beneath the convent (no admission) have revealed traces of a Roman villa which seems to have had a terrace on the hillside similar in form to the Spanish Steps.

From the Piazza there is a good view of the long and straight **Via Sistina**, which descends to Piazza Barberini (see Rte 10) and then ascends the Quirinal Hill as Via delle Quattro Fontane. This handsome thoroughfare was laid out by Sixtus V as the 'Strada Felice' which ran for some 3km via Santa Maria Maggiore all the way to Santa Croce in Gerusalemme. In this street most of the illustrious visitors to Rome between the days of Napoleon and 1870 seem to have lodged. Nikolai Gogol (1809–52), lived at No. 126; No. 48 housed in succession Giovanni Battista Piranesi (1720–78), Bertel Thorvaldsen (1770–1844), and Luigi Canina (the architect and archaeologist (1795–1856). At the top end it still has some well known hotels and elegant shops. Between Via Sistina and Via Gregoriana is the charming and bizarre PALAZZO ZUCCARI, built by the artist as his residence and studio. Reynolds lived here in 1752–53 and Winckelmann in 1755–68. In 1900 it was bought by Enrichetta Hertz who left her library, with the palace, to the German government. The BIBLIOTECA HERTZIANA is now one of the most famous art history libraries in the country.

In the other direction, Viale della Trinità dei Monti leads along the edge of the hill to the **VILLA MEDICI** (Pl. 4; 1), the seat of the French Academy since 1803. Here students who win the Prix de Rome at the École des Beaux-Arts in Paris for painting, sculpture, architecture, engraving, or music are sent to study for three years at the expense of the French Government. The grounds are normally open to the public on one or two days of the week (admission, see p 47). Important exhibitions are held in the Villa.

The palace built by Annibale Lippi for Cardinal Ricci da Montepulciano, c 1540, was bought by Ferdinando dei Medici, later Grand Duke of Tuscany in 1576. Here also lived Cardinal Alessandro (later Leo XI). The villa was modified by Bartolomeo Ammannati for the Medici, who here housed their famous collection of ancient Roman sculpture, the masterpieces of which were later transferred to the Uffizi in Florence. In 1801 it was bought by Napoleon and the French Academy, founded in 1666 by Louis XIV, was transferred here. In the 17C Velazquez was a tenant, and Galileo was confined here by the Inquisition from 1630–33.

The villa is famous for its inner *FAÇADE on the garden front decorated with numerous ancient Roman statues, medallions, columns, and bas-reliefs (including four delicately carved panels dating from 43 AD). The beautiful 16C *GARDEN has long vistas through hedged walks, and fine views over Rome. The formal garden has several fountains and fragments of ancient sculpture, including the head of Meleagar which might even be an original by Skopas.

Among the ilexes in front of the Villa Medici the *FOUNTAIN, with an ancient Roman red granite vase, was designed in 1589 by Annibale Lippi. The cannon ball is said to have been shot from Castel Sant'Angelo by Queen Christina of Sweden, when late for an appointment with the painter Charles Errard who was staying at the French Academy. The view is familiar from many paintings, although it is now somewhat impaired by trees in the foreground.

The gently sloping Viale della Trinità dei Monti ends at a monument by Ercole Rosa (1883) to the Brothers Cairoli, who died at Villa Glori in October 1867 in Garibaldi's attempt to rouse the Romans against the papal government. From this point Viale D'Annunzio descends to Piazza del Popolo while Viale Mickiewicz ascends to the Pincio.

The *PINCIO (46m; Pl. 3; 2) was laid out as a Romantic park by Giuseppe Valadier in 1809–14 on the Pincian Hill. Adjoining the Villa Borghese, it forms the largest public garden in the centre of Rome and it is especially crowded on holidays. It was the most fashionable Roman 'passeggiata' in the last century when the aristocracy and foreign visitors came here in their carriages to hear the band play and admire the sunset. Joseph Severn describes his walks here with John Keats in 1820–21 (while staying above the Spanish Steps), during which they frequently met Pauline Borghese, Napoleon's sister. The *view from the terrace of the Piazzale Napoleone is dominated by the dome of St Peter's.

The Pincio was known as the *Collis Hortulorum* of ancient Rome since it used to be covered with the monumental gardens of the Roman aristocracy and Emperors. On part of the hill was the villa of L. Licinius Lucullus, built after 63 BC. Here, in the same villa, later the property of Valerius Asiaticus, Messalina, the third wife of the Emperor Claudius, murdered its owner. In the 4C it was owned by the Pinci, from whom the name of the hill is derived. Recent excavations have found traces of 1C walls here.

Piazzale Napoleone may be reached also by a fairly steep broad path which rises from the right-hand (NE) side of Viale della Trinità dei Monti near the Cairoli monument. At the top of the path is a terrace on which is the CASINA VALADIER (1813–17), still a fashionable restaurant and open-air café. Among the habitués of its most sumptuous period have been Richard Strauss, Mussolini, Farouk, Gandhi, and Chiang Kai-shek. The view from its terrace is even better than that from Piazzale Napoleone, into which the pathway leads.

The park is intersected by broad avenues passing between magnificent trees, many of them remarkable specimens of their kind. One of these avenues, Viale dell'Obelisco, runs E to join Viale delle Magnolie in the Villa Borghese (see Rte 9). The obelisk which gives the avenue its name was placed here in 1822; it was originally erected by Hadrian on the tomb of his favourite Antinous, which was probably near Santa Croce in Gerusalemme. Throughout the park are busts of celebrated Italians from the days of ancient Rome to the present time. Of the fountains, the most notable are the Water Clock, in Viale dell'Orologio, and the Fountain of Moses, reached from there by a subsidiary walk.

The Pincio is bounded on the N and E by massive walls, which define its limits by a right angle. Part of these walls is the *Muro Torto*, or *Murus Ruptus*, the only portion of Aurelian's wall that was not fortified by Belisarius against the Goths. The wall has for centuries seemed on the point of collapsing. When Belisarius proposed to fortify it, the Romans prevented him, saying that it would be defended by St Peter. Viale del Muro Torto, at the foot of the Pincio, is a busy road running outside the wall from Piazzale Flaminio to Porta Pinciana.

9

Villa Borghese and Villa Giulia

Immediately N of the Aurelian wall is the magnificent *VILLA BORGHESE (Pl. 11; 5, 6, 7, 8), Rome's most famous public park, with a circumference of 6km, in which is the suburban villa which houses the celebrated Museo Borghese (see below). The main entrance to the park is on the WSW, from Piazzale Flaminio, just outside Porta del Popolo. There are four other entrances: S, from Piazzale Brasile, outside Porta Pinciana; SE, from Via Pinciana; NE, from Via Mercadante; and N from Viale delle Belle Arti (see below). Traffic is excluded from the main area of the park.

The Villa owes its origin, in the 17C, to Cardinal Scipione Borghese, Paul V's nephew (see below). In the 18C Prince Marcantonio Borghese (father of Prince Camillo Borghese who married Pauline Bonaparte) employed Jacob More from Edinburgh to design the gardens. Early in the 19C the property was enlarged by the addition of the Giustiniani Gardens and in 1902 it was bought by the State and handed over to the city of Rome, and opened to the public. The Villa (c 688 hectares) is now connected with the Pincio and the Villa Guilia, so that the three form one great park, intersected in every direction by avenues and paths, with fine oaks, giant ilexes, umbrella pines and other trees, as well as statues, fountains, and terraces.

From the classical main gateway on Piazzale Flaminio (Pl. 11; 7), by Canina (1835), Viale Washington ascends to the FOUNTAIN OF AESCULAPIUS by Luigi Canina, 1830–34, with a Roman statue. From here a road leads (right) to the PORTICO EGIZIANO, another imposing entrance, in the form of pylons. Straight on is a monument to Victor Hugo (1905), presented by the Franco-Italian League. On the left of the avenue is the **Giardino del Lago**, with hedged walks and arbours, laid out in 1785 by Jacob More and Cristoforo Unterberger, *'all'inglese'*.

The Giardino del Lago

On an island in the little lake is a TEMPLE OF AESCULAPIUS by Antonio and Mario Asprucci. Seven statues by Vincenzo Pacetti (partly Roman) have been replaced by copies. The originals are to be exhibited in the Casina di Raffaello (see below), together with other recently restored statuary from the garden including four Tritons (removed here in 1909 from the Fontana del Moro in Piazza Navona where they were replaced by copies in 1874). A huge neo-classical monument to the Dutch Jurist Jan van der Capellen made in 1790 by Giuseppe Ceracchi and erected in the gardens in 1845 will also probably be housed here, and a Roman sarcophagus with the myth of Phaeton.

From Piazza delle Canestre the broad Viale delle Magnolie, connecting these gardens with the Pincio, runs SW, and Viale San Paolo del Brasile runs SE past a monument to Goethe (by Gustav Eberlein), and the 17C CASINA DELLE ROSE, abandoned for years but now destined to be restored as a club for military officers (which is hopefully to be removed from Palazzo Barberini). In Piazzale Brasile is a monument, in Carrara marble, to Byron after Thorvaldsen (1959). Beyond is Porta Pinciana, at the top of Via Vittorio Veneto (see Rte 10).

From Piazza delle Canestre an avenue leads NE past the so-called CASINA DI RAFFAELLO, reconstructed by Asprucci in 1792. The interior (with decorations by Felice Giani) is to be used as a museum of sculptures from the garden. Beyond is the attractive **Piazza di Siena**, a rustic amphitheatre created by Mario and Antonio Asprucci in c 1792, with tall pine trees, where important equestrian events are held. Beside it is a monument to Umberto

I, by Davide Calandra. At the end of the avenue is a reproduction of the Temple of Faustina.

On the left 'LA FORTEZZUOLA' dates from the 16C; the crenellations were added in the 19C. In 1926 it became the studio of the sculptor and musician Pietro Canonica (born 1869) who lived here until his death in 1959. He left the house and a large collection of his sculpture to the Commune of Rome as the **Museo Canonica** (admission, see p 46). The first room contains portraits of Donna Franca Florio (1903) and Princess Emily Doria Pamphili (1901); and 'Dopo il Voto', a statue of a young nun exhibited in Paris in 1893. Room II has the model for a monument to Alexander II of Russia (destroyed in the Revolution of 1917), and various funerary monuments. Room III. Equestrian statue of Simon Bolivar (1954), and the King of Irak (1933), and several war memorials. The gallery at the right of the entrance contains original models of portraits, notably Lyda Borelli (1920), Alexander II of Russia (1913), Luigi Einaudi (1948), the Duke of Portland (1896), Margaret of Savoy (1903), and casts of portraits of the English royal family made in 1902–22. The house and small studio are also sometimes open, with some fine works of art collected by Canonica (some from Palazzo Reale in Turin).

Viale dei Cavalli leads right past the 18C FONTANA DEI CAVALLI MARINI, by Christopher Unterberger, a marble basin supported by four seahorses. A road to the left leads to the **Palazzina** or **Casino Borghese** (approached directly from Porta Pinciana by the Viale del Museo Borghese). The Palazzina was begun for the Borghese in 1608 by Flaminio Ponzio, Paul V's architect, and continued after his death in 1613 by Jan van Santen (Giovanni Vesanzio). It was altered for Marcantonio IV Borghese by Antonio Asprucci and Christopher Unterberger in 1775–90 when the splendid interior decoration was carried out. At the rear of the building is a beautiful formal garden.

The villa, which housed the *MUSEO AND GALLERIA BORGHESE (Pl. 12; 5, 7; admission, see p 46), a collection of sculpture and paintings founded by Cardinal Scipione Borghese, has been fenced off since 1984 and is undergoing lengthy structural repairs. Meanwhile only the ground floor is open with the collection of sculpture, which includes classical works, as well as some masterpieces by Gian Lorenzo Bernini and Canova. A selection of the paintings is exhibited in Trastevere at the ex Istituto di San Michele (described in Rte 21), and it is not known when this remarkably important collection will be returned here. The entrance to the Museum is at present at the rear of the building, reached from Via Raimondo and Parco dei Daini (Viale Giovanni Vasanzio; see Pl. 12; 5).

The Cardinal acquired numerous works of art through the good offices of his uncle Paul V, including Raphael's Deposition which he carried off from the church of San Francesco in Perugia. The collection was added to by later members of the family, but much of the sculpture was sold in 1807 to Napoleon I by Camillo Borghese, husband of Pauline Bonaparte, and is now in the Louvre. For nearly two centuries the paintings were housed in Palazzo Borghese; they were brought here in 1891. The collections were acquired by the State in 1902.

Ground Floor. The present (temporary) entrance leads into Room IV (see the Plan). In the PORTICO are fragments of a triumphal frieze of Trajan. The **Salone** has a ceiling fresco by Mariano Rossi (1774), representing M. Furius Camillus at the Capitol breaking off peace negotiations with Brennus; on the pavement, five fragments of a Roman mosaic (early 4C) with gladiators and wild beasts (found in 1834 at Torre Nuova, near Rome). The sculpture

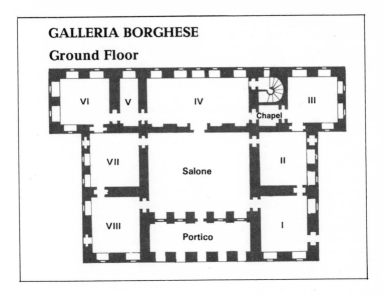

GALLERIA BORGHESE

Ground Floor

includes: the colossal figure of a satyr; colossal heads of Hadrian and Antoninus Pius; and statues of Augustus and Bacchus.

Most of the other ceilings on this floor were decorated at the time of Marcantonio Borghese (c 1750–60) by Giovanni Battista Marchetti, with numerous assistants. **Room I**. *Pauline Borghese, sister of Napoleon, as Venus Victrix, by Canova (1805), justly one of his best known works; *St John the Baptist, plaster sketch by Jean-Antoine Houdon for a colossal marble statue, never executed, which was to have been a pendant to his St Bruno in Santa Maria degli Angeli. The bust of Clement XII is by Pietro Bracci.

Room II. Panels of a sarcophagus representing the Labours of Hercules and the Birth of Apollo and Diana; frieze depicting the arrival of the Amazons at Troy; *David, a statue carved by Bernini at the age of 25 (1623–24); the face is a self-portrait. The paintings here include: Annibale Carracci, Samson in prison; Nicolò dell' Abate, landscape with deer hunt; Girolamo da Carpi (or Garofalo), landscape with procession of magicians; Guido Reni, Moses; Pier Francesco Mola, Liberation of St Peter.

Room III. *Apollo and Daphne, by Bernini, made in 1624; the dramatic moment of capture is well portrayed. The paintings include: Cigoli, Joseph and Potiphar's wife; Giovanni Baglione, Judith and Holofernes; and, over the doors, two landscapes by Paul Brill. In the **Chapel**, frescoed by Claude Deruet (d 1660), is exhibited a fragment found in Rome in 1980 thought to be Michelangelo's first version of the head of Christ for the Rondanini Pietà (now in Milan).

Room IV. Busts of Roman emperors, in porphyry and alabaster, carved in the 17C. The decoration of the room is a notable example of 18C skill and taste in the ornamental arrangement of a great variety of precious marbles, and the incorporation of bas-reliefs and paintings into the design. Here are exhibited vases in marble from Luni, with the Seasons, by Maximilien Laboureur. The Rape of Proserpine is another early masterpiece by Bernini (formerly in the Villa Ludovisi), and the bozzetto in bronze of Neptune was made by him for a fountain group now in the Victoria and Albert Museum, London. Also here is a bronze replica by Antonio Susini of the Farnese bull (now in the Museo Nazionale in Naples).

Room V. Hermaphrodite, a replica of a famous Hellenistic prototype; in the niche above, alabaster vase on red porphyry base; bust of Titus; and Sappho, after a 5C Greek original. On the floor is a Roman mosaic of a fishing scene, and above the doors, landscapes by Paul Brill. **Room VI**. Bernini, *Aeneas and Anchises, carved at the age of 15 (1613) jointly with his father (Pietro Bernini); colossal figure of Truth (on loan from the Bernini estate), sculpted by Bernini for the vestibule of his palace in Via del Corso, but left unfinished. The paintings include: Dosso Dossi, saints Cosmas and Damian and Garofalo, Conversion of St Paul. **Room VII** has paintings by Tommaso Conca representing the gods and religions of ancient Egypt. The sculpture includes a youth riding on a dolphin, intended for a fountain (period of Hadrian), and an archaic Greek statue of a *young girl (head restored). **Room VIII**. *Dancing faun, discovered in 1824 at Monte Calvo (Sabina) and restored under the direction of Thorvaldsen. Paintings by Giovanni Honthorst, Giorgio Vasari, Taddeo Zuccari, and Perino del Vaga.

From Room IV, a spiral staircase leads to the upper floor which has been closed for many years (and the paintings removed to the ex-Istituto di San Michele, see Rte 21).

Viale dell'Uccelliera runs NW to Viale del Giardino Zoologico, in which is the entrance to the **Zoological Gardens** (Pl. 11; 6), established in 1911 and enlarged in 1935 (it now has an area of about 12 hectares). The collection is strong in bears and large cats. Admission, see p 47. In Via Ulisse Aldovrandi, on the N side of the Zoo, and accessible from there also, are the MUSEO ZOOLOGICO (1932) and the MUSEO AFRICANO with an interesting SHELL COLLECTION in an annexe (sometimes open on Saturday).

Viale del Giardino Zoologico continues to the exit of Villa Borghese on Viale delle Belle Arti. In this avenue, on the right, is the **Palazzo delle Belle Arti** (Pl. 11; 5), built in 1911 by Cesare Bazzani, and enlarged in 1933. It contains the *GALLERIA NAZIONALE D'ARTE MODERNA (admission see p 46), the most important collection extant of 19–20C Italian art, founded in 1883. The Gallery has been undergoing lengthy structural restoration and rearrangement for many years. In 1993 only twelve of the seventy-three rooms were open. There are long-term plans to arrange all the 20C works in the right wing and all the 19C works in the left wing, with contemporary art in an annexe under construction. Exhibitions are frequently held here.

In the central **Hall** have been hung four large paintings of *Spring by Galileo Chini (1914; representative of Italian Art Nouveau). The rooms so far open in the **Right Wing** contain 20C Italian works displayed chronologically. **Room I** is to be arranged with paintings by Giacomo Balla, including: Portrait in the open, 1902; Villa Borghese, Il Parco degli Daini, 1910; Line of Velocity + Form + Noise, 1915; Bridge of Velocity, 1913/14; the Stream of Borghetto, 1938; and the Queue in the street for lamb, 1942.

Room II will contain works representing the Futurists: Umberto Boccioni (Ungracious Portrait, Horse + Rider + house); Gino Severini, Girl + Road +

Atmosphere, 1913; Boccioni, Portrait of Maestro Busoni, Silvia; Enrico Prampolini, Figure + Window, 1914; and works by Alberto Magnelli. **Room III**. The Twenties. Piet Mondrian, Large Composition A, 1919; Laszlo Moholy-Nagy, Yellow Cross Q.7; Marcel Duchamp, La Boîte-en-valise; Giorgio de Chirico, Hector and Andromaca; Roberto Melli, Study of a head, 1919; Carlo Carrà, Oval of the apparitions, 1918; Giorgio Morandi, Still Life, 1918 (a good work of the Metaphysical period).

The **Veranda** exhibits sculpture (1920–30). Libero Andreotti, The Pardon; Arturo Martini, Relief of Orpheus; Francesco Messina, Boy at the sea; Adolfo Wildt, Bust of Arturo Toscanini. Numerous busts by Bruno Innocenti, Francesco Messina, Arturo Martini, and others. Libero Andreotti, Affrico and Mensola; works by Giacomo Manzù.

The **Salone** is divided into sections. **A.** Ardengo Soffici, Washing the Boy; Gino Severini, Group of Things, 1930, Still Life, 1929; Giorgio de Chirico, Self-portrait, 1925, Battle of Gladiators, 1933–34, Horseman with red hat, Still Life, 1929; Alberto Savinio, Autumn, 1935. **B.** Carlo Carrà, Horses, 1927, Boy on a horse, 1936; Mario Sironi, Solitude, 1925. **C.** Felice Carena, Bathers, 1925; Virgilio Guidi, Head of a girl; Ubaldo Oppi, *Fishermen of Santo Spirito; Virgilio Guidi, *In the Tram; Antonio Donghi, *Hunter, 1929; Francesco Trombadori, *Still life with basket of fruit. **D.** Felice Casorati, *Portraits, *Apples; Massimo Campigli, *Sailors' wives, 1934.**E.** Works by Giorgio Morandi, and Ottone Rosai, and Arturo Tosi. **F.** Giacomo Balla, Pessimism and Optimism, 1923; and works by Fortunato Depero, Gerardo Dottori, and Enrico Prampolini. **G.** Works by Mario Mafai (including a self-portrait of 1942); Scipione, Portrait of his mother, 1930, Portrait of the poet Ungaretti. **H.** Works by Fausto Pirandello; Emanuele Cavalli, *The Bride, 1934; Giuseppe Capogrossi, Female Portrait, *The Storm. The sculpture in the Salone includes The Sisters (or The Stars) by Arturo Martini.

Room IV. Works by Riccardo Francalancia, Antonio Donghi, Mario Broglio, Roberto Melli (The Checked Dress), Filippo De Pisis (*Still Lives, A road in Paris, etc.). **Room V**, Amerigo Bartoli, Friends at the café, 1929; Gregorio Sciltian, Bacchus at the Hostelry; Gino Severini, The Married couple, 1939; Afro, Self-portrait, 1935; and works by Alberto Zivieri. **Room VI**. The 'Sei' of Turin (Enrico Paulucci, Carlo Levi, Gigi Chessa, Francesco Menzio, Nicola Galante, and Jessie Boswell). Walter Richard Sickert, Portrait of Baron Aloisi; Wassily Kandinsky, Angular Line, 1930, Joan Miró, Seated woman, 1935; Carlo Levi, Portrait of a friend, 1930; works by Pio Semeghini; Maurice Utrillo, Quai d'Anjou, 1925.

Steps lead up from the Veranda (see above) to a room with paintings by Renato Guttuso. Other rooms in this wing will eventually display art from 1945–72 including works by Lucio Fontana, Alberto Burri, Ettore Colla, Umberto Mastroianni, and Alberto Giacometti.

In the **Left Wing**, which will display 19C art, only three rooms are at present open. The first two contain European art including works by: De Chirico; Gustav Klimt (The Three Ages of Man, 1905); Dante Gabriele Rossetti (Mrs William Morris); Rodin (bust of the sculptor Dalou, *Bronze Age, Bozzetto for a ballerina); Amedeo Modigliani; Degas; Vincent Van Gogh (The Gardener, and 'L'Arlesienne); and Paul Cézanne. The third room has a display of sculptures by Vincenzo Gemito (1852–1929), including a bust in gilded bronze of Cesare Correnti (1880).

Other artists represented in the collection (but whose works are not at present on view) include: Giovanni Fattori, Aristide Sartorio, Ettore Ximenes, Ercole Rosa, Vincenzo Vela, Adolfo Wildt, Achille d'Orso ('Prosimus Tuus' or 'weary tiller'), Marco Calderini,

Federico Zandomeneghi, Giovanni Boldini (Portrait of Giuseppe Verdi), Giuseppe de Nittis (*Bois de Boulogne), Edoardo Gordigiani, Urbano Nono, Giovanni Battista Amendola, Antonio Mancini, Edoardo Dal Bono, Ettore Tito, Gaetano Previati, Leonardo Bistolfi, Teodoro Matteini, Andrea Appiani, Filippo Agricola, Vincenzo Podesti, Natale Schiavoni, Henry Raeburn, George Romney, Pietro Tenerani, Antonio Canova, Tommaso Minardi, Lorenzo Bartolini, Domenico Induno, Giacinto Gigante, Ippolito Caffi, Massimo d'Azeglio, Francesco Hayez, Il Piccio, Giuseppe Molteni, Filippo Palizzi, Gioacchino Toma, Michele Cammarano, Domenico Morelli, Giovanni Duprè, Giulio Monteverde (Edward Jenner experimenting on a young boy), Antonio Fontanesi, Giacomo Favretto, Tranquillo Cremona, Paolo Troubetzkoy, Medardo Rosso, Giuseppe Pellizza, Luigi Galli, Norberto Pazzini, and Luigi Serra.

European 19C prints and drawings from the collection of Luigi Sprovieri, include works by: Hogarth, Gillray, Cruikshank, Rowlandson, Blake, *Goya, Flaxman, Richter and German artists; Japanese artists: Hiroshige, Utamaro, and Hokusai. Other 19C European prints and drawings include works by: Prud'hon, Géricault, Delacroix, Ingres, Corot, Millet, Courbet, Fantin-Latour, Rodin, Manet, Degas, Sisley, Renoir, Pissarro, Toulouse-Lautrec, Gauguin, Edvard Münch, Egon Schiele, Whistler, Beardsley, Burne-Jones, William Morris, Fattori, and Signorini.

The collection dedicated to the group of Tuscan artists known as the *Macchiaioli* includes works by Antonio Puccinelli, Giovanni Fattori (*Portrait of his first wife), Giuseppe Abbati, Silvestro Lega (*The visit), Odoardo Borrani, Vincenzo Cabianca, Cristiano Banti, Adriano Cecioni, Telemaco Signorini, Vito d'Ancona, and Odoardo Borrani.

Outside the Gallery Viale delle Belle Arti widens into Piazza Thorvaldsen, in which, on the right, is a copy of Thorvaldsen's Jason, a gift from the city of Copenhagen. Above the steps is a statue of Simon Bolivar (1934). On the hill above, in Via Antonio Gramsci, is the **British School at Rome** (Pl. 11; 5), established in 1901 as a School of Archaeology. After the 1911 International Exhibition of Fine Arts in Rome, the site where the British Pavilion had stood was offered to the School by the Commune of Rome. The pavilion designed by Sir Edwin Lutyens, with a façade based on the west front of St Paul's Cathedral, was reproduced in permanent materials. In 1912, the School widened its scope to the study of the Fine Arts, Literature, and History of Italy. Scholarships are awarded, and an annual exhibition is held in June of the artists' work. The researches of the School are published annually in 'The Papers of the British School'.

This district, known as the VALLE GIULIA, was laid out at the beginning of the century after Viale delle Belle Arti had been opened. Numerous foreign academies and cultural institutes have been established here: on the left of the Viale are the Belgian, Dutch, Swedish, and Romanian Academies; on the right, in Via Gramsci, beyond the British School, is the Faculty of Architecture of Rome University, and the Austrian Academy.

Farther along Viale delle Belle Arti stands *Villa Giulia, or correctly *Villa di Papa Giulio* (Pl. 11; 5), built in 1550–55 for pope Julius III by Vignola, Vasari, and Bartolomeo Ammannati, with some help from Michelangelo. In the 17C the villa was used to house guests of the Vatican, including Queen Christina of Sweden in 1665. Since 1889 it has been the home of the *MUSEO NAZIONALE ETRUSCO DI VILLA GIULIA (admission, see p 47), devoted mainly to pre-Roman works found in Lazio, Umbria, and southern Etruria. In 1908 the Barberini collection was donated to the museum, and later acquisitions include the Castellani and Pesciotti collections (in 1919 and 1972). Material from excavations in progress at the Etruscan sites of northern Lazio is also exhibited here. Villa Poniatowsky (1870) in a park to the right of the Villa has been acquired by the State, and there are long-term plans to use it to enlarge the museum.

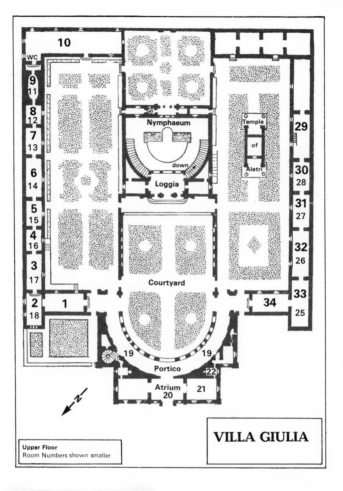

This charming suburban villa has lost much of its 16C decoration, including many pieces of ancient sculpture (which were taken to the Vatican). The façade is of two orders, Tuscan on the ground floor and Composite above. The porch, in rusticated masonry, leads to an ATRIUM, with Corinthian columns and niches for statues. This opens into a semicircular **Portico**, with Ionic columns and arches. The delightful vaulted ceiling is painted with vine trellises, birds and putti, and the wall panels are painted in the Pompeian style (attributed to Paolo Venale). Beyond lies the COURTYARD (part of which has recently been restored), enclosed by walls with Ionic columns, niches, and reliefs. Some of the delicate stucco decorations by Ammannati on the LOGGIA survive. The *NYMPHAEUM, which has lost much of its original decoration, was frequently copied in later 16C Italian villas.

Two curved staircases lead down from the loggia to the first level, with fountains adorned with statues symbolising the Tiber and the Arno. On the lower level is a ceiling relief of the miraculous finding of the Acqua Vergine and four marble caryatids. Behind the portico is an aedicula or shrine, with a statue of Hygieia, a Roman copy of a 5C Greek original. The garden extends on either side of the courtyard. On the right is a reconstruction of the Temple of Aletrium (Alatri) by Count Adolfo Cozza (1891), according to the account of Vitruvius and the evidence of the remains (see below). There is a café open at the back of the gardens.

On the left of the Atrium at the entrance, is the library, with frescoes attributed to Taddeo Zuccari and Prospero Fontana. A temple relief illustrating the Seven against Thebes from Pyrgi (460 BC) was formerly exhibited here. The museum was arranged in galleries flanking the garden in 1960. Some of the rooms and show-cases are now in need of renovation (and the labelling is erratic); part of the museum has been closed for this reason. The entrance is on the left of the semicircular portico. Rooms 1–5 contain finds from the necropolis of **Vulci** (see Rte 40), where some 15,000 tombs were found, mostly dating from the 9–5C BC. **Room 1**. Two stone sculptures of a Man astride a sea-horse and a Centaur showing Greek influence, found at the tomb entrances. **Room 2** contains fine bronze objects, including ossuaries, buckles, and razors, a statuette of a warrior in prayer with a pointed helmet, large shield, and long plaits (9C from Sardinia), bronze armour dating from the end of the 6C BC, and an *urn in the shape of a hut (mid 7C BC). **Rooms 3 and 4**. Attic red and black figure vases imported from Greece or Iona, and local Etruscan-Corinthian ware, including a large amphora by the 'Painter of the Bearded Sphinx', and a black-figure hydra showing women at a fountain. **Room 5**. Three terracotta models of a temple, a stoa, and a tower, terracotta heads and figurines from Hellenistic Vulci, forming part of a *Stipe* (trench for a votive offering). More recent finds include seated figures of children. Stairs lead down to the reconstruction of a *tomb from the necropolis at Cerveteri, with two chambers, containing beds and the belongings of the dead.

Room 6. Tomb furniture from the Villanovian and archaic necropolis of **Bisenzio-Vesentium**, including 8C geometric pottery, and a small bronze rustic chariot decorated with figurines which was used as an incense burner (late 8C). **Room 7**. Finds from the sanctuary of Portonaccio at **Veio** (see Rte 36) discovered in 1916 and 1939, including the celebrated group of *APOLLO AND HERAKLES. These colossal statues in polychrome terracotta (restored) formed part of a votive group representing the contest between Apollo and Herakles for the sacred Hind in the presence of Hermes and Artemis, and are a splendid example of Etruscan sculpture of the late 6C or early 5C BC. They were probably the work of Vulca, a celebrated sculptor of Veio, who is said to have been summoned to Rome by Tarquinius Superbus to execute the statue and decorations for the Temple of Jupiter Capitolinus. Of the other figures in the group there remain only the hind (removed) and the *head of Hermes. From the same temple is the statue of Latoma holding Apollo as a child, and the antefixes with the head of a gorgon and the head of a Maenad.

Rooms 8–10 house finds from the necropolis at **Cerveteri** (the ancient **Caere**; 7–1C BC; see Rte 39). **Room 8**. Terracotta votive heads, sarcophagus 'of the Lions'. Here are displayed copies of the three famous gold-leaf plaques from Pyrgi, the Etruscan port of Cerveteri (see Rte 39; the originals belong to the museum but are kept in the vaults), with inscriptions in

Etruscan and Phoenician referring to the dedication of the sanctuary to the Phoenician 'Astarte' and the Etruscan 'Uni'. **Room 9**. Terracotta *sarcophagus (6C), representing a husband and wife feasting upon a couch; this remarkable and rare sculpture bears witness to the skill of the Etruscan artists, evident in the expressive rendering of the features, especially the hands and feet.

Room 10. Collection of skyphoi (drinking cups), kylixes (cups on stems), vases for perfume and wine, and amphorae (7C–2C). Case 2: Protocorinthian skyphoi, with geometric decoration, and a Corinthian krater, with warriors on horseback and chariots. Case 3: Bucchero ware. Case 6: collection of small aryballoi (vases for perfume). Cases 7–10: rare Attic kylix, with lively figures of satyrs dancing, Story of Polyphemus, Vine motif, etc. Cases 14–17: small red-figured kylix, showing two exploits of Theseus and a young cithara player. Case 19: Attic red-figured psykter (global vase with cylindrical support), showing Zeus enthroned on one side, and Theseus fighting the Minotaur on the other. Case 20: Attic red-figured krater, with hoplite running, and, on the neck, athletes, and Herakles struggling with Kyknos. Cases 21–24: Etruscan and Faliscan vases; silver-painted vases from Bolsena.

Upper Floor. Rooms 11–18 contains the **Antiquarium**; many of the objects here are of unknown provenance. **Room 11**. Bronze plates from a triumphal chariot, with hoplites and horsemen fighting (6C); buckles. **Room 12**. Ploughman at work, found at Arezzo; bronze statuettes, including elongated votive figurines. **Rooms 13 and 14** contain bronze domestic objects including mirrors, candelabra, cistae (see below), horse-bits, strigils and small containers for unguents in leather and metal used by athletes. **Room 15**. Statuette of Veiovis, 1C AD, found in 1955 at Monterazzone, near Viterbo. Case 4: *CHIGI VASE found at Formello (Veio), of exquisite workmanship and the finest extant example of the Protocorinthian style (first half of the 7C BC); among the subjects depicted are a lion-hunt, a hare-hunt, a troop of soldiers, and the Judgment of Paris.

Room 16. Vases. **Room 17**. Fragment of a krater of Assteas, depicting a comic scene: Ajax, fleeing from Kassandra, clings to the statue of Pallas Athena. **Room 18**. Etruscan Biga from Castro. Dating from the 6C BC this two-wheeled chariot was found in 1967 in a tomb beside the skeletons of two horses (also exhibited here). The chariot, with bronze decorations, is particularly well preserved.

Stairs lead up to the hemicycle (**19**) with the **Castellani Collection of Ceramics** (many of them from Cerveteri). This was amassed in the 19C by Augusto Castellani, a member of a firm of goldsmiths. The rooms have a good view of the courtyard and garden of the villa. Case 1: alabaster vases imported from Greece and Cyprus, Etruscan vases showing Oriental influence. Case 2: black- and red-figure vases, many decorated with animals. Case 3: two pitchers, one with the rape of Persephone, the other with Herakles and the dog Cerberus before Eurystheus. Case 4: black-figured Attic vases; Laconian krater decorated with lotus-flowers. Case 5: two amphorae signed by Nikosthenes (540–510 BC). Case 6: group of miniature kylixes. Case 7: amphora with large handles, red- and black-figured. Case 8: red-figured Attic vases; pitcher with two young men and leveret. Case 10: red-figured Attic vases, and pelike showing Dionysus, Satyrs, and Maenads. Case 11: examples of Faliscan, Campanian, and Apulian ware. Case 12: ceramics from Egnatia in Apulia, white- and yellow-figured. Part of the hemicycle is also used for exhibitions.

On the right **Room 20** contains the PESCIOTTO collection, with vases from the Villanovian and archaic periods (8–6C BC), including incised bucchero ware and bronzes. Room 21 is closed for restoration, and the two small rooms beyond (22; also closed) contain the **Castellani** *jewellery collection, beautifully arranged. This is one of the finest collections of antique jewellery in existence, dating from the Minoan period, with splendid examples of Hellenistic and Roman, as well as Oriental, works. The exhibits are complemented by a remarkable series of copies or reworkings made by the renowned Castellani jewellers in the 19C.

In 1993 Rooms 25–33 were closed, and so it was necessary to go down the spiral staircase from the hemicycle and cross the courtyard to Room 34. The description below may, therefore, be changed when the following rooms are reopened. Rooms 25–29 exhibit material from the **Ager Faliscus**, the area between Lake Bracciano and the Tiber (see Rte 35). The Falisci were an Italic people akin to the Latins but much influenced by their Etruscan neighbours. **Room 25** contains finds from Capena, including an Etrusco-Campanian *dish with a war elephant and her baby, evidence of the impression made in Italy by the elephants of Pyrrhus. Three huge bronze shields, decorated with quadrupeds and floral motives, from Narce. Vases, mirrors and other relics from Corchiano and Monte Sant'Angelo.

Rooms 26–29 are devoted to the necropolis of Falerii Veteres (Civita Castellana). **Room 26**. Cinerary urn in the form of a small house. Psykter (wine-cooler) showing the fight of the Centaurs and the Lapiths. Krater with scenes of the devastation of Troy. Oinochoe, with a battle of Amazons, and Actaeon being devoured by his hounds; two similar bowls, with Dionysos and Ariadne and a Faliscan inscription (resembling Latin): 'Today I drink wine, tomorrow I shall have none'. *Amphora with volutes, showing Eos and Kephalos and Boreas and Orithyia. Large stamnos (two-handled jar) with two men feasting, a girl flute-player, and two young men, drunk, in the background (c 440 BC); twin stamnoi with Dionysos carrying the Thyrsos, and Eros, with a nude girl seated on a panther skin.

Room 27. Black-figured kylix with Dionysos and Maenads on the outside; red-figured kylix, with men and boys conversing, signed by Hieron. *Rhytons (drinking horns) shaped respectively like a knuckle-bone and a dog's head, masterpieces of Greek ceramic art of the first half of the 5C BC; the first is signed by Syriskos and the second attributed to Brygos. Large *krater (mid 5C) with girls dancing; krater from S Italy with Belerophon and the Chimaera. **Room 28**. Amphorae and stamnoi from Volsinium (Bolsena), painted and with floral decoration. Stamnos, with a scene from the worship of Dionysos Perikonios at Athens. Red-figured *krater with Herakles and the Nemean lion; *krater of the end of the 5C, with Herakles being received into Olympos.

In **Room 29**, on two levels, are sculptures and architectonic terracottas from temples near Falerii Veteres. To the right: part of the decoration from the Temple of Apollo at Lo Scasato (4–2C), with notable antefixes of Persian Artemis and a winged genius. To the left: decoration of the pediment and entablature from one or both temples in the neighbourhood of Sassi Caduti, and decorative cover-slab from the temple which replaced them, including a representation of flute-players. Below are large figured terracottas which decorated the pediments of each temple. They offer striking examples of the influence of Greek sculpture, and especially good are: *Apollo; fine head of Mercury; female head. In glass cases are excellent examples of temple decoration and cult statues: antefixes with heads of Maenads, of

Silenus, and part of an acroterion with two warriors, from Sassi Caduti (early 5C); portraits from the *stipes* of the Temple at Vignale, the acropolis of Falerii Veteres; female head in peperino, crowned in bronze-leaf, from Celle; head of Zeus from Scasato.

Room 30 contains material from the **Temple of Diana at Nemi** (4–2C BC), the famous sanctuary of the Golden Bough in the sacred wood beside the lake (see Rte 30): lower portion of a cover-slab in gilded bronze, votive objects, terracotta pediment of the temple. Male head from Antemnae (late 4C). **Room 31**. Coffin formed from the trunk of an oak-tree (from Gabii); antefix with Maenad's head, from Lanuvium; terracotta model, perhaps of a temple, from Velletri. **Room 32**. Collection from the Tomba delle Ambre, at Satricum in the territory of the Volsci, including sculptures from the temple of Mater Matuta (6C BC), and a votive stipe of the 7C BC.

Room 33. Works from **Palestrina**, the ancient **Praeneste** (see Rte 31), a flourishing centre of Latin and Volscian civilisation. Since the trade and industry of Etruria and Latium were derived from the same sources, the culture here naturally had much in common with the Etruscan culture. The material includes finds from the Barberini and Bernardini Tombs, two important examples of the Oriental period (7C BC). The *Barberini Collection* was formed of objects unearthed between 1855 and 1866 from tombs in the locality of Colombella, just S of the town of Praeneste. It was acquired by the State in 1908, and includes the contents of a large tomb covered with marble slabs of the Oriental period (7C BC), and the contents of deep-laid tombs of the 4–2C BC. The *Bernardini Tomb*, discovered in 1876, a trench-tomb lined with tufa and covered by a tumulus, exactly corresponds with the style of the Barberini tombs and with that of the Regolini-Galassi tomb in the Vatican.

The tombs of the Oriental period yielded gold and silver articles, bronzes and ivories, in which Egyptian, Assyrian, and Greek art are mingled. Notable among the goldsmith's work: two *pectorals, or large buckles, of gold granulated work, decorated with cats' heads, chimaeras, and sphinxes; patera in silver-gilt with Pharaoh in triumph, horses, and an Assyrian king's hunt; Caldaia, for heating or cooling water, in silver-gilt, with six serpents on the brim, and decorated with horsemen, foot-soldiers, farmers and sheep attacked by lions. Ivories: cups; lion with dead man on his back; mirror-handles(?) shaped like arms. Bronzes: conical vase-stand with fantastic animals in repoussé; throne in sheet-bronze, with ornamental bands and figures of men and animals.

The contents of the 4–2C tombs include a full collection of bronze mirrors and **cistae**, which contained the mirrors, strigils, spatulae and other implements for the care of the body. The cistae are usually cylindrical, with engraved decoration in repoussé or pierced work, lids adorned with small figures, and feet and handles of cast metal. These toilet boxes were virtually unique to Praeneste (see Rte 31). Among them is the *CISTAE FICORONI, the largest and most beautiful yet discovered. It is named after Francesco Ficoroni who bought it and gave it to the Kircher Collection (now incorporated in the Prehistoric and Ethnographic Museum). On the body of the cista is a representation of the boxing match between Pollux and Amykos, king of the Bebryces, an elaborate design pure in its lines and evidently inspired by some large Greek composition, possibly a wall-painting contemporary with those by Mikon in the Stoa Poikile at Athens. The names of both the maker and the buyer of the cista are recorded in an archaic Latin inscription: *Novios Plautios med Romai fecid, Dindia Macolnia fileai dedit;* and it was no doubt a wedding present.

Room 34. Goldsmith's work; bronze helmet inlaid with silver, from Todi; Attic *bowl signed by Pampheios, showing Odysseus evading Polyphemos; head from Cagli.

Beyond the Villa Giulia Viale delle Belle Arti goes on past the red-brick church of SANT'EUGENIO (1951), built to celebrate the 25th anniversary of the episcopal consecration of Pius XII in 1942, to the Via Flaminia, on which is the elegant PALAZZINA OF PIUS IV, attributed to Pirro Ligorio, who designed the Casina of Pius IV in the Vatican gardens. The busy Via Flaminia (traversed by buses and trams) leads back to Piazza del Popolo. (see Rte 7).

10

The Quirinal Hill and Palazzo Barberini

To the E of the Victor Emmanuel Monument, beside the two small churches in front of Trajan's Column (see Rte 4), steps lead up to Via IV Novembre (with the entrance to the Markets of Trajan, described in Rte 4). Beyond is the LARGO MAGNANAPOLI (Pl. 4; 5), at the beginning of the busy Via Nazionale. In the centre of the square is a little group of palm trees, with some remains of the Servian Wall; in the ancient PALAZZO ANTONELLI (No. 158; restored) are other remains in several rooms off the courtyard, including an arch for a catapult. On the right, behind the church of SANTA CATERINA DA SIENA (closed for restoration), with a good Baroque interior, rises the conspicuous Torre delle Milizie.

At the beginning of Via Panisperna, in a fine position high up on the right, is the tall façade of **Santi Domenico e Sisto** (ring for admission at the college next door; bell by the gate), preceded by a scenographic staircase (1654) by Vincenzo della Greca. Inside is a huge fresco (1674–75) by the Bolognese painter, Domenico Canuti. In the first S chapel, sculptured group (Noli me tangere) by Antonio Raggi, and in the third N chapel, a Madonna and Child thought to be an early work by Antoniazzo Romano (formerly attributed to Benozzo Gozzoli).

Via Nazionale (Pl. 4; 5, 4) leads from Largo Magnanapoli towards Piazza della Repubblica and the Station. On the right it skirts the extensive garden of the VILLA ALDOBRANDINI, built in the 16C for the Duke of Urbino, acquired by Clement VIII (Ippolito Aldobrandini), and given by him to his nephews. The villa was a famous meeting place for the Roman aristocracy during the Napoleonic era. Now owned by the State, it contains an international law library. A splendid Roman fresco of a marriage scene found on the Esquiline in 1605 was kept in one of the garden pavilions here until 1838, when it was moved to the Vatican museum (where it is still known as the 'Aldobrandini Marriage'). Via Nazionale skirts the villa wall as far as Via Mazzarino, in which (right) is an open gate and steps which lead up past impressive 2C ruins to the garden.

Farther on in Via Mazzarino, to the left, is the church of SANT'AGATA DEI GOTI (if closed, ring at No. 16), built by an Arian community in 462–70, but much restored. The Byzantine plan remains despite the disappointing 20C restorations, with antique columns and decorative capitals with pulvins. In the apse is a well-preserved 12–13C Cosmatesque tabernacle. The picturesque 17C court is hung with ivy. The original fabric of the church can be seen on leaving the church by the door in the right aisle.

Farther along Via Nazionale, on the right, is the huge neo-classical head office of the BANCA D'ITALIA by Gaetano Koch (1886–1904), behind a row of palm trees and colossal lamp-posts. On the left is the Teatro Eliseo. Just beyond Via Milano (with a road tunnel on the left; see Rte 8), rises the monumental **Palazzo delle Esposizioni** (Pl. 4; 5), erected in 1878–82 to a design by Pio Piacentini. As an important exhibition centre, it has been radically restored, and a new system of illumination has been installed.

Beyond the palace, on a much lower level, is the little church of **San Vitale** (usually closed), dedicated in 416 and several times restored. It has a fine portico with old columns and 17C doors. In the interior is a carved wood ceiling, and the walls are decorated with effective 17C trompe l'oeil frescoes with landscapes by Cavalier d'Arpino, Gaspard Dughet, Andrea Pozzo and others.

From Largo Magnanapoli Via XXIV Maggio climbs the Quirinal Hill. This street was named to commemorate the day on which in 1915 Italy declared war on Austria. In a house here the poetess Vittoria Colonna used to meet with Michelangelo and others.

Near the beginning, on the left, is the entrance to the church of **San Silvestro al Quirinale**, on an upper floor (ring at No. 10 on the right, 9.00–13.00), from which the cardinals used to march in procession to shut themselves in the Quirinal when a conclave was held in summer. The INTERIOR was rebuilt in 1524 on a Latin cross. NORTH SIDE. The first chapel, with pretty floor tiles, has two fine landscapes by Maturino and Polidoro da Caravaggio, who also painted the St Catherine and Mary Magdalene flanking the altar. In the vault, frescoes by Cavalier d'Arpino. Second chapel, Nativity by Marcello Venusti. SOUTH SIDE, second chapel, Pius V and Cardinal Alessandrino by Giacinto Gemignani, with, in the centre, a 13C Madonna and Child by a Roman artist. The domed Bandini chapel at the end of the NORTH TRANSEPT contains tondi by Domenichino, and statues of Mary Magdalene and St John the Evangelist by Alessandro Algardi (1628; probably his first Roman commission). The altarpiece of the Ascension is by Scipione Pulzone.

The street ascends between two of the most attractive of Rome's princely residences. On the left is the entrance to VILLA COLONNA, the garden dependency of Palazzo Colonna (see Rte 8); on the right (behind a high wall), on the site of the BATHS OF CONSTANTINE, is **Palazzo PallaviciniRospigliosi** (Pl. 4; 5; admission only to the garden Casino, see p 45), built in 1613–16 probably by Carlo Maderno. It later passed to Cardinal Mazarin who enlarged it. In 1704 it was purchased by the Pallavicini-Rospigliosi family who still live here. In the 19C the beautiful gardens were greatly altered and diminished. The GALLERIA PALLAVICINI (open only with special permission) on the first floor contains some important paintings of Italian and foreign schools (15–18C). The collection was founded by Nicolò Pallavicini (friend of Rubens) and his son Cardinal Lazzaro, and includes works by Botticelli, Lorenzo Lotto, Annibale and Ludovico Carracci, Guido Reni, Guercino, Federico Barocci, and Rubens (Christ and the Apostles).

In the charming little hanging garden is the *Casino Pallavicini (adm see p 45) designed by Giovanni Vesanzio. The fine façade (recently restored) is decorated with numerous good reliefs of mythological subjects from Roman sarcophagi (2–3C AD). The pavilion contains Guido Reni's celebrated *fresco (1613–14) of Aurora scattering flowers before the chariot of the Sun, which is escorted by the Hours. It was greatly admired by travellers to Rome in the 19C. On the walls are four frescoes of the Seasons by Paul Brill, and two 'Triumphs' by Antonio Tempesta. The ceiling frescoes in the two side rooms are by (left) Giovanni Baglione, and (right) Passignano. Here are hung a number of 17C paintings and the sinopia of a fresco of the Allegory of Night by Giovanni da San Giovanni, from the ballroom of the palace.

At the top of Via XXIV Maggio is the spacious and dignified **PIAZZA DEL QUIRINALE** (beware of fast traffic), with its two palaces: the Quirinal in front, and Palazzo della Consulta, to the right. The balustrade on the W side, overlooking Via della Dataria, provides a view across roof-tops to the dome of St Peter's in the distance. The piazza occupies the summit of the **Quirinal** (61m), the highest of the Seven Hills. It received its name from a Temple of Quirinus, or from *Cures*, an ancient Sabine town NE of Rome from which, according to legend, the Sabines under their king Tatius settled on the hill. The name of Quirinus was a title of Romulus, after he had been deified; the festival in his honour was called *Quirinalia*.

In the middle of the square, on a high pedestal, flanking an obelisk, are two famous colossal groups of the **Dioscuri** (Castor and Pollux), standing by their horses, over 5.5m high. They are Roman copies, dating from the Imperial era, of Greek originals of the 5C BC. The two groups were found nearby in the Baths of Constantine and placed here by Domenico Fontana under Sixtus V (1585–90), who was responsible for the recutting of the false inscriptions on the bases, 'Opus Phidiae' and 'Opus Praxitelis', which probably date from c AD 450. The statues appear in numerous representations of the city from medieval times. They were formerly called the horse-tamers, and the square was known as Monte Cavallo. The OBELISK (shaft 14.5m; restored in 1984), originally in front of the Mausoleum of Augustus, was brought here by Pius VI in 1786; Pius VII added the great basin (now a fountain) of dark grey granite, until then used as a cattle-trough in the Roman Forum.

At the corner of Via XXIV Maggio, where Via della Dataria begins, is a part of the SCUDERIE PONTIFICIE, or Papal Stables, built in 1722. The **Palazzo della Consulta**, the seat of the supreme court of the Papal States (Santa Consulta) and later of the Italian Ministry of Foreign Affairs, is now the seat of the Corte Costituzionale, a supreme court for matters concerning the constitution. The façade is by Ferdinando Fuga (1739).

PALAZZO DEL QUIRINALE (Pl. 4; 3) has been the official residence of the President of the Republic since 1947. The President's guards, who have to be over six feet tall, have splendid crimson and blue uniforms. The stately front of the palace projects into the piazza, while its flank, known as the 'manica lunga' ('long sleeve'), is in Via del Quirinale. The building was begun in 1574 by Flaminio Ponzio and Ottavio Mascherino, under Gregory XIII, on the site of a villa belonging to Cardinal d'Este, and was continued by Domenico Fontanaga, Carlo Maderno, Bernini (who worked on the 'manica lunga'), and Fuga: it was not completed until the time of Clement XII (1730–40). The principal entrance is by Maderno; the tower on the left of it was added in the time of Urban VIII.

From 1592 the Quirinal was the summer residence of the popes, and some conclaves were held here. Sixtus V died in the palace in 1590. Pius VII left the palace as prisoner of Napoleon, and from its balcony Pius IX blessed Italy at the beginning of his pontificate. From 1870 to 1947 it became the residence of the Kings of Italy. Victor Emmanuel II died here on 9 January 1878.

The INTERIOR can be visited by appointment after written application to the 'Ufficio Intendenza del Quirinale'. On the grand staircase is Melozzo da Forlì's magnificent *fresco of Christ in Glory, with angels, formerly in the church of the Santi Apostoli. At the top of the stairs is the SALA REGIA, decorated in 1616–17, with a frieze designed by Agostino Tassi and executed by Lanfranco and Saraceni. This and the adjoining CAPPELLA PAOLINA are by Carlo Maderno. The chapel has fine stucco decoration by Martino Ferrabosco. The CAPPELLA DELL' ANNUNCIATA was decorated between 1609 and 1612, under the direction of Guido Reni (who executed the scenes of the life of the Madonna and the prophets, in the pendentives), by Lanfranco, Francesco Albani, and Antonio Carracci. The GALLERY OF ALEXANDER VII has frescoes carried out under the direction of Pietro da Cortona (1656–57) by Grimaldi, Lazzaro Baldi, Ciro Ferri, Mola (Joseph and his brothers, which is considered his most successful fresco), Maratta, Gaspard Dughet, Antonio Carracci and others. The extensive garden was designed by Mascherino.

Via del Quirinale skirts the 'manica lunga' (see above) of the palace. On the right, beyond a public garden with an equestrian statue of Charles Albert by Romanelli (1900) rises the church of *SANT'ANDREA AL QUIR-INALE (open 8.00–12.00, 16.00–19.00, except Tuesday), a masterpiece by Bernini (1658–70), and his pupil Mattia De Rossi. The simple FAÇADE of a single order balances the fine domed elliptical INTERIOR, with columns, pilasters, and frames in pink and grey marble, and gilded and stuccoed decorations. Cherubim look down from the lantern. Each chapel is lit by windows high up behind the altars. The fine 17C altarpieces include (first chapel on the right), St Francesco Saverio by Baciccia, and, in the second chapel, Deposition by Giacinto Brandi. The high altarpiece, with the Crucifixion of St Andrew, by Borgognone, is surmounted by a splendid group of angels and cherubim sculpted by Raggi. On the left of the high altar is an altarpiece by Carlo Maratta. The sacristy has a pretty frescoed ceiling by Giovanni De La Borde (approved by Bernini). The lavabo here is attributed to Bernini.

Beyond a public park, on the right, is another small oval church, *SAN CARLO ALLE QUATTRO FONTANE (San Carlino; open 9.00–12.30, 16.00–18.00, Saturday afternoon and Sunday closed), a masterpiece by Borromini which provides an interesting contrast to the former church by Bernini. The tall curved FAÇADE (1665–68; cleaned in 1993) is well adapted to the cramped site on the corner of a narrow street. The INTERIOR (1638) has convex and concave surfaces in a complicated design using triangles in a unifying scheme. The symbolism throughout is of the Holy Trinity. In the chapel to the left of the altar, Rest on the flight into Egypt, attributed to Annibale Carracci or Giovanni Francesco Romanelli. The small *CLOISTER which can be entered from the church is also designed by Borromini. From here is the entrance to the *CRYPT, (not at present open to the public), designed in a fantastical play of curves linked by a heavy continuous cornice. It is thought Borromini intended this as the place of his own burial.

At this point Via del Quirinale ends at the carfax known as the **Quattro Fontane** (Pl. 4; 4), with its four vistas ending in Porta Pia and the obelisks of the Quirinal, Pincio, and Esquiline, typical of the Rome of Sixtus V. The four small fountains (which give the busy cross-roads its name), dating from 1593, personify Fidelity, Strength, the Aniene, and the Tiber. Via delle Quattro Fontane leads right to Via Nazionale and left to Piazza Barberini.

Via Venti Settembre leads straight on, beyond the cross-roads, past PALAZZO DEL DRAGO, by Domenico Fontana (1600), and the large Ministry of Defence, to Piazza San

Bernardo (see below), where this route is rejoined after a detour to the NW. At No. 7 in this street, on the left, is the Scottish Presbyterian church of ST ANDREW, with a war memorial (1949) to the London Scottish.

To the left Via delle Quattro Fontane descends all the way to Piazza Barberini. Half-way down, on the right, is *PALAZZO BARBERINI (Pl. 4; 3), one of the grandest palaces in Rome (being restored). It was begun by Carlo Maderno for Urban VIII in 1624. The windows of the top storey, the stairs, and some doorways were executed from a design by Borromini. The central block is attributed to Bernini. The garden flanks one side of the street where the huge stone pilasters and iron grille were added in the 19C by Francesco Azzurri.

In 1949 the palace became the property of the State, and one wing houses part of the *GALLERIA NAZIONALE D'ARTE ANTICA (admission, see p 46), a national gallery of paintings divided in two parts; the other section is in Palazzo Corsini (see Rte 21). The right wing of the palace has for years been occupied by offices and club rooms of the armed forces. It seems that at long last these are to be moved, so that the gallery, at present over-crowded with paintings, can expand into this part of the palace, and the 17C works be re-hung. After the State had purchased Palazzo Corsini with the picture-gallery of Cardinal Neri-Corsini, it was presented with the collections of Prince Tommaso Corsini and later acquired the Torlonia and other collections. The combined collections, opened to the public in 1895, are pre-eminent in Italian Baroque painting; there are also some good examples of the 15–16C, and a large selection of foreign works.

Across the garden, planted with palm trees, a door on the left beneath the portico leads into the palace. A monumental flight of stairs probably designed by Bernini leads up to the **First Floor**, with the entrance to the gallery (and the ticket office). A door on the right leads through a vestibule into the Hall (see below), with the 'Madonna Avvocata' by the 12C Roman school, acquired in 1987. **Room I**. Simone and Machilone, Crucifix; Giovanni Baronzio, Scenes from the life of Christ; Bonaventura Berlinghieri, Crucifixion; Nicolò di Pietro, Coronation of Mary; 'Maestro dell'Incoronazione di Urbino', Birth of St John the Baptist. **Room II**. Filippo Lippi, Madonna and Child, *Annunciation and donors. **Room III**. Piero di Cosimo, *Mary Magdalene; Francesco di Giorgio Martini, Pietà, a terra-cotta group restored in 1985 (and formerly attributed to Giacomo Cozzarelli); circle of Filippino Lippi, Madonna enthroned between Saints Peter and Paul. **Room IV**. Lorenzo di Viterbo, Madonna and Saints Peter and Michael; L'Alunno, Madonna and Child with Saints; Perugino, St Nicholas of Tolentino; and works by Antoniazzo Romano.

Room V. Michele Giambono, Madonna and Child; 'Maestro di San Sebastiano', Pilgrims at a sanctuary (a very unusual work); 15C Provençal school, Addolorata; Francesco Pagano (attributed), Saints Sebastian and Catherine; Giacomo Francia, Pietà; Marco Palmezzano, St Jerome; Calisto Piazza da Lodi, St Catherine of Alexandria; Andrea Solario, Lute-player; Bartolomeo Veneto, *Portrait of a man. **Room VI**. The Creation of the Angels in the vault is by Andrea Camassei. Here is hung the famous portrait of a lady by Raphael known as *'La Fornarina'. The sitter may be Raphael's mistress, the daughter of a Sienese bakerwoman, although the painting has also been attributed to the master's pupil, Giulio Romano. Also here: Baldassare Peruzzi, *Ceres; Sodoma, Rape of the Sabines, Marriage of St Catherine; Brescianino, Lady with a turban; Beccafumi, Madonna and

Child with the young St John; Andrea del Sarto, *Holy Family; Vincenzo Tamagni, Marriage of the Virgin.

Room VII. On the ceiling, *Divine Providence by Andrea Sacchi (1630–33). Girolamo Genga, Marriage of St Catherine. In the CHAPEL frescoed with New Testament scenes by Pietro da Cortona and Giovanni Francesco Romanelli, are displayed two portaits: Henry VIII by Holbein (possibly a replica), and Erasmus, by Quentin Metsys. Sodoma, Three Fates; Siciolante da Sermoneta, Francesco II Colonna; Bronzino, Stefano Colonna. **Room VIII**. Giovanni Busi (Il Cariani), *Madonna and Child with St Anna and the young St John the Baptist; Girolamo da Carpi, Portrait of a Man (being restored); Niccolò dell'Abate, Portrait of a young man; Lorenzo Lotto, Mystical Marriage of St Catherine; El Greco, Adoration of the Shepherds and Baptism of Christ; Tintoretto, Christ and the adulteress; Titian, Venus and Adonis (replica of a painting in the Prado); Dosso Dossi, Saints John the Evangelist and Bartholomew with two donors.

Room IX has a ceiling painting of the Chariot of the Sun by Giuseppe Chiari. Marcello Venusti, Prayer in the Garden; 'Master of the Manchester Madonna', Pietà (a monochrome painting, derived from Michelangelo); Jacopino dal Conte, Deposition; Jacques De Backer, Dead Christ supported by an angel; Scipione Pulzone, Cardinal Ricci, Portrait of a Lady; Federico Zuccari, Portrait of a man; Luca Cambiaso, Venus and Adonis. **Room X** has ceiling frescoes by Pietro da Cortona and his pupils (including Francesco Romanelli). Here are displayed works by Bartolomeo Passarotti; a portable tabernacle by Annibale Carracci, and a landscape by Paul Brill. Beyond two small rooms, **Room XII** contains works by Ventura Salimbeni and Domenico Feti (Jacob's Dream). **Room XIII**. Carlo Saraceni, Madonna and Child with St Anne, Santa Cecilia and an angel; Orazio Gentileschi, St Francis supported by an angel; Giovanni Baglione, Sacred and Profane Love; Caravaggio, *Narcissus, Judith and Holofernes, and St Francis in meditation (attributed); Carlo Saraceni, St Gregory the Great.

Room XIV Orazio Borgianni, Self-portrait; Bartolomeo Manfredi, Bacchus and a drinker; Orazio Riminaldi, Sacrifice of Isaac. **Room XV**. Massimo Stanzione, Deposition; Luca Giordano, Portrait of a capomaestro; Mattia Preti, Resurrection of Lazarus; Salvator Rosa, Allegories of Poetry and Music; Giuseppe De Ribera, St Giacomo. **Room XVI**. Guido Reni, *Portrait of a lady, supposed to be Beatrice Cenci, Sleeping Putto (a fresco); Giovanni Lanfranco, Music; Guercino, Flagellation; Guido Reni, Mary Magdalen; Guercino, Et in Arcadia Ego. **Room XVII**. Alessandro Algardi, bust of St Philip Neri (in bronze); two paintings by Gian Lorenzo Bernini (David with the head of Goliath and Portrait of Urban VIII); works by Nicolas Poussin; marble bust of Nano del Duca di Créqui by Duquesnoy; Lanfranco, Transfiguration. **Room XVIII**. Baciccio, Pietà, Clement IX, Portrait of Gian Lorenzo Bernini; two huge paintings by Andrea Camassei; Pier Francesco Mola, Portrait of a Lady; Sassoferrato, Portrait of Ottaviano Prati; Pietro da Cortona, Guardian Angel.

The **Salone** has a magnificent ceiling fresco of *THE TRIUMPH OF DIVINE PROVIDENCE, by Pietro da Cortona, his main work, painted between 1633 and 1639 to celebrate the glory of the Papacy of Urban VIII and the Barberini family. It is a *tour de force*, particularly in the organisation of the space, and the reduction of the composition into the angles. On the walls are hung seven cartoons by the school of Pietro da Cortona showing scenes from the life of Urban VIII, executed for tapestries manufactured in the Barberini workshops active in Rome from 1627–83 (and now in the Vatican).

Also four cartoons for mosaics in the Cappella Colonna in St Peter's by Andrea Sacchi, Bernini and Carlo Pellegrini, and Giovanni Lanfranco.

The **Second Floor** has been closed since 1990. Here are the impressive **18C collection** of paintings and the delightful 18C Barberini apartments, arranged with period furniture. In the entrance corridor are Roman paintings by Placido Costanzi, Sebastiano Conca, Pietro Bianchi, and others. ROOM 1 (right), bozzetti by Sebastiano Conca, and small works by Carlo Maratta. ROOM 2. Pierre Subleyras, Madonna reading, Female nude; works by Francesco Trevisani; larger works by Marco Benefial (Pyramus and Thisbe) and Francesco Mancini. ROOM 3 contains bozzetti for frescoes in Roman churches by Baciccio, and Andrea Pozzo (the dome and vault of Sant'Ignazio, see Rte 7). ROOM 4. Portraits by Ignazio Stern, Pompeo Batoni, and Angelica Kauffmann. ROOM 5. Works by Francesco Solimena, Gaspare Traversi, Giuseppe Bonito (a Neapolitan artist), and Sebastiano Conca (Adoration of the Magi). ROOM 6 contains works by Giuseppe Maria Crespi, Donato Creti, Alessandro Magnasco, and portraits by Vittore Ghislandi and Pietro Antonio Rotari. ROOM 7. Giovanni Battista Piazzetta, Judith; Giovanni Battista Tiepolo, Old Faun and young satyr.

ROOM 8, frescoed with chiaroscuri in 1780–90 contains the Cervinara collection of charming small 18C French paintings, including: Nicolas Lancret, Le Faucon, Family Group; Jean Baptiste Greuze, Portrait of a girl; Jean-Honoré Fragonard, *Annette et Lubin; Hubert Robert, Landscapes; François Boucher, Le Matin, Le Soir, La petite jardinière; and Louis-Leopold Boilly, La Fête du Grand-Père. ROOM 9 contains interesting views of Rome by Gaspar van Wittel, and ROOM 10 views of ancient ruins by Giovanni Paolo Pannini. In ROOM 11 are more works from the Cervinara collection, by Francesco Guardi (the Giudecca Canal), and Hubert Robert (Bridge with washerwomen). ROOM 12. Views of Venice by Luca Carlevarijs, and Canaletto; Bernardo Bellotto, The Schlosshof in Vienna. The last room, with a pretty ceiling, is reserved for recently restored works.

Other rooms contain the exceptionally valuable **Numismatic Collection**, made by Victor Emmanuel III.

Also on this floor (but closed) are five rooms containing the **Dusmet Collection** which was left to the State in 1949. ROOM I. 16C majolica from Asia Minor. ROOM II. 17–18C Chinese porcelain, and a Tien Lungli vase; 16C Flemish tapestries. ROOM III Neri di Bicci (attributed), Death of the Virgin, Madonna and Child (tabernacle); 14C Sienese school, Diptych of San Vescovo and San Monaco; 14C artist from the Marches, Bishop Saint. ROOM IV Terracotta works: Leone Leoni, Deposition; Francavilla, statuettes of Moses and Aaron; 16C Florentine school, Pietà; Susini, Christ in the Garden. ROOM V. 16C Flemish tapestries. Guercino (attributed), Visitation of St Julian; Annibale Carracci, Self-portrait; Lorenzo Costa, Annunciation. The 18C **Barberini Apartments**, with Rococo decorations, contain furniture, porcelain, costumes, etc.

Opposite the palace was the SCOTS COLLEGE from 1604 until 1962 when it moved to Via Cassia (see Rte 36). The buildings dating from 1869, and the church of St Andrew (1645–76), deconsecrated in 1962, are now incorporated in a bank.

Via delle Quattro Fontane ends in **Piazza Barberini**, which was transformed between the Wars into one of the busiest traffic centres in the city. Here converge Via del Tritone (from the Corso), Via Sistina (from the Pincio), Via Vittorio Veneto, Via San Nicola da Tolentino, and Via Barberini. Isolated in the centre of the square in this unpleasant setting is Bernini's masterpiece, the *Fontana del Tritone* (1642–43), with four dolphins supporting a shell on which is seated a Triton who blows water through a shell held up in his hands. On the N side, at the beginning of Via Veneto, is the little reconstructed FONTANA DELLE API, designed by Bernini a year later, bearing the Barberini device of the bee and with an inscription stating that the water is for the use of the public and their animals.

Here begins the broad and tree-lined **VIA VENETO** (Pl. 4; 3, 1), which climbs in two sweeping curves to Porta Pinciana. Officially called Via

Vittorio Veneto, it was opened in 1886 on part of the site of the beautiful park of the VILLA LUDOVISI which was obliterated, and which gave its name to this aristocratic district of the city, laid out at the turn of the century. The street with its luxury hotels, great mansions, and famous cafés was especially fashionable for its ambience of 'la dolce vita' in the sixties.

On the right is the church of the **Cappuccini** or **Santa Maria della Concezione** (Pl. 4; 3), architecturally simple and unpretending in accordance with Franciscan ideals and in strong contrast to the Baroque works of the time (1626). Its founder was Cardinal Antonio Barberini. In the very dark INTERIOR all the pictures are labelled. SOUTH SIDE, first chapel, Guido Reni, *St Michael; to the left, Honthorst, Mocking of Christ; third chapel, Domenichino, St Francis in Ecstasy, and Death of St Francis; fifth chapel, Andrea Sacchi, St Anthony raising a dead man. An inscription on the pavement (*hic jacet pulvis, cinis et nihil*) marks the grave of Cardinal Barberini in front of the high altar.

NORTH SIDE, fifth chapel, Andrea Sacchi, The Virgin and St Bonaventura; first chapel, Pietro da Cortona, St Paul having his sight restored. A CEMETERY (entered down the stairs to the right of the church) has five subterranean chapels lined with the bones and skeletons of over 4000 Capuchins, arranged in patterns. On the floor of two of these chapels is earth brought from Palestine. On All Souls' Day (2 November) this gruesome scene is illuminated.

Opposite the church, a street with steps ascends to **Sant'Isidoro** with a pink façade by Carlo Bizzaccheri (1704). The church (1620, by Antonio Casoni) was attached to a college for Irish students, founded by Luke Wadding (1588–1657), the distinguished Irish Franciscan, who instigated the Irish rebellion of 1641 against the confiscation of Ulster. His tomb is in the church, which contains several works by Carlo Maratta, and a chapel in the right transept designed by Gian Lorenzo Bernini with sculptures attributed to his son Paolo.

Farther up Via Veneto, by its second curve (right) is PALAZZO PIOMBINO, or PALAZZO MARGHERITA, a huge building by Gaetano Koch (1886–90) standing in a garden, now the United States Embassy. Queen Margherita lived here after the death of Umberto I in 1900. At 2 Via Boncompagni is the United States Information Service Bureau. Farther on, Via Lombardia leads left from Via Veneto to the **Casino dell'Aurora** (No. 46; no admission), a relic of the famous Villa Ludovisi which belonged to Cardinal Ludovisi, nephew of Gregory XV. The first Roman scene in Henry James' 'Roderick Hudson' takes place in the gardens here. The garden-house contains a fine ceiling painting of Aurora and Fame by Guercino (1621). Via Veneto ends at **Porta Pinciana**, a handsome fortified gateway erected by Honorius c 403 and since enlarged. Opposite is one of the entrances to the Villa Borghese (Rte 9).

On the city side of Porta Pinciana, Via di Porta Pinciana branches left from Via Veneto and, passing the grounds of the Villa Medici, runs into Via Francesco Crispi, which ends in Largo del Tritone. Beyond the gate, the broad Corso d'Italia skirts a long stretch of the Aurelian Wall (272–79) with some eighteen turrets as far as Piazza Fiume on the site of the demolished Porta Salaria, and continues to Porta Pia (Rte 19).

Via Barberini, opened in 1926, ascends from Piazza Barberini. On the left, in a side street called after it, is the church of **San Nicola da Tolentino** (closed for restoration; but ring at the Armenian College at No. 17), rebuilt in 1620 by Carlo Buti, and finished by Martino Longhi the Younger and Giovan Maria Baratta, who built the façade in 1670. The high altar was designed by Alessandro Algardi. The second chapel on the left is thought to be the last work of Pietro da Cortona (1668) and contains sculptures by Ercole Ferrata, Cosimo Fancelli, and Antonio Raggi.

Via Barberini ends at Largo Santa Susanna, another traffic centre, where it is joined on the left by Via Leonida Bissolati, with numerous tourist agencies. The square is dominated by the building of the UFFICIO GEOLOGICO (1873, by Raffaele Canevari), containing the GEOLOGICAL MUSEUM (admission by appointment after written application), with a collection of minerals, marbles (archaeological and modern), and fossils.

Adjoining Largo Santa Susanna on the SE is the busy PIAZZA SAN BERNARDO, with its fountain and three churches. It is, in effect, a widening of Via Venti Settembre. On its NW side is the church of **Santa Susanna** (Pl. 4; 4; open 17.00–19.00; fest. 10.00–12.00, 16.30–19.00), a Paulist church, probably dating from the 4C, restored in 795, and remodelled in the 15C and 16C. It is now the American National church. The façade is by Maderno (1603), and is by many considered his masterpiece; in the good late Mannerist interior (1595) are large frescoes by Baldassare Croce. Opposite, at the beginning of Via Torino, is the round church of **San Bernardo alle Terme** built into one of the two circular halls flanking the exedra of the Baths of Diocletian (see below) in the 16C (in an unattractive colour). The domed interior contains eight colossal stucco statues of saints by Camillo Mariani (c 1600–05), and a neo-classical monument to the sculptor Carlo Finelli (died 1853) by Rinaldo Rinaldi.

The **Fontana dell'Acqua Felice** is fed by an aqueduct (1585–87) from Colonna in the Alban Hills. The fountain dates from the time of Sixtus V and is by Domenico Fontana; the unsuccessful figure of Moses is attributed to Prospero Antichi or Leonardo Sormani. The bas-relief of Aaron is by Giovanni Battista della Porta, and that of Gideon by Flaminio Vacca and Pier Paolo Olivieri; the four lions are copies of Egyptian antiques removed by Gregory XVI to the Egyptian Museum founded by him in the Vatican.

The church of ***SANTA MARIA DELLA VITTORIA** (Pl. 4; 4), is a fine edifice by Maderno (1620), with a façade by Giovanni Battista Soria. Originally dedicated to St Paul, it was renamed from an image (burned in 1833) of the Virgin that gave victory to the Catholic army over the Protestants at the battle of the White Mountain, near Prague, on 8 November 1620 (Thirty Years War). The INTERIOR (being restored) is considered one of the most complete examples of Baroque decoration in Rome, rich in colour and glowing with marbles. It has good stucco work and a fine organ and cantoria by a pupil of Bernini, Mattia De Rossi. The frescoes are by Giovanni Domenico Cerrini.

The second S chapel has an altarpiece of the Madonna and St Francis by Domenichino. The *CORNARO CHAPEL (fourth chapel on the N side; push-button light), by Bernini, is a splendid architectural achievement, using the shallow space to great effect. Over the altar is his famous sculptured group representing the Ecstasy of St Theresa, and below is a gilt bronze relief of the Last Supper. At the sides are expressive portraits of the Venetian family of Cornaro, by pupils and followers of Bernini. The last half-hidden figure on the left is said to be a portrait of Bernini. The fresco, by Luigi Serra (1885), in the apse of the church, commemorates the triumphal entry into Prague of the Catholic army.

Via Venti Settembre continues to Porta Pia (see Rte 19), passing on the left a building built in 1902 to house the Ministry of Agriculture and Forests; and on the right, the colossal TREASURY building by Raffaele Canevari (1870), containing a NUMISMATIC MUSEUM (adm see p 47; document required). Interesting is a collection of wax seals by Benedetto Pistrucci, who designed the St George and dragon on the English sovereign. The short Via Servio Tullio, opposite, leads N to Piazza Sallustio, where, behind Villa Maccari (right), is a considerable fragment of a villa which used to stand in the GARDENS OF SALLUST, laid out in 40 BC, on which the historian C. Sallustius Crispus lavished the wealth he had accumulated during his African governorship. Here also are the foundations of the Trinità dei Monti obelisk, showing where it stood in the Middle Ages.

The short Via Orlando runs from Piazza San Bernardo past the Grand Hotel opened in 1894 (when it was the first hotel in Italy with electric light), to the large circular **PIAZZA DELLA REPUBBLICA** (Pl. 5; 3), formerly *dell' Esedra* (from the exedra of the Baths of Diocletian, the buildings of which may be seen on the opposite side). The semicircular porticoed fronts of the palazzi on either side of the entrance to the piazza (by Koch; 1896–1902), follow the line of the exedra. The abundant FOUNTAIN OF THE NAIADS (1870) is supplied by the Acqua Marcia. Four groups of reclining nymphs and the central Glaucus were sculpted by Mario Rutelli (1901–11).

The *Baths of Diocletian** were built in 298–306 by Diocletian and Maximian. The largest of all the ancient Roman baths, they could accommodate over 3000 people at once. They covered a rectangular area, c 380m by 370m, corresponding to that now bounded SE by Piazza dei Cinquecento, SW by Via Torino, NW by Via Venti Settembre, and NE by Via Volturno. The main buildings included a calidarium, tepidarium, and frigidarium. The calidarium, which survived into the late 17C, occupied part of the present piazza. The tepidarium and the huge central hall of the baths are now occupied by the church of Santa Maria degli Angeli (see below). The frigidarium was an open-air bath behind this hall. Numerous large and small halls, nymphaea, and exedrae were located within the precincts.

The only entrance to the baths was on the NE side, near the present Via Volturno. On the SW side the closed exedra was flanked by two circular halls: one of these is now the church of San Bernardo alle Terme (see above; the other is at the corner of Via Viminale and Via delle Terme. A third (octagonal) hall, on the corner of Via Parigi at the NW angle of the main complex, has recently been restored and is open to the public (see below). In the 16C a Carthusian convent was built in the ruins, and the baths were plundered for their building materials in the 16–19C. In 1889 the Museo Nazionale Romano (see below) was opened in seven splendid vaulted rooms of the baths around the SE transept of Santa Maria degli Angeli and in four more rooms in and near the frigidarium, and in part of the convent, including the cloisters. Most of this area has been inaccessible for decades.

Along the modern Via Parigi stand conspicuous remains of buildings demolished to make way for the Baths. At the beginning of the street is a Roman column, surmounted by a caravel, a gift from Paris (1961). On the corner of Via Parigi is the **Octagonal Hall of the Baths of Diocletian**, which formerly housed a planatarium and has recently been restored to display some works from the Museo Nazionale Romano (see below). The rectangular exterior hides a domed octagonal *interior (open 10.00–13.00, 15.00–18.00), a splendid Roman architectural work. The hall is thought to have connected the open-air gymnasium and gardens of the Baths of Diocletian with the heated calidarium. Roman foundations can be seen through the glass panel in the centre of the hall.

Here are displayed Roman statues and busts (mostly dating from the 2C to 3C AD), many of them found in the Baths of Caracalla, Diocletian, and Trajan. Also temporarily displayed here (to be moved to the ex Collegio Massimo when it opens, see below) are two famous bronzes: the *Boxer resting, a magnificent work signed by Apollonius, dating from the 1C BC, and the Hellenistic '*Prince' (early 2C BC). Also temporarily displayed here (and also to be moved to the ex Collegio Massimo) is the marble *Aphrodite or Venus of Cyrene, an original Greek work of the 4C BC, possibly by a predecessor of Praxiteles, representing the goddess just risen from the sea; near her right leg is her cloak, supported by a dolphin; the head and arms are missing. The statue was found in the Baths at Cyrene.

SANTA MARIA DEGLI ANGELI (Pl. 5; 3; open 7.30–12.30, 16.00–18.30) occupies the great central hall of the baths, converted into the church of the Carthusian convent. The work of adaptation was carried out in 1563–66 for Pius IV by Michelangelo, who may also have designed the cloisters and other conventual buildings. Michelangelo placed the entrance of the church at the short SE side of the rectangle and thus had at his disposal a nave of vast proportions. The effect was spoiled by Vanvitelli who, instructed by the Carthusian fathers in 1749, altered the orientation. He made the entrance in the long SW side and so converted the nave into a transept. To compensate for the loss of length, he built out on the NE side an apsidal choir, which broke into the monumental SW wall of the frigidarium. The façade on Piazza della Repubblica, with Vanvitelli's doorway, incorporates an apsidal wall, all that is left of the calidarium. Excavations during the restoration of the floor in 1970 revealed further remains of the baths.

In the disappointing INTERIOR, the circular VESTIBULE stands on the site of the tepidarium. Here are the tombs of Carlo Maratta (died 1713; right) and Salvator Rosa (died 1673; left). By the entrance into the transept is (right) a fine colossal statue of St Bruno, by Houdon (1766). The vast TRANSEPT is nearly 100m long, 27m wide and 28m high. The eight monolithic columns of red granite, nearly 14m high and 1.5m in diameter, are original; the others, in brick, were added when the building was remodelled. To the right: in the pavement, a meridian dating from 1703; tomb by Antonio Muñoz, of Marshal Armando Diaz (died 1928), Italian commander-in-chief in the First World War. The huge paintings include (left): Mass of St Basil, by Subleyras; Fall of Simon Magus, by Pompeo Batoni. In the CHOIR, on the right, Romanelli, Presentation in the Temple; Domenichino, Martyrdom of St Sebastian; left, Pomarancio, Death of Ananias and Sapphira (painted on slate); Carlo Maratta, Baptism of Christ. In the apse, on the left, monument of Pius IV, from Michelangelo's design, which inspired also the monument of Cardinal Serbelloni opposite. The door to the sacristy in the left transept leads to impressive remains of the FRIGIDARIUM of the Baths of Diocletian (see above).

Viale Einaudi leads past a garden with a monument by Azzurri, erected in memory of 548 Italian soldiers ambushed at Dogali, Eritrea, in 1887. It incorporates an Egyptian obelisk found in the Isaeum Campense (its companion is in Florence) inscribed with hieroglyphs recording the glories of Ramesses the Great or Sesostris, the Pharaoh of the time of Moses. (The monument, first erected in front of the old railway station was moved here in 1924; in 1936–44 it was decorated with the Lion of Judah plundered from Addis Ababa).

Beyond, is the present entrance to the *MUSEO NAZIONALE ROMANO (Pl. 5; 4; admission see p 47), one of the great museums of the world, which has been all but closed for many years. Most of the masterpieces are to be exhibited in the nearby ex Collegio Massimo in Piazza dei Cinquecento, and the Ludovisi collection will probably be moved to Palazzo Altemps (see Rte 6). Meanwhile in 1994 only two rooms here, and the cloister, were open (and the octagonal hall, described above). The huge collection of epigraphs and sarcophagi is one day to be arranged here.

The Museum was founded in 1889, and includes archaeological finds made in Rome since 1870, part of the Kircherian collection formerly in the Collegio Romano, and the Ludovisi collection formed by Cardinal Ludovico Ludovisi, nephew of Gregory XV (Alessandro Ludovisi; pope 1621–23). This was originally housed in Villa Ludovisi and was moved to the new palace in Via Vittorio Veneto on its completion in 1890. In 1901, after the palace had become the residence of Queen Margherita, the State bought the collection from the Prince of Piombino, Rodolfo Boncompagni-Ludovisi.

The present entrance is through a garden, to the right of the church of Santa Maria degli Angeli. Beyond the ticket office, a corridor displays mosaics, including one of a skeleton with an inscription in Greek ('Know Thyself') and busts and herms. On the right a room contains the *Ludovisi Throne, the only work from the famous Ludovisi collection at present on view. This is a large throne thought to have been intended for the statue of a divinity, and usually considered to be an original work of the 5C BC found in the Villa Ludovisi. The back and sides are adorned with reliefs. The central subject is apparently the birth of Aphrodite, who rises from the sea supported by two Seasons; on the right side is the representation of a young woman sitting clothed on a folded cushion; she is taking grains from a box and burning them in a brazier; on the left side is a naked flute girl, also sitting on a folded cushion, playing a double pipe. Doubts about the authenticity of the three fine reliefs were raised in 1988 by a well-known art critic.

In the room beyond is displayed the *Discus-thrower from the Lancelotti collection, the finest and best-preserved replica of the famous statue of Myron (sold to Hitler in 1938, but recovered ten years later).

The *GREAT CLOISTER was built in 1565 and is ascribed to Michelangelo, who died the year before. It has a perimeter of 320m, and the arcades, having alternate square and oval windows, are supported by 100 travertine columns. The fountain in the cloister garden dates from 1695; it is shaded by four cypresses, one of which is the original. Seven colossal heads of animals (probably from the Forum of Trajan) surround the fountain. In the cloister and garden are sculptures and inscriptions of relatively minor importance.

WING I. Statues of Roman generals with carved breastplates; group of seated man and woman; nude youth, possibly the emperor Heliogabalus; three female statues. WING II. Near the angle with Wing I, Granite slab with relief of Egyptian deities. At the corner of WING III, *pilasters with inscriptions relating to the Ludi Saeculares, celebrated in the reigns of Augustus (17 BC) and of Septimius Severus (AD 204). The earlier inscription records the festival ordained by Augustus, during which the Carmen Saeculare of Horace was sung at the Capitol. Between the pilasters, Nilotic mosaic. WING IV. Statue of Jupiter standing with chlamys over his left arm; headless Herakles with club and lion-skin, after Lysippos; athlete, after Polykleitos. In the garden, along the cloister wings, Inscriptions; Base from the Temple of Hercules at Tivoli; landmarks delimiting the land bordering the Tiber, with records of the consuls, censors, and *curatores alvei et riparum Tiberis.*

The vast **Piazza dei Cinquecento** (Pl. 5; 4), by far the largest square in Rome, is the terminus or junction of many bus services. The ex **Collegio Massimo** (Pl. 5; 4) has been restored as the new seat of the *MUSEO NAZIONALE ROMANO (see above), but is still not open to the public. The building, which used to house the Collegio Massimiliano Massimo, was built in 1883–87 by Camillo Pistrucci. It is to contain the masterpieces of classical sculpture, and an indication of the likely arrangement is given below, but may well be altered when all the floors are opened. Only the main works are mentioned, as it is to be hoped that all the exhibits will be well labelled. On the **Ground Floor** will be displayed art from the time of Sulla to Augustus, including portraits, and some Greek originals. A room dedicated to Augustus will contain the celebrated *statue of Augustus as Pontefex Maximus, one of the finest portraits of the emperor, found in the Via Labicana; an *altar from Ostia, with reliefs of the origins of Rome (Mars and Rhea Silvia, Romulus and Remus suckled by the she-wolf, etc.); the altar is dated 1 October AD 124. Also to be exhibited here are the two bronzes at present in the Octagonal Hall of the Baths of Diocletian (see above). Another room will display the Daughter of Niobe, from the Gardens of Sallust, a Greek original of the 5C BC of the school of Kresilas, and the Ludovisi throne (at present exhibited in the old seat of the Museum, and described above).

On the **First Floor** will be exhibited sculptures found in Imperial villas (including Hadrian's Villa outside Tivoli, and Nero's Villa outside Subiaco). A room will contain statues of the Muses, the Crouching Venus, and the *'Maiden of Anzio', a masterpiece of Greek art dating from the end of the 4C or beginning of the 3C BC by a sculptor of the school of Lysippos who had come under the influence of Praxiteles. It represents a young girl approaching an altar and carrying implements for a sacrifice, and was discovered in the Imperial villa at Anzio in 1878. The *Ephebus of Subiaco, a Roman copy of an original of the 4C BC (probably one of the Niobids), and a young girl or nymph sleeping, both come from Nero's villa at Subiaco. A section will be devoted to portraits found in Hadrian's Villa, and another to busts of emperors, including Lucius Verus and Vespasian (one of the best surviving Roman portraits, found at Ostia), and female portarits of the 3C and 4C AD. On this floor also will be exhibited the famous *Discus-thrower from the Lancelotti collection (at present in the old seat, see above). In another room will be displayed the bronzes from the ships salvaged from Lake Nemi (see Rte 30).

The **Second Floor** is to be devoted to *wall-paintings and *mosaics from the Republican era onwards. The rectangular room from the Imperial Villa at Prima Porta of Livia, wife of Augustus, will be reconstructed, the walls of which were decorated with splendid *frescoes of an orchard and flower garden. It constitutes the masterpiece of naturalist decoration of the second style of Roman painting. Deatched and restored in 1952–53, the frescoes were saved just in time from complete decay. The stuccoed and painted decoration of a building of the Augustan age discovered in the grounds of the Villa Farnesina near the banks of the Tiber will also be displayed here. The paintings are second in importance only to those from Pompeii and Herculaneum. The *ceilings decorated in stucco are masterpieces of their kind, with friezes decorated with festoons and cupids, interspersed with landscapes and mythological scenes. Other decorations come from the Villa of Antoninus Pius at Castel Di Guido. The mosaics include some from the Villa of Septimius Severus at Baccano. The **Basement** will have rooms for the coin collection, medals and jewellery.

Other masterpieces which will probably be exhibited include: Apollo by the school of Pheidias, or perhaps by Kalamis, found in the Tiber; Dancer wearing a chiton, and Juno, possibly the portrait of an empress as the goddess, both found on the Palatine (5C BC); Peplophoros, probably a Greek original of the first half of the 5C BC, found in Piazza Barberini; the 'Torso Valentini', a hero or athlete, a remarkable work of the early 5C BC, formerly in the courtyard of Palazzo Valentini; the head of Hypnos, attributed to Praxiteles, from Hadrian's Villa; bronze statue of a young man leaning on a lance, perhaps Pollus or one of the Seleucids, in the identical pose as the Alexander the Great of Lysippos; the Apollo of Anzio, by an unknown Attic predecessor of Praxiteles; head of the goddess of Butrinto, discovered in 1929 at Butrinto in Albania (the arrangement of the hair somewhat resembles that of the Apollo of Anzio); 'Dancer of Tivoli', Roman copy of a Hellenistic original; young satyr turning round to look at his tail, a Hellenistic work; Goddess personifying a seaport, accompanied by a child merman (1C BC; recalling 4C); marble altar (1C AD) found near Ponte Sant'Angelo, the front and sides with plane-branch decoration surmounted by a bull's head; sepulchral altar, comprising an ossuary and a cippus, with reliefs depicting a nuptial scene, and figures of maenads dancing and of youths carrying implements for a sacrifice; half-length figure of a chief Vestal, from the House of the Vestals in the Roman Forum; head of a maiden, with hair in tight curls, from the tomb of Sulpicius Platorinus; head of a princess of the Julio-Claudian gens wearing a diadem, possibly Agrippina, mother of Nero; Antoninus Pius as a young man; Commodus as a youth; head of Sabina, wife of Hadrian (with traces of colour still visible); the head of Hadrian, found beneath the Stazione Termini; Dionysos, from Hadrian's Villa, Hadrianic copy of a 4C Greek original; and head of a dying Persian, of the school of Pergamon, one of a series of sculptures set up at Pergamon to commemorate the victory of Attalos I over the Gauls; terracottas from Ariccia; and polychrome marble intarsia panels from the basilica of Giunio Basso on the Esquiline (early 4C AD).

The **Stazione di Termini** (Pl. 5; 4; called after the Baths of Diocletian), on the SE side of the square, with its twelve main and numerous subsidiary platforms, is one of the largest and most modern railway stations in Europe. Its reconstruction, begun in 1938 and delayed by war, was completed 12 years later, and it was formally opened on 20 December 1950. Strictly functional in design, the station extends from Via Giovanni Giolitti on the SW to Via Marsala on the NE. The façade is a plain white rectangular block, pierced horizontally by nine continuous lines of windows. In front is a gigantic quasi-cantilever construction sweeping upwards and outwards and serving as a portico for vehicles. The older and more conventional wings had been partly completed when the war stopped building operations in 1942. A covered way through the station connects the streets on either side. The Stazione di Termini is also the starting-point of the Underground railway.

In front of the station (left), is the best preserved fragment of the so-called SERVIAN WALL, formed of massive blocks of tufa. This wall was actually built after the invasion of the Gauls in 390 BC and was restored in the last days of the Republic. Further fragments of the wall were unearthed during the reconstruction of the station. Beneath the station have been found also remains of a private house and of some baths, with good mosaics, dating from the 2C AD.

11

The Esquiline Hill and Santa Maria Maggiore

The **Esquiline** (65m), the highest and most extensive of the Seven Hills of Rome, was formerly a region of vineyards and gardens, and had few inhabitants. It has four summits: most of the *Oppius* or OPPIAN HILL is covered by a park (the *Parco Oppio*), on the site of the Baths of Titus and of Trajan and Nero's Domus Aurea. The *Cispius*, extending to the NE, is crowned by the basilica of Santa Maria Maggiore. The other two summits are the *Subura*, above the low-lying district of that name, and the *Fagutalis*, named from a beech grove. According to the erudite Varro, the name 'Esquiline' was derived from the word *excultus*, which referred to the ornamental groves planted on the hill by Servius Tullius, including the *Querquetulanus* (oak grove) and *Fagutalis*.

Although most of the hill was considered an unhealthy place to live, the region between the modern Via Cavour and the slopes of the Oppian Hill, called the *Carinoe*, was a fashionable residential district. Pompey lived here, in a small but famous house, occupied after his death by Antony. The site of the villa of Maecenas was afterwards occupied by the Baths of Titus. The villa was eventually acquired by Nero, who incorporated it in his famous Domus Aurea. Virgil had a house near the gardens of Maecenas. Propertius lived in the vicinity and Horace may have done so: he was certainly a constant visitor at the villa of his patron.

Via Cavour (Pl. 8; 2), opened in 1890 and now an important traffic artery of the city, runs direct from Via dei Fori Imperiali (Rte 4) to Piazza dei Cinquecento and the railway station. At the beginning on the left is the base of the massive TORRE DEI CONTI, all that remains of a great tower erected after 1198 by Riccardo dei Conti, brother of Innocent III. It was damaged by an earthquake in 1348 and reduced to its present state by Urban VIII in the 17C. Via Cavour now passes through the ancient *Subura*, the scarcely noticeable hill of which was one of the four summits of the Esquiline included in the Septimontium, the city that succeeded Roma Quadrata. The district was connected to the Roman Forum by the Argiletum.

At the first important cross-roads Via degli Annibaldi (right) provides an interesting glimpse of the Colosseum, and Via dei Serpenti (left) leads to the **Madonna dei Monti**, a fine church by Giacomo della Porta (who also designed the fountain nearby). The 17C INTERIOR contains stuccoes by Ambrogio Buonvicino and frescoes by Cristoforo Casolani. SOUTH SIDE: first chapel, frescoes by Giovanni da San Giovanni; third chapel, Paris Nogari, Christ carrying the Cross. The DOME was decorated in 1599–1600 by Cesare Nebbia, Orazio Gentileschi, and others. In the chapels on the NORTH SIDE: Adoration of the Shepherds by Girolamo Muziano and two paintings by Cesare Nebbia; and an Annunciation by Durante Alberti.

On Via Cavour, at the end of a high wall, a flight of steps, called Via San Francesco di Paola ascends to the right, on the site of the ancient Via Scelerata, so called from the impious act of Tullia, who drove her chariot over the dead body of her royal father Servius Tullius. On the right is the base, with bands of black and white stone, of a medieval tower. To the right is Piazza San Francesco di Paola, with a large 17C palace which houses the administrative offices of the Istituto Centrale del Restauro, which now has its main laboratories in the ex-Istituto di San Michele (see Rte 21). The steps pass beneath an archway above which is an attractive Doric loggia, once part of the house of Vannozza Catanei, mother of Lucrezia Borgia.

At the top is a square in front of the basilica of **SAN PIETRO IN VINCOLI** (Pl. 5; 7; open 7.00–12.30, 15.30–18.00), or *Basilica Eudoxiana*, traditionally founded in 442 by the Empress Eudoxia, wife of Valentinian III, as a shrine for the chains of St Peter. The church was restored in 1475 under Sixtus IV by Meo del Caprina, who was responsible for the FAÇADE, with its beautiful colonnaded portico. During 1956–59 remains of previous buildings, some going back to Republican times, were discovered beneath the church.

The two chains with which St Peter was supposed to have been fettered in the Tullianum are said to have been taken to Constantinople. In 439 Juvenal, Bishop of Jerusalem, gave them to the Empress Eudoxia, wife of Theodosius the Younger. She placed one of them in the basilica of the Apostles at Constantinople, and sent the other to Rome for her daughter Eudoxia, wife of Valentinian III. The younger Eudoxia gave the chain to St Leo I (pope 440–61) and built the church of San Pietro in Vincoli for its reception. Later the second chain was sent to Rome. On being brought together, the two chains miraculously united.

The basilican INTERIOR, much affected by restoration, preserves its twenty ancient columns with Doric capitals (the Ionic bases were added in the 17C). The NAVE, almost four times as wide as the aisles, has a ceiling-painting by Giovanni Battista Parodi, representing the cure of a person possessed by an evil spirit by the touch of the holy chains. SOUTH AISLE. First altar, Guercino, St Augustine; second altar, Domenichino designed the tomb on the left and painted the portraits above both tombs; the altarpiece is a copy of his Deliverance of St Peter, now in the sacristy.

At the end of the aisle is the TOMB OF JULIUS II, the famous unfinished masterpiece of Michelangelo, who was so harassed while working on the monument that he called it the 'tragedy of a sepulchre'. Hindered by his quarrels with Julius and by the jealousy of that pope's successors, Michelangelo finally abandoned work on the tomb, and the great pontiff, who had contemplated for himself the most splendid monument in the world, lies uncommemorated in St Peter's. Some forty statues were to have decorated the tomb, including the two slaves now in the Louvre, and the four unfinished slaves in the Accademia gallery in Florence. No idea of the original design of the monument (for which many drawings survive) can be gained from this very unsatisfactory grouping of statues and niches. Only a few magnificent fragments remain here, notably the powerful figure of *Moses, Michelangelo's most strongly individualised work, in whose majestic glance is seen the prophet who spoke with God. The satyr-like horns represent the traditional beams of light, an attribute of the prophet in medieval iconography. The beautiful figures on either side of *Leah and *Rachel, symbols of the active and contemplative life (Dante, 'Purgatorio', xxvii, 108), are also by Michelangelo. The rest is his pupils' work: an ineffectual effigy of the Pope, by Maso del Bosco; a Madonna, by Alessandro Scherano; a Prophet and Sibyl, by Raffaello da Montelupo.

The SACRISTY has a pretty 16C frescoed vault by Paris Nogari and a small 15C marble bas-relief of the Madonna and Child. In the vestibule is the original painting of the Deliverance of St Peter by Domenichino. In the last

Michelangelo's statue of moses in San Pietro in Vincoli

chapel of this aisle, *St Margaret, by Guercino. The bishop's throne in the APSE, which is frescoed by Giacomo Coppi, is a marble chair brought from a Roman bath. The baldacchino over the high altar is by Virginio Vespignani (19C). In the confessio below are the Chains of St Peter, displayed in a tabernacle with beautiful bronze *doors attributed to Caradosso (1477). Stairs lead down to a tiny CRYPT (usually closed), in which is a fine late 4C

Roman sarcophagus with figures representing scenes from the New Testament, containing the relics of the seven Maccabee brothers.

NORTH AISLE. Second altar, 7C mosaic *icon of the bearded St Sebastian, well preserved (coin-operated light, on right); first altar, Pomarancio, Descent from the Cross; (near the W wall) tomb of Cardinal De Cusa, with a good coloured relief (1465), attributed to Andrea Bregno. On the end wall (covered with scaffolding) to the right of the entrance door, is the little tomb of the brothers Pollaiuolo with two expressive portrait busts attributed to Luigi Capponi. Above is a very worn fresco of the plague of 1476 by an unknown 15C artist, and to the left, an early fresco of the Head of Christ (behind glass).

The CLOISTER (entrance at 16 Via Eudossiana, on the right, now the University Faculty of Engineering), is attributed to Giuliano da Sangallo. The arches have sadly been enclosed, but the lovely well-head by Simone Mosca survives.

The narrow and pretty Via delle Sette Sale leads out of the piazza on the left of San Pietro in Vincoli. This unexpectedly rural street passes between two of the summits of the Esquiline, the Cispius (left) and the Oppius (right). The park which now covers the Oppian Hill contains scattered remains of the huge BATHS OF TRAJAN, built after a fire in 104 by Apollodorus of Damascus and inaugurated in 109. The conspicuous ruins include an exedra which was decorated as a nymphaeum, and a hall with two apses. Between Via Terme di Traiano and Viale del Colle Oppio is a nymphaeum (well below ground level) on a basilican plan, probably part of Nero's Domus Aurea, restored by Trajan.

At 2 Via Terme di Traiano is the entrance (kept locked; for admission ask at the Auditorium of Maecenas, see below) to the so-called SETTE SALE, in fact a remarkable large vaulted building with nine sections, the reservoir of the Baths of Trajan. Excavations have shown that a house was built above the reservoir in the 4C. The rest of the park is occupied by Nero's Domus Aurea, see Rte 13.

At the end of Via delle Sette Sale, by its junction with Viale del Monte Oppio, is the church of **SAN MARTINO AI MONTI** (Pl. 5; 5, 6), the church of the Carmelites, built c 500 by St Symmachus and dedicated to Saints Sylvester and Martin. It replaced an older church founded in the 4C by Pope St Sylvester I, who came from Mount Soracte to cure Constantine of an illness. It was rebuilt in the 9C and given its present appearance c 1650 by Filippo Gagliardi. It stands on remains of the old church and incorporates part of a Roman edifice. In this church were proclaimed, in the presence of Constantine, the decisions of the Council of Nicaea, and the heretical books of Arius, Sabellius, and Victorinus burnt.

In the INTERIOR the broad nave is divided from the aisles by 24 ancient Corinthian columns which support an architrave, and the presbytery is raised above the crypt. The fine 17C decoration, with statues, stucco medallions, and frescoes, is by Paolo Naldini and Filippo Gagliardi. In the lower side aisles are frescoes of the life of Elijah and landscapes of the Roman Campagna by Gaspard Dughet, and (left aisle) interesting views of the interiors of St John Lateran and St Peter's before reconstruction, by Filippo Gagliardi. The Council of Pope Sylvester is by Galeazzo Leoncino.

The tribune, with a double staircase, leading to the high altar, and the tabernacle are by Gagliardi, who also designed the elaborate stucco decoration of the CRYPT. Here on the left a door (key in the sacristy) leads to stairs which descend to a private chapel of the 3C, with traces of frescoes and mosaics, incorporated in eight large halls of a Roman building. In the left aisle, second altar, St Albert by Girolamo Muziano, and (first altar), Vision of St Angelo by Pietro Testa.

A door on the right of the apse leads out to a busy cross-roads with two heavily restored medieval towers, from which the church of Santa Prassede may be reached (see below). Viale del Monte Oppio ends at the Largo Brancaccio, on the busy 19C Via Merulana. Here (right) is PALAZZO BRANCACCIO (1896, on a design by Luca Carimini) which houses the Istituto Italiano per il Medio ed Estremo Oriente. On the second floor is the **MUSEO NAZIONALE DI ARTE ORIENTALE** (closed in 1994), founded in 1957 and the most important collection of Oriental art in Italy. The arrangement may change when the museum reopens.

ROOM I. Pre-Mohammedan Iran. Prehistoric ceramics, decorated with animal and geometric motifs, terracotta vases. Luristan bronzes, weapons, and horsebits. ROOMS II and III. Mohammedan Iran. ROOM III. 9–15C glazed pottery, finely coloured. On the wall, a 16C gold-embroidered cope, with hunting motif; 9–10C Oriental-type vases (Tang), 12–18C Mohammedan ceramics, including exquisite tiles. Indian and Siamese stelae and images, 8C BC sculpture from Afghanistan, of the god Durga killing the demon buffalo. ROOMS IV and V (G. Auriti donation). Chinese, Japanese, and Korean bronzes, ceramics, and Buddhas. ROOM VI contains Japanese screen paintings. ROOM VII. Sculpture, and 18C paintings on decorated vellum from Tibet. ROOMS. VIII and IX. Architectural fragments and sculpture from Swat, in NE Pakistan; ROOMS X–XII are used as offices and for exhibitions. The last ROOMS (XIII–XVI) complete the collections from Swat, including material from recent Italian excavations of necropoli (14–4C BC).

To the S in Largo Leopardi is the so-called **Auditorium of Maecenas** (adm see p 45). An Augustan apsidal building, this was in the gardens of Maecenas, and may have been a nymphaeum. The unusual apse has tiered seats in a semicircle. Traces of red landscape paintings can be seen in the apse and wall niches. The building is adjoined by a stretch of the Servian Wall.

Via Leopardi leads NE to the large 19C **Piazza Vittorio Emanuele** (Pl. 5; 6) surrounded by porticoes and planted with plane trees, cedars of Lebanon, and oleanders. It is now the scene of Rome's most important food market, particularly noted for fish. In the garden of the square are the impressive ruins of a fountain, known as the 'TROFEI DI MARIO' (no admission) built at the time of Alexander Severus (restored in 1986). This was formerly the terminal of an aqueduct (either the Acqua Claudia or the Aniene Nuovo), and the marble panoplies known as the 'Trophies of Marius' were removed from here to the balustrade of Piazza del Campidoglio in the 16C. Near the fountain is the curious PORTA MAGICA or *Porta Ermetica* (restored in 1989), with an alchemist's prescription for making gold, dating from 1680. This was removed earlier this century from the villa of Massimiliano Palombara.

In the N corner of the square is the church of **Sant'Eusebio**, founded in the 4C and rebuilt in 1711 and 1750. The ceiling painting, the Triumph of St Eusebius, is by Raphael Mengs; in the apse are fine, elaborately carved 16C stalls. In the sacristy, in the right aisle, is the carved top of the tomb of St Eusebius (15C) from the earlier church.

Via Carlo Alberto leads NW from the square to Santa Maria Maggiore, passing the ARCH OF GALLIENUS, the middle arch of a triple gate erected in the time of Augustus and dedicated in AD 262 in honour of Gallienus and his consort Salonina by the city prefect M. Aurelius Victor; it occupies the site of the Porta Esquilina of the Servian Wall. On the left is the church of **Santi Vito e Modesto** (4C; restored in 1900 and again in 1977). It contains frescoes by Antoniazzo Romano, and excavations have revealed traces of the Servian Wall and a Roman aqueduct. Farther on, on the right, is

Sant'Antonio Abate, the church of the Russo-Byzantine rite, with a doorway attributed to the Vassalletto (1262–66). The interior was redesigned c 1730.

At the end of Via Merulana is **Piazza Santa Maria Maggiore**, occupying the highest point (55m) of the Cispian summit of the Esquiline. In the square rises a fluted cipollino column 14.5m high, from the basilica of Maxentius. It was set up here in 1613 for Paul V by Carlo Maderno (who designed the fountain), and crowned with a statue of the Virgin.

Dominating the square is the ornate porticoed façade of ***SANTA MARIA MAGGIORE** (Pl. 5; 6; open 7.00–20.00; 7.00–19.00 in winter), once also called the *Basilica Liberiana*, which, more completely than any other of the four patriarchal basilicas, retains its original interior magnificence. A basilica was built here by Pope Liberius (352–66) on the site of a Roman edifice. This was reconstructed by Pope Damasus (366–84) and again by Sixtus III (432–40). The present church almost certainly dates from the time of Sixtus III. Nicholas IV (1288–92) added the polygonal apse and transepts, Clement X (1670–76) rebuilt the apse, and Benedict XIV ordered Ferdinando Fuga to carry out further alterations and add the main façade.

According to a 13C legend, the Virgin Mary appeared on the night of 4–5 August c 358, to Pope Liberius and to John, a patrician of Rome, telling them to build a church on the Esquiline on the spot where they would find in the morning a patch of snow covering the exact area to be built over. The prediction fulfilled, Liberius drew up the plans and John built the church at his own expense. The original title was therefore Santa Maria della Neve. The church was afterwards called *Santa Maria del Presepe*, after a precious relic of the Crib of the Infant Jesus. In 366 supporters of the antipope Ursinus barricaded themselves in the church and surrendered only when the partisans of Pope Damasus I took off the roof and pelted them with tiles. In 1075 Gregory VII (Hildebrand) was carried off from Mass by the rebel Cencio, but was rescued next day by his supporters. In 1347 Rienzo was crowned here as Tribune of Rome.

Excavations (admission only with special permission) carried out in 1967–72 beneath the nave revealed a large Roman building with remains of frescoes including a remarkable rural calendar with illustrations for each month. Two important ceremonies are held in the basilica annually. On 5 August the legend of the miraculous fall of snow is commemorated in a pontifical Mass in the Borghese Chapel (see below). On Christmas morning there is a procession in honour of the Santa Culla, or Holy Crib, which culminates in the exposure of the relic on the high altar. Santa Maria Maggiore has the privilege of extraterritoriality.

Exterior. The fine ***CAMPANILE**, the highest in Rome, was given its present form in 1377 by Gregory XI, and the polychrome decoration has been restored. The APSIDAL FAÇADE (restored in 1993), completed c 1673, is approached by an imposing flight of steps from Piazza dell'Esquilino. The right-hand section, with its dome, is by Flaminio Ponzio; the central and left sections by Carlo Rainaldi; the left-hand dome by Domenico Fontana. The MAIN FAÇADE, masking one of the 12C, was designed by Fuga (1743); it is approached by steps and is flanked by two grandiose wings.

The PORTICO is surmounted by a loggia of three arches, above which are statues. In the portico is a bronze statue of Philip IV of Spain, on a model by Bernini. Here tickets may be purchased to visit the UPPER LOGGIA (small groups are usually conducted 9.30–18.00). A monumental staircase leads up past a bronze statue of Pope Paul V by Paolo Sanquirico (1605) to the open loggia, from which there is a good view (including the basilica of San Giovanni Laterano at the end of the long straight Via Merulana on the right). From the loggia can be seen the mosaics (recently restored) on the earlier façade, dating from the time of Nicholas IV (1294–1308). The upper part, signed by Filippo Rusuti, depicts Christ Pantocrator with angels and Saints. The four scenes below, illustrating the Legend of the Snow (see above), were probably completed by assistants. The four 18C statues of angels by Pietro Bracci were originally over the high altar of the church.

The vast but well-proportioned **interior** (86m long), which still preserves its basilican form, is divided into nave and aisles by 36 columns of shining Hymettian marble and four of granite, all with Ionic capitals supporting an architrave, the whole discreetly rearranged and regularised by Ferdinando Fuga. Over the triumphal arch and in the nave are *mosaics, dating from the time of Sixtus III (432–40), the most important mosaic cycle in Rome of this period, of exquisite workmanship, in the classical tradition. The small rectangular biblical scenes high up above the architrave in the nave are difficult to see with the naked eye. On the left, scenes from the life of Abraham, Jacob, and Isaac; right, scenes from the life of Moses and Joshua (restored; in part painted); over the triumphal arch, scenes from the early life of Christ. The coffered *CEILING, attributed to Giuliano da Sangallo, is said to have been gilded with the first gold brought from America by Columbus, presented to Alexander VI by Ferdinand and Isabella. The fine Cosmatesque pavement dates from c 1150. At the W end (A) is the monument of Clement IX (1670), designed by Carlo Rainaldi, with a statue of the Pope by Domenico Guidi and statues of Faith and Charity by Cosimo Fancelli and Ercole Ferrata. The tomb (B) of Nicholas IV (1574), with sculptures by Leonardo Sormani, was designed by Domenico Fontana.

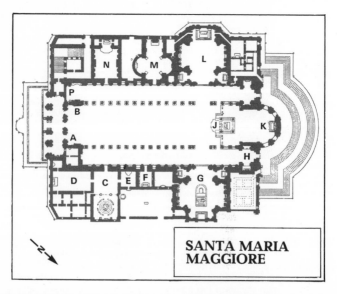

SANTA MARIA
MAGGIORE

SOUTH AISLE. From the baptistery (C), with a high relief of the Assumption by Pietro Bernini, is the entrance to the SACRISTY (D), designed, like the baptistery, by Flaminio Ponzio (early 17C). By the entrance, the Santarelli monument has a bust by Alessandro Algardi. In the vault of the Cappella San Michele (E), by a side door, are traces of 15C frescoes (restored in 1981) including two Evangelists by the circle of Piero della Francesca and a Pietà attributed to Benozzo Gozzoli. A column in the adjoining courtyard celebrates the conversion of Henry IV of France. The Cappella delle Reliquie (F), designed by Ferdinando Fuga, has ten red porphyry columns, and a 15C wood Crucifix. The *Sistina Chapel (G), or Chapel of the Holy Sacrament, on a domed Greek-cross plan, is a work of extraordinary magnificence carried out for Sixtus V by Domenico Fontana (1585). It is a veritable church in itself decorated with statues, stuccoes (by Ambrogio Buonvicino), and late 16C Mannerist frescoes by Cesare Nebbia, Giovanni Battista Pozzo, Paris Nogari, Lattanzio Mainardi, and Giacomo Stella. The marble decoration was brought from the Septizodium (demolished by Sixtus V) and set up here by Carlo Maderno. Here are the sumptuous tombs of Sixtus V, with a statue by Valsoldo, and of Pius V with a statue by Leonardo Sormani da Sarzana. The temple-like baldachino, with four gilt bronze angels by Sebastiano Torrigiani, covers the original little Cosmatesque Chapel of the relics, redesigned by Arnolfo di Cambio (late 13C), with figures of the crêche by his assistants. In the chapel (H), at the end of the aisle (closed for restoration), is the beautiful *tomb of Cardinal Consalvo Rodriguez (died 1299), a masterpiece by Giovanni Cosmati, showing the influence of Arnolfo di Cambio. The mosaic of the Madonna enthroned, with saints, fits well with the architectonic lines of the tomb, which was completed by the beginning of the 14C.

The CONFESSIO (J), reconstructed in the 19C by Vespignani, contains a kneeling statue of Pius IX by Ignazio Jacometti. The baldacchino over the HIGH ALTAR, with four porphyry columns, is by Fuga; a porphyry sarcophagus which contains the relics of St Matthew and other martyrs serves as the high altar; the fragment of the Crib of the Infant Jesus is kept below in the Confessio in a reliquary adorned with reliefs and silver statuettes. At the foot of the sanctuary steps, in the S aisle, is the simple pavement tomb of the Bernini family, including Gian Lorenzo.

The mosaic of the APSE (K) dating from the time of Nicholas IV (1288–94), is signed by Iacopo Torriti (1290–95). It represents the *Coronation of the Virgin, with angels, saints, Nicholas IV, Cardinal Iacopo Colonna, etc. It is the culminating point of all the mosaics in the church, which commemorate the declaration at the Council of Ephesus (5C) that the Virgin was the Mother of God (Theotókos). The Virgin is seated on the same throne as Christ, a composition probably derived from the 12C mosaic in the apse of Santa Maria in Trastevere. Below, between the windows, are more mosaics by Torriti of the life of the Virgin, notably, in the centre, the Dormition of the Virgin. The four reliefs, below the windows, are from the old ciborium by Mino del Reame.

NORTH AISLE. Balancing the Sistina Chapel is the even more sumptuous **Borghese Chapel**, or CAPPELLA PAOLINA (L). This chapel, erected by Paul V, was designed by Flaminio Ponzio (1611). The best known contemporary artists were employed to decorate it, including Cigoli, Cavalier d'Arpino, Guido Reni, Baglione, and Passignano, and the sculptors Stefano Maderno, Francesco Mochi, and Nicolas Cordier. On the altar, surrounded with lapis lazuli and agate, is a Madonna and Child with crossed hands, now thought to date from the 12–13C, although it has also been attributed to a Byzantine artist working before the 10C. The tombs of Clement VIII and Paul V, with statues by Silla Longhi, are on either side. The SFORZA CHAPEL (M), erected by Giacomo della Porta to a design by Michelangelo, contains an Assumption, by Sermoneta. In the CESI CHAPEL (N), probably designed by Guidetto

Guidetti (c 1550), are two Cesi tombs, by Guglielmo della Porta and an altarpiece of the Martyrdom of St Catherine, by Sermoneta. The tomb of Cardinal Philippe de Levis de Quelus and his younger brother Archbishop Eustache (1489), above the Porta Santa (P) is in the style of Giovanni Dalmata.

Just out of Piazza Santa Maria Maggiore Via Santa Prassede leads to the inconspicuous side entrance of the church of *SANTA PRASSEDE (Pl. 5; 6; open 7.00–12.00, 16.00–18.30), built by St Paschal I in 822 and still enveloped on all sides by medieval and later buildings. An oratory is said to have been erected here about AD 150 by St Pius I, and a church is known to have been in existence here at the end of the 5C. Paschal's 9C church was restored in 1450, 1564, 1832, and 1869. The building is dedicated to Praxedes, sister of Pudentiana (see below) and daughter of Pudens, in whose house St Peter is traditionally supposed to have first found hospitality at Rome. Here in 1118 the Frangipani attacked Pope Gelasius II with arrows and stones, driving him to exile in France, where he died.

The main W entrance, on the old Via San Martino ai Monti, is kept locked: it is preceded by a medieval porch with two reversed Doric capitals. The only part of the exterior visible is the Zeno Chapel, beside the S entrance. In the INTERIOR the NAVE has sixteen granite columns and six piers supporting an architrave made up from ancient Roman fragments. The effective trompe l'oeil frescoes date from the late 16C (by Paris Nogari, Baldassarre Croce, Ciampelli, and others). In the nave a large porphyry disc with an inscription indicates the well where St Praxedes is supposed to have hidden the bones of Christian martyrs. The CHOIR is approached by steps of rosso antico.

The fine Baroque baldacchino by Francesco Ferrari (1730) partially hides the splendid 9C *mosaics (coin-operated light on right): on the entrance-arch (outer face) the New Jerusalem, whose doors are guarded by angels, (inner face) Christ and saints; on the apse-arch, the Agnus Dei with the seven golden candlesticks, the symbols of the Evangelists, and 24 Elders; in the semi-dome, Christ between (right) Saints Peter, Pudentiana, and Zeno, and (left) Saints Paul, Praxedes, and Paschal; below, the Lamb, the flock of the Faithful and a dedicatory inscription; above, the monogram of Paschal I. On the left and right of the sanctuary are six Roman *COLUMNS of very unusual design incorporating the form of acanthus and laurel leaves. In the CRYPT beneath are four palaeochristian sarcophagi, including one with the remains of Saints Praxedes and Pudentiana, and a 13C Cosmatesque altar, with a damaged fresco above of the Madonna between Saints Praxedes and Pudentiana.

In the S aisle is the Byzantine *Chapel of St Zeno (coin-operated light on left), the most important work of this date in Rome, built in 817–24 by St Paschal as a mausoleum for his mother, Theodora. The entrance is flanked by two ancient porphyry columns with 9C Ionic capitals which support a rich 1C architrave from some pagan temple, elaborately sculptured; on this rests a Roman marble urn (3C). Above is a double row of 9C mosaic busts; in the inner row, the Virgin and Child, Saints Praxedes and Pudentiana, and other saints, in the outer, Christ and the Apostles, and four saints (the lowest two perhaps added in the 13C). The exquisite vaulted interior, the only chapel in Rome entirely covered with mosaics, was known as the 'Garden of Paradise'. The pavement is perhaps the oldest known example of opus sectile. Over the door, Saints Peter and Paul uphold the throne of

God; on the right, Saints John the Evangelist, Andrew, and James, and Christ between St Paschal and Valentine(?); inside the altar-niche, Madonna between Saints Praxedes and Pudentiana; on the left, Saints Praxedes, Pudentiana, and Agnes, and four female half-lengths including Theodora (with the square nimbus). In the vault, Christ and four angels. The bases of the four supporting columns date from the 9C, except for the one on the right of the altar which is a fine 5C Roman work. In a niche on the right are fragments of a column brought from Jerusalem after the 6th Crusade (1228), and said to be that at which Christ was scourged.

In the adjoining funerary chapel is the *tomb of Cardinal Alain Coëtivy (1474) by Andrea Bregno. Outside, on a nave pillar, is the tomb of Giovanni Battista Santoni (died 1592), one of the earliest works of Bernini. At the E end of the aisle a chapel contains the tomb of Cardinal Pantaleon of Troyes (died 1286), with Cosmatesque fragments, attributed to Arnolfo di Cambio, marble architectural fragments, and a 16C Crucifix. In the second chapel in the S aisle are two paintings by Ciro Ferri, and ceiling frescoes by Borgognone.

NORTH AISLE. First chapel, altarpiece by Giuseppe Severoni; second chapel, St Charles Borromeo by Stefano Parrocel, and two paintings on the side walls by Ludovico Stern. Here is preserved the chair used by St Charles Borromeo. Third chapel, frescoes by Cavalier d'Arpino, and an altarpiece of Christ bearing the Cross, by Federico Zuccari. Against the left wall (in a frame) is the top of the table used by St Charles Borromeo. The fourth chapel was decorated with frescoes and mosaics in 1933. In the SACRISTY, the altarpiece is by Ciampelli. On the right wall is a good painting of the *Flagellation, attributed to Giulio Romano, and a Deposition by Giovanni de Vecchi. To the right a spiral staircase (no admission) leads up to the campanile with 9C wall-paintings.

Behind the apse of Santa Maria Maggiore is **Piazza dell'Esquilino** with an obelisk, nearly 15m high, set up by Sixtus V in 1587. Like its twin in Piazza del Quirinale it once stood outside the entrance to the Mausoleum of Augustus. Via Cavour (see above) cuts across the piazza. Opposite Santa Maria Maggiore Via Agostino Depretis runs NW towards Via Nazionale (see Rte 10). Via Urbana, on the left, leads in a few metres to **SANTA PUDENZIANA** (Pl. 5; 5), one of the oldest churches in Rome, thought to have been built c 390 above a Roman thermal hall of the 2C. It was rebuilt several times later, notably in 1589. The church is dedicated to Pudentiana, sister of Praxedes (see above), and daughter of the Roman senator Pudens, a legendary figure who is supposed to have given hospitality to St Peter in his house on this site. The church is now well below the level of the modern street. The FAÇADE was rebuilt and decorated in the 19C; the fine campanile probably dates from the late 12C. The good doorway preserves a beautiful medieval frieze in relief.

In the disappointing INTERIOR the nave and aisles are divided by Roman columns built up into piers. The dome was painted by Pomarancio. The precious *MOSAIC in the apse, the earliest of its kind in Rome, dates from 390. It was damaged by a 16C restoration, which removed the two outermost Apostles at each end and cut the others in half. It shows Christ enthroned holding an open book between the Apostles and two female figures representing the Church of the Jews and the Church of the Heathen crowning St Peter and St Paul. The Roman character of the figures is marked; the magisterial air of Christ recalls the representations of Jupiter, and the Apostles, in their togas, resemble senators. Above is a jewelled Cross and the symbols of the Evangelists, and buildings (including houses, thermae, and a basilica) representing Jerusalem and Golgotha.

In the chapel at the end of the left aisle an altar, presented by Cardinal Wiseman, encloses part of the legendary communion-table of St Peter; the rest of it is in St John Lateran. The marble group of Christ entrusting the keys to St Peter is by Giovanni Battista della Porta. The Cappella Caetani, opening off the aisle, is a rich Baroque work by Francesco da Volterra, finished by Carlo Maderno. The altar relief is by Pietro Paolo Olivieri. Behind the apse are fragments of frescoes and a statuette of the Good Shepherd.

Through a door in the left aisle (apply to sacristan, but usually closed) is a courtyard, showing part of 2C baths, and, up some stairs, the ORATORIUM MARIANUM (also kept locked), containing 11C frescoes and brick stamps of Hadrian's time, discovered during excavations. The building incorporates part of the baths said to have been erected by Novatian and Timotheus, the brothers of Pudentiana and Praxedes, above the so-called house of Pudens. The baths extend on to the pavement in Via Balbo; the frescoes are also visible from here. Excavations under the church in 1933 revealed Republican mosaics and walls, with a 2C house; these, however, have been closed since 1970 when they were badly flooded.

Via Urbana continues to the undulating Via Panisperna in which is the church of **San Lorenzo in Panisperna** (Pl. 5; 5), the traditional site of the martyrdom of the saint, in a delightful court of old houses, and a villa to the left (part of the Ministry of the Interior, see below). The church contains a vast fresco of the martyrdom by Pasquale Cati. The huge PALAZZO DEL VIMINALE (1920), now the Ministry of the Interior fronts Piazza del Viminale on Via Agostino Depretis.

On the parallel Via Napoli, on the corner of Via Nazionale, is the American Episcopal church of **St Paul's** ('within the Walls'; open for services on Thursday at 10.30, and on fest. 8.30, 10.30, and 18.00 or 19.30), an interesting building by George Edmund Street (1879). The conspicuous red-and-white exterior, in travertine and red brick, is in a Romanesque style (the mosaics are by George Breck, former director of the American Academy in Rome). In the interior the *mosaics in the large apse and choir are by Edward Burne-Jones. The figures in the lower register include portraits of J.P. Morgan, Archbishop Tait, General Grant, Garibaldi, and Abraham Lincoln. On both walls of the nave are ceramic tiles designed by William Morris. The stained glass windows were made by the English firm of Clayton and Bell.

In Via Viminale is the **Teatro dell'Opera**, built in 1880 by Achille Sfondrini for Domenico Costanzi. The Roman première of Verdi's 'Falstaff' was performed here in 1893. It was acquired by the Comune of Rome in 1926, and restored and enlarged by Marcello Piacentini in 1959–60. It is the most important lyric theatre in Rome.

12

St John Lateran and Santa Croce in Gerusalemme

On the edge of the Celian Hill, around the busy **PIAZZA DI SAN GIOVANNI IN LATERANO** (Pl. 10; 3) are assembled some of the most important monuments in Christian history, including the first church of Rome. Here in 1588, on a line with Via di San Giovanni and Via Merulana, Domenico Fontana set up a red granite **Obelisk**, the oldest in the city. It had been erected by Thothmes IV in front of the Temple of Ammon at Thebes (15C BC), and was brought to Rome by Constantius II (357) to decorate the Circus Maximus, where it was discovered in three pieces in 1587. It is the tallest obelisk in existence (31m high, 47m with the pedestal), though one metre had to be sawn off during its reconstruction. On the W side of the square is the OSPEDALE DI SAN GIOVANNI, the main hospital in Rome for emergencies ('pronto soccorso'; car accidents, etc.). Excavations in 1959–64 beneath the hospital revealed remains of a villa, thought to be that of Domizia Lucilla, mother of Marcus Aurelius.

The church of *ST JOHN LATERAN (*San Giovanni in Laterano*; Pl. 10; 3; open 7.00–18.00; summer 7.00–19.00) is the cathedral of Rome and of the world ('Omnium urbis et orbis Ecclesiarum Mater et Caput'). Founded by Constantine, it was the first Christian basilica to be constructed in Rome. The original five-aisled church with an apse, on a basilican plan, was probably built between 314 and 318, and was dedicated to the Redeemer and later to Saints John the Baptist and John the Evangelist. It served as a model for all subsequent Christian churches. Partly ruined by the Vandals, it was restored by St Leo the Great (440–61) and Hadrian I (772–95) and, after the earthquake of 896, by Sergius III (904–11). Nicholas IV (1288–92) enlarged and embellished the building to such an extent that it was considered the wonder of the age; Dante described it with admiration when Boniface VIII proclaimed the first Holy Year in 1300 from the loggia of the E façade.

The church was destroyed by fire in 1308 and rebuilt by Clement V (1305–14) soon afterwards; it was decorated by Giotto. In 1360 it was burnt down again and its ruin was lamented by Petrarch. Under Urban V (1362–70) and Gregory XI (1370–78) it was entirely rebuilt by the Sienese Giovanni di Stefano. Martin V (1417–31), Eugenius IV (1431–47) and their successors added to its splendour (Sixtus V employing Domenico Fontana, and Clement VIII, Giacomo della Porta). In 1646–49 Innocent X commissioned Borromini to rebuild the church yet again, and in 1734 Clement XII added the E façade. The ancient apse was entirely reconstructed in 1875–85 and the mosaics reset after the original designs.

The basilica derives its name from the rich patrician family of Plautius Lateranus, who, having been implicated in the conspiracy of the Pisoni, was deprived of his property and put to death by Nero. Recent excavations in the neighbouring Via Aradam have revealed a large Roman building thought to be the house of the Pisoni and Laterani expropriated by Nero. The property afterwards passed to Constantine as the dowry of his wife Fausta. In this 'Domus Faustae' church meetings were probably held as early as 313. The Emperor presented it, together with the land occupied by the barracks (excavated in 1934–38 beneath the nave of the present basilica) built in the 2C for his private horseguards, 'the Equites Singulares', to St Melchiades (pope 311–14), for the purpose of building a church for the see of Rome.

Until 1870 the popes were crowned here, and it has been the seat of five General Councils: in 1123, 1139, 1179, 1215, and 1512. Under the Lateran Treaty of 11 February 1929, this basilica, with those of San Paolo fuori le Mura and Santa Maria Maggiore, was accorded the privilege of extraterritoriality. After the ratification of the treaty the pope, for the first time since 1870, left the seclusion of the Vatican. On 24 June 1929, Pius XI officiated at St John Lateran, and the annual ceremony of blessing the people from the loggia was later resumed. The Pope traditionally attends the Maundy Thursday celebrations in the basilica.

Exterior. The NORTH FRONT, on Piazza di San Giovanni in Laterano, built by Domenico Fontana in 1586, has a portico of two tiers. It was damaged in a bomb explosion in 1993, and is covered for restoration. Beneath it, on the left, is a statue of Henry IV of France, by Nicolas Cordier (c 1610), erected in gratitude for his gifts to the chapter. The two towers behind date from the time of Pius IV (1560). The principal or EAST FRONT, overlooking the vast Piazza di Porta San Giovanni, is a theatrical composition by Alessandro Galilei (1734–36). It consists of a two-storeyed portico surmounted by an attic with sixteen colossal statues of Christ with the Apostles and saints. On Maundy Thursday the pope gives his benediction from the central loggia. Beneath the PORTICO, the bronze central doors were first used for the Curia, and later the church of Sant' Adriano in the Forum. On the left (A) is a statue of Constantine, from his Baths on the Quirinal. On the right is the entrance (only open on the first Sunday of the month) to the Museo Storico Vaticano in the Lateran Palace (see below).

The **interior**, 130m long, with two aisles on either side of the nave, preserves in part its original 4C proportions, although it was entirely remodelled by Borromini in 1646–49. In the niches of the massive piers which encase the verde antico pillars are colossal statues of the apostles made in the early 18C by Lorenzo Ottoni, Camillo Rusconi, Giuseppe Mazzuoli, Pierre Legros, Pierre Monnot, Angelo de Rossi, and Francesco Moratti. Above them are stuccoes designed by Algardi with scenes from the Old and New Testaments. Higher still are paintings of prophets (1718) by Domenico Maria Muratori, Marco Benefial, Giuseppe Nicola Nasini, Giovanni Odazzi, Giovanni Paolo Melchiorri, Sebastiano Conca, Benedetto Luti, Francesco Trevisani, Andrea Procaccini, Luigi Garzi, Giuseppe Chiari, and Pierleone Ghezzi. The rich ceiling is by Flaminio Boulanger and Vico di Raffaele, and the marble pavement is of Cosmatesque design.

The outer aisles were also decorated by Borromini, and the funerary monuments reconstructed and enclosed in elegant Baroque frames. RIGHT AISLES. INNER AISLE. On the nave piers: Boniface VIII proclaiming the Jubilee of 1300 (B), a fragment of a fresco from the exterior loggia now considered to be by the hand of Giotto; cenotaph of Sylvester II (died 1003; C), by the Hungarian sculptor William Fraknoi (1909); beneath is a curious medieval memorial slab to the pope; tomb (D) of Alexander III, the pope of the Lombard League; tomb (E) of Sergius IV, with a medieval figure of a Pope; tomb (F) of Cardinal Ranuccio Farnese, by Vignola. In the OUTER AISLE, enclosed in Borromini's Baroque frames, tomb (J) of Cardinal Antonio de Chaves (1447) attributed to Isaia da Pisa, and tomb (H) of Cardinal Casati (1290), by the Cosmati. Over the window-screen outside the Cappella Massimo (I) is a fragment of the original altar with a statuette of St James, attributed to Andrea Bregno. The CAPPELLA TORLONIA (K), richly decorated by Raimondi (1850), is closed by a fine iron balustrade, and has a sculptured altarpiece (Descent from the Cross) by Pietro Tenerani. Beyond is the tomb (L) of Giulio Acquaviva (1574), made cardinal at the age of 20 by Pius V. The tomb of Paolo Mellini (1527) is in the embrasure of the Porta Santa (M; opened only in Holy Years), with a damaged fresco.

LEFT AISLES. At the beginning of the OUTER AISLE (K) is a sarcophagus with the cast of a recumbent figure of Cardinal Riccardo degli Annibaldi (1276) by Arnolfo di Cambio (the original is now exhibited in the cloisters, see below). The CAPPELLA CORSINI (L), a graceful early 18C structure by Alessandro Galilei, contains above its altar a mosaic copy of Guido Reni's painting of St Andrea Corsini; on the left, tomb of Clement XII (Lorenzo Corsini; died 1740), a porphyry sarcophagus from the Pantheon, and in the vault below (apply to sacristan), a Pietà by Antonio Montauti. In the aisle, tombs of the Archpriest Gerardo da Parma (1061; U) and of Cardinal Bernardo Caracciolo (died 1255; V); at the end, beyond the pretty CAPPELLA LANCELLOTTI (W), by Francesco da Volterra (1585–90, rebuilt 1675 by Giovanni Antonio de Rossi), is the tomb of Cardinal Casanate (1707; X), founder of the library that bears his name.

The TRANSEPTS (closed during restoration work in 1993 after damage from a bomb explosion) were built under Clement VIII (1592–1605) by Giacomo della Porta, and the large frescoes of the conversion of Constantine, his gift to the pope, and the building of the basilica, completed in 1600 under the direction of Cavalier d'Arpino (by Giovanni Battista Ricci, Paris Nogari, Cristoforo Roncalli, Orazio Gentileschi, Cesare Nebbia, Giovanni Baglione, and Bernardo Cesari). In the central space is the PAPAL ALTAR, reconstructed by Pius IX, containing many relics, including the heads of Saints Peter and Paul, and part of St Peter's wooden altar-table. Above is the Gothic *baldacchino by Giovanni di Stefano (1367), frescoed by Barna da Siena. In the enclosure in front of the confessio (M) is the *tomb-slab of Martin V (died 1431), by Simone Ghini.

In the right transept are the great organ (1598; by Luca Blasi), supported by two columns of giallo antico, and the tomb (N) of Innocent III (died 1216), by Giuseppe Lucchetti (1891), erected when Leo XIII brought the ashes of his great predecessor from Perugia. In the corner, to the right in the little Cappella del Crocifisso (O), is a kneeling statue of Boniface IX (Cosmatesque; late 14C). In the left transept is the tomb of Leo XIII (P), by Giulio Tadolini (1907). At the end is the Altar of the Holy Sacrament (Q), by Pier Paolo Olivieri (from the time of Clement VIII), flanked by four antique bronze columns. On the right is the CAPPELLA DEL CORO (R), with fine stalls of c 1625.

The APSE was reconstructed, at the expense of Leo XIII, by Virginio and Francesco Vespignani in 1885 when the fine apse mosaics were destroyed and substituted by a copy. The original mosaics were designed by Iacopo Torriti and Iacopo da Camerino (1288–94) from an antique model. Beneath the Head of Christ (the copy of a mosaic fabled to have appeared miraculously at the consecration of the church) the Dove descends on the bejewelled Cross. From the hill on which it stands four rivers flow to quench the thirst of the faithful. On either side are (left) the Virgin with Nicholas IV and Saints Peter and Paul, and (right) Saints John the Baptist, John the Evangelist, and Andrew; the figures of St Francis of Assisi (left) and St Anthony of Padua (right) were added by Nicholas IV. At their feet flows the Jordan. Kneeling at the feet of the Apostles (in the frieze below) are the tiny figures of Torriti and Camerino.

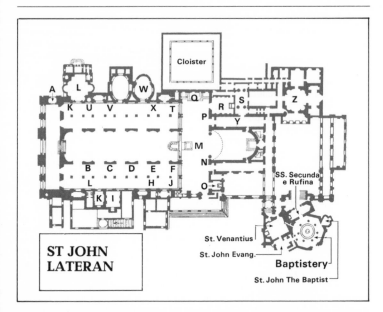

Cloister

A L W Q S Z
K U V X T R P Y
M
B C D E F N
L H J O
K I SS. Secunda e Rufina

St. Venantius

ST JOHN LATERAN

St. John Evang.

Baptistery

St. John The Baptist

The doorway beneath Leo XIII's tomb admits to the SACRISTY (Z), reached by a corridor (Y) containing the tombs of Andrea Sacchi and the Cavalier d'Arpino, and (behind the apse) two fine statues of St Peter and St Paul by Deodato di Cosma. On the left is the OLD SACRISTY (S), with a beautiful Annunciation by Marcello Venusti, after Michelangelo.

In the left aisle (T) is the entrance to the peaceful *cloister (open 9.00–17.00, 9.00–18.00 in summer), the masterpiece of Iacopo and Pietro Vassalletto (c 1222–32), a magnificent example of Cosmatesque art. The columns, some plain and some twisted, are adorned with mosaics and have fine capitals. The frieze is exquisite. In the centre is a well-head dating from the 9C. Many interesting fragments from the ancient basilica are displayed around the cloister walls. On the NORTH SIDE are various pieces of Cosmati work. EAST SIDE: 27. Large marble inscription (1072) recording the restoration of the basilica by Pope Alexander II; 38. Papal throne, an antique marble chair with Cosmati decorations from the time of Pope Nicholas IV. A door from this walk leads into the little MUSEUM which contains two Florentine tapestries (1595–1608), an early 16C ex-voto of Tommaso Inghirami, numerous gifts, including a French cope, given to Pius IX, the *cope of Boniface VIII (13C English workmanship), and a model of the Colonna dell'Immacolata (1854) in Piazza di Spagna. At the end of the east side is the tomb effigy of Giovanni Cardelli who died in 1465.

SOUTH SIDE. 73. 6C head of a Byzantine empress (on a 2C Roman bust; removed); 84. Inscription recording the papal bull of Sixtus IV (1475); 81. Two half-columns decorated with palm leaves. The *tomb of Cardinal Riccardo Annibaldi, has been removed for restoration. It was the first important work of Arnolfo di Cambio in Rome (c 1276), and has been reconstructed from fragments, which include reliefs and the recumbent statue. 103. Roman sarcophagus, with four portraits; various pavement tomb-slabs, carved in relief. WEST SIDE: 167–68. Four small columns supporting a marble slab; 188. Head from the tomb of Lorenzo Valla (died 1465); bronze door with an inscription of 1196. NORTH SIDE. 201. Roman cippus, reused in the 16C; 229. Circular altar dating from the 5C AD.

Beside the N front of the basilica, in the SW corner of Piazza di San Giovanni in Laterano, is the ***BAPTISTERY OF ST JOHN**, or *San Giovanni in Fonte*, built by Constantine c 315–24, though not, as legend states, the scene of his baptism as the first Christian emperor (337). It is a centrally planned octagonal building, although the original baptistery, designed for total immersion, and derived from classical models, may have been circular. It was remodelled by Sixtus III (432–40), and its design was copied in many subsequent baptisteries. It was restored again by Hadrian III in 884.

In the INTERIOR (closed for restoration after damage by a bomb explosion in 1993, but usually open 8.00–12.00, 16.00–18.00; winter 8.00–12.00, 15.00–17.00; the chapels are unlocked by the sacristan) are eight columns of porphyry erected by Sixtus III; they support an architrave which bears eight smaller white marble columns. In the centre is the green basalt font. The 17C decorations were added by Urban VIII, and the harsh frescoes of scenes from the life of St John the Baptist on the drum of the cupola are modern copies of works by Andrea Sacchi. The CHAPEL OF ST JOHN THE BAPTIST was founded by the martyred pope, St Hilary (461–68). It preserves its original doors (once thought to come from the Baths of Caracalla), which resound musically when opened. The CHAPEL OF SAINTS CYRIAN AND JUSTINA (or SAINTS SECUNDA AND RUFINA) occupied the narthex of Sixtus III, altered to its present form in 1154. Over the door is a relief of the Crucifixion after Andrea Bregno (1492). In one of the apses is a beautiful 5C *mosaic with vine tendrils on a brilliant blue ground. High up on the wall can be seen a fragment of the original marble intarsia decoration of the baptistery. A door leads out into a courtyard from where can be seen the outer face of the narthex with two beautiful huge antique columns supporting a fine Roman architrave.

The CHAPEL OF ST VENANTIUS, added by Pope John IV in 640 contains mosaics commissioned by Pope Theodore I (642–49): in the apse, the head of Christ flanked by angels and the Madonna with Saints and Pope Theodore, and on the triumphal arch the martyrs whose relics Pope John brought from Dalmatia and (high up) views of Jerusalem and Bethlehem. Remains of 2C Roman baths built above a 1C villa, with a mosaic pavement, may also be seen here. The structure of the original baptistery can be seen in the walls and beneath the apse. The CHAPEL OF ST JOHN THE EVANGELIST, dedicated by St Hilary, with bronze doors of 1196, is decorated with a vault *mosaic (5C) of the Lamb surrounded by symbolic birds and flowers. The altar has alabaster columns. On the left, Luigi Capponi, St Leo praying to St John.

Adjoining the basilica, and facing Piazza di Porta San Giovanni, is the **LATERAN PALACE** (Pl. 10; 3), used by the popes before the move to Avignon in 1309. The old palace, which dated from the time of Constantine, was almost destroyed in the fire of 1308 which devastated St John Lateran. On the return from Avignon in 1377 the Holy See was transferred to the Vatican. In 1586 Sixtus V demolished or displaced what the fire had left and ordered Domenico Fontana to carry out a complete reconstruction. It was intended to make the new Lateran the summer palace of the popes, but the Quirinal was preferred. The interior was restored in 1838. Under the Lateran Treaty of 1929, the palace was recognised as an integral part of the Vatican City. It is now the seat of the Rome Vicariate and offices of the Rome diocese. Since 1991 the **Museo Storico Vaticano** has been housed here (entrance from the portico at the main (E) façade of the basilica of San Giovanni in Laterano; opening times, see p 47). The Papal Apartments, with late-Mannerist frescoes (by Giovanni Guerra and others) and some good ceilings contain interesting 17C and 18C tapestries (Gobelins and Roman works made in San Michele). The historical museum is displayed on three sides of a loggia. It illustrates the history of the Papacy from the 16C to the present day, with historical paintings, etc.; Papal ceremonies of the past; and the Papal guards disbanded by Paul VI in 1970.

On the E side of Piazza di Porta San Giovanni are three survivals from the old Lateran Palace: the Scala Santa, the Sancta Sanctorum, and the Triclinium. Domenico Fontana, architect of the new Lateran, designed the building in 1589 which houses the **Scala Santa** and **Chapel of the Sancta Sanctorum** (open 6.15–12.15, 15.00–18.45; 15.30–19.15 in summer). The staircase from the old Lateran Palace was, from the 15C, identified with the staircase of Pilate's house which Christ descended after his condemnation. A legend related how it had been brought from Jerusalem to Rome by St Helena, mother of Constantine. The twenty-eight Tyrian marble steps are protected by boards and only worshippers on their knees are allowed to ascend them. In the vestibule are 19C sculptures by Ignazio Jacometti. The vault and walls of the Scala Santa and the side staircases were decorated at the end of the 16C under the direction of Giovanni Guerra and Cesare Nebbia.

At the top is the *Sancta Sanctorum (or Chapel of St Lawrence), the private chapel of the pope which preserved the most sacred relics, removed from the old Lateran Palace. Mentioned in the *Liber Pontificalis* in the 8C, it was rebuilt in 1278 and is never open, but usually visible through the grating. It is not at present visible since it is undergoing the first restoration in its history, during which the conservative Roman frescoes and mosaics carried out for Pope Nicholas III (1277–80) have been cleaned. Protected by a silver tabernacle presented by Innocent III is the relic which gives the chapel its particular sanctity. This is an ancient painting on wood of Christ which could date from as early as the 5C (many times repainted and restored). It is said to have been begun by St Luke and an angel: hence its name 'Acheiropoeton', or the picture made without hands. The precious relics and their reliquaries are exhibited in the Vatican Museums. The chapel has a beautiful Cosmatesque pavement. The other rooms in the building have been occupied by a Passionist convent since 1953.

To the E of the Scala Santa is the **Tribune** erected by Fuga for Benedict XIV in 1743 and decorated with good copies of the mosaics from the TRICLINIUM OF LEO III, the banqueting hall of the old Lateran Palace. In the centre, Christ sending forth the Apostles to preach the Gospel; on the left, Christ giving the keys to St Sylvester and the labarum, or standard of the Cross, to Constantine; on the right, St Peter giving the papal stole to Leo III and the banner of Christianity to Charlemagne. A fragment of the original mosaic is in the Museum of Christian Art in the Vatican.

The huge Piazza di Porta San Giovanni is often used for political demonstrations, and here the festival of San Giovanni is celebrated with a traditional fair on the night of 23–24 June. **Porta San Giovanni** (Pl. 10; 3), built in 1574 by Giacomo del Duca, superseded the ancient PORTA ASINARIA, on the site of the PORTA COELIMONTANA of the Servian Wall. To the W of the modern gateway, between two fine towers, may be seen the old gate with its vantage-court, excavated in 1954. Outside the gate the busy Via Appia Nuova leads out of the city through the extensive southern suburbs towards the Alban Hills.

From Piazza di Porta San Giovanni Viale Carlo Felice leads E. The first turning on the left is Via Conte Rosso, which runs N to the VILLA WOLKON-SKY, formerly the German Embassy, and now the residence of the British ambassador. The Embassy has been transferred to its old site in Via Venti Settembre. Viale Carlo Felice ends in Piazza Santa Croce in Gerusalemme, a busy traffic centre, in an unattractive part of the city. Here is the church of **SANTA CROCE IN GERUSALEMME** (Pl. 10; 2), one of the 'Seven Churches' of Rome, occupied by Cistercians since 1561. According to tradition, this church was founded by Constantine's mother, St Helena. It was in fact probably built some time after 326 within part of the large Imperial palace erected for St Helena in the early 3C on the SW extremity of the city. The principal edifice was known as the *Sessorium*, and the church took the name of *Basilica Sessoriana*. Here was enshrined a relic of the True Cross saved in Jerusalem by St Helena. It was rebuilt in 1144 by Lucius II, who added the campanile, and completely modernised by Benedict XIV in 1743–44.

The impressive theatrical *FAÇADE and oval *VESTIBULE were built to a very original design by Domenico Gregorini and Pietro Passalacqua in 1744. The 18C INTERIOR has the nave and aisles separated by granite columns, some of them boxed in pilasters. The Cosmatesque pavement was restored in 1933. The vault paintings of St Helena in Glory, and the Apparition of the Cross towards the E end are by Corrado Giaquinto (1744). Near the W door is the epitaph of Benedict VII (died 983), who is buried here. The second S altarpiece of St Bernard introducing Vittore IV to Innocent II is by Carlo Maratta. Above the high altar, with the basalt tomb which encloses the remains of Saints Caesarius and Anastasius, is a graceful 18C baldacchino. In the apse is a large fresco cycle of the Invention of the Cross attributed to Antoniazzo Romano. The tomb on the E wall of Cardinal Quiñones (died 1540) is by Iacopo Sansovino.

A stairway at the end of the right aisle leads down through the GREGOR-IAN CHAPEL, built by Cardinal Carvajal in 1523, with an early 17C Roman bas-relief of the Pietà, to the CHAPEL OF ST HELENA (closed for restoration in 1993). It contains a statue of the saint, originally a figure of Juno found at Ostia, copied from the Barberini statue in the Vatican. The altar is reserved for the pope and the titular cardinal of the basilica. The vault *mosaic, the original design of which is probably by Melozzo (c 1480), was restored by Baldassarre Peruzzi and later by Francesco Zucchi. It represents Christ and the Evangelists, Saints Peter and Paul, St Sylvester (who died here at Mass), St Helena, and Cardinal Carvajal. The fragments of 12C frescoes found here were detached in 1968. At the end of the left aisle in the CHAPEL OF THE RELICS, by Florestano Di Fausto (1930), are preserved the pieces of the True Cross, together with other greatly venerated relics. There are long term plans to open a small MUSEUM here to exhibit fragments of 12C frescoes detached from the roof of the nave, a 14C fresco of the Crucifixion from the Chapel of the Crucifix, and French 14C statues of Saints Peter and Paul formerly in the Gregorian Chapel.

On the right of the basilica are remains of the AMPHITHEATRUM CASTRENSE (no adm), a graceful edifice, built of brick by Heliogabalus or Alexander Severus for amusements of the Imperial court, incorporated with the Aurelian Wall by Honorius. To the left of the basilica, in the gardens of the ex-Caserma dei Granatieri rises a large ruined apsidal hall known since the Renaissance as the 'TEMPLE OF VENUS AND CUPID'. It was built in the early 4C by Maxentius or Constantine.

In the barracks here are two military museums, and a fine **Museum of Musical Instruments** (adm see p 47), inaugurated in 1974, with a remarkably representative display dating from Roman times to the 19C, most of it collected by the tenor Evangelista Gorga (1865–1957). The attractive building of c 1903, in the Art Nouveau style, looks N to a section of the Aurelian Wall. On the other side of the building, near the basilica, are more Roman ruins. The collection is beautifully displayed in rooms on the first floor (some of which are sometimes closed because of lack of custodians).

ROOM 1. Archaeological material, including Roman works in terracotta and bronze. ROOM 3. Exotic instruments from the Far East, America, Africa, and Oceania. ROOM 4. Instruments used for folk-dances and folk-songs made in Naples, Russia, Spain, etc. In the centre of ROOM 5 is the pianoforte built by Bartolomeo Cristofori in 1722. Also displayed here are other 18C pianos, and a late 17C German clavichord. ROOM 6. Military instruments and instruments used by street musicians: hunting horns; 19C walking sticks which could become violins and flutes; a portable 18C harpsichord; 19C processional organs; hurdy-gurdies; Aeolian harps; and accordians. ROOM 7. Church music (an organ, bells, and a 'marina' trumpet). ROOM 9. A unique organ built by Montesanti, with pipes and reeds of 1777; a glass harmonica; spinets, and lutes. ROOMS 11–15 are arranged in roughly chronological order with instruments from the 11C to 18C. ROOM 11 contains the oldest known German harpsichord made in 1537 by Mueller. In ROOM 13 is the elaborate Barberini harp. ROOMS 16–18 contains mechanical instruments (musical boxes, etc.).

To the E of the barracks, across Viale Castrense and outside the Aurelian Wall, excavations in 1959 revealed remains of the extensive CIRCUS VARIANUS, wellpreserved, and dating from the reign of Heliogabalus (218–22). From Piazza Santa Croce Via di Santa Croce leads NW towards Via Conte Verde and Piazza Vittorio Emanuele. On the left it passes the end of the Villa Wolkonsky (see above). Via Statilia, skirting the N side of the villa, runs parallel to a fine series of arches of the AQUEDUCT OF NERO, an extension of the Acqua Claudia (see below), and built by Nero to provide water for his various constructions on the Palatine and Oppian Hills.

The ugly Via Eleniana leads N from Piazza Santa Croce to the large and busy PIAZZA DI PORTA MAGGIORE, in an unattractive part of the city. On the W side of this square is the beginning of Via Statilia, with some arches of the Acqua Claudia, restored to carry the Aqua Marcia (1923). On the E side is the **Porta Maggiore**, or *Porta Prenestina* (Pl. 10; 2), built by Claudius in AD 52, formed by the archways carrying the Acqua Claudia and the Anio Novus over the Via Prenestina and the Via Casilina (or Labicana, see below). The Porta Prenestina was a gate in Aurelian's Wall; it was restored by Honorius in 405. The ancient Via Prenestina and Via Labicana which pass under the arches can still be seen. Also here are foundations of a guard-house added by Honorius. On the outside of the gate, is the unusual **Tomb of the Baker** (M. Virgilius Eurysaces, a public contractor, and his wife Atistia), discovered in 1838. This pretentious monument, built entirely of travertine, dates from c 30 BC. The circular openings represent the mouths of a baker's oven; above is a frieze illustrating the stages of bread-making.

The **Acqua Claudia** and the **Anio Novus**, or *Acqua Aniene Nuova*, were two of the finest Roman aqueducts. Both were begun by Caligula in AD 38; the Acqua Claudia was completed by Claudius in AD 47, and the Anio Novus in 52. They were restored by Vespasian in 71 and by Titus in 81. The water of the Acqua Claudia was derived from two copious springs near Sublaqueum (Subiaco); its length was 74 kilometres. The Anio Novus was the longest of all the aqueducts (95km) and the highest; some of its arches were 33m high. Outside the Porta Maggiore are two main roads: VIA PRENESTINA on the left, leading to Palestrina (Praeneste), and, on the right, VIA CASILINA, anciently Via Labicana. Via Casilina passes through Labico (Labicum), which gave it its original name.

At 17 Via Prenestina, about 130m from the gate, is the entrance to the *Basilica di Porta Maggiore** (admission only with special permission, see p 45), unearthed in 1916. It is approached by a modern staircase beneath the railway. This remarkable building of the 1C AD, in near perfect preservation. has the rudimentary form of a cult building, with a central porch, an apse at the east end, a nave and two arched aisles with no clerestory. This became the basic plan of the Christian church. The ceiling and walls are covered with exquisite stuccoes representing landscapes, mythological subjects, scenes of early childhood, etc.; the principal design of the apse is thought to depict the Death of Sappho. The purpose for which the building was built is still under discussion: it may have been a type of funerary hall, or have been used by a mystical sect, perhaps the Pythagoreans.

From Piazza di Porta Maggiore, the long and straight Via Giovanni Giolitti runs parallel to the railway and Stazione Termini towards Piazza dei Cinquecento (over 1km from Porta Maggiore). About 300 metres from Porta Maggiore it passes on the right the so-called **Temple of Minerva Medica** (Pl. 6; 7), now surrounded by ugly buildings. This large ten-sided domed hall is a remarkable survival from the 4C (the ruin is conspicuous on the approach to Rome by train). It was probably the nymphaeum of the GARDENS OF LICINIUS, but was given its present name after the discovery inside it of a statue of Minerva with a serpent, which probably occupied one of the nine niches round its walls. The cupola, which collapsed in 1828, served as a model for many classical buildings.

Beyond the temple Viale Manzoni leads left past the end of Via di Porta Maggiore. Near Via Luzzatti is the entrance to the **Hypogeum of the Aureli**, a series of tomb-chambers discovered in 1919. For admission, apply to the Pontificia Commissione di Archeologia Sacra, 1 Via Napoleone III. On the floor of the first room is a mosaic dedication showing that the vault belonged to freedmen of the Gens Aurelia. The well-preserved wall-paintings (AD 200–250), include the Good Shepherd, the Christian symbol of the peacock, and some landscapes of obscure significance, suggesting a mixture of Christian and gnostic beliefs.

Via Giovanni Giolitti continues to (right) **Santa Bibiana** (Pl. 6; 5), about 600 metres from Porta Maggiore. This was a 5C church rebuilt by Bernini in 1625, interesting as his first architectural work. It contains eight columns from pagan temples, including (left of entrance) that at which St Bibiana was supposed to have been flogged to death. On the architrave are frescoes by (right) Agostino Ciampelli and (left) Pietro da Cortona. The *statue of the saint, set in an aedicula above the altar, is a fine early work by Bernini.

Just beyond on the left is Piazza Guglielmo Pepe, in which are six arches of an ancient aqueduct. Via Santa Bibiana leads under the railway to PORTA SAN LORENZO (Pl. 6; 5). Immediately N, in the Aurelian Wall, is PORTA TIBURTINA, built by Augustus and restored by Honorius in 403. The triple attic carried the waters of the Acquae Marcia, Tepula, and Julia. Farther N, in Piazzale Sisto V, is an arch formed out of a section of the Aurelian Wall by Pius V and Sixtus V at the end of the 16C to carry the waters of the Acqua Felice.

13

The Oppian and Celian Hills

The **Oppian Hill** (Pl. 4; 8), just NE of the Colosseum, is one of the four summits of the Esquiline and one of the seven hills of the primitive Septimontium of Rome. On its slopes is the PARCO OPPIO, with its main entrance in Via Labicana. Near the entrance of the park are traces of the BATHS OF TITUS and the extensive ruins of a wing of the *DOMUS AUREA of Nero (Pl. 4; 8; Nero's 'Golden House'), overlaid by those of the BATHS OF TRAJAN. This has been closed, partly for conservation reasons, since 1984; for special permission to visit, see p 45. Excavations unearthed the vast ramifications of the palace buildings which were buried by the construction of the baths. These subterranean rooms were known to and visited by artists of the Renaissance, who examined the murals and scratched their names on the walls. The type of decoration known as 'grottesques' takes its name from the Domus Aurea, and clearly inspired Raphael when decorating his Loggia in the Vatican.

Nero already had one palace, the Domus Transitoria on the Palatine, which was destroyed in the fire of AD 64. Even before its destruction he had planned to build another palace (the Domus Aurea) which, with its outbuildings and gardens, was to extend over part, or all of the Palatine, much of the Celian and part of the Oppian Hills, an area of about 50 hectares which invaded the heart of the city. He is reputed to have commented when it was completed that at last he was beginning to be housed like a human being. He employed Severus as architect, and Fabullus as painter, and produced what has been called the first expression of the Roman revolution in architecture. The understanding and use of vaulted spaces in the palace was quite new. It is thought that nearly all the rooms were vaulted, although some of the ceilings in the wing that survives are no longer intact. The atrium or vestibule, with the colossal statue of the emperor (see Rte 4), was on the summit of the Velia; the main part of the palace was on the site of the so-called Domus Tiberiana on the Palatine (Rte 3); the gardens, with their lake, were in the valley now occupied by the Colosseum.

This grandiose edifice did not long survive the tyrant's death in 68, and his successors hastily demolished or covered up his buildings, and restored the huge area they had occupied to the city. In 72 Vespasian obliterated the lake to build the Colosseum; Domitian (81–96) buried the constructions on the Palatine (except the cryptoporticus) to make room for the Flavian palaces. Trajan (98–117) destroyed the houses on the Oppian to build his baths; and Hadrian (117–78) built his Temple of Venus and Rome on the site of the atrium, and moved the statue.

Of the Baths of Titus, which occupied the SW corner of the Oppian Hill, hardly anything remains. The much larger BATHS OF TRAJAN are better preserved. There survive some remains of the central hall towards the SE, with exedrae and parts of the wall that surrounded the baths. A well-preserved feature was formerly part of the Domus Aurea, adapted by Trajan; this is a reservoir called 'Le Sette Sale' (see Rte 11). The architect of the baths was Apollodorus of Damascus, whose designs were a model for later builders of Imperial baths.

The remains of the Domus Aurea include a NYMPHAEUM, with an interesting vault mosaic (the only one surviving in the rooms of the palace so far excavated) depicting Ulysses and Polyphemus, and a long CRYPTOPOR-TICUS decorated with grotesques, on the vault of which artists left their signatures in the 16C. The most important group of rooms are designed around an octagonal ATRIUM, which has a particularly original design and structure. It is lit from the side rooms as well as from the wide central opening in the dome. The southern prospect of the rooms would have opened on to an extensive garden, looking across the valley where the Colosseum now stands. A great porphyry vase and the famous Laocoön (both now in the Vatican) were found here in the 16C. Numerous rooms have frescoed decorations, including one with paintings of birds, and another with well-preserved perspectives, and scenes of Rome. Painted stucco decorations as well as some mosaic floors also survive.

At the bottom of the hill, on the E side of the Colosseum and between Via Labicana and Via San Giovanni in Laterano (Pl. 9; 1) are remains of the LUDUS MAGNUS, the principal training school for gladiators constructed by Domitian, and excavated in 1960–61. Part of the curved wall of a miniature amphitheatre used for training can be seen. Via San Giovanni in Laterano continues past a new office block (beneath which were found remains of houses built before AD 64 with fine mosaics) to *SAN CLEMENTE (Pl. 9; 2; open 9.00–12.00, 15.30–18.00; fest. 10.00–12.30, 15.30–18.00), one of the best preserved of the medieval basilicas in Rome. It is dedicated to St Clement, the fourth pope. It consists of two churches superimposed, raised above a large early Imperial building owned possibly by the family of T. Flavius Clemens.

The LOWER CHURCH, mentioned by St Jerome in 392, was the scene of papal councils under St Zosimus in 417 and under St Symmachus in 499. Restored in the 8C and 9C, it was destroyed in 1084 during the sack of Rome by the soldiers of Robert Guiscard. Eight centuries later, in 1857, it was rediscovered by Father Mullooly, prior of the adjoining convent of Irish Dominicans, and was excavated in 1861. The UPPER CHURCH was begun in 1108 by Paschal II, who used the decorative marbles from the ruins of the old church. In the 18C it was restored by Carlo Stefano Fontana for Clement XI.

The **upper church** is entered by the side door in Via San Giovanni in Laterano (B). The façade (A) is turned towards the E and looks onto an atrium with Ionic columns surrounding a courtyard with a little fountain, outside of which is a gabled porch of four 12C columns. The typically basilican INTERIOR has a nave with a large apse, and aisles separated by two rows of seven columns, and a pre-Cosmatesque pavement. The walls of the nave were decorated with a cycle of paintings in 1713–19 under the direction of Giuseppe Chiari, who also executed the Triumph of St Clement on the ceiling. The SCHOLA CANTORUM (C), from the lower church, contains two ambones, candelabrum, and a reading-desk, all characteristic elements in the arrangement of a basilican interior. The *screen of the choir and sanctuary, with its transennae, marked with the monogram of John II (533–35), the choir raised above the confessio, the high altar with its tabernacle, the stalls of the clergy, and the bishop's throne, are also well preserved. In the PRESBYTERY is the delicate baldacchino (D) borne by columns of pavonazzetto.

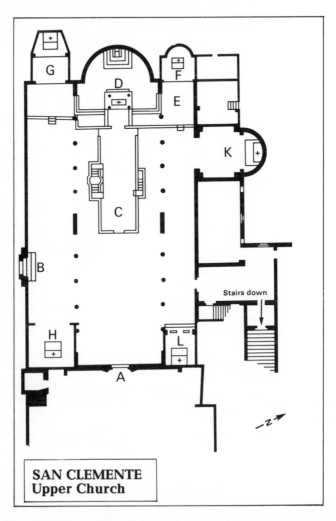

**SAN CLEMENTE
Upper Church**

The early 12C *mosaics in the apse are especially fine; on the triumphal arch, Christ and the symbols of the Evangelists, and below (on the right), Saints Peter and Clement, with the boat and oars, Jeremiah, and Jerusalem, and on the left, Saints Paul and Laurence, Isaiah, and Bethlehem. In the apse-vault, the dome of Heaven with the Hand of God above the Crucifix. The twelve doves on the Cross represent the Apostles. Beside the Cross are the Madonna and St John. From the foot of the Cross springs a vine with acanthus leaves, encircling figures of St John the Baptist, the Doctors of the Church, and other saints, while the rivers of Paradise flow down from the Cross, quenching the thirst of the faithful (represented by stags) and watering the pastures of the Christian flock. Below are the Lamb of God and twelve companions. On the apse wall below are impressive large 14C frescoed figures of Christ, the Virgin, and the Apostles. To the right is a beautiful wall-tabernacle, probably by Arnolfo di Cambio.

In the RIGHT AISLE (E), tombs of Archbishop Giovanni Francesco Brusati, by Luigi Capponi (1485), and of *Cardinal Bartolomeo Roverella, by Andrea Bregno and Giovanni Dalmata (1476). In the BAPTISTERY (F), late 16C frescoes attributed to Iacopo Zucchi, and a 16C statue of St John the Baptist; in the chapel of St Cyril (K), Madonna, attributed to Sassoferrato (one of several versions). In the chapel by the W door (L) are three paintings of scenes from the life of St Dominic, attributed to Sebastiano Conca.

LEFT AISLE. In the chapel to the left of the presbytery (G), Our Lady of the Rosary, by Sebastiano Conca, and tomb of Cardinal Antonio Venier (died 1479), incorporating columns from a 6C tabernacle. The chapel of St Catherine (H) contains *frescoes by Masolino da Panicale, probably with the help of his pupil, Masaccio (before 1430; being restored): on the left entrance pier, St Christopher; on the face of the arch, Annunciation; in the archivolt, the Apostles; in the vault, the Evangelists and Fathers of the Church; behind the altar, Crucifixion; right wall, Life of St Ambrose; left wall, Life of St Catherine of Alexandria. To the right above, outside the chapel, is a sinopia for the beheading of St Catherine (found during restoration) and, on the aisle wall, the sinopia for the Crucifixion.

Off the right aisle is the entrance to the **lower church** (open at the same time as the upper church, see above) the apse of which was built above a mithraeum (3C). This formed part of a late 1C apartment house. Below this again are foundations of the Republican period. The staircase, which has miscellaneous fragments of sculpture, descends to the frescoed NARTHEX.

At the foot of the steps a catacomb (see below) can be seen through a grate in the floor. On the right wall is a *fresco (late 11C) of the Legend of St Clement (A), who was banished to the Crimea and there executed by drowning in the Black Sea. The scenes include the Miracle of a Child found alive in a church at the bottom of the sea (full of fish). Below are St Clement and the donor of the fresco. Farther on, to the right, Translation of St Cyril's body (B) from the Vatican to San Clemente (11C). An archway leads into the aisled church which has a wide NAVE obstructed by the foundation piers of the upper church, and is unequally divided by a supporting wall. Immediately to the left is a 9C fresco (C) of the Ascension, with the Virgin in the centre surrounded by the Apostles, St Vitus, and St Leo IV (with square nimbus). In the corner (D), very worn frescoes of the Crucifixion, the Marys at the Tomb, the Descent into Hell, and the Marriage at Cana.

Farther along, on the left wall of the nave is the Story of St Alexis (E; 11C): the saint returns home unrecognised and lives for seventeen years beneath a staircase; before dying he sends the story of his life to the Pope, and is thus recognised by his wife and father. Above, lower part of a fresco of Christ amid angels and saints. Farther on, Story of Sisinius (F): the heathen Sisinius follows his Christian wife in secret, hoping thereby to capture the Pope, but he is smitten with a sudden blindness; below, Sisinius orders his servants to seize the Pope, but they, also struck blind, carry off a column instead (this fresco more probably depicts the building of the church, as is

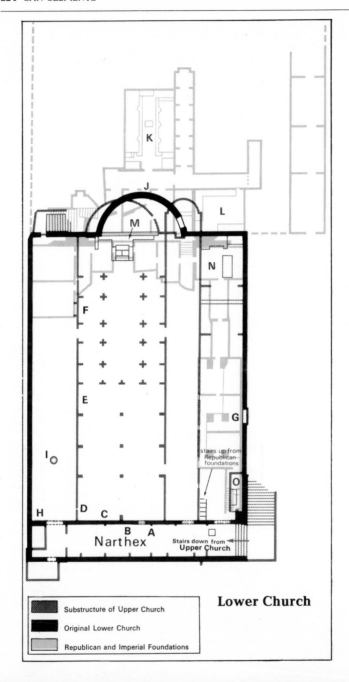

Lower Church

Substructure of Upper Church

Original Lower Church

Republican and Imperial Foundations

explained by the painted inscriptions, which are among the oldest examples of Italian writing). Above, St Clement enthroned by Saints Peter, Linus, and Anacletus, his predecessors on the pontifical throne (only the lower part of the fresco survives).

RIGHT AISLE. In a niche, Byzantine Madonna (G; 5C or 6C), which may have been originally a portrait of the Empress Theodora; female saints with the crown of martyrdom; and a beardless Christ. The frescoes, much damaged, probably depict the Council of Zosimus, the Story of Tobias, and the Martyrdom of St Catherine. At the end, a sarcophagus of the 1C AD with the story of Phaedra and Hippolytus, and a Byzantine figure of Christ (7C or 8C; almost totally obliterated). LEFT AISLE. Faded frescoes (H) of uncertain subjects. In the floor (I) is a circular recess, perhaps an early baptismal piscina. At the end, remains of a tomb perhaps that of St Cyril (869), the apostle of the Slavs.

From the end of the left aisle a 4C staircase descends to the 1C level with a 'palazzo', and a Mithraic temple of the late 2C or early 3C. Around the corner at the bottom (right) is the pronaos of the TEMPLE (J), with stucco ceiling ornaments (very damaged); opposite is the TRICLINIUM (K) with benches on either side and an altar in the centre showing Mithras, in his Phrygian cap, sacrificing a bull to Apollo, and in the niche behind is a statue of Mithras (removed); the vault imitates the roof of a cavern. At the far end of the corridor, to the right, is the presumed MITHRAIC SCHOOL (L; closed), where catechumens were instructed, with a mosaic floor and stuccoed vault.

From the pronaos, a door (left) leads to the 1C 'PALAZZO', probably belonging to Flavius Clemens, which lies beneath the lower basilica. A long narrow passage (M) divides the temple area from the thick tufa wall of the building constructed after Nero's fire on Republican foundations. Only two sides of this building have been excavated. Immediately to the right at the bottom of a short flight of steps is a series of rooms; the last two (sometimes closed) are the best-preserved rooms of the palace, showing the original brickwork. The second side of the building is reached by returning to the opening from the corridor; beyond a room (N) with spring water which has been channelled away by tunnels, are seven more vaulted rooms, the last of which (O) has a small catacomb (probably 5C or 6C, as it is within the city walls). A staircase (right) leads up to the lower church and exit.

Opposite San Clemente is Via dei Querceti at the foot of the high wall of the fortified 12C monastery and church of **SANTI QUATTRO CORONATI** (Pl. 9; 2; open 9.30–12.00, 16.30–18.00; Sunday 9.30–10.45, 16.00–17.45), which is reached from here by the steep Via dei Santi Quattro (left). This unexpectedly rural street leads up to the entrance to this remarkable castellated building of the Middle Ages. The original 4C or 5C foundation, on a huge scale, was destroyed by Norman soldiers in 1084, and the present church was erected on a smaller scale in 1110 by Paschal II. It was well restored in 1914 by Antonio Muñoz. Its dedication recalls the tradition of five Pannonian sculptors who refused to make a statue of Aesculapius, and of four soldiers (the Coronati; Saints Severus, Severinus, Carpophorus, and Victorinus) who refused to worship it when finished by other hands. The church is specially venerated by sculptors and marble masons.

The entrance gate passes beneath the unusual CAMPANILE, dating from the 9C, a squat fortified tower. The small court which succeeds the 5C atrium has a portico with 16C frescoes, and beyond is a second court, once part of the nave, whose columns have survived. On the right of the portico is the **Chapel of St Sylvester** (ring for the key at the monastery of the closed order of Augustinian nuns; first door on the right). It was built in 1246, and contains a delightful *fresco cycle of the same date (particularly well preserved), illustrating the story of the life of Constantine. The first scene is on the left wall: Constantine catches leprosy; the sick Emperor asleep dreams of Saints Peter and Paul who suggest he calls Pope Sylvester; three mounted messengers ride towards Mount Soratte in seach of the Pope. The messengers climb the mountain to reach the hermitage of the Pope; the Pope returns to Rome and shows the emperor the effigies of Saints Peter and Paul; Constantine is baptised by total immersion; Contantine, cured of leprosy, presents his Imperial tiara to the Pope; the Pope rides off wearing it, led by Constantine; the Pope brings back to life a wild bull; finding of the True Cross; the Pope liberates the Romans from a dragon. The floor is Cosmatesque, and the 16C frescoes in the presbytery are attributed to Raffaellino da Reggio.

At the back of the second court is the entrance to the **church**. The aisled INTERIOR has a disproportionately wide apse, and a 12C matroneum, or women's gallery. The 12C pavement is in opus alexandrinum. On the W wall and that of the S aisle are remains of 14C frescoes. In the right aisle is an altarpiece of the Adoration of the Shepherds by the 16C Flemish school, and in the left aisle an altarpiee of St Sebastian tended by holy women by Giovanni Baglione, and (at the W end) an Annunciation by Giovanni da San Giovanni. Against the left pillar of the apse is a beautiful 15C tabernacle attributed to Andrea Bregno or Luigi Capponi. The apse is effectively decorated with frescoes by Giovanni da San Giovanni (1630), depicting the history of the Quattro Coronati and the glory of all saints. The tomb of the four martyrs is in the 9C crypt (usually closed). From the N aisle is the entrance to the delightful tiny *CLOISTER (ring for adm) of the early 13C, with a 12C fountain and lovely garden. It is one of the most secluded spots in Rome. On the left is the 9C chapel of Santa Barbara interesting for its architecture and fine corbels made from Roman capitals, and with remains of medieval frescoes in the vault.

The monastery of the Santi Quattro Coronati is on the edge of the **Celian Hill** (51m), which extends to the S and W towards the Palatine. Next to the Aventine, it is the southernmost of the Seven Hills of Rome and the most extensive after the Esquiline. It is supposed originally to have been called *Mons Querquetulanus* from the oak forests that covered its slopes. It received its name of Mons *Coelius* from Caelius (or Coelius) Vibenna, an Etruscan who is said to have helped Romulus in his war against the Sabine king Tatius, and to have settled here afterwards. Tullus Hostilius lived on the hill and transferred to it the Latin population of Alba Longa. It became an aristocratic district in Imperial times. Devastated by Robert Guiscard in 1084, it remained almost uninhabited for centuries. Even today it is sparsely populated, but its ruins and churches are of great interest.

Via dei Querceti leads up to Via Annia and (right) Piazza Celimontana (where traces of *insulae* were excavated in 1991) in front of the huge 19C OSPEDALE DEL CELIO, a military hospital. Excavations in the extensive gardens here in 1991 (during work on new pavilions) revealed remains of an ancient Roman *domus*, thought to be that of the Simmachi. Just S of the military hospital, near a conspicuous survival of the Claudian aqueduct, Via Santo Stefano leads left to **SANTO STEFANO ROTONDO** (Pl. 9; 4; entrance at No. 7), one of the largest and oldest circular churches in existence. It was finally reopened in 1990 after a long restoration (8.30–13.00, 14–16.00; summer: 8.30–13.00, 16.00–18.30; Saturday 8.30–12.30; closed fest.). It dates from the time of Pope St Simplicius (468–83). The original plan included three concentric rings, the largest 65m in diameter, intersected by the four arms of a Greek Cross. This complex design was almost certainly taken from eastern models, perhaps the church of the Holy Sepulchre in Jerusalem, as well as ancient Roman buildings. The outer ring and three of the arms were pulled down by Nicholas V in 1450, so that the diameter was reduced to 40m. The vestibule is formed by the one remaining arm of the Greek Cross.

The circular nave has a double ring of antique granite and marble columns, thirty-four in the outer and twenty-two in the inner series, while two Corinthian columns in the centre and two pillars support three arches (recently covered with a bright white intonaco). An incongruous wooden floor has been laid following the recent restorations (a mithraeum of the 2–3C AD was found beneath the floor in 1973). On the left of the entrance is an antique Roman throne, said to be that of St Gregory the Great. In the first chapel on the left is a small 7C mosaic depicting Christ *above* the jewelled Cross, with Saints Primus and Felician, showing Greek influence. In the second chapel is a fine 16C tomb. The Renaissance altar by Bernardo Rossellino was reconstructed in the centre of the church in 1990. The walls were covered with frescoes by order of Gregory XIII by Antonio Tempesta and Niccolò Circignani with vivid scenes of martyrdom in chronological order, in the spirit of the Counter Reformation.

On the summit of the hill, across Via della Navicella is the church of **SANTA MARIA IN DOMNICA** (Pl. 9; 3, 4), or *della Navicella*, an ancient foundation and the senior diaconate of Rome; its title is a corruption of Dominica, i.e. Chief. The alternative name is derived from the Roman stone *BOAT, which Leo X had made into a fountain in front of the church. The boat was probably a votive offering from the CASTRA PEREGRINA, a camp for non-Italian soldiers, situated between Via Santo Stefano and Via Navicella.

The present church, restored by St Paschal I (pope, 817–24), and practically rebuilt by Cardinal Giovanni de' Medici (Leo X) in the 16C from the designs of Andrea Sansovino, has a graceful portico. In the interior (being restored; if closed, ring at the door on the right) the nave contains eighteen granite columns; over the windows is a frieze by Perino del Vaga from designs by Giulio Romano. On the triumphal arch, flanked by two porphyry columns, is a beautifully coloured 9C *mosaic of Christ with two angels and the Apostles, and Moses and Elijah below; in the semi-dome, St Paschal kisses the foot of the Madonna and Child surrounded by a throng of angels. In the nave are some interesting Roman sarcophagi.

On the left of the church is the main entrance of the **Villa Celimontana** or VILLA MATTEI (Pl. 9; 3), built for Ciriaco Mattei in 1582 and celebrated for its splendid gardens (now a public park, adm 7.00–dusk). It houses the Società Geografica Italiana. In the grounds are ancient marble fragments found on the spot, and a granite Roman obelisk, probably from the Temple of Isis Capitolina, presented by the Senate to Mattei in 1582. It formed a pair with that in Piazza della Rotonda. The terrace of the casino and the belvedere at the end of an avenue provide fine views. There is an exit from the park opposite the church of Santi Giovanni e Paolo (see below).

To the N of Santa Maria in Domnica is the entrance to the former Trinitarian hospice of the church of SAN TOMASO IN FORMIS. The doorway is surmounted by a mosaic (c 1218) of Christ between two Christian slaves, one white, the other a Negro. In the hospice St John of Matha, founder of the Trinitarians, died in 1213. On the left of Via Claudia, which descends from Santa Maria in Domnica to the Colosseum, are remains of the TEMPLE OF CLAUDIUS, built by Nero's mother Agrippina, fourth wife of Claudius, to whom she dedicated the temple (AD 54). Nero converted it into a nymphaeum for his Domus Aurea, and Vespasian rebuilt it in 69.

The ARCH OF DOLABELLA AND SILANUS (AD 10; restored in 1986), a single archway that Nero afterwards used for his aqueduct to the Palatine, leads into the picturesque Via di San Paolo della Croce, which runs between two garden walls (above which can be seen orange trees) to Piazza dei Santi Giovanni e Paolo. Here is the church of **SANTI GIOVANNI E PAOLO** (Pl. 9; 3; open 8.00–11.30, 15.30–17.30; closed Sunday morning), beside the 12C convent built above remains of the Temple of Claudius (see above). The travertine blocks of the temple are clearly visible in the base of the beautiful tall *CAMPANILE (45m), the first two storeys of which were begun in 1099–1118, and the five upper storeys completed by the middle of the 12C.

The church occupies a site traditionally connected with the house of John and Paul, two court dignitaries under Constantine II, who were martyred by Julian the Apostate. Two Roman apartment houses (2–3C AD) were incorporated in the original sanctuary, founded before 410 by the senator Byzantius and his son Pammachius, a friend of St Jerome. This was demolished by Robert Guiscard in 1084, and rebuilding was begun by Paschal II (1099–1118) and continued by Hadrian IV (Nicholas Breakspeare, the only English pope; 1154–59), who was responsible for the apse and the campanile. Excavations carried out in 1949 on the initiative of Cardinal Spellman revealed the palaeochristian façade and some of the ancient constructions beneath the convent.

The 12C Ionic PORTICO has eight antique columns and is closed by an iron grille (1704). Above is a 13C gallery and the paleochristian façade with five arches. The 13C Cosmatesque doorway is flanked by two lions. The INTERIOR, hung with chandeliers, with granite piers and columns, was restored in 1718 for Cardinal Paolucci by Antonio Canevari; Cardinal Cusani was responsible for the ceiling (1598); the floor, in opus alexandrinum, was restored in 1911. A tomb-slab in the nave (protected by a railing) commemorates the burial-place of the two martyrs. Their relics are preserved in a porphyry urn under the high altar. In the third S chapel (by Filippo Martinucci, 1857–80) is the altar-tomb of St Paul of the Cross (1694–1775), founder of the Passionists, whose convent adjoins the church. The apse has frescoes by Pomarancio. In a store-room (unlocked by the sacristan) on the left of the high altar can be seen a remarkable 12C fresco originally over the altar of the church.

From the end of the right aisle (apply to the sacristan) steps lead down to the **House of Saints John and Paul** (temporarily closed, but restored and normally open at the same time as the church, see above), an interesting two storeyed construction, with twenty rooms, originally part of three buildings: a Roman palace, a Christian house, and an oratory, decorated with frescoes of the 2C or the 3–4C. Near the foot of the stairs is a well-shaft. Behind it to the right is a NYMPHAEUM with a striking fresco of Peleus and Thetis (or Proserpine) and a Nereid, and boats manned by cupids. Beyond a foundation wall of the basilica are two rooms. Off the first (left) is the

TRICLINIUM with pagan frescoes of peacocks and other birds and youths bearing garlands. A small adjoining room (reached by a flight of steps) has architectural frescoes.

The series of rooms to the left of the entrance has more frescoes, some with Christian subjects, including a large standing figure praying in the early Christian manner, with arms extended and eyes raised. The MEDIE-VAL ORATORY (near the road) has been closed during excavation work (and a fresco of the Passion has been removed for restoration). An iron staircase leads up to the CONFESSIO, decorated with 4C frescoes the significance of which is not entirely clear. On the end wall is a praying figure, perhaps one of the martyrs, between drawn curtains, and at whose feet are two other figures. On the right, Saints Priscus, Priscillian, and Benedicta (who tried to find the remains of the martyrs and were themselves killed) awaiting execution with eyes bound, probably the oldest painting of a martyrdom. Stairs lead down from a room N of the Confessio to another series of rooms which were part of the BATHS in a private house.

Remains of the 'CLAUDIANUM', two storeys of a huge Roman portico, connected with the Temple of Claudius (see above), can be seen beside the convent (ring for admission at the convent on the right of the portico).

In the piazza outside the church are some arches of Roman shops dating from the 3C. The pretty CLIVO DI SCAURO (the ancient *Clivus Scauri* probably opened in the 1C BC) descends beneath the medieval buttresses of the church spanning the road. Here can be seen the tall façade of a Roman house incorporated in the left wall of Santi Giovanni e Paolo, and the fine •apse, a rare example of Lombard work in Rome, dating from 1216. Farther down on the left are remains of the 6C basilican hall of the library erected by Agapitus I, and, beneath the Chapels of Sant'Andrea and Santa Barbara (see below), a Roman edifice of the 3C AD.

A short road on the left leads up to the church of **SAN GREGORIO MAGNO** (Pl. 9; 3), a medieval church altered and restored in the 17C and 18C. A monastery was founded here by St Gregory the Great (590–604) on the site of his father's house, and dedicated to St Andrew. This was demolished in 1573 except for the two chapels of Santa Barbara and Sant'Andrea (see below).

The •EXTERIOR (staircase, façade, and atrium) is by Giovanni Battista Soria (1633) and is considered his masterpiece. In the ATRIUM are several fine tombs, including (near the entrance) that of Sir Robert Peckham (died 1569), a self-exiled English Catholic, and a memorial to Sir Edward Carne (died 1561), an envoy of Henry VIII and Mary I; and, beyond the gate leading to the chapels (see below), those of Canon Guidiccioni (1643) and (on the right, beside the convent door) the brothers Bonsi (1481), the latter by Luigi Capponi.

The INTERIOR (if closed ring at the convent on right of atrium) has sixteen antique columns and a restored mosaic pavement; it was rebuilt in 1725–34 by Francesco Ferrari. At the end of the right aisle is the CHAPEL OF ST GREGORY, with a fine altar-frontal sculptured by Luigi Capponi. The predella is an early 16C painting, depicting St Michael overcoming Lucifer, the Apostles with St Anthony Abbot, and St Sebastian. A small room on the right contains a chair of the 1C BC known as the throne of St Gregory. Off the left aisle is the SALVIATI CHAPEL, by Francesco da Volterra and Carlo Maderno; on the right is an ancient fresco of the Madonna (repainted in the 14C or 15C) which is supposed to have spoken to St Gregory; on the left, a fine tabernacle, of the school of Andrea Bregno (1469). On either side of the apse are 15–16C statues of Saints Andrew and Gregory.

On the left of the church (reached through a gate in the atrium) is a pretty group of three chapels (restored but still closed in 1994) surrounded by ancient cypresses. The chapel on the right was built in 1603 and dedicated to **Santa Silvia**, mother of Gregory. It contains her statue by Nicolas Cordier, and a *fresco of an angel choir by Guido Reni (still awaiting restoration). The other two chapels belonged to the medieval monastery and were built above a Roman edifice (visible from the Clivus Scauri, see above); they were restored in 1602. In the centre is the chapel of **Sant'Andrea**, preceded by a portico with four antique cipollino columns. Inside is a *Flagellation of the saint (right) by Domenichino, and the saint on the way to his martyrdom, by Guido Reni; the peasant-woman on the left repeats the well-known type of Beatrice Cenci. On the entrance wall, Saints Silvia and Gregory by Giovanni Lanfranco, and on the back wall (beneath the roof) an 11C mural which has recently been discovered.

The third chapel, of **Santa Barbara**, contains a statue of St Gregory by Nicolas Cordier. The 3C table is supposed to be the one at which he served twelve paupers daily with his own hands, among whom an angel once appeared as a thirteenth; this legend gave the alternative name to the chapel, the *Triclinium Pauperum*. It was in this convent in 596 that St Augustine received St Gregory's blessing before setting out, with forty other monks, on his mission to convert the English to Christianity. A fresco on the left, by Antonio Viviani (1602) commemorates the famous incident of the fair-haired English children, 'non Angli sed Angeli', which culminated in St Augustine's mission.

From Piazza di San Gregorio a flight of steps descends to the tree-lined VIA DI SAN GREGORIO, now a busy road with fast traffic. On the line of the ancient *Via Triumphalis* it follows the declivity between the Celian and Palatine Hills to the Colosseum. The area to the S, with the Baths of Caracalla, is described in Rte 14.

14

The Baths of Caracalla to Porta San Sebastiano

Bus No. 118 every 20–40 minutes from the Colosseum via Via delle Terme di Caracalla (for the Baths of Caracalla) and Via di Porta San Sebastiano (with request stops outside the Tomb of the Scipios and at Porta San Sebastiano). On the return, No. 118 can be taken from outside Porta San Sebastiano via Via di Porta Latina back to Piazzale Numa Pompilio.

PIAZZA DI PORTA CAPENA (Pl. 9; 3) is a busy road junction at the beginning of Via di San Gregorio (which leads to the Colosseum) and adjoining the rounded end of the Circus Maximus (see Rte 15). It occupies the site of the PORTA CAPENA, a gate in the Servian Wall, and the original starting point of the Appian Way. After Aurelian had built his much more extensive walls, the stretch of the road between Porta Capena and Porta Appia (now Porta San Sebastiano; see below) became known as the 'urban section' of the Appian Way. This part of the Via Appia is now called Via delle Terme di Caracalla as far as Piazzale Numa Pompilio, and, beyond that square, Via di Porta San Sebastiano. On the NE side of Piazza di Porta Capena is the VIGNOLA, a charming little 16C palace moved here from near Via Santa Balbina in 1911 and reconstructed using the original masonry. The 4C STELE OF AXUM was stolen from the ancient capital of Ethiopia by Mussolini during the Italian occupation in 1935–36 and erected here in 1937. Despite the peace treaty of 1947 and numerous international protests, the monument has never been returned. On the modern Viale Aventino rises the huge building begun in 1938 by Mario Ridolfi and Vittorio Cafiero to house the Ministero per l'Africa Italiano. Since 1951 it has been the seat of the 'FAO' (United Nations Food and Agriculture Organization).

Viale Guido Baccelli leads through the PARCO DI PORTA CAPENA, formerly the 'Passeggiata Archeologica' opened in 1910. There is now an open-air sports stadium here. In Via Santa Balbina is the church of **Santa Balbina** (Pl. 9; 5; open 9.00–12.00, 15.00–17.00), entered through the ex-convent on the right of the portico. Founded in the 5C, the church has been rebuilt, and was restored in 1930. The pleasant interior has a wood ceiling bearing the name of Cardinal Marco Barbo (1489). The transennae in the pretty windows, and the schola cantorum, were installed in 1931. In the floor are set numerous good Roman black-and-white mosaics (1C AD) found in Rome in 1939. The 13C Cosmatesque episcopal chair in the apse is in excellent condition. The apse fresco of the Glory of Christ is by Anastasio Fontebuoni (1523). The fresco fragments include a good Madonna enthroned with four Saints and the Redeemer above, attributed to the school of Pietro Cavallini. The bas-relief of the Crucifixion (1460) is attributed to Mino da Fiesole and Giovanni Dalmata, and the *tomb of Stefanus de Surdis (1303) is by Giovanni Cosmati.

In Via delle Terme di Caracalla is the entrance to the huge *BATHS OF CARACALLA (Terme di Caracalla), or Thermae Antoninianae (Pl. 9; 5; adm see p 45), the best preserved and most splendid of the Imperial Roman baths in the city. They could accommodate some 1600 bathers. The romantic sun-baked ruins are on a vast scale.

Begun by Antoninus Caracalla in 212, the baths were opened in 217 and finished under Heliogabalus and Alexander Severus. After a restoration by Aurelian they remained in use until the 6C, when the invading Goths damaged the aqueducts. The baths, built on an artificial platform, have always been above ground, but excavations in this century greatly enlarged the area accessible to the public. In the 16–17C, the Belvedere Torso, the Farnese Hercules, the Farnese Flora, and many other statues were found among the ruins, and the mosaic of the athletes, now in the Vatican, also came from here. Shelley composed a large part of his 'Prometheus Unbound' in this romantic setting. From 1937 to 1993 opera performances were given here in summer; these have now been forbidden for conservation reasons.

The massive brick-built baths are an architectural masterpiece. Their remarkably complex design (see the plan) included huge vaulted rooms, domed octagons, exedrae, porticoes, etc. as well as an intricate heating system and hydraulic plant. Of the elaborate decoration only a few architectural fragments and some floor-mosaics remain, revealing the Baroque taste of the 3C in the introduction of divinities on the fine Composite capitals.

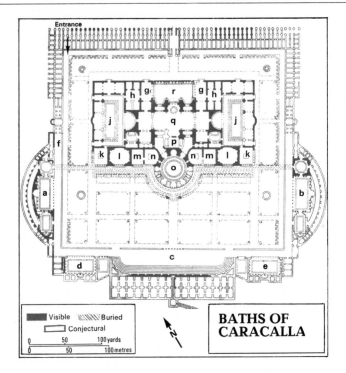

An enclosed garden, now planted with pines, laurel, and cypresses, surrounds the main buildings of the baths (see below). Along the boundary wall were two huge exedrae with an apsidal central hall (a and b), and in the middle of the S side a shallow exedra in the form of a STADIUM (c) with tiers of seats concealing the huge water cisterns. On either side were two halls (d and e), probably libraries. The present entrance skirts the boundary wall on the W side past remains of one of the exedrae (a), and older buildings below ground level, including a MITHREUM (f), the largest discovered in Rome (admission only with special permission). Excavations and restorations (including conspicuous reconstructions) have been carried out in the area of the stadium (c) and one of the libraries (d), and on the E side of the garden where a house and triclinium of the time of Hadrian have been discovered. This area is still fenced off.

The main buildings of the **Baths** (220 x 114m) are symmetrically arranged around the huge central hall (q) and the piscina (r; see below). The bathers normally entered through a VESTIBULE (g) to reach the APODYTERIA (h) or dressing rooms. The two PALESTRAE (j), for sports and exercises before bathing, consisted of an open courtyard with porticoes on three sides and a huge hemicycle opposite five smaller rooms. The pavement here has remains of fine polychrome geometric mosaics. The series of rooms (k, l, m, and n) to the S, which may have included a Turkish bath (LACONICUM; l) led to the circular CALIDARIUM (o), 34m across, only part of one side of which remains. It had high windows on two levels designed to admit the sun's rays for many hours of the day, and was formerly covered with a dome. From here the bathers passed into the TEPIDARIUM (p) and the large vaulted central hall (q). Beyond is the NATATIO (r) with an open-air piscina. This has niches on two levels for statues and two hemicycles.

Opposite the Baths, in Piazzale Numa Pompilio, is the church of **Santi Nereo ed Achilleo** (Pl. 9; 5; open in summer, 10.00–12.00, 16.00–18.00, ring for custodian), on the site of the Oratory of the Fasciola, named from the bandage which is supposed to have fallen from the wounds of St Peter after his escape from the Mamertine prison. In 524 the oratory was enlarged into a church by John I, when he brought here the bodies of Nereus and Achilleus, the Christian servants of Flavia Domitilla, who had been martyred at Terracina. The church was enlarged by Leo III c 800, and again by Sixtus IV (1471–84), and was rebuilt by Cardinal Baronius in 1597.

The aisled INTERIOR has frescoes by Pomarancio. The ancient ambo and the 15C candelabrum come from other churches; the fine plutei and the high altar, which covers the body of St Domitilla, are of 13C Cosmati work. The mosaic on the choir-arch, of the time of Leo III (815–16), shows the Transfiguration, with a Madonna and an Annunciation at the sides. On the bishop's throne in the apse is carved a fragment of St Gregory's 28th homily, which he delivered from this throne when it stood in the first church dedicated to Saints Nereus and Achilleus in Via Ardeatina.

On the other side of the piazza is the rebuilt church of SAN SISTO VECCHIO, with its convent, historically interesting as the residence in Rome of St Dominic (1170–1221). The campanile dates from the 13C. The façade and interior were designed by Filippo Raguzzini in 1735–27. It contains remains of a fresco cycle of 13–14C.

From Piazzale Numa Pompilio roads lead to four of the gates in the Aurelian Wall: Via Druso NNE to Porta Metronia, Via di Porta Latina SE to Porta Latina ('one way' from the gate), Via di Porta San Sebastiano SSE to Porta San Sebastiano ('one way' to the gate), and the continuation of Via delle Terme di Caracalla S to Porta Ardeatina, adjoining the Bastione del Sangallo.

Via di Porta San Sebastiano, on the line of the urban section of the Appian Way, is a beautiful road (disturbed by fast traffic) running between high walls behind which are fine trees and gardens. On the right, beyond a walled public garden, is the ancient church of **San Cesareo** (Pl. 9; 6; closed many years ago for restoration) rebuilt at the end of the 16C, with a façade attributed to Giacomo della Porta. Inside is some fine *Cosmati work, including the high altar, the bishop's throne, the transennae, the candelabrum, the ambo, and the fronts of the side-altars. The two angels beneath the high altar are probably from a 15C tomb by Paolo Romano. The beautiful wooden ceiling, gilded on a blue ground, bears the arms of the Aldobrandini Pope, Clement VIII. The apse mosaic of the Eternal Father was designed by Cavalier d'Arpino. The baldacchino dates from the time of Clement VIII.

Below the church (reached by a stair to the left of the entrance; apply to sacristan), is a large black-and-white *mosaic of the 2C AD (suffering from humidity). The fantastic sea-monsters, animals, and figures may have decorated the floor of Roman baths. Two apses and the base of a large column, dividing the excavated area, suggest that the first part was later adapted as a church.

Beyond the church, on the right, at No. 8 is the **House of Cardinal Bessarion** (closed indefinitely for restoration since 1984), the famous scholar (1389–1472), whose tomb is in the church of the Santi Apostoli. The delightful house and garden are a good example of a 15C home. The loggia and several of the rooms are decorated with contemporary frescoes, which have been restored and the false additions removed. From the loggia with landscape scenes is the entrance to the first large room which has wall-paintings of garlands and ribbons which cast painted shadows, and a fragment (in a niche) of a 15C fresco of the Coronation of the Virgin and two saints. The walls of the room on the right have an over-all pattern of acanthus leaves and pomegranates. The house is furnished in the Renaissance style. The rooms downstairs are used as reception rooms by the Commune of Rome.

About 500 metres farther along the road is (left; No. 9) the **Tomb of the Scipios** (closed indefinitely for restoration; for information enquire at the Museo delle Mura, see below). The ticket formerly included admission to the Columbarium of Pomponius Hylas. The charming entrance beside two old columns and a little fountain leads into a beautifully kept garden. The tomb, one of the first to be built on the Appian Way, was discovered in 1780. The excavated area is dominated by a threestoreyed house of the 3C which retains traces of paintings and mosaics and was built above the tomb of the Scipios. In front is a COLUMBARIUM, reached by a staircase below ground level, containing numerous niches with funerary urns. To the right of the house, a short passage leads to a small Christian CATACOMB, with a chapel attached. Store-rooms contain archaeological material found during excavations.

The **tomb** itself is reached from the left of the house. It was built for L. Cornelius Scipio Barbatus, consul in 298 BC, and great-grandfather of Scipio Africanus. Many other members of the gens Cornelia were buried here also, up to the middle of the 2C BC, although Scipio Africanus was buried at Liternum (Patria, near Naples), where he died. The sarcophagus of Scipio Barbatus and the funerary inscriptions found here were replaced by copies when they were removed to the Vatican. The other tombs include those of his son, Lucius Scipio (consul 259 BC), the conqueror of Corsica, of Cornelius Scipio Asiaticus, of Cn. Scipio Hispanus (praetor 139 BC) and Aula Cornelia his wife; also an inscription to Publius, possibly the son of Scipio Africanus.

When the Tomb of the Scipios is open the caretaker usually conducts visitors through an attractive little public park to the *Columbarium of Pomponius Hylas (for admission enquire at the Museo delle Mura), which is one of the best preserved in existence. The steep original staircase, with a small mosaic inscription, with the name of the founder and his wife Pomponia Vitalis, leads down to the 1C chamber with niches and funerary urns, and decorated with stucco and paintings.

A gate leads out of the park into the pretty rural Via di Porta Latina, in which to the left is the picturesque church of *San Giovanni a Porta Latina, in a quiet cul-de-sac, with a large cedar and ancient well. It has a narthex of four Roman columns, and a beautiful 12C campanile. The church, founded c 550, was rebuilt by Hadrian I in 772, and several times restored, but the interior retains its beautiful 11C basilican form. The apse has three lovely windows of selenite, and 12C frescoes (restored in 1940).

In the other direction Via di Porta Latina leads to the gate, past the little octagonal chapel of **San Giovanni in Oleo**, traditionally marking the spot where St John the Evangelist stepped out unharmed from a cauldron of boiling oil. Rebuilt during the reign of Julius II, it has an interesting design, usually attributed to Bramante (or to Sangallo and his school). It was restored in 1658 by Borromini, who added the frieze. The interior (ring at No. 17) contains stuccoes and paintings by Lazzaro Baldi.

Porta Latina is an opening in the Aurelian Wall (see below) with two towers built by Belisarius. Outside the gate Viale delle Mura Latine skirts the wall to Porta San Sebastiano, and Via di Porta Latina runs SE to Via Appia Nuova.

In Via di Porta San Sebastiano, at No. 13 are other interesting columbaria discovered in the last century in the VIGNA CODINI, now private property (no adm). The largest had room for some 500 urns, another in the form of a horse-shoe has vaulted galleries decorated with stuccoes and paintings. Near the end of the road is the so-called triumphal ARCH OF DRUSUS, in fact the arch that carried the aqueduct for the Baths of Caracalla over the Appian Way. Only the central of three openings survives; it is decorated with Composite columns of giallo antico.

Porta San Sebastiano (Pl. 9; 8), the *Porta Appia* of ancient Rome, is the largest and best preserved gateway in the Aurelian Wall. It was rebuilt in the 5C by Honorius and restored in the 6C by Belisarius. The two medieval towers at the sides rest on basements of marble blocks. The interior has been restored as a **Museum of the Walls** (*Museo delle Mura*; adm see p 47). For the history and description of the Aurelian Walls, see p 20. It was at the Porta San Sebastiano that the senate and people of Rome received in state the last triumphal procession to enter the city by the Appian Way, that of Marcantonio Colonna II after the victory of Lepanto in 1571.

The museum is arranged in the rooms on two levels above the gate, and in the two towers. It contains prints, models, etc. illustrating the history of the walls. The ramparts along the inner face of the walls, traversing nine defensive towers, are open for some four hundred metres, as far as Via Cristoforo Colombo (see Pl. 9; 8). They provide a very unusual view of rural Rome, skirting overgrown fields and woods, beyond which (towards the end of the walkway) can just be seen, above the trees, the tops of the Victor Emmanuel Monument, the Baths of Caracalla, and the dome of St Peter's. The BASTIONE DEL SANGALLO, a formidable structure built for Paul III in 1537 by Antonio da Sangallo the Younger, which is beyond Via Cristoforo Colombo, is not yet accessible.

The next stretch of the Appian Way outside the gate is described in Rte 17.

15

The Theatre of Marcellus and Piazza Bocca della Verità

The broad and traffic-ridden **Via del Teatro di Marcello** (Pl. 3; 8), skirting the W base of the Capitoline Hill, was opened in 1933. It descends past (right) the severe façade of the MONASTERO DI TOR DE' SPECCHI (open to visitors on 9 March every year), founded in 1425 by St Francesca Romana. The Oratory is decorated by Antoniazzo Romano. Beyond rises the Theatre of Marcellus (described below). In Via Montanara is the pretty deconsecrated church of SANTA RITA by Carlo Fontana, moved here in 1937 from the foot of the Capitol Hill, below Santa Maria in Aracoeli. It has an interesting oval interior. Beyond opens the handsome PIAZZA CAMPITELLI, with a fountain (1589) designed by Giacomo della Porta. Facing the church are three fine palaces: the 16C Palazzo Cavalletti (No. 1), Palazzo Albertoni, and Palazzo Capizucchi (Nos 2 and 3), both dating from the late 16C and attributed to Giacomo della Porta.

The charming façade (now much blackened) of **Santa Maria in Campitelli** (Pl. 3; 8) was erected by Carlo Rainaldi when the church was rebuilt (1662–67) in honour of a miraculous image of the Madonna, which was believed to have halted an outbreak of pestilence. The fine INTERIOR (closed 12.00–17.00) has an intricate perspective effect using numerous arches, columns, and a heavy cornice. In the second chapel on the right is St Anne, St Joachim, and the Virgin by Luca Giordano (light on the right); the ornate high altar surrounds the miraculous image of the Madonna in pietra dura perhaps dating from the 11C. In the first chapel on the left are two tombs of the Altieri family, inscribed respectively 'Nihil' and 'Umbra'; in the left transept, Birth of St John the Baptist, by Baciccia.

Via Cavalletti and Via de' Delfini leads E out of the piazza to the picturesque Piazza Margana, where several houses are hung with old vines. Via de' Funari leads out of the N side of the piazza through an area of charming old streets to **Santa Caterina dei Funari** (Pl. 3; 6), a church with a fine façade by Guidetto Guidetti (1564) and an original campanile. The interior (which has been closed for restoration for many years) contains 16C paintings by Girolamo Muziano, Scipione Pulzone, Livio Agresti, Federico Zuccari, and Marcello Venusti, and a fine stuccoed and painted *chapel by Vignola.

Across Via Caetani (described in Rte 5) is the huge **Palazzo Mattei**, which comprised five palaces of the 16C and 17C. The fine façades in Via dei Funari and Via Michelangelo are by Carlo Maderno. In the little Piazza Mattei, Nos 19 and 17 open onto courts, and a third door gives access to a staircase (left) finely decorated with 17C stuccoes surrounding antique reliefs. Inside are frescoes by Domenichino, Lanfranco, and Albani. Part of the buildings, now owned by the State, are used by the Centro Italiano di Studi Americani. A MUSEUM OF GRAMOPHONES (entrance at No. 32) is closed for rearrangement. It includes a number of early instruments invented by Edison. The charming *Fontana delle Tartarughe (in Piazza Mattei), by Taddeo Landini (1584), on a design by Giacomo della Porta, was restored in 1658 perhaps by Bernini, when the tortoises (now replaced by copies) were added. At the SW angle of the piazza is PALAZZO COSTAGUTI (no adm), with ceilings on the first floor painted by Albani, Domenichino, Guercino, Lanfranco, and others.

On the right of the church of Santa Maria in Campitelli the narrow old Via della Tribuna di Campitelli leads past an old house (harshly restored) with Ionic columns set into its façade to Via Sant'Angelo in Pescheria which continues to the site of the **GHETTO** and remains of an entrance to the **Portico of Octavia** (Pl. 3; 8), once a rectangular portico (circa 119m by 132m) with about three hundred columns, which enclosed two temples, dedicated to Jupiter and Juno. Erected by Quinto Cecilio Metello in 146 BC, it was reconstructed by Augustus in honour of his sister Octavia c 23 BC, and restored by Septimius Severus (AD 203). The southern extremities of the area of the portico have been exposed, and remains of columns to the W, and the stylobate to the E can also be seen.

The entrances consisted of two propylaea with eight columns and four piers; the one on the SW survives (partly covered for restoration) and serves as a monumental entrance to the church of **Sant'Angelo in Pescheria**, founded inside the portico in 755. An arch was added, and the pediment repaired in the Middle Ages. The church (usually closed) was rebuilt in the 16C and contains a fresco of the Madonna enthroned with angels, attributed to Benozzo Gozzoli or his school, and an early 12C Madonna and Child. From this church Cola di Rienzo and his followers set out to seize the Capitol on the night of Pentecost, 1347. Here from 1584 until the rule of Pius IX the Jews were forced to listen to a Christian sermon every Saturday.

The portico was used from the 12C as a fish market for the city up until the destruction of the Ghetto in 1888 (see below).

The area roughly occupied by the old Ghetto, between Piazza Cairoli and the Theatre of Marcellus, and Via del Portico d'Ottavio and the Tiber is now recognised as the site of the CIRCUS OF FLAMINIUS (221 BC). To the right of the Portico of Octavia are three Corinthian columns of the TEMPLE OF APOLLO MEDICO, built in 433 BC and restored by the consul C. Sosius, in 33 BC. Beyond it are the ruins of the TEMPLE OF BELLONA, built in 296 BC.

These two temples are close outside the imposing remains of the cavea of the *THEATRE OF MARCELLUS** (Pl. 8; 1). The theatre, together with remains of the temples, are now surrounded by a fence; for admission ask next door at the archaeological offices of the Comune at 29 Via Portico d'Ottavia. The theatre, planned by Julius Caesar, was dedicated in 13 or 11 BC by Augustus to the memory of his nephew (Octavia's son) and son-in-law, Marcellus, who had died in 23 BC at the age of nineteen. It was restored by Vespasian and Alexander Severus. The building was pillaged in the 4C for the restoration of Ponte Cestio. It was fortified in the early Middle Ages and made into a stronghold by the Faffo. Renaissance architects frequently studied the theatre. In the 16C it was converted into a palace by Baldassarre Peruzzi for the Savelli; he inserted a façade into the curved exterior of the cavea. It later passed in turn to the Orsini and the Sermoneta families. The theatre was restored in 1932, when numerous houses and shops on the site were demolished. The cavea originally had at least two tiers of forty-one arches, the first with Doric and the second with Ionic engaged columns probably crowned by an attic of the Corinthian order. Only twelve arches in each of the first two tiers survive; the upper stage has disappeared in the course of various alterations. It could probably have held some 15,000 spectators.

The **Ghetto** occupied the district to the W, where from 1556 onwards the Jews were segregated and subject to various restrictions on their personal freedom, although to a lesser degree than in other European countries. The walls were torn down in 1848, and the houses demolished in 1888 before the area S of Via del Portico d'Ottavia was reconstructed around the new synagogue. Many Jewish people still live in the area between Lungotevere Cenci, Via Catalana, and Via del Portico d'Ottavia. In Via del Portico d'Ottavia are several medieval houses, and a shop with an ancient Roman architrave framing the door. No. 13 (in very poor repair) has a fine court with loggie. At the end (No. 1) is the CASA DI LORENZO MANILIO, dating from 1468 (2221 years after the foundation of Rome), decorated with ancient Roman sculptural fragments. The inscription carved in bold stone lettering was set up by Manilio, and includes (on the side facing Piazza Costaguti) the patriotic invocation 'Have Roma'. Via della Reginella here is a survival from the old Ghetto.

On the left opens PIAZZA DELLE CINQUE SCOLE (laid out in the last century when the Ghetto was demolished) with a fountain from Piazza Giudea by Giacomo della Porta. Here is the interesting PALAZZO CENCI, which belonged to the family of Beatrice Cenci, and was renewed in the 16C. A short narrow road on the right leads up to MONTECENCI, an artificial mound (probably on Roman remains) with a pretty little piazza between Palazzo Cenci and the church of SAN TOMMASO DEI CENCI (usually closed). An antique altar is incorporated into its façade. It contains a chapel frescoed by Sermoneta (1575) and two carved Roman brackets supporting a side altar.

Piazza delle Cinque Scole continues to the river; on the left, on Lungotevere Cenci, rises the monumental **Synagogue** (Pl. 3; 8) built by Vincenzo Costa and Osvaldo Armanni in 1899–1904, with a **Jewish Museum** (adm see p 46), illustrating the history of the community in the city. In 1993 a marble *aròn* of 1523, incorporating some Roman fragments (demolished in 1908–10), was reconstructed and temporarily exhibited in the vaults of the synagogue.

The debris from the demolitions of the Theatre of Marcellus became known as Monte Savello which gave its name to the traffic-ridden piazza to the S. This faces the *ISOLA TIBERINA (Pl. 3; 8), a pretty little island in the Tiber, reached from here by *Ponte Fabricio, the oldest Roman bridge to have survived in the city, and still in use for pedestrians. The inscription over the fine arches records the name of the builder, L. Fabricius and the date, 62 BC. The bridge is also known as the Ponte 'dei Quattro Capi' from the two herms of the four-headed Janus on the parapet. Remains of the 'Ponte Rotto' (see below) can be seen upstream.

Isola Tiberina and the Ponte Rotto

The island, which provides an easy crossing place on the Tiber, is thought to have been settled early in the history of Rome. A temple of Aesculapius was dedicated here in 291 BC (after a plague in 293 BC) and ever since the island has been associated with the work of healing. It is now largely occupied by the hospital of the Fatebenefratelli, founded in 1548, and modernised by Cesare Bazzani in 1930–34. On the right is the church of SAN GIOVANNI CALIBITA founded in the 11C and reconstructed in 1640. In the 18C interior is a ceiling painting by Corrado Giaquinto. On the left is a tall medieval tower, formerly part of an 11C fortress, and Piazza San Bartolomeo. The island was formerly encircled with a facing of travertine, a portion of which still remains at the extremity, which can sometimes be reached through the archway on the left of San Bartolomeo. It is in the form of a ship with the serpent of Aesculapius carved on it in relief. There are long-term plans to open a museum illustrating the history of the island in the interesting medieval building here, now owned by the Comune.

The church of SAN BARTOLOMEO, on the site of the temple of Aesculapius, was built in the 10C in honour of St Adalbert, Bishop of Prague, and several times restored, notably by Orazio Torriani in 1624; the tower is Romanesque. The interior contains fourteen antique columns, and an interesting sculptured well-head on the chancel steps, probably from the original church. There is a hall crypt beneath the transept. The S side of the island is joined to Trastevere (Rte 21) by the **Ponte Cestio**, probably built by L. Cestius in 46 BC, restored in AD 370, and rebuilt in 1892 (the centre arch to its original design and measurements).

In Piazza di Monte Savello is the apse of the church of **San Nicola in Carcere** (Pl. 8; 1; open 7.30–12.00, 16.30–19.00; fest. 10.30–13.00), the side door of which can usually be reached from here by a walkway. This 11C church, probably on the site of an older sanctuary, was reconstructed and consecrated in 1128. It was remodelled in 1599 by Giacomo della Porta and detached from the surrounding buildings in 1932. It occupies the site of three Republican temples in the FORUM HOLITORIUM, the vegetable and oil market which extended from the Capitoline Hill to the Tiber. The temples are thought to have been dedicated to *Janus*, *Juno Sospita*, and *Spes*. The first, to the right of the church, was Ionic hexastyle, with columns on three sides only, the remains of which can be seen incorporated in the S wall of the church; the second, now incorporated in the church, was Ionic hexastyle peripteral; the third, on the left of the church was Doric hexastyle peripteral. The INTERIOR of the church has fine antique columns from the temples with diverse capitals. At the end of the left aisle is an altarpiece of the Ascension, by Lorenzo Costa.

The main door of the church faces the wide and busy Via del Teatro di Marcello, across which is a medieval fortified mansion (over-restored). A path with steps (called Via di Monte Caprino) leads up from here to the Capitol Hill. Vico Jugario, a road on the site of the Roman road which connected the Forum Holitorium with the Roman Forum, skirts the foot of the Capitol to Piazza della Consolazione past Sant'Omobono.

At the beginning of Vico Jugario on the left can be seen the arcades of a portico built of peperino in the Rebublican era. On the right, around the church of Sant'Omobono (usually locked), is the **Area Sacra di Sant'Omobono** (Pl. 8; 1; closed, but partly visible through the railings). Excavations begun in 1937 and continued in the 1960s (and still not completed) have revealed interesting remains on seven different levels, the oldest dating from c 1500 BC. Traces of hut dwellings of the 9–8C BC, similar to those on the Palatine have also been found. The archaeological evidence has provided new light on the origins of Rome and the presence of the Etruscans here in the 7C and 6C BC. Two archaic temples (mid 6C BC) dedicated to Fortuna and Mater Matuta and traditionally founded by Servius Tullius rest on an artificial mound c 6 metres high in which were found Bronze Age and Iron Age sherds and imported Greek pottery of the 8C BC. In front of the temples are two archaic altars, possibly dedicated to Carmenta. The most conspicuous remains mostly date from after 213 BC when the temples were reconstructed. The material found on the site, including a terracotta group of Hercules and Minerva from one of the temples, is kept in the Antiquarium Comunale.

In Piazza della Consolazione beyond, is the church of **Santa Maria della Consolazione**. The façade is by Martino Longhi the Elder (1583–1606); the upper part was added in the same style in the 19C. In the first chapel to the right are frescoes by Taddeo Zuccari (1556) of the life of Christ (including the *Flagellation) and the Crucifixion (much damaged). In the apse, Birth of Mary and the Assumption by Pomarancio, and over the altar, the Madonna della Consolazione, a 14C fresco repainted by Antoniazzo Romano. In the first chapel on the left, is a marble relief of the Marriage of St Catherine by Raffaello da Montelupo (1530). The cliff above, on the Capitoline Hill, is thought to be the Tarpeian Rock (see Rte 1).

Via del Teatro di Marcello continues between ugly municipal public offices set up by the Fascist regime in 1936–37 to **Piazza della Bocca della Verità** (Pl. 8; 3), an open space with a picturesque group of buildings now sadly disturbed on all sides by busy traffic. This occupies part of the site of the *Forum Boarium*, or cattle-market, the oldest market of ancient Rome, and here in a little garden stand two ancient Roman temples and a fine fountain by Carlo Bizzaccheri (1717), opposite the medieval church of Santa Maria in Cosmedin.

On the right of the temples is the eccentric **Casa dei Crescenzi** (no admission), a unique example of a mansion built by a wealthy Roman in the Middle Ages. Formerly a tower guarding the river, it dates from c 1100 and the inscription over the door states that it was erected by one Nicolaus, son or descendant of Crescentius and Theodora, probably members of the Alberic family, the most powerful clan in Rome at the end of the 10C. It is constructed mainly from fragments of classical buildings (or medieval copies of Roman works). The bricks of the lower storey are formed into half-columns, with rudimentary capitals. A fragment of the upper storey and its arcaded loggia survives. It is now used by the 'Centro Studi per la Storia dell'Architettura', and concerts are occasionally held here.

The *Temple of Portunus** (no admission), dedicated to the god of harbours, was formerly called the *Temple of Fortuna Virilis*. It dates from the end of the 2C BC. In 872 it was consecrated as the church of *Santa Maria Egiziaca*. This pseudoperipteral temple, with four fluted Ionic columns in front of the portico and two at the sides, escaped alteration in the Imperial period and survives as a precious example of the Greco-Italian temples of the Republican age.

The little round *Temple of Hercules Victor** was for long known as the *Temple of Vesta*. It also dates from the end of the 2C BC (restored under Tiberius) and is the oldest marble edifice to survive in Rome. An inscription from the base of a cult statue found here confirmed its dedication to Hercules Victor. This charming little building consists of a circular cella of solid marble, surrounded by twenty fluted columns. The original ones are those in Greek marble; after severe damage in the 1C AD the temple was restored and some of the columns and capitals replaced, using Luni marble. One of the columns is missing on the N side but the base is left. The exquisite capitals were restored in 1991. In the Middle Ages the temple became the church of *Santo Stefano delle Carrozze* and later *Santa Maria del Sole*. The original roof and ancient entablature have not survived. The entrance to a side conduit of the Cloaca Maxima (see below) can be seen under a travertine lid beside the fountain.

*SANTA MARIA IN COSMEDIN** (Pl. 8; 3; open 9.00–12.00, 15.00–17.00) is a fine example of a Roman medieval church, preceded by a little gabled porch and arcaded narthex. The building incorporates two earlier structures, the arcaded colonnade of the Imperial Roman *Statio Annonae*, or market inspector's office, and the side-walls of a porticoed hall, part of an early Christian welfare centre, or *diaconia* (c 600). Near by was a monumental altar and a temple, both dedicated to Hercules, the latter restored by Pompey. The oratory was enlarged into a basilican church by Hadrian I (772–95), and assigned to Greek refugees driven from Constantinople by the iconoclastic persecutions, and became known as the *Schola Graeca*. Its other name, 'in Cosmedin', probably comes from a Greek word meaning decoration, referring to the embellishments of Hadrian. At that period it had a matroneum and three apses. Cardinal Alfano, chamberlain of Calixtus II, rebuilt the church c 1123, closed the galleries, and added the schola cantorum.

The fine tall CAMPANILE of seven storeys also dates from this time. The church was over-restored and the pretty 18C façade torn down in 1894–99; it is again being restored.

Beneath the PORTICO, to the left, is the famous BOCCA DELLA VERITÀ, a large cracked marble disc representing a human face, the open mouth of which was believed to close on the hand of any perjurer who faced the ordeal of placing it there. It is in fact a slab that once closed an ancient drain. To the right is the tomb of Cardinal Alfano (see above). The principal doorway is the work of Johannes de Venetia (11C).

The fine INTERIOR with a nave and two aisles each ending in an apse closely reproduces the 8C basilica with some 12C additions. The arcades are supported on antique columns with good capitals grouped in threes between piers. In the first part of the nave remains of the Statio Annonae and diaconia (see above) can be seen. High up on the walls are the remains of frescoes of the 11C. The schola cantorum, rood-loft, paschal candelabrum, episcopal throne, and pavement (1123) are the *work of the Cosmati. The baldacchino over the high altar (an antique porphyry bath) is by Deodatus, third son of the younger Cosmas (1294). The paintings in the apses are restored. In the SACRISTY, to the right of the entrance, is a fragment of a mosaic of 706 on a gold ground, representing the Adoration of the Magi, formerly in the oratory of John VII at St Peter's. In the chapel to the left of the sacristy, over the altar, is a Madonna and Child attributed to the late 15C Roman school. The tiny crypt (closed for restoration), reached from either aisle, was built into part of the altar dedicated to Hercules, the columns of which remain.

From the Lungotevere Aventino, W of Piazza della Bocca della Verità, the iron *Ponte Palatino* crosses the Tiber to Trastevere (Rte 21). In the bed of the Tiber, upstream, is a single arch of the PONS AEMILIUS, the first stone bridge over the Tiber (the piers were built in 179 BC, and were connected by arches in 142 BC). From the 13C onwards it was repaired numerous times, and has been known as the PONTE ROTTO since its final collapse in 1598. From the parapet of the Ponte Palatino the mouth of the Cloaca Maxima (see below), may be seen under the quay of the left bank, when the river is low.

On the E side of Piazza della Bocca della Verità is Via del Velabro, which perpetuates the name of this ancient district of Rome. The *Velabrum*, once a stagnant marsh left by the inundations of the Tiber, extended between the river and the Palatine, and included the Forum Boarium (see above). The derivation of the name is uncertain. The Velabrum is famous in legend as the spot where the shepherd Faustulus found the twins Romulus and Remus. It was drained by the **Cloaca Maxima**, which was an extensive system serving the valleys between the Esquiline, Viminal, and Quirinal Hills, as well as the Roman Forum. At first a natural watercourse to the Tiber, it was canalised by Tarquinius the Elder and Servius Tullius (c 616–535 BC), and arched over in c 200 BC; it is still in use.

In the peaceful Via del Velabro (Pl. 8; 3) is the massive four-sided **Arch of Janus**, which formed a covered passage at a cross-roads (quadrivium) and provided shelter for the cattle-dealers. Poorly proportioned, it is a work of decadence, dating perhaps from the reign of Constantine, and is built partly of ancient fragments, with numerous niches for statues. To the left is *SAN GIORGIO IN VELABRO (Pl. 8; 1) an ancient church severely damaged in a terrorist bomb explosion in 1993, which destroyed the 9–12C Ionic portico. The area is cordoned off while restoration and reconstruction is in progress. The church was built over a diaconia established here c 600 perhaps in the 9C or earlier. The campanile dates from the 12C. The church was further restored in 1926.

The beautiful plain grey INTERIOR is basilican, with nave and aisles separated by sixteen ancient columns. The pretty windows were restored in this century. The irregularity of the plan which can be seen from the wood ceiling suggests an earlier construction was incorporated in the 9C building. In the apse is a fresco attributed to Pietro Cavallini (c 1296; repainted) of Christ with the Madonna and Saints Peter, Sebastian, and George. The altar, with some Cosmatesque decoration, and the canopy, date from the 13C.

To the left of the church is the ornate little ARCUS ARGENTARIORUM (AD 204), which was erected by the money-changers (argentarii) and cattle-dealers in honour of the emperor Septimius Severus, Julia Domna, and their children. The portrait and name of Geta were effaced as a mark of his disgrace.

To the left of the arch, a street leads to the church of **San Giovanni Decollato** (ring at No. 22). The interior has fine stucco and fresco decoration dating from 1580–90. The altarpiece of the decapitation of St John is by Vasari. In front of the W door is the entrance to the oratory with remarkable *frescoes by the 16C Roman Mannerists, Jacopino del Conte, Francesco Salviati, Pirro Ligorio, and others. There is also a 16C cloister. On the other side of the road, reached by a raised pavement, is SANT'ELIGIO DEI FERRARI (open for services on Sunday) with an interesting Baroque interior.

Via San Teodoro to the NE corresponds to the ancient *Vicus Tuscus*, skirting the Palatine on the W. On the right, well below the level of the road, is the small round domed church of **San Teodoro** (Pl. 8; 2; open for services on fest. at 11.30), beside which was found the bronze she-wolf (now in Palazzo dei Conservatori). The first church was built on the site of the great granary warehouse known as the *Horrea Agrippiana*, later turned into an early Christian diaconia. It is preceded by a delightful courtyard. The present church dates from c 1453 and it contains an early mosaic in the apse of the old oratory (Christ and saints, c 600), much restored. Remains of earlier buildings, including the Roman structures, have been found beneath the foundations.

From Piazza della Bocca della Verità Via dei Cerchi runs SE. On the left, in Piazza di Sant'Anastasia (reached also from Via di San Teodoro; see above) is the church of SANT'ANASTASIA (closed for restoration), dating from 492 and several times restored. The classical façade is by Luigi Arrigucci. Inside, under the high altar, is a recumbent statue of St Anastasia, begun by Francesco Aprile and finished by Ercole Ferrata. Beneath the church are remains of an Imperial building.

Via dei Cerchi skirts the NE side of the Circus Maximus (with a good view from below of the ancient buildings on the S slopes of the Palatine, see Rte

3), and Via del Circo Massimo borders its SW side. In Piazzale Romolo e Remo is a seated bronze statue, by Ettore Ferrari, of Giuseppe Mazzini, unveiled at the centenary (1949) of the Roman Republic.

The **CIRCUS MAXIMUS** (Pl. 8; 4) lies in the Valle Murcia, between the Palatine and the Aventine Hills; now planted with grass, it is used as a public park. This was the first and largest circus in Rome. According to Livy, it dates from the time of Tarquinius Priscus (c 600 BC), who is said to have here inaugurated a display of races and boxing-matches after a victory over the Latins; but the first factual reference to the circus is in 329 BC. The circus was altered and enlarged on several occasions. In the time of Julius Caesar its length was three stadia (1875 Roman feet), its width one stadium, and the depth of the surrounding buildings half a stadium. The resultant oblong was rounded at one end and straight at the other. Tiers of seats were provided all round except at the straight end; here were the *carceres*, or stalls for horses and chariots. In the centre, running lengthwise, was the *spina*, a low wall terminating at either end with a *meta* or conical pillar denoting the turnings of the course. The length of a race was seven circuits of the *spina*. Though primarily adapted for chariot races, the circus was used also for athletic contests, wild-beast fights, and (by flooding the arena) mock sea battles. It could accommodate from 150,000 to 385,000 spectators; its capacity varied from one reconstruction to the next. The circus was destroyed by fire under Nero (AD 64) and again in the time of Domitian. A new circus was built by Trajan; Caracalla enlarged it and Constantine restored it after a partial collapse. The last games were held under the Ostrogothic king Totila in AD 549.

The extant remains belong to the Imperial period. Some seats and part of the substructure of the stairways can be seen at the curved E end, around the medieval tower near Piazza di Porta Capena, as well as some shops. In the centre of this curve are fragmentary decorative columns of a triumphal arch commemorating Titus's conquest of Jerusalem in AD 80–81, which formed the entrance gate. Excavations have been in progress here since 1984. The obelisks now in Piazza del Popolo and outside the Lateran once stood in the circus. At the W end of the Circus, on Via dell'Ara Massima, are remains of a large Roman public building (2C AD) with a 3C MITHREUM beneath (admission only with special permission from the Comune).

16

The Aventine Hill

The **AVENTINE HILL** (40m; Pl. 8; 3, 5) rises on the SW side of the Circus Maximus (see Rte 15). A secluded residential area with beautiful trees and gardens, it is one of the most peaceful places in the centre of Rome. The southernmost of the Seven Hills of Rome, it was not at first included within the precincts of the city and remained outside the *pomoerium*, or line of the walls, throughout the Republican era. For centuries it was sparsely populated. It has two summits: the Aventine of ancient Rome, which extends SW of Via del Circo Massimo in the direction of the Tiber, and the 'Piccolo

Aventino', to the S. These are divided by Viale Aventino, which runs SW from the Porta Capena towards the Testaccio. It was to the Aventine that C. Gracchus, after failing to obtain his re-election as tribune, withdrew with his colleague Fulvius Flaccus for their last stand against the Senate. In the Imperial era the Aventine became an aristocratic district, and in the early Middle Ages it was already covered with elegant mansions.

From Via del Circo Massimo, Clivio dei Publici or Via di Valle Murcia (bordered by a rose garden) mount the hill to Via di Santa Sabina. At the top of the rise the road passes (right) the Clivio di Rocca Savelli, a pedestrian lane which leads back down the hill past the wall of the 12C Savelli castle. Beyond is the delightful walled garden (open to the public) known as the **Parco Savello**, planted with orange trees, and beautifully kept. It has a good view of Rome to the N and NW (steps in the far corner lead down to the Clivio di Rocca Savelli, see above). A door in the wall leads into Piazza Pietro d'Illiria, with a splendid wall fountain.

Here is the church of ***SANTA SABINA** (Pl. 8; 3; open 6.30–12.45, 15.30–19.00), perhaps the most beautiful basilica in Rome which survives from the early Christian period. It was built by Peter of Illyria (422–32), a priest from Dalmatia, on the legendary site of the house of the sainted Roman matron Sabina, near a temple of Juno. It was restored in 824 and in 1216. In 1219 Honorius III gave it to St Dominic for his new Order. It was disfigured in 1587 by Domenico Fontana and skilfully restored by Antonio Muñoz in 1919 and 1937.

The church has a small 15C PORTICO, and a door on the left leads into a VESTIBULE with sculptural and architectural fragments. On the far left is a remarkable wooden *DOOR of the early 5C, with eighteen panels carved with Scriptural scenes, probably not in the original order. These include one of the oldest representations of the Crucifixion in existence.

The beautifully proportioned classical INTERIOR is modelled on the basilicas of Ravenna. Of its mosaic decoration which formerly covered the nave walls and apse, only one section remains, above the doorway, showing seven hexameters in classical gold lettering on a blue ground, with the founder's name (430), and, at the sides, figures of the Church of the Jews (ex-circumcisione), and the Church of the Gentiles (ex-gentibus). The wide and tall nave is divided from the aisles by twenty-four fluted Corinthian *columns from a neighbouring 2C building. The spandrels of the arcades are decorated with a splendid 5C marble inlay in 'opus sectile', and the beautiful large windows, thirty-four in all, have their transennae of varied design based on original fragments.

In the centre of the NAVE is the unusual mosaic tombstone of Fra' Muñoz de Zamora (died 1300), perhaps by Iacopo Torriti. The schola cantorum, ambones, and bishop's throne (in the choir) have been reconstructed from ancient fragments. The unattractive apse fresco by Taddeo Zuccari was repainted by Vincenzo Camuccini in 1836. Below the RIGHT AISLE can be seen an ancient column, older than the church. Adjacent to it, the Chapel of St Hyacinth is frescoed by the Zuccari; and at the end of the aisle is the tomb of Cardinal Auxias de Podio (1485), of the school of Andrea Bregno. Beneath the nave excavations have revealed remains of a small temple and an edifice of the early Imperial period with a fine marble pavement. The Baroque Elci Chapel, in the LEFT AISLE, contains, over its altar, the *Madonna of the Rosary with Saints Dominic and Catherine, by Sassoferrato. In the convent is St Dominic's room, now a chapel. The beautiful *CLOISTER (1216–25), with 103 columns, is entered from the portico.

Beyond the convent is another little public park with orange trees, pine trees, a palm tree, and bougainvillea. From the parapet the view over Rome includes: in the foreground, the long orange façade of the ex-Istituto di San Michele, St Peter's with the Janiculum Hill to the left, and to the right the dome of Sant'Andrea della Valle, the little spiral tower of Sant'Ivo, the dome of the Pantheon, the Synagogue, the French Academy (on the skyline surrounded by trees), the Victor Emmanuel Monument, the Capitol Hill, and the Torre Milizie (just behind the tree on the extreme right).

The church of **Sant'Alessio** (Pl. 8; 3; until 1217, *San Bonifacio*), near which the Crescentii built a convent in the 10C, is preceded by an attractive courtyard, and retains its fine Romanesque campanile. The interior of the church (if closed, ring at the door on the left) was modernised by Tommaso de Marchis in 1750, but two tiny mosaic columns remain on either side of the wooden bishop's throne in the apse. At the W end of the left aisle, set in an altar of 1700 by Andrea Bergondi, is a portion of the wooden staircase beneath which St Alexis is supposed to have lived and died.

The street ends at the delightful **Piazza dei Cavalieri di Malta**, with elaborate decorations by Giovanni Battista Piranesi, seen against a background of cypresses and palms. He also designed the monumental entrance in the square to the **Priorato di Malta**, or Maltese Villa (Pl. 8; 5), the residence of the Grand Master of the Knights of Malta. There is a remarkable view of the dome of St Peter's at the end of an avenue through the keyhole in the doorway. The villa (admission rarely granted), contains a Chapter Hall with portraits of the Grand Masters, from Gerard (1113) onwards, and an altarpiece from the church by Andrea Sacchi. The beautiful garden, planted with palm trees and bay hedges, has a superb view from a terrace looking over the Tiber towards Monte Mario.

On the left, a drive leads to the back of the villa and the church of **Santa Maria del Priorato**, or *Aventinense* (admission as for the Villa), a Benedictine foundation once incorporated in the residence of the patrician senator Alberic, who was the virtual ruler of Rome in 932–54. It passed into the hands of the Templars, and from them to the Knights of Malta. It was rebuilt in 1765 by Piranesi. The fine FAÇADE of a single order crowned with a tympanum, has rich decorative details. The harmonious INTERIOR is striking, with fine stucco decoration; the Rococo high altar by Tommaso Righi is cleverly lit. On the right is the 15C tomb of Baldassorre Spinelli, an ancient Roman sarcophagus with reliefs of the Muses, beyond which is a statue of Piranesi by Giuseppe Angelini. In the left aisle is the tomb of Bartolomeo Carafa (died 1405) by Paolo Salviati, and a medieval marble reliquary, in the form of a pagan cinerary urn (?10–12C).

On the W side of the Priorato, facing Via della Marmorata, is the ancient brick ARCO DI SAN LAZZARO, which may have had some connection with the storehouses (*Emporia*) in this neighbourhood. In Piazza di Sant' Anselmo, just S of the Priorato, is the large Benedictine Seminary (1892–96), with the church of SANT' ANSELMO, built in 1900 in the Lombard Romanesque style. Mass is held here with Gregorian chant at 9.30 on Sunday.

From Piazza Sant' Anselmo, Via di Sant'Anselmo and Via Icilio (left) lead towards Santa Prisca (beyond Piazza Albinia; see the Plan), on the other side of the hill. The church of **Santa Prisca** (Pl. 8; 5; open 8.00–12.00, 16.00–19.00), possibly dating from the 4C, is said to occupy the site of the house of Aquila and Prisca, who entertained St Peter. In the INTERIOR the pretty frescoes in the nave are by Fontebuoni, follower of the Zuccari brothers. Right aisle: baptismal font made from a large Doric capital, with a bronze cover and the Baptism of Christ, by Antonio Biggi. Left aisle (near the entrance door): fragment of a 15C Tuscan fresco (Annunciation). In the sacristy are three detached 17C fresco fragments by the school of Maratta. Beneath the church (entered from the beginning of the right aisle, but closed indefinitely), besides a nymphaeum (with a small museum) and the crypt, is a MITHRAEUM, found in 1958. The interesting remains include frescoes and a statue of Mithras slaying the Bull and the lying figure of Saturn.

Via di Santa Prisca continues down to the wide and busy Viale Aventino. In Piazza Albania (right) are extensive remains of the Servian Wall (c 87 BC). Across the square Via San Saba leads up to the 'Piccolo Aventino' and the steps preceding the church of **San Saba** (Pl. 8; 6; open 7.00–12.00, 16.00–18.30), with a little porch and walled forecourt. Beneath the church were found fragments of frescoes (now exhibited in the sacristy corridor), belonging to the first church founded in the 7C by Palestinian monks escaping from the Eastern invasions. The present church may date from c 900, although it has been rebuilt several times and was restored in 1943. In 1463, under Cardinal Piccolomini, the loggia was added above the portico and the four original windows bricked in.

In the PORTICO are sculptural fragments, some Oriental in character (including a knight and falcon), and a large Roman sarcophagus with figures of a bridegroom and Juno Pronuba. The fine DOORWAY is by Giacomo, the father of Cosma, who also probably designed the floor. In the INTERIOR, the right aisle has remains of a schola cantorum, a patchwork of Cosmatesque work. On the left- hand side of the church is a short fourth aisle, formed by wide decorated arches, within which are remains of 13C frescoes of St Nicholas of Bari. High up on the arch over the apse is an Annunciation, also added for Cardinal Piccolomini. In the apse, above the Bishop's throne is a fine Cosmatesque marble disc and a 14C fresco of the Crucifixion.

Porta San Paolo and the area farther S are described in Rte 25.

17

The Appian Way and the Catacombs

The **Appian Way** from Porta San Sebastiano to the church of Domine Quo Vadis is now an unattractive traffic ridden road, extremely unpleasant to explore on foot. Beyond the church the road, although very narrow (beware of fast cars), becomes prettier and passes the side entrance to the catacombs of St Calixtus and then descends to San Sebastiano. A short way beyond San Sebastiano is the Circus of Maxentius and the Tomb of Cecilia Metella, the two most interesting monuments on the road. Beyond the tomb the bus leaves the Appian Way. The remaining four kilometres as far as the Casal Rotondo are the most beautiful and characteristic section of the road, although in the last few decades some of the monuments have been vandalised and rubbish of all sorts now abounds. It is not advisable to visit this stretch of the road (one-way for cars leaving Rome) if you are on your own after dark.

Public transport. The Appian Way may be reached from the Colosseum by Bus No. 118. This runs by Via San Gregorio, Via delle Terme di Caracalla, Via di Porta San Sebastiano, Porta San Sebastiano, and Via Appia Antica as far as the Tomb of Cecilia Metella. There are request stops for the main monuments along the route, including the catacombs of San Callisto and San Sebastiano. The service is infrequent (every 20–40 mins). Bus No. 218, starting from St John Lateran joins Via Appia Antica outside Porta San Sebastiano and then branches off beyond the church of Domine Quo Vadis to the Fosse Ardeatine and Catacombs of St Domitilla. The only public transport back to the city from Casal Rotondo is reached by taking Via di Casal Rotondo to Via Appia Nuova where Bus No. 664 can be taken back towards the centre of the city. At the bus terminus is the 'Colli Albani' station of the underground railway (Line A) for the Station and Piazza di Spagna. The Appian Way is cut in two by the Rome Circular Road (Grande Raccordo Annulare) near the seventh Roman mile.

The ***APPIAN WAY** (*Via Appia Antica*, Pl. 9; 8) begins outside Porta San Sebastiano, in the Aurelian Wall, continuing the line of its urban section (see Rte 14). Called by Statius the queen of roads (*regina viarum*), it was the most important of the consular Roman roads. It was built by the censor Appius Claudius in 312 BC as far as Capua, and later extended to Beneventum (Benevento) and Brundusium (Brindisi). In 37 BC Horace, Virgil, and Maecenas travelled the three hundred and seventy kilometres to Brindisi in fifteen days.

The Appian Way served for the first few kilometres as a patrician cemetery, and was lined on either side by a series of family graves. Some of the tombs, usually in the form of a tower or tumulus, can still be seen, although often only their concrete core survives. The solid bases were sometimes used in the Middle Ages as the foundations of watch-towers and fortalices. The ancient paving, of massive polygonal blocks of grey basaltic lava from the Alban Hills, with *crepidines* or sidewalks, has been almost totally covered with asphalt in recent years up to the third milestone. The road was reopened at the end of the 18C and many of the monuments lining the road were erected by Luigi Canina in 1852. The Via Appia was also used by the early Christians for their underground cemeteries, and it is now mostly visited for its famous catacombs. Although the road survives as far as the twelfth Roman milestone and its junction with the modern Via Appia Nuova, little or no attempt has been made to preserve it in recent years, and beyond its crossing with the Grande Raccordo Annulare it has been totally abandoned. Despite the institution of a regional archaeological park here in 1988, there are no signs that conservation work is in progess.

The initial section of the Appian Way, the ancient *Clivus Martis* is now a busy unattractive road, not recommended for walkers. It gently descends from Porta San Sebastiano, and about 120m from the gate is the site of the FIRST MILESTONE (marked by a column and an inscription; see the Plan on pp 250-251). The road passes under an ugly fly-over bearing a new fast road (where excavations have revealed Roman remains), and then under the main Rome-Civitavecchia railway. It crosses the brook *Almone* (or *Marrana della Caffarella*), where the priests of Cybele, the Magna Mater, used to perform the annual ceremony of washing the image of the goddess. Tombs appear here and there. On the left nearly 1km from the gate, is a conical Roman mound with a house on the top, and the little church of **Domine Quo Vadis**.

This stands on the spot where, according to tradition, St Peter on his way from the city met an apparition of Jesus and so returned to Rome and martyrdom (the story was the subject of a novel by Sienkiewicz).

By the church Via Ardeatina branches off to the right to (1km) the Fosse Ardeatine (see below). At this fork is the entrance for cars to the catacombs of St Calixtus (see below). The drive, along a beautiful cypress avenue, passes the fields and farm of the monastery.

About 100 metres from the church of Domine Quo Vadis is a turning to the left, called Via della Caffarella. Less than a kilometre along this lane is a path (left), leading to the so-called TEMPLE OF THE DEUS REDICULUS (now private property), by a mill near the Almone brook. The 'temple' is really a sumptuous tomb of the 2C, once identified as that of Annia Regilla, wife of Herodes Atticus (see below).

After making a short ascent the Appian Way passes a trattoria (No. 87; left) which incorporates remains of the so-called COLUMBARIUM OF THE FREED-MEN OF AUGUSTUS, where some 3000 inscriptions were found. At No. 101 is the little HYPOGEUM OF VIBIA (no adm), with interesting pagan paintings of the 3C AD. Beyond (No. 103) is the site of the SECOND MILESTONE. At No. 110, on the right, is the entrance to the **Catacombs of St Calixtus**, the first official cemetery of the early Christian community, and usually considered the most important of the Roman Catacombs.

The Catacombs

For **admission times**, see p 45. The Catacombs most often visited (St Calixtus and San Sebastiano on the Via Appia, and St Domitilla on Via delle Sette Chiese) all have guided tours in several languages, and tend to be crowded with large tour groups which can impair the visit if you are on your own. In some catacombs explanatory films are shown before the visit. Routes often vary and are shortened at the height of the tourist season. The catacombs have some steep stairs and unlevel narrow corridors (often poorly illuminated) and the visit is therefore not normally advisable if you have difficulty in walking. The catacombs of St Agnes on Via Nomentana, and of Priscilla on Via Salaria, of no less interest, are usually less crowded. For permission to visit the catacombs not regularly open to the public (see the Index), apply to the Pontificia Commissione di Archeologia Sacra.

The catacombs were used by the early Christians as underground cemeteries outside the walls of Rome. They were often situated on property donated by wealthy Romans, after whom the cemetery was named (i.e. Domitilla, Agnese, Priscilla, and Commodilla). They were easily quarried in the soft tufa, and provided space for the tombs of thousands of Christians since burial within the walls was forbidden (pagan Romans were cremated). They were in use from the 1C up until the early 5C. Many martyrs were buried here and the early Christians chose to be buried close to them. Later they became places of pilgrimage until the martyrs' relics were transferred to various churches in Rome. They were pillaged by the Goths (537) and the Lombards (755), and by the 9C they were abandoned. They received their name from the stone quarries ('ad catacumbas') on the site of the cemetery of San Sebastiano. In the 16C Antonio Bosio visited the catacombs, but they were not systematically explored until 1850 when the famous archaeologist G.B. De Rossi carried out excavations (first at St Calixtus), and the Pontificia Commissione di Archeologia Sacra was set up. They were opened to the public and became one of the most famous sights of Rome, when visits by candle-light fired the romantic imagination of 19C travellers. The popular belief that they were used as hiding places by the early Christians has been totally disproved.

The catacombs are a system of galleries of different sizes, often arranged on as many as five levels, and sometimes extending for several kilometres. In the walls simple rectangular niches (*loculi*) were cut in tiers where the bodies were placed wrapped in a sheet. The openings were closed with slabs of marble or terracotta on which the names were inscribed (at first in Greek, later in Latin), sometimes with the date or the words 'in pace' added (almost all of these have now disappeared). Terracotta lamps were hung above the tombs to provide illumination in the galleries. A more elaborate type of tomb was the *arcosolium*, which was a niche surmounted by an arch and often decorated. Small rooms or *cubicula* served as family vaults. The shallowest of the galleries are 7–8m beneath the surface, while the deepest are some 22m below ground level. Openings in the vaults, some of which survive, were used for the removal of earth during the excavations. Most of the tombs were rifled at some time over the centuries in the search for treasure and relics, but the inscriptions and paintings which survive are of the greatest interest.

The *CATACOMBS OF ST CALIXTUS (adm see p 45) were named after St Calixtus (San Callisto) who was appointed to look after the cemetery by Pope Zephyrinus (199–217), and who enlarged it when he himself became pope in 217. It was the official burial place of the bishops of Rome. It was first investigated in 1850 by G.B. De Rossi (see above) and is not yet fully explored. The monastery, in a beautiful open landscape, is surrounded by an extensive farm.

Visitors are conducted by an English-speaking priest to a small basilica with three apses, the ORATORY OF SAINTS SIXTUS AND CECILIA, where the dead were brought before burial in the catacombs. Here are inscriptions and sculptural fragments from the tombs, and a bust of De Rossi. Pope St Zephyrinus is generally supposed to have been buried in the central apse.

The catacombs excavated on five levels are reached by an ancient staircase. The tour usually remains on the second level, from which several staircases can be seen descending to other levels. The *PAPAL CRYPT preserves the tombs with original Greek inscriptions of the martyred popes, St Pontianus (230–35), St Anterus (236), St Fabian (236–50), St Lucius (253–54), martyred under Valerian's persecution, St Stephen I (254–57), St Dionysius (259–69), and St Felix I (269–75). In honour of the martyred popes, Pope St Damasus (366–84) set up the metrical inscription seen at the end of the crypt.

In the adjoining crypt is the CUBICULUM OF ST CECILIA, where the body of the saint is supposed to have been buried after her martyrdom at her house in Trastevere in 230. It is thought that it was moved by Paschal I in 820 to the church built on the site of her house. Here has been placed a copy of Maderno's statue of the saint in the church. On the walls are very worn 7–8C frescoes: Head of Christ, St Urban, and other saints. Beyond the crypt, a 3C passage leads down a short flight of stairs, with Christian symbols carved on stone slabs, to the CUBICULA OF THE SACRAMENTS, with symbolic frescoes. In the first cubicle are frescoes of the Raising of Lazarus, and opposite, the Miracle of the Loaves and Fishes. On the end wall, a fine double sarcophagus, with a lid in the form of a roof. The other cubicles have similar frescoes, several depicting the story of Jonah. Farther on is the CRYPT OF ST EUSEBIUS, martyred in 310. In the adjoining cubicles are the sepulchral inscriptions of Pope St Gaius (283–96) and two sarcophagi with mummified bodies. Next is the TOMB OF POPE ST CORNELIUS (251–53), with a contemporary Latin inscription containing the word 'martyr', and fine 6C Byzantine paintings. Adjoining is the CRYPT OF LUCINA, the oldest part of the cemetery.

Near the Catacombs of St Calixtus are further burial-places, including the Catacomb of the Holy Cross, discovered in 1953. Here are believed to have been the tombs of Saints Marcus and Marcellianus and the HYPOGEUM OF ST DAMASUS.

Just beyond the Catacombs of St Calixtus, **Via Appia Pignatelli** branches off to the left, a road opened by Innocent XII (1691–1700) to link the Appian Way with the Via Appia Nuova. Near the beginning, on the left, are the **Catacombs of Praetextatus** (admission only with special permission; see p 45). Above ground are pagan, below

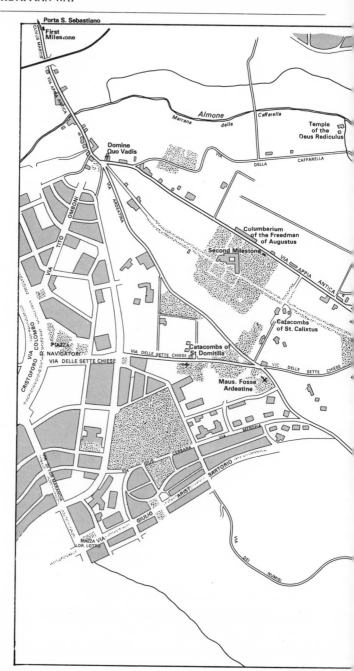

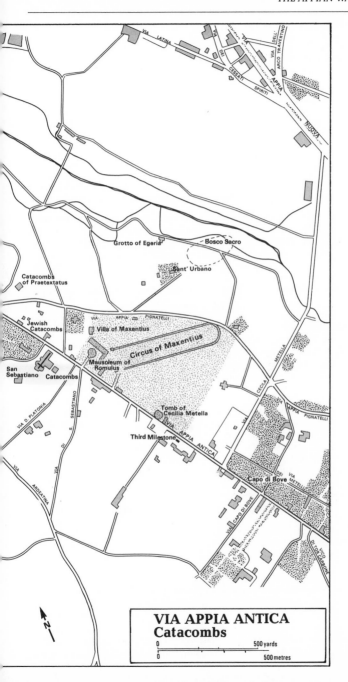

VIA LATINA
VIA DEI CESSATI
VIA DELLI
ARCO TRAVERTINO
APPIA
SPIRITI
NUOVA

Grotto of Egeria
Bosco Sacro
Sant' Urbano

Catacombs of Praetextatus

VIA APPIA PIGNATELLI
Jewish Catacombs
Villa of Maxentius
Circus of Maxentius
METELLA
CECILIA

San Sebastiano
Catacombs
Mausoleum of Romulus

VIA D. PLATONIA
VIA DI S. SEBASTIANO
Tomb of Cecilia Metella
VIA APPIA PIGNATELLI
VIA APPIA ANTICA
Third Milestone
VIA DEI METELLI

VIA ARDEATINA
Capo di Bove
VIA CAPO DI BOVE
D. VICO CARBONE

N

VIA APPIA ANTICA
Catacombs

| 0 | | 500 yards |
| 0 | | 500 metres |

ground Christian sarcophagi. Here were buried several Christian martyrs. In the crypt is the large SPELUNCA MAGNA, in which were buried the martyred companions of St Cecilia. In a cubicle excavated in 1850 are 2C paintings.

The next turning to the left, Vicolo Sant'Urbano leads to a villa (now a restaurant) in the park of which is the church of *Sant'Urbano. This was originally a temple forming part of the villa of the wealthy Herodes Atticus, patron of arts and man of letters of the time of the Antonines, famous above all for his numerous buildings in Greece. The temple was converted into a church in the 9C or 10C and was restored in 1634, when four fluted columns from the pronaos were incorporated into the wall of the church. Inside (apply at the villa for the key) are remains of stucco ornamentation and interesting *frescoes by a certain Bonizzo (1011): over the door, Crucifixion; on the end wall, Christ blessing, with saints and angels; on the other walls, Life of Jesus, and Lives of St Cecilia and her companions, and of St Urban.

Not far away, on a hill looking towards the Alban Hills, is the BOSCO SACRO (sacred wood), once mistakenly identified as the place where Numa Pompilius used to consult the nymph Egeria. On the other side of the hill is the so-called GROTTO OF EGERIA, watered by a branch of the Almone. The Fountain of Egeria was near the Porta Capena.

In the Appian Way, at No. 119A, is the entrance to the **Jewish Catacombs** (adm only with special permission; see p 45), excavated in 1857. The tombs, in the form of loculi or niches, are for the most part cut on end and date from the 3C to the 6C. Among the symbols are the cornucopia (Plenty), the palm-leaf (Victory), and the seven-branched candlestick. The epitaphs are mostly in Greek.

The road now descends to a small piazza in which, on the left, is a column set up by Pius IX in 1852 to commemorate his restoration of the Via Appia. On the right are the **BASILICA AND *CATACOMBS OF SAN SEBASTIANO** (entrance to the left of the church; admission, see p 45). The basilica, one of the seven pilgrimage churches of Rome, was originally dedicated to Saints Peter and Paul and called the *Basilica Apostolorum*. It was built in the first half of the 4C over the cemetery into which the bodies of the Apostles had been temporarily moved from their tombs in St Peter's and San Paolo fuori le Mura; this is said to have occurred in 258 during the persecution of Valerian. At a later date St Sebastian, who suffered under Diocletian in 288, was buried here. After the 9C the association with the Apostles was forgotten and the church was named after St Sebastian. From the 3C to the 9C this was the most venerated area of subterranean Rome. The catacombs have two special claims to fame: they are the only ones that have always been known, visited, and therefore damaged, and they were originally the only underground burial place to receive the name of catacombs: *ad catacumbas* (literally, by the caves, since they were built in an abandoned stone quarry here).

In the ticket office are fragments of sarcophagi, inscriptions, etc. Visitors are conducted by an English-speaking guide; the order of the tour is sometimes changed. A stair with fragments of terracotta lids of sarcophagi with Imperial seals lead down to the CRYPT OF ST SEBASTIAN (restored) which contains a copy of a bust of St Sebastian, attributed to Bernini. Beyond are the catacombs excavated on four levels. The CHAPEL OF SYMBOLS has carved Christian symbols. An area below the basilica (the walls of which can be seen) known as the 'PIAZZUOLA' has three elaborate pagan *tombs of the early 2C. They each have a façade with a terracotta tympanum. The first, on the right, has a fresco above the tympanum of a pastoral scene and a banquet. The marble inscription names this as the sepulchre of M. Clodius Hermes. The interior has a vault fresco with a Gorgon's head, and decorative frescoes on the walls, including a beautiful composition with a vase of fruit and flowers flanked by two birds. The floor preserves a mosaic. The centre tomb has a magnificent stucco vault, dating from the early 2C, terminating in a shell design decorated with lotus and acanthus leaves and a peacock. It is believed both pagan and Christian burials took place in this composite tomb on several levels. The tomb to the left has a well-preserved stucco vault which descends to a lunette finely decorated with a grape and vine design. The cubicles here are also decorated with stucco.

From here ascends a steep staircase to the TRICLIA, a room reserved for the funerary banquets held in honour of the Apostles, Peter and Paul. There is a bench around the wall, and remains of red-painted decorations and fragments of pictures. The walls are inscribed with graffiti invoking the Apostles, including one dating from 260.

The **church** is usually shown at the end of the tour of the catacombs. It originally had a nave and two aisles; the aisles were walled up in the 13C. In 1612 it was rebuilt for Cardinal Scipio Borghese by Flaminio Ponzio; the façade has a portico with six Ionic columns, taken from the preceding 15C portico. The 17C wood *ceiling is by Vasanzio. Off the S side is the apsidal CHAPEL OF THE RELICS containing a stone which was once believed to bear the imprint of Christ's feet, and other relics, and the CAPPELLA ALBANI built as a sepulchral chapel for Clement XI by Carlo Fontana. On the high altar are four columns of verde antico. On the third N altar, St Francis of Assisi, attributed to Girolamo Muziano. In a chapel off this side, late 14C wooden Crucifix (restored). Beyond this chapel (beside the stairs up from the catacombs) is the glass door (kept locked) which admits to the ARCHAE-OLOGICAL MUSEUM (admission only with special permission) arranged in the ambulatory (where the construction of the 4C basilica can be seen clearly). Another chapel on the N side has a recumbent *statue of St Sebastian, by Antonio Giorgetti, from a design by Bernini. Near the entrance is a stone from the catacombs with an inscription in honour of the martyr Eutychius, by Pope St Damasus.

Other parts of the catacombs not usually shown include the PLATONIA, the tomb of St Quirinus, and the CHAPEL OF HONORIUS III, with 13C paintings, and an apsidal cubiculum with graffiti which indicate that this was the temporary grave of St Peter.

Just short of San Sebastiano, Via delle Sette Chiese, on the right, leads to Via Ardeatina (600m) and (250m farther) the Catacombs of St Domitilla (see below). In Via Ardeatina (bus, see above), a little to the left of its junction, is the **Mausoleo delle Fosse Ardeatine**, scene of one of the most horrifying events of the Second World War, during the German occupation of Rome. On 24 March 1944, as a reprisal for the killing on the previous day of 32 German soldiers by the Resistance Movement in Via Rasella, the Germans shot 335 Italians. The victims, who had no connection with the killing of the German soldiers, included priests, officials, professional men, about a hundred Jews, a dozen foreigners, and a boy of fourteen. The Germans then buried the bodies here under an avalanche of sand artificially caused by exploding mines. Local inhabitants provided a medico-legal commission with the means of exhuming and identifying the bodies after the German retreat. The scene of the massacre, below a huge tufa cliff, now has cave chapels. The 335, reinterred after identification, are commemorated by a huge single concrete slab placed in 1949 over their mass grave, with a group of standing figures, in stone, by Francesco Coccia (1950).

The ***CATACOMBS OF ST DOMITILLA** (adm see p 45), or Catacombs of Saints Nereus and Achilleus, farther along Via delle Sette Chiese, are among the most extensive in Rome and may be the most ancient Christian cemetery in existence. Here were buried St Flavia Domitilla (niece of Flavia Domitilla, sister of Domitian) and her two Christian servants, Nereus and Achilleus, as well as St Petronilla, another Christian patrician, perhaps the adopted daughter of St Peter. The catacombs contain more than 900 inscriptions.

At the foot of the entrance stairway is the aisled BASILICA OF SAINTS NEREUS AND ACHILLEUS, built in 390–95 over the tombs of the martyred saints. There are traces of a schola cantorum, and ancient columns probably from a pagan temple. The area below the floor level has sarcophagi and tombs. By the altar is a rare small column, with the scenes of the martyrdom of St Achilleus carved in relief. The adjoining chapel of St Petronilla (shown during the tour of the catacombs) with a fresco of the saint, contained the sarcophagus of the saint until the 8C, when it was removed to St Peter's.

A friar conducts groups from the basilica to the **catacombs**, excavated on two levels. The CEMETERY OF THE FLAVIANS (the family of Domitilla) had a separate entrance on to the old Via Ardeatina. At this entrance is a vaulted vestibule probably designed as a meeting-place for the service of Intercession for the Dead, with a bench along the wall, and a well for water. A long gallery slopes down from here, having niches on either side, with 2C frescoes of flowers and genii. From the original entrance a gallery leads to another HYPOGEUM, with four large niches decorated with 2C paintings (Daniel in the lions' den, etc.). At the foot of a staircase is another ancient section; here is a cubicle with paintings of winged genii and the earliest representation of the Good Shepherd (2C). On the upper level is the CUBICULUM OF AMPLIATUS, with paintings in classical style. Other sections contain more paintings, including the Madonna and Child with four Magi; Christ and the Apostles; and a Cornmarket.

The Appian Way now leaves behind the area of the catacombs, and becomes more attractive and interesting for its Roman remains. On the left, in a hollow, at No. 153, are the extensive ruins of the **VILLA OF MAXENTIUS** (admission, see p 45), built in 309 by the Emperor Maxentius. This includes a palace, a circus, and a mausoleum built in honour of his son Romulus (d 307). The ***Circus** is the best preserved of the Roman circuses, and one of the most romantic sites of ancient Rome. From it is the best view of the Tomb of Cecilia Metella (see below). The circus was excavated by Nibby in 1825 for the Torlonia, and restored in the 1960s and 1970s.

The stadium (c 513 x 91m) was probably capable of holding some 10,000 spectators. The main entrance was on the W side with the 12 *carceres* or stalls for the chariots and quadrigae, and, on either side, two square towers, with curved façades. Two arches, one of which has been restored, connected the towers to the long sides of the circus and provided side entrances. In the construction of the tiers of seats amphorae were used to lighten the vaults (these can still clearly be seen). In the centre of the left side is the conspicuous emperor's box, which was connected by a portico to his palace on the hill behind (see below). At the far end was a triumphal arch where a fragment of a dedicatory inscription to Romulus, son of Maxentius, was found which identified the circus with Maxentius, previously attributed to Caracalla. In the centre, restored in 1971, is the round *meta* and the *spina*, the low wall which divided the area longitudinally (and where the obelisk of Domitian, now in Piazza Navona, originally stood). The course was seven laps around the *spina*. The spina and the carceres were both somewhat obliquely disposed to equalise as far as possible the chances of all competitors, although it is likely that the circus was never actually used since Maxentius fell from power in 312.

On the hillside to the left, towards Via Appia Pignatelli, are the overgrown remains (fenced off) of the **Palace** which include fragments of baths, a basilica, and a cryptoporticus. The conspicuous high wall near the W end of the circus belongs to the quadriporticus around the **Mausoleum of Romulus**, which faces the Via Appia. Some of the pilasters of the quadriporticus survive, as well as much of the outer wall. In the centre is the circular tomb preceded by a rectangular pronaos which lie beneath a derelict house. The entrance is in front of a palm tree: beyond the pronaos is the mausoleum with niches in the outside wall for sarcophagi, and a huge pilaster in the centre also decorated with niches. The upper floor, probably covered with a cupola, has been destroyed. Nearby, beside the Via Appia is the so-called TOMBA DEI SEMPRONII, probably dating from the Augustan era. It is not open to the public while excavations are still in progress.

The road rises to the famous *TOMB OF CECILIA METELLA, a massive circular tower of the Augustan period, 29.5m (100 Roman ft) in diameter, rising from a square base, and extremely well preserved (admission, see p 47; informed custodian). Much of the marble facing is still intact as is also part of the elegant frieze surrounding the upper part, with garlands of fruit and bucrania (hence the name *Capo di Bove* given to the adjacent ground). A relief represents a soldier with Gallic shields and a prisoner from Gaul kneeling at his feet. Also on the side nearest the road is the inscription to Cecilia, daughter of Quintus Metellus Creticus and wife of M. Licinius Crassus (elder son of the triumvir and one of Caesar's generals in Gaul). In the 13C the Caetani transformed the tomb into a crenellated tower to serve as the keep of their castle which they built across the roadway and included a Gothic church, the ruins of which can be seen on the other side of the road. The interior of the tomb (now inhabited by pigeons), constructed with small flat bricks, is particularly interesting; the roofless room on the right contains a collection of inscriptions and fragments from other tombs. The THIRD MILESTONE has recently been set up outside the enceinte of the castle, just to the left of the road, beneath the two-light windows.

A short distance farther on is Via Cecilia Metella, where the bus coming from the Colosseum diverges left from the Appia Antica to Via Appia Pignatelli and Via Appia Nuova. The Via Appia, lined by numrerous ancient tombs, becomes more and more interesting as the view of the Campagna opens out. To the left can be seen the imposing aqueduct of the Acqua Marcia and the Acqua Claudia.

About 4km from Porta San Sebastiano is the **ancient section of the Appian Way**, excavated in 1850–59 between the third and eleventh milestones. This is the best preserved part of the whole road, even though in recent years it has been neglected and partly used as a rubbish dump. For ten Roman miles or more it was bordered with tombs on both sides, and the picturesque remains of some of these were recovered and others reconstructed in the last century by Antonio Canova and Luigi Canina. Some of the original sculptures have been removed to the Museo Nazionale Romano and replaced here by casts (easily identified by their yellow tint); other monuments have been vandalised. In this century part of the area bordering the road has been occupied by luxurious private villas.

On a brick pilaster, on the left, opposite the site of the FOURTH MILE-STONE, are fragments of a tomb of a member of the Servilian gens. An inscription records that this was a gift made by Canova in 1808, who, contrary to the general practice of his time, felt that objects found during excavations should be left in situ. Beyond is the so-called TOMB OF SENECA (left; replaced by casts), immediately followed by the SEPOLCRO ROTONDO, a cella with four 'loculi', and the TOMB OF THE CHILDREN OF SEXTUS POMPEIUS JUSTUS (partly replaced by casts). Beyond this, set back from the road, is a so-called TEMPLE OF JUPITER, square with apsidal niches. On the right, in the Proprietà Lugari (near a clump of huge umbrella pines), is a superb monument in the form of a shrine (supposed to be that of St Urban), surrounded by the ruins of what was probably a villa.

In the next 550 metres are the scant remains of the TOMBS OF THE LICINII, of HILARIUS FUSCUS (the five busts replaced by casts), of the FREEDMEN OF THE CLAUDIAN GENS, and of Q. APULEIUS PAMPHILIUS. Beyond a sepulchre in the form of a temple is the TOMB OF THE RABIRII (the three busts replaced by casts). Beyond more tombs, one in peperino (decorated with festoons), and another with four busts (casts) the road crosses Via Erode Attico. At a point marked by a group of gigantic pines, near the FIFTH MILESTONE, the road makes a bend, probably to avoid some earlier tumuli, one of which (now surmounted by a tower) passes for the burial-place of one of the legendary *Curiatii*, while two others, surrounded by pines, about 350m farther on (right), represent those of the *Horatii*. In the field to the right of the first are the remains of an *Ustrinum* (cremation place). A gate on the left opens on a by-road leading to the estate of Santa Maria Nuova, built over ruins (see below), and, farther on, on the same side, is a great pyramidal tomb. Then, opposite the second of the graves of the Horatii, an inscription of the 1C BC marks the tomb of M. Caecilius, in whose family grave (according to Eutropius) was buried Pomponius Atticus, the friend of Cicero.

Just beyond are the magnificent and picturesque ruins of the *Villa of the Quintilii**, now part of the property of Santa Maria Nuova (see above). The ruins sprawl across fields through which sheep are grazed. These are so extensive as to suggest a town rather than a villa and in fact they used to be called *Roma Vecchia*. The villa, of which the principal mass dates from the time of Hadrian, belonged under Commodus to the wealthy brothers Quintilii, Maximus, and Condianus, consuls under Antoninus Pius (AD 151) and writers on agriculture, who were put to death by Commodus for the sake of their possessions, including the villa. This was kept in repair until the 4C. Near the road are the remains of a nymphaeum (converted in the 15C into a castle), a hippodrome, and an aqueduct, and, a little in front of them, a cryptoporticus. But the greater portion of these ruins lies nearer the Via Appia Nuova, where there are high walls with windows and boldly executed arcades, also the floor of a small amphitheatre of later date and traces of thermae. Beyond the Via Appia Nuova is a fine monument, converted into a tower by the Saracens.

The road now becomes more deserted, and the monuments more widely scattered. The **Casal Rotondo**, 8km from Porta San Sebastiano, is a large round tomb on a square base, with an incongruous modern house and an olive garden on the summit. This was the largest tomb on the Appian Way, and dates from the Republic; it was enlarged in early Imperial times. It is said to have been erected to the memory of the poet Messala Corvinus by his son Valerius Maximus Cotta. The stylobate is 120 Roman ft (c 36m) in diameter. Attached to a wall close by are fragments of the tomb. Facing this monument is a smaller one attributed to the Aurelian gens. Just beyond the Casal Rotondo are cross-roads, on the far side of which was the SIXTH MILESTONE. Here also the Rome–Naples railway passes diagonally below in a short tunnel.

Via di Torricola, on the right leads towards the Via Ardeatina; 4.5km before this intersection is the **Santuario del Divino Amore**, at Castel di Leva. The sanctuary, crowded with pilgrims on Whit Monday, was inaugurated in 1745 to enshrine a picture of the Virgin painted by an unknown 14C artist in the surviving tower of the CASTEL DI LEVA, a castle of the Orsini which passed to the Savelli before its destruction in the 15C. The painting, credited with miraculous powers of protection, is said to have saved the life of a pilgrim attacked here by mad dogs.

On the left Via di Casal Rotondo, bearing left after a short distance slopes down to the Via Appia Nuova. This is a convenient point at which to leave the Appian Way; otherwise it can still be followed as far as the Grande Raccordo Annulare.

Beyond the Casal Rotondo is a tomb with reliefs of griffins and a columbarium. Opposite another columbarium, on the right of the road, is a tomb with four busts (casts). Some way farther on (about 1km from the Casal Rotondo) is the TORRE IN SELCE, a pyramidal tumulus with a medieval tower, 107m above sea-level. The remainder of the road is less interesting, and has been abandoned to rubbish and prostitutes; it soon becomes impracticable for cars.

Beyond inscriptions of M. Julius Pietas Epelides and C. Atilius Eudos, a jeweller, the road swerves a little and begins to descend, and the arches of an aqueduct by which the water of a sulphur spring near Ciampino was formerly conveyed to the villa of the Quintilii, are prominent. Near this point the Appian Way is cut in two by the Circular Road (*Grande Raccordo Anulare*; radius 11–16km), linking all the consular highways that lead out of Rome. The first section was opened in 1951 and it has only recently been completed. Its total length is 68km. It is already too narrow to carry the volume of traffic passing round Rome, and is always very busy.

On the other side of the Circular Road the Appian Way is totally abandoned. It passes the TORRE ROSSA (a 12–13C structure on a Roman base) and, at about the end of the eighth Roman mile, a sepuchral chamber (or possibly a sanctuary of the mysteries), known as the 'Pillars of Hercules'.

Farther along Via Appia, beyond the TORRACCIO DEL PALOMBARO (a monument preserved through having been turned into a church in the 10C), is a path that leads on the right to LA GIOSTRA, a little hill upon which are ruins, once identified with the ancient Latin city of *Tellene*, but now thought to be a 4C Roman fortified outpost. Then come other tombs, more or less ruined (including one called the RUZZICA D'ORLANDO); and at the NINTH MILESTONE is what is left of the VILLA OF GALLIENUS, with a fine circular ruin that is regarded as the mausoleum of that emperor. The road is here totally blocked by refuse: it crosses the Rome–Terracina railway and, a little beyond the TWELFTH MILESTONE, joins the busy Via Appia Nuova.

18

San Lorenzo fuori le Mura

The **Basilica of San Lorenzo** in Piazzale del Verano is reached by numerous buses and trams from the centre of the city (i.e. No. 71 from Piazza San Silvestro, No. 11 from the Colosseum, etc.).

The basilica of ***SAN LORENZO FUORI LE MURA** (Pl. 6; 4) is one of the seven pilgrimage churches of Rome and consists of two churches placed end to end. It is open 6.30–12.00, 15.30–18.30, but it is often used for funerals. Beside the 4C covered cemetery basilica of *San Lorenzo* (to the E) Pelagius II built a new church in 579. The church of the *Madonna* dates from the time of Sixtus III (pope, 432–40). These churches were united in 1216, when Honorius III demolished their apses; they were skilfully restored in 1864–70. San Lorenzo was the only church in Rome to suffer serious damage during the Second World War, when it was partly destroyed in an air raid on 19 July 1943. The façade and the S wall of the church of the Madonna were rebuilt after the war, and the basilica was reopened for worship in the summer of 1949.

The simple Romanesque CAMPANILE dates from the 12C. The reconstructed 13C NARTHEX of six antique Ionic columns has a carved cornice and a mosaic frieze. Inside are two unusual tombs, a tablet (1948) commemorating repairs ordered by Pius XII after war damage, and a monument to the statesman Alcide De Gasperi (died 1954) by Giacomo Manzù; the 13C frescoes depict the lives of Saints Laurence and Stephen.

The basilican 13C INTERIOR has a chancel and no transept. Twenty-two Ionic columns of granite support an architrave, and the floor is paved with a 12C Cosmatesque mosaic. On the right of the entrance is the tomb of Cardinal Fieschi, a large Roman sarcophagus converted to its present use in 1256; it was rebuilt from the original fragments after the bombardment. Near the end of the nave on the right is a Cosmatesque ambone and the twisted stem of a paschal candlestick.

The baldacchino in the CHOIR is by Augusto and Sassone, sons of the mastermason Paolo (1147; upper part modern). The episcopal throne dates from the 13C. Inside the triumphal arch is a 6C mosaic of Christ with saints, and Pelagius offering the Church, reset during the Byzantine revival. The raised *CHANCEL incorporates the 6C church (except for its apse). The Corinthian columns support an entablature of antique fragments, and above, an arcaded gallery.

Stairs lead down to the level of the earliest basilica, with some of the original pillars. In its former choir, now beneath the high altar, are preserved the remains of Saints Laurence, Stephen, and Justin. The original narthex, at the end, is now the mausoleum of Pius IX (died 1878), rebuilt by Cattaneo in 1881 and decorated by Lodovico Seitz. The lunette mosaics are good; the coats of arms commemorate the families that subscribed to the tomb. In the sacristy, off the right aisle, is the entrance to the *CLOISTER built in 1187–91, with varied columns, and inscriptions and fragments on the walls, and pagan sarcophagi (a ridiculous fountain has recently been installed here). Off the cloister are the extensive CATACOMBS OF ST

CYRIACA (closed indefinitely) where the body of St Laurence is said to have been placed after his death in 258.

To the right of the church is the entrance to the huge municipal cemetery called **Campo Verano** (Pl. 6; 4), on the site of the estate of the emperor Lucius Verus. It was designed by Giuseppe Valadier in 1807–12, with a church and quadriporticus by Virginio Vespignani. The four colossal allegorical figures at the entrance date from 1878. Among the tombs is that of Goffredo Mameli (died 1849), the soldier-poet (first avenue to the left). On the high ground beside Via Tiburtina is a memorial of the battle of Mentana (1867). In the zone of the new plots is a First World War memorial, by Raffaele De Vico.

PIAZZALE SAN LORENZO, a busy traffic centre and bus and tram terminus, is traversed by Via Tiburtina, on the site of the ancient Roman road to Tibur (now Tivoli). Viale Regina Elena leads NW between the Istituto Superiore di Sanità with a research centre for chemical microbiology, and (left) the **Città Universitaria** (Pl. 6; 3, 4), one of the most interesting examples of Fascist architecture. The extensive series of faculty buildings were designed on a monumental scale by Marcello Piacentini and completed in 1935, in which year the seat of the University of Rome was transferred here from its cramped quarters in Palazzo della Sapienza. Numerous other buildings have been built in this century (some by Giovanni Michelucci) as the university has expanded. The entrance is in Piazzale Aldo Moro.

Behind a bronze statue of Minerva, by Arturo Martini, rises the RECTOR'S PALACE (with a fresco by Mario Sironi in the Aula Magna), and the UNIVERSITY LIBRARY, founded by Alexander VII (with more than 1,000,000 vols). In the Faculty of Letters are three study collections (open by appointment, Monday–Friday, 9.00–13.00): the MUSEO DELLE ORIGINI, which illustrates the pre-history of Italy (founded in 1942, it was reopened in 1991); the MUSEO DELLE ANTICHITÀ ETRUSCHE E ITALICHE, and the MUSEO DELL'ARTE CLASSICA (formerly the Museo dei Gessi), with more than 1000 casts of Greek and Hellenistic statuary. The Botanical Institute has an important Herbarium. The chapel of DIVINA SAPIENZA, is also by Piacentini (1950). To the S, at the junction of Viale delle Scienze with Via dei Marrucini, is the building of the National Council of Research, by Dagoberto Ortensi.

Across Viale delle Science is the Air Ministry by Roberto Marino (1931), and beyond Viale dell'Università is the **Policlinico** (Pl. 6; 1, 3), a large teaching hospital, designed by Giulio Podesti (1893). To the W are the buildings (entrance on Viale Castro Pretorio), opened in 1975, of the **Biblioteca Nazionale Centrale Vittorio Emanuele II** (Pl. 6; 1). The National Library, the largest in Italy (open weekdays 9.00–18.30, Saturday 9.00–13.30) was founded in 1877 with the contents of the library of the Jesuit Collegio Romano (its former seat), and later enriched with the books from 70 monastic libraries. It now has about 4,500,000 volumes (a copy of every book published in Italy has to be sent here), 1935 incunabula, and 6500 manuscripts.

The library is on the site of the CASTRA PRETORIA, the huge Roman barracks of the Praetorian Guard. The *Praetoriae Cohortes*, or emperor's bodyguard, originally nine or ten cohorts (9000–10,000 men), were instituted by Augustus and concentrated into a permanent camp here by Sejanus, minister of Tiberius in AD 23; some portions of his building survive. In later Imperial times the Praetorian Guard acquired undue influence in the conduct of affairs of state. As Gibbon pointed out, emperor after emperor had to bribe them on his accession with a 'donative'; on one occasion, after the death of Pertinax in 193, they put up the Roman Empire for sale by auction; it was bought by Didius Julianus, who enjoyed his purchase for 66 days. Centuries later the Castro Pretorio passed into the hands of the Jesuits, who renamed it *Macao*, after their most successful foreign mission. It was again used as barracks in this century.

Via San Martino della Battaglia leads SW to PIAZZA DELL' INDIPENDENZA (Pl. 5; 4), on the site of the *Campus Sceleratus*, where vestals who had forgotten their vows of chastity were buried alive. Via Solferino continues to Piazza dei Cinquecento in front of the Railway Station (Rte 10).

19

Porta Pia and Via Nomentana (Sant'Agnese fuori le Mura)

The important church of **Sant'Agnese fuori le Mura**, a long way from the centre of the city along a relatively uninteresting road, may be reached from Piazza Venezia by Bus No. 60.

Porta Pia (Pl. 5; 2), restored in 1989, a high isolated arch, was Michelangelo's last architectural work, commissioned by Pius IV in 1561. The exterior face is by Virginio Vespignani (1868). It stands at the beginning of Via Nomentana. The ancient *Porta Nomentana*, walled up by Pius IV, is in Piazza della Croce Rossa to the right. The N tower has been preserved. The Castro Pretorio here and the area to the S are described in Rte 18. It was by the Porta Pia that the Italian troops under General Raffaele Cadorna entered Rome on 20 September 1870 and so brought to an end the temporal power of the popes. The actual breach was, however, a few steps to the left of the gate, in Corso d'Italia (commemorative stones). In the small courtyard of the gateway is the MUSEO STORICO DEI BERSAGLIERI (admission on request), which documents the wars of independence, the African campaign, and the First World War. Outside the gate is a monument of 1932.

Inside the gate, on the left, is VILLA PAOLINA, seat of the French Embassy to the Vatican. It was the home of Pauline Bonaparte from 1816–24, and was once famous for its garden. On the other side of Via XX Settembre is the BRITISH EMBASSY, a conspicuous building surrounded by water, by Sir Basil Spence opened in 1971, on the site of the VILLA TORLONIA damaged by a terrorist's bomb in 1946.

The wide **Via Nomentana** (Pl. 12; 8) runs NE from Porta Pia, traversing a residential district of the city, with palaces and villas, many with beautiful gardens. It follows the line of the ancient Roman consular road to Nomentum, now Mentana, c 20km NE of Rome. Any of the buses here pass the church of Sant'Agnese fuori le Mura (see below). On the right, in Via dei Villini, at No. 32 are the CATACOMBS OF NICOMEDES, named after a martyr of the reign of Domitian (adm only with special permission).

Beyond Viale Regina Margherita on the left is Villa Paganini (a public garden), and on the right is the garden of **Villa Torlonia** (Pl. 12; just beyond 8), which became the private residence of Mussolini after 1929. Since 1978 it has been open to the public (9.00–dusk) as a municipal park (13.5 hectares). It is in an abandoned state and the buildings have been vandalised. By the entrance gate, near a grove of palm trees, is a neo-classical villa built by Giuseppe Valadier in 1806. This may be restored for use by the University of Rome. Several neo-Gothic garden buildings built here in 1840 by Giuseppe Japelli are in urgent need of restoration. The stained glass made in 1916–19 for the delightful little Art Nouveau CASINA DELLE CIVETTE, was removed and restored in 1987. There are long-term plans to restore the building and use it as a musuem. There is also a theatre built in 1841–74. Beneath the house and grounds are JEWISH CATACOMBS (2C or 3C), which originally extended for over 9km, but are now mostly caved in (and closed indefinitely). For the other Villa Torlonia, see Rte 20.

About 2km from Porta Pia, opposite a fountain of the Acqua Marcia, stands the church of *SANT'AGNESE FUORI LE MURA, in an important group of palaeochristian buildings. These consist of the ruins of a large cemetery basilica built probably after Constantine's death by his elder daughter Constantia in 337–50 on her estate next to the tomb of the martyred St Agnes (304). Above the crypt sanctuary and catacombs Honorius I (625–38) built a second church, when the Constantinian basilica was already in ruins. Next to the basilica (and with an entrance from its S aisle) Constantia built her mausoleum in which she and her sister Helena were buried. According to a Christian tradition, St Agnes, having refused the advances of a praetor's son, was exposed in the Stadium of Domitian, where her nakedness was covered by the miraculous growth of her hair. She was then condemned to be burned at the stake, but the flames did not touch her, so that she was finally beheaded by Diocletian. The *Pallium* worn by the Pope is made of the wool of lambs blessed annually on the day of her festival, 21 January.

The most direct entrance is on Via Sant'Agnese, but you can also enter through the gate of the convent of the Canonici Lateranensi on Via Nomentana, from which the campanile of the basilica of Honorius and the small colonnaded front can be seen. On the right of the court is a hall (originally a cellar) into which Pius IX and his entourage fell unharmed after the collapse of the floor of the room above in 1855. Beyond a fine tower is the entrance to the 7C **Basilica of Sant'Agnese fuori le Mura** (open 9.00–12.00, 16.00–18.00; Sunday 16.00–18.00), restored in 1479 by Giuliano Della Rovere (Julius II), by Cardinal Varallo after the sack of 1527, and by Pius IX in 1856. It is reached by a staircase of forty-five white marble steps (1590), the walls of which are covered with inscriptions from the catacombs, including St Damasus's record of the martyrdom of St Agnes (on the right near the bottom).

In the INTERIOR of the church (best light in the afternoon) the nave and aisles are separated by fourteen ancient Roman columns of breccia and pavonazzetto. There is a narthex for the catechumens, and a matroneum was built over the aisles and the W end in 620. The carved and gilded wood ceiling dates from 1606 (restored in 1855). In the second chapel on the right, over a Cosmati altar, is a fine relief of St Stephen and St Laurence, by Andrea Bregno (1490), and a bust of Christ once attributed to Michelangelo and probably the work of Nicolas Cordier.

On the high altar, in which are preserved the relics of St Agnes and St Emerentiana, her foster-sister, is an antique torso of Oriental alabaster restored in 1600 as a statue of St Agnes, beneath a baldacchino (1614) supported on four porphyry columns. On the left of the altar is a fine candlestick, thought to be a neo-Attic work of the 2C. In the apse is the original plain marble decoration and an ancient episcopal throne. Above, a *mosaic (625–38), representing St Agnes between Popes Symmachus and Honorius I, two restorers of the basilica, a model of which is held by Honorius. The simplicity of the composition, against a dull gold background is striking.

In the left aisle is the entrance to the *Catacombs of St Agnes, the best-preserved and among the most interesting Roman catacombs (open at the same time as the church, see above). They were discovered in 1865–66. Visitors are conducted. The atmosphere in these catacombs, not normally visited by travellers in large groups, offers a striking contrast to that in the more famous catacombs on the Appian Way (see Rte 17) which are usually crowded with tours. These contain no paintings but there are numerous inscriptions and many of the loculi are intact. They may date from before 258 but not later than 305; the oldest zone extends to the left of the basilica. A chapel was built where the body of St Agnes was found, and a silver coffer provided in 1615 by Pope Paul V.

On the other side of the entrance court a path leads to the round mausoleum of Constantia, known as the church of *SANTA COSTANZA (open at the same time as Sant'Agnese, see above; if closed apply at the sacristy in Sant'Agnese; it is often in use for weddings). This was built probably before 354 by Constantia as a mausoleum for herself and her sister Helena. The charming INTERIOR is annular in plan: twenty-four granite columns in pairs with beautiful Corinthian capitals and pulvinated imposts support the dome, which is 22.5m in diameter. Sixteen clerestory windows provide light. On the barrel-vaulting of the encircling ambulatory are remarkable palaeochristian *mosaics (4C), pagan in character. They are designed in pairs on a white ground. Those flanking the entrance have a geometric design, and the next, a circular motif with animals and figures. Vintage scenes and vine tendrils with grapes follow, and the 4th pair have roundels with a leaf design, busts, and figures. On either side of the sarcophagus are leaves, branches, amphorae, and exotic birds. Over the sarcophagus only a fragment remains of a mosaic with a star design. The two side niches also have fine mosaics (5C or 7C). Constantia's magnificent porphyry sarcophagus was replaced here by a cast when it was removed to the Vatican.

Two small gates on the right of the mausoleum lead into an overgrown garden and orchard with the remains of the huge **Constantinian basilica** (see above), identified in 1954. They include the outer walls with a round window in the apse, sustained on the outside by huge buttresses. In plan it was typical of the early cemetery basilicas of Rome, such as San Lorenzo fuori le Mura, San Sebastiano, etc.

Beyond the church of Sant'Agnese Via Nomentana continues NE towards the river Aniene. On the right, incorporated in the garden wall of the Villa Blanc, is a 2C circular tomb looking like a small copy of the Mausoleum of Cecilia Metella. The gardens of the **Villa Blanc** were designated a public park in 1974, but are still not open to the public and are in a state of abandon. The villa, built in an eclectic style with Art Nouveau elements, is in urgent need of repair.

Farther on, to the left, in Via Asmara (No. 6), is the entrance to the CATACOMBS OF THE CIMITERO MAGGIORE (adm only with special permission), with interesting frescoes. The road crosses the river Aniene by the modern Ponte Tazio. The Aniene, the ancient *Anio*, rises near Tivoli, where it falls in cascades on its way to the Campagna. Here the river is quiescent. On the right of the new bridge is the Roman *Ponte Nomentano, rebuilt by Narses in 552 and guarded by a medieval watch-tower. Beyond the river is the dismal modern QUARTIERE DI MONTE SACRO, named after the *Mons Sacer* (37m), which rises to the right. This was the scene in 494 BC of the first secession of the plebs, who were induced to return to Rome by the fable of the belly and its members recited to them by Menenius Agrippa.

20

Via Salaria (Villa Torlonia and the Catacombs of Priscilla)

The **Catacombs of Priscilla**, a long way from the centre of the city, can be reached from the Station by Bus No. 319 (nearest stop, Via di Priscilla).

PIAZZA FIUME (Pl. 12; 7) is on the site of the Roman *Porta Salaria*. The gate no longer exists but the bases of two tombs in the square define its width. Here begins **Via Salaria** (Pl. 12; 7, 5, 4, 2), one of the oldest Roman roads, which takes its name from its association with the salt trade between the Romans and the Sabines. It runs (now the modern N4) via Rieti and Antrodoco to Ascoli Piceno and the Adriatic near San Benedetto del Tronto. Some 300 metres outside the gate it passes the large park with umbrella pines (right) of *Villa Torlonia (Pl. 12; 5, 6), formerly *Albani*, built in 1760 by Carlo Marchionni for Cardinal Alessandro Albani, whose valuable collection of classical sculpture was arranged here by Winckelmann in 1765. By order of Napoleon 294 pieces of this collection were removed to Paris; after Waterloo nearly all of them were sold at Munich instead of being returned. The original collection, however, continued to increase. In 1852 it passed into the possession of the Chigi and in 1866 it was bought, with the villa, by Princess Alessandra Torlonia. Visitors are sometimes admitted, but only after previous written application to the Amministrazione Torlonia, 30 Via della Conciliazione. There are two villas of the same name, the one described here, and the former residence of Mussolini, in Via Nomentana (Rte 19).

The CASINO surrounded by a formal garden, has a hemicycle with forty Doric columns. In the PORTICO are niches with busts of Roman emperors. Beyond an ATRIUM with caryatids, the first gallery has a collection of herms. On the STAIRCASE are Roman reliefs and a frieze of Diana slaying the Niobids, possibly reproduced from the composition of Pheidias for the throne of Zeus Olympios. On the first floor the OVAL HALL has the statue of an athlete, signed by Stephanos (1C BC). In the GREAT HALL the ceiling *painting of Parnassos is by Raphael Mengs. Here is displayed the Albani Pallas, wearing the diplax or folded mantle with a clasp (the head, from another statue, has a wolf's head headdress), a statue of the Attic school. In the RIGHT WING are paintings, including works by Alunno (Madonna and saints, signed and dated 1475),

Perugino (polyptych), Giovanni Paolo Pannini, Honthorst, Pompeo Batoni, Van Dyck (Crucifixion), Taddeo Zuccari, Tintoretto, Ribera, and Guercino.

The LEFT WING has a celebrated *relief of Antinous, from Hadrian's villa, the only piece brought back from Paris in 1815; the so-called Leucothea, a relief dating from the beginning of the 5C BC; a 5C *relief of a battle scene, showing the influence of Pheidias; the *Apollo auroktonos, ancient copy after Praxiteles; a bust of Quintus Hortensius; and the *Apotheosis of Hercules, in the style of the Tabula Iliaca in the Capitoline Museum. The so called Aesop is a naturalistic nude statue of a hunchback, possibly a portrait of a court dwarf of the time of Hadrian. The paintings include sketches by Giulio Romano of the story of Psyche in Palazzo del Te at Mantua, and works by Borgognone, Luca Giordano, and Gaspare Vanvitelli. On the ground floor is the STANZA DELLA COLONNA, a room with 12 fine columns (one fluted, in alabaster), in which is displayed a *sarcophagus, with a scene of the marriage of Peleus and Thetis, considered by Winckelmann to be one of the finest in existence. The CAFFEEHAUS contains Roman mosaics.

Opposite Villa Torlonia is the circular MAUSOLEUM OF LUCILIUS PETO, dating from the time of Augustus. Behind the mausoleum, on the corner of Via Po and Via Livenza, a 4C HYPOGEUM was discovered in 1923, 9m below ground level. It contains frescoes and mosaics, and may have been a cult sanctuary or possibly a monumental fountain (it is not normally open to the public). Via Salaria continues to the road junction with Viale Regina Margherita (right) and Viale Liegi (left) which leads to the **Parioli** (see p 291), a fashionable residential district of the city.

In this area are a number of catacombs not normally open to the public, but sometimes open to visitors with special permission (see Rte 17). In Piazza Verdi is the ISTITUTO POLIGRAFICO DELLO STATO (Government printing works, 1930). Beside a church are the CATACOMBS OF PANFILO (Pl. 12; 5), visited in 1594 by Antonio Bosio and further excavated in this century. They contain frescoes, and tombs decorated with lamps and statuettes. At 13 Via Bertoloni are the CATACOMBS OF SANT'ERMETE (Pl. 11; 4), with a large underground basilica, containing an 8C fresco of the Madonna and angels with Saints Hermes and Benedict, the earliest known painting of the last.

On the other side of Via Salaria, at 2 Via Simeto, is the entrance to the CATACOMBS OF SANTA FELICITÀ or MASSIMO (Pl. 12; 5), with a small underground basilica.

Via Salaria continues past St George's English School (left), and now widens with a line of pines down the centre. Via Panama skirts the wall of the vast expanse of VILLA ADA (formerly Savoia; Pl. 12; 1, 2), the garden wall of which extends for a long way along Via Salaria. This was once the private residence of Victor Emmanuel III, and is now the embassy of the United Arab Republic. Part of the grounds are open as a public park.

On the other side of Via Salaria, on the corner with Via Taro, is the entrance to the CATACOMBS OF THE GIORDANI (Pl. 12; 4; adm only with special permission), believed to be the *Catacombs of Trasone* before excavations were carried out in 1966–69. These are the deepest catacombs in Rome, with five tiers of galleries, and contain a fine 4C mural of a woman in prayer. Farther on, between Nos 2 and 4 VIA ANAPO (Pl. 12; 4) is the entrance to another CATACOMB, formerly thought to be the cemetery of the Giordani. This contains interesting frescoes of Old and New Testament scenes, dating from the 3C and 4C. Adm only with special permission.

At 430 Via Salaria is the entrance to the **Catacombs of Priscilla** (Pl. 12; 2; adm see p 45), the most important catacombs on Via Salaria, and among the most interesting in Rome. Visitors are taken in groups by an English-speaking nun. The tour is on the road level, although there are further catacombs (unlit) below. The exit is usually on the other side of Via Salaria. The dating and significance of the various areas of the catacombs are still under discussion. Several parts were found to have a layer of lime, formed after centuries of earth had been packed against the walls, and this was removed in some places, and the frescoes beneath saved. It is now thought a villa of the Roman family of Acilii existed above the cemetery, to which the cryptoporticus (with cross-vaulting and remains of Pompeian-style frescoes) and a nymphaeum probably belonged. Many popes were buried here between 309 and 555.

The so-called GREEK CHAPEL (from the Greek inscriptions found here) is an interesting funerary chapel with frescoes of biblical scenes and good stucco decoration. A banquet scene on the apse arch includes the figure of a woman. These paintings, once thought to date from the 2C, were probably not in fact executed before the end of the 3C. In the area of the 'arenario' (probably a pozzolana stone quarry) is the CUBICULUM OF THE VELATI with late 3C scenes from the life of the deceased woman including a woman and child, once taken to be the Madonna and Child and so erroneously thought to be one of the earliest known representations of this familiar subject.

21

Trastevere

TRASTEVERE (Pl. 7; 2, 4), the area 'across the Tiber' (*trans Tiberim*), has been, since the Middle Ages, essentially the popular district of Rome, and its inhabitants seem to retain the characteristics of the ancient Romans, who are said to have been proud and independent. This area of the city has been distinguished by its numerous artisans' houses and workshops since Roman times. In the last decade or so it has become a fashionable place to live, and it now has a cosmopolitan atmosphere.

In earliest Republican days this bank of the Tiber was occupied by Lars Porsena in his attempt to replace the Tarquins on the Roman throne; and here was the scene of the exploits of Horatius, Mutius Scaevola, and Cloelia. Under the Empire, though it was still called the 'Ripe Veientana', it became densely populated by artisans and dock workers. On the higher ground, and along the water-front, suburban villas were built by the aristocracy. These included the houses of Agrippa and of Clodia, both of which have been identified with the late-Republican villa excavated in 1880 next to the Farnesina (and then destroyed), the magnificent wall-paintings of which are preserved in the Museo Nazionale Romano. Trastevere was the stronghold of independence during the Risorgimento; here Mazzini found support for his Republic of 1849, and here Giuditta Tavani Arquati, with her family made an attempt to incite the city on Garibaldi's behalf in 1867. In July, the lively festival of '*Noi Antri*' ('we others') takes place here.

The **Tiber**, or *Tevere* (418km long), is the most famous though not the longest of the rivers of Italy. It is said originally to have been called *Albula* and to have received the name of *Tiberis* from Tiberinus, king of Alba Longa, who was drowned in its waters. It rises in the Tuscan Apennines, NE of Arezzo and, fed by numerous mountain streams, is liable to sudden flooding. Its swift waters are discoloured with yellow mud, even far from its source: hence the epithet *flavus* given to it by the Roman poets. The deposits brought down by the river have appreciably advanced the coastline; long ago the port of Ostia was rendered useless by silting up. The salt marshes near the river-mouth have been drained in a reclamation scheme. There are long-term plans to clean its polluted waters.

PONTE GARIBALDI (Pl. 7; 2), a modern bridge, with small obelisks, leads to the busy Piazza Gioacchino Belli, named after the Roman dialect poet and containing a monument to him, by Michele Tripisciano (1913). Here begins the wide and traffic-ridden VIALE TRASTEVERE. On the left is the over-re-stored 13C PALAZZETTO ANGUILLARA, with its corner tower, the last of many which once guarded Trastevere. The picturesque courtyard is a modern reconstruction using ancient material. The building is now the CASA DI DANTE (tablet), where readings from the 'Divina Commedia' have been given by leading Italian men of letters since 1914 (now on Sunday from November–mid March, 10.30–12.00). The Library (open Monday, Wednesday, and Friday 17.00–20.00) has the best collection in Italy of works relating to the poet.

On the other side of the Viale is the church of **SAN CRISOGONO** (Pl. 7; 4), founded in the 5C and rebuilt by John of Crema between 1123 and 1130. It was reconstructed by Giovanni Battista Soria in 1623 and restored in 1866. The CAMPANILE dates from the 12C. In the INTERIOR (open 7.00–11.30, 16.00–19.00) are twenty-two ancient Roman Ionic columns separating the nave from the aisles; the triumphal arch is supported by two huge monolithic porphyry columns. The baldacchino by Giovanni Battista Soria rests on four columns of yellow alabaster. The 13C opus sectile pavement has been restored. A mosaic in a square frame in the apse, attributed to the school of Pietro Cavallini, depicts the Madonna and Child betwen Saints James and Chrysogonus. Beneath the church (entered through the sacristy in the left aisle, down a steep spiral iron staircase unlocked by the sacristan on request) is an interesting 5C PALAEOCHRIS-TIAN CHURCH, on the site of a late-Imperial Roman edifice later adapted for Christian use. The annular crypt was added by Gregory III (731–41); its mural decoration survives, as well as later frescoes and a number of fine sarcophagi.

Behind the church is the huge hospital of SAN GALLICANO, a remarkable utilitarian building by Filippo Raguzzini (1724). The handsome long low façade, with the two floors divided by a balcony, incorporates a church in the centre.

The description below follows a somewhat circuitous route through old Trastevere to the church of Santa Cecilia (Pl. 8; 3); the direct approach to this church is via Via dei Genovesi which runs left from Viale Trastevere.

Across Viale Trastevere the old Via della Lungaretta leads E on the line of the last stretch of the ancient Roman Via Aurelia. The first turning on the right, in Piazza del Drago (Via di Monte Fiore), leads to the GUARDROOM OF THE SEVENTH COHORT OF VIGILES (Roman firemen). Remains can be seen from the street: the interior (entrance at 9 Via della VII Coorte) can only be seen with special permission. It contains interesting graffiti refer-ring to reigning emperors, from Severus to Giordian III, and a bath or nymphaeum. The barracks were built on the site of a 2C private house.

Via della Lungaretta continues to Piazza in Piscinula (Pl. 8; 3). In the far corner on the right is the small church of SAN BENEDETTO, with a charming 11C roofed campanile. (If closed, ring at the door to the right of the façade.) On the left of the vestibule, a fine doorway leads into an ancient cross-vaulted cell, in which St Benedict is said to have lived. To the left of the entrance door is a detached 13C fresco of St Benedict (restored). Inside, eight antique columns with diverse capitals divide the nave from the aisles. The fine pavement is Cosmatesque. Above the altar is a 15C painting of St Benedict, and a damaged fresco of the Madonna and Child (15C). Opposite is the medieval CASA DEI MATTEI (restored), with a 15C loggia, and 14C cross-mullioned windows.

Via dell'Arco dei Tolomei leads out of the other side of the piazza through an arch, and Via dei Salumi diverges left. A short way along on the right is Vicolo dell'Atleta (interesting house at No. 14 where the bronze horse now in the Capitoline Museum, and the statue of the Apoxyomenos now in the Vatican, were found), which leads to Via dei Genovesi, and its extension (left), Via Augusto Jandolio. Immediately opposite is a house (Nos 9, 10) with wooden eaves (characteristic of this area). To the left, at the end of the street, can be seen the church of Santa Maria in Cappella (No. 6), dating from 1090 (and now propped up with scaffolding), with a contemporary campanile. The lovely old Vicolo di Santa Maria in Cappella leads to PIAZZA DEI MERCANTI (with fine 15C houses, including one on the right recently over-restored). The piazza now has several restaurants (not cheap).

In the piazza to the right is the church of **SANTA CECILIA IN TRASTEVERE** (Pl. 8; 3; usually open 10.00–12.00, 16.00–18.00), on the site of the house of St Cecilia and her husband St Valerian, whom she converted to Christianity. This building was adapted to Christian use probably in the 5C, and the body of St Cecilia was transferred here and a basilica erected by Paschal I (817–24). The church, radically altered from the 16C onwards, was partly restored to its original form in 1899–1901. The slightly leaning campanile dates from 1120.

St Cecilia, a patrician lady of the Gens Cornelia, was martyred in 230, during the reign of Alexander Severus. She was shut up in the calidarium of her own baths (see below), to be scalded to death. Emerging unscathed, she was beheaded in her own house, but the executioner was so maladroit that she lived for three days afterwards. She was buried in the Catacombs of St Calixtus, where her body remained until its reinterment in her church in 820. As the inventor of the organ, she is the patron saint of music. On 22 November churches hold musical services in her honour.

Beyond an elaborate FAÇADE attributed to Ferdinando Fuga (1725) is the ATRIUM, with a fountain made from a large antique marble basin for ceremonial ablutions in a lovely garden. The PORTICO with four antique Ionic columns bearing a frieze of 12C mosaic medallions, precedes the Baroque façade of the church. The INTERIOR, an aisled 18C hall whose piers (1823) enclose the original columns, contains a ceiling fresco of the Coronation of St Cecilia by Sebastiano Conca. WEST WALL. On the left of the door, *monument of Cardinal Niccolò Forteguerri (died 1473), the assistant of Pius II and Paul II in their suppression of the great feudal clans, a beautiful work attributed to Mino da Fiesole (recomposed in 1891). On the other side of the door, tomb of Cardinal Adam Easton (died 1398), a distinguished English churchman who was appointed cardinal in 1381, deposed by Urban VI (c 1386), and reappointed by Boniface IX in 1389. It bears the arms of England and may be the work of Paolo Taccone.

SOUTH AISLE. In the first chapel, fresco of the Crucifixion (?14C). The CORRIDOR on the right (closed for restoration in 1993), with landscapes (very ruined) by Paul Brill and a marble figure of St Sebastian attributed to Lorenzetto, leads to the ancient CALIDARIUM (closed indefinitely), where St Cecilia was to be scalded to death by steam but was miraculously preserved. The steam conduits are still visible. On the altar is the Beheading of St Cecilia, and opposite, Saints Cecilia and Valerian, by Guido Reni. Also off the south aisle opens the CAPPELLA DEI PONZIANI, with ceiling-frescoes and, on the walls, Saints George, Catherine of Alexandria, Sebastian, and

James, all by Pastura. The 18C CAPPELLA DELLE RELIQUE is by Luigi Vanvitelli. The last chapel contains the theatrical tomb (1929) of Cardinal Rampolla, who was responsible for the excavations beneath the church. In a small room preceding it a tondo of the Madonna by Perugino was stolen in 1993. In the chapel at the end of the aisle is a very damaged 12–13C fresco detached from the portico showing the Discovery of the Body of St Cecilia.

In the SANCTUARY is a fine *baldacchino (1293), signed by Arnolfo di Cambio. Beneath the altar is a celebrated *statue of St Cecilia, by Stefano Maderno. The body of the saint is represented lying as it was found when her tomb was opened in 1599, on which occasion the sculptor was present. The luminous 9C *mosaic (restored in 1993) in the APSE shows Christ blessing by the Greek rite, between (right) Saints Peter, Valerian, and Cecilia, and (left) Saints Paul, Agatha, and Paschal (the last with the square nimbus); below are the flock of the Faithful and the Holy Cities. The CRYPT is decorated in the Byzantine style by Giovanni Battista Giovenale (1899–1901), with luminous mosaics by Giuseppe Bravi. Behind a grille are the sarcophagi of St Cecilia, St Valerian and his brother St Tiburtius, St Maximus, and the Popes Lucius I and Urban I. The statue of St Cecilia is by Cesare Aureli. In the NORTH AISLE, the fourth, third, and second altarpieces are by Giovanni Baglione, and the first altarpiece is by Giovanni Ghezzi.

The ROMAN EDIFICES BENEATH THE CHURCH are entered from the W end of the N aisle (open at the same time as the church). The excavations have not yet been fully explained, but are generally thought to consist of two Roman houses (possibly including the house of St Cecilia), probably united in the 4C for Christian use. Some scholars also believe there are remains here of a palaeochristian basilica. In the various rooms are mosaic pavements and a number of Christian sarcophagi. A 2C room with eight huge basins in the floor was probably used as a tannery. A *lararium* with Republican columns contains a niche with a relief of Minerva in front of an altar. A frescoed room (not yet open to the public) was discovered in 1991 with an ancient large font for total immersion.

Inside the CONVENT (also entered from the W end of the N aisle; shown on Tuesday and Thursday 10.00–11.15, Sunday 12.00–12.30), in the Nun's choir can be seen the splendid *fresco of the Last Judgment (restored in 1980) by Pietro Cavallini, a masterpiece of medieval Roman fresco painting (c 1293). This used to be the inside façade of the old church.

From Piazza Santa Cecilia, Via di San Michele leads right. It is fronted by the long bright orange façade of the huge building of the **ex Istituto San Michele a Ripa** (Pl. 8; 3), seat of the Ministero per i Beni Culturali e Ambientali since 1983, and of the Istituto Centrale del Restauro since 1976. Restoration of this huge complex has almost been completed and it is used for exhibitions and conferences, and paintings from the Galleria Borghese are temporarily exhibited here (see below).

The site was purchased in 1686 by Monsignor Tommaso Odescalchi, nephew of Innocent XI, who here founded a hospice and training centre for orphans and vagabond children, built by Carlo Fontana. In 1701 Fontana added a prison building. The façade of the huge building facing the Tiber was completed after Fontana's death by Nicola Michetti. In 1734 Ferdinando Fuga added a women's prison (the prison buildings were in use up to 1870). Numerous artisans' workshops were later installed here, and a renowned tapestry manufactory. The buildings were purchased by the State in 1969 and restoration work was begun in 1973. It is also now the headquarters of the International Center for the Study of the Preservation and Restoration of Cultural Property created by 'UNESCO' in 1956.

The entrance at 22 Via San Michele leads into a large courtyard with a fountain. To the left is a second courtyard, off which is the CHIESA GRANDE (open 9.00–19.00; fest. 9.00–13.00; closed Monday), which at present houses a selection of about two hundred **paintings from the Galleria Borghese** while the upper floor of the Villa Borghese (see Rte 9) is closed to the public. The church was begun in 1713 on a Greek-cross plan by Carlo Fontana, and finished in 1835 by Luigi Poletti, who added the neo-classical choir. The statue of the Saviour here is by Adamo Tadolini.

The paintings are all labelled. On the right of the entrance: Perugino, *St Sebastian; copy of Raphael's painting of the Fornarina attributed to Raffaellino dal Colle; Raphael, *Portrait of a Man, *Lady with a unicorn, possibly the portrait of Maddalena Strozzi; Lorenzo di Credi, tondo of the Madonna and Child; Niccolò dell'Abate, Portrait of a lady; Andrea del Sarto, *Madonna and Child with the young St John; Bronzino, *St John the Baptist; Vittore Carpaccio, Courtesan; Brescianino, Venus and two putti; Lucas Cranach, Venus and Cupid. On the right wall at the entrance to the transept: landscapes by Paul Brill and *Lamentation by Rubens. In the right transept: two self-portraits, and the portrait of a boy by Gian Lorenzo Bernini; four tondos of mythological subjects (Venus, Adonis, Vulcan, and Diana) by Francesco Albani; Guercino, Sampson; Domenichino, Diana the huntress. Six paintings by Caravaggio: *Madonna of the Serpent, painted for the Palafrenieri (the Papal Grooms), who hung it in St Peter's; it was later criticised for its excessive realism and removed from the church. Also here, *David with the head of Goliath; Boy with a basket of fruit; Boy crowned with ivy; St Jerome; and St John the Baptist.

In the centre of the church: small paintings by Marcello Venusti, Scarsellino, and Garofalo. Girolamo Savoldo, Portrait of a Young Man, *Tobias and the Angel; Alessandro Allori, Cosimo I (copy from Bronzino). In the left transept: Dosso Dossi, *Circe, Apollo and Daphne; Palma Vecchio, Lucrezia; Michele di Ridolfo del Ghirlandaio, Leda; Paolo Veronese, *Preaching of the Baptist; Parmigianino, Portrait of a man; Federico Barocci, Eneas fleeing from the fire of Troy; Correggio, *Danaë; Sassoferrato (copy from Titian), Three Ages of Man; Lorenzo Lotto, Portrait of the widower Mercurio Bua; Titian, Scourging of Christ, St Dominic, Venus blindfolding Cupid. In the last section are two Roman scenes attributed to Canaletto.

Masterpieces of the collection not at present on view include: Deposition (or Christ carried to the Sepulchre) by Raphael, signed and dated 1507; Sacred and Profane Love (being restored) by Titian; Portrait of a Man by Antonello da Messina; and Madonna and Child by Giovanni Bellini.

At the far end of the building of the ex Istituto San Michele, the Tiber is crossed by PONTE AVENTINO. The original bridge at this point, the *Pons Sublicius*, was the first bridge across the Tiber; it is said to have been built by Ancus Marcius, fourth king of Rome, to connect the Janiculum with the city. From the bridge there is a good view of the Roman PORT lining the opposite bank of the Tiber along Lungotevere Testaccio. Here in 193–174 BC an EMPORIUM was constructed, backed by the PORTICUS AEMILIA. This was a wharf with extensive storehouses some 500 metres in length.

To the right, on this side of the Tiber, the PORTA PORTESE, built by Urban VIII (1623–44) replaces the former *Porta Portuensis*, dating from the time of Honorius. The famous **Porta Portese 'flea' market** is farther S, near Stazione Trastevere. Open only on Sunday mornings, it is the largest general open market in Rome, noted for clothes.

From Piazza di Santa Cecilia (see above) Via di Santa Cecilia leads to Via dei Genovesi, which leads left to the church of SAN GIOVANNI BATTISTA DEI GENOVESI (1481; restored). The remarkable 15C *cloister is entered along Via Anicia on the left (ring at No. 12, Tuesday and Thursday, 14.00–16.00; summer, except August, 15.00–18.00). It has an arcaded lower gallery and a trabeated upper storey, with a beautiful garden of orange trees. Via Anicia continues past (right), the church of SANTA MARIA DELL'ORTO, with an unusual façade attributed to Vignola crowned with obelisks, and an ornate interior, with 17C and 18C works.

Via Anicia ends in Piazza San Francesco d'Assisi, in which is the church of **San Francesco a Ripa** (Pl. 7; 4), built in 1231 to replace the old hospice of San Biagio, where St Francis stayed in 1219. The last chapel on the left has the famous *statue of Beata Lodovica Albertoni, showing her in a state of mystical ecstasy. It is a late work by Bernini, displayed effectively by concealed lighting. Above is an altarpiece by Baciccia. The CELL OF ST FRANCIS (apply at the sacristy), contains relics (displayed in an ingenious reliquary), and a 13C painting of the saint, in the style of Margaritone d'Arezzo.

Via Tavolacci rejoins Viale Trastevere, across which Via Morosini leads past the right side of the Ministero di Pubblica Istruzione. Via Roma Libera is the first road to the right, and here, at No. 76 is the old people's HOSPICE OF REGINA MARGHERITA (formerly the convent of San Cosimato). Visitors are admitted to see the beautiful 12C cloister with twin columns, and in a garden on the left, the church of SAN COSIMATO dating from the 10C, rebuilt in 1475. It has a good doorway, and contains (on the left of the altar) a 15C fresco of the Virgin with Saints, and the tomb of Cardinal Alderano Cybo (died 1550), ascribed to Iacopo Sansovino (this is now a second altar in a chapel to the left). The second cloister has 15C octagonal columns. From Via Roma Libera the original narthex can be seen, and beyond is Piazza San Cosimato with a large market.

Via di San Cosimato leads N via Piazza San Calisto to **Piazza di Santa Maria in Trastevere** (Pl. 7; 4), the characteristic centre of Trastevere. The handsome *FOUNTAIN, of Roman origin, was restored by Carlo Fontana (1692). Palazzo di San Calisto on the left of the church, was rebuilt in the 17C by Orazio Torriani.

The large basilica of *SANTA MARIA IN TRASTEVERE (Pl. 7; 4) was constructed by Julius II (337–52), and was probably the first church in Rome dedicated to the Virgin. According to legend a 'taberna meritoria' or hostel for veteran soldiers existed near the site, and some sort of Christian foundation is known to have existed here under St Calixtus (pope, 217–22). The great basilica of Julius II was rebuilt by Innocent II in 1140, and slightly modified later. A careful restoration programme of the church and its works of art has been in progress since 1983. The campanile is Romanesque.

The FAÇADE bears a 12–13C mosaic of the Madonna surrounded by ten female figures with lamps (two of which are extinguished), of uncertain significance. The PORTICO added by Carlo Fontana in 1702 (and recently restored) contains an interesting lapidary collection, including Roman inscriptions and reliefs from sarcophagi, and medieval fragments including some from a schola cantorum. The worn frescoes of the Annunciation date from the 15C. The three doorways are made up from Roman friezes.

In the splendid 12C *INTERIOR (open 7.00–12.45, 15.00–18.45) are twenty-one vast ancient columns from various Roman buildings, some with fine bases and (damaged) capitals. The opus sectile pavement is made up of old material; the wood *CEILING was designed by Domenichino (1617), who painted the central Assumption. The decoration on the walls of the nave and triumphal arch was carried out when the church was remodelled by Pius IX in the 19C. The charming tabernacle at the beginning of the S aisle is by Mino del Reame. In the N AISLE is the tomb of Innocent II (died 1143), erected by Pius IX in 1869, and the *AVILA CHAPEL, designed by Antonio Gherardi (1680–86), with a remarkable Baroque dome and very unusual altar.

The CHOIR is preceded by a marble screen made up of transennae and plutei, many of them remade in the 19C. Near a Paschal candlestick here is the spot on which a miraculous fountain of oil is supposed to have flowed throughout a whole day in the year of Christ's Nativity in the 'taberna meritoria'. The baldacchino over the high altar is by Virginio Vespignani. The *MOSAICS of the triumphal arch and apse (1140; restored in 1993) are particularly fine; on the arch, the Cross with the symbolic Alpha and Omega between the seven candlesticks and the Evangelical emblems; at the sides, Isaiah and Jeremiah, with the rare and touching symbol of the caged bird (Christus Dominus captus est in peccatis nostris). In the semi-dome, Christ and the Virgin enthroned beneath the hand of God bearing a wreath and the monogram of Constantine. On the right, Saints Peter, Cornelius, Julius, and Calepodius; on the left Saints Calixtus and Laurence, and Pope Innocent II with a model of the church. Lower are six rectangles with mosaic *scenes from the Life of Mary, by Pietro Cavallini (c 1291), and, beneath them a mosaic rectangle with Saints Peter and Paul presenting the donor, Bertoldo Stefaneschi, to the Madonna (1290). Beneath the mosaics in the apse are late 16C frescoes by Agostino Ciampelli (to be restored).

To the right of the choir are the Armellini monument (1524) with sculptures by Michelangelo Senese, and the WINTER CHOIR, with decorations after Domenichino's designs. The chapel was restored by Henry of York in the 18C. The huge 16C organ is to be restored. To the left of the choir is the ALTEMPS CHAPEL, decorated with frescoes and stuccoes by Pasquale Cati (1588), with an interesting scene of the Council of Trent. On the altar is a photograph of a precious *painting of the Madonna 'della Clemenza', flanked by angels, displayed since its restoration in a little room on the left (seen through a glass door). This remarkable Byzantine work is thought to date from the 8C, or earlier. On the left wall outside the chapel is the tomb of Cardinal Stefaneschi (died 1417) by 'Magister Paulus', beside the monument to Cardinal Filippo d'Alencon (died 1397) which includes his effigy and the relief of the Dormition of the Virgin, also attributed to 'Magister Paulus' or a follower of Orcagna. The SACRISTY, approached by a passage with two exquisite tiny 1C Roman mosaics from Palestrina, one of marsh *birds and the other a port scene, contains a Madonna with Saints Sebastian and Roch of the Umbrian School (very worn).

Via della Paglia skirts the N side of the church. To the right opens Piazza Sant'Egidio, where, at No. 1B a **Folklore Museum** was opened in 1978 (adm see p 46). On the first floor are drawings and engravings by Bartolomeo Pinelli, and (in the gallery to the right) 19C paintings including works by Ippolito Caffi, and Gino Severini (1903). At the end are a series of charming life-size tableaux of Roman scenes by Orazio Amato (1884–1952) based on paintings by Pinelli. Beyond a room with more engravings wooden stairs lead up to the reconstructed studio of the poet 'Trilussa' (Carlo Alberto Salustri, 1871–1950). Two more rooms have water-colours of Rome by Ettore

Rooster Franz (1878), and in the last room are some objects from the studio of the musician Maestro Alessandro Vessella (1860–1929). The building is also used as a cultural centre.

Via della Scala leads out of the piazza past the ornate church of SANTA MARIA DELLA SCALA (1592), containing (over the first altar on the right), St John the Baptist by Honthorst, and a ciborium over the high altar by Carlo Rainaldi (1647). If closed, the church can be entered through the Carmelite Monastery (right) which adjoins the PHARMACY OF SANTA MARIA DELLA SCALA, administered by the monks. The old 17C pharmacy upstairs may sometimes be seen on request (ring at the door on the left). Via della Scala ends at PORTA SETTIMIANA (Pl. 7; 2), incorporated in the Aurelian Wall and rebuilt by Alexander VI (1492–1503; covered for restoration).

The street to the right, just before the gate, is Via Santa Dorotea. At No. 20 is the medieval CASA DELLA FORNARINA, the supposed house of Raphael's mistress. Other houses of this type may be seen in Vicolo dei Moroni. Via di Ponte Sisto leads to **Ponte Sisto** (pedestrians only), erected for Sixtus IV (1471–84), probably by Baccio Pontelli, to replace the ancient *Pons Janiculensis* (or the *Pons Antoninus*).

The unusual and attractive VIA GARIBALDI leads uphill from the gate towards the Janiculum (Rte 22). At the end of the first straight section of the road (before a sharp turn to the left) is the entrance at No. 27 to the convent of **Santa Maria dei Sette Dolori**. The church was begun by Borromini in 1643, and its unfinished façade (1646) can be seen through the gate. The vestibule and interior of the church are entered through the convent; door to the right of the façade. The church is oblong with rounded ends, with two apses in the middle of the long sides, and a continuous series of pillars connected by a heavy cornice. The disappointing interior decoration was added later in the 17C. The Janiculum hill is described in Rte 22.

Porta Settimiana marks the beginning of **Via della Lungara** (Pl. 7; 2, 1), the longest of the 'rettifili', or long straight streets built by the Renaissance popes. It was laid out c 1507 by Julius II to connect Trastevere with the Borgo. On the left is the building which houses the **Museo Torlonia**, considered to be the most important private collection of ancient sculpture in existence. For years closed 'for restoration' the interior was converted into flats in the 1970s and the works put in store. In 1977 the palace and collection were officially sequestered, and interminable bureaucratic procedures took place in an attempt by the State to acquire the collection. It now seems that at last the State has drawn up a plan with the Torlonia to rearrange the collection here and reopen it to the public. For further information apply to the Amministrazione Torlonia, 30 Via della Conciliazione.

The museum was founded by Gian Raimondo Torlonia (1754–1829) with sculptures from Roman collections, to which were added later the yields from excavations on the family estates at Cerveteri, Vulci, Porto, etc. There are over 620 pieces of sculpture, some over-restored, including a few Greek originals. The most important works include the 'Giustiniani Hestia', a splendid statue attributed to Kalamis (5C BC), and a bas-relief of Herakles liberating Theseus and Peirithöos (school of Pheidias; 4C BC). There are numerous Roman copies of works by Greek sculptors, notably Kephisodotos, Polykleitos, Praxiteles, and Lysippos. Of the Roman originals perhaps the most striking is a portrait statue of Lucilla, daughter of Marcus Aurelius. The Roman iconographic collection contains over one hundred busts of the Imperial era. The valuable Etruscan paintings (4C BC) are from Vulci. There is also a very fine collection of sarcophagi.

At the end of Via Corsini (No. 24) is the **Orto Botanico** (adm see p 47), founded on the Janiculum in 1660, but on this site only since 1883 when Tommaso Corsini donated the gardens of Palazzo Corsini, on the slopes of the hill, to the State. One of the most important botanical gardens in Italy, it covers some 12 hectares and is beautifully kept. It is famous for its palms and yuccas. A rare collection of orchids is kept in one of the 19C green houses.

In Via della Lungara, just beyond Via Corsini, on the left, is **PALAZZO CORSINI** (Pl. 7; 1, 2), built by Cardinal Domenico Riario in the 15C, and rebuilt by Ferdinando Fuga for Cardinal Neri Maria Corsini, nephew of Clement XII in 1732–36. Cardinal Corsini's fine collection of paintings was acquired by the State in 1883 and became part of the **GALLERIA NAZIONALE D'ARTE ANTICA** (which is now divided between this palace and Palazzo Barberini; admission, see p 46). The original Corsini collection (Inventory nos 1–606) has been returned here. The present arrangement is extremely crowded, but more rooms may eventually be opened to the public. The pictures are all labelled. The palace was the residence of Queen Christina of Sweden, who died here in 1689. In 1797 General Duphot was killed near here in a skirmish between the French democratic party and the papal dragoons, and in 1800 Madame Letizia, mother of Napoleon, came to live in the palace.

On the **First Floor** is a VESTIBULE with neo-classical sculptures by John Gibson, Antonio Solà, Pietro Tenerani, etc. **Room I**. Portraits of the Corsini, and a bust of Clement XII Corsini by Pietro Bracci. Pompeo Batoni, Nativity; Sebastiano Conca, Adoration of the Magi; Francesco Trevisani, Nymphs and Satyrs; two 18C bronze statuettes. **Room II**. 558. Giovanni da Milano, Madonna and Child and scenes from the Life of Christ; *464. Murillo, Madonna and Child, one of the finest versions by the painter of this familiar subject; works by David Teniers the Younger, and Marten van Cleve; 111. Van Dyck, Madonna and Child, probably painted during his stay in Italy; 388. Rubens, St Sebastian tended by angels; 350. Pourbus the Younger, Portrait of a man; 347. Joos van Cleve, Portrait of Bernardo Clesio; 354. Perino del Vaga, Portrait of Cardinal Alessandro Farnese; 318. Federico Barocci, Self-portrait; 140. Titian, Philip II; 193. Jacopo Bassano, Adoration of the Shepherds; 99. Andrea del Sarto, Madonna and Child; 488. Franciabigio, Portrait of a man; 221. 16C Roman school, La Fornarina; 116. Fra Bartolomeo, Holy Family; 397, 396, 395. Fra Angelico, triptych; 436. Francesco Francia, St George and the dragon; 686. Alessandro Algardi, Baptism of Christ (small bronze).

Room III (ahead). Works by Michelangelo Cerquozzi and Simon Vouet; 441. Gerard Seghers, Judith with the head of Holofernes; *107. Orazio Gentileschi, Madonna and Child; *433. Caravaggio, St John the Baptist. **Room IV**. Works by Callot, Van Bloemen, Luca Carlevaris, Gaspard Dughet (386. Landscape), and Jan de Momper (73, 75. Landscapes). **Room V** survives from the old Palazzo Riario. It is decorated by a follower of the Zuccari. Queen Christina of Sweden is supposed to have died in this room in 1689; her portrait as Diana by Justus van Egmont (c 1656) was placed here in 1991. A terracotta bust of Alessandro VII Chigi attributed to Bernini is also exhibited here, as well as works by Jan Miel and Michael Sweerts. **Room VI**. In the centre is the Corsini throne, dating from the 2C or 1C BC and present in the palace since 1700. 1696. Sarzana, Hagar and the angel; 186. Francesco Furini, Andromeda; 371. Baciccio, Portrait of Cardinal Corsini.

Room VII has a splendid view of the palm trees in the Botanical Gardens (see above). Here are displayed: 276. Guercino, Adoration of the Shepherds; 273. Sassoferrato, Madonna and Child; 279, 287. Guercino,

Madonna and Angel, and Annunciation; 79. Donato Creti, Jacob's Dream; works by Giovanni Lanfranco; 191. Guido Reni, Salome with the head of the Baptist. **Room VIII**. Works by Luca Giordano, including (394.) Jesus in the Temple; works by Salvator Rosa, including (484.) Prometheus; Mattia Preti, 117. Tribute Money, 1154. Eneas and Anchises.

The palace also houses the **Accademia Nazionale dei Lincei**, founded by 'Prince' Federico Cesi in 1603 for the promotion of learning, and said to be the oldest surviving institution of its kind. Galileo was a Lincean. The administrative offices are in the Villa Farnesina (see below). With it are incorporated the BIBLIOTECA DELL'ACCADEMIA (1848), with 100,000 volumes and other publications, the BIBLIOTECA CORSINIANA, founded in 1754 by Monsignor Lorenzo Corsini, with a valuable collection of incunabula, manuscripts, and autographs, and the FONDAZIONE CAETANI, whose object is to promote scientific knowledge in the Muslim world. The library may be visited (9.00–13.00; also 15.00–18.30 on Friday; entered from the ground floor to the right, up a spiral staircase). A series of rooms lead to a terrace overlooking the garden.

Opposite Palazzo Corsini is the entrance to the graceful Renaissance *VILLA FARNESINA (Pl. 7; 2), built by Baldassare Peruzzi (1508–11), as the suburban residence of Agostino Chigi, 'the Magnificent', the banker who controlled the markets of the East. It is surrounded by a lovely garden, once much larger. Admission, see p 47. Here Agostino Chigi entertained in grandeur Pope Leo X, cardinals, ambassadors, artists, and men of letters, and here he died on 10 April 1520, four days after Raphael. At a celebrated banquet in a loggia overlooking the Tiber (demolished in the 19C) silver plates and dishes were thrown into the river after every course (although it was later learned that a net had been in position to recover them). In 1590 the villa passed to Cardinal Alessandro Farnese, and received its present name, and through the Farnese it was inherited by the Bourbons of Naples in 1731. Since 1927 it has been the property of the State, and houses the administrative offices of the Accademia dei Lincei (see above).

Detail of the ceiling of the Loggia of the Galatea in Villa Farnesina

The painted decoration in the villa was carried out between 1510 and 1519, and was beautifully restored in the 1970s and 1980s. On the ground floor is the festive *LOGGIA OF CUPID AND PSYCHE, which formerly opened directly on to the garden. The ceiling has famous frescoes illustrating the legend of Apuleus in a beautiful painted pergola with festoons of fruit and flowers. The decorative programme was provided by Raphael (who probably also made the preparatory cartoons), and the paintings executed by his pupils, Giulio Romano, Francesco Penni, Giovanni da Udine, and Raffaellino del Colle. To the right is the LOGGIA OF THE GALATEA. The ceiling is frescoed with the constellations forming the horoscope of Agostino Chigi, by Peruzzi. The lunettes, with scenes from Ovid's 'Metamorphoses' are by Sebastiano del Piombo, although the colossal monochrome charcoal head here, a striking work, is now ascribed to Peruzzi. On the walls: the giant Polyphemus by Sebastiano del Piombo, and the celebrated *Galatea by Raphael, a superb composition (covered for restoration in 1993). This interrupts the decorative sequence and seems to have been painted just after the works by Sebastiano. The other scenes were added in the 17C by Gaspard Dughet. A little room off the loggia (door unlocked), known as the SALA DEL FREGIO, contains a beautifully painted frieze with mythological scenes by Peruzzi.

On the upper floor is the *SALA DELLE PROSPETTIVE, the drawing room, with charming trompe l'oeil views of Rome and mythological subjects by Peruzzi. The bedroom, known as the SALA DELLE NOZZE DI ALESSANDRO E ROSSANA, contains *frescoes by Sodoma.

Wall-paintings and stuccoes found in a Roman house in the grounds of the Villa are kept in the Museo Nazionale Romano. On the second floor of the Villa Farnesina is the **Gabinetto Nazionale delle Stampe** (open 9.00–13.00 except Sunday and Monday), with an exceptionally fine collection of prints and drawings housed in a series of beautiful rooms. Exhibitions are held here periodically. In 1975 this institute was merged with the Calcografia Nazionale as the ISTITUTO NAZIONALE PER LA GRAFICA, and there are plans to move it to Palazzo Poli, in Piazza di Trevi.

Via della Lungara continues along the right bank of the Tiber past the REGINA COELI prison (1881–1900) and the 16C Palazzo Salviati to Piazza della Rovere (Pl. 2; 5). The Borgo beyond is described in Rte 23.

22

The Janiculum Hill

The Janiculum is traversed by Bus No. 41 from Corso Vittorio Emanuele (Via Paola), near the Tiber (Pl. 2; 5). By foot the prettiest approach is from Trastevere (Via Garibaldi, or Vicolo del Cedro behind Piazza Sant'Egidio; see Rte 21).

The **JANICULUM** (82m; Pl. 7; 1, and 1; 8; in Italian, *Gianicolo*), not counted as one of the Seven Hills of Rome, is a ridge rising steeply from the Tiber and approximately parallel to its course for the whole of its length. It is now mostly covered with parks and gardens, and has wonderful *views from the ridge. It has two important churches, San Pietro in Montorio at its southern end and Sant'Onofrio to the north.

Its highest point, to the S, is Porta San Pancrazio; to the N it reaches almost as far as Piazza San Pietro. Its ancient name was *Mons Aureus* which referred to the yellow sand which covers its surface. The name of *Mons Janiculus* is derived from the old Italian deity Janus, who, according to legend, founded a city on the hill; his temple was in the Roman Forum. Numa Pompilius, the Sabine successor of Romulus, was buried on the Janiculum, and Ancus Marcius, the fourth king, is said to have built the Pons Sublicius over the Tiber to connect the Janiculum with the city of Rome. The hill provided a natural defence against the Etruscans, but it does not appear to have been fortified until the time of the Republic. Part of it was included within the Aurelian Wall, and it was completely surrounded by Urban VIII when he built his wall in 1642. It was the scene of Garibaldi's stand against the French troops of Marshal Oudinot in 1849. The *views from the ridge are famous.

Via Garibaldi (Pl. 7; 1, 2) mounts the hill from Trastevere. Above the church of Santa Maria dei Sette Dolori (described in Rte 21), on the right, is the former entrance gate to the BOSCO PARRASIO, where in 1725 the academy of **Arcadia** was established. It was founded in 1690 to carry on the work of the academy inaugurated by Queen Christina of Sweden ten years before for the discussion of literary and political topics. The object of Arcadia was to eliminate bad literary taste and to purify the Italian language, and it exercised a profound influence on Italian literature during the 18C. In 1786 Goethe was admitted as a 'distinguished shepherd'. Later its importance waned and in 1926 it was absorbed into the Accademia Letteraria Italiana. The paintings which belong to the academy are at present kept at the Museo di Roma. The garden can sometimes be seen on request at 32 Via di Porta San Pancrazio. Beyond a lovely circular dining-room with a dome (1725, by Antonio Canevari) is an amphitheatre, beyond which steps wind down through a small wood, circling a giant Roman pine.

Via Garibaldi continues to mount, in sweeping curves (if you are on foot you can take a short cut via steps to the right of the road), until it reaches a terrace. Here is the church of ***SAN PIETRO IN MONTORIO** (Pl. 7; 3, 4), built on a site wrongly presumed to have been the scene of St Peter's crucifixion. Mentioned in the 9C, the church was rebuilt in the late 15C at the expense of Ferdinand of Aragon and Isabella of Castile. The apse and campanile, damaged in the siege of 1849, were restored in 1851. Raphael's Transfiguration (now in the Vatican) adorned the apse from 1523 to 1809. In front of the fine simple façade (attributed to the school of Andrea Bregno) is a group of palm trees and a terrace with a view towards the Victor Emmanuel Monument, and, in the distance among the trees of its garden, the Villa Medici.

INTERIOR (lights in each chapel). SOUTH SIDE: first chapel, *Scourging of Christ, a superb work by Sebastiano del Piombo (1518) from designs by Michelangelo, and other frescoes by the same artist; second chapel, Madonna della Lettera, a detached fresco fragment formerly attributed to Pomarancio, but now thought to be by Giovanni Battista Lombardelli, and above, *Coronation of the Virgin, and four Virtues, attributed to Baldassarre Peruzzi. The fifth chapel has an altarpiece of the Conversion of St Paul by Vasari, and a balustrade and two tombs by Bartolomeo Ammannati. In front of the high altar are the tombstones of Hugh O'Neill of Tyrone and Roderick O'Donnell of Tyrconnel (1608), leaders in the Irish revolt against James I. Here also was buried Beatrice Cenci, beheaded as a parricide at Ponte Sant' Angelo in 1599.

NORTH SIDE. The fifth chapel, designed by Daniele da Volterra, contains a Baptism of Christ attributed to Giulio Mazzoni. The fourth chapel has stucco work attributed to Stefano Maderno; the Descent from the Cross and other frescoes are by Dirk Baburen (1617), a pupil of Caravaggio. Third chapel, altarpiece after Antoniazzo Romano. The second chapel (Raimondi) is an early work by Bernini, with an unusual relief of the Ecstasy of St Francis, executed by his pupils Francesco Baratta and Andrea Bolgi.

On the right of the church is a courtyard with the famous ***Tempietto** by Bramante (usually dated 1499–1502, or 1508–12), erected on the supposed exact site of St Peter's martyrdom. This jewel of the Renaissance, a miniature circular building with sixteen Doric columns of granite, combines all the grace of the 15C, with the full splendour of the 16C. The interior may sometimes also be seen (ring at the convent, 8.00–12.00, 16.00–19.00). Stairs designed by Bernini lead down to a crypt with pretty stuccoes by Giovanni Francesco Rossi. To the right of the court is the SPANISH ACADEMY.

Via Garibaldi continues to a neo-classical monument by Giovanni Jacobucci (1941), which commemorates the defenders and deliverers of Rome in 1849–70, and incorporates the tomb of Goffredo Mameli. Farther on is the fountain of the **Acqua Paola**, constructed for Paul V (as the handsome inscription states), by Giovanni Fontana and Flaminio Ponzio (1612), using marble from the Roman Forum. The water, which flows abundantly from the subterranean Aqueduct of Trajan (from Lake Bracciano), falls into a large granite basin added by Carlo Fontana in 1690, beneath six columns (four of which are from the façade of Old St Peter's). On the right of the road is a subsidiary entrance to the Passeggiata del Gianicolo (see below). At the top of the hill is the **Porta San Pancrazio** (Pl. 7; 3), built by Urban VIII, breached by Oudinot in 1849, and rebuilt by Virginio Vespignani in 1857. This gate, once known as the *Porta Aurelia*, was the starting-point of the Via Aurelia (see Rte 39).

From the gate Viale delle Mura Gianicolensi leads S to the VILLA SCIARRA, a Romantic park laid out in the early 20C, and now a public park (open 9.00–dusk). It has particularly fine wistaria which flowers in early spring. Beyond is the residential district of **Monteverde**.

In front of Porta San Pancrazio Via di San Pancrazio leads SW to the ruins of the VASCELLO, a Baroque villa where Goffredo Mameli and Luciano Manara were killed in a last sally in 1849. Farther on is an entrance to the ***VILLA DORIA PAMPHILJ** or *Belrespiro*, by far the largest park in Rome (9km round). It was laid out in 1644–52 for Prince Camillo Pamphilj, nephew of Innocent X. The beautiful park is owned partly by the State and partly by the Commune of Rome and is open to the public (daily, sunrise to sunset). Many of the 19C garden buildings are in need of restoration. Some of the statues have been vandalised (and others removed for safety). The views take in the Campagna as well as the city, and the umbrella pines are a feature of the park. The grounds were cut in two in 1960 by the Via Olimpica. The CASINO DEL BEL RESPIRO, built by Alessandro Algardi and Giovanni Francesco Grimaldi in 1644–52, with a formal garden, was used for receptions by the Italian State (but may become a sculpture museum). On Via Aurelia Antica (No. 183) is the VILLA VECCHIA decorated with exquisite stuccoes by Francesco Nicoletti in 1749–51 (restored in 1986).

Via di San Pancrazio passes the basilica of **San Pancrazio**, on the site of the tomb of St Pancrazio, who, according to Christian tradition, was martyred under Diocletian in

304. A Christian cemetery and 5C oratory existed here, and the present large basilica was built by Honorius I in 630, and remodelled in the 17C. The Baroque interior incorporates the apse, part of the transept and the annular crypt of the 7C church. The 4C CATACOMBS OF SAN PANCRAZIO (adm from the church) contain Oriental inscriptions.

Beyond Porta San Pancrazio is the beginning of the *Passeggiata di Gianicolo (Pl. 7; 1), a wide avenue laid out in 1884 (with fine pine trees) across the Villa Corsini above the fortifications of Urban VIII. At Piazzale del Gianicolo the road is joined by that from the Acqua Paola (see above). Here stands the conspicuous equestrian Statue of Garibaldi, by Emilio Gallori, erected in 1895 on the site of the hero's exploits of 1849. Around the base are four bronze groups: in front, Charge of Manara's Bersaglieri (Rome, 1849); behind, Battle of Calatafimi (1860); at the sides, Europe and America. The statue itself is 7m high.

The Passeggiata now goes downhill. On the right is the VILLA LANTE, built by Giulio Romano in 1518–27, and owned by Finland since 1950. On the left is the bronze equestrian STATUE OF ANITA GARIBALDI, by Mario Rutelli, presented by the Brazilian Government in 1935 to honour her Brazilian origin, and incorporating her tomb. Farther on is a BEACON, by Manfredo Manfredi, presented to Rome in 1911 by Italian residents in Argentina. A cannon shot is fired from here every day at 12 o'clock.

From this point there is an especially fine *view of Rome. On the extreme left is the dome of St Peter's, then Castel Sant'Angelo, San Giovanni dei Fiorentini, Palazzo di Giustizia and the modern Prati district, with the green slopes of the Villa Borghese, the Pincio, and the gardens of the Villa Medici behind, among which the French Academy and the Trinità dei Monti stand out. To the right is the façade of Montecitorio with its clock. Below the hill is the prison of Regina Coeli, and beyond the river the spiral campanile of the Sapienza, the dome of the Pantheon, and the Quirinal. Farther to the right is Sant'Andrea, and, in the distance, the bell-tower and domes of Santa Maria Maggiore. Then come the Torre delle Milizie, the triple-arched loggia of the Palazzo Farnese, the Victor Emmanuel Monument, the bell-tower of Palazzo Senatorio on the Capitoline Hill, and the dome of the Synagogue. Behind them are the statues crowning the façade of St John Lateran. Among the trees of the Janiculum, on the extreme right, is the Acqua Paola. The Alban, Tiburtine, and Praenestine Hills fall away gradually on the right.

The avenue continues downhill. A stairway on the right ('Rampa della Quercia'), avoiding a sweep of the road, leads down to TASSO'S OAK, the dead battered trunk (now supported by iron girders) of the tree beneath which Tasso used to sit (tablet; 1898), and around which St Philip Neri played 'sapiently' with the Roman children ('si faceva co' fanciulli fanciullo sapientemente').

Near the end of the avenue a short flight of steps leads up to the little Piazzale di Sant'Onofrio, with ilex trees and a fountain. Here is the church of SANT'ONOFRIO (Pl. 1; 8; open 8.00–12.00 only), founded by Blessed Nicolò da Forca Palena in 1419 and restored by Pius IX in 1857. A graceful L-shaped Renaissance portico connects the church and monastery. In the lunettes beneath the portico are three frescoes from the life of St Jerome (Baptism, Chastisement for reading Cicero, Temptation), by Domenichino, and over the door, a Madonna by Claudio Ridolfi. By the convent entrance is the tomb of the founder.

The dark INTERIOR (if closed, ring the bell to the right) is paved with numerous tombstones. On the left: the first chapel contains a monument to Tasso, by Giuseppe de Fabris (1857), and the third chapel, the tombstone of Cardinal Mezzofanti (died 1849), who could speak 50 or 60 languages. In the pretty apse over the main altar are repainted frescoes by the school of Pinturicchio; above them, scenes from the life of the Virgin. The fresco of St Anne teaching the Virgin to read, on the right, above the monument of Giovanni Sacco (died 1505), is by a pupil of Andrea Bregno. In the second chapel on the right, Madonna di Loreto, attributed to Annibale Carracci (or his school); in the vault pendentives above the altar in the first chapel, *Annunciation, by Antoniazzo Romano (light).

The **Monastery**, now occupied by American friars of the Atonement, has a charming 15C cloister, with frescoes of the life of St Onophrius, by Giuseppe Cesari, Sebastiano Strada, and Claudio Ridolfi. In the atrium is a monument to the 'Arcadian' poet, Alessandro Guidi (died 1712). In the upper corridor, above a Della Robbia frieze, is a fresco of the Virgin with a donor, much repainted, attributed to Giovanni Antonio Boltraffio. Torquato Tasso (1544–95), the epic poet, spent his last days and died here. The MUSEO TASSIANO (adm only by appointment with the Cavalieri del Santo Sepolcro, 33 Via della Conciliazione) occupies two rooms, containing the poet's death-mask, mementoes, MSS, and editions and translations of his works.

The steep Salita di Sant'Onofrio leads down to Piazza della Rovere (Pl. 1; 6), the end also of Via della Lungara. A gentler descent is by the road to the left, which passes the buildings of the pontifical NORTH AMERICAN COLLEGE, transferred from Via dell'Umiltà in 1953. PONTE PRINCIPE AMEDEO (1942) crosses the Tiber, and on the left is the road tunnel known as the *Traforo Principe Amedeo*, which leads under the Janiculum to Largo di Porta Cavalleggeri. In front is PORTA SANTO SPIRITO, an unfinished gateway begun in 1540 by Antonio da Sangallo. It leads by Via dei Penitenzieri into the *Città Leonina*, or Rione of the Borgo (see Rte 23).

23

The Borgo and Castel Sant'Angelo

The **BORGO** (Pl. 1; 4, 6 and Pl. 2; 5), the district on the right bank of the Tiber between the Janiculum to the S and Monte Mario to the N, was known in ancient Rome as *Ager Vaticanus*. It was the stronghold of the papacy from 850, when Leo IV surrounded it with a line of walls, until 1586, when it was formally incorporated in the city of Rome.

The **Ager Vaticanus** was chosen by Caligula (AD 37–41) for his circus, which was enlarged by Nero (54–68). The site of the CIRCUS OF NERO, just S of the basilica of St Peter's, was identified during excavations in this century. In the adjoining gardens many Christians were martyred under Nero in AD 65, including St Peter who was buried in a pagan cemetery near by. Over his grave the first church of St Peter's was built (c AD 90) to commemorate his martyrdom. Also within the Ager Vaticanus Hadrian built his mausoleum (now Castel Sant'Angelo) in 135.

Inscriptions found on the temples of Cybele and Mithras suggest that paganism retained its hold with great tenacity here up until the late 4C. Despite this tendency, churches, chapels and convents were built round the first church of St Peter and the district, attracting Saxon, Frank, and Lombard pilgrims, came to be called the *Borgo* (borough), a name of Germanic origin from 'borgus' meaning small fortified settlement. In 850 Leo IV (847–55) surrounded the Borgo with walls 12m high, fortified with circular towers, to protect it from the incursions of the Saracens: hence the name *Civitas Leonina* or *Città Leonina*. Remnants of Leo IV's wall survive to the W of St Peter's. The Leonine City became the papal citadel: within its walls John VIII was besieged in 878 by the Duke of Spoleto; in 896 Arnulph of Carinthia attacked it and Formosus crowned him emperor. Gregory VII, took refuge in the Castel Sant'Angelo from the Emperor Henry IV, and was rescued by Robert Guiscard in 1084. After the coronation in 1167 of Barbarossa in St Peter's, the Romans besieged the Leonine City (and it was attacked again twelve years later).

During the 'Babylonian captivity' (1309–78) the Borgo fell into ruin, but when the popes returned from Avignon to Rome they chose the Vatican as their residence in place of the Lateran. In the 15C Eugenius IV and Sixtus IV, and early in the 16C Julius II and Leo X, were active in developing and embellishing the Borgo as well as the Vatican. The original area of the Borgo was enlarged to the N of Borgo Angelico. However, after the sack of Rome in 1527 the Borgo became one of the poorest and least populated districts of Rome, and in 1586 Sixtus V relinquished the papal claim to this area, so that it was united to the city of Rome.

Five (originally seven) streets in the Leonine City have the prefix Borgo. Borgo Sant'Angelo and Borgo Santo Spirito run respectively N and S of Via della Conciliazione. In the construction of that street, the central Borgo Nuovo and Borgo Vecchio were destroyed. The remaining streets, the Borghi Angelico, Vittorio, and Pio survive between the Castel Sant'Angelo and the Vatican.

The celebrated ***Ponte Sant'Angelo** (Pl. 2; 5; pedestrians only, but closed for restoration in 1993), the ancient *Pons Aelius* or *Pons Adrianus*, was built by Hadrian (P. Aelius Hadrianus) in 134 as a fitting approach to his mausoleum, known since the Middle Ages as the Castel Sant'Angelo. It was transformed by Gian Lorenzo Bernini when he designed the ten ***statues of angels with the symbols of the Passion** on the balustrade. These were executed in 1688 by his pupils, including, Ercole Ferrata, Pietro Paolo Naldini, Cosimo Fancelli, and Antonio Raggi; two of the angels are copies of the originals which were removed to the church of Sant'Andrea delle Fratte. At the end towards the castle, the statues of St Peter and Paul, by the school of Lorenzetto and Paolo Taccone (1464), were set up by Clement VII in 1534. The three central arches are part of the original structure; the end arches were restored and enlarged in 1892–94 during the construction of the Lungotevere embankments. When the Tiber is in flood it sometimes rises to the top of the arches. Upstream is PONTE VITTORIO EMANUELE (1911), decorated with monumental sculptures in travertine, and bronze victories.

Facing the bridge is ***CASTEL SANT'ANGELO** (Pl. 2; 5), an enormous circular structure begun by Hadrian c AD 130 as a mausoleum for himself and his family. It was completed in 139, a year after his death, by his successor Antoninus Pius. In the early Middle Ages the tomb was surrounded with ramparts and became the citadel of Rome. In its general plan, the castle follows the design of Hadrian's mausoleum. The curtain walls of the inner ward, between the medieval bastions, are original; so is the entrance (no longer in use), except that the Roman threshold was lower. The round tower is Hadrian's, without its marble facing and its statues. Above it are the Renaissance and later additions, such as the arcaded galleries. The former papal apartments occupy the area of the earthen tumulus. The central tower was the base of Hadrian's quadriga, now replaced by a bronze angel. The pentagonal outer ward, added in the 16C, used to have five bastions (two of them were demolished during the construction of Piazza Pia and of the Lungotevere). The ditch between the two fortifications, planted with trees and covered with lawns, is a public park.

The castle, particularly interesting for its architecture, now contains the *MUSEO NAZIONALE DI CASTEL SANT'ANGELO (admission, see p 45), inaugurated in 1925. The fifty-eight rooms, some of which have fine 16C stuccoes and frescoes, contain a collection of paintings, furniture, tapestries, etc., and a military museum. The views of Rome and the Tiber are superb. The interior is a labyrinth of rooms, staircases, courtyards, and terraces. The various features are numbered with arabic numerals, which correspond to the numbers given in the description below, and constant reference should be made to the four plans within the text. Some rooms are often closed, and sometimes certain areas of the castle are temporarily inaccessible; the works of art are frequently rearranged. There is a small café on the Gallery of Pius IV (60). There is a lift reserved for the staff, and the disabled.

History. The mausoleum consisted of a base 89m square, supporting a round tower 64m in diameter, of peperino and travertine overlaid with marble. Above this was an earthen tumulus planted with cypress trees. At the top was an altar bearing a bronze quadriga driven by a charioteer representing Hadrian, as the Sun, ruler of the world. Inside the building was a spiral ramp (still in existence), which led to a straight passageway ending in the cella, in which was the Imperial tomb. Hadrian and Sabina (his wife), and his adopted son L. Aelius Caesar, were buried in the mausoleum; and succeeding emperors until Septimius Severus. When Aurelian built his wall round Rome, he carried it on the left bank of the Tiber above the Porta Settimiana. He built the Porta Aurelia Nova on the city side of the Pons Aelius and made Hadrian's mausoleum into a bridgehead on the other side of the river. He surrounded his bridgehead with a wall strengthened with towers.

The mausoleum was gradually transformed into a castle. Theodoric (474–526) used it as a prison and for a time it became known as the *Carceri Theodorici*. According to legend, St Gregory the Great, while crossing the Pons Aelius at the head of a procession to pray for the cessation of the plague of 590, saw on the top of the fortress an angel sheathing his sword. The vision accurately announced the end of the plague and from then onwards the castle has born its present name.

In the following centuries the possession of Castel Sant'Angelo was contested between popes and antipopes, the imperial forces and the Roman barons (Alberic, Crescentii, etc.). In 1084 Gregory VII was rescued from Henry IV's siege by Robert Guiscard. By the late 12C the castle was established as papal property. It was from here that Cola di Rienzo, at the end of his first period of dictatorship, fled to Bohemia on 15 December 1347. In 1378 the castle was severely damaged by the citizens of Rome, resentful of foreign domination. In the reign of Boniface IX rebuilding began. Alexander VI had Antonio da Sangallo il Vecchio complete the four bastions of the square inner ward (see below) which had been begun by Nicholas V. Julius II built the south loggia, facing the river. When Clement VII and some 1000 followers (including 13 cardinals and 18 bishops) took refuge here in 1527 from the troops of Charles V, Benvenuto Cellini took part in its defence. In a famous passage of his 'Autobiography' he describes his gifts of valour and marksmanship. Paul III built the north loggia and decorated the interior with frescoes. The outer ward, with its defensive ditch, was added by Pius IV. Urban VIII provided the castle with cannon made of bronze taken from the ceiling of the Pantheon portico, and he employed Bernini to remodel the outworks.

From 1849 to 1870 the castle was occupied by French troops. Under the Italian Government it was used as barracks and as a prison until 1901 when the work of restoration was begun, and in 1933–34 the castle was adapted for use as a museum and the surrounding area was cleared.

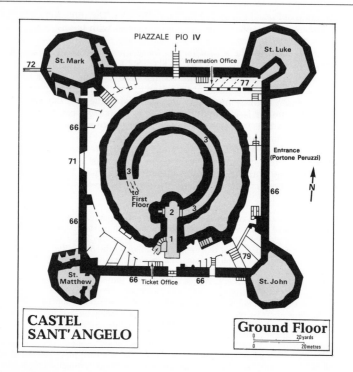

PIAZZALE PIO IV

Information Office

St. Mark

St. Luke

72

77

66

3

71

Entrance
(Portone Peruzzi)

3
to First Floor

66

N

66

2

3

1

79

66

St. Matthew

66 Ticket Office 66

St. John

CASTEL SANT'ANGELO

Ground Floor

0   20 yards
0   20 metres

Since 1993 the castle has been entered from the gardens on the E side. A ramp leads down to the PORTONE PERUZZI (see the plan above), an entrance gate to the castle built in 1556 by Giovanni Sallustio Peruzzi for Paul VI. It was adapted in 1628 for the use of barracks built by Urban VIII, and was demolished in 1892 when the Lungotevere was built and moved to this side of the castle. Inside the gate a street leads right past an information office and didactic display in a hall beneath the Chapel of the Crucifix (77). The delightful cobbled street continues between the foot of Hadrian's splendid round tower and the medieval castle walls to the TICKET OFFICE. The usual entrance (closed since 1991; see below) to the interior is reached by steps which descend to a spacious VESTIBULE (1), with models of the castle. On the left is the shaft (2) of a lift built for the infirm Leo X and, in front, a niche for a statue of Hadrian. On the right is a *spiral ramp (3; also closed for restoration), 125.5m long, which rises gently to the sepulchral cella (see below). The ramp is in a remarkable state of preservation; the floor has remains of mosaic decoration. Along it are four ventilators, the last but one of which was converted into a prison, mentioned by Benvenuto Cellini.

At present the entrance to the castle from the ticket office is by an outside stair which leads up past a small guard-house to the bastions (described below). A drawbridge (63) leads across to the castle, with a small guard-room (62) at the foot of the **Staircase of Alexander VI** (5), which cuts diametrically across the circular Roman building. By means of a bridge (6) built in 1822 by Valadier in place of a drawbridge the staircase passes above the Roman SEPULCHRAL CELLA (7), of which only the travertine wall blocks survive, with some fragments of marble decoration. Here were kept the urns containing the Imperial ashes. Hadrian's porphyry sarcophagus was annexed by Innocent II (1130–43) for use as his own tomb in the Lateran, where it was destroyed by the fire of 1360.

At a landing lit by a round window (9) the staircase of Alexander VI originally turned to the right. Paul III closed this section and opened one to the left (10; by Antonio da Sangallo the Younger), to give access to the **Courtyard of the Angel** (11), named from the marble statue of an angel (13) by Raffaello da Montelupo, removed here from the terrace at the top of the castle.

At the end of the court are the STAIRCASE OF URBAN VIII and the façade by Michelangelo (restored in 1988) of the MEDICI CHAPEL, built c 1514 for Leo X (12). On the right is a series of rooms (14, 15, II–VII, on two levels) which house a **Museum of Arms and Armour** (partly closed for restoration in 1993). The collection has material from the Stone Age to the 20C, and includes 15–18C arms found during excavations within the castle precincts. There is a display of prehistoric weapons, 14–17C defensive arms, swords, pikes, and firearms. The 19–20C material includes exotic arms from Africa and China, and 19C uniforms. Also off the Court of the Angel are the ROOMS OF CLEMENT VIII (16, 17) and the Hall of Justice (18) which are usually open only for exhibitions. The HALL OF JUSTICE (18) is so called because it was the seat of the tribunal of the 16–17C. It was built in Roman times above the sepulchral cella, and has a fresco of Justice attributed to Domenico Zaga.

Another door in the courtyard leads into the HALL OF APOLLO (19), named after the mythological grotesques on the ceiling attributed to Luzio Luzi. On the right is a trap-door covering a cellar 9m deep; adjacent is the top of the lift-shaft seen from the spiral ramp (see above). On the right is the CHAPEL OF LEO X (20), with a relief of the Madonna and Child attributed to Raffaello da Montelupo. Opposite are the ROOMS OF CLEMENT VII (21, 22). The first room (21) is decorated with a frieze by Giulio Romano, and has a coffered ceiling. The paintings include: two detached frescoes of the 15C Lombard school; 15C Tuscan school, Madonna enthroned; Niccolò l'Alunno, St Sebastian and St John the Baptist; Zavattari brothers, Polyptych; Carlo Crivelli, Christ blessing, St John the Baptist; Lorenzo Lotto, *St Jerome. ROOM 22: Martino Spanzotti, Pietà; Bartolomeo Montagna, *Madonna and Child; Luca Signorelli, Madonna and Saints; Giampietrino, Mocking of Christ.

A passage (23) leads right out of the Hall of Apollo into the large **Courtyard of Alexander VI** (24), with a fine marble well. Theatrical performances were given here in the time of Leo X and Pius IV. A small staircase (26) leads up to the charming BATHROOM OF CLEMENT VII (27) decorated with stuccoes and frescoes attributed to Giovanni da Udine. This room communicates with a small dressing-room on the next floor (closed). The COURTYARD OF LEO X (28) with a loggia is also usually closed; below it is a 15C casemate. Adjacent is a small triangular courtyard from which stairs lead to a chamber which had a stove for heating the bath water and the air which circulated between the hollow walls.

On the right side of the Courtyard of Alexander VI is a semicircular two-storeyed building, the rooms of which (25) were formerly used as prison cells. In the second room from the right Benvenuto Cellini was imprisoned during the first period of his captivity. A staircase leads down from the courtyard to the **historical prisons** (30). Two large underground OIL STORES (31) contain 84 jars, with a capacity of c 22,000 litres. The oil not only served to feed the garrison, but also as a defence, since boiling oil could be poured on attackers. The five GRAIN SILOS (32) were later used as prison cells. Other macabre prison cells open off a corridor; numerous bones found under the floors indicate that the prisoners were buried where they died. Benvenuto Cellini is said to have passed the second period of his captivity in the last cell.

Stairs lead back up to the Courtyard of Alexander VI, and from there a staircase (33) continues up to the semicircular **Gallery of Pius IV** (35), a terrace with a splendid *view. A series of small rooms here were used originally as quarters for the household of the papal court and later as political and military prison cells. The first (36: closed) is a reconstruction of a political prison in the first half of the 19C. In the rest (37; often closed) is an interesting muster of uniforms, decorations, and medals of the various Italian states before the Unification. To the left is the LOGGIA OF PAUL III (34), with another fine view, built by Antonio Sangallo the Younger and decorated with stuccoes and Mannerist grotesques in 1543–48. The LOGGIA OF JULIUS II (38), on a design by Giuliano da Sangallo, faces S and the Ponte Sant'Angelo.

A staircase leads from here to the **Papal Apartments** (39–49), decorated for Paul III in 1542–49. They are appropriately furnished, and the contents are mainly from the Contini donation. The SALA PAOLINA or DEL CONSIGLIO

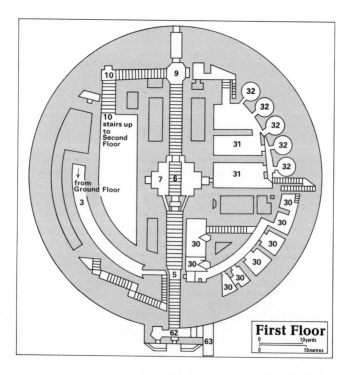

First Floor

(39) is adorned with *stuccoes by Girolamo da Sermoneta and Baccio da Montelupo. The walls are decorated by Pellegrino Tibaldi, Domenico Zoga, Perino del Vaga, Polidoro da Caravaggio, Giovanni da Udine, and others. On the right is an amusing trompe-l'oeil fresco of a courtier entering the room through a painted door. In the floor are the coat of arms of Innocent XIII who restored the room. The CAMERA DEL PERSEO (40) takes its name from the beautiful frieze by Perino del Vaga and his bottega (restored in 1982). The wooden ceiling is intaglio work of the 16C. The tapestries come from State collections and include one showing an episode in the life of Julius Caesar. The painting of Christ carrying the Cross is by Paris Bordone.

The CAMERA DI AMORE E PSICHE (41; seen beyond a railing) has another frieze (recently restored) by Perino del Vaga and his bottega, illustrating the story of Cupid and Psyche in seventeen episodes. It has a fine carved gilt 15C ceiling, a large 16C canopied bed, a clavichord, and other furniture. The paintings include: Christ carrying the Cross by Sebastiano del Piombo, and a Girl with a unicorn by a 16C artist. The statuette is attributed to Jacopo della Quercia.

From the Sala Paolina a corridor (43) frescoed in the Pompeian style by Perino del Vaga and his bottega leads to the HALL OF THE LIBRARY (44), with ceiling frescoes by Luzio Luzi and stuccoes by Sicciolante da Sermoneta (16C). The marble chimneypiece is by Raffaello da Montelupo. The furniture includes four cassoni and a 15C wardrobe. The ROOM OF THE MAUSOLEUM OF HADRIAN (45) is named after a frieze by Luzi and his

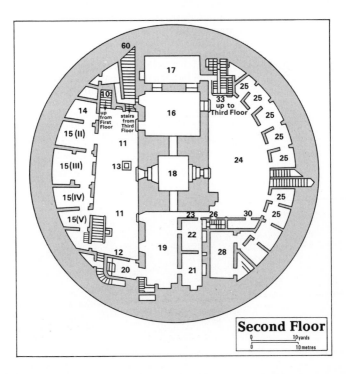

Second Floor

0 _____ 10 yards

0 _____ 10 metres

school. The three paintings of Bacchanals are 17C copies of works by Bellini, Poussin and Jordeans. The fine painting of the Madonna between saints Roch and Sebastian is a copy from Lorenzo Lotto. A case contains 15–17C ceramics. Beyond Room 46 a short flight of stairs leads up to the APPARTAMENTO CAGLIOSTRA (47–49; usually closed), three 16C rooms decorated with grotteschi by Luzi and containing a collection of majolica (15C 'alberelli', floor tiles, Deruta and Faenza ware).

A small vestibule leads out of the Hall of the Library into the central ROOM OF THE SECRET ARCHIVES or of the TREASURY (50). The walnut cupboards in this room were used for the archives inaugurated by Paul III. In the middle are some large chests in which Julius II, Leo X, and Sixtus V kept the Vatican treasury. A Roman staircase ascends to the ROUND HALL (51), situated beneath the statue of the angel and above the last room. Formerly used as a political prison, it now contains the armature of Verschaffelt's angel (see below), a cast of the head, and the original sword. A short staircase leads to the HALL OF THE COLUMNS (usually closed) which contains a charming 15C polychrome wood group of the Deposition, and a wooden model of the Archangel Michael attributed to Pietro Bracci. The two adjoining rooms (52–53) are only open for exhibitions.

The staircase continues up to the **terrace** (54) at the top of the castle, scene of the last act of 'Tosca'. On a small higher terrace (no admission) is a huge bronze *angel in the act of sheathing his sword (4m high) by Peter Anton Verschaffelt (1752). This commemorates the vision of Gregory the Great in 590 (see above) after which the castle is named. The *Campana della Misericordia* used to announce the execution of capital sentences.

The *view from the terrace is superb. On the left, in front, is the Palace of Justice, with the Trinità dei Monti just visible behind. Farther to the left, the Prati district; in the distance, the green park of the Villa Borghese and of the Pincio. Across the Tiber, the Ministry of Finance, with the orange Quirinal building in front; then Palazzo della Consulta, with Santa Maria Maggiore behind it. To the right, on the skyline, the Torre delle Milizie, with the cupola of the Pantheon in front. Next comes the Victor Emmanuel Monument, with St John Lateran behind it. In the background, the Castelli Romani. Continuing to the right, the bell-tower of Palazzo Senatorio on the Capitol Hill; in front, the two cupolas of Sant'Andrea della Valle and San

View towards St Peter's from Castel Sant'Angelo

Carlo ai Catinari. Then can be seen the Aventine, with San Paolo fuori le Mura in the background. Farther right, beyond Ponte Sant'Angelo, is Trastevere and the Janiculum; St Peter's and the Vatican; Monte Mario. Immediately below, Ponte Sant'Angelo and Ponte Vittorio Emanuele, with the Lungotevere.

From the terrace the descent is sometimes signposted by a modern staircase which passes three rooms of the APPARTAMENTO DEL CASTEL-LANO, beyond which stairs continue down to the Gallery of Pius IV and the Courtyard of the Angel. Otherwise visitors return from the terrace down the same staircase to the Hall of the Library (44), which should be crossed diagonally, and left by a door on the left of the fireplace. Stairs lead from here to the loggia of Paul III, from which another flight of stairs continues down to the Courtyard of Alexander VI. After this the route follows Paul III's staircase (10), and Alexander VI's staircase (5) to the exit.

The **ramparts** are traversed by open walkways (66) which encircle the Roman structure and connect the four **bastions** of the square inner ward (signposted to the right from the drawbridge near the entrance; 63). The first part of the walkway passes above a terrace with four 15C bombards and piles of marble and stone cannon balls, once part of the castle's ammunition store. Beyond the BASTION OF ST MATTHEW are the MILLS (71) used from the time of Pius IV to grind flour for the castle. The BASTION OF ST MARK is closed for restoration. Here can be seen the beginning of the COVERED WAY (*Corridoio* or *Passetto*; 72) which connects the castle with

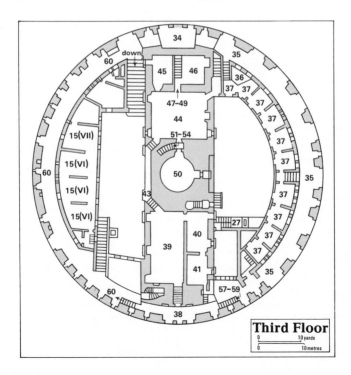

Third Floor

the Vatican. This was built in 1277–80 by Nicholas III above Leo IV's 9C defensive wall of the Borgo. It was reconstructed by Alexander VI, who used it as an escape route from the Vatican in 1494. It was again used in 1527 when Clement VII took refuge in the castle from the troops of Charles V.

Between the bastions of St Mark and St Luke is a passageway (closed) leading into the public gardens (Piazzale Pio IV). Just before the BASTION OF ST LUKE is the CHAPEL OF THE CRUCIFIX or of Clement XII (77), in which condemned criminals had to attend mass before execution. The circuit continues above the reconstructed gate of 1556 (the present entrance to the castle) to the BASTION OF ST JOHN, beyond which steps lead down to ground level. The exit is past two vaulted oil stores (79), where architectural and sculptural fragments found in the castle have been arranged, including Roman and Byzantine pieces. Also displayed here is a model of Hadrian's tomb.

Beside Castel Sant'Angelo, on the river front, is the huge **Palazzo di Giustizia** (Pl. 2; 3), the Palace of Justice, known as the 'Palazzaccio'. A colossal ornate building in solid travertine, decorated with sculptures by Enrico Quattrini and Ettore Ximenes, it was built between 1889 and 1910. It was evacuated in 1970 because it was in danger of collapse, but it has been partially reopened. New judiciary offices and law courts have been built by Giuseppe Perugini, and others in the CITTÀ GIUDIZIARIA (Pl. 15; 7), in Piazzale Clodio.

To the N, beyond Piazza Cavour, an important traffic centre and terminus for buses, are the PRATI and TRIONFALE districts. In Via Pompeo Magno is the church of SAN GIOACCHINO (Pl. 2; 3), erected by Raffaele Inganni in 1890 to commemorate the sacerdotal jubilee of Leo XIII (Gioacchino Pecci). The church has bronze capitals and an aluminium cupola painted inside to represent a star-strewn sky.

About 500m N is Piazza Mazzini. In Viale Mazzini to the right is the church of CRISTO RE built in 1930 by Marcello Piacentini, with a sculpture by Arturo Martini over the central door. It contains frescoes by Achille Funi and sculptures by Corrado Vigni and Alfredo Biagini. Next to it is the headquarters of the R.A.I. (the Italian State-owned radio and television network). About 700m farther N is the **Museo dell'Arma del Genio** (Pl. 15; 6; adm see p 46), illustrating Italian military transport, bridge building, and communications. It includes a military aircraft of 1909, and models of historical fortifications, and armoury from Roman times to the present day. **Monte Mario** which rises to the NW is described in Rte 24.

From Castel Sant'Angelo the unattractive cold **Via della Conciliazione** (Pl. 1; 6) leads towards St Peter's. The approach to the great basilica was transformed by this broad straight thoroughfare, typical of Fascist urban planning, which was completed in 1937. In its construction two characteristic streets of the Città Leonina, the Borgo Nuovo (opened in 1499) and Borgo Vecchio (known as the Spina di Borgo), and the buildings between them were destroyed, except for one palace which was moved (see below). The colonnaded piazza in front of St Peter's was not originally designed to be seen from a distance; its impact is therefore lessened by this monumental approach.

Via della Conciliazione first passes (right) the Carmelite church of SANTA MARIA IN TRASPONTINA (1566–87). Beyond is *PALAZZO TORLONIA (formerly Giraud), a delightful reproduction of the Palazzo della Cancelleria, built by Andrea Bregno in 1495–1504 for Cardinal Adriano da Corneto. Then comes PALAZZO DEI CONVERTENDI, built in the second half of the 17C, and re-erected in its present position in 1937. It originally occupied the site of a house built by Bramante for Raphael, who died in it in 1520. On the S side of the street is PALAZZO DEI PENITENZIERI built (probably) by Baccio

Pontelli for Cardinal Domenico della Rovere in 1480. It is now occupied by the Penitentiaries, whose office it is to hear confessions in St Peter's. Via della Conciliazione ends in Piazza Pio XII, in front of Piazza San Pietro (described in Rte 27).

Parallel to Via della Conciliazione to the N is Borgo Sant'Angelo which is skirted by the wall (in urgent need of restoration) which supports the covered way which connects Castel Sant'Angelo with the Vatican (see above). BORGO PIO, one street further N is the prettiest street to have survived in the Borgo. Partly closed to traffic, it is a local shopping street and has several pizzerie.

On the other side of Via della Conciliazione is Borgo Santo Spirito. Here a flight of steps leads up to the little church of SAN MICHELE E MAGNO (open on Sunday morning), founded in the 8C and retaining a 13C campanile. Inside is the tomb of Raphael Mengs (died 1779). On the corner of Via dei Penitenzieri is **Santo Spirito in Sassia** (Pl. 1; 6), a church founded in 726 for Saxon pilgrims by Ine, king of Wessex, who died in Rome in the same year. The church was rebuilt in 1540 by Antonio da Sangallo the Younger: the design of the FAÇADE was probably his, but the work itself was done in 1585 by Ottavio Mascherino. The CAMPANILE, entirely Tuscan in character, is one of the most graceful in Rome. It is ascribed to Baccio Pontelli.

In the INTERIOR the wood ceiling dates from 1534–49. On the W wall are two interesting paintings in elaborate frames: Visitation by Francesco Salviati, and the Conversion of Saul, attributed to Marco da Siena. SOUTH SIDE. First chapel, Pentecost by Jacopo Zucchi; second chapel, Assumption by Livio Agresti. The interesting little porch in front of a side door with two columns has 16C frescoes and a pretty ceiling. It supports the organ of 1546–52. The huge apse was covered with frescoes by Jacopo and Francesco Zucchi in 1583. NORTH SIDE. The third chapel has a 16C Crucifix and frescoed decorations in Roman style imitating precious marbles with figures in grisaille. On the second altar, Coronation of the Virgin by Cesare Nebbia.

It was from the ramparts of the Leonine City near here that Benvenuto Cellini, according to his own statement, shot the Constable de Bourbon in 1527; a plaque on the outer wall of the church, however, attributes the deed to Bernardo Passeri, another goldsmith. Adjoining the church are the buildings of the huge **Arcispedale di Santo Spirito**, founded by Innocent III c 1198 as a hospital and hostel, and rebuilt for Sixtus IV by various architects (c 1473–78). The first building, the Palazzo del Commendatore (i.e. the house of the director of the hospital), with a spacious courtyard, dates from c 1567. The harmony of the proportions of the main building was spoilt by Alexander VIII, who added a storey, and by Benedict XIV, who blocked up the arches of the portico. The portal is an effective example of the early Renaissance style. The chapel (adm by special permission only) contains an altar with a baldacchino of the time of Clement VIII (1592–1605) and an altarpiece (Job) by Carlo Maratta. The river front, the Lungotevere in Sassia, was rebuilt and extended in 1926 in harmony with the old style.

The hospital contains several institutions devoted to the history of medicine: the LANCISIANA LIBRARY (founded 1711; in the Palazzo del Commendatore), the HISTORICAL MEDICAL ACADEMY, and the NATIONAL MUSEUM OF THE HISTORY OF MEDICINE, unique in Italy (admission, see p 47), opened here in 1933. It includes anatomical drawings by Paolo Mascagni (1752–1815), the collection of the surgeon Giuseppe Flajani (1741–

1808), surgical instruments, and the reconstruction of a 17C pharmacy, and of an alchemist's laboratory.

24

Monte Mario and Ponte Milvio

The foot of Monte Mario (Piazza Maresciallo Giardino) is reached by Bus No. 90 from the Corso. Bus 186 (weekdays) from Piazza Venezia for the Foro Italico.

Monte Mario (139m; Pl. 15; 5) is the ancient *Clivus Cinnoe* and the medieval *Monte Malo*. Its present name is taken from the Villa Mario Mellini built on the summit. Via di Villa Madama climbs the E slope of the hill to *Villa Madama** (Pl. 15; 3). This suburban villa, begun for Cardinal Giuliano de' Medici (Clement VII) by Giulio Romano was designed by Raphael. It was altered by Antonio da Sangallo the Younger. Later it came into the possession of 'Madama' Margaret of Parma and was afterwards owned by the kings of Naples. Today it is used by the Italian Government as accommodation for prominent visitors. For permission to see the interior application must be made in writing to the Foreign Office, Viale della Macchia della Farnesina.

The beautiful loggia, decorated with stucco reliefs by Giovanni da Udine and paintings by Giulio Romano (1520–25) after Raphael's designs, rivals and even excels the famous loggia of the Vatican. In one of the rooms is a frieze of Cupids by Giulio Romano. There is a lovely *view of Rome from the balcony of the main façade. The attractive hanging *garden served as a model for many Italian gardens.

On the S slope of the hill is the round church of SANTA MARIA DEL ROSARIO, built in 1650 by Camillo Arcucci (Pl. 15; 7, 5; 109m; *view). Beyond the ditches of the Fort of Monte Mario, a road leads right to the summit at the VILLA MARIO MELLINI, now incorporated in the **Astronomical and Meteorological Observatory** (Pl. 15; 5), with a COPERNICAN MUSEUM (adm, see p 46), founded in 1873, with mementoes of Copernicus, astrolabes, sextants, quadrants, telescopes, etc. and a large collection of globes.

At the foot of Monte Mario, extending along the river front is the **Foro Italico** (Pl. 15; 4, 2), an ambitious sports centre built in 1928–31 by the former Accademia Fascista della Farnesina, one of the most impressive building projects carried out by Mussolini (altered during work on preparations for the World Cup in Italy in 1990). It was designed by Enrico Del Debbio, and finished by Luigi Moretti in 1936. Facing the entrance is PONTE DUCA D'AOSTA (1939).

A marble monolith, 17m high, inscribed 'Mussolini Dux', rises at the entrance in front of an imposing avenue paved with marble inlaid with mosaics designed by Gino Severini, Angelo Canevari, and others (partly restored in 1990). It ends in a piazza decorated with a fountain and with a huge marble sphere. On either side of the avenue are marble blocks, with inscriptions recording events in the history of Italy. At the end, beyond the piazza, is the STADIO OLIMPICO, finished for the Olympic Games in 1960, with accommodation for 100,000. It was reconstructed for the World Cup in 1990, with little respect for the setting. To the right is the STADIO DEI MARMI, capable of seating 20,000 spectators, with 60 colossal statues of athletes. There are open-air and enclosed swimming-pools, the latter with mosaics by Giulio Rossi and Angelo Canevari. Another building has mosaics by Gino Severini. There are also lawn-tennis and basket-ball courts, running tracks, gymnasium and fencing halls, and other facilities.

Lungotevere Maresciallo Diaz continues along the Tiber passing the Casa Internazionale dello Studente, and, behind it, the ITALIAN FOREIGN OFFICE (1956), known as the 'Farnesina' from the name of the road here. The sculpture is by Arnaldo Pomodoro (1968). Farther back is the FRENCH MILITARY CEMETERY, with the graves of 1500 French who died in the Second World War. The Lungotevere ends at Piazzale Milvio (Pl. 15, just beyond 2), where several roads converge.

To the right, between the Via Cassia (N 2 to Viterbo, Siena, and Florence) and Via Orti della Farnesina, is the church of the GRAN MADRE DI DIO, designed by Cesare Bazzani in 1933. Ahead Viale di Tor di Quinto continues along the river to PONTE FLAMINIO, opened in 1951, a seven-arched entrance to the city from the north. Along it runs Corso di Francia, which passes above the VILLAGGIO OLIMPICO, built to accommodate athletes in 1960, and now a residential district.

Ponte Milvio or **Ponte Molle** (*Pons Milvius*), over the Tiber, was built by the censor M. Aemilius Scaurus in 109 BC. It was here that Cicero captured the emissaries of the Allobroges in 63 BC during the Catiline conspiracy; and it was from this bridge that the Emperor Maxentius was thrown into the Tiber and drowned after his defeat by his co-emperor Constantine on 28 October 312 (see below). Remodelled in the 15C, by Nicholas V, who added the watch-towers, it was restored in 1805 by Pius VII, who commissioned Giuseppe Valadier to erect the triumphal arch at the entrance. Blown up in 1849 by Garibaldi to arrest the advance of the French, it was again restored in 1850 by Pius IX. The bridge was reopened to pedestrians after its restoration in 1985.

Across Ponte Milvio is Piazza Cardinal Consalvi, with a shrine containing a statue by Paolo Taccone, erected by Pius II in 1462 on the spot where he had met Cardinal Bessarion returning from the Morea (Peloponnese) with the head of St Andrew. The straight Via Flaminia returns from here to Piazza del Popolo and the centre of the city.

A short way along Via Flaminia which runs parallel with Viale Tiziano ('one way' going out of the city) is Piazza Apollodoro. To the left is the PALAZZETTO DELLO SPORT, an adventurous and striking construction by Pier Luigi Nervi and Annibale Vitellozzi, designed for the Olympic Games in 1960. Beyond is the Villaggio Olimpico (see above). A little to the S is the STADIO FLAMINIO, designed in reinforced concrete by Pier Luigi and Antonio Nervi in 1959 on the site of the old Stadio Nazionale. In addition to the football ground, which can accommodate 45,000 spectators, there are gymnasiums, a fencing school, and a swimming-pool. On the right of Piazza Apollodoro in Via Guido Reni, is the church of SANTA CROCE, built by Pius X in 1913 to commemorate the 16th centenary of the Edict of Milan (March 313), which conceded civil rights and toleration to Christians throughout the Roman Empire.

Further S, on the left Viale Tiziano widens to form Piazzale Manila, from which Viale Maresciallo Pilsudski leads NE and then E towards the exclusive **PARIOLI** residential district (Pl. 11; 2, 3), the centre of which is at Piazza Euclide, with the huge church of the SACRO CUORE IMMACOLATO DI MARIA by Armando Brasini (1923).

On the right are the remains of the BASILICA OF ST VALENTINE, built by St Julius I (pope 337–52) over the tomb of the saint; adjoining are the CATACOMBS OF ST VALENTINE (adm only with special permission). Farther on (left) is the Corso di Francia (see above), and still farther the entrance to the PARCO DI VILLA GLORI (Pl. 11; 1). This park was converted in 1923–24 by Raffaello De Vico into the **Parco della Rimembranza**, to commemorate the heroism of Enrico and Giovanni Cairoli, who were killed in 1867. The park, planted with cypresses, oaks, elms, maples, horse-chestnuts and other trees, has a column to the dead of 1867 and preserves the trunk of the almond tree beneath which Enrico Cairoli died. A clump of oak trees commemorates heroes of the First World War. There is a fine *view of the Tiber valley. Beyond is the mineral spring called ACQUA ACETOSA; the well-head (1661) usually attributed to Bernini, is probably by Andrea Sacchi.

Via Flaminia continues to the graceful little circular church of SANT'AN-DREA IN VIA FLAMINIA by Vignola (1550–55), erected by Julius III to commemorate his deliverance from Charles V's soldiers while he was a cardinal. It is now between Via Flaminia and Viale Tiziano. Further S, on the left, is the beginning of Viale delle Belle Arti, which passes Villa Giulia (Rte 9). On the right, beyond Piazzale delle Belle Arti, is PONTE DEL RISORGIMENTO (1909–11), the first bridge to be built in the city in rein-forced-concrete, with a single span of 100m.

At the corner of Viale delle Belle Arti is the Palazzina of Pius IV (see Rte 9), and where Via di Villa Giulia leads left, is a fountain of Julius III, beneath an imposing façade, originally of only one storey, by Bartolommeo Amman-nati (1553); the second part was added by Pirro Ligorio in 1562. In Piazza della Marina is the vast MARINE MINISTRY, by Giulio Magni (1928), which has another façade on the Tiber. Via Domenico Alberto Azuni leads to Ponte Matteotti. Beyond the wooded grounds on the left of Villa Strohl Fern is Piazzale Flaminio (Pl. 2; 2), the starting-point of the Via Flaminia. On the E side are the main entrance to the Villa Borghese (Rte 9), and the beginning of Viale del Muro Torto, which runs outside the Aurelian Wall to Porta Pinciana.

Porta del Popolo opens into Piazza del Popolo (Rte 7).

25

Porta San Paolo and San Paolo fuori le Mura

The UNDERGROUND (line B) from the Station and Colosseum runs to Porta San Paolo ('Piramide') and the basilica of San Paolo fuori le Mura ('San Paolo'). BUS 673 from the Colosseum via Porta San Paolo, or No. 170 from the Station, Piazza Venezia, and Largo Argentina, both terminate at San Paolo fuori le Mura.

The well preserved **Porta San Paolo** (Pl. 8; 7), the *Porta Ostiensis* of ancient Rome, preserves its inner side, with two arches from the time of Aurelian. The outer face, rebuilt by Honorius in 402, has been restored. The gate houses the MUSEO DELLA VIA OSTIENSE (admission, see p 47), which illustrates the history of the road to Ostia. It includes milestones and reliefs (some only casts), together with models of Ostia and its port in Imperial times. Among the tomb paintings are three frescoed lunettes from a tomb of the Servian period. On the S side of the gate the square is called Piazzale Ostiense, an important traffic centre, with a station of the underground, and the railway station for the branch line to Ostia and Lido di Ostia. The new direct line from Tiburtina station to Fiumicino airport also stops here.

On the W side of the square, across the line of the city wall, is the *Pyramid of Gaius Cestius (died 12 BC), praetor, tribune of the plebs, and member of the college of the Septemviri Epulones, who had charge of solemn banquets. This is a tomb in the form of a tall pyramid of brick faced with marble, 27m high with a base 22m square. An inscription records that it was built in less than 330 days. It was included in the Aurelian walls in the 3C, and remains one of the most idiosyncratic and best preserved monuments of ancient Rome. Adm only by special permission.

Beyond the pyramid to the left extends the so-called **Protestant Cemetery** (Pl. 8; 7; open 7.00 until dusk; visitors ring at 6 Via Caio Cestio), romantically set with dark green cypresses. The earliest recorded grave dates from 1738.

It was of the OLD CEMETERY (left of the entrance), that Shelley wrote 'it might make one in love with death to think that one should be buried in so sweet a place'. The tomb in the far corner is that of John Keats (1796–1821; 'Here lies one whose name was writ in water'); close by lies his friend Joseph Severn (1793–1879); behind, John Bell (1763–1820), the surgeon. In the NEW CEMETERY lie the ashes of Percy Bysshe Shelley (1792–1822; 'cor cordium'), with a monument by Onslow Ford (1891). Close by lies his friend Edward Trelawny (1792–1881). Here are buried also J. Addington Symonds (1840–93), the historian of the Renaissance; John Gibson (1790–1886), the sculptor; William Howitt (1792–1879) and his wife Mary (1799–1888), R.M. Ballantyne (1825–94), and Julius Goethe (died 1830), the only son of the poet.

Just beyond the Protestant Cemetery, at the end of Via Caio Cestio, and across Via Nicola Zabaglia is the **Rome British Military Cemetery**, where 429 members of the three Services are buried. The cemetery is beautifully sited along the line of the city wall. If the gates are locked, telephone the Area Office (address and telephone number are given on a notice).

To the N of the British Military Cemetery and W of Via Nicola Zabaglia rises **Monte Testaccio** (Pl. 8; 7), an isolated mound 54m high and some 1000m round, entirely composed of potsherds (testae) dumped here from the Augustan period up to the middle of the 3C AD, from the neighbouring storehouses of the Republican port which lined the Tiber between Ponte Testaccio and Ponte Sublicio (now Ponte Aventino; see Rte 21). Among the finds here was a hoard of amphorae, used to import oil from Spain, with official marks scratched on them, which are of fundamental importance to our knowledge of the economic history of the late Republic and early Empire. The top of Monte Testaccio (entered from the corner facing Via Galvani and Via Zabaglia) commands a fine view. The neighbourhood was the scene of jousts and tournaments in the Middle Ages. The district of **Testaccio**, near the 'ex-Mattatoio', a huge slaughter-house built in 1888–91, has recently become a centre of cultural activities with several small theatres and a cinema complex. It is also renowed for its restaurants (of all categories).

From Piazzale Ostiense the broad uninteresting VIA OSTIENSE leads almost due S through a depressing part of the town. It is not recommended to walkers; bus No. 23 follows it to (2km) the basilica of San Paolo. It crosses under the Pisa railway; beyond, to the left, are the Mercati Generali and, to the right, the headquarters of the Gas Works. Some distance farther, on the left, is the site of an oratory marking the spot where, according to tradition, St Peter and St Paul greeted each other on the way to martyrdom. To the E extends the modern *Quartiere della Garbatella*. In the middle of the road just before San Paolo is a small necropolis known as the SEPOL-CRETO OSTIENSE, which contained pagan and perhaps Christian tombs. The site, seen through railings (adm only by special permission) extended over a wide area; another part is visible left of the road. Here the narrow and long Via delle Sette Chiese, passing the CATACOMBS OF COMMODILLA, (adm by special permit), branches off to join, eventually, Via Ardeatina and the Appian Way (Rte 17).

*SAN PAOLO FUORI LE MURA (2km from Porta San Paolo; Pl. 8; 7; open 7.00–18.30) is the largest church in Rome after St Peter's. The present building, third on the site, is a cold 19C reconstruction, replacing the ancient basilica virtually destroyed by fire in 1823. In plan and dimensions, if not in spirit, the new basilica follows the old one almost exactly. One of the four great patriarchal basilicas, it commemorates the martyrdom of St Paul and is believed to contain the Apostle's tomb.

San Paolo fuori le Mura (wood cut made in 1875)

According to Christian tradition the Roman matron Lucina buried the body of Paul in a vineyard on this spot. A small shrine existed here when in 384 a large basilica was begun by Valentinian II and Theodosius the Great at the request of Pope Damasus. It was enlarged by Theodosius' son Honorius and decorated with mosaics by Galla Placidia, sister of Honorius. The basilica was further embellished by Leo III (Pope, 795–816) and it became the largest and most beautiful church in Rome. In the 9C it was pillaged by the Saracens and John VIII (872–82) enclosed it in a fortified village known as *Giovannipolis*. It was restored c 1070 by Abbot Hildebrand, later Gregory VII. The façade, overlooking the Tiber, was preceded by a colonnaded quadriporticus. Before the Reformation the King of England was *ex officio* a canon of San Paolo and the abbot, in return, was decorated with the Order of the Garter. This great basilica was almost entirely destroyed by fire on the night of 15–16 July 1823.

Leo XII ordered the reconstruction, which was directed by Pasquale Belli, Bosio, and Camporese, and afterwards by Luigi Poletti. In the rebuilding it was decided to use new materials, instead of repairing the damaged stucture. The transept was consecrated by Gregory XVI in 1840 and the complete church by Pius IX in 1854. In 1891 an explosion in a neighbouring fort broke most of the stained glass which was replaced by slabs of alabaster. A service took place here in March 1966 performed by Pope Paul VI and Dr Ramsey, Archbishop of Canterbury, when they issued a joint declaration of amity. It is one of the three basilicas of Rome which has the privilege of extraterritoriality.

EXTERIOR. The Romanesque campanile was pulled down to make way for the unattractive CAMPANILE by Luigi Poletti on Via Ostiense. Poletti was

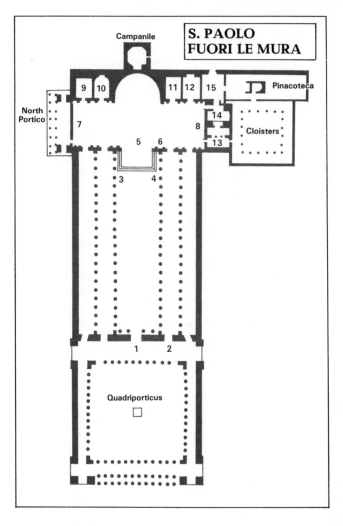

S. PAOLO FUORI LE MURA

Campanile

9 10   11 12 15   Pinacoteca

North Portico

7   14

8   Cloisters

5 6   13

3   4

1   2

Quadriporticus

also responsible for the NORTH PORTICO which incorporates twelve Hymettan marble columns from the old basilica. On one of the nearest columns, beneath the frieze, is a 4C inscription of Pope Siricius (384–99). The façade (right) is preceded by a great QUADRIPORTICUS with 146 enormous monolithic granite columns, added by Guglielmo Calderini (1892–1928) in keeping with the frigid 'air of conscious bravado' throughout the rebuilt church. The elaborate frescoes on the façade date from 1885. The central bronze doors (1) are by Antonio Maraini (1928–30). The PORTA SANTA (2) has the bronze *doors (recently restored; seen from the inside of the basilica) which belonged to the old basilica. They were made at Constantinople by

Staurakios in 1070, and inlaid with silver in fifty-four panels of scenes from the Old and New Testament.

INTERIOR. The nave and transept form in plan a tau or Egyptian cross, 132m by 65m; the height is 30 metres. The highly polished marble, alabaster, malachite, lapis, and porphyry give an impression of neo-classical splendour. The NAVE, with double aisles separated from one another by eighty columns of Montórfano granite, is the new part of the basilica. In the centre of the ceiling, which is richly decorated with stuccoes in white and gold, are the arms of Pius IX. The paintings executed in the mid 19C between the windows depict scenes in the life of St Paul (by Pietro Gagliardi, Francesco Podesti, Guglielmo De Sanctis, Francesco Coghetti, and Cesare Mariani); under these (and in the aisles), forming a frieze, are the portraits in mosaic of all the 263 popes from St Peter to Paul VI. In the outermost aisles are niches with statues of the Apostles. The six huge alabaster columns beside the doors were presented by Mohammed Ali of Egypt. The statue of St Peter (3) is by Giacometti and of St Paul (4) by Revelli.

The *TRIUMPHAL ARCH, a relic of the old basilica, is supported by two colossal granite columns. Its mosaics (much restored) are due to Galla Placidia. They represent Christ blessing in the Greek manner, with angels; Symbols of the Evangelists; the Elders of the Apocalypse; Saints Peter and Paul. On the other face of the arch are the remains of mosaics by Pietro Cavallini. Over the HIGH ALTAR, supported by four porphyry columns, is a splendid *tabernacle (5) by Arnolfo di Cambio and his companion Pietro (Oderisi?, 1285). The old tradition which places the tomb of St Paul beneath the altar is well founded. Excavations before the rebuilding in 1823 revealed a 1C tomb, surrounded by Christian and some pagan burials. When the grating of the confessio is opened, the inscription 'Paolo Apostolo Mart', dating from the time of Constantine, may be seen. The huge 12C paschal *candlestick (6) is by Nicolò di Angelo and Pietro Vassalletto.

The magnificent ceiling of the TRANSEPT is decorated with the arms of Pius VII, Leo XII, Pius VIII, and Gregory XVI, as well as with those of the basilica (an arm holding a sword). The walls are covered with rare marbles. The Corinthian pilasters are made up of fragments of the old columns. The great *mosaic of the APSE was executed c 1220 by Venetian craftsmen sent by Doge Pietro Ziani at the request of Pope Honorius III. It was heavily restored in the 19C after damage in the fire. The subjects are Christ blessing in the Greek manner, with Saints Peter, Andrew, Paul, and Luke; at the feet of Christ, Pope Honorius III; below this, a gem-studded Cross on the altar, angels and apostles. On the inner face of the arch, Virgin and Child with St John blessing Pope John XXII.

At either end of the transept is an altar of malachite and lapis lazuli, presented by Nicholas I of Russia: the Conversion of St Paul (7) is by Vincenzo Camuccini, and the mosaic (8), a copy from the Coronation of the Virgin, by Giulio Romano. The Chapel of St Stephen (9) has a statue of the saint by Rinaldi, and paintings of his expulsion from the Sanhedrin, by Coghetti, and of his stoning, by Podesti. The Chapel of the Crucifix (10), by Carlo Maderno was the only chapel salved in the fire; on the altar, Crucifix attributed to Tino da Camaino. In a niche to the right of the door, statue of St Bridget by Stefano Maderno; to the left, statue of a Saint in wood. In this chapel, in 1541, St Ignatius de Loyola and the first Jesuits took the corporate oaths formally establishing their society as a religious order. The Chapel of the Choir or of St Laurence (11), is by Guglielmo Calderini; it contains a

15C marble triptych, and frescoes by Viligiardi. Chapel of St Benedict (12), a sumptuous work of Poletti, with a reproduction of the cella of an ancient temple; the 12 fluted columns are from Veio.

The SALA DEL MARTIROLOGIO (13), has badly damaged 13C frescoes, and a bust of Poletti. The BAPTISTERY (14; designed by Arnaldo Foschini in a Greek cross in 1930) leads into the VESTIBULE (15) preceding the S door of the church, which contains a colossal statue of Gregory XVI by Rinaldi, and 13C mosaics from the old basilica.

A door to the right off the vestibule leads to the *Cloisters (open daily 9.00–13.00, 15.00–18.00) belonging to the old Benedictine convent. They have coupled colonnettes of different forms decorated with mosaics, with tiny couchant animals (most of which have now disappeared) between the columns. In the centre is a rose garden. The cloisters were begun under Abbot Pietro da Capua (1193–1208) and finished after 1228, and are the work, at least in part, of the Vassalletti. Along the walls are placed inscriptions and sculptured fragments: XIV. Statue of Boniface IX; XVII. Sarcophagus with the story of Apollo and Marsyas; XIX. An inscription recording the suicide of Nero (probably a 17C forgery); XX. Statue of a prophet. The painted wood roof is noteworthy. Off the Cloister is the CHAPEL OF RELIQUARIES, with a gilded silver cross, and the PINACOTECA, with works by Antoniazzo Romano (Madonna and four Saints) and Bramantino (Flagellation), as well as old prints showing the damage caused by the fire.

From San Paolo the road continues S. After a short distance, a road to the right leads via Viale Marconi to Via del Mare (for Ostia, see Rte 28). For EUR and the Monastery of Tre Fontane (Rte 26) Via Laurentina forks left from Via Ostiense under the railway, and soon joins Via Cristoforo Colombo.

26

The district of EUR (Esposizione Universale di Roma)

Approaches. EUR is easily reached in 12 minutes from the Stazione Termini by the Metropolitana, on which it is the penultimate station. The line ends at Tre Fontane (Laurentino). It is also reached by numerous buses, including No. 714 from Stazione Termini, and No. 761 from San Paolo fuori le Mura.

For motorists the quickest route is by Via Cristoforo Colombo (c 6km), which starts at Porta Ardeatina (reached from the Colosseum by Via di San Gregorio and Viale di Caracalla). It passes through the arches of the Aurelian Wall with its gallery, and a sepulchre to the left. It continues as a ten-lane highway, and passes straight through the middle of EUR.

The VIA OLIMPICA, a road 15km long, built for the Olympic Games of 1960 links the two important sporting centres of EUR and Foro Italico (Rte 24), avoiding the centre of the city. Crossing the Tiber by Ponte Marconi it runs by way of the Circonvallazione Gianicolense, and passing across the Villa Doria Pamphilj reaches the Piazzale degli Eroi. Beyond the Foro Italico it turns E to recross the Tiber by the new Ponte Tor di

Quinto. From here it passes the Centro Sportivo dell'Acqua Acetosa and joins the Via Salaria (Rte 20).

Esposizione Universale di Roma (now always abbreviated to **EUR**; Plans 13, 14) was begun in 1938 to the designs of Marcello Piacentini. An ambitious project to symbolise the achievements of Fascism, it was to have been opened in 1942. Its buildings were only partly completed, however, and the site suffered some war damage. After 1952 the original buildings were restored, new ones were added, and Government offices and public institutions were moved to the site, which has also developed as an exclusive residential district, deserted at night. The monumental white marble buildings are spaciously set out between wide avenues and empty roads, in a setting which recollects the metaphysical paintings of De Chirico. Many of the buildings are now in need of restoration. Some of the huge buildings house museums, which are didactic in arrangement, and mostly visited by school parties.

Via Cristoforo Colombo passes over the Centro Sportivo delle Tre Fontane, before reaching Piazza delle Nazioni (Pl. 14; 1), with twin palaces whose façades form two hemicycles. Viale della Civiltà del Lavoro leads right to the PALAZZO EUR and, at the end, the PALAZZO DELLA CIVILTÀ ITALIANA built in 1938–43 by Giovanni Guerrini, Ernesto Bruno La Padula, and Mario Romano, now called PALAZZO DEL LAVORO (Pl. 13; 2). Known as the 'square Colosseum', it has statues symbolising the arts beneath the lowest arches. At the opposite end of Viale della Civiltà is PALAZZO DEI CONGRESSI, by Adalberto Libera (1938–54), with paintings by Gino Severini in the atrium.

Beyond is the vast Piazza Marconi (Pl. 14; 3), in the centre of which is a stele of Carrara marble (45m) by Arturo Dazzi (1938–59), dedicated to Marconi. On the right are two edifices with symmetrical fronts (PALAZZI DELL'ESPOSIZIONI), while between them, farther back, is the GRATTACIELO ITALIA (1959–60). On the left, joined by a huge colonnade, are two palazzi of similar design.

The one to the left facing the colonnade contains the **Museo Nazionale delle Arti e delle Tradizioni Popolari** (Pl. 14; 3; adm, see p 46). The museum is being rearranged. It contains material collected by Lamberto Loria (1855–1913) for the Museo di Etnografia Italiana, founded in Florence in 1906, and illustrates with models, reconstructions, etc. the various aspects of Italian life. On the ground floor are exhibits relating to transport. The sections on the upper floor include furniture from rural houses, toys, crib figures, carnival and theatrical costumes, musical instruments used during local festivals, and puppets. There is a large collection of 19C and early 20C jewellery. A section on religious festivals includes ex-votoes. On the stair-landing is a gondola of 1882. The great hall with frescoes of 1941, exhibits arts and crafts, with reconstructions of artisans' workshops. The next section illustrates agricultural life. The sections on seafaring and pastoral life are closed for rearrangement.

To the right of the colonnade is the PALAZZO DELLE SCIENZE which contains the **Museo Preistorico ed Etnografico Luigi Pigorini** (Pl. 14; 3). For adm, see p 47. The museum, one of the most important of its kind in the world, is derived from the collection formed in the late 17C by Father Anastasius Kircher in the Collegio dei Gesuiti. From 1871 onwards it was greatly enlarged by Luigi Pigorini and in 1876 it became the Museo Preistorico del Nuovo Regno d'Italia. After 1913 the protohistoric objects went to Villa Giulia, classical and Christian antiquities to the Museo Nazionale Romano, and medieval exhibits to Palazzo di Venezia.

The MUSEO PREISTORICO is arranged geographically to indicate the way civilisation developed regionally through the Stone, Bronze, and Iron Ages. Most of the exhibits are Italian, of the prehistoric period. They include material from all parts of the peninsula, so that a complete idea may be obtained of the growth of its civilisation and of the commercial and artistic influences of the East and of the countries bordering on the Aegean. The descriptive labels, maps, and diagrams are very informative. The most interesting exhibits include: material from cemeteries in the Lazio area; finds of the Italian School in Crete; curious Sardinian statuettes of priests and warriors in bronze; a tomb from Golasecca, representative of the western civilisation of Northern Italy. The objects found in the cemeteries of western and southern Etruria (Vetulonia, Tarquinia, Vulci, Veio, etc.) are particularly interesting; among them are well-tombs (10–8C BC), with ossuaries resembling those of Villanova, closed with a flat lid or shaped like a house, and trench-tombs (8–7C BC) showing the influence of Greek commerce, especially on pottery.

The ETHNOGRAPHICAL COLLECTION includes material from the Americas, Africa, and Oceania collected by Lamberto Loria, Vittorio Bottego, Guido Boggiani, and Enrico Hillyer Giglioli. There is a pre-Columbian archaeological collection from Mexico and the Andes, and artefacts made by the Invits of the Arctic Circle. The collections from Oceania and Africa are at present closed: the African collection includes material from Angola and Zaire. Much of the material which belonged to Loria was collected by him in New Guinea.

Farther along the colonnade, on the right, at Viale Lincoln, is the entrance to the **Museo dell'Alto Medioevo** (adm see p 46), which is on the first floor of the Palazzo delle Scienze. A disappointing and small collection made in 1967, it contains Italian material from the fall of the Roman Empire to the 10C AD. ROOM I. Head of a Byzantine Emperor and Empress, gold fibula, all of the late 5C found on the Palatine. ROOM II. Pottery, glass and gold work (including beautiful jewellery) found in a 7C tomb at Nocera Umbra. ROOM III. Contents of a 7C tomb at Castel Trosino, including more very fine jewellery (B, 115, 16), a blue glass rhyton (119), a gold dagger case (F), glass containers (37–45), and fragments of a shield (T). ROOMS IV–V. Collection of 7–10C church reliefs and friezes. ROOM VI. Finds from the site of Santa Cornelia, near Formello, excavated by the British School in 1963–65. Three distinct constructions were found: an early Roman house, a cult building of c 780, and a monastic complex of 1100. ROOM VI. 8–9C pottery from the Roman Forum. ROOM VII. Finds from San Rufina, on the Via Cornelia, including mosaics. ROOM VIII. Coptic materials and fabrics of the 5–8C.

Beyond the colonnade Viale della Civiltà Romana, leads to the piazza flanked by two symmetrical buildings again joined by a colonnade, the building of which was financed by the Fiat organisation. Here the **Museo della Civiltà Romana** (Pl. 14; 4) was inaugurated in 1955. The entrance is in the right wing (admission, see p 46). The museum was created to house the exhibits from the Archaeological Exhibition of 1911 and from the Mostra Augustea della Romanità of 1937. They consist entirely of plaster-casts of famous statues and monuments, and reconstructions of buildings which illustrate the history of ancient Rome and the influence of Roman civilisation throughout the world. They are displayed in fifty-nine rooms of monumental proportions, which have been undergoing lengthy structural repairs for many years.

Each room illustrates a period of the history of Rome, in chronological sequence. Room VI, origins of the city; Room VII, the conquest of the Mediterranean; Room VIII, Julius

Caesar; Room IX, Augustus (including a reproduction of the pronaos of the temple of Augustus at Ancyra); Rooms X–XIV, the Roman emperors; Room XV, Christianity; Rooms XVI–XIX, the Roman army. The other rooms are closed, except for the room (XXXVII) in the opposite wing of the museum (reached by returning to the entrance and crossing the piazza) where a celebrated *model of Rome as it was in the 4C is displayed. It was made in 1937 on a scale of 1:250.

Other rooms in the museum are devoted to the navy; ports; central administration; the Imperial court; the 'triumphs' celebrated in Rome for victorious generals; the provinces of the Roman empire; the eleven 'regions' of Italy; methods of construction (quarries and mines); baths and aqueducts; theatres, amphitheatres and circuses; fora, temples, and basilicas; military architecture; Roman roads; education; funerary monuments; domestic architecture; the family; religion; portraits; law; libraries; music; science and letters; medicine; artisans; agriculture; hunting and fishing; commerce; and art. In Room LI is a complete collection of *casts made in 1860 from Trajan's Column, and in Room LIX the reconstruction of part of the Column of Marcus Aurelius.

Viale dell'Arte leads left; the second turning to the right is Viale Europa. Here are the ministries of Foreign Trade and Finance, built after the war. On the corner of Via Cristoforo Colombo is the Ministry of Postal Services and Communications. Here is the well-arranged **Museo Storico delle Poste e delle Telecommunicazioni** (Pl. 13; 4; adm see p 47). The postal display begins with a casket of 1300 used by the Pontifical Post Office of Urbino and 17C letter boxes, including a 'bocca di leone', and there is a fine copy of the Peutinger Table on tile. Later postal history (pioneer air-mail flights; Ethiopian military cancellers, etc.) is well chosen. Here also is displayed the electronic calculator invented by Entrico Fermi, and made in 1956. The history of telegraph and telephone is copiously illustrated by original appliances, including apparatus used by Marconi in his 1901 experiments between Cornwall and Newfoundland.

Viale Europa ends in steps which lead up to the massive church of SANTI PIETRO E PAOLO (Pl. 13; 3), with a cupola almost as large as that of St Peter's. Dating from 1938–55, it was designed by Arnaldo Foschini. The first turning right at the foot of the steps leads to the PISCINA DELLE ROSE in Viale America and a large open-air theatre. Parallel to this road is a lake about 1km long, divided into three basins, the sides of which are planted with a thousand cherry trees from Japan. This area is perhaps the most successfully planned within the EUR complex. Bridges lead to the *Palazzo dello Sport* (Pl. 13; 6), designed by Pier Luigi Nervi and Marcello Piacentini for the Olympic Games of 1960, and an outstanding work of modern architecture. Constructed of prefabricated concrete, it is covered by a fine rib-vaulted dome 100 metres in diameter, and seats 15,000 spectators. The well designed VELODROMO OLIMPICO, for cycling events, is about 500m E.

About 1km E of the point where Via Cristoforo Colombo crosses Via delle Tre Fontane, and reached by the latter and Via Laurentina, is the **Abbazia delle Tre Fontane** (Pl. 14; 2). This was built on the traditional site of the martyrdom of St Paul, whose severed head, rebounding three times, is supposed to have caused three fountains to spring up. A monastic community from Asia Minor was established here by 641. St Bernard is believed to have stayed here on his visit to Rome in 1138–40. Three churches were built, but the locality was afterwards abandoned as malarial. In 1868 it was acquired by the Trappists, who drained the ground and planted large groves of eucalyptus. A eucalyptus liqueur is distilled in the community. This and chocolate made by the monks are on sale.

An ilex avenue leads to a medieval fortified gate, with a frescoed vault. A small garden contains classical fragments, and is filled with the sound of doves and a fountain. Ahead is the porch of *Santi Vincenzo ed Anastasio*. It was founded by Honorius I (625), rebuilt by Honorius III (1221), and restored by the Trappists. The spacious plain interior preserves its marble windows. In the nave are poorly restored frescoes of the Apostles (16C).

On the right on high ground, is **Santa Maria Scala Coeli**, an old church with an octagonal interior, rebuilt by Giacomo della Porta (1582). The design can best be appreciated from the outside. It owes its name to the legend that St Bernard, while celebrating mass, saw in a vision the soul for which he was praying ascend by a ladder from purgatory to heaven. The Cosmatesque altar which was the scene of this miracle is still preserved in the crypt. The mosaics in the left-hand apse (Saints with Clement VIII and his nephew Aldobrandini) are by Francesco Zucchi from designs by Giovanni de' Vecchi.

From the left of this church an avenue leads to **San Paolo alle Tre Fontane**, a 5C church, rebuilt by Della Porta in 1599, with a good façade. Inside to the right is the pillar to which St Paul is supposed to have been bound; on the floor are two Roman mosaic pavements from Ostia.

27

The Vatican City. St Peter's and the Vatican Museums

The **VATICAN CITY** (*Città del Vaticano*; Pl. 1; 5, 6) lies on the right bank of the Tiber. Through the Lateran Treaty (*Il Concordato*) signed at the Lateran Palace on 11 February 1929, the Vatican City has the status of an independent sovereign state. With an area of 43 hectares (less than half a square kilometre) and a population of about 550, it is, in size, the smallest independent state in existence. The States of the Church before the unification of Italy in 1870 extended for 44,547 square kilometres. As the residence of the Pope and the site of St Peter's, the most important Roman Catholic church, it attracts visitors from all over the world. The decorations in the Vatican Palace include the famous frescoes in the Sistine Chapel and the 'Stanze' which are the masterpieces of Michelangelo and Raphael. The Vatican museums are unique in their scope, quality, and abundance.

There are three **entrances to the Vatican City**, protected by members of the Swiss Guard, and not open to the general public. The PORTONE DI BRONZO, in the colonnade to the right of St Peter's, is the official entrance to the Holy See. The ARCO DELLE CAMPANE, to the left of St Peter's is the entrance for cars, and is also used for access to the Audience Hall, and for the organised tours of the gardens and City, and of the necropolis below St Peter's. The CANCELLO DI SANT'ANNA, in Via di Porta Angelica, is used for the Polyglot Printing Press, the offices of the *Osservatore Romano*, etc. The **entrance to the Vatican Museums and the Sistine Chapel** (see p 318) is in Viale Vaticano. For admission to St Peter's, see p 308.

Dress. You are not allowed inside St Peter's or the Vatican City wearing shorts, mini-skirts, or with bare shoulders.

An **Information Office** is open every day (8.30–19.00) in Piazza San Pietro to the left of the façade of the basilica.

The Concordat defined the limits of the Vatican State. They are (counter- clockwise) St Peter's Colonnade, Via Porta Angelica, Piazza del Risorgimento, Via Leone IV, Viale Vaticano (which almost encircles the area), Via della Sagrestia, and St Peter's Colonnade. The city is surrounded by a high wall, skirted by Viale Vaticano for the whole of its length. On the N side, Viale Vaticano rises fairly steeply, past (left) the entrance to the Vatican Museums, to the top of the hill, known as *Monte Vaticano*. At the top Viale Vaticano bears left and after another left incline, still accompanied by the wall, descends towards St Peter's Colonnade.

The Lateran Treaty also granted the privilege of extraterritoriality to the basilicas of St John Lateran (with the Lateran Palace), Santa Maria Maggiore and San Paolo fuori le Mura, and to certain other buildings, including the Palazzo della Cancelleria, and to the Pope's villa at Castel Gandolfo. Special clauses in the treaty provided for access to St Peter's and the Vatican Museums. Under the treaty, Italy accepted canon law on marriage and divorce and made religious teaching compulsory in secondary as well as primary schools (clauses which were modified in 1984). Italy also agreed to pay 750 million lire in cash and the income from 1000 million lire in Italian State 5 per cent bonds, in final settlement of the claims by the Holy See for the loss of papal property taken over by the Italian Government. After the execution of the Lateran Treaty the Pope, for the first time since 1870, emerged from the Vatican. On 24 June 1929, Pius XI visited St John Lateran. A new Concordat was signed between the Italian Government and the Vatican on 18 February 1984 in Villa Madama. This made religious instruction in schools optional, and contained modifications to the Lateran Treaty regarding marriage, etc.

By the Vatican City law of Pius XI, dated 7 June 1921, the Pope is head of the legislature, executive, and judiciary. He delegates the Cardinal Secretary of State to represent the Vatican in international relations, and nominates the General Council and the Governor of the Vatican. The State has its own postage-stamps, and its own currency. Its newspaper, the *Osservatore Romano*, has a world-wide circulation. It owns a radio transmitting station (prominent in the Second World War) and has its own railway-station, now used only for merchandise.

Security. Within the Vatican City policing is carried out by the SWISS GUARD, a corps founded in 1506, which retains the picturesque uniform said to have been designed by Michelangelo. The Noble Guards and Palatine Guards established in the 19C were disbanded by Pope Paul VI in 1970, and the Pontifical Gendarmes transformed into a private corps.

The Hierarchy. The Sovereign Pontiff is Bishop of Rome, successor to St Peter, and, as such, the head of the Roman Catholic Church and the Vicar of Christ. He enjoys the *primatus jurisdictionis*, that is, the supreme jurisdictional power over the whole Church. He is assisted by the Sacred College of Cardinals and by the Roman Curia. The SACRED COLLEGE OF CARDINALS was limited by Sixtus V to 70, but after the consistory of March 1962 the number was increased to 87. John XXIII created 46 new cardinals, and gave them all episcopal dignity. At present there is no limit to the number of cardinals who can be appointed. The College consists of six Cardinal Bishops (whose dioceses are the suburbicarian sees of Ostia, Velletri, Porto and Santa Rufina, Albano, Frascati, and Palestrina), nearly 70 Cardinal Priests, and 14 Cardinal Deacons. The ROMAN CURIA comprises the twelve SACRED CONGREGATIONS, which deal with the central administration of the Church, the three *Tribunals*, and the six *Offices* (which includes the *Segretario di Stato*).

Conclave (from the Latin, a room that may be locked). On the death of a pope, cardinals under the age of 80 are confined in a chosen locality, usually the Sistine Chapel, to elect a new pope. The place chosen is locked both inside and outside and it includes rooms for the cardinals and their attendants. The internal guardian is the Camerlengo; the external guardian the Commander of the Swiss Guard. The cardinals meet twice daily before the voting procedure takes place. The result of the vote is indicated by the colour of the smoke which issues from a vent above the Sistine Chapel. If the smoke is black the election is still in doubt; if white, the new pope has been elected. The old practice of burning the voting papers (mixed with damp straw for the black) to produce the smoke, was discontinued after the conclave of 1958. The new pope is proclaimed by the senior cardinal-deacon from the central balcony on the façade of St Peter's, from where also he gives his blessing. The ceremony, discontinued in 1870, was revived by Pius XI after the concordat. Since the proceedings take some time, there is always an interregnum between the death of a pope and the election of his successor; John Paul I died on 29 September and John Paul II was elected on 16 October 1978.

Holy Year. The Roman Catholic Church adapted the secular Jewish idea of the jubilee, giving it an exclusively religious meaning; the remission of the temporal punishment of sins substituted the remission of debts. The first Holy Year was proclaimed from the balcony of St John Lateran on 22 February 1300, by Boniface VIII. The pope gave a plenary indulgence to those confessed communicants who, on the occasion of every centenary of the birth of Christ, visited the four major basilicas, St Peter's, San Paolo fuori le Mura, St John Lateran, and Santa Maria Maggiore, within a specified time. In 1343 Clement VI reduced the interval from 100 to 33 years and Paul II (1464–71) to 25 years. This quarter-century interval has been maintained, with few exceptions, ever since: i.e. in 1900, 1925, 1950, and 1975. In addition to the regular celebrations, a Jubilee has occasionally been proclaimed for a special reason, as in 1933, when Pius XI commemorated the 19th centenary of the Crucifixion, or in 1983/4 when John Paul II commemorated the 1950 years since the Death and Resurrection of Christ.

A Holy Year is usually inaugurated on the preceding Christmas Eve with the opening of the Holy Doors (*Porte Sante*) of the four major basilicas. The Holy Door of St Peter's is opened by the Pope; the other three are opened by their archpriests. The Pope used to use a silver hammer and a temporary wall in front of the door would fall inwards. In 1983 the Pope used a bronze hammer and the Porta Santa was unlocked for him. In the ceremony the Pope crosses the threshold bareheaded and carrying a torch, followed by cardinals and attendants. At the end of the Holy Year the Holy Doors are reclosed by the Pope.

Papal Audiences. General Audiences usually take place at 10 or 11 o'clock on Wednesday mornings in the New Audience Hall, reached under the colonnade to the left of the façade of St Peter's. A special section is set aside for newly married couples. Audiences are now also sometimes held in St Peter's, or in the Piazza (when the Pope is transported by jeep). Application to attend an audience can be made in writing to the Prefetto della Casa Pontificia, Città del Vaticano, 00120 Rome. Otherwise you can apply in person on the Monday or Tuesday before the audience at the Portone di Bronzo (open 9.00–13.00) in the colonnade to the right of St Peter's. At the far end of the Corridore del Bernini is the Scala Regia, the staircase leading to the Sala Regia. At a table at the entrance you are asked to fill in a form and take it to the office of the Prefettura, on the first floor reached by the Scala Pia.

A. St Peter's

*PIAZZA SAN PIETRO (Pl. 1; 6), the masterpiece of Gian Lorenzo Bernini (1656–67), is one of the most superb conceptions of its kind in civic architecture, and is a fitting approach to the world's greatest basilica. Partly enclosed by two semicircular colonnades, it has the form of an ellipse adjoining an almost rectangular quadrilateral. At the end, above a triple flight of steps, rises St Peter's, with the buildings of the Vatican towering on the right. Each of the two colonnades has a quadruple row of Doric columns, forming three parallel covered walks. There are in all 284 columns and 88 pilasters. On the Ionic entablature are 96 statues of saints and martyrs. In the middle of the piazza, on a tall plinth, is an **Obelisk**, devoid of hieroglyphics, 25.5m high. It was brought from Alexandria (where it had

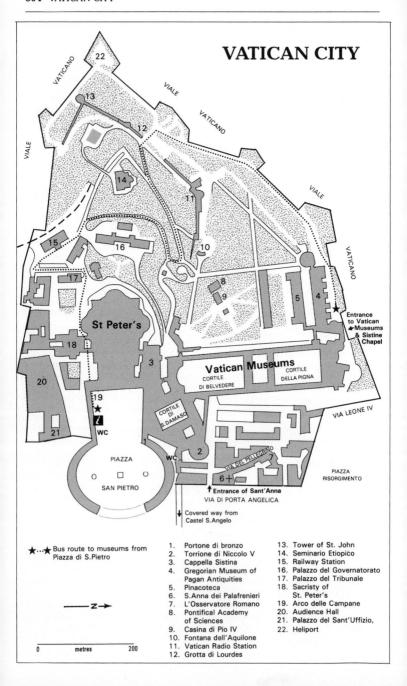

VATICAN CITY

★···★ Bus route to museums from
Piazza di S.Pietro

0   metres   200

1. Portone di bronzo
2. Torrione di Niccolo V
3. Cappella Sistina
4. Gregorian Museum of
   Pagan Antiquities
5. Pinacoteca
6. S.Anna dei Palafrenieri
7. L'Osservatore Romano
8. Pontifical Academy
   of Sciences
9. Casina di Pio IV
10. Fontana dell'Aquilone
11. Vatican Radio Station
12. Grotta di Lourdes

13. Tower of St. John
14. Seminario Etiopìco
15. Railway Station
16. Palazzo del Governatorato
17. Palazzo del Tribunale
18. Sacristy of
    St. Peter's
19. Arco delle Campane
20. Audience Hall
21. Palazzo del Sant'Uffizio,
22. Heliport

been set up by Augustus) in AD 37, and it is thought that Caligula placed it on the spina of his circus, later called the Circus of Nero.

In 1586 Sixtus V ordered its removal from the S of the basilica to its present site and put Domenico Fontana in charge of operations. No fewer than 900 men, 150 horses, and 47 cranes were required. The task was completed on 18 September 1586. It is said that the Pope forbade the spectators, under pain of death, to speak while the obelisk was being raised into position. A sailor called Bresca, seeing that the tension on the ropes had not been correctly assessed and that they were giving way under the strain, transgressed the order, and shouted 'acqua alle funi!' ('wet the ropes!'). The Pope rewarded him by granting his family the privilege of supplying St Peter's with palms for Palm Sunday. The incident, now discredited as an 18C fabrication, is said to have been the origin of the industry, still flourishing at Bordighera, of exporting palm. Round the foot of the obelisk is a plan of the mariner's compass, giving the names of the winds. The globe which surmounted the obelisk until 1586, when it was replaced by a Cross, is now in Palazzo dei Conservatori.

The two abundant *fountains are supplied by the Acqua Paola. The one on the right was designed by Carlo Maderno (1614; a similar fountain had existed in the piazza since 1490). It was moved to its present site and slightly modified by Bernini in 1667, when the second fountain was begun. Between the obelisk and each fountain is a round porphyry slab from which you have the illusion that each of the colonnades has only a single row of columns. In this piazza on 13 May 1981 a Turk, Mehmet Ali Agca, made an attempt on the life of John Paul II.

Covered galleries, also decorated with statues, unite the colonnades with the portico of St Peter's. The gallery on the right, known as the *Corridore del Bernini* and leading to the Scala Regia, is closed by the famous PORTONE DI BRONZO, the official entrance to the Holy See. It was kept closed from 1870 to 1929. The left-hand colonnade is skirted outside by Via della Sagrestia, one of the frontier streets of the Vatican City. A great staircase, of three flights, leads up to the portico of the basilica. At the foot are colossal statues of St Peter, by Giuseppe de Fabris, and of St Paul, by Adamo Tadolini, set up here by Pius IX.

**ST PETER'S, or the *Basilica di San Pietro in Vaticano* (Pl. 1; 5, 6), is perhaps the most imposing church of Christendom. Though neither a cathedral nor the mother church of the Catholic faith, it is the composite work of some of the greatest artists of the 16C, and a masterpiece of the late Italian Renaissance. Orientated towards the west and approached through its monumental piazza, the church has its fitting culmination in Michelangelo's dome.

History. According to the Liber Pontificalis, Pope St Anacletus built an oratory (c AD 90) over the tomb of St Peter, close to the Circus of Nero, near which he had been martyred. Modern research, however, has revealed that there may have been a confusion of names, and that Pope St Anicetus (155–66) was probably responsible for the oratory. On the site of this oratory Constantine, at the request of Pope St Sylvester I, began a basilica c 319–22, which was consecrated on 18 November 326. The basilica was 120m long and 65m wide, about half the size of the present edifice. It was preceded by a great quadrangular colonnaded portico. The nave and double aisles were divided by 86 marble columns, some of which were said to have been taken from the Septizonium on the Palatine (if so, this was long before the demolition of that building by Sixtus V). It contained numerous monuments of popes and emperors, and was decorated with frescoes and mosaics, and was visited by pilgrims from all over Europe. Charlemagne was crowned here by Leo III in 800. Some of its relics are preserved (see

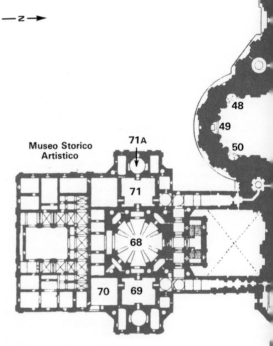

ST PETER'S

0	10	20	30 yds
0	10	20	30 ms

— z →

Museo Storico
Artistico

71A

71

68

70   69

48

49

50

1

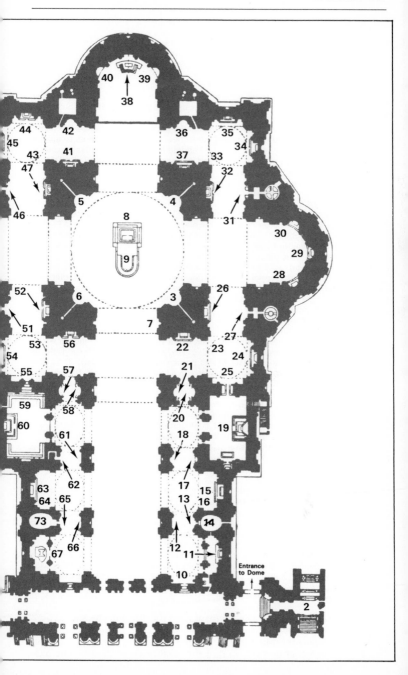

below). Its façade is shown in Raphael's fresco of the 'Incendio di Borgo' in the 'Stanze' in the Vatican.

In the middle of the 15C the old basilica showed signs of collapse, and Nicholas V, recognising its importance to the prestige of the Roman Catholic faith, decided to rebuild it. He entrusted the work to Bernardo Rossellino, Leon Battista Alberti, and Giuliano da Sangallo, but on the Pope's death in 1455, building work was virtually suspended for half a century. Julius II decided on a complete reconstruction, and he employed Bramante, who started work in 1506. Most of the old church was dismantled, and much was destroyed which could have been preserved: Bramante was nicknamed 'Bramante Ruinante'. The new basilica was on a Greek-cross plan surmounted by a gigantic central dome and flanked by four smaller cupolas. By the time of Bramante's death in 1514, the four central piers and the arches of the dome had been completed.

Leo X employed Raphael to continue the building (on a Latin-cross plan) in collaboration with Fra Giocondo (died 1515) and Giuliano da Sangallo (died 1516). On Raphael's death in 1520 Baldassarre Peruzzi reverted to Bramante's design. Neither Adrian VI, the austere theologian who regarded art as hostile to the Church, nor Clement VII (1523–34), overwhelmed by political disturbances brought about by the Reformation, and culminating in the sack of Rome (1527), were interested in the completion of the basilica. However, under Paul III the work received fresh impetus from Antonio da Sangallo the Younger. He made a huge wood model in 1539 of the basilica readopting the Latin-cross plan (this remarkable work, 736cm x 602cm, and 468cm high, survives and was restored in 1994). At his death in 1546, Michelangelo, then seventy-two years old, was summoned by Paul III. He decided on the original Greek-cross plan, and developed Bramante's idea with even greater audacity. He took Brunelleschi's Florentine cupola for his model, and substituted Bramante's piers with new, stronger, ones. His plan for the façade was derived from the Pantheon. Confirmed in his appointment by Paul III's successors, he continued to direct the work until his death in 1564. Vignola and Pirro Ligorio then took over the work, and were followed by Giacomo della Porta (assisted by Carlo Fontana), who completed the dome in 1590, and added the two smaller domes.

In 1605 Paul V demolished what had been left of the old basilica, pulled down the incomplete façade and directed Carlo Maderno to lengthen the nave towards the old Piazza San Pietro. The present façade and portico are Maderno's work. Thus, after many vicissitudes, the basilica was completed on a Latin-cross plan. On 18 November 1626, the 1300th anniversary of the original consecration, Urban VIII consecrated the new church. Bernini, who succeeded Maderno in 1629, and was commissioned to decorate the interior, wanted to erect two campanili by the façade, but the one that he completed began to crack on its sinking foundations and was pulled down (much to Borromini's satisfaction). Alexander VII kept Bernini as architect of St Peter's, and under him the piazza was begun in 1656. The sacristy was built in the 18C.

In 1940 systematic excavations were begun beneath St Peter's. The ancient cemetery in which St Peter was buried after his crucifixion was discovered beneath the Vatican Grottoes. On 23 December 1950, the Pope announced that the tomb of St Peter had been identified (see below).

Dimensions. The exterior length of the church, including the portico, is 211.5m; the cross on the dome is 136.5m above the ground. The façade is 115m long, and 45.5m high. Inside, the church is 186m long and 137m wide across the transepts. The nave is 60m across (including the aisles) and 44m high; the diameter of the dome is 42m, or 1.5m less than that of the Pantheon. The total area is 49,737 sq m (St Paul's in London is 26,639 sq m).

Admission. The basilica is open daily from 7.00–19.00 (18.00 in winter). You are not allowed to enter the church wearing shorts or mini-skirts, or with bare shoulders. Mass is held on Sunday at 7, 8, 9, and 10 o' clock (Sung Mass at 10.30), and frequently during the week. Holy Communion can be taken in the Cappella del Santissimo Sacramento throughout the day on Sunday.

Exterior. At the top of the triple flight of steps rises the long **façade**. Its great size impairs the view of the dome from the piazza. Eight columns and four pilasters support the entablature. A dedicatory inscription on the frieze records its erection in 1612, during the pontificate of Paul V. The attic, almost without ornament, is surmounted by a balustrade on which are statues of Christ, St John the Baptist, and eleven of the Apostles (St Peter's statue is inside), and two clocks, by Giuseppe Valadier (near the ends). Under the left-hand clock are the six bells of the basilica, electrically operated since 1931. The oldest bell dates from 1288; the largest (1786) is 7.5m round and weighs 9.75 tonnes. Above the doors and extending beyond them on either side is a row of nine large windows with balconies. The central balcony is that from which the senior cardinal-deacon proclaims the newly elected pope and from which the new Pope gives his blessing. Below the balcony is a relief, by Ambrogio Bonvicino, of Christ handing the keys to St Peter.

The **portico** is prolonged by vestibules at both ends connecting with the covered galleries of the piazza. The pavement was designed by Bernini. The vault is magnificently decorated in stucco, by Martino Ferrabosco; in the lunettes below it are 32 statues of canonised popes. Of the five entrances to the church, that on the extreme right is the PORTA SANTA, opened only in Holy Years. The panels on the door are by Vico Consorti (1950). The door on the right of the main door is by Venanzio Crocetti (1968). The bronze central *DOOR, from Old St Peter's, was decorated by Filarete in 1439–45 with reliefs of Christ, the Virgin, Saints Peter and Paul and their martyrdom, and events in the life of Pope Eugenius IV. Around them is a frieze of classical and mythological subjects, animals, fruits, and portraits of emperors. The door to the left is by Giacomo Manzù, (1963), with sculptures depicting the death of religious figures and abstract themes of death, and the door on the extreme left is by Luciano Minguzzi (1977).

High up on the wall between the doors are three framed inscriptions: the one on the left commemorating the donation by Gregory II of certain olive trees to provide oil for the lamps over the tomb of St Peter; the Latin epitaph of Adrian (772–95), attributed to Charlemagne; and the bull of Boniface VIII proclaiming the first jubilee or Holy Year (1300). In the tympanum, above the central entrance (that is, looking backwards, against the light) is the famous *NAVICELLA, a mosaic representing Christ walking on the waters, executed by Giotto for the old basilica. It has frequently been moved, and has suffered from resetting and restoration; it is now virtually a copy of the original. The equestrian statue of Charlemagne (1), at the left end of the portico, is by Agostino Cornacchini; that on the right, of *Constantine (2) by Bernini, is beyond a door which gives access to the corridor leading to the Scala Regia. This is often open for visitors leaving the Sistine Chapel.

The immensity of the **interior** is disguised by the symmetry of its proportions. The work of Bernini for this majestic church, which had begun with the approach and his decorations on Ponte Sant'Angelo and was continued in the piazza, culminates in the magnificent baldacchino and exedra in the tribune. As the shrine of St Peter, the church has a ceremonial air, with temporary pews beneath the gilded coffered ceiling designed by Bramante. The coloured marble of the walls and pavement is the work of Giacomo della Porta and Bernini.

Nave. The first part of the nave, with its aisles and three side chapels, is Maderno's extension, which transformed the plan of the church from a Greek to a Latin cross. The round slab of porphyry let into the pavement in front of the central door is that on which the emperors used to kneel for their coronation in front of the altar of the old basilica. Farther on are metal lines indicating the lengths of the principal churches of Europe. The nave is separated from the aisles by colossal piers, each decorated with two fluted

Corinthian pilasters, supporting great arches. In the niches between the pilasters of the nave and transepts are statues of the founders of the religious orders. The aisles have sumptuous decorations by Bernini. Over the spaces between the piers are elliptical cupolas, three on either side, decorated with elaborate mosaics. In addition to these six minor cupolas there are four circular domes over the corner chapels in the main body of the church, where the sessions of the second Vatican Council took place in 1962–65.

Michelangelo's *dome is an architectural masterpiece. Simple and digni- fied, and flooded with light, it rises immediately above the site of St Peter's tomb. Four pentagonal **piers** support the arches on which rests the drum of the cupola. The piers are decorated with balconies and niches designed by Bernini. Each balcony has two spiral columns taken from the saint's shrine in the old basilica (another of these columns is the Colonna Santa; see below). The niches are filled with colossal statues, which give each of the piers its name. Beginning from the right (NE) and going counter-clockwise, they are:*St Longinus (3), by Bernini; St Helena (4), by Andrea Bolgi; St Veronica (5), by Francesco Mochi; and St Andrew (6), by François Duques- noy. On the balconies are reliefs referring to the 'Reliquie Maggiori'; these precious relics, which are displayed in Holy Week, are preserved in the podium of the pier of St Veronica. They are the lance of St Longinus, the soldier who pierced the side of Christ on the Cross, presented to Innocent VIII; a piece of the True Cross, collected by St.Helena; and the cloth of St Veronica, with the miraculous image of Christ. The head of St Andrew, presented to Pius II in 1462 by Thomas Paleologos, despot of the Morea, was recently returned to the Greek Orthodox Church at Patras.

The Latin inscription on the frieze of the dome is a continuation of the Greek inscription in the tribune. In the pendentives of the dome are huge mosaics of the Evangelists (the pen held by St Mark is 1.5m long). On the frieze below the drum is inscribed in letters nearly 2m high: 'Tu es Petrus et super hanc petram aedificabo ecclesiam meam et tibi dabo claves regni caelorum.' The dome is divided into sixteen compartments, corresponding to the windows of the drum, by ribs ornamented with stucco; in these compartments are six bands of mosaic by Cavalier d'Arpino, representing saints, angels, and the company of Heaven; in the lantern above is the Redeemer.

Under a canopy against the pier of St Longinus, facing inwards, is the famous bronze **statue of St Peter** (7), seated on a marble throne. It was once believed to date from the 5C or 6C, but, since its restoration in 1990, is considered to be the work of Arnolfo di Cambio (c 1296). The extended foot of the statue has been worn away by the kisses of the faithful. The statue is robed on high festivals. Above is a portrait in mosaic of Pius IX (1871).

Over the high altar rises the great **baldacchino** (8), designed by Bernini and unveiled on 28 June 1633, by Urban VIII. This colossal Baroque structure, a combination of architecture and decorative sculpture, is cast of bronze taken from the Pantheon. Four gilt bronze solomonic columns rise from their marble plinths, which are decorated with the Barberini bees. The columns resemble in design the Colonna Santa (see below) but are deco- rated with figures of genii and laurel branches. They support a canopy from which hang festoons and tassels and on which angels (by Duquesnoy) alternate with children. From the four corners of the canopy ascend ornamental scrolls, which support the globe and cross. Inside the top of the canopy is the Dove in an aureole.

The **High Altar**, at which only the Pope may celebrate, is formed of a block of Greek marble found in the Forum of Nerva and consecrated by Clement VIII on 26 June 1594. It covers the altar of Calixtus II (d 1123) which in turn encloses an altar of Gregory the Great (d 604). It stands over the space which is recognised as the tomb of St Peter.

In front (9) is the CONFESSIONE, built by Maderno and encircled by perpetually burning lamps. During excavations in 1940 it was discovered that the foundations of the confessione were hollow. When they were opened, they led into the ancient Roman necropolis below the Vatican Grottoes. Here was found the Tropaion of Gaius (see below).

South aisle. Above the Porta Santa is a mosaic of St Peter (10), designed by Ciro Ferri (1675). The CAPPELLA DELLA PIETÀ (11) is named after **Michelangelo's *Pietà** (1499; restored and protected by glass since its damage in 1972). This exquisite work was made at the age of 25 for the French ambassador, Cardinal Villiers de la Groslay. It is perhaps the most moving of all Michelangelo's sculptures and is the only one inscribed with his name (on the ribbon falling from the left shoulder of the Virgin). The mosaic decorations of the cupola, by Pietro da Cortona and Ciro Ferri, depict the Passion. The triumph of the Cross is by Lanfranco. Under the first arch of the aisle are a monument to Queen Christina of Sweden (12), by Carlo Fontana (1689), and opposite, a statue of Leo XII (13), by De Fabris (1836). Beneath it is the entrance to the small CAPPELLA DEL CROCIFISSO (14; usually closed), with a Crucifixion ascribed to Pietro Cavallini.

The CAPPELLA DI SAN SEBASTIANO (15) has an altar mosaic of the saint's martyrdom, after Domenichino. The monument to Pius XI (d 1939; 16) is by Francesco Nagni. Opposite is a monument to Pius XII (d 1958) by Francesco Messina. Under the next arch are a fine Baroque monument to Innocent XII (d 1700; 17), by Filippo Valle, and one by Bernini (18) of the Countess Matilda of Tuscany (d 1115), whose remains were moved from Mantua in 1635. The iron grille of the *CAPPELLA DEL SANTISSIMO SACRAMENTO (19) was designed by Borromini. Over the altar is a gilt bronze ciborium by Bernini, modelled on Bramante's 'tempietto' at San Pietro in Montorio. The two angels also form part of this unfinished composition. Behind is the Trinity, by Pietro da Cortona. Over the altar on the right is a mosaic of the Ecstasy of St Francis, after Domenichino. Under the next arch are the interesting monument (20) to Gregory XIII (d 1585), the reformer of the calendar (by Rusconi; 1723), and the unfinished tomb (21) of Gregory XIV (d 1591). Opposite, on the pier of St Longinus (22), is a *mosaic of the Communion of St Jerome, after Domenichino.

The CAPPELLA GREGORIANA (23) was built by Gregory XIII from designs by Michelangelo, with a cupola 42m above the floor. The chapel is dedicated to the Madonna del Soccorso, an ancient painting on part of a marble column from the old basilica, placed here in 1578 (24). Beneath the altar is the tomb of St Gregory Nazianzen, and on the right is that of Gregory XVI (d 1846), by Luigi Amici (1855; 25). Under the next arch is a mosaic (26) of the Mass of St Basil, after Subleyras. Opposite is the tomb of Benedict XIV (27), by Bracci; the statue of the Pope (d 1758) shows him proclaiming the Holy Year of 1750.

The **south transept** was used for the sessions of the council in 1869–70. Its three altars are decorated with mosaics: St Wenceslas (28), after Angelo Caroselli; the Martyrdom of Saints Processus and Martinian, St Peter's gaolers, after Valentin (29); and the Martyrdom of St Erasmus (30), after Nicolas Poussin (1629). In the arch beyond are the splendid *monument of Clement XIII (31), by Canova, and, against the pier of St Helena, the Altar of the Navicella (32), with a mosaic of Christ walking on the waters, after Lanfranco; the subject is the same as that of Giotto's mosaics in the portico.

The CAPPELLA DI SAN MICHELE (33) contains mosaics of St Michael (34), after Guido Reni, and of *St Petronilla (35), by Cristofari after Guercino. This chapel, in the SW corner of the basilica, has a round cupola, decorated with mosaics of angels, and pendentives with mosaics of the Doctors of the Church, after Romanelli and Sacchi. To the left (36) is the monument of Clement X (d 1676), by De Rossi and others; opposite, on the pier of St Helena, is a mosaic of St Peter raising Tabitha, after Placido Costanzi (37).

Two porphyry steps from the old basilica lead to the **tribune**, the most conspicuous object in which is the *CHAIR OF ST PETER (38), an ambitious and theatrical composition by Bernini (1665). This enormous gilt bronze throne is supported by statues of four Fathers of the Church: Saints Augustine and Ambrose, of the Latin Church (in mitres), and Saints Athanasius and John Chrysostom, of the Greek Church (bareheaded). It encloses an ancient wooden chair inlaid with ivory, said to have been the episcopal chair of St Peter. A circle of flying angels surrounds a great halo of gilt stucco in the centre of which, providing the focal point of the whole church, is the *DOVE set in the window above the throne.

On the right of St Peter's Chair is the fine *monument to Urban VIII (died 1644), also by Bernini, with statues of the pope and allegorical figures of Charity and Justice (39). The design of the tomb is clearly influenced by the Medici tombs in Florence by Michelangelo. The use of different materials in the sculpture give an effective colour to the monument. On the left is the monument to Paul III (died 1549; 40), by Guglielmo della Porta, a less successful attempt at the same type of tomb sculpture and design. Beyond the tribune, on the pier of St Veronica, is a mosaic of St Peter healing the paralytic, after Francesco Mancini (41); opposite is the monument to Alexander VIII (died 1691; 42), by Arrigo di San Martino; the bronze statue of the pope is by Giuseppe Bertosi, and the other sculptures are by Angelo De Rossi.

North aisle. The CAPPELLA DELLA COLONNA (43), one of the corner chapels with round cupolas, was decorated in 1757 with figures of angels carrying garlands and with symbols of the Virgin. The lunettes have mosaics after Francesco Romanelli. In this chapel is the tomb of St Leo the Great (died 461; 44); above is a *relief by Alessandro Algardi (1650), representing St Leo arresting the progress of Attila with the help of Saints Peter and Paul. On the altar (left, 45) is an ancient and greatly venerated representation of the Virgin painted on a column from the old basilica. In the middle of the chapel is the tombstone of Leo XII (died 1829). Under the next arch is the monument of Alexander VII (died 1667; 46), Bernini's last work in St Peter's. Although the design is original, the execution is not very careful. Opposite is a mosaic (47), Apparition of the Sacred Heart, after Carlo Muccioli, set here in 1922 by Benedict XV in place of an oil-painting on slate (Punishment of Simon Magus, by Francesco Vanni).

The **north transept** contains confessionals for foreigners, served by the Penitentiaries, who hear confessions in ten languages. The three altars are decorated with mosaics: St Thomas (48), after Vincenzo Camuccini; Crucifixion of St Peter (49), after Guido Reni; and St Joseph (50). In front of the central altar is the tomb of Palestrina (1594) by Achille Funi.

Over the door to the sacristy (see below) is the neo-classical monument to Pius VIII (died 1830), by Pietro Tenerani (51); opposite, against the pier of St Andrew, a mosaic (52) of Ananias and Sapphira, after Pomarancio. The CAPPELLA CLEMENTINA (53) is the fourth of the corner chapels with round cupolas; the cupola is decorated with mosaics after Pomarancio; in the pendentives are four Doctors of the Church. The chapel is named after Clement VIII (died 1605), who ordered Giacomo della Porta to decorate it for the jubilee of 1600. It contains the tomb of St Gregory the Great (died 604; 54), beneath the altar. Above it is a mosaic of a miracle of St Gregory, after Andrea Sacchi. To the left of the altar is a monument to Pius VII (died 1823), by Thorvaldsen, a classical work showing the influence of Canova (55).

On the E side of the pier of St Andrew is a mosaic of the Transfiguration (56), after Raphael, four times as large as the original in the Vatican. Opposite, beneath the aisle arch, are the monuments of *Leo XI, who reigned for only 27 days (died 1605; 57), by Algardi, and of Innocent XI (died 1689; 58), by Pierre Monnot (the urn decorated with a relief of the liberation of Vienna by John Sobieski). The CAPPELLA DEL CORO (59; closed) is richly decorated in stucco by Giovanni Battista Ricci after designs by Giacomo della Porta. It is closed by a fine gate with the arms of Clement XIII. It is furnished with elegant classical stalls by Bernini, and two large organs. The altarpiece (60), after a painting by Pietro Bianchi, represents the Immaculate Conception. In the pavement is the simple tombstone of Clement XI (died 1721).

Under the next arch is the bronze *monument to Innocent VIII (died 1492; 61), by Antonio Pollaiuolo, the only monument from the old basilica to be re-created in the new. The Pope is represented by two bronze statues; one recumbent on the urn, the other seated and holding in the left hand a spearhead, in allusion to his reception from the sultan Bajazet II of the spear that pierced the side of Christ. Opposite (62) is the monument to St Pius X (died 1914), by Pier Enrico Astorri. The ceremony of the canonisation of Pius X took place on 26 May 1954.

The CAPPELLA DELLA PRESENTAZIONE (63) is named after its altar-mosaic of the Presentation of the Virgin, after Francesco Romanelli; beneath the altar is the tomb of St Pius X. The cupola is decorated with a mosaic, after Carlo Maratta, exalting the glory of the Virgin. On the right is a monument to Pope John XXIII, by Emilio Greco. On the left is the monument to Benedict XV (died 1922; 64), by Pietro Canonica. Under the next arch are the Stuart monuments: above the door on the right (now used as an exit from the cupola, see below) is the monument (65) to Clementina Sobieska (died 1735), wife of James Stuart, the Old Pretender (she is here called Queen of Great Britain, France, and Ireland), by Filippo Barigioni; on the left is the *monument to the last Stuarts (66), by Canova, with busts of the Old and Young Pretenders (died 1766 and 1788) and of Henry, Cardinal York (died 1807). George IV contributed to the expense of this monument.

In the BAPTISTERY (67) the cover of a porphyry sarcophagus, placed upside-down, is used as the font. It formerly covered the tomb of the Emperor Otho II (973–83; in the Grottoes). According to a tradition (now discredited), the sarcophagus came from the sepulchral cella of Hadrian's mausoleum (Castel Sant'Angelo) and was the emperor's own. The present metal cover is by Carlo Fontana. The mosaics reproduce paintings of the Baptism of Christ, by Carlo Maratta; of St Peter baptising the centurion Cornelius, by Andrea Procaccini; and of St Peter baptising his gaolers Saints

Processus and Martinian, by Giuseppe Passeri. At the end of the nave can be seen the back of the doors by Giacomo Manzù, with a dedicatory inscription.

The *treasury (open 9.00–17.30), or MUSEO STORICO ARTISTICO, is entered by the door under the monument to Pius VIII (51). In the vestibule is a large stone slab with the names of the popes buried in the basilica, from St Peter to Pius XII. A corridor leads to the entrance of the treasury, rearranged in 1975 in dark modern exhibition rooms (the harsh illumination has been justly criticised). The treasury was plundered in 846 by the Saracens, and again during the sack of Rome in 1527 by Imperial troops, and was impoverished by the provisions of the Treaty of Tolentino (1797), which Pius VI was forced to conclude with Napoleon. It still, however, contains objects of great value and interest. The exhibits include vestments, missals, reliquaries, pyxes, patens, chalices, monstrances, crucifixes, and other sacred relics, as well as candelabra and ornaments.

ROOM I. The *Colonna Santa, a 4C Byzantine spiral column, one of twelve from the old basilica (eight decorate the balconies of the great piers of the dome in St Peter's; the remaining three are lost). The column was once thought to be that against which Christ leaned when speaking with the doctors in the Temple. The gilt bronze cock (9C) used to decorate the top of the campanile of the old basilica. ROOM II (Sagrestia dei Beneficiati; 71). Here is displayed the *Crux Vaticana, the most ancient possession of the treasury, dating from the 6C, the gift of the emperor Justinian II. It is made of bronze and set with jewels. Also here are the so-called *dalmatic of Charlemagne, now usually considered to date from the 11C or the early 15C; a Byzantine case with an enamelled Cross; fragment of a Byzantine diptych in ivory; copy (1974) of the ancient Chair of St Peter, now incorporated in Bernini's decoration in the tribune of St Peter's.

In the CAPPELLA DELLA SAGRESTIA DEI BENEFICIATI (71A) is displayed a beautiful *ciborium by Donatello (c 1432), from the old basilica. It encloses a painting of the Madonna 'della Febbre' (the protectress of malaria) attributed to Lippo Memmi. Over the chapel altar is St Peter receiving the keys, by Girolamo Muziano. A plaster-cast of Michelangelo's Pietà in St Peter's is also displayed here. ROOM IV. *Monument of Sixtus IV, a masterpiece in bronze by Antonio Pollaiuolo (1493). It can be seen to advantage from the raised platform. ROOM V. Ceremonial ring of Sixtus IV (1471–84); reliquary bust of St Luke the Evangelist (13–14C), and a wood Crucifix probably dating from the 14C.

A passage containing illuminated manuscripts, including one from the Giulia choir (1543) and a 17C ivory Crucifix leads to ROOM VI. Here are displayed a Cross and candelabra by Sebastiano Torrigiani; a Crucifix and six candelabra (1581) made by Antonio Gentili for Cardinal Alessandro Farnese and presented by him to the basilica in 1582; and two huge *candelabra of the 16C, traditionally attributed to Cellini. ROOM VII. Model of an angel in clay by Bernini (1673) used for one of the angels flanking the ciborium in the Cappella del Sacramento; 13C Slavonic icon in a jewelled silver frame, and reliquaries. ROOM VIII. Gilt bronze tiara (early 18C) for the statue of St Peter; on high festivals this statue is attired in full pontificals. Gold chalice set with diamonds (18C), bequeathed to the Vatican by Henry Stuart, Cardinal York; platinum chalice, presented by Charles III of Spain to Pius VI, interesting as the first recorded use of platinum for such a purpose. ROOM IX. *Sarcophagus of Junius Bassus, prefect of Rome in 359. This was found near St Peter's in the 16C, and is superbly carved.

From the entrance to the museum, a second corridor leads right, off which is the SACRISTY (68; open only 7.00–12.00), built for Pius VI by Carlo Marchionni (1776–84). It is an octagonal hall with a cupola supported by pilasters of yellow Siena marble and grey marble columns from Hadrian's Villa near Tivoli. To the left is the SAGRESTIA DEI CANONICI (69; special permit required, but sometimes open in the morning), with a chapel containing a Madonna and Saints by Francesco Penni, and an early Madonna with St John by Giulio Romano. The adjoining CHAPTER HOUSE (70) contains paintings of saints by Andrea Sacchi.

Ascent of the Dome. Admission daily 8.00–one hour before the basilica closes, except Christmas Day and Easter Day, and when the Pope is in the basilica (often on Wednesday morning). The entrance is from outside the basilica at the right end of the portico. The dome was completed as far as the drum by Michelangelo; the vault and the lantern were added by Giacomo della Porta in 1588–90. Clement VII covered the vault with strips of lead reinforced with bronze ribs.

A lift (or staircase) ascends to the ROOF from which there is a close view of the spring of the dome, whose Cross is 92m above. The two side cupolas by Giacomo della Porta are purely decorative and have no opening into the interior of the church. On the roof are buildings used by the *sampietrini*, masons and others employed on the maintenance of the fabric. Two stairways lead to a curving corridor from which is the entrance into the first circular gallery around the interior of the drum of the dome (53m above the ground and 67m below the top of the dome). From here there is an impressive view of the pavement far below and of the interior of the dome; the decorative details and mosaics are on a vast scale. The higher circular gallery is closed to the public.

Signs indicate the way on up via a spiral staircase with lancet windows, and a curving narrow stair between the two shells of the dome. The first big window has a view S, with the roof of the huge Audience Hall (1971) directly below. Iron stairs continue up to the tiny marble stairs which emerge on the loggia around the pretty LANTERN, 537 steps above the pavement of the basilica. There is a *view of the Vatican City and gardens, and beyond, on a clear day, of the whole of Rome and of the Campagna from the Apennines and the Alban hills to the sea. The Cross surmounting the copper ball (2.5m in diameter, just large enough to hold 16 people) is 132.5m above the ground. Another staircase leads down and out onto the roof with a view from the parapet, beside the huge statues on the façade, of Piazza San Pietro. The exit is at present inside St Peter's, under the Sobieska monument, next to the baptistery (65).

The **Vatican Grottoes** are open on weekdays 8.00–17.00 or 18.00, except when the Pope is in the basilica. The entrance is at present by the pier of St Longinus (3) although one of the other three entrances at the piers are sometimes used (see the Plan). The exit is on the outside of the church, to the right of the portico. In the space between the level of the existing basilica (30m above sea-level) and that of the old one (27m) the Renaissance architects built the so-called SACRED GROTTOES and placed in them various monuments and architectural fragments from the former church. They were used for the burial of numerous popes. Excavations were carried out below the level of the old basilica from 1940 to 1957.

The grottoes, which follow the outline of the basilica above them (except for their annexes), are in two adjoining sections. The OLD GROTTOES have the form of a nave with aisles (corresponding to Maderno's nave but extending beyond it); on either side are the annexes discovered during the excavations. The NEW GROTTOES are in the form of a horse-shoe, with extensions. The centre is immediately below the high altar of St Peter's. Four of the extensions reach to points below the four piers of St Longinus, St Helena, St Veronica, and St Andrew.

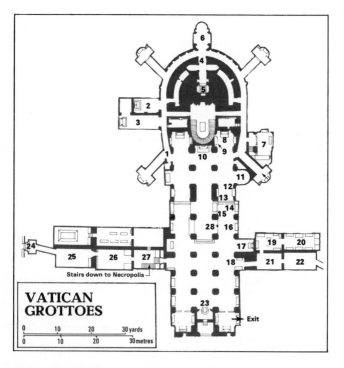

Stairs lead down from the church to the **New Grottoes** and a horse-shoe corridor, lined with fine reliefs attributed to Matteo del Pollaiuolo of the life of St Peter which decorated the tabernacle over the high altar of the old basilica. Beyond a modern chapel is the 14C chapel of the Madonna della Bocciata (2) and the 15C chapel of the Madonna delle Febbri (3). The Clementine Chapel (4) is immediately beneath the centre of the church above. Here the rear wall was breached during the excavations for St Peter's tomb. Behind is the foundation of the altar of Calixtus II enclosing that of Gregory I. The Tropaion of Gaius (see below) is therefore beneath (5). Openings to the left and right show the structure of the foundations more clearly (visible only when the grille is opened on a guided tour of the necropolis, see below). Opposite the chapel is (6) the tomb of Pius XII (died 1958). Another chapel (7) has the unfinished tomb of Paul II (died 1471) by Mino da Fiesole, Giovanni Dalmata, and others.

The area of the **Old Grottoes** lies at the W end of the right aisle. Immediately to the right is a chapel (8) with a 15C altar of the Virgin, and the tomb (9) of Pius VI (died 1799) in an early Christian sarcophagus. At the W end of the nave, flanked by two lions and two angels, can be seen the TOMB OF ST PETER (10). Continuing down the aisle, the route passes the tomb of Pope John XXIII (died 1963; 11). Beyond on the left (12) is the tomb of Christina of Sweden (died 1689), and opposite (13), the tomb of Queen Charlotte of Cyprus (died 1487). After a short flight of steps are more tombs: on the left (14) Innocent IX (died 1591), and right (15) Benedict XV (died 1922), followed by (16) Marcellus II (died 1555), and (28) John Paul I (died 1978). The chapel (17) beyond has a relief of the Madonna attributed to Isaia da Pisa. Here is the plain tomb slab of Paul VI (died 1978).

A turning left leads away from the Old Grottoes, passing some mosaics, and (left) (18) the tomb of Julius III (died 1555) into the N ANNEXE, a series of rooms (19–22; sometimes closed) containing interesting inscriptions and fragments from the old basilica. In the two rooms to the left (19 and 20; sometimes unlit) is the sarcophagus of Anicius Probus, Prefect of Rome in 395. At the W end of the grottoes (23) is a kneeling *statue of Pius VI by Canova, removed from the confessione of the basilica in 1980. The present exit is through a corridor where some column bases from Constantine's basilica can be seen, and the cenotaph of Calixtus III with good reliefs. The corridor leads out to the portico of the church beside the equestrian statue of Constantine I by Bernini (keyed 2 on the plan of St Peter's).

*Necropolis and St Peter's Tomb**. You can apply in writing or in person to the Ufficio Scavi (beneath the Arco della Campana, left of St Peter's) for permission to join the groups of fifteen which are conducted on most days (9.00–12.00, 14.00–17.00; the visit takes c 1½hrs). A double row of mausoleums, dating from the 1C AD, running from E to W, were discovered below the level of the old basilica. The extreme W series of these is on higher ground and adjoins a graveyard which is immediately beneath the high altar of the present church. Constantine significantly chose to erect his basilica above this necropolis, a most difficult undertaking because of the slope of the hill. He had to level the terrain and make use of supporting foundation walls. A baldacchino in the presbytery covered the TROPAION OF GAIUS, a funerary monument in the form of a small aedicule or niche, referred to c 200, and probably built by Pope Anicetus.

This monument was discovered during excavations. It backs on to a supporting wall plastered with red, dating from the same period. An empty space beneath it is believed to be St Peter's tomb. This was probably a mound of earth covered by brick slabs, and it shows signs of the interference which history records. That this was a most revered grave is evident from the number of other graves which crowd in on it, without cutting across the tomb. In front of the red wall, on which a Greek inscription is taken to name the saint, is a later wall, scratched with the names of pilgrims invoking the aid of Peter. Bones, obviously displaced, of an elderly and powerfully built man, were found beneath this second graffiti wall and declared by Paul VI to be those of St Peter. The site of the Circus of Nero, the most likely place of St Peter's martyrdom, lay along the S flank of the basilica, and extended as far as Via Sant'Uffizio.

You are usually asked to enter the Vatican City through the Arco delle Campane, and meet in Piazza dei Protomartiri Romani. The visit normally starts at the S ANNEXE (24) of the Old Grottoes, through two rooms (25 and 26) with 14–15C tomb slabs and sarcophagi. A third room (27) has transennae and architectural fragments of the 4–9C, and part of the nave foundation wall of the old basilica; from here stairs lead down to the necropolis. (If, however, work on the excavations prevents this route being used, the group is taken into St Peter's and through the New Grottoes (5), from which these stairs can also be reached.)

The necropolis is well preserved and was in use until Constantine's reign. Among the eighteen loculi cleared the one purely Christian mausoleum provides the most ancient mosaics yet discovered on a Christian subject. Here, on the vault richly decorated with a vine pattern, Christ is depicted as Helios, the sun-god. On the walls the sinopie remain of mosaics which have become detached from the surface (on the left, Jonah, and ahead, fishermen). In the other mausoleums Oriental cults and those of Greece and Rome are combined. Christians were also buried in the mausoleum of the Caetenii, with the grave of Aemilia Gorgonia; in the magnificent stuccoed mausoleum of the Valerii, with reliefs in niches, where the inscription of Valerinus Vastulus, despite the pagan sarcophagus (3C), specifies his Christian burial; and in the so-called Egyptian chamber. The paintings of peacocks in the mausoleum of the family of P. Aelius Tyrannus, the marble bust of the woman in that of the Valerii, and the remarkable sarcophagus of Q. Marcius Hermes and his wife, mirror the tastes and wealth of the families of freedmen to whom the loculi belonged. Among the many sarcophagi is one for a child, with figures of the mourning parents.

B.   The Vatican Museums

Admission. The Vatican Museums and Galleries are open Monday–Saturday from 8.45 to 14.00; usually in July, August, and September, and during the Easter period they are open from 8.45–17.00 (the ticket office closes one hour before closing time). They are also open free on the last Sunday of the month, unless it is a holiday (see below). The museums and galleries covered by the ticket (13,000 lire, 8000 lire for students in 1994), for one single visit, are the Gregorian Museum of Pagan Antiquities and the Pio Christian Museum, the Picture Gallery, the Pio-Clementino Museum (sculpture), the Chiaramonti Museum (sculpture), the Egyptian Museum, the Etruscan Museum, the Museum of Pagan Antiquities, the exhibition rooms of the Library, the Museum of Christian Art, the Borgia Rooms and the Gallery of Modern Religious Art, the Raphael Rooms, the Sistine Chapel, the Chapels of Nicholas V and of Urban VIII, the Room of the Chiaroscuri, the Hall of the Immaculate Conception, the Gallery of Maps, the Gallery of Tapestries, and the Ethnological Missionary Museum. The Etruscan Museum is closed Wednesday and Saturday, and the Ethnological Museum is only open on Wednesday and Saturday.

The Vatican collections are closed on Sundays (except the last in the month) and on: New Year's Day, 6 January, 11 February (anniversary of the founding of the Vatican City State), Easter Monday, 1 May, Ascension Day, Corpus Christi, 29 June, 15 August, 1 November, 8 December, Christmas Day and Boxing Day, and whenever special reasons make it necessary.

A **bus service** runs daily, except Sunday and Wednesday (if a Papal audience is being held), every half hour (between 8.45 and 12.45, and between 8.45 and 13.45 in July–September and the Easter period) from the Arco delle Campane (left of the façade of St Peter's) through the Vatican gardens (described at the end of this Route) to a side entrance to the Museums, at the ambulatory (5 minutes; 2000 lire). This is recommended not only as the most convenient way of reaching the museums from St Peter's, but also it provides the opportunity of seeing part of the Vatican City and gardens, which can otherwise be seen only on an organised tour (see below). The bus can also be taken back from the Museums to St Peter's (10.00, 10.30, etc; last bus at 14.00).

Facilities are provided for the **disabled** in the Vatican Museums.

There is a self-service **Restaurant** and **Café** below the courtyard outside the *Quattro Cancelli*.

The ****VATICAN PALACE** contains some of the world's greatest art treasures. The extensive buildings and interior courts cover an area of 5.5 hectares. Most of the palace is open to the public, as the apartments reserved for the Pope and the papal court are contained in a relatively small area. The gardens and city can only been seen on an organised tour (see below). As well as the remarkable Greek and Roman sculpture museums, the gallery of paintings, the library, the Egyptian and Etruscan collections, ethnological material, etc. the palace contains the famous Sistine Chapel frescoed by Michelangelo and the 'Stanze' decorated by Raphael. Because of the number of different museums it contains and the vast extent of the halls and galleries on two floors, it is not practicable to see them all in a single visit. You are strongly recommended not to attempt to see too much, and to plan to return at least two or three times. Over two million people a year visit the Sistine Chapel, which is the exclusive goal of almost all the tour groups which enter the palace. Some of the other areas of the palace remain comparatively peaceful, and a number of the galleries with exceptional masterpieces receive many less visitors simply because they are not 'on the way' to the Sistine (see 'Plan of Visit', below).

History. In the days of Pope St Symmachus (498–514) a house was built beside the first basilica of St Peter. This house was not the residence of the popes as, until the migration to Avignon in 1309, they lived in the Lateran Palace; but it was used for state occasions and for the accommodation of foreign sovereigns. In it Charlemagne stayed in 800 and Otho II in 980. By the 12C it had fallen into disrepair. Eugenius III (1145–53) was the first of numerous popes to restore and enlarge it. In 1208 Innocent III built a fortified residence here which was added to by his successors. When Gregory XI returned from Avignon in 1378 he found the Lateran uninhabitable and so took up residence in the Vatican. On his death in the same year, the first conclave was held in the Vatican. A covered way which connected the Vatican Palace to Castel Sant'Angelo was used in emergencies (see Rte 23).

Nicholas V transformed the house into a palace which he built round the Cortile dei Pappagalli. In 1473 Sixtus IV added the Sistine Chapel. Innocent VIII had Giacomo da Pietrasanta build the Belvedere Pavilion on the N summit of the Vatican hill. Alexander VI decorated a suite of rooms on the first floor of the palace of Nicholas V and they became known, after his family name, as the Appartamento Borgia; he also added the Borgia Tower. Julius II began to form the famous collection of classical sculpture, which he installed in the courtyard of the Belvedere Pavilion. He also commissioned Bramante to unite this pavilion with the palace of Nicholas V by means of long corridors, thus creating the great Courtyard of the Belvedere.

Leo X decorated the E side of the palace with open galleries looking on to the Courtyard of St Damasus, one of which became known as the Loggia of Raphael. Paul III employed Antonio da Sangallo the Younger to build the Cappella Paolina and the Sala Regia. Under Pius IV and Gregory XIII various additions were made by Pirro Ligorio. Sixtus V assigned to Domenico Fontana the construction of the block overlooking Piazza San Pietro and of the great Library, which was built at right angles to the long corridors and thus divided the Courtyard of the Belvedere in two. The Scala Regia of Bernini was begun under Urban VIII and completed under Alexander VII. The Museum of Pagan Antiquities was founded by Clement XIII.

Clement XIV converted the Belvedere Pavilion into a museum which his successor Pius VI enlarged; hence its name 'Pio-Clementino'. The architect was Michelangelo Simonetti, who altered the courtyard and added several rooms. Pius VI was also the founder of the Picture Gallery. Pius VII (Chiaramonti) founded the Sculpture Gallery which bears his name and added the New Wing (by Raffaele Stern), which paralleled the Library. Its construction divided the Courtyard of the Belvedere into three. From now on the sections became known as the Courtyard of the Belvedere (retaining the old name; nearest the pontifical palace), the relatively small Courtyard of the Library, and, nearest to the Belvedere Pavilion, the Courtyard of the Fir Cone (Pigna; after a bronze fir cone placed in it by Paul V). Gregory XVI was responsible for the Etruscan and Egyptian Museums. Pius IX closed the fourth side of the Courtyard of St Damasus and built the Scala Pia. Leo XIII restored the Borgia Rooms and reopened them to the public.

Under Pius XI were built the new Picture Gallery and the new entrance to the Vatican Museums in the Viale Vaticano, both of them dating from 1932. A new building was opened in 1970 by Paul VI to house the former Lateran museums (the Gregorian Museum of Pagan Antiquities and the Pio Christian Museum); in 1973 the Ethnological Missionary Museum was opened beneath, and a Historical Museum was built under the gardens (this has since been transferred to the Lateran Palace). An extensive series of galleries in and around the Borgia apartments were opened in 1973 as a Museum of Modern Religious Art.

The most convenient way of reaching the Vatican Museums from St Peter's is by the Vatican bus service (see above). Otherwise, from St Peter's it is a long and rather unpleasant walk along Via di Porta Angelica (Pl. 1; 4) to the right (N) of Bernini's colonnade in Piazza San Pietro. At the beginning of the street is the battlemented covered way to Castel Sant'Angelo (see Rte 23). The site of Porta Angelica was the modern Piazza del Risorgimento. On the left is the Cancello di Sant'Anna, one of the entrances to the Vatican City. The road skirts the city wall, and turns left out of Piazza del Risorgimento.

Continuing along the wall, Viale Vaticano leads left to the **entrance to the Vatican Museums** (Pl. 1; 3, 4). The ENTRANCE HALL has a ticket office for tour groups (for individual visitors see below), an information office, and lifts for the museums. The monumental *DOUBLE STAIRCASE, built in 1932 by Giuseppe Momo, has independent ascending and descending spirals, carved out of the hill, to connect the street level with that of the museums. The bronze balustrade is by Antonio Maraini.

The AMBULATORY at the top of the staircase, with mosaics and busts, has the ticket office for individual visitors (separate office for students), the bus terminus from St Peter's, a bank, a post office, telephones, bookstalls, cloakrooms, etc. Beyond the TICKET GATES a short flight of steps mounts to the VESTIBULE decorated with three mosaics from Hadrian's Villa. In summer (and on fine days) visitors are directed instead outside to the CORTILE DELLE CAROZZE where the *base of the Column of Antoninus Pius has been placed since its restoration. A monolithic block of Greek marble it has high reliefs on three sides with the Apotheosis of Antoninus and his wife Faustina, who are being conducted to Heaven by a winged Genius personifying Rome, and delightful scenes of cavalcades (AD 138–61). It was found in 1703 in Via della Missone, near Montecitorio. On the right is the entrance to the new building which houses the Gregorian Museum of Pagan Antiquities and the Pio Christian Museum. Beyond is an open court (below which is a self-service restaurant and café). On the left is a vestibule known as the **Quattro Cancelli**, from which the various museums and galleries are signposted.

Plan of visit. The collections are so extensive and their layout is so complicated that it is not practicable to see them all in a single visit. To add to the complication four one-way itineraries have been imposed by the Vatican authorities and you are expected to chose one of the four 'tours' depending on the time at your disposal. This is primarily to regulate the flow of people to the Sistine Chapel and tour groups have to take the signposted routes. If you are not in a tour these can be disregarded to some extent, but if you want to see one particular collection only, the one-way systems are usually a hindrance, and in some cases access from one part of the museums to another is no longer possible.

The number of guided tours in the Vatican can seriously impede the other visitors' enjoyment of the museum. If you have time, it can be a good idea to go straight to the Sistine Chapel at opening time in order to enjoy it in comparative peace, and then return to the Quattro Cancelli to begin the detailed tours described below. However, you are now often able to leave the museums through the Sistine Chapel by the Scala Regia (usually closed on Wednesdays) which descends directly to the portico of St Peter's. The museums which are not 'on the way' to the Sistine Chapel are usually comparitively deserted (anyway before 11 o'clock): these include the Picture Gallery, the Gregorian Museum of Pagan Antiquities, the Etruscan Museum, the Chiaramonti Museum, and the New Wing.

The four separate tours suggested below can at present be made taking into account the one-way systems.

I. Quattro Cancelli—Simonetti staircase—Egyptian Museum—Chiaramonti Museum—New Wing—Pio-Clementino Museum—upstairs to the Room of the Biga—Etruscan Museum—return to the Quattro Cancelli.

II. A very long and tiring route which should, if time permits, be taken in two stages. Quattro Cancelli—upstairs to the Gallery of the Candelabra—Gallery of Tapestries and Gallery of Maps—Hall of the Immaculate Conception—Raphael Rooms—Room of the Chiaroscuri—Chapel of Nicholas V—Chapel of Urban VIII—Borgia Rooms and Gallery of Modern Religious Art—Sistine Chapel—Museum of Christian Art—Sistine Hall and Library—Quattro Cancelli.

III. Quattro Cancelli—Vatican Picture Gallery—Quattro Cancelli.

IV. Vestibule—Gregorian Museum of Pagan Antiquities—Pio Christian Museum—Ethnological Missionary Museum—Vestibule.

The itineraries described below follow the above scheme.

I. The Egyptian Museum, Chiaramonti Museum, New Wing, Pio-Clementino Museum, and Etruscan Museum

The Vatican Palace houses the largest collections of ancient sculpture in the world. These collections owe their origin to the Renaissance popes, and in particular to Julius II. However, many of the pieces were later dispersed, in particular by Pius V who made numerous gifts to the city of Rome and to private individuals. The popes of the late 18C and early 19C tried to reassemble the old collections and formed new ones.

The contents of the sculpture galleries are mainly Greek originals, Roman originals, or Roman copies of Greek originals executed in the 1C and 2C AD. In some cases the Roman sculptor when copying a Greek model placed a contemporary portrait head on his copy; later restorers often made additions in marble, stone, or plaster and also, in some cases, put heads on statues to which they do not belong. In addition, all the male sculpture was ludicrously disfigured by prudish plaster additions, and there are few undraped female statues (this does not apply to the Gregorian Museum of Pagan Antiquities).

The **Vatican Inventory Numbers** given in the following description are inconspicuously marked on the right side or back of the works themselves. The other more prominent numbered labels (some of them missing or difficult to decipher), usually in red, attached below each work have been ignored in the description below. In each room the keyed plans to the most important works also carry the Vatican Inventory Numbers.

The one-way systems (see above) make it, at present, obligatory to approach the sculpture galleries through the Egyptian Museum.

The Egyptian Museum

The **EGYPTIAN MUSEUM** occupies rooms in the lower floor of the Belvedere Pavilion adjoining the Pio-Clementino Museum. The entrance is at the top of the first flight of the Simonetti Staircase outside the Hall of the Greek Cross (described below). The museum was founded by Gregory XVI in 1839 and was arranged by Father Luigi Maria Ungarelli, one of the first Italian Egyptologists to continue the scientific research of Jean-François Champollion. The rooms were decorated in the Egyptian style in the 19C by Giuseppe De Fabris. The collection was beautifully rearranged in 1989 (and it is well labelled).

Room I. Funerary stelae and tomb reliefs arranged in chronological order from c 2600 BC–600 AD. **Room II**. Wooden painted mummy cases (1000 BC); two marble sarcophagi (6C BC); jewellery, ornaments, figurines, etc. found in tombs (1500–525 BC), canopic jars (1500–500 BC); model of a boat (2000 BC); and funerary masks and a painted cloth from the Roman period. **Room III**. *Statuary from the Serapeum of the Canopus of the Egyptian delta, built by Hadrian in his villa at Tivoli after his journey to Egypt in 130/31 (see Rte 33), including Serapis, a colossal bust of Isis, and statues of Antinous. The arrangement of the statues has been reconstructed. **Room IV**. Colossal grey marble statue personifying the Nile (1C AD); two statues of Hapy, the god representing the Nile in flood; and works from the Serapeum in the Campus Martius.

Room V, the **Hemicycle**, conforms in shape to the Niche of the Bronze Fir Cone (described below). *Head in sandstone of Mentuhotep II (c 2060–2040 BC), the oldest portrait in the museum; statues in black granite of the lion-headed goddess Sekhmet (1390–1352 BC); colossal *statue of Queen Tuaa, mother of Rameses II, brought to Rome by Caligula; colossal granite statue of Ptolemy Philadelphos (284–242 BC) and his wife Arsinoe; black bust of Serapis (2C AD). **Rooms VI and VII** contain the Grassi collection of small bronzes of sacred animals and gods, terracotta statuettes from Alexandria, lamps, utensils, Islamic ceramics, Syrian glass from Palestine (1–5C AD), etc. **Room VIII**. Material from Mesopotamia and Persia (3000–1000 BC). **Room IX**. Exquisite *bas-reliefs from Mesopotamia (884–626 BC).

The **Niche of the Bronze Fir Cone**, reached from the hemicycle, is the apse at the N end of the extensive **Courtyard of the Fir Cone** (*Cortile della Pigna*; open if fine), one of the three sections into which Bramante's Courtyard of the Belvedere was eventually divided. Here Paul V (1605–21) placed the colossal bronze FIR CONE, over 4m high (recently restored), found near the Thermae of Agrippa. It formed the centrepiece of a fountain (there are holes in the top of the scales) beside the Temple of Isis, and was made by a certain P. Cincius Salvius, in the 1C AD. In the Middle Ages it was in the portico of Old St Peter's, together with the two bronze gilt peacocks (here replaced by copies; originals in the New Wing), on either side of it. The fir cone was seen by Dante ('Inferno', XXXI, 53) and gave its name to a district of the city, the *Quartiere della Pigna*. Also here are seated black granite statues of the goddess Sekhmet, and, in the courtyard below, two lions once part of a monument to Nectanebo I (XXXth Dynasty), removed by Gregory XVI from the Fontana dell'Acqua Felice. An incongruous sculpture, donated by Arnaldo Pomodoro, was installed in the centre of the courtyard in 1990.

From the landing outside Room IX of the Egyptian Museum stairs lead down to the Chiaramonti Sculpture Gallery, and a door into the Courtyard of the Fir Cone.

The Chiaramonti Museum

The **CHIARAMONTI SCULPTURE MUSEUM** is reached by stairs leading down from the landing outside the Egyptian Museum and near the Round Vestibule (see below). This gallery is named after its founder Pius VII (Chiaramonti) and it was arranged by Canova who designed the lunette frescoes with scenes from the life of Pius VII as patron of the arts (by Francesco Hayez, Philippe Veit, etc.). The New Wing and the Gallery of Inscriptions are extensions of this museum. The Chiaramonti gallery, in Bramante's E corridor, is 300 metres long. It flanks and overlaps the Courtyard of the Fir Cone. The exhibits are divided into 59 sections, numbered with roman numerals (odd numbers on left, even numbers on right).

Section I. 1195. Sarcophagus of C. Junius Euhodus and his wife Metilia Acte, a priestess of the Magna Mater at Ostia, with a relief of the story of Alcestis; the faces of Alcestis and her husband Admetus are portraits of the Roman couple (2C AD). **Section II**. 1211. Herm of Hephaistos (Vulcan); the head may be derived from a statue by Alkamenes; Roman copy of a 5C Greek original. **Section IV**. 1246. Statue of Hygieia, part of a group of Hygieia and Asklepios, Roman copy of a 4C original by the sons of Praxiteles in the Asklepieion on the island of Kos. **Section V**. 1252. Antoninus Pius, wearing armour. **Section IX**. 1314. Herakles with his son Telephos; the statue of Herakles is after a 4C original, that of Telephos after a 3C original; the group is a Roman synthesis.

Section X. 1343. Sepulchral monument of P. Nonnius Zethus and his family (1C AD), a square marble block with eight conical cavities for the various members of the family. The reliefs of a mill being turned by a donkey and of baking implements probably indicated the man's trade. **Section XI**. 1359. Portrait bust of Cicero; 1365. Sarcophagus lid. **Section XII**. 1370. Relief from a 3C sarcophagus, with a mule in blinkers turning a wine-press. **Section XIII**. 1373. Hermes, from an original of the 5C BC; 1376. Ganymede and the eagle, copy of a 3C Hellenistic original. **Section XV**. Portrait bust of Pompey.

Section XVI. *1434. Head of Athena, copy of a Greek original of the 5C BC; the eyes are restorations but they indicate the skill with which Greek artists caught the expression of the human eye. The whites of the eyes were probably of ivory, the pupils of semi-precious stone, and the lashes and brows of bronze. **Section XVII**. 1441. Silenus with a panther, copy of a 3C Hellenistic original. **Section XIX**. 1487. Portrait-head of a priest of Isis (1C BC); 1488. Head of a Roman of the late Republican period. **Section XX**. 1507. Athena, from a Greek original of the 5C BC. **Section XXI**. 1509. Eros bending his bow, probably a copy of a bronze original by Lysippos; *statue of a boy. **Section XXIII**. *1558. Fragment of a relief of Penelope in her characteristic attitude: sitting on a chair and resting her head on her right hand; from a Greek original of the 5C BC. **Section XXVI**. Head of the Discobolos of Myron, Roman copy of the 5C Greek original; *head from a Palmyran sepulchral relief, in the limestones typical of Palmyran sculpture, which was a fusion of Syrian and Hellenistic-Roman styles; 2C AD.

Section XXIX. 1639. Colossal head of Augustus; 1641. Statue of Tiberius; 1642. Head of Tiberius. **Section XXXI**. 1669. Relief of the Three Graces, Archaic period. **Section XXXII**. 1697. Dacian prisoner of high rank, Roman art of the 2C AD. **Section XXXV**. 1751. Roman pontiff in the act of sacrifice (1C BC). **Section XXXVI**. 1765. Resting athlete, Roman copy of a 4C Greek original. **Section XXXVII**. 1771. Statue of Herakles; from a Greek original of the 4C BC. **Section XL**. 1839. Statue of the Muse Polyhymnia, Roman copy of a Hellenistic original of the 3C or 2C BC; 1841. Statue of Artemis (Diana), Roman copy of a 4C Greek original. **Section XLIII**. *1901. Statuette of Ulysses, part of a group of Ulysses offering wine to Polyphemus, Roman copy of a 3C Greek original. **Section XLV**. Colossal head of Trajan.

Section XLVII. 1975. Portrait bust of a lady of the Julio-Claudian gens; the hair is typical of the fashion of the age of Augustus (1C AD); portrait statue of a Roman thought to be Sulla (1C BC). **Section LVIII**. 663. Personification of Winter; the female figure is wrapped in a cloak and holds a pine branch in her left hand; she is reclining near a stream where cupids are catching waterfowl and fishes; a Hellenistic-Roman work of the 2C AD; 664. Sepulchral relief of a Roman family (1C BC). **Section LIX**. 2166. Personification of Autumn, a companion piece to Winter (above); the female figure is surrounded by cupids gathering grapes; 664. Sepulchral relief of a Roman family (1C BC).

At the end of the Chiaramonti Museum is a gate (closed), beyond which is the **Gallery of Inscriptions** (*Galleria Lapidaria*), open only to scholars. It occupies the remaining part of Bramante's E corridor. The gallery was founded by Clement XIV and reorganised and classified by the celebrated epigraphist Monsignor Gaetano Marini (1742–1817). It contains over 5000 pagan and Christian inscriptions from cemeteries and catacombs.

On the right a door leads into the **NEW WING**, or *Braccio Nuovo*, an extension of the Chiaramonti sculpture gallery constructed by Raffaele Stern (1817–22) for Pius VII. It contains some of the most valuable sculptures in the Vatican. The impressive hall, 70m long and 8m wide, has a vaulted coffered ceiling and an apse in the middle of the S side, facing the Courtyard of the Library. The floor is inlaid with mosaics of the 2C AD from a Roman villa at Tor Marancia.

2296. Caryatid, copy of one of the caryatids of the Erechtheion on the Acropolis of Athens (5C BC); 2293. Head of a Dacian, from the Forum of Trajan (2C AD); 2292. Silenus carrying the infant Dionysos, copy of an original ascribed to Lysippos. *2290. The **Austus of Prima Porta** is one of the most famous portraits of the emperor, found in Livia's villa at Prima Porta. The emperor, who appears to be about 40 years old, is wearing a cuirass over his toga; he holds a sceptre in his left hand; his raised right hand shows that he is about to make a speech. The head is full of character and the majestic pose suggests the influence of Polykleitos. The cuirass, a remarkably delicate piece of work, is decorated with scenes that date the statue. The central scene depicts the restoration by the Parthians in 20 BC of the eagles lost by Crassus at Carrhae in 53 BC. The small cupid riding a dolphin, placed as a support for the right leg, may be a portrait of Gaius Caesar, grandson of Augustus. *2284. 'Modesty', probably Mnemosyne, copy of a Greek original of the 3C BC; 2282. Statue of Titus.

In the recess, 2276. Priestess of Isis; 2309. *Bust of Julius Caesar; alabaster cinerary urn said to be that of Livilla, daughter of Germanicus. The two bronze gilt peacocks (recently restored), probably stood at one of the entrance gates to Hadrian's Mausoleum (see above). The six tombstones were found near the Mausoleum of Augustus; five of them belong to the Julian family and the sixth to Vespasian's. 2272. Wounded Amazon (see below); 2265. Bust of Trajan; 2268. Selene (the Moon) approaching the sleeping Endymion, copy of a Hellenistic original of the 4–3C BC; 2266. Statue of a tragic poet (the head of Euripides does not belong), copy of a 4C original (?Aeschylus); *2261. Portrait bust of a Roman (1C AD).

On the opposite wall: *2255. **Demosthenes**. This is a replica of the original statue by Polyeuctos of Athens, set up in Athens in 280 BC to the memory of Demosthenes, the orator and statesman. The hands were originally joined, with the fingers crossed. The mouth plainly suggests the stutter from which the great Athenian suffered. Portrait bust of Ptolemy of Numidia (1C AD); *2252. Wounded Amazon, a replica of one of the statues from the Temple of Diana at Ephesos, by Polykleitos. According to the Elder Pliny, this statue won the prize in a competition in which Polykleitos, Pheidias, Kresilas, and Phradmon entered. The arms and feet were restored by Thorvaldsen; 2247. Bust of Hadrian wearing armour; 2246. Statue of Hera, copy of a 5C Greek original (attributed to Alkamenes); 2244. Fortune, copy of a 4C Greek statue (the head, though Roman, is from another figure; the oar and globe are Roman additions); 2243. Portrait bust of an unknown Roman of the 2C AD; 2242. statue of a man, a Greek portrait of the 4C BC; *2240. Statue of Artemis, from a 4C original.

In the apse. *2236. Bust of a man of the late Republican era, possibly Mark Antony; bust of Marcus Aurelius as a young man; statuettes of athletes; 2226. Statue of Diana; in the floor, mosaic of Diana of the Ephesians. *2300. **The Nile**, a fine Hellenistic work, found in 1513, with a statue of the Tiber (now in the Louvre), near the Temple of Isis (recently restored). The river-god, who reclines near a sphinx and holds a horn of plenty, has the calm benevolent expression of a benefactor who enjoys his munificence. The sixteen children who frolic over him are supposed to symbolise the sixteen cubits which the Nile rises when in flood. The plinth is decorated with characteristic scenes of life on the banks of the Nile.

2225. Statue of Julia, daughter of Titus; *2223. The **Giustiniani Athena**, after a Greek original of the 4C BC; this is the best existing copy of an original in bronze attributed to Kephisodotus or to Euphranor; it portrays the goddess's twofold function as the divinity of the intellect and of arms. 2222. Portrait bust of an unknown Roman of the 1C AD, possibly Cn. Domitius Ahenobarbus; 2221. Statue of a man wearing a toga, with the head of Claudius; *2219. **Resting Satyr**, copy of the famous statue by Praxiteles (replica in the Gallery of Statues; others in the Museo Gregoriano Profano and in the Capitoline Museum); 2218. Bust of Commodus (180–92);

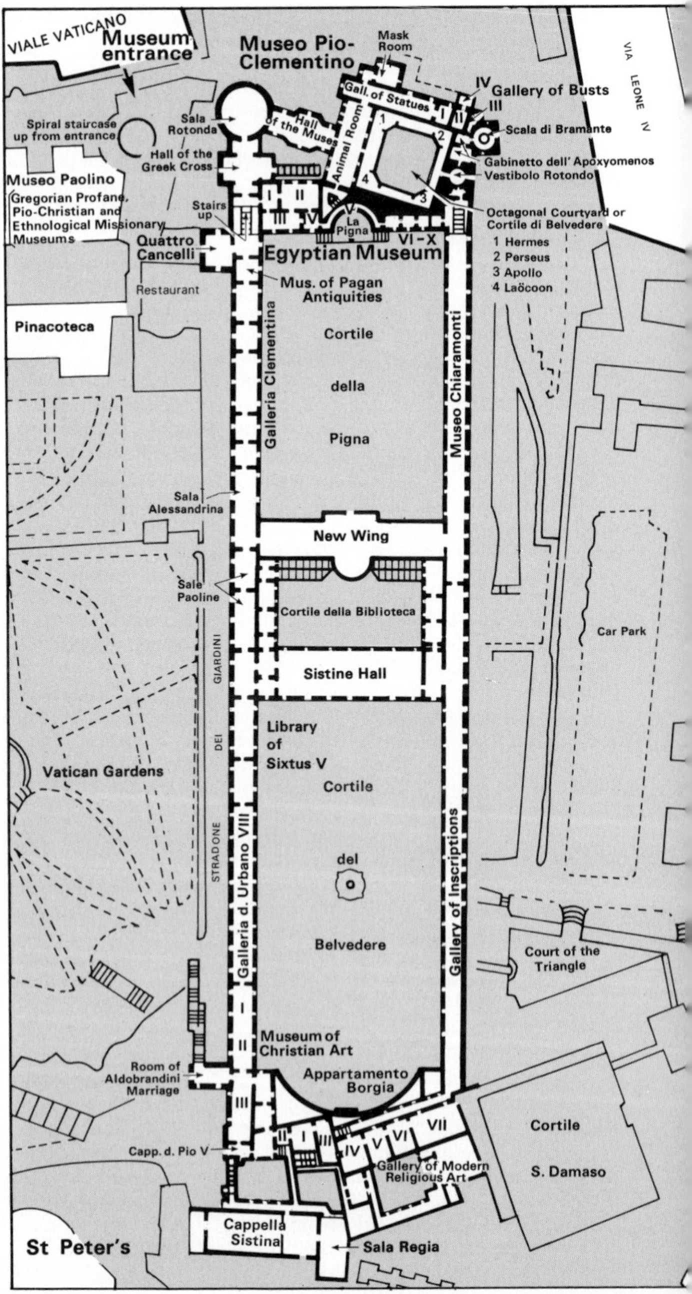
VIALE VATICANO
Museum entrance
Museo Pio-Clementino
Mask Room
Gall. of Statues
Hall of the Muses
Animal Room
IV Gallery of Busts
III
Scala di Bramante
Gabinetto dell' Apoxyomenos
Vestibolo Rotondo
Octagonal Courtyard or Cortile di Belvedere
1 Hermes
2 Perseus
3 Apollo
4 Laöcoon
VIA LEONE IV
Spiral staircase up from entrance
Sala Rotonda
Hall of the Greek Cross
Museo Paolino
Gregorian Profane, Pio-Christian and Ethnological Missionary Museums
Stairs up
La Pigna
VI–X
Quattro Cancelli
Egyptian Museum
Mus. of Pagan Antiquities
Restaurant
Pinacoteca
Galleria Clementina
Cortile della Pigna
Museo Chiaramonti
Sala Alessandrina
New Wing
Sale Paoline
Cortile della Biblioteca
Car Park
Sistine Hall
GIARDINI DEI STRADONE
Library of Sixtus V
Vatican Gardens
Cortile del Belvedere
Gallery of Inscriptions
Galleria d. Urbano VIII
Court of the Triangle
Museum of Christian Art
Room of Aldobrandini Marriage
Appartamento Borgia
Cortile S. Damaso
Capp. d. Pio V
Gallery of Modern Religious Art
Cappella Sistina
St Peter's
Sala Regia

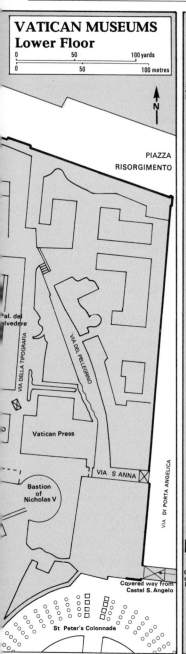

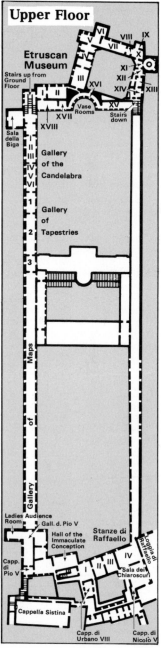

2217. Statue of an athlete with the head of Lucius Verus; the body is a copy of a 5C Greek original; 2216. Bust of the emperor Philip the Arabian (244–49); *2215. **Doryphoros of Polykleitos** (removed for restoration), copy of the famous bronze statue of a young spear-bearer. Polykleitos, the greatest sculptor of the school of Argos and Sikyon, devoted himself especially to the study of the proportions of the human body. Innumerable copies were made of the Doryphoros, with a head of the dolichocephalic type, and a youthful male form of beautiful proportion. Head of a Dacian, from Trajan's Forum (see No. 2293 above); *statue of Domitian, wearing a cuirass.

It is now necessary to return through the Chiaramonti Sculpture Museum to the landing outside the exit from the Egyptian Museum. Ahead is the present entrance to the Pio-Clementino Museum.

Pio-Clementino Museum

This sculpture gallery occupies the Belvedere Pavilion, which was adapted as a museum by Michelangelo Simonetti. The present entrance is from the landing outside the exit from the Egyptian Museum.

In the first vestibule is the *sarcophagus (1191.), in peperino, of Lucius Cornelius Scipio Barbatus, from the Tomb of the Scipios; the sarcophagus is in the form of a Doric altar but the general character is Etruscan. The archaic inscription, in Saturnine verse, is said to be by Ennius. Above are two inscriptions, also from the Tomb of the Scipios, to the son of Scipio Barbatus, who conquered Corsica in 259 BC.

Ahead is the **Round Vestibule** (*Vestibolo Rotondo*). Here are a large bowl of pavonazzetto and sculptural fragments. Beyond is the **Gabinetto dell'Apoxyomenos**. *1185. APOXYOMENOS, a finely built athlete scraping the oil from his body with a strigil, from a bronze original by Lysippos; this was the masterpiece of the sculptor's maturity (c 330 BC) and illustrated his canon of proportions. The statue was found in Trastevere (Vicolo dell'Atleta) in 1844. Above, Archaic Latin inscriptions from the Tomb of the Scipios; to the right, inscriptions, among them that of Lucius Mummius Achaicus, the conqueror of Greece (146 BC). In the ATRIUM beyond are three circus scenes (3C AD) and a funerary niche (957.) from near Todi (late 1C AD). Through a glass door here can be seen the *STAIRCASE OF BRAMANTE, which ascends to the floor above. The design is masterly; at each revolution the order changes, starting with Tuscan at the bottom and ending with Corinthian at the top.

From the Round Vestibule is the entrance to the **Octagonal Courtyard of the Belvedere** (there is another, larger, courtyard of the Belvedere, to the S), where Julius II placed the first classical sculptures which formed the nucleus of the great Vatican collections. When Pius VI had the museum enlarged in 1775, Michelangelo Simonetti made the courtyard into an octagon by forming the recesses (gabinetti) in the four corners.

To the left is the **Gabinetto dell'Apollo**. Here is the famous *APOLLO BELVEDERE (1015.), a 2C Roman copy of a bronze original probably by Leochares (4C BC). The slender elegant figure of the young god is stepping forward to see the effect of the arrow that he has just shot. The statue has been greatly admired as one of the masterpieces of classical sculpture since it was brought to the Vatican in 1503. It was beautifully restored in 1982. Under the adjoining colonnade: *relief of a procession, from the Ara Pacis

Augustae, an original fragment not returned to the altar on its reconstitution in 1937–38; nearly all the heads are restorations.

The **Gabinetto del Laocoonte** contains the famous group of *LAOCOÖN (1059.) and his two sons in the coils of the serpents, a vivid and striking illustration of the story related by Virgil in the Aeneid. Laocoön, priest of Apollo, warned his fellow Trojans against the trickery of the Greeks and entreated them not to admit the wooden horse into the city. In punishment Apollo or Athene sent serpents to crush him and his young sons to death in their coils. This group, of Greek marble, was found on the Esquiline Hill, in 1506, and was at once recognised as that described by Pliny, though it is not carved from a single block, as he states, but from at least three pieces. It was purchased by Julius II after its discovery and brought to the Vatican. It is ascribed to the Rhodian sculptors Agesander, Polydoros, and Atheno-doros (c 50 BC). The violent realism of the conception as well as the extreme skill and accurate detail with which the agonised contortions of the bodies are rendered are typical of the sculpture of the late Hellenistic period. One of the best known classical sculptures, it influenced Renaissance and Baroque artists, and was particularly admired in the 19C (Byron, in 'Childe Harold' describes 'Laocoön's torture dignifying pain'). The group acquired its present appearance in a restoration in 1960. Its more familiar appearance as restored by Montorsoli (on the advice of Michelangelo) is preserved in a plaster-cast which can be seen from a window of the Gregorian Profane Museum (see below).

Flanking the doorway beyond are two *molossian dogs of the school of Pergamon. **Gabinetto dell'Hermes**. *907. Hermes (formerly thought to be Antinous), perhaps Hermes Psychopompos, the conductor of souls to the underworld, copy of an original by Praxiteles. The head is reminiscent of that of his famous Hermes at Olympia. It was restored in 1984. In the portico beyond (niche), Venus Felix and Cupid: the body is copied from the Venus of Knidos in the Mask Room; the inscription on the plinth states that the group was dedicated to Venus Felix by Sallustia and Helpis. It has stood in the courtyard since Julius II began the collection here. Also here is a small marble funerary urn in the shape of a house or shrine, and beyond, a sarcophagus with a battle of the Amazons, Achilles, and Penthesileia grouped in the centre, 3C AD.

The **Gabinetto del Canova** contains three neo-classical statues by Antonio Canova placed here when most of the classical masterpieces were taken to Paris by Napoleon in 1800, after the Treaty of Tolentino. 969. Perseus, inspired by the Apollo Belvedere and the boxers, Creugas and Damoxenes (968, 970.).

Beneath the following portico, sarcophagus of Sextus Varius Marcellus, father of Heliogabalus; sarcophagus with curved ends and a relief of a Bacchic procession. Beneath the porticos are six granite basins, the four smaller ones from the Baths of Caracalla.

The door flanked by the two hounds leads out of the courtyard and into the **Animal Room** (*Sala degli Animali*). Most of the animal statues are by Francesco Antonio Franzoni (1734–1818), who made them for this room for Pius VI. Some are entirely Franzoni's work; others were made up by him from ancient fragments. The Roman pieces include: (in the room on the left), sow with a litter of twelve, perhaps of the Augustan period; (under the far window) 511. Colossal head of a camel (fountain head), copy of a Hellenistic original of the 2C BC; *490. Meleager with his dog and the head of a boar, copy of a 4C original by Skopas; 464. Triton and nereid, with cupids, perhaps a Hellenistic original of the 2C BC; 461. Head of a minotaur, copy of a 5C Greek original. In the room on the right, 437. Mithras slaying the bull (2C AD); (on the wall behind), *421, 423. Mosaics with animals, from Hadrian's Villa at Tivoli (2C AD). In the pavement of each room, mosaics with animals and plants (2C AD).

The **Gallery of Statues** (right) is part of the original Belvedere Pavilion built by Innocent VIII. Remains of paintings by Pinturicchio may still be seen on the walls. To the right: *769. EROS OF CENTOCELLE, replica of a Greek original of the early 4C BC. Also called the 'Genius of the Vatican', it is probably a statue of Thanatos, the god of death, from an original attributed to Kephisodotos. It was found at Centocelle by Gavin Hamilton. 767. Discobolos of Polycletus, replica of the second half of the 5C BC; 762. Seated statue of Paris, possibly a copy of an original by Euphranor (4C BC); 756. Apollo Kitharoidos, restored as Minerva, late 5C; 754. Seated statue of Penelope (so called; with a head from another antique statue); *750. APOLLO SAUROCTONOS, representing the god watching a lizard that he is about to kill, an attractive composition, copy of the famous bronze original by Praxiteles; 748. So-called Mattei Amazon, from an original attributed to Kresilas (head from another statue); 747. Satyr; 745. Muse, restored as Urania, belonging to the series found at Tivoli (see above). On either side of the door (735, 588.) a pair of seated statues of Poseidippos and Menander(?), the comic poets, copies of Hellenistic originals; 573. Roman, traditionally identified as the emperor Macrinus (AD 217–18); 571. Aesculapius and Hygieia, of Alexandrian type; 567. Two children of Niobe, fragment of the well-known Florentine group; 563. Danaid, or nymph holding a cup.

*561. RESTING SATYR, one of several known replicas of the famous statue of Praxiteles. At the end of the room: *551, 547. The BARBERINI CANDELABRA, a famous pair, with representations of divinities, from Hadrian's Villa at Tivoli, Roman works in neo-Attic style (2C AD); *548 Sleeping Ariadne, copy of a Hellenistic original of the 3C or 2C BC; below, 549. Sarcophagus with a gigantomachia, 2C AD after a Hellenistic original of the 2C BC; 540. Relief of Bacchus and Ariadne, from Hadrian's Villa; 544. Hermes, copy of a 5C Greek original (school of Myron); 541. Statue of Augustus of the 1C AD with the head of Lucius Verus (AD 161–69). On the bases of several of the statues are inscriptions relating to the gens Julia-Claudia found near the Mausoleum of Augustus.

At the end is the **Gallery of Busts** divided by arches into four little rooms. ROOM I. To the right (above) 711. Caracalla; 704. Marcus Aurelius; 703. Antoninus Pius; (below) 723. Trajan; 718. Nero idealised as Apollo; 716. Old man wearing a crown of vine-leaves, possibly a priest of Dionysos, Hellenistic, 2C BC; 715. Head of Augustus as one of the Fratres Arvales, and as a boy (714); Julius Caesar; column with three dancing Hours, found near the Ara Pacis; 598. Porphyry bust of a youth perhaps Philip the Arabian, emperor in 244–49; *592. Portrait group, Cato and Porcia, probably from a Roman tomb, 1C BC. ROOM II. 702. Apollo; 698. Saturn, after an original of the 5C or 4C BC; (above) 689. Colossal bust of Serapis; 697. Isis; 694. Head of Menelaus, from a group of Menelaus with the body of Patroclus (see Pasquino). In the middle of the room, base in the form of a rectangular chest standing on legs of winged lions, the lid decorated with flowers and foliage; on the sides, reliefs of uncertain significance.

ROOM IV (the recess to the left). 641. Mask of Jupiter Ammon, copy of a 4C original; 637. Woman in the attitude of prayer, Augustan after a 5C original *636. Bust of Antinous, an exquisite portrait; 626. Head of Juno, after a Greek original of the 5C BC. ROOM III. *671. Seated statue of Zeus (Jupiter Verospi), copy of a Hellenistic original (the lower part is a restoration); 784. Celestial globe; 654. Head of one of the Diadochoi wearing the regal fillet; 653. Augur; 651. Mithras in Phrygian cap; 675. Pan.

The so-called **Open Loggia** (*Loggia Scoperta*), usually closed to the public, skirts the N side of the Belvedere Pavilion as far as the Mask Room. 858. Fragment of relief depicting a youth taking part in a Bacchic procession, 3C AD; 862. Frieze, in two sections, with scenes of farm activities and of the sale of bread in a baker's shop, 3C AD; over the door to the Mask Room, sepulchral relief of Galatea, a priestess of Isis, with her husband, 2C AD.

The **Mask Room** (*Gabinetto delle Maschere*; usually locked, but visible through a glass door), entered also from the Gallery of Statues, derives its name from four *mosaics of theatrical masks in the pavement. They came from Hadrian's Villa and date from the 2C AD. The border is of the time of Pius VI and bears his coat of arms. Opposite the entrance, *812. VENUS OF KNIDOS, a fine copy of the famous statue of Praxiteles. The head belongs to another copy of the statue; the limbs are mainly restorations. The goddess is about to bathe; she has a towel and, near by, a pitcher (hydria). On the left, 810. The Graces, from an original perhaps of the 2C BC. In the niche opposite, 801. Satyr, in rosso antico, from a bronze original (Hellenistic, 2C BC). On the wall between the doors, 815. Venus at her bath, copy of a larger original by Doidalsas, a Bithynian sculptor of the 3C BC (being restored).

From the Animal Room (see above) is the entrance to the **Hall of the Muses** (*Sala delle Muse*), an octagon with a vestibule at either end, built in 1782 by Michelangelo Simonetti (the paintings are by Tommaso Conca). FIRST VESTIBULE. Herms (including, 322. Sophocles). Reliefs (above): 321. Pyrrhic dance, a 4C Attic work; Birth of Bacchus. OCTAGON, a magnificent hall with 16 columns of Carrara marble. Seven of the statues of the Nine Muses in this room were found, together with that of Apollo, in a villa near Tivoli, and are thought to be copies of originals, apparently of bronze, by Praxiteles or his school, but possibly they do not all belong to the same group. 317. Erato; 312. Calliope; 310. Apollo Kitharoidos, an expressive figure; 308. Terpsichore. Nos. 303 and 293 (Euterpe and Urania) were not found with the rest and were not, in fact, originally intended as muses. 299. Melpomene; 295. Thalia; 291. Clio; 287. Polyhymnia. The statues alternate with herms: Metrodorus; so-called Alcibaides; 315. Homer; 314. Socrates; Strategos (Alcibaides?); 305. Plato (not Zeno); 302. Euripides; 301. Epicurus; 289. Demosthenes. In the centre, *1192. BELVEDERE TORSO, found in the Campo dei Fiori at the time of Julius II, and bearing the signature of Apollonios, an Athenian sculptor of the 1C BC. The figure is sitting on a hide laid over the ground. Greatly admired by Michelangelo, Raphael, and other Renaissance artists, it may represent Hercules, Polyphemus, Prometheus, Sciron, Marsyas, or Philoctetes. SECOND VESTIBULE. Herm of Pericles, copy of a 5C original by Kresilas; herms of Bias and Periander.

The domed **Circular Hall** (*Sala Rotonda*) was also designed by Simonetti (c 1782), modelled on the Pantheon. In the pavement, mosaic from Otricoli, representing a battle between Greeks and centaurs, tritons, and nereids; in the centre of the room, a huge monolithic porphyry vase found in the Domus Aurea; *257. Jupiter of Otricoli, a colossal head of majestic beauty, attributed to Bryaxis (4C BC); 256. Antinous (d AD 130) as Bacchus, from a Greek prototype of the 4C BC (the drapery, which was originally of bronze, was restored by Thorvaldsen); 255. Faustina the Elder (died 141), wife of Antoninus Pius; *254. Female divinity, perhaps Demeter, wearing the peplos, after a Greek original of the late 5C BC. 253. Head of Hadrian, from his mausoleum; 252. Hercules, colossal statue in gilded bronze, an early Imperial copy of a work of the school of Skopas; 251. Bust of Antinous; 249. Juno (the Barberini Hera), a Roman copy of a cult-image in the manner of the late 5C; 248. Marine divinity (from Pozzuoli), believed to personify the Gulf of Baiae, an interesting example of the fusion of marine elements and human features; *246. Nerva (or Galba), after a statue representing Jupiter; 245. Bust of Serapis, after a work by Bryaxis; 243. Claudius as Jupiter; 242. Head of Claudius; 241. Juno Sospita from Lanuvium, dating from the Antonine period; 240. Head of Plotina (died 129), wife of Trajan; 258. Head of Pertinax(?); 259. Genius of Augustus; 260. Head of Julia Domna (died 217), wife of Septimius Severus.

Hall of the Greek Cross (*Sala a Croce Greca*), another neo-classical room by Simonetti. To the left of the doorway, 199. C. Caesar, nephew of Augustus, sacrificing. *238. Sarcophagus in porphyry of St Helena, mother of Constantine, decorated with Roman horsemen, barbarian prisoners, and fallen soldiers; *237, Sarcophagus of Constantia, daughter of Constantine, in porphyry, decorated with vine-branches and children bearing grapes, peacocks, and a ram (Christian symbols); this sarcophagus was once in the church of Santa Costanza, in Via Nomentana, built by Constantine as a mausoleum for his daughter. 236, 239. Two granite sphinxes; and, in the pavement, mosaics: *basket of flowers, shield with the head of Minerva and the phases of the moon.

Ahead is the landing of the Simonetti Staircase. It ascends to a second landing outside the Gallery of the Candelabra (see below) and the Room of the Biga (right).

The **Room of the Biga** (with glass doors, usually locked) is a circular domed hall by Giuseppe Camporese. *2368. BIGA, or two-horsed chariot, a reconstruction in 1788 by Francesco Antonio Franzoni from ancient fragments; only the body of the chariot and part of the offside horse are original. The chair was used as an episcopal throne in the church of San Marco during the Middle Ages. The bas-reliefs suggest that the biga was a votive chariot dedicated to Ceres and that it dates from the 1C AD. Along the wall, from the left, 2344. Charioteer; with the head from another statue; *2346. Discobolos, a copy of Myron's work with the head wrongly restored; 2347. Hermes (so-called Phokion), from a 5C original (head a copy of a head of a 4C strategos); *2349. Discobolos, from a bronze original by Naucides, nephew and pupil of Polykleitos, a fine example of Peloponnesian sculpture of the 5C BC; *2355. Roman in the act of sacrifice (early Empire), with voluminous draperies; *2363. Bearded Dionysos, called Sardanapalus, a work of the early 4C BC, attributed to Kephisodotos. 2364, 2356, 2348, 2341. Sarcophagi of children (3C AD); the first three have circus scenes, with cupids as competitors; the fourth represents the chariot race between Oinomaos and Pelops.

The Simonetti Staircase continues up to the Etruscan Museum.

The Etruscan Museum

The *ETRUSCAN MUSEUM (closed on Wednesday and Saturday), reached by a staircase from the landing outside the Room of the Biga, was founded in 1837 by Gregory XVI and its official name is the *Museo Gregoriano Etrusco*. One of the most important collections of its kind in existence, many of the objects come from Southern Etruria, but there are also outstanding examples of Greek and Roman art, and a notable collection of Greek vases. In 1989 the Giacinto Guglielmi collection of finds from Vulci was acquired (including Attic vases and Etruscan material) but is not yet on view. It is undergoing a complete rearrangement, and only seven rooms are at present open. Apart from the first two rooms, the exhibits are subdivided according to material (i.e. bronze, stone, terracotta, precious objects, and ceramics). At the top of the stairs, outside the entrance, is a beautiful krater in grey stone.

Room I displays Early Iron Age material (9–8C BC). In the case on the left are finds from Etruria including Villanovan cinerary urns, and in the case on the right objects from Latium Vetus (S of the Tiber), including a reconstructed chariot and weapons of the late 8C BC.

Room II has interesting frescoes (restored in 1991) by Federico Barocci and Taddeo Zuccari, with good stuccoes. The room contains objects found in 1836 in an Etruscan necropolis S of Cerveteri where a small group of tumulus chamber-tombs were unearthed; the most important is the *REGOLINI-GALASSI TOMB, named after its discoverers. Three important people were buried here in 650 BC, including a princess (called Larthia), a warrior of high rank, and a priest-king who was cremated. Their funeral equipment includes: gold jewellery (a gold *clasp, with repoussé decoration, necklaces, and bracelets); ivories; cups; plates; and silver ornaments (of Greco-Oriental provenance); a bronze libation bowl, with six handles in the shape of animals; and a reconstructed throne. Also here were found a cremation *urn; a series of fictile statuettes; a bronze incense-burner in the shape of a wagon; a bronze stand with repoussé figures; two five-handled lebetes; silverware including a drinking cup and jug; and small dishes of Eastern origin. The biga has been reconstructed, as well as a funeral carriage with a bronze bed and funeral couch. The two cases on the window wall contain finds from tombs in the immediate vicinity of the Regolini-Galassi Tomb, including Bucchero vases in relief, and ceramics from another tomb in the necropolis.

Room III. The frescoes were painted for Pius IV by Niccolò Pomarancio and Santi di Tito. It contains a rich collection of bronze objects in common use. In glass cases: incense-burner, tripod, buckles, jars, small throne, etc. Two statuettes of children wearing the bulla. In the centre, *Mars of Todi, wearing armour, a bronze statue dating from the beginning of the 4C, but inspired by Greek art of the 5C. In the glass cases to the left, mirrors and candelabra; to the right, mirrors, cistae, paterae, sheet bronze, vases, etc. Among them is a *mirror engraved with Herakles and Atlas, and another with Chalchas, the soothsayer, both designs derived from Greek models of 5–4C BC. The collection of *cistae* mostly from Palestrina, which were used as 'beauty cases', includes a fine oval *cista, decorated with a battle between Greeks and Amazons, and the handle formed by a satyr and a nymph riding on swans (from Vulci). Patera with the figure of Eos (Aurora) carrying away Kephalos.

Two steps lead up to **Room IV**, recently rearranged to exhibit works in stone. The two lions (late 6C BC) used to guard a tomb at Vulci. The sarcophagus of Circeo has a polychrome relief of a procession from the Tomba dei Sarcophaghi at Cerveteri (late 5C or early 4C BC) with the defunct lying on the roof (restored in 1990). Beyond some small inscribed funerary cippi of the Volsinii type (4–3C BC), is a cippus from Todi with a bilingual inscription in Latin and Celtic on both sides. A sarcophagus from Tuscania has a relief of the Battle of the Centaurs. Beyond is a female sandstone seated statue from Chiusi (3–2C BC), and cippi in the form of pine cones from Palestrina. The sculpted heads include some from Vulci. A sarcophagus from Tarquinia (2C BC) shows the Thebans. The works from Vulci (4C BC) include two horses' heads and a funeray cippus in the form of a capital.

Rooms V–XV are closed for rearrangement; at present the hemicycle (Room XVI) and the last two rooms (XVII and XVIII), all three of which contain vases, are approached from Room III.

Rooms V–XV all have extensive views over Rome, towards Monte Mario. The arrangement of the material will probably change when these rooms are reopened. They contain finds from Vulci, including a bronze incense-burner supported by the figure of a youth; Bucchero jar with incised decoration and a 6C inscription; red-figured •hydria, perhaps by the Athenian Euthymides c 520. Jewellery, mostly from Vulci, includes a necklace with pomegranate drops; coronets and diadems used as funerary wreaths; bulla in gold, on a chain, found at Ostia; silver and bronze clasp in the Daedalic style (7C BC). Objects in terracotta include cinerary urns, antefixes, statues, votive objects, etc. Etruscan portrait heads of both sexes and all ages date from the Archaic period to the 1C AD. They were probably ex-votos, as were the models of legs, feet, etc. The animated expression of the heads is heightened by the colouring. Some of the urns bear traces of their original colour. The fronts are decorated with reliefs of funeral or mythological scenes after Greek models, or scenes of combat, abduction, or the chase. There are also lids of sarcophagi in the shape of beds on which the deceased are lying. A group of terracotta statues from a temple in Tivoli includes part of a frieze with male and female heads flanked by figures of children.

The **Antiquarium Romanum**. Three reliefs showing Hercules fighting the lion, the hydra, and the bull; Roman scales; bronze weight in the shape of a crouching pig, marked C (i.e. 100 Roman pounds); armour in bronze and iron; rings, pins, keys, etc. Antefixes and friezes in terracotta, and architectonic fragments; ivory and bone objects, including a doll with movable limbs (4C AD), also bronze statuettes. Fragmentary bronze male torso; ceramics from Arezzo, finely decorated; Roman lamps; Roman glass vases, some of which still have their lids. Terracotta wall reliefs, alabaster phials of Greek and Eastern origin found in Etruscan tombs, and ivory work. Bronze head of a woman (1–2C AD); portrait of a Roman wearing a laurel crown (3C AD); fragment of a bronze portrait-statue of a Roman (1C BC). The FALCIONI collection contains bronze, gold, and terracotta objects coming from the neighbourhood of Viterbo.

The •STAIRCASE OF BRAMANTE (described above) which descends to the Pio-Clementino Museum, can be seen through a glass door. The STAIRCASE OF ASSYRIAN RELIEFS has reliefs and inscriptions of the 9–7C BC; also some Cufic sepulchral inscriptions of the 11–12C AD. The staircase goes down to the landing near the Round Vestibule (see above).

The hemicycle (XVI) and Rooms XVII and XVIII contain a valuable •**Collection of Greek, Italic, and Etruscan vases**. Most of them come from the Etruscan tombs of Southern Etruria, discovered during excavations of the first half of the 19C. At the time of their discovery the vases were all indiscriminately called Etruscan. In fact many of them are Greek in origin and illustrate the importance of the commercial relations between Greece and Etruria; from the end of the 7C to the late 5C many Greek vases were imported. By the middle of the 4C the Greek imports were largely replaced by the products of Magna Graecia, Lucania, and Campania.

The **Hemicycle (Room XVI)** has charming 18C frescoes with views of Rome, the Vatican, and scenes of the Papal States. The building which houses the sacristy of St Peter's can also be seen, built at about this time. (In the Cortile della Pigna a building 12 metres below ground level was opened in 1981 to house the Secret Archives of the Vatican Library.) The hemicycle has a splendid display of ATTIC VASES. At the right end: case of black-figure oinochoë; the black-figure amphorae (500–490 BC) include one with a battle scene and chariot by the 'Edinburgh Painter'. Displayed in a case on its own is a *hydria of the Leagros group (c 500 BC). Another case has four black-figure amphorae showing athletes in the presence of Athena by the 'Berlin Painter' (500–480 BC). Beyond the door are kylixes of the 6C BC, including one with red-figure and black-figure decorations. In another case, black-figure *amphora signed by Exekias, who worked in 530–520 BC. One side shows Achilles and Ajax playing with dice; on the other side Castor and Pollux are being welcomed on their return home by their parents, Tyndareus and Leda. The red-figure amphorae (being restored) is attributed to the 'Kleophrades Painter' (510–500 BC). The wall case has red-figure vases including three signed hydria. In a case on its own is a red-figure amphora attributed to the 'Hector Painter' showing Hector carrying out libations before a battle, and taking leave of his parents Priam and Hecuba. In the last case are red-figure amphorae, and a *kylix by the famous 5C vase painter Duris, with Oedipus trying to solve the riddle of the Sphinx.

Room XVII, frescoed by Pomarancio, contains the private collection left to the museum in 1967 by Astarita of Naples. Exhibited on its own is a large krater of the late Corinthian period showing Ulysses and Menaleus asking for the return of Helen. **Room XVIII**. Black-figure vases from Vulci and Cerveteri (6C BC), attributed to the 'Madrid Painter' and the 'Vatican Painter', and works in the Corinthian style (650–615 BC).

The Simonetti Staircase leads back down to the Quattro Cancelli.

II. Gallery of Tapestries, Raphael Rooms, Borgia Rooms and Gallery of Modern Religious Art, Sistine Chapel, Museum of Christian Art, Sistine Hall and Library

From the Quattro Cancelli the Scala Simonetti leads up two flights of stairs to the landing outside the Room of the Biga. Here is the beginning of Bramante's long West Gallery with the Gallery of the Candelabra, the Gallery of Tapestries, and the Gallery of Maps.

The **Gallery of the Candelabra** (80m long) is named after the pairs of marble candelabra, of the Roman Imperial period, placed on either side of the arches which divide it into six sections. The ceiling has frescoes by Domenico Torti and Ludovico Seitz illustrating events in the pontificate of Leo XIII. In the pavement are marbles from the Emporia, the warehouses of ancient Rome.

Section I. 2422. Sarcophagus of a child, Roman, 3C AD; pair of candelabra from Otricoli, with reliefs of Bacchic rites and of Apollo and Marsyas, Roman, 2C BC. **Section II**. Pan extracting a thorn from a satyr's foot, copy of a 2C Hellenistic original; 2505. Diana of the Ephesians, 3C AD; 2513. Sarcophagus with the legend of Orestes, 2C AD; 2487, 2482. Candelabra of the 2C AD from a Roman villa later used in the churches of Sant'Agnese fuori le Mura and Santa Costanza; 2465. Sarcophagus with the story of

Protesilaos and Laodamia; 2445. Ganymede carried off by the eagle, after a bronze original by Leochares.

Section III. On the walls, fragments of frescoes from a Roman villa at Tor Marancia (near the Catacombs of Domitilla), with flying figures, 2C AD; 2580. Mosaic of fish, fruit, etc.; Apollo from an archaic Greek type; 2555. Satyr with young Dionysos on his shoulders (1C AD).

Section IV. Statuette of Maritime Victory, from a Hellenistic original (the head is from another figure); portrait statue of a woman (with substituted head), 1C AD; *2698. Sarcophagus with Dionysos and Ariadne and Dionysiac scenes, 2C AD; *2684. Fisherman, a realistic work of the school of Pergamon (3C BC); 2673. Upper part of a statue of Cronos (Saturn), copy of a 4C original; *2672. Tyche (Fortune) of Antioch, from a bronze by Eutychides, a pupil of Lysippos; *2655. Boy with goose, from a bronze by Boethus of Chalcedon, 3C BC; *2635. Sarcophagus with the slaughter of the Niobids, a fine work of the 2C AD; 2622. Boy of the Julio-Claudian family, 1C AD.

Section V. *2784. Girl running in a race during a Peloponnesian religious festival, Roman copy of a Greek bronze original of the 5C BC; 2760. Young satyr playing the flute. **Section VI**. 2834. Artemis, from a Praxitelean original; the head (which does not belong) is a copy of a 5C bronze; 2826. Statuette of a woman wearing a cloak, copy of a Hellenistic original of the 4C or 3C BC; sarcophagus with Diana and Endymion; 2807. Youth wearing the Phrygian cap, after an original of Praxiteles; Niobid, copy of a Hellenistic original of the 4C or 3C BC; *2794. Fighting Persian, statuette after an original bronze belonging to the series of statues given by Attalos I of Pergamon to the Athenians which were placed on the Acropolis in Athens; 2796. Sarcophagus with the rape of the daughters of Leukippos.

The **Gallery of Tapestries** (*Galleria degli Arazzi*) is divided into three rooms, and contains the so-called 'New School' series of tapestries executed after Raphael's death from cartoons by his pupils, some of which were copied from drawings he had left. Also displayed here are Roman and Flemish tapestries. ROOM 1. Raphael 'New School' tapestries, woven in Brussels in the 16C: *149. Adoration of the Shepherds; *151. Adoration of the Magi; 148. Presentation at the temple. 209, 210, 211. Tapestries illustrating the life of Urban VIII, the most important product of the Barberini workshop active in Rome, 1627–83. ROOM 2. Raphael 'New School' tapestries: *152. Resurrection of Christ; 156–54. Massacre of the Innocents (from a cartoon attributed to Tomaso Vincidor); 146. Christ appearing to Mary Magdalene; 147. Supper at Emmaus. 215, 213, and 212. More 17C Roman tapestries illustrating the life of Urban VIII (see above). ROOM 3. 79. Death of Julius Caesar, Flemish (1594).

The *Gallery of Maps (Galleria delle Carte Geografiche)* was decorated at the time of Gregory XIII, the reformer of the calendar. The walls are decorated with numerous *maps and plans painted in 1580–83 by Antonio Danti, on designs drawn by his brother Ignazio, the Dominican cosmographer, architect, and painter. They are extremely important to our knowledge of 16C Italy and represent various regions of the country and the neighbouring islands, as well as the papal territory of Avignon. There are also several town plans and views of seaports, including one (on the end wall) of *Venice. The ceiling was decorated with stuccoes and frescoes by a group of painters under the direction of Girolamo Muziano. Along the walls are herms of Socrates, Plato, and others. From the windows is a fine view of the Vatican gardens.

Beyond the Gallery of Maps is the **Gallery of Pius V** in which are more tapestries of the late 15C: 33. Scenes of the Passion; *34. The Creed. On the right, 157. Religion, Grace, and Charity, woven in 1525 in Brussels; 143. Coronation of the Virgin, woven in Brussels in the 16C from a cartoon of the 'New School' of Raphael.

To the right is the **Ladies' Audience Room** (*Sala delle Dame*; closed indefinitely), added by Paul V (1605–21). This room was formerly used as a private audience chamber for ladies, who were not admitted into the pontifical apartments. The frescoes, by Guido Reni, represent the Transfiguration, Ascension, and Pentecost.

At the end of the gallery is the CHAPEL OF ST PIUS V; to the left is the SOBIESKI ROOM. The floor is inlaid with mosaics from Ostia, and there is a painting by Jan Alois Mateiko (1883) depicting the Liberation of Vienna by John Sobieski on 12 September 1683.

Beyond is the **Hall of the Immaculate Conception**, a room decorated with frescoes by Francesco Podesti (1858) which illustrate the definition and proclamation of the dogma of the Immaculate Conception pronounced by Pius IX on 8 December 1854. On the ceiling are the arms of Pius IX; the floor has 2C mosaics from Ostia. Beyond are the Stanze of Raphael.

**Stanze of Raphael

This series of rooms was built by Nicholas V, and the walls were originally painted by Andrea del Castagno, Piero della Francesca, and Benedetto Bonfigli. Julius II employed a group of great artists to continue the decoration, including Luca Signorelli, Perugino, Sodoma, Bramantino, Baldassarre Peruzzi, Lorenzo Lotto, and the Flemish painter Jan Ruysch. Bramante, the Urbinese architect of St Peter's, recommended his fellow-citizen, Raffaello Sanzio, and the Pope sent for him, and set him to work immediately on his arrival in Rome in 1508. The result proved so satisfactory that Julius dismissed all the other painters, ordered their works to be destroyed, and commissioned Raphael to decorate the whole of this part of the Vatican.

The Stanze are the painter's masterpiece; they show the extraordinary development which took place in his art during the years between his coming to Rome and his early death in 1520. When Raphael arrived, the court of Julius II was an intellectual centre of the first rank; the College of Cardinals and the Curia included among their members many celebrated savants, humanists, and men of letters; and a crowd of artists, led by Bramante and Michelangelo, were at work in the city. In this highly cultured environment Raphael, who had great powers of assimilation, acquired an entirely new manner of painting. He began work in the Stanza della Segnatura (II), with the frescoes of Astronomy, Apollo, Adam and Eve, and Judgment of Solomon, which were probably his trial works; he then carried out the other frescoes in this room. After this he decorated, successively, the Stanza d'Eliodoro (III), the Stanza dell'Incendio (I), and the Stanza di Costantino (IV). A careful restoration programme is under way of the frescoes.

The entrance to the Stanze has been altered. A covered balcony from the Hall of the Immaculate Conception leads direct to the farthest room, the

Sala di Costantino (IV), so that the rooms now have to be visited in reversed chronological order, as described below.

IV. **Sala di Costantino**, painted almost entirely in the time of Clement VII (1523–34), after Raphael's death, by Giulio Romano with the assistance of Francesco Penni and Raffaellino del Colle. On the wall facing the window is the VICTORY OF CONSTANTINE OVER MAXENTIUS near the Pons Milvius, for which Raphael had made some sketches. The reddish tint which suffuses the picture is characteristic of Giulio Romano. To the right are figures of St Urban, Justice, and Charity; to the left, St Sylvester, Faith, and Religion.

On the entrance wall: CONSTANTINE ADDRESSING HIS SOLDIERS AND THE VISION OF THE CROSS, by Giulio Romano, perhaps from Raphael's design; to the right of this, St Clement, Temperance, and Meekness; to the left, St Peter, the Church, and Eternity. On the wall opposite the entrance: The BAPTISM OF CONSTANTINE by St Sylvester (a portrait of Clement VII), by Francesco Penni, and at the sides (right) St Leo, Innocence, and Truth, and (left) St Damasus, Prudence, and Peace. On the window wall: CONSTANTINE'S DONATION OF ROME TO SYLVESTER, by Raffaellino del Colle. At the sides: (right) Gregory VII(?) and Fortitude; (left) St Sylvester and Courage. Below are other scenes from the life of Constantine. On the ceiling, the Triumph of Christianity, by Tomaso Laureti. In the floor is a 2C Roman mosaic with the Seasons.

It is now necessary to interrupt the visit to the Stanze in order to see the Room of the Chiaroscuri and the Chapel of Nicholas V. From the Sala di Costantino a door leads into the **Room of the Chiaroscuri** or the *Room of the Grooms* (*Sala dei Palafrenieri*). This room has a magnificent carved and gilded *ceiling, with the Medici arms, but the frescoes by Raphael were obliterated by Pius IV, and the existing monochrome frescoes were added under Gregory XIII. The little adjoining **Chapel of Nicholas V** is entirely decorated with *frescoes by Fra Angelico, painted between 1448 and 1450. These represent scenes from the lives of the deacon saints Stephen (upper section) and Laurence (lower section); especially fine is the painting of St Stephen preaching. On the ceiling are the four Evangelists and on the pilasters the Doctors of the Church.

The *Loggia of Raphael** (formerly reached from the Sala di Costantino) has been closed to the public for many years (adm to scholars only with special permission). The long gallery of thirteen bays overlooks the Courtyard of St Damasus with a fine view of Rome beyond. Situated on the second floor of the palace, it was begun by Bramante about 1513 and completed after Bramante's death by Raphael and his pupils. The vault of each bay has four little paintings, so that there are fifty-two in all. The grotteschi of the borders are considered to have been inspired by those in the Domus Aurea of Nero, which were discovered in 15C and known to Raphael. The designs were carried out by Giulio Romano, Giovanni da Udine, Franceso Penni, Perino del Vaga, Polidoro da Caravaggio, and others. Controversial restoration work was carried out on the paintings in 1978.

The subjects of the paintings in the vaults are (beginning at the other end of the Loggia): I. Separation of light from darkness; Separation of land and water; Creation of sun and moon; Creation of the animals. II. Creation of Eve; the Fall; Expulsion from Paradise; Adam and Eve at work. III. Building the Ark; the Deluge; Leaving the Ark; Noah's Sacrifice. IV. Abraham and Melchisedek; God's covenant with Abraham; Abraham and the three angels; Flight of Lot. V. God appearing to Isaac; Abimelech spying on Isaac and Rebecca; Isaac blessing Jacob; Jacob and Esau. VI. Jacob's dream;

Jacob and Rachel at the well; Jacob reproaching Laban; Jacob's journey. VII. Joseph telling his dream to his brethren; Joseph sold by his brethren; Joseph and Potiphar's wife; Joseph interpreting Pharaoh's dream. VIII. Moses in the bulrushes; the Burning Bush; Pharaoh drowned in the Red Sea; Moses striking the rock. IX. Moses receiving the Tables of the Law; Worship of the Golden Calf; Moses and the pillar of fire; Moses showing the Tables of the Law to the people. X. Crossing of Jordan; Fall of Jericho; Joshua making the sun stand still; Joshua and Eleazar dividing Palestine among the twelve tribes. XI. Samuel anointing David; David and Goliath; Triumph of David; David and Bathsheba. XII. Crowning of Solomon; Judgment of Solomon; Queen of Sheba; Building of the Temple. XIII. Nativity; the Magi; Baptism of Christ; Last Supper.

A door leads back into the Raphael Stanze from the Room of the Chiaroscuri. ROOM III. **Stanza d'Eliodoro**, painted by Raphael in 1512–14; the subjects were nearly all chosen by Julius II. On the principal wall (right) is the EXPULSION OF HELIODORUS FROM THE TEMPLE at Jerusalem, alluding to Julius II's success in freeing the States of the Church from foreign powers. The picture illustrates a story in the Apocrypha (Maccabei II, 3): King Seleucus sends his treasurer Heliodorus to Jerusalem to steal the Temple treasure, but the crime is avenged by a horseman assisted by two angels with whips. In the middle of the crowd on the left is Julius II, carried on the sedia gestatoria (the front bearer is a portrait of the engraver Marcantonio Raimondi). In the centre of the composition, under the vault of the temple, the high priest Onias renders thanks to God before the Ark of the Covenant.

On the left is the MASS OF BOLSENA, representing the famous miracle which took place at Bolsena in 1263. A Bohemian priest, who had doubts about the doctrine of Transubstantiation, was convinced when he saw blood drop from the Host on to the altar cloth (the stained corporal is preserved in the cathedral at Orvieto.) This alludes to the vow made by Julius II when, on his first expedition against Bologna in 1506, he stopped at Orvieto to pay homage to the relic. He is shown kneeling opposite the priest, in place of Urban IV, the contemporary pope. The warm colours and, especially, the harmony of reds in the composition show how much Raphael was influenced by the Venetian painters (Sebastiano del Piombo and Lorenzo Lotto arrived in Rome at this time).

On the long wall is LEO I REPULSING ATTILA, a subject originally selected by Julius II and taken up again at the suggestion of Leo X, when considerable changes were made in the design. It was executed partly by Raphael's school. The scene representing the banks of the Mincio, where the historic event took place, was replaced by the environs of Rome, and the figure of the Pope, on a white mule, was brought from the back of the picture into the foreground in order to accentuate the allusion to the battle of Ravenna (11 April 1512), at which Leo X, then a cardinal, was present, and which resulted in the expulsion of the French from Italy. Attila, mounted on a white horse, and the Huns behind him, are struck with terror by a vision of St Peter and St Paul.

On the fourth wall is the LIBERATION OF ST PETER, alluding to the captivity of Leo X after the battle of Ravenna. Three night scenes, with remarkable light effects, illustrate three different episodes: in the middle, the interior of the prison is seen through a high barred window, with St Peter waking up as the angel frees him from his chains; on the left are the guards outside the prison; and on the right St Peter escaping with the angel.

The decoration of the lower part of the walls, with caryatids and four herms, is attributed to Perino del Vaga. The ceiling paintings of God appearing to Noah, Jacob's dream, the Burning Bush, and Abraham's Sacrifice are generally attributed to Peruzzi.

ROOM II. The **Stanza della Segnatura**, where the pope signed bulls and briefs, has the most beautiful and harmonious frescoes in the series. It was painted entirely by Raphael in 1508–11. On the long wall opposite the entrance is the famous DISPUTA or DISPUTATION ON THE HOLY SACRAMENT, representing a discussion on the Eucharist but essentially intended as a Glorification of Catholicism. Given an extremely difficult subject, Raphael succeeded in making the relatively limited space occupied by the composition, which is divided into two zones, appear far larger than it is. In the celestial zone Christ appears between the Virgin and St John the Baptist; above is God the Father surrounded by angels; beneath, the Holy Dove between the four angels holding the book of the Gospels; on the left are St Peter, Adam, St John the Evangelist, David, St Lawrence, and Jeremiah(?); on the right, St Paul, Abraham, St James, Moses, St Stephen, and Judas Maccabaeus. In the middle of the terrestrial zone is a monstrance with the Host on an altar. On the right are Saints Augustine and Ambrose, and on the left Saints Gregory and Jerome; they are surrounded by an assembly of Doctors of the Church, popes, cardinals, dignitaries, and the faithful. Certain figures are thought to be portraits of Duns Scotus, and Saints Dominic, Francis, Thomas Aquinas, and Nicholas of Bari. The man pointing upward with his right hand is said to be Pietro Lombardo; on the right is the head of Dante crowned with laurel, and, beyond him (in a black hat), Savonarola; on the extreme left is Fra Angelico in the black Dominican habit and, in the foreground, Bramante.

Beneath the picture are three monochrome paintings by Perino del Vaga: a pagan sacrifice, St Augustine and the child on the seashore, and the Cumaean Sibyl showing the Virgin to Augustus.

On the wall nearest the Courtyard of the Belvedere is the PARNASSUS. Apollo is playing the violin in the shade of laurels surrounded by the nine Muses and the great poets. Calliope is seated on the left, and behind her are Melpomene, Terpsichore, and Polyhymnia; on the right, also seated, is Erato, and behind her are Clio, Thalia, Euterpe, and Urania. In the group of poets on the left is the figure of the blind Homer, between Dante and Virgil; lower are Alcaeus, Corinna, Petrarch, and Anacreon, with the voluptuous form of Sappho seated beside them. In the group on the right are Ariosto(?), Ovid, Tibullus, and Propertius, and, lower, Sannazaro, Horace, and Pindar, seated.

Below the picture are two monochrome scenes: that on the left is thought to show Alexander placing Homer's poems in the tomb of Achilles (or, possibly, the discovery of a sarcophagus containing Greek and Latin MSS on the Janiculum in 181 BC). The subject of the scene on the right is either Augustus preventing Virgil's friends from burning the Aeneid, or Roman consuls ordering the burning of Greek works considered harmful to the Roman religion. Below these again is some very fine painted intarsia-work by Fra Giovanni da Verona.

On the wall facing the Disputa is the splendid SCHOOL OF ATHENS, symbolising the triumph of Philosophy, and forming a pendant to the triumph of Theology opposite. The setting is a portico, representing the palace of Science, a magnificent example of Renaissance architecture, inspired by Bramante. The remarkable vaulting, well depicted in light and shade, recalls the Baths of Caracalla. At the sides are statues of Apollo and Minerva. On the steps are the greatest philosophers and scholars of all ages gathered round the two supreme masters, Plato and Aristotle. Plato (probably intended as a portrait of Leonardo da Vinci) points towards heaven, symbolising his system of speculative philosophy, while Aristotle's calm gesture indicates the vast field of nature as the realm of scientific research.

At the top of the steps, on Plato's side, is the bald head and characteristic profile of Socrates; near him, in conversation, are Aeschines, Alcibiades (represented as a young warrior), Xenophon, and others. The beckoning figure next to Xenophon is presumably Chrysippus. At the foot of the steps on the left is Zeno, an old man with a beard, seen in profile; near him Epicurus, crowned with vine-leaves, is reading a book; in the foreground Pythagoras is writing out his harmonic tables, with Averroes, in a turban, and Empedocles looking over his shoulder. The young man sitting down is Federico Gonzaga, who was included by order of Julius II; the handsome youth standing up is Francesco Maria della Rovere; beside him, his foot resting on a block of marble, is a figure which may represent Anaxagoras, Xenocrates, or possibly, Aristoxenus. The seated figure of Heracleitus, isolated in the centre foreground, was not part of the original composition; obviously inspired by Michelangelo's work in the Sistine Chapel (the first section of the vault was uncovered in 1510), it has also recently been suggested that it was intended as a portrait of him.

On the right, around Aristotle, are the students of the exact sciences; standing at the foot of the steps is Ptolemy, with his back to the spectator, and, because of a confusion with the Egyptian kings of the same name, wearing a crown. Opposite him is Zoroaster, holding a sphere. On the extreme right of the composition, Raphael has introduced portraits of himself and Sodoma. To the left is Archimedes or Euclid (with the features of Bramante), surrounded by his disciples and bending over a blackboard on which he is tracing figures with a compass. The solitary figure on the steps is Diogenes, also thought to be a portrait of Michelangelo.

The monochromes beneath the picture are by Perino del Vaga, and represent Philosophy, astrologers in conference, and the Siege of Syracuse with the Death of Archimedes.

On the fourth wall, above the window, are the three CARDINAL VIRTUES, Fortitude, Temperance, and Prudence. On the left of the window, Justinian publishing the Pandects, representing CIVIL LAW, and beneath, Solon haranguing the Athenians, by Perino del Vaga. On the right, Gregory IX (in the likeness of Julius II) handing the Decretals to a jurist (1227), to represent CANON LAW. The prelates around the Pope are portraits of Raphael's contemporaries; on the left, in front, is Giovanni de' Medici, afterwards Leo X, then Cardinal Antonio Del Monte, Alessandro Farnese (Paul III), and others.

Beneath is Moses bringing the Israelites the Tables of Stone, by Perino del Vaga. The ceiling was also painted by Raphael: above the Disputa, Theology; above the Parnassus, Poetry; above the School of Athens, Philosophy; and above the window wall, Justice. In the pendentives, Adam and Eve, Apollo and Marsyas, Astronomy, and the Judgment of Solomon. The small central octagon is attributed to Bramantino. The floor, in opus alexandrinum, shows the arms of Nicholas V and Leo X, and the name of Julius II.

I. **Stanza dell'Incendio**. On the ceiling is the Glorification of the Holy Trinity by Perugino, Raphael's master (the only work not destroyed when Raphael took over the decoration of the Stanze). The walls were painted in 1517 by Raphael's pupils (Giulio Romano, Francesco Penni, and perhaps

Perino del Vaga) from his own designs. The subjects chosen were events of the times of Leo III (795–816) and Leo IV (847–55), most of which, however, allude to episodes in the history of Leo X.

Facing the window is the INCENDIO DI BORGO, illustrating the fire that broke out in Rome in 847, and was miraculously extinguished when Leo IV made the sign of the Cross from the loggia of St Peter's. This was probably intended as an allusion to the achievement of Leo X in restoring peace to Italy. In the background flames threaten the old church of St Peter's (the façade of which is shown); on the right, the Pope leaves the Vatican. On the left is a scene of the Burning of Troy, with naked figures scaling the walls and Aeneas carrying his father Anchises on his back, followed by his wife Creusa and their son Ascanius.

Opposite the entrance wall is the CORONATION OF CHARLEMAGNE BY LEO III in 800, an obvious reference to the meeting of Leo X and Francis I at Bologna in 1516, since Leo and Charlemagne have the features of the later pope and king. On the opposite wall the subject is the VICTORY OF LEO IV OVER THE SARACENS AT OSTIA (849), in allusion to the Crusade against the Turks proclaimed by Leo X, who is again represented in the figure of Leo IV. The two cardinals behind him are portraits of Cardinal Bibbiena and Giulio de' Medici. On the window wall is the OATH OF LEO III, made in St Peter's on 23 December 800. On this occasion the Pope cleared himself of charges that had been brought against him. This alludes to the Lateran Council held by Leo X.

The monochrome figures below the paintings represent Godfrey de Bouillon, Ethelwulf of England (called Astolfo), Charlemagne, Lothair I and Ferdinand of Castile.

From the Stanza dell'Incendio a door leads into the **Chapel of Urban VIII**, richly decorated with frescoes and stuccoes by Pietro da Cortona.

Outside the chapel a stairway leads down (right) to the Borgia Rooms and the Museum of Modern Religious Art. It is possible at this point to proceed direct (left) to the Sistine Chapel instead of approaching it through the Borgia Rooms and the Museum of Modern Religious Art. However, it is well worth visiting the first six Borgia Rooms to see Pinturicchio's frescoes, even if you do not intend to continue through the fifty subsequent galleries of modern religious art.

The Borgia Rooms and Gallery of Modern Religious Art

The six **BORGIA ROOMS** (*Appartamento Borgia*) are named after Alexander VI (Borgia), who adapted this suite in the palace of Nicholas V for his personal use, and had it decorated with *frescoes by Pinturicchio and his school (1492–95). The first two rooms are immediately beneath the Hall of the Immaculate Conception; the other rooms are beneath the Stanze of Raphael. After the death of Alexander VI, the Borgia Rooms continued to be used as papal apartments until Julius II abandoned them in 1507. Leo XIII had them restored by Lodovico Seitz in 1889–97 and opened them to the public. Incongruous modern paintings were hung here in 1973.

Room I, of the Sibyls, is square and has twelve lunettes each with a sibyl accompanied by a prophet. The juxtaposition of sibyls and prophets illustrates an ancient belief that the sibyls foretold the coming of the Messiah. Here Caesar Borgia was imprisoned by Julius II in 1503, in the very room where he had had his cousin Alfonso of Aragon murdered in 1500. **Room II** (left) contains copes designed by Matisse.

Room III, of the Creed, is named after the scrolls on which are written the sentences of the Creed, held by the twelve Apostles depicted in the lunettes. Each Apostle is accompanied by a prophet holding an appropriate inscription. These frescoes are attributed to Pier Matteo d'Amelia, a successor of Pinturicchio.

Room IV, of the Liberal Arts, symbolises the seven liberal arts: the *Trivium* (grammar, dialectic, rhetoric) and the *Quadrivium* (geometry, arithmetic, astronomy, music) which were the basis of medieval learning. The paintings are attributed to Antonio da Viterbo, a pupil of Pinturicchio. The Arch of Justice, in the middle, was painted in the 16C. The ceiling is decorated with squares and grotesques alternating with the Borgia bull. The fine chimneypiece is by or after Sansovino. The hidden treasure of Alexander VI was found in this room.

Room V, of the Saints. The walls and the vault are covered with more splendid *frescoes by Pinturicchio, his masterpiece. The room is divided by an arch into two cross-vaulted areas forming six lunettes. On the ceiling, Legend of Isis; Osiris and the bull Apis (in reference to the Borgia arms; see above), with reliefs in gilded stucco. Above the door, Madonna and Child with saints (medallion). Entrance wall, the Visitation; Saints Paul the Hermit and Anthony Abbot in the desert (right); End wall, *Disputation between St Catherine of Alexandria and the emperor Maximian; the saint was once thought to be a portrait of Lucrezia Borgia or Giulia Farnese. The figure behind the throne is a self-portrait by Pinturicchio, and in the background is the Arch of Constantine. Window wall, Martyrdom of St Sebastian, with a view of the Colosseum. On the exit wall, Susanna and the Elders; Legend of St Barbara.

Room VI, of the Mysteries of the Faith. The frescoes, partly by Pinturicchio, represent the Annunciation, Nativity, Adoration of the Magi, *Resurrection (the kneeling pontiff is Alexander VI), Ascension, Pentecost, and Assumption of the Virgin. The last fresco includes a portrait of the donor, perhaps Francesco Borgia. In the ceiling are stuccoes and paintings of prophets.

Room VII, of the Popes, formerly decorated with portraits of popes. The frescoes and stucco decoration of the splendid vaulted ceiling were commissioned by Leo X from Perino del Vaga and Giovanni da Udine.

The **Gallery of Modern Religious Art** was arranged in 1973 in the Borgia Apartments, and in fifty or so rooms, lavishly renovated. The works were presented to the Pope by invited artists from all over the world. They include: Pietro Annigoni, Francis Bacon, Giacomo Balla, Bernard Buffet, Carlo Carrà, Marc Chagall, Salvador Dalí, Giorgio De Chirico, Filippo de Pisis, Max Ernst, Paul Gauguin, Renato Guttuso, Wassily Kandinsky, Paul Klee, Oskar Kokoschka, Fernand Léger, Carlo Levi, Giacomo Manzù, Marino Marini, Arturo Martini, Henry Matisse, Henry Moore, Giorgio Morandi, Edvard Munch, Ben Nicholson, José Clemente Orozco, Pablo Picasso, Auguste Rodin, Georges Rouault, David Alfaro Siqueiros, Mario Sironi, Ardengo Soffici, Graham Sutherland, Maurice Utrillo, Maurice de Vlaminck, and numerous others. They are arranged in no particular order, but they are fully labelled, and a hand list is available at the door.

Stairs lead up from the last gallery to the Sistine Chapel.

**The Sistine Chapel

The present entrance to the **SISTINE CHAPEL** is in the W wall, to the right of the altar.

The chapel takes its name from Sixtus IV who had it rebuilt by Giovanni de' Dolci in 1473–81 as the official private chapel of the popes, and for the conclaves for the election of the popes which are still held here. It is famous for its superb frescoes by Michelangelo, perhaps the greatest pictorial decoration in Western art. The hall is a rectangle 40m long, 13m wide, and nearly 21m high, lit on either side by six windows, placed rather high up.

Ceiling frescoes. The barrel-vaulted ceiling is entirely covered by the celebrated FRESCOES OF MICHELANGELO. He is known to have been reluctant to take up this commission from Julius II, but having accepted, he completed the vault between 1508 and 1512. The complex design, which has received various theological interpretations, combines Old and New Testament figures, as well as themes from pagan prophecy and Church history. The powerful sculpturesque figures are set in an architectural design with an effect of high relief and rich colour on a huge scale. Work on the ceiling was begun at the main entrance, in the area farthest from the altar: the development in the artist's skill and his facility in the technique of fresco painting can be seen in the later figures at the altar end. The scaffolding was taken down and the first half of the ceiling revealed in 1510 to the wonder of all who came to see it.

Restoration of the frescoes was begun in 1980 and the ceiling was completed in 1990. Work on the Last Judgment, on the wall above the altar, was finished in 1994. The chapel was kept open to the public throughout this remarkable operation. The frescoes had been discoloured by dirt and candle smoke, and damaged by poor restorations in the past. Their brilliant original colour has been restored. Important details about the way in which Michelangelo worked on this great commission have also been discovered. The holes for the scaffolding have been found beneath the windows which would seem to confirm that the scaffolding bridge from which the whole ceiling was painted was without support on the ground. The lunettes were painted in three days directly onto the fresh plaster, without the help of a preliminary cartoon or the transfer of a preparatory sketch. There is now considerable concern about the conservation of the frescoes, since up to 20,000 people a day enter the chapel.

Looking towards the high altar, on the lower curved part of the vault are the Hebrew Prophets and pagan Sibyls sitting on architectonic thrones with mouldings in warm grisaille. Above the Last Judgment is the splendid figure of Jonah issuing from the whale. Nearest the altar, on the left side: the Libyan Sibyl; Daniel writing; the Cumaean Sibyl; Isaiah, in deep meditation; and the Delphic Sibyl. At the far end above the entrance is Zachariah. On the right side, from the altar end: Jeremiah; the Persian Sibyl; Ezekiel, with a scroll; the Erythrean Sibyl; and Joel.

Along the centre of the vault itself are nine scenes from Genesis, from the Creation to events in the life of Noah. Again beginning from the altar, these are: Separation of Light from Darkness; Creation of the Sun, Moon, and Planets; Separation of Land and Sea and the Creation of the fishes and birds; Creation of Adam, perhaps the most beautiful work on the ceiling; Creation of Eve; Temptation and Expulsion from Paradise; Sacrifice of Noah; the Flood; and the Drunkenness of Noah. These are framed by decorative pairs of nudes, Michelangelo's famous 'ignudi', the most idiosyncratic elements in the ceiling and a remarkable celebration of the nude figure. In the lunettes over the windows are figures representing the forerunners of Christ. In the spandrels on either side of the prophet-sibyl sequence are scenes of Salvation from the Old Testament; over the altar, Moses and the Brazen Serpent (right) and the Death of Haman (left); at the other end, Judith and Holofernese (right) and David and Goliath (left).

More than twenty years later, in 1535–41, Michelangelo was commissioned by Paul III to paint his great fresco (20m by 10m) of the **Last Judgment** on the altar wall. This involved the walling-up of two windows and the destruction of two frescoes (both by Perugino) on the side walls. An extremely complex restoration operation was begun on this wall in 1990 (and was completed in 1994). The fresco had deteriorated, and had been blackened by candle smoke and incense, and by the glues used as varnishes in restorations from the late 16C up to the 18C.

The unity of the conception is extraordinarily fine, and the crowded composition, with innumerable nude figures, contains a remarkable sense of movement and high relief. The strong colour of the background, produced by Michelangelo's liberal use of lapis lazuli, has re-emerged during restoration work. In the upper centre is the enigmatic figure of Christ, beardless, and probably derived from classical models. Near him are the Madonna and (probably) Adam, and on the right St Peter with the keys. At Christ's feet are seated St Laurence and St Bartholomew with his flayed skin (the caricature of a face seen in the folds of the skin is a self-portrait of Michelangelo). In the lunettes high up above the figure of Christ are two groups of angels with the instruments of the Passion.

Beneath, in the central zone, on the left, are the elect ascending to heaven with the help of angels; in the centre is a group of angels with trumpets; on the right the damned are being hauled down into hell. In this group is the famous figure of a soul in despair (known as the *Disperato*) looking down into the abyss. In the lowest zone, on the left, there is a scene representing the Resurrection of the Body; in the centre is a cave full of devils; on the right is the entrance to hell, with the boat of Charon (as in Dante's description) and Minos, the guide to the infernal regions. According to Vasari Minos has the features of Biagio da Cesena (with ass's ears) who was master of ceremonies to Paul III and had objected to the nudity of Michelangelo's figures. Pius IV also protested about this and at one time intended to destroy the fresco, but in the end he commissioned Daniele da Volterra to paint clothes on some of the figures.

A graceful marble screen by Mino da Fiesole, Giovanni Dalmata, and Andrea Bregno divides the chapel into two unequal parts, a larger choir and a small nave. The same artists were responsible for the cantoria. The 15C mosaic pavement is a fine example of opus alexandrinum.

The *frescoes on the long walls** were painted in 1481–83 by some of the greatest artists of the time. They depict parallel events in the lives of Moses (left) and of Christ (right). There are six (originally seven) on either side; the two nearest the altar were eliminated to make room for Michelangelo's Last Judgment. On the left (south) wall, beginning from the altar: Pinturicchio, Moses and Zipporah his wife in Egypt and the Circumcision of their son; Botticelli, *Burning Bush, with Moses slaying the Egyptian and driving the Midianites from the well; school of Ghirlandaio, Passage of the Red Sea; Cosimo Rosselli, Moses on Mount Sinai and the Worship of the Golden Calf; Botticelli, *Punishment of Korah, Dathan, and Abiram (in the background are the Arch of Constantine and the Septizonium); Luca Signorelli and Bartolomeo della Gatta, Moses giving his rod to Joshua, and Mourning for the death of Moses.

Right (north) wall, beginning from the altar: Perugino(?) and Pinturicchio, Baptism of Christ; Botticelli, Cleansing of the Leper and the Temptation in the Wilderness (in the background, the hospital of Santo Spirito); Domenico Ghirlandaio, *Calling of Peter and Andrew; Cosimo Rosselli and Piero di Cosimo, Sermon on the Mount and Healing the Leper; Perugino, *Christ giving the keys to St Peter; Cosimo Rosselli, Last Supper. On the East wall are two frescoes, the Resurrection by Domenico Ghirlandaio, and St Michael defending the body of Moses by Salviati, overpainted at the end of the 16C by Arrigo Fiammingo and Matteo da Lecce. In the niches between the windows are twenty-eight portraits of the first popes, by Fra Diamante, Domenico Ghirlandaio, Botticelli, and Cosimo Rosselli. The celebrated tapestries designed by Raphael, now in the Vatican Pinacoteca, were first exhibited in the Sistine Chapel in 1519.

Through the main door of the Sistine Chapel the sumptuous **Sala Regia** (admission, see below) can sometimes be seen. It was begun by Antonio da Sangallo the Younger in 1540, but not completed until 1573, and originally intended for the reception of ambassadors. The rich stucco decorations of the ceiling are by Perino del Vaga; those of the walls by Daniele da Volterra. The large frescoes are by Vasari, Salviati, and the Zuccari. They depict Gregory VII releasing the emperor Henry IV from excommunication; Charles V at the battle of Tunis; Return of Gregory XI from Avignon; Reconciliation of Alexander III and Barbarossa; Battle of Lepanto; Massacre of St Bartholomew. Here the first official meeting since the Reformation took place between the Pope and the Archbishop of Canterbury in 1966.

A special permit from the Governor of the Vatican City is needed in order to visit the following rooms. The AULA DELLE BENEDIZIONI is situated above the portico of St Peter's. From the central window of this vast hall the Pope blesses 'Urbi et Orbi'. The **Sala Ducale** was designed by Bernini, and is decorated with landscapes by Paul Brill. The **Cappella Paolina**, by Antonio da Sangallo the Younger, has two remarkable *frescoes by Michelangelo (Conversion of St Paul and Crucifixion of St Peter), painted in 1542–45 and 1546–50.

If you do not wish to continue the tour of the museums, you are often able to leave the chapel by the SCALA REGIA (when open; usually closed on Wednesdays), an imposing staircase built by Bernini which descends past a statue of Constantine to the portico of St Peter's. Otherwise the exit from the Chapel is by a small door in the N wall of the nave, which leads to the Museum of Christian Art.

Museum of Christian Art

The **MUSEUM OF CHRISTIAN ART** (*Museo Sacro*) was founded by Benedict XIV in 1756, and enlarged in the 19C, partly by the acquisitions of Pius IX but mainly by finds made during excavations in the catacombs by De Rossi and his successors. In 1934 more rooms were added, and the museum was rearranged to illustrate the historic development of the Christian minor arts.

Beyond a room in which is exhibited a 4C Greek relief of a horseman presented to Pius IX by Ferdinand II of the Two Sicilies is the **Chapel of St Pius V**, decorated by Giacomo Zucchi to designs by Vasari. There is a portrait of St Pius V in the apse on the right. In the wall case is part of the *treasury of the Sancta Sanctorum*, the pope's private chapel in the old Lateran Palace. The relics were preserved in precious reliquaries inside a case made of cypress wood for Leo III (795–816). The 9–12C works include: an enamelled *Cross presented by St Paschal I (817–24), containing five pieces of the True Cross; a large Greek Cross of gold filigree work containing a small piece of the True Cross, decorated with precious stones and still partly covered with the balsams with which it was anointed every year by the Pope; a 9C case in the form of a Cross; and the Reliquary of Santa Prassede.

The **Room of the Addresses** (*degli Indirizzi*), was so called because in the time of Pius XI, the address or congratulatory documents sent to Leo XIII and Pius X were kept here. Here is displayed a splendid collection of liturgical objects in ivory, enamel, majolica, silver, metal, etc. In the cases opposite the window: *ivories, including diptychs and triptychs (9–15C). The *Ramboyna diptych (c 900) has Christian scenes with the representation of the Roman wolf in the bottom of the left-hand panel. A five-panelled wooden *tablet with Christ blessing was part of the cover of a New Testament (the other half is in the Victoria and Albert Museum, London). Another *book cover from the Convent of St Gall, Switzerland, is illustrated with the Nativity. The collection of enamels includes Limoges enamels (12–16C). Other cases display 14–16C silver Crosses and 18–19C missals. On the window wall: Church silver; Crosses and amulets; 16C German, French and Roman silver; hammers used to open the Porta Santa in Holy Years; Roman silver made by Santi Lotti (1629–59); glass; seals and cameos.

The **Room of the Aldobrandini Marriage** (left) was built by Paul V in 1611 and restored by Pius VII in 1817. The ceiling frescoes are by Guido Reni. In the pavement is a 2C geometric mosaic; in the octagon in the centre is Achilles with the body of Hector. On the upper part of the walls are *frescoes of the 1C BC, with scenes from the Odyssey, found on the Esquiline in 1848. Lower down are paintings of famous women of antiquity, five of them from Tor Marancia, and paintings of children, from Ostia (1C AD). On the end wall is the *ALDOBRANDINI MARRIAGE (*Nozze Aldobrandine*), a masterpiece of Augustan art inspired by a Greek model of the 4C or 3C BC, found on the Esquiline in 1605 and kept in one of the garden pavilions of the Villa Aldobrandini until its removal to this room in 1838 by Gregory XVI. The painting of a marriage scene combines realism and symbolism. Two cases contain 3–5C gilt-engraved glass found in the catacombs.

The **Room of the Papyri** dates from 1774 when 6–9C papyri from Ravenna were displayed here (now replaced by facsimiles). The frescoes are by Raffaello Mengs and his assistant Christopher Unterberger.

The last room displays **Early Christian Antiquities** from the Catacombs of St Calixtus, St Domitilla, St Sebastian, and other cemeteries. These include a collection of glass, some of the finer specimens gilded, engraved 4C glass from Ostia, and 2–3C multicoloured glass. Christian and pagan lamps (1–4C), some with symbols of the Good Shepherd, the fish, the peacock, and the monogram of Christ; terracottas; bronze lamps (3–5C); fabrics including 11–13C Church embroideries; objects in gold. An inlaid enamel *reliquary of the 9C comes from the church of the Santi Quattro Coronati.

Beyond is the first of the exhibition rooms of the Vatican Library.

The Vatican Library

The **VATICAN LIBRARY** (*Biblioteca Apostolica Vaticana*) was founded by Nicholas V with a nucleus of some 350 volumes, which he increased to 1200. Sixtus IV brought the total to 3650. The library was pillaged in the sack of 1527. Before the end of the 16C Sixtus V commissioned Domenico Fontana to build the great Sistine Hall. Later popes adapted numerous rooms in Bramante's W corridor to house the steadily increasing collection of gifts, bequests, and purchases. Among the most important acquisitions were the Biblioteca Palatina of Heidelberg (1623), the Biblioteca Urbinas (1657, founded by Federico, Duke of Urbino), Queen Christina of Sweden's library (1690), the Biblioteca Ottoboniana bought in 1748 (formerly the property of Alexander VIII Ottoboni), the Jesuit Library (1922), the Biblioteca Chigiana (1923), and the Biblioteca Ferraioli (1929). There are now about 60,000 MSS, 7000 incunabula, and 1,000,000 other printed books. Leo XIII added a reference library; Pius X reorganised the manuscripts and provided a study-room; and Pius XI carried out further reorganisation. A disastrous collapse in December 1931 of part of the ceiling of the Sistine Hall was repaired two years later. The Library can be used by scholars (with a letter of introduction), on weekdays between 8.00 and 13.30. The VATI-CAN ARCHIVES are open on weekdays 8.00–13.30 to scholars who have a special permit from the Prefecture.

The exhibition rooms of the Library are the Gallery of Urban VIII, the Sistine Rooms, the Sistine Hall, the Pauline Rooms, the Alexandrine Room, the Clementine Gallery, and the Museum of Pagan Antiquities. All the rooms, except the Sistine Hall, are in Bramante's W corridor. The literary contents are not normally visible, as they are kept in cupboards; but in the Sistine Hall there is usually an exhibition (changed annually) of valuable MSS and printed books.

The first room is the **Gallery of Urban VIII**. By the entrance wall are two statues: on the left the sophist Aelius Aristides (AD 129–89) dating from the 3C and on the right the Greek orator Lysias, dating from the 2C. Here are shown astronomical instruments, sailing directions dating from the early 16C, and the Farnese Planisphere (1725), given to Leo XIII by the Count of Caserta.

Beyond are the two **Sistine Rooms**, part of the Library of Sixtus V (see below). In the first, paintings of St Peter's as planned by Michelangelo, and of the erection of the obelisk in Piazza San Pietro. Over the doors of the second room, Sixtus V proclaiming St Bonaventura Doctor of the Church in the church of the Santi Apostoli (Melozzo's frescoes are seen in their original place on the wall of the apse); Canonisation of San Diego in Old St Peter's.

The *Sistine Hall, named after its founder Sixtus V, was built in 1587–89 by Domenico Fontana across the great Courtyard of the Belvedere, cutting it into two. It was later paralleled by the New Wing, the construction of which created a small central courtyard, known as the Courtyard of the Library. Beneath this an underground deposit was constructed in 1983 to house the precious collection of Vatican manuscripts, and incunabula. The Sistine Hall is 71m long, 15m wide, and 9m high; it is divided into two vaulted aisles by seven columns. The decorations of the hall embody two main themes, the glorification of literature and of the pontificate of Sixtus V. At the ends of the aisles and in the lunettes over the windows are paintings, most of them views of Rome in the time of the pope and some of them illustrating events of his reign, such as his coronation on the steps of St Peter's, and the papal processions to the Lateran and to Santa Maria Maggiore, the latter for the inauguration of the special Holy Year of 1585. *Exhibitions here of the precious possessions of the library are changed annually.

Under the arches of the hall are displayed some of the gifts (vases, etc.) made to the popes by various foreign rulers. In the VESTIBULE (left), which is divided into two small rooms, is a pair of colossal enamel and gilt candelabra used at Napoleon I's coronation and presented by him to Pius VII. Above the doors are paintings of the Lateran Palace before and after its reconstruction by Domenico Fontana. Here are displayed the largest and smallest MSS in the Vatican Library, namely the Hebrew Bible of Urbino (1295) and the Masses of SS Francis and Anne, decorated with 16C miniatures.

Beyond the two PAULINE ROOMS, added by Paul V, and decorated in the Mannerist style of 1610–11 (with a press designed by Bramante for sealing papal bulls), is the ALEXANDRINE ROOM, adapted in 1690 by Alexander VIII, and decorated with scenes in the life of Pius VII by De Angelis. It contains an early embroidered cope and altar cloth (11–12C).

The **Clementine Gallery**, in five sections, was added to the Library by Clement XII in 1732; in 1818, under Pius VII, it was decorated by De Angelis with paintings of scenes in the life of that pope. The first two rooms contain a collection of plans of Rome, including one by Antonio Tempesta (1606), and valuable 16–17C Italian and German bookbindings, and bozzetti by Bernini. The last room has a bronze head of a Muse (Roman copy of a Hellenistic original), and two bronze hippogriffs of the Imperial period. On either side of the entrance are two Mithraic divinities.

Beyond is the main hall of the **Museum of Pagan Antiquities of the Library** (*Museo Profano della Biblioteca*), a museum and coin collection begun by Clement XIII in 1767, with additions from excavations in 1809–15. It was completed in the time of Pius VI, when it was decorated by Valadier. The ceiling paintings symbolise Time. In the cupboards in the right wall; carved Roman ivory, busts in semi-precious stones, a miniature torso, and a mosaic from Hadrian's Villa at Tivoli. Beyond, Roman bronze statuettes (1–3C AD) and plaques with inscriptions. In the cupboards on the left wall: head and arm of a chryselephantine statue of Minerva, claimed to be a 5C Greek original; Etruscan bronzes and carved Roman ivory. Beyond, Etruscan and Roman objects found in Rome and the Pontine Marshes. On the end wall in a niche to the left, *bronze head of Augustus; on right, bronze head of Nero (removed).

Beyond the Museum of Pagan Antiquities of the Library is (left) the Quattro Cancelli.

III. The Vatican Picture Gallery

The *VATICAN PICTURE GALLERY, *Pinacoteca Vaticana*, is reached by the passageway from the open court beyond the Quattro Cancelli. The gallery owes its origin to Pius VI, but under the Treaty of Tolentino (1797), he was forced to surrender the best works to Napoleon. Of these, seventy-seven were recovered in 1815. The present building in the Lombardic Renaissance style, by Luca Beltrami, was opened in 1932.

Room I. BYZANTINE SCHOOL AND ITALIAN PRIMITIVES. Antonio Veneziano, 16. St James, 19. Mary Magdalene; 18. Jacopo da Bologna, Death of St Francis; 17. Vitale da Bologna, Madonna and Child; 20. 12C Roman school, Christ in Judgement; 23. Giunta Pisano, St Francis, and panels illustrating his life; *526. Giovanni and Niccolò (Rome; late 11C), Last Judgment, the oldest picture in the gallery; 2. Margaritone d'Arezzo, St Francis of Assisi; (window wall) 14. Giovanni del Biondo, Madonna and Child with saints; 169. Taddeo di Bartolo, Death of the Virgin; 9. Giovanni Bonsi, Madonna and saints, signed and dated 1371; *146–150, 158–161. Bernardo Daddi, Legend of St Stephen. Also works by Niccolò di Pietro Gerini, and the Florentine school.

Room II. In the centre, *120. The STEFANESCHI TRIPTYCH, by Giotto and assistants. This altarpiece for the Confessio of Old St Peter's painted on both sides, represents Christ enthroned, the martyrdom of Saints Peter and Paul (at the foot of the throne is the donor, Cardinal Stefaneschi); on the back, St Peter accepting the triptych from the Pope; at the sides, four Apostles; on the predella, other Apostles. Around the walls is an exquisite series of small paintings: 168, 166, 163, 170. Pietro Lorenzetti, Christ before Pilate, St John the Baptist, St Peter, the Virgin; 165. Simone Martini, Redeemer; *174. Bernardo Daddi, Madonna of the Magnificat; 102, 97, 101. Mariotto di Nardo, Nativity, St Nicholas freeing three knights, Annunciation; works (136, 138) by Sano di Pietro; 132. Giovanni di Paolo, Nativity; 234. Sassetta, Vision of St Thomas Aquinas; 193. Lorenzo Monaco, Stories from the life of St Benedict; 247–50. Gentile da Fabriano, Stories from the life of St Nicholas of Bari; 2139. Sassetta, Madonna and Child; (window wall) 263. Francesco di Gentile, Madonna and Child.

Room III. FRA ANGELICO AND OTHERS. Masolino da Panicale, 260. Crucifixion, 245. Transition of the Virgin; Fra Angelico, *251, 252. Scenes from the life of St Nicholas of Bari, 253. Madonna and Child with saints; 243. Filippo Lippi, Coronation of the Virgin, a triptych; 262. Benozzo Gozzoli, St Thomas receiving the Virgin's girdle.

Room IV. MELOZZO AND PALMEZZANO. 269. Remaining fragments of a *fresco of the Ascension, with eight angel musicians, by Melozzo da Forlì, formerly in the church of the Santi Apostoli; another part is in the Quirinal. *270. Melozzo, Sixtus IV conferring on the humanist Platina the librarianship of the Vatican in the presence of Giuliano Della Rovere (afterwards Julius II), his brother Giovanni, and Girolamo and Raffaele Riario, a fine fresco transferred to canvas. On the right wall, Marco Palmezzano, *619, 273. Madonna and saints.

Room V. 15C ARTISTS. 286. Francesco del Cossa, predella with Miracles of St Vincent Ferrer; 275. Lucas Cranach, Pietà; 294. Giovanni Battista Utili, Madonna and Child.

Room VI. POLYPTYCHS. Carlo Crivelli, 297. Madonna (dated 1482), 300. Pietà. Vittorio Crivelli, Madonna with saints (dated 1481); Niccolò l'Alunno, 299. Crucifixion, 307. Polyptych of Montelparo; Antonio Viviani, St Anthony Abbot (in relief) and other saints (signed and dated 1469).

Room VII. UMBRIAN SCHOOL. 312. Pinturicchio, Coronation of the Virgin; 313. Umbrian 15C school, Madonna with St John; 316. Lo Spagna, Adoration of the Magi ('Madonna della Spineta'); Perugino, *317. Madonna enthroned with saints (318. Resurrection), 319–321. Part of predella with saints Benedict, Flavia, and Placidus; 326. Giovanni Santi (father of Raphael), St Jerome.

Room VIII, the largest room in the gallery, is devoted to the works of RAPHAEL. It contains three of his most famous paintings, two predellas, and ten tapestries made from his original cartoons. *334. The Coronation of the Virgin, belongs to his early Perugian period and was his first large composition, painted in 1503, when he was twenty years old. In a table case: 335. Predella to the above, with the Annunciation, Adoration of the Magi, and Presentation in the Temple. *329. The MADONNA OF FOLIGNO, is a mature work painted about 1511. It was a votive offering by Sigismondo Conti in gratitude for his escape when a cannon-ball fell on his house during the siege of Foligno. He is shown with St Jerome, and in the background is Foligno during the battle. It was kept in the Convent of Sant'Anna in Foligno from 1565 until it was stolen by Napoleon in 1797.

*333. The TRANSFIGURATION, Raphael's last work, was commissioned in 1517 by Cardinal Giuliano de' Medici for the cathedral of Narbonne. From 1523 to 1809 it was in the church of San Pietro in Montorio. It was restored in 1972–77. The superb scene of the transfiguration of Christ is shown above the dramatic episode of the healing of the young man possessed of a devil. It is not known how much of the painting had been finished by the time of Raphael's death in 1520, and, although the composition is Raphael's, it seems likely that the lower part was completed by his pupils Giulio Romano and Francesco Penni.

The ten celebrated *TAPESTRIES represent scenes from the Acts of the Apostles. Intended for the Sistine Chapel, they were commissioned by Leo X and woven in Brussels by Pieter van Aelst from cartoons drawn by Raphael in 1515–16. They are being restored, one by one. Seven of the cartoons (the other three have been lost) are in the Victoria and Albert Museum, London, though some scholars believe that these seven, which were bought in 1630 by Charles I of England, are 17C copies and that all the originals have been lost. Other tapestries from the same cartoons, but of inferior quality, are in Hampton Court Palace near London, in the Palazzo Ducale at Mantua, and in the Palazzo Apostolico at Loreto.

The tapestries were first exhibited in 1519 in the Sistine Chapel. They have borders of grotesques and broad bases decorated with bronzecoloured designs; most of this work is by Giovanni da Udine. The subjects are: A. Blinding of Elymas (this tapestry was cut in halves during the sack of Rome in 1527), B. Conversion of St Paul, C. Stoning of St Stephen, D. St Peter healing the paralytic, E. Death of Ananias, F. St Peter receiving the keys, G. The miraculous draught of fishes, H. St Paul preaching in Athens, I. Inhabitants of Lystra sacrificing to Saints Paul and Barnabas, L. St Paul in prison at Philippi. These tapestries belong to the so-called 'Old School' series. Ten of the 'New School' series are in the Gallery of Tapestries (see above). Also displayed here is (80.) a 16C Flemish tapestry of the Last Supper (after Leonardo's fresco in Milan).

Room IX. LEONARDO DA VINCI AND OTHER 15–16C MASTERS. *337. LEONARDO DA VINCI, ST JEROME (removed for restoration); 340. Lorenzo di Credi, Madonna; 339. 16C Lombard school, Christ at the Column, portrait of Bramante(?); *290. Giovanni Bellini, Pietà.

Room X. TITIAN, VERONESE, FRA BARTOLOMEO. 347. Girolamo Genga, Madonna and saints; 346. Veronese, Allegory; 349. Moretto, Madonna and Child enthroned with saints; 351. Titian, Madonna of San Niccolò de' Frari; *445. Doge Niccolò Marcello; 352. Veronese, St Helena; 354. Paris Bordone,

St George and the Dragon; 355. Garofalo, Apparition of the Virgin to Augustus and the Sibyl; *359. Giulio Romano and Francesco Penni, 'Madonna of Monteluce'; 336. Lombard 16C school 'Madonna della Cintura'.

Room XI. BAROCCI and others. 363. Vasari, Stoning of St Stephen; 365. Cavalier d'Arpino, Annunciation; 368. Muziano, Raising of Lazarus; 372. Cola dell'Amatrice, Assumption of the Virgin; Barocci, 375. Head of the Virgin; 376. Annunciation, *377. Rest on the Flight into Egypt, 378. The Blessed Michaelina, 380. St Francis receiving the stigmata. In the centre, 742. Marble bas-relief of Cosimo I by Pierino del Vaga.

Room XII. 17C MASTERS. There is a fine view of the cupola of St Peter's from the window. 381. Valentin, Martyrdom of Saints Processus and Martinian (mosaic in St Peter's); *382. Sacchi, Vision of St Romuald; 383. Guercino, Incredulity of St Thomas; *384. Domenichino, Communion of St Jerome (signed and dated 1614, his first important work; mosaic in St Peter's), 385. Caravaggio (copy), Denial of St Peter; *386. Caravaggio, Descent from the Cross, 1602 (copy in St Peter's Sacristy); Guido Reni, 387. Crucifixion of St Peter (mosaic in St Peter's). *389. Virgin in glory with saints; 388. Giuseppe Maria Crespi, Holy Family; Guercino, 391. Mary Magdalene, 392. St Margaret of Cortona; 394. Nicolas Poussin, Martyrdom of St Erasmus (signed); 381. Valentin de Boulogne, Martyrdom of saints Processo and Martiniano; *395. Guido Reni, St Matthew.

Room XIII. MARATTA, RIBERA, VAN DYCK, and others. *396. Sassoferrato, Madonna and Child; 1059. Orazio Gentileschi, Judith; *775. Van Dyck, St Francis Xavier; 1931. Pier Francesco Mola, Vision of St Bruno; 405. Pietro da Cortona, Appearance of the Virgin to St Francis; 408. Ribera (or his pupil Henry Somer), Martyrdom of St Laurence; 410. Pietro da Cortona, David and a lion; 415. Pompeo Batoni, Appearance of the Virgin to St John Nepomuc. In the centre, wood model of Michelangelo's dome of St Peter's, by Giacomo della Porta and Vanvitelli.

Room XIV. FLEMISH, DUTCH, GERMAN, FRENCH, AND ITALIAN PAINTERS (17–18C). Daniel Seghers, 416, 418. Small religious pictures with flower borders; 421. Rosa da Tivoli, Hunter; 419. Matthias Stomer, Orpheus, Pluto, and Proserpina; 784. Rubens, Triumph of Mars, mainly executed by his pupils; 432–439. Donato Creti, Astronomical Observations; 815. Nicolas Poussin, Gideon; 423. Van Bloeman, Horses; 460. Carlo Maratta, Clement IX.

Room XV. 446. Bernardino Conti, Francesco Sforza, 447. Pieter Meert, Philosopher; 448. Sir Thomas Lawrence, George IV of England; 451. David Teniers the Younger, Old man; 1210. Muziano, idealised portrait of Gregory XII, who abdicated in 1415; 455. Pompeo Batoni, Pius VI; 457. Scipione Pulzone, Cardinal Guglielmo Sirleto; 458. Giuseppe Maria Crespi, Benedict XIV, painted while still a cardinal (the papal robes were added afterwards); *460. Carlo Maratta, Clement IX.

Room XVI. Works by Wenceslao Peter (1742–1829), including Paradise and a self-portrait.

IV.   The Gregorian Museum of Pagan Antiquities, Pio Christian Museum, and Ethnological Missionary Museum

The **GREGORIAN MUSEUM OF PAGAN ANTIQUITIES** is reached from the vestibule by the entrance to the museums. This striking building was designed by a group of Italian architects headed by Fausto and Lucio Passarelli, and opened in 1970. Using the latest methods of display, it contains the collections that were in the Lateran, comprising the ***Gregorian Museum of Pagan Antiquities** (*Museo Gregoriano Profano*), consisting of Roman and neo-Attic sculpture, and some Greek originals, the **Pio Christian Museum**, and the **Ethnological Missionary Museum**, as well as additional material. The Museo Profano was founded by Gregory XVI (1831–46) to house the overflow of the Vatican Museums and the yields of excavations during his pontificate at Rome, Ostia, Veio, and Cerveteri. It was enriched by further excavations up to 1870, and at the end of the 19C by a collection of pagan inscriptions. John XXIII was responsible for its removal from the Lateran to the Vatican.

The numbers used in the description below refer to the plan on p 354.

Near the entrance (left) are Roman copies of original Greek sculpture (torsos, statuettes, and heads), and (ahead) MARSYAS (1), a marble copy of a bronze by Myron which formed part of a group placed at the entrance to the Acropolis in Athens in the mid 5C BC. Marsyas is attracted by the sound of the double flute, which Athena had invented and just thrown away. He is foiled in his attempt to pick up the instrument by Athena's commanding gesture (the statue of Athena is a cast).

To the right (2) are displayed some *Greek originals (formerly in part of the Etruscan Museum). These include: a superb sepulchral stele, showing a young man with his young slave handing him a strigil and a flask of oil (5C BC); two heads (fragments from one of the metopes and from the N frieze of the Parthenon), and the fragment of a horse's head from the W pediment of the Parthenon, probably one of Athena's horses. The head of Athena is also a 5C original from an acrolith; it was made to wear a helmet, probably of bronze. The eyes are of polished grey stone in which were set glass pupils; the eyebrows and eyelashes were made of thin strips of bronze, and the ears had gold earrings. Two relief fragments of horsemen, perhaps part of a frieze, resemble in style the Parthenon frieze. The relief of dancing nymphs is an Attic work of the 4C. Stairs (3) lead up to an area which contains the Lateran collection of PAGAN INSCRIPTIONS (open only to scholars with special permission).

There follow a series of HERMS (4), and, on the floor, the *HERACLITUS MOSAIC (5) of an unswept floor from the triclinium of a house on the Aventine, showing the remains of a banquet. It is signed 'Heraclitus', and may be a copy of a celebrated work by Sosus of Pergamon. Other works in this section include: round altar, with a faun playing for two dancing women; triangular tripod base, with reliefs of dancing figures taking part in Dionysiac rites, a neo-Attic work in Pentelic marble of the 1C BC, after a 4C original; copy of the Resting Satyr of Praxiteles (others in the Museo Pio-Clementino and the Capitoline Museum); colossal statue of Poseidon (Neptune), after a bronze original by Lysippos (with several restorations); colossal statue of Zeus.

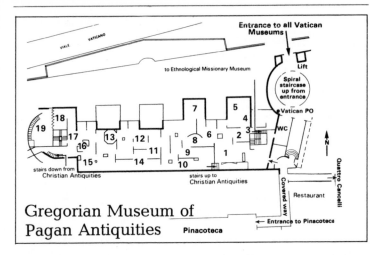

Gregorian Museum of
Pagan Antiquities   Pinacoteca

In the next section, by the windows, is a relief of Medea and the daughters of Pelias whom she is inducing to kill their father, neo-Attic copy of a late 5C BC original. It is one of a series of four relating to the dramatic competitions in Athens. The best copy of the second (Orpheus and Eurydice) is in the Naples Museum, a third (Herakles, Theseus, and Peirithöos) is in the Museo Torlonia.

Beyond a marble statue of Sophocles from Terracina, with fine drapery (a copy of a 4C work) are the remains of the large circular VICOVARO MONUMENT (6), dating from the early 1C AD. In the next recess is the CHIARAMONTI NIOBID (7), a fine Roman copy of an original by Leochares of the 4C BC. The head of a Muse, crowned with ivy, is in the manner of Praxiteles (good copy of a 4C BC original). The torso of a statue of Diana is a Roman copy of a Greek original of the 4C BC; the motion expressed in the drapery is particularly fine. Also here are two Roman orators in togas (1C AD), and fine Roman portrait heads (the last two perhaps portraits of Virgil).

The following sections contain Roman sculpture in chronological order, beginning with the late Republican era. Opposite two statues of the sleeping Silenus (copies of Hellenistic works), found in the Roman Theatre at Caere (see below), are a series of funerary reliefs: the first with portraits of parents and a young son, and the second with five busts of members of the Furia family. The circular altar dedicated to Piety comes from Veio; it is decorated with garlands, citharae, and the attributes of Vulcan (1C AD).

Around to the left are a group of STATUES FROM THE ROMAN THEATRE AT CAERE (8), mainly of the Julio-Claudian family: Agrippina, mother of Nero and wife of Claudius, as a goddess; colossal seated statue of Claudius as Jupiter; relief with figures symbolising three Etruscan cities of Vetulonia, Vulci, and Tarquinia, found with the statue and believed to have been part of his throne; colossal head, probably of Augustus; colossal seated statue of Tiberius idealised as Jupiter; series of inscriptions found with the statues, explaining their identity; Drusus and elder, with a cuirass decorated with bas-reliefs of two griffins and above, a gorgon; altar dedicated to C. Manlius, a censor of Caere, by his clients (1C AD); statue of an Emperor in a cuirass, decorated with reliefs.

Next comes the so-called ALTAR OF VICOMAGISTRI (9), 1C AD, found near the Cancelleria. The relief is of a sacrificial procession, followed by four figures carrying statuettes of lares and by priestly officials known as *vicomagistri*. Two statues of young boys wearing togas, belonging to the Julio-Claudian family (one with a 3C head); more Roman portrait busts and heads.

To the left is an area with CINERARY URNS (10), among which are an urn with finely carved reliefs, with the head of Medusa in the centre, and below a cock-fight, and festoons with eagles and genii at the sides. A covered urn has good reliefs and an inscription relating to Quinto Volusio Antigono. The next section has architectural fragments, and some exquisite decorative reliefs with small Bacchic scenes and vine-leaves (1C AD). The area is dominated by two large CANCELLERIA RELIEFS (11), dating from the Flavian period (AD 70–96). The frieze on the left (damaged) represents the return to Rome of Vespasian (who appears on the extreme right of the third panel). Surrounding the Emperor are vestals, the Roman Senate and people, and the seated figure of Rome. The frieze on the right represents the departure from Rome of Domitian who appears (restored as Nerva) in the second panel from the left, surrounded by (left) Minerva, Mars, and Victory, and (right) Rome with soldiers.

Beyond more portrait busts is sculpture from the TOMB OF THE HATERII (12), near Centocelle. Two similar niches have well-modelled portrait busts of a man and woman. Three reliefs illustrate a woman's funeral: the body lying in state, surrounded by relatives and mourners in the atrium of a house; the funeral procession, passing buildings on the Via Sacra; and the sepulchral monument of the Haterii, with a view of the inside and the apparatus used in its construction. Above, high relief with three busts of gods of the underworld; triangular pillar, beautifully carved, with candelabrum, rose branches, and birds. Relief of a procession of Roman magistrates in front of a temple (1C AD); one of the heads was restored (erroneously) by Thorvaldsen to represent Trajan.

Towards the windows, large funerary relief of a woman (the head is a portrait) lying on a bed with a small dog. A sepulchral relief of a chariot race (with a side view of the circus seen from above) shows the organisers of the games, in whose memory the relief was made, on the left (early 2C AD). Two columns are carved with a papyrus motif and lotus leaves around the base.

To the right, colossal STATUE OF A DACIAN (13), dating from the time of Trajan, found in 1841 in Via dei Coronari, on the site of a sculptor's studio of the Imperial era.

A series of capitals and antifixes follow, with two fragments of an architectural frieze from the forum of Trajan, with cupids and griffins and a neo-Attic amphora.

The next sections contain *PAGAN SARCOPHAGI (14), with mythological scenes. Among them, several depicting the story of Adonis, of Hippolytus and Phaedra (with scenes of the wild boar hunt), of Orestes, and of the slaughter of the family of Niobe. Farther on, is a fine sarcophagus dating from the 3C AD, with a scene of the triumph of Dionysos (Bacchus): he is represented as a victor on his return from India in a triumphal carriage drawn by two elephants, being crowned by Nike (Victory).

Beyond is a colossal statue of Antinous as the god Vertumnus (with finely modelled drapery; the head is modern); fragment of a relief with two boxers, presumably part of a large monument (2C AD).

Fragment of the large oval PLOTINUS SARCOPHAGUS (15), with figures in relief in philosophical discussion(?), and part of a lion hunt; on the wall behind, sepulchral relief with the deceased man reading from a large scroll, surrounded by his family and pupils (3C AD); on the right, funerary monument in high relief of a warrior saluting his wife who is seated; a horse stands ready, and a snake is depicted in the tree above. Fragments of draped IMPERIAL PORPHYRY STATUES (16). Towards the windows, relief of a nymph feeding an infant satyr from a large horn-shaped vessel, while in a grotto near by a young Pan plays the syrinx. Known as the Amaltheia relief, this was originally part of a fountain. To the right is the STATUE OF DOGMAZIO (17). Another area (18) contains Roman religious sculpture, including statues of Mithras and the bull (3C AD), Diana of the Ephesians, and Asklepios.

To the right of the stairs are fragments of a group with a boy riding a horse, and a naiad on a sea centaur. Upstairs a walkway passes above a MOSAIC OF ATHLETES FROM THE BATHS OF CARACALLA (19) and a black marble statue of a stag (Roman copy of a 4C Greek original). A corridor has Hebrew inscriptions, and, beyond, a balcony overlooks a second fine mosaic from the Baths of Caracalla (and there is a view of the dome of St Peter's from here).

The rest of the upper floor is occupied by the **PIO CHRISTIAN MUSEUM**, founded by Pius IX in 1854 with objects found mainly in the catacombs, and displayed by subject matter. The display begins at the other end of the mezzanine floor, at the entrance to the building. The first section is devoted to the valuable collection of Christian sarcophagi of the 2–5C, of the highest importance for the study of early Christian iconography; some famous sarcophagi owned by the Vatican but not on view here are represented by casts (numbered with Roman numerals). At the beginning on the left wall, are fragments of sarcophagi representing the Nativity and Epiphany (124, 190.) of the 4C AD. Farther on (right) is a sarcophagus showing the Crossing of the Red Sea.

Three steps lead up to the next section: in the middle, cast of the sarcophagus of Junius Bassus (the original is in the Treasury of St Peter's). Round the corner to the left is a sarcophagus (164.) with five niches showing Christ triumphant over death, Cain and Abel, Peter taken prisoner, the Martyrdom of Paul, and Job. Another short flight of steps ascends past (right) 152. Sarcophagus of the husband and wife Crescentianus and Agapene, found in the Vatican necropolis. At the top of the stairs (left) is a large sarcophagus (104.) with episodes from the Bible. To the right: panels (184, 189, 178, 175, 183A.) with scenes from the Old and New Testaments; cast of the sarcophagus from Sant'Ambrogio in Milan. The next part of the gallery contains more sarcophagi (including one from St Calixtus) and some mosaic fragments. Three steps lead up to the last section of the museum. On the left is a well-preserved sarcophagus (150.) with traces of the original polychrome decoration. At the end, 191A. Sarcophagus illustrating the Good Shepherd.

On the right wall begins the collection of epigraphs from the **Museum of Christian Inscriptions**, the largest and most important collection of Christian inscriptions in existence. The whole collection was arranged and classified by G.B. De Rossi (1822–94) in four series. FIRST SERIES. Inscriptions from public monuments connected with Christian worship. Fragment of the sepulchral inscription of Publius Sulpicius Quirinus (Cyrenius), Governor of Syria, who took the census at the time of the birth of Christ;

inscriptions of Pope St Damasus (366–84). SECOND SERIES. Dated sepulchral inscriptions. Dogmatic inscriptions, including the (fish) acrostic. Inscriptions relating to the ecclesiastical hierarchy, virgins, catechumens, senators, soldiers, officials, and workers, etc. THIRD SERIES. Chi-Rho and other symbols and representations of Christian dogma. The FOURTH SERIES are arranged topographically (2–6C). Inscriptions from the cemetery of Priscilla, the cemetery of Praetextatus, Sant'Agnese fuori le Mura, Ostia, tombs near the Vatican, San Lorenzo fuori le Mura, San Pancrazio, and Monte Mario.

The statue of the Good Shepherd is a fine work dating from the late 3C. A passage continues past (177.) a sarcophagus from San Lorenzo fuori le Mura, and the cast of a seated statue of the martyred doctor St Hippolytus. On the left of his chair is a list in Greek of the saint's works, and on the right a paschal calendar for the years 222–334. The original was moved by Pope John XXIII to the entrance of the Biblioteca Vaticana, in the Belvedere Court (see below). On the balcony overlooking a mosaic from the Baths of Caracalla (see above) is a fragment of the tombstone of Abercius, bishop of Hierapolis (Phrygia), who lived in the reign of Marcus Aurelius (161–80), discovered by Sir William Ramsay and presented to Leo XIII. The Greek text is in three parts: in the first part Abercius says that he is a disciple of Christ the Good Shepherd, in the second he mentions his journey to Rome and the East, in the third he asks the faithful to pray for him and threatens defilers of his grave.

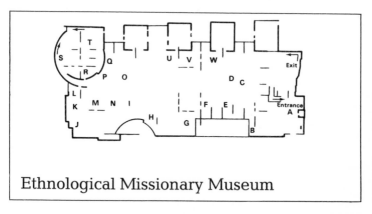

Ethnological Missionary Museum

The *ETHNOLOGICAL MISSIONARY MUSEUM** (only open on Wednesday and Saturday) occupies the whole of the area below ground level. It was established by Pius XI in 1927 as a development of the Vatican Missionary Exhibition of 1924–26. The primitive and more recent cultures of each country have been arranged according to subject matter; labelling is kept to a minimum. The countries are indicated by a letter (see the plan). The exhibits illustrate the ways of life and religious customs in: China (A), with fine Buddhist sculpture and religious figures of the Ming and T'ang dynasties; Japan (B), with ceremonial masks and paintings of martyrs;

Korea (C); Tibet, Mongolia (D); Indochina (E), where examples of local art and manufacture show the adaptation of European sacred art to the local genius; *Indian sub-continent (F), illustrating Shivaism and Vishnuism; Indonesia, Philippines (G); Polynesia (H); *Melanesia (I), with protective spirits, ceremonial masks and costumes, and the reconstruction of a hut of the spirits from New Guinea; Australia (J); North Africa (K); Ethiopia (L); Madagascar (M); West Africa (N), with statuettes of tribal gods; Central Africa (O); East Africa (P); Southern Africa (Q); Christian Africa (R); South America (S), including ancient wood sculpture from Colombia; Central America (T); North America (U); Persia (V); Middle East (W); and Christian art from countries penetrated by the missions. A mezzanine floor contains study collections open to scholars.

The PADIGLIONE DELLE CARROZZE, built by Paul VI in 1973 houses carriages and the first automobiles used by the popes. The **Historical Museum** has been transferred to the Lateran Palace.

V. The Vatican City and Gardens

Tours of part of the Vatican City and gardens are organised at the Information Office to the left of St Peter's façade. Tickets should be booked at least one day in advance. The tours, partly by bus and partly on foot (c 2 hrs) depart at 10.00 on Tuesday, Friday and Saturday (Lire 16,000); the tours on Monday and Thursday include the Sistine Chapel (3 hrs; Lire 25,000). From November to February there are tours usually only on Saturday of the gardens and city (Lire 12,000). Individual visitors are not admitted to the city or gardens (except with a special permit).

The **Vatican Gardens**, laid out in the 16C, cover the N and W slopes of the Vatican Hill. The ARCO DELLE CAMPANE is protected by a sentry of the Swiss Guard, armed with a rifle instead of the halberd carried by the guard at the Bronze Door. The square beyond is Piazza dei Protomartiri Romani, the site of the martyrdom of the early Christians near the Circus of Nero. On the left is the CAMPOSANTO TEUTONICO, dating from the 8C, and probably the oldest medieval cemetery; it is still reserved for the Germans and Dutch. In the adjacent COLLEGIO TEUTONICO are a small museum and a library. Beyond, against the wall of the city, is the new AUDIENCE HALL (1971), by Pier Luigi Nervi. Designed in the shape of a shell it has seating for 8000 people.

In the pavement in front of the first arch of the passage beneath the sacristy of St Peter's a slab marks the former site of the obelisk in Piazza San Pietro. A road leads beneath the sacristy to Piazza Santa Marta. Here, on the right, is a fine view of the left transept of St Peter's; on the left is the PALAZZO DELL'ARCIPRETE DI SAN PIETRO. At the W end of the square is the PALAZZO DEL TRIBUNALE.

Opposite the majestic W end of St Peter's is the little church of SANTO STEFANO DEGLI ABISSINI, built by Leo III as Santo Stefano Maggiore. In 1479 Sixtus IV conceded it to Coptic monks; it was rebuilt by Clement XI.

A road ascends past the STUDIO DEL MOSAICO, with an exhibition room, and (right) the modern Governor's Palace (PALAZZO DEL GOVERNA-TORATO), built in 1931 as the seat of the civic administration of the Vatican City. To the S is the little-used VATICAN RAILWAY STATION. On the first floor a PHILATELIC AND NUMISMATIC MUSEUM was opened in 1990. It preserves all the postage stamps and coins issued by the Vatican since 1929.

Viale dell'Osservatorio continues up through the gardens past the SEMI-NARIO ETIOPICO. At the W extremity of the city is a stretch of the wall built by Nicholas V on the site of the ancient walls put up by Leo IV. Here the TOWER OF ST JOHN, once an observatory, is now used as a guest-house. On the westernmost bastion of the city walls is the HELIPORT. The road passes a reproduction of the Grotto of Lourdes, presented by the French Catholics to Leo XIII.

A road leads down through exotic vegetation past the VATICAN RADIO STATION, designed by Marconi, and inaugurated in 1931. Since 1957 Vatican Radio has transmitted from a station at Santa Maria di Galeria, 25km outside Rome. The FONTANA DELL'AQUILONE, by Giovanni Vesanzio, has a triton by Stefano Maderno. Nearer the huge Museum buildings is the *Casina of Pius IV, two small buildings by Pirro Ligorio (1558–62), which are a masterpiece of Mannerist architecture. In the villa, now the seat of the PONTIFICAL ACADEMY OF SCIENCES, Pius IV held the meetings which received the name of *Notti Vaticane*; at them were held learned discussions on poetry, philosophy, and sacred subjects. Pius VIII and Gregory XVI used to give their audiences here.

Towards St Peter's a group of buildings include the FLORERIA, formerly the MINT (Zecca), founded by Eugenius IV, and the FONTANA DEL SACRA-MENTO. The STRADONE DEI GIARDINI is an avenue which skirts Bramante's W corridor of the Vatican Museums. The exit is usually through Piazza del Forno (overlooked by the Sistine Chapel), around St Peter's, and through the Arco delle Campane.

The northern part of the city, normally closed to visitors, is entered through the ARCO DELLA SENTINELLA, beyond which is the Borgia Tower and a series of small courtyards, in the heart of the Vatican Palace, including the CORTILE DEI PAPPAGALLI (so called from its frieze of parrots, now almost obliterated). The larger CORTILE DI SAN DAMASO is overlooked by the Loggia of Raphael. On the other side of the huge museum buildings (and entered from the Cancello di Sant'Anna on Via di Porta Angelica) are various offices of the Vatican State, including the POLYGLOT PRINTING PRESS, the POST OFFICE, the CASA PARROCHIALE, and the *Osservatore Romano* newspaper. Also here are the barracks of the Swiss Guard, a restoration centre for tapestries, and the restored church of San Pellegrino. In 1956 a Pagan necropolis (tombs of 1–4C) was discovered beneath the car park. The cemetery was alongside Via Triumphalis, the line of which is now followed by Via del Pellegrino. It can only be visited with special permission. Beside the Cancello di Sant'Anna is SANT' ANNA DEI PALAFRENIERI, the parish church of the Vatican City, built in 1573 by the Papal Grooms (Palafrenieri della Corte Papale) to the designs of Vignola.

To the S of St Peter's Colonnade, outside the Vatican City, but granted the privilege of extraterritoriality is **Palazzo del Sant'Uffizio**. The Holy Office, commonly known as the Inquisition, was established here in 1536 by Paul III to investigate charges of heresy, unbelief, and other offences against the Catholic religion. In Rome and the Papal States the Holy Office exercised a severe control over heresy and the suspicion of heresy but never, so far as is known, ordered the death of anyone found guilty, and the excessive rigours of the Spanish Inquisition were condemned by the Renaissance popes. The preparation of the Index of Prohibited Books was originally entrusted to the Congregation of the Holy Office. In 1571 Pius V established a special Congregation of the Index, which survived until its suppression by Benedict XV in 1917, when these duties were resumed by the Holy Office. The tribunal was formally abolished by the Roman Assembly in February 1849, but it was re-established by Pius IX a few months later. To the right is the former PALAZZO DEL MUSEO PETRIANO, now used by Vatican Radio.

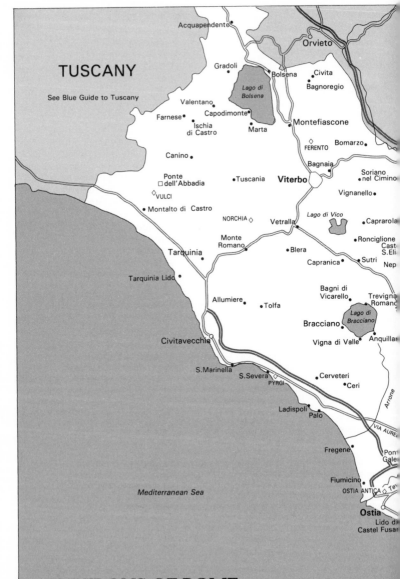

TUSCANY

See Blue Guide to Tuscany

ENVIRONS OF ROME
(& northern Lazio)

0   30 kilometres

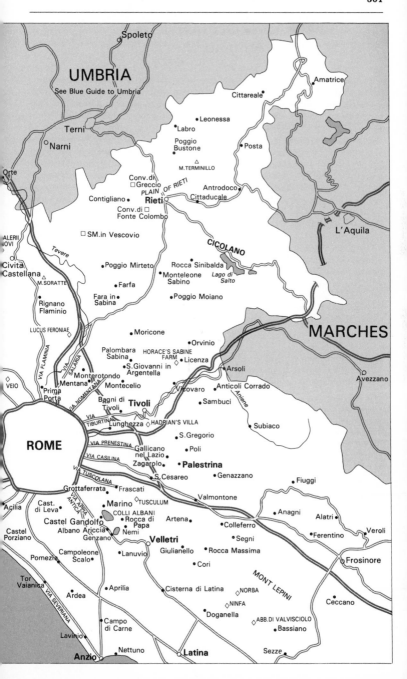

ENVIRONS OF ROME
(including northern Lazio)

The routes described below cover the whole of northern Lazio: the immediate environs of Rome with its province, as well as the provinces of Rieti and Viterbo. Important Roman remains close to Rome include the vast excavations of the Roman city of Ostia and Hadrian's famous Villa at Tivoli, one of the most interesting classical sites known, both of them still in beautiful settings, as well as the huge Sanctuary of Fortune in the centre of the town of Palestrina. Just outside Cerveteri and Tarquinia are Etruscan tombs of the highest importance, and both towns have fine Etruscan museums. Viterbo, Tuscania, and Tarquinia are interesting medieval towns. Some of the most beautiful and famous gardens in Italy are in northern Lazio: these include the Villa Lante at Bagnaia, Palazzo Farnese at Caprarola, the Villa d'Este at Tivoli, the Villa Aldobrandini in Frascati, and the park at Bomarzo. Lovely unspoilt countryside can still be found in the province of Rieti, around the Lago di Nemi in the Alban Hills, and in 'Alto Lazio' (the Lago di Vico, Lago di Bolsena, and near Tuscania and Vulci).

Many of the main towns are still reached on the line of the ancient Roman roads. Most of the places are well served by public transport, details of which are given at the beginning of each route. The bus services are run by 'CO.TRA.L' (*Consorzio Trasporti Pubblici Lazio*; information, Tel. 06/46954444). The countryside looks its best in the spring, when the Campagna is in flower, and in autumn, when the hills are ablaze with colour.

The Province of Rome (8438sq km) is one of five that make up the modern region of **Lazio**; the others are Rieti (2737sq km), Viterbo (2934sq km), Frosinone (3064sq km), and Latina (2250sq km): the last two are both described in 'Blue Guide Southern Italy'.

The **Roman Campagna** (40–70m above sea level), the country surrounding Rome, is an undulating plain, with indeterminate limits, extending from the Tyrrhenian Sea to a semicircle of hills some distance inland. These are the Monti della Tolfa and Monti Sabatini, to the NW of Rome, the Monti Tiburtini and Monti Prenestini, to the E, and the Monti Lepini and Monti Ausoni, to the SE. The area is traversed by the Tiber, into which flow the Aniene and other tributaries. In the Tertiary Age the plain was occupied by a gulf of the sea in which volcanic eruptions formed numerous islands. In the centre the islands became the Alban Hills. In the NW they formed a series of ranges, one behind the other, with craters which are now filled up by lakes: the Monti Sabatini, with the Lago di Bracciano, the Monti Cimini, with the Lago di Vico, and the Monti Volsini, with the Lago di Bolsena. The lava from the eruptions spread as far as the hills where Rome later was built.

The name of *Campania Romana*, dating from the time of Constantine and replacing that of *Latium*, was used to distinguish the area from that of the *Campania Felix*, which surrounds Naples. In the widest sense of the term, the Roman Campagna includes the *Agro Pontino*, formerly the Pontine Marshes. In a more restricted sense it is taken to comprise the area between the sea, the Monti Sabatini, and the Alban Hills, corresponding roughly to that of the *Agro Romano*, or administrative division of the Commune of Rome, with an area of 2074sq km.

The Campagna was the focus of almost all the people who were to form the Italic race. In the early days of Rome the growing of corn was the main activity of the Campagna, but after their Mediterranean conquests the Romans were able to import cereals, and gardens and orchards were planted here, sustained by irrigation. The ruins of villas, aqueducts, and cisterns found in every part of the Agro Romano testify to the productivity of the farms that once surrounded the city. In the early days of the Empire the farms began to be displaced by large landed estates (*latifundia*), fertility declined, and maleria increased, so that the population dwindled. During later centuries some of the popes tried without success to help the area with schemes of repopulation and agricultural centres to provide food for the city.

By the time of the Unification of Italy the Agro Romano was a vast malarial desert. In 1878 the Government began to drain the marshes and stagnant waters and reclaim a belt extending to 10km from the centre of the city. The estates of the suppressed religious organisations were divided up, and in 1883 a principle of compulsory cultivation was established, and a law to this effect regarding the whole of the Agro Romano was passed in 1921. In the years following the First World War, and under the Fascist regime, land reclamation took place on a large scale. The area now sustains cornfields, pasture-land, orchards, vineyards, and olive groves.

28

Ostia Antica

ROAD, 23km. VIA DEL MARE (N 8) from Viale Marconi (beyond San Paolo fuori le Mura). This fast 'superstrada' reaching the coast (28km) at the W end of the Lido di Ostia, was opened in 1928, when the Lido became Rome's seaside resort. It runs parallel to the old Via Ostiense for the whole of its length. The *Via Ostiensis*, one of the earliest consular roads, dates from the victorious campaign of the Romans against the inhabitants of Veio to secure their salt supply (5C BC). It ran to Ostia, and from there, under the name of *Via Severiana*, it followed the coast to Laurentum (near Castel Fusano), Antium (Anzio), and Terracina, where it joined the Via Appia.

RAILWAY. *Ferrovia Roma-Lido* from Porta San Paolo c every half hour for Ostia Antica. From the station of Ostia Antica, Via Ostiense and Via del Mare are crossed by a footbridge; straight ahead is the entrance to the excavations.

Outside Porta San Paolo (Pl. 8; 7) Via Ostiense leads S. After 1.5km, just before the Basilica of San Paolo, Lungotevere San Paolo branches right. This joins Viale Marconi, and off this (right) begins the Via del Mare proper. The road runs parallel to Via Ostiense, which is on the left. Farther to the left many prominent buildings of EUR (Rte 26) are conspicuous. To the right is a road to the racecourse of Tor di Valle. 12km Crossing of the Grande Raccordo Anulare (Rome Circular Road). 13km MEZZOCAMMINO; on a hill are the remains of a Roman villa and between the two roads is the tomb of a Roman knight. The road runs close to the Tiber for a very short period. 18km ACILIA. Here excavations were begun in 1976 of the ancient city of FICANA, founded at the end of the 8C BC. Conquered by Ancus Marcius, the fourth king of Rome, it had probably disappeared by the 2C BC. From here three parallel roads continue to the sea. 23km Turning right for 'Scavi di Ostia Antica'; you should take care not to miss the turn as otherwise the fast main road continues (with no more exits) straight on to Lido di Ostia (now usually called just 'Ostia'), an ugly modern suburb of Rome on the coast, with a complicated system of one-way roads.

The extensive ****excavations of the Roman city of OSTIA ANTICA**, in a beautiful park of umbrella pines and cypresses, are one of the most interesting and beautiful sights near Rome. The excavations give a remarkable idea of the domestic and commercial architecture prevalent in the Empire in the late 1C and 2C AD (hardly any of which has survived in Rome itself). The remains are as important for the study of Roman urban life as those of the older cities of Pompeii and Herculaneum. They are open every day from 9 to one hour before sunset (the Museum closes one hour earlier). At least half a day is needed for the visit, and it is a splendid place to picnic (refreshments can be bought in the village of Ostia Antica, close to the entrance to the excavations). Some of the *mosaics discovered in the ruins are occasionally covered with wind-blown sand. In the description below only the most important monuments are mentioned as the ruins are well labelled (also in English).

Ostia, now called **Ostia Antica**, is named after the *ostium*, or mouth of the Tiber. The river formerly flowed past the city on the N in a channel, the *Fiume Morto*, dry since a great flood in 1557. According to legend, Ostia was founded by Ancus Marcius, fourth king of Rome, to guard the mouth of the river Tiber. The surviving remains are not, however, older than the 4C BC, and the city, which was probably the first colony of Rome, may have been founded about 335 BC. It was originally a fortified city (*Castrum*), whose walls survive in part; later it became a much larger commercial city (*Urbs*), also surrounded with walls. Its first industry was the extraction of salt from the surrounding marshes, but it soon developed into the commercial port of Rome and, shortly before the outbreak of the First Punic War (264 BC), it also became a naval base. The link between the port and the capital was the *Via Ostiensis*, which, carrying as it did all Rome's overseas imports and exports until the construction of the Via Portuensis, must have been one of the busiest roads in the ancient world.

The commerce passing through Ostia was vital to the prosperity and even the existence of Rome. One of its most important functions was the organisation of the *Annona*, for the supply of produce, mainly corn, to the capital. At the head of the Annona was originally the *Quoestor Ostiensis*, who had to live at Ostia. He was appointed by lot and his office, according to Cicero, was burdensome and unpopular. By 44 BC the Quoestor was replaced by the *Procuratores Annonoe*, answerable to the Praefectus Annonae in Rome. The organisation involved the creation of a large number of commercial associations or guilds covering every aspect of trade and industry. Numerous inscriptions referring to these associations have been found in the Piazzale delle Corporazioni. Ostia suffered a temporary setback in 87 BC, when it was sacked by Marius, but Sulla rebuilt it soon afterwards and gave it new walls.

As the city continued to thrive, it outgrew its harbour and the construction of another port became, by the 1C AD, an imperative necessity. Planned by Augustus, this was built by Claudius, to the NW of Ostia, and later enlarged by Trajan (Porto; see below). For a time Ostia remained the centre of the vast organisation for the supply of food to the capital. It added to its temples, public buildings, shops and houses, and it received special marks of favour from the emperors.

The decline of Ostia began in the time of Constantine, who favoured Porto. The titles conferred by the emperor on the newer seaport must have been particularly galling to the inhabitants of Ostia. But even in the 4C, though it had become a residential town instead of a commercial port, it was still used by notable people travelling abroad. In 387 St Augustine was about to embark for Africa with his mother, St Monica, when she was taken ill and died in a hotel in the city. In the following centuries Ostia's decline was accelerated by loss of trade and by the increase of malaria. Its monuments were looted: columns, sarcophagi and statues stolen from the ruins have been found as far afield as Pisa, Amalfi, Orvieto, and Salerno. An attempt to revive the city was made by Gregory IV, when he founded the borgo of Ostia Antica. In 1756 the city, which at the height of its prosperity had had a population of some 80,000, had 156 inhabitants; half a century later only a few convicts of the papal Government lived here; Augustus Hare, writing in 1878, speaks of one human habitation breaking the utter solitude.

Excavations of the site began on a small scale at the beginning of the 19C, under Pius VII. Further work was instituted in 1854 under Pius IX, but systematic excavations did not begin until 1907. They have been continued with few interruptions, until the present day. The work carried out in 1938–42 by Guido Calza and others brought to light many monuments of great interest. The excavated area has been doubled and is now c 34 hectares, or two-thirds of the area of the city at its greatest extent.

DOMESTIC ARCHITECTURE. One result of research has been the great increase in knowledge of the various types of house occupied by Romans of the middle and lower classes. Since it is not likely that the domestic architecture of Ostia differed radically from that of the capital, the examples that have been unearthed of the lower-grade house at Ostia may be taken as typical of such dwellings in Rome itself. The middle- and lower-class house at Ostia (*Insula*) was in sharp contrast to the typical Pompeian residence (*Domus*), with its atrium and peristyle, its few windows and its low elevation. This occurs only rarely at Ostia.

The ordinary Ostia house usually had four storeys and reached a height of 15m, the maximum permitted by Roman law. It was built of brick, probably not covered with stucco, and had little in the way of adornment. Sometimes bricks of contrasting colours were used. The entrance doors had pilasters or engaged columns supporting a simple pediment. There were numerous rooms, each with its own window. The arches over the windows were often painted in vermilion. Mica or selenite was used instead of glass for the windows. The façades were of three types: living-rooms with windows on all floors; arcaded ground floor with shops, living-rooms above; and ground floor with shops opening on the street, living-rooms above. Many of the houses had balconies, which were of varying designs. The apartment houses contained numerous flats or sets of rooms designated by numbers on the stairs leading to them. They too, were of different types; some were of simple design and others were built round a courtyard. The rare *Domus*, built for the richer inhabitants, were usually on one floor only and date mostly from the 3C and 4C. They were decorated with apses, nymphaea, and mosaic floors. The rooms often had columns and loggias.

RELIGION. In Ostia, as elsewhere in the Roman world, different religious cults flourished without disharmony. As well as temples dedicated to the traditional deities such as Vulcan, Venus, Ceres, and Fortuna, there was a popular cult of the emperors and a surprisingly large number of eastern cults, such as the Magna Mater, Egyptian and Syrian deities, and especially Mithras. Singularly few Christian places of worship have been found.

The city of Ostia appears to have been divided into at least five *Regiones*, the precise limits of which are not yet determined. The various monuments have been classified according to the region to which they are believed to have belonged. As a result, the streets and buildings are marked with signs indicating (*a*) the number of the region, (*b*) the number of the block (*c*) the type of construction, such as temple, warehouse, dwelling-house (insula), residence (domus), etc., (*d*) the traditional name of the street or building.

The entrance to the excavations leads into VIA OSTIENSE, outside the walls. Parallel on the S is Via delle Tombe. This street is also outside the walls, in conformity with Roman law, which prohibited intramural burials. In it are a few terracotta sarcophagi and sealed graves, as well as columbaria for the urns holding the ashes from cremations.

The entrance to the city is by the PORTA ROMANA, with remains of the gate of the Republican period; some fragments of a marble facing of the Imperial era have been found and placed on the inner walls of the gate. The **Piazzale della Vittoria** is dominated by a colossal STATUE OF MINERVA VICTORIA, dating from the reign of Domitian and inspired by a Hellenistic original. The statue may once have adorned the gate. On the right of the square are the remains of HORREA (warehouses), later converted into baths. In the THERMAE OF THE CISIARII on the far side of the warehouses are several mosaics, one with scenes of life in Ostia.

Here begins the **Decumanus Maximus**, the main street of Ostia. It runs right through the city and is c 1200m long. A little way along this street, on the right, is a flight of steps leading to a platform, on the second storey of the BATHS OF NEPTUNE. From the platform can be seen the tepidarium and

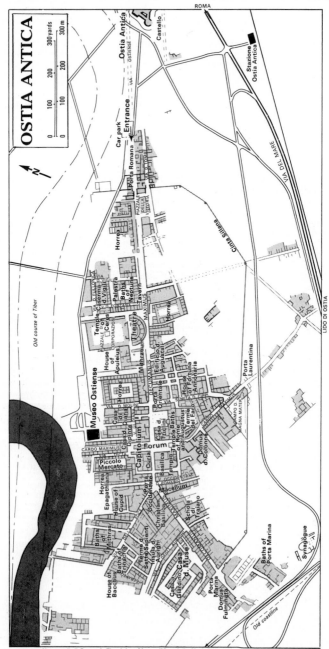

OSTIA ANTICA

ROMA

Necropoli di Porto & Fiumicino Airport (Mus. delle Navi Romane)

calidarium, remains of columns, and the floor of the large entrance hall with a *mosaic of Neptune driving four sea-horses and surrounded by Tritons, nereids, dolphins, etc. In an adjoining room is another mosaic: Amphitrite escorted by Hymen. The platform provides a fine view of the excavations (in the distance straight ahead can be seen the buildings of Fiumicino airport). Adjoining is the PALAESTRA (Gymnasium) a large colonnaded courtyard surrounded by rooms.

Just before the Baths of Neptune is VIA DEI VIGILI (Street of the Firemen), the construction of which involved the demolition of some earlier buildings, to which belonged a mosaic (displayed nearby) representing the Four Winds and Four Provinces (Sicily, Egypt, Africa, Spain). The street leads to the CASERMA DEI VIGILI (Firemen's Barracks), built in the 2C AD. It has an arcaded courtyard, a shrine dedicated to Fortuna Santa, and an AUGUSTEUM, or shrine for the cult of the emperors.

An archway leads into VIA DELLA FONTANA, one of the best-preserved streets in Ostia. Here is a typical apartment house, with shops and living-rooms over them. To the right the street joins VIA DELLA FULLONICA, named from its well-equipped fullers' workshop, complete with courtyard for cloth-drying.

The street rejoins the Decumanus Maximus at the TAVERN OF FORTU-NATUS in which is a mosaic pavement with the broken inscription: 'Dicit Fortunatus: vinum cratera quod sitis bibe' ('Fortunatus says: drink wine from the bowl to quench your thirst'). The next street to the right (W) is VIA DELLE CORPORAZIONI; in it is a well-preserved apartment house, with paintings on the walls and ceilings. On the other side of the street is the *Theatre, built by Agrippa, enlarged by Septimius Severus in the 2C. The theatre is a semicircular building of the usual Roman type. It has two tiers of seats (originally three), divided by stairways into five sections or *Cunei*. It could accommodate 2700 people. A tufa wall with some marble fragments and three marble masks survive from the stage, behind which some cipol-lino columns have been set up, which once decorated the third tier of the auditorium. In the main façade, towards the Decumanus Maximus, is a series of covered arcades, formerly shops. Between the arcades and the street are areas paved with travertine and, at either end, a fountain. Into the fountain on the E side was built a CHRISTIAN ORATORY in honour of St Cyriacus and his fellow-martyrs of Ostia.

Behind the theatre extends the spacious *PIAZZALE DELLE CORPORAZIONI (Square of the Guilds). In this square were 70 offices of commercial associations ranging from workers' guilds to corporations of foreign representatives from all over the ancient world. Their trade-marks are preserved in the mosaic floors of the brick-built arcade running round the square. The trade-marks of the foreign representatives are historically valuable, as they tell where the merchants came from (e.g. Carthage, Alexandria, Narbonne, etc.) and what their trade was. Equally informative are the inscriptions relating to the citizens, some of whom were employed in ship repair and construction, in the maintenance of docks, warehouses, and embankments, as dockers, salvage crews, and customs and excise officials. In the middle of the square are the stylobate and two columns of a small temple in antis known as the TEMPLE OF CERES, and the bases of statues erected to the leading citizens of Ostia.

Beyond the square is a handsome house of the Pompeian type, rare at Ostia, with an atrium and rooms decorated with mosaics. It is called the HOUSE OF APULEIUS. Beside it is a MITHRAEUM, one of the best preserved of the many temples dedicated to Mithras in the city. It has two galleries for the initiated, on the walls of which are mosaics illustrating the cult of the god. There are also casts of the marble relief of Mithras which was found here, with several inscriptions. In front are four small tetrastyle TEMPLES, erected in the 2C BC on a single foundation of tufa. They are supposed to have been dedicated to Venus, Fortuna, Ceres, and Hope. In the square in front of the temples are the remains of a Nymphaeum and of a Sanctuary of Jupiter.

From the Decumanus Maximus can be seen, on the right, large WARE-HOUSES (HORREA) for the storage of corn. They have over 60 small rooms, some of them arranged round a central colonnaded courtyard. At the corner of the next street on the right, VIA DEI MOLINI, so called after a building in it containing millstones, are the remains of a REPUBLICAN TEMPLE. Here is the PORTA ORIENTALE, the East Gate of the original fortified city, or Castrum; to the left are the original tufa walls. At this point the Decumanus Maximus has been excavated down to the level of the ancient city and is liable to flooding in bad weather.

A street on the W side of Via dei Molini, VIA DI DIANA, takes its name from a house called the *CASA DI DIANA. The façade is characteristic: shops on the ground floor, rooms with windows on the first floor, and a projecting balcony on the second floor. The house is entered through a vaulted corridor. On the ground floor is a room (left) whose ceiling and walls have been restored with fragments of frescoes. The small interior courtyard has a fountain and a relief of Diana. At the back of the premises are two rooms converted into a Mithraeum. Opposite the entrance to the Casa di Diana Via dei Lari opens into PIAZZETTA DE LARI, with a round marble altar dedicated to the Lares of the Quarter.

In Via di Diana beyond the Casa di Diana, is (left) the THERMOPOLIUM, which bears a striking resemblance to a modern Italian bar. Just outside the entrance, under the balcony, are two small seats. On the threshold is a marble counter, on which is a small stone basin. Inside the shop is another counter for the display of food dishes; above are wall-paintings of fruit and vegetables. On the rear wall is a marble slab with hooks for hats and coats. Beyond is a delightful court and fountain.

At the end of Via di Diana (right) is an apartment house, originally of four storeys, called the CASA DEI DIPINTI. A staircase leads up to the top floor from which there is a fine view of the excavations. The ground floor (entered around the corner from Via dei Dipinti) has been closed for many years: the corner room has a mosaic floor and 'architectural' wall-paintings; beyond is a fine *hall painted with mythological scenes, human figures, and land-scapes. In the garden of the house are numerous *Dolii*, large terracotta jars for the storage of corn and oil. At the end of the street is the Museum, which contains the principal finds from the excavations.

The ***Museo Ostiense** is housed in a building dating from 1500 and origi-nally used by the authorities concerned with the extraction of salt; it was given its neo-classical façade in 1864.

Room I (left). *Bas-reliefs showing scenes of everyday life (including various arts and crafts, the scene of a birth, a surgical operation, etc.); by the window, two bas-reliefs with the plan of a temple and the topographical plan of a city. **Room II**. Architectural and decorative terracotta fragments; statue of Fortune (2C AD). Off the Atrium (with a statue of Apollo Kitharoi-dos of 2C AD) are (left) Rooms III and IV with works relating to Eastern cults. **Room III**. In the niche at the end, *Mithras slaying the bull, from the Baths of Mithras, signed by Kritios of Athens (first half of the 2C BC); in the niche to the right, group of 18 cult statues found in the Sanctuary of Attis (AD 140–70); circular *altar with reliefs of the Twelve Gods, a neo-Attic work of the 1C BC. **Room IV**. Recumbent figure of a priest of Cybele (second half of 3C AD); Egyptian-Roman relief in black basalt of Asklepios; stele with a boy initiated in the cult of Isis (early 4C AD).

Steps descend from the Atrium into Room VI. To the left is **Room V** with sculpture inspired by Greek art of 5C BC: inscribed bases testifying to the presence of Greek artists; head of Hermes; votive relief (an original Greek-Italiot work of the first half of 5C BC); three heads of Athena, from originals of the Phidias type, the Kressilas type, and the Kephisodotos type (first half of 4C BC); upper part of a herm of Themistocles, copy of an original of the 5C; Omphalos Apollo, from the 5C original; head of an unknown man.

Room VI contains sculpture inspired by Greek art of the 4C and 3C BC: two copies of Eros drawing his bow (one a replica of an original by Lysippos); cult statue of Asklepios(?); two herms of Hermes (of the Alcamene type); Dionysos (with elements inspired by Praxiteles). In the centre, fragment of a group of Wrestlers dating from the Trajan era on a Hellenistic model. **Room VII**. Sculpture inspired by Hellenistic works. Head of a satyr and of a barbarian of the Pergamene type (2C BC); two heads of Korai; head of Victory (Giulio-Claudian era); Perseus with the head of Medusa; Cupid and Psyche from the House of Cupid and Psyche; replica of the crouching Venus of Doidalsas (3C BC); statue of the Three Graces.

The glass cases between Room VI and Room VIII contain Attic pottery (including a fragment of a red-figure cup showing Orpheus dating from the second half of 5C BC), Aretine vases, and 'terra sigillata' ware. **Room VIII** (SALA GUIDO CALZA). Roman sculpture from the 1C BC to the mid-2C AD. Headless male *statue, nude except for the drapery over the left arm, signed with the name of the donor C. Cartilius Poplicola, whose sarcophagus is near Porta Marina. This statue is regarded as the best extant copy of the type known as the 'Hero in Repose'; portraits of Augustus, Trajan (including a statue of him wearing a cuirass), Hadrian, Sabina, wife of Hadrian, and a group of portraits of members of the family of Marcus Aurelius. Herm of Hippocrates (from an original of 3C BC); funerary statue of Giulia Procula; relief (fragment of an architectural frieze) showing the sacred geese in front of the Temple of Juno Moneta on the Capitoline. The small cases between Room VIII and Room X contain kitchen pottery, terracotta statuettes, and oil lamps.

Room IX (left of Room X). Roman sarcophagi of the 2–3C AD. The *sarcophagus of a boy, from the Isola Sacra Necropolis, is a magnificent example of the Attic type, dating from the 2C AD; on the lid is the figure of a boy lying on a couch decorated with bas-reliefs; and the three sides have reliefs of Dionysiac rites with a charming frieze of putti (illustrating the direct influence sarcophagi of this type had on artists of the Renaissance). On the back is the scene of a wrestling match which was left in a rough, unfinished state. The *sarcophagus from Pianabella (c 160 AD) has scenes from the Iliad, and another sarcophagus has a scene of Lapiths and Centaurs. **Room X**. Roman sculpture (end of 2C to 4C AD). Maxentius(?) as Pontifex Maximus, found in the Edificio degli Augustali; statue of Fausta, sister of Maxentius (AD 310–312); Giulia Domna, in the semblance of Ceres, bust of Septimius Severus, her husband; statue in grey marble of Iside Pelagia, with two fragments of a serpent, also in grey marble, at her feet.

Room XI. Roman art of the 4–5C AD. Magnificent opus sectile *panels found in an edifice near Porta Marina. The design includes various portraits, and a head thought to be that of Christ (with a halo), and two scenes of a lion attacking a horse. Relief showing scribes recording an orator's speech (thought to have a Christian significance), and two portrait busts in marble tondos. Between Room IX and Room XII cases display Roman glass (including a cup engraved with the figure of Christ, the Cross, and the Monogram, 4–5C), and objects in bone, ivory, bronze, and lead. **Room XII** (partly in restoration) displays Imperial wall paintings and mosaic fragments.

Parallel with Via dei Dipinti, on the W is the wide **Cardo Maximus** with arcaded shops, which runs from the Tiber to the Forum and from there to the Porta Laurentina. To the W of this street and also parallel is the narrow VIA TECTA, on the brick walls of which have been affixed many of the best preserved inscriptions found in the ruins. Via Tecta runs beside a grain warehouse called the PICCOLO MERCATO; some of its rooms form the Antiquarium Ostiense housing archaelogical material (no adm). In the S wall have been incorporated several layers of the tufa blocks of the primitive city walls. The Cardo Maximus runs S to the **Forum**, which is traversed from E to W by the Decumanus Maximus. At the N end of the Forum is the *Capitolium, the city's most important temple, dedicated to Jupiter, Juno, and Minerva. This prostyle hexastyle building, dating from the first half of the 2C, had six fluted white marble columns. The pronaos is reached by a wide flight of steps, in front of which is an altar (reconstructed). In the cella are niches and a plinth for statues of the deities. During the Barbarian invasions the temple was stripped of nearly all its marble facing, but a magnificent slab of African marble is still in place on the threshold and a few surviving marble fragments have been placed to the E of the building under a colonnade, which defined the sacred area.

Opposite the Capitolium, on the S side of the Forum, are the remains of the 1C TEMPLE OF ROME AND AUGUSTUS. Like the Capitolium it had six fluted marble columns across the front, but with two side staircases. Fragments of the pediment have been placed on a modern wall to the E; the cult statue of Rome as Victory, dressed as an Amazon, has been placed inside the temple on a plinth, and a headless statue of Victory near the rearranged pediment fragments.

On the E side of the Forum are the BATHS OF THE FORUM, built in the 2C and restored in the 4C. When restored the baths were decorated with mosaics and cipollino columns; some of the columns have been re-erected. The FRIGIDARIUM survives, together with a series of rooms warmed by hot air. Off the N side is the town FORICA (public lavatory), with its 20 seats all but completely preserved. Also on the E side, at the corner where the Decumanus Maximus enters the Forum, is the CASA DEI TRICLINI, so called from the couches in each of the three rooms on the right wing of the central courtyard. Behind the courtyard is a room with a high podium decorated with coloured marbles.

Opposite, on the W side of the Forum, is the BASILICA, or law courts and place of assembly. The façade towards the Forum had a portico of marble arches with a decorated frieze. Fragments of this decoration and of the columns have been preserved. To the S of the Basilica is the TEMPIO ROTONDO, dating from the 3C and probably an AUGUSTEUM, or temple erected to the worship of the emperors. The peristyle was paved with mosaics and surrounded by marble-faced niches. It was reached by a flight of steps (preserved), which led to the pronaos; this comprised a portico with brick piers faced with marble and with cipollino columns. In the cella are seven niches, three rectangular and four circular. Between the niches are column bases; to the right are the remains of a spiral staircase that led to the dome.

Also on the W side, N of the Decumanus Maximus, is the CURIA, or senate house. The inscriptions on the walls are lists of *Augustales*, citizens of Ostia belonging to the cult of the emperors. Beside the Curia is the CASA DEL LARARIO, or House of the Shrine of the Lares, a combination of a house and shopping centre.

Leaving the Forum the Decumanus Maximus continues to the PORTA OCCIDENTALE, the West Gate of the original Castrum; the ancient walls are well seen in Via degli Horrea Epagathiana, a turning on the right. In this street are the *HORREA EPAGATHIANA ET EPAPHRODITIANA, warehouses in a remarkable state of preservation, and used as a sherd store (no adm). They were built by two Eastern freedmen, Epagathus and Epaphroditus, whose names are preserved on a marble plaque above the entrance; this is a brick portal with two engaged columns supporting a pediment. The inner courtyard was surrounded by an arcade of brick piers, repeated on the upper floor. On the walls of the vestibule and courtyard are four intact aediculae. In a large vaulted room at the rear of the Horrea are further remains of the primitive town wall.

The region to the W of the Decumanus Maximus was excavated in 1938–42. The Decumanus Maximus now forks. The right fork is VIA DELLA FOCE (Street of the River Mouth); it has been excavated for c 270m. The left fork is the continuation of the Decumanus Maximus (see above) and runs SW to the Porta Marina, or Sea Gate.

In Via della Foce, on the left, a long passageway leads to the MITREO DELLE PARETI DIPINTE, built in the 2C into a house of the Republican period. The Mithraeum is divided into two sections by partly projecting walls with ritual niches. The two stucco-faced galleries of the inner section also have niches. In the rear wall is the brick-built altar, with a marble cippus on which is a bust of Mithras. On the N wall are paintings of initiation rites.

A short street to the right leads to the SACRED AREA OF THREE REPUBLICAN TEMPLES. The central and largest is the prostyle hexastyle TEMPLE OF HERCULES INVICTUS. The pronaos, paved with mosaics, is reached by a flight of nine steps as wide as the façade. Inside the cella was a small marble column carved to represent the club of Hercules with the lion skin thrown over it. The temple, which may date from the time of Sulla, was given an altar in the 4C AD by Hostilius Antipater, Praefectus Annonae. On the N side of the Sacred Area is a TETRASTYLE TEMPLE (dedication unknown) of the same date as the first. Between the Temple of Hercules and Via della Foce is the TEMPLE OF THE AMORINI, named after a round marble altar with winged cupids found there. It was built in the early Republican and rebuilt in the Imperial period. Its final form was distyle in antis.

Behind the temple is a street leading to the ***House of Cupid and Psyche**, a Domus dating from the end of the 3C. It is named after a marble group found in it and now in the Museum. On the W side of the central atrium are four rooms, one with a pavement of coloured marbles (and a copy of the statue); on the E is an attractive nymphaeum in a courtyard with columns and brick arches. At the N end of the Atrium is a large room paved with opus sectile, and preserving some marble mural facing. Farther along Via della Foce is VIA DELLE TERME DI MITRA (right). The BATHS OF MITHRAS date from the time of Trajan and were rebuilt in the 2C. They had elaborate systems for heating and for pumping water. In the basement is a Mithraeum, in which was found the group of Mithras and the Bull, now in the Museum.

Roman temples 'in antis', after Vitruvius, architect and surveyor to Augustus ('De architectura', before AD 27), published by Carlo Amati in 1829

On the left side of the main street are three blocks of small apartment houses; then follows a complex of two apartment blocks with baths between them. The INSULA DI SERAPIDE is named after a figure of Serapis in an aedicula in the courtyard. The TERME DEI SETTE SAPIENTI were so called from a satirical painting of the Seven Sages found in one of the rooms. The Sages are distinguished by name (in Greek); to each of them is attached a frank inscription on the subject of health. The baths have a round central hall (once domed), paved with a beautiful *mosaic with five concentric rows of hunting scenes, including what appears to be a tiger. In a room next to a marble plunge pool is a painting of Venus Anadyomene. A passage leads to the extensive INSULA DEGLI AURIGHI, an apartment block with a large central courtyard. Two small paintings of charioteers belonging to opposing factions in the E wall of the arcade give the house its name. Off the N walk is a flat of six rooms with interesting paintings. Beyond the E side of the courtyard is a shrine presumably of Mithras.

Farther along Via della Foce, on the left, is a group of buildings of Hadrian's time. The BATHS OF TRINACRIA preserve good mosaics, and interesting installations for heating and conducting the water. On the other side of Via Serapeo is the HOUSE OF BACCHUS AND ARIADNE, with rich floral mosaics. The SERAPEUM, behind, was dedicated in AD

127, and included a temple, with courtyard flanked by porticoes and cult rooms. To the W, originally connected with the Serapeum, is a fine domus, with more mosaics.

Beyond the Insula degli Aurighi is VIA DEGLI AURIGHI, which runs E to join the extension of the Decumanus Maximus. In this street are the INSULA DELLE CELLE (left), a type of warehouse with small rooms, and, opposite, a modest hotel with a stable called ALBERGO CON STALLA. This inn also faces a street named after the INSULA DELLE VOLTE DIPINTE (no adm), with painted ceilings. Across the street is the *Casa delle Muse (closed for many years), dating from the time of Hadrian. This house has a central courtyard with a covered arcade. The restored wooden roof of the arcade rests on the ancient brick cornice. In a room to the E are paintings of Apollo and the Muses; in one to the N are panel paintings of divinities and satyrs. On a wall of the arcade are some graffiti, one of them representing the lighthouse of Ostia.

To the right is the CASA A PARETI GIALLE, or House with the Yellow Walls. This looks on to a vast square of four large apartment houses built round a garden and known as the CASE A GIARDINO. The scale of construction, the provision of a private garden, and the absence of shops all indicate that the flats in these buildings were intended for the wealthier inhabitants of Ostia.

The Decumanus Maximus, and its extension from the fork outside the West Gate, continues SW and runs for 350m to the Porta Marina and, beyond it, to the sea-coast. The PORTA MARINA, or Sea Gate, was an opening in the walls built by Sulla, remains of which may be seen. Just inside the gate is a wine-shop, the CAUPONA DI ALEXANDER, and, outside, a large square. The extension of the Decumanus Maximus beyond the gate, built in the time of Augustus, ran through an earlier cemetery (see below). On this section is the SANTUARIO DELLA BONA DEA, a small prostyle tetrastyle temple, whose four column bases survive. Farther towards the sea is the DOMUS FULMINATA, with a small monument recording the fact that the house had been struck by lightning. Opposite, Via di Cartilio Poplicola leads to the BATHS OF PORTA MARINA past the TOMB OF L. CARTILIUS POPLICOLA, a prominent citizen. The surviving fragment of its decorative frieze shows a trireme with the helmeted head of a goddess. This and another tomb close by attest to the existence of a cemetery in the Republican era.

On the outskirts of the town towards the shore, and between the sea and the ancient Via Severiana (on the SW side of this street), is the most ancient Jewish **Synagogue** known from monumental remains. It was in continuous use from the 1C to the 5C AD. Ritual carvings and poorly preserved mosaics have been found; several Ionic columns have been re-erected. It was discovered in 1961–63 when the new road to Fiumicino airport was constructed.

The Decumanus Maximus returns past the charming FONTANA A LUCERNA. In a street to the S beyond the junction with Via degli Aurighi is a block of shops with windows beside their doors. Close by is the SCHOLA DI TRAIANO, seat of an Ostian corporation named after a statue of Trajan found in it. In the courtyard, which has stuccoed brick columns, is a long basin provided with niches. The central room has a headless statue of Fortuna and a mosaic pavement. The school overlays earlier constructions, among them a 1C Domus; its nymphaeum has been partly restored. On the opposite side of the main street is the SCHOOL OF THE NAVAL SMITHS, with a temple. The arcade of the courtyard in front of the temple was evidently a marble store: unused and partly finished columns, bases and capitals have been found in it. The store appears to have belonged to Volusianus, a senator of the 4C, as his name is carved on some of the column shafts. Adjoining is the CHRISTIAN BASILICA, an unpretentious structure with two aisles divided by columns and ending in apses. Vico del Dionisio leads S to the CORTILE DI DIONISIO, surrounded by several houses, and to the MITREO DELLE SETTE PORTE, a Mithraeum which displays in seven arches the seven grades of the Mithraic cult.

The Decumanus Maximus continues to (right) the MACELLUM, or market, which occupies the area between the Decumanus and a street running S, VIA OCCIDENTALE DEL POMERIO. The market has numerous shops; two fish-shops open on to the Decumanus. Behind them is the market-place. Via Occidentale del Pomerio and Via del Tempio Rotondo behind the Tempio Rotondo at the S end of the Forum lead to the S continuation of the Cardo Maximus. On the right here is the DOMUS DI GIOVE FULMINATORE, a house of the Republican period remodelled in the 4C, with a striking phallic 'doormat' mosaic. Beside it is the DOMUS DELLA NICCHIA A MOSAICO, another Republican house, twice rebuilt. It is named after a semicircular niche faced with polychrome mosaic in the tablinum. Adjoining is the NINFEO DEGLI EROTI, with well-preserved marble floor and walls and niches in which were found two copies of the Eros of Lysippos. The next building is the DOMUS DELLE COLONNE, a large corner house, with façades on the Cardo Maximus and on Via della Caupona del Pavone (right). In the centre of the courtyard is a stone basin with a double apse and short white marble columns; beyond is the large tablinum with its entrance between two columns.

In the side street is an ancient wine-shop, the 3C CAUPONE DEL PAVONE. One of its rooms is decorated with paintings of flying bacchanals and muses; beyond is the bar, with a counter and small basins. On the opposite side of the street is the DOMUS DEI PESCI, evidently a Christian house. A vestibule has a mosaic with a chalice and fishes. A large room on the S side, with two marble columns, has a fine mosaic *floor.

The Cardo Maximus passes on the right the PORTICO DELL'ERCOLE; opposite is a fulling mill. Adjoining are the TERME DEL FARO. In a floor of the frigidarium of the baths is a mosaic with fishes, sea monsters, and a lighthouse (pharos), after which the baths were named. One of the rooms has a white marble pool and frescoed walls in the 3C style. A ramp leads from the Cardo to the triangular CAMPO DELLA MAGNA MATER, one of the best preserved sacred areas of the Roman world. At the W corner is the prostyle hexastyle TEMPLE OF CYBELE. At the E corner the SANCTUARY OF ATTIS has an apse flanked by telamones in the shape of fauns. On the same side is the TEMPLE OF BELLONA, dating from the time of Marcus Aurelius, and, opposite, the SCHOLA DEGLI HASTIFERES, seat of an association connected with the cult of Bellona. The sanctuary is close to the PORTA LAURENTINA, which retains the tufa blocks of Sulla's circumvallation (c 80 BC).

To the S of the Porta Laurentina, along the line of the ancient Via Laurentina, is (500m) the CEMETERY OF THE PORTA LAURENTINA, first excavated in 1865 and systematically explored in 1934–35. Many of the inscriptions relate to freedmen. Beyond the motorway, in the locality called PIANABELLA, excavations begun in 1976 have revealed a necropolis and Christian basilica.

A short distance back along the Cardo Maximus, the SEMITA DEI CIPPI leads to the right (N). This street is flanked by two cippi and contains a 3C Domus (CASA DEL PROTIRO), its reconstituted portal prettily flanked by cypresses.

To the N a right turn leads into a street named after the HOUSE OF FORTUNA ANNONARIA, which has a garden in its peristyle. On the W side of the peristyle is a large room with three arches, columns, and a nymphaeum. At the end of the street, on the right, is another temple of Bona Dea, with a Mithraeum next door, notable for its mosaic pavement. Also in the street is the DOMUS REPUBLICANA, with four Doric columns; it is adjoined by the EDIFICIO DEGLI AUGUSTALI, the headquarters of the Augustales. This building has another entrance in Via degli Augustali, which leads to the Decumanus Maximus, and the main entrance.

Across the road from the entrance to the excavations is the borgo of **OSTIA ANTICA**, a fortified village whose walls are still standing, founded by Gregory IV in 830 and given the name of *Gregoriopolis*. There are now some modern houses outside the walls which enclose a tiny picturesque hamlet beside the castle and church. The *CASTLE (closed many years ago for restoration), is a splendid building erected in 1483–86 by Baccio Pontelli for Julius II while still a cardinal. It houses archaeological collections from the excavations, medieval material, and frescoes by Baldassarre Peruzzi. The church of SANTA AUREA, by Baccio Pontelli or Meo del Caprina, contains the body of the martyred St Aurea (died 268), and, in a side chapel, a fragment of the gravestone of St Monica (who died at Ostia in 387; see above), mother of St Augustine. The Episcopal Palace has fine frescoes by Baldassarre Peruzzi (1508–13). It is the residence of the Bishop of Ostia, holder of one of the six suburbicarian sees allotted to the cardinal bishops.

Via del Mare continues to **LIDO DI OSTIA**, (61,600 inhab.), now usually called just **OSTIA**, on the coast. It can also be reached direct from EUR in Rome by a 'superstrada' (Via Cristoforo Colombo), built in 1936, in 27km. The lido became Rome's seaside resort after the First World War, and under the Fascist regime was planned as a district of the capital. Ostia is now an ugly suburb of Rome with numerous high-rise blocks of flats, and is still used as a resort by thousands of Romans in summer. It has some monumental edifices erected in 1916–40, but has been ruined by indiscriminate new buildings. On the sea-front, in Piazza Anco Marzio, a monument by Pietro Consagra was set up in 1993 to the writer and film director Pier Paolo Pasolini found murdered on 2 November 1975 at the IDROSCALO, a former seaplane station near the mouth of the Tiber, W of the esplanade (where another neglected monument stands). Nearby survives the Tor San Michele built in 1568 by Nanni di Baccio Bigio in 1568 on a design by Michelangelo.

To the E is the **Lido di Castel Fusano** in a beautiful pine forest. The first pines were planted here c 1710, and in 1755 the property was acquired by the Chigi family and was afterwards let as a royal chase. In 1932 it was bought by the Commune of Rome and in 1933 part of it was opened as a public park. There are long-term plans to connect it, as one huge nature reserve of some 6000 hectares, to the forests of Castel Porziano and Capocotta to the S (see Rte 29). This is the largest coastal forest in the country.

From Ostia Antica (see above) a branch road (signposted for Fiumicino) skirts the fence protecting the excavations, curving right on a spur from Via del Mare. It passes close to the remains of the synagogue (described above). Beyond the Tiber and a set of traffic lights, the road passes a huge old industrial building and at a pedestrian crossing (traffic lights) a narrow road (inconspicuous sign for 'necropoli di Porto') leads right. The first by-road left ends at the entrance to the **Necropoli di Porto** or **Isola Sacra** (open every day 9.00–17.00, or 18.00 in summer), in a pretty group of trees. This was the necropolis of the port of Claudius and the later port of Trajan, later known as Porto (see below), particularly important for its 2–3C tombs. It is situated on the **Isola Sacra**, a tract of land made into an island by the cutting of the Fossa Traiana from Porto to the sea. Only part of the site has been excavated as much of it is under cultivation (and some of the tombs are at present being restored).

Since the necropolis was the burial-place of the middle- and lower-class inhabitants of Porto such as merchants, artisans, craftsmen, and sailors, there are no elaborate mausolea. The tombs, which have been preserved by the sand that covered them for centuries, are arranged in groups. They have or had barrel vaults of brick and masonry faced with stucco; some of them had gable roofs. Internally they are decorated with stuccoes, paintings, and mosaics. Sarcophagi and urns in columbaria have been found, often in the same tomb, evidence of the simultaneous practice of burial and cremation. Many of the sarcophagi are adorned with mythological reliefs; terracotta reliefs have representations of arts and crafts, indicating the trade of the deceased. Nearly every tomb has a name inscribed over the door. The tombs of the wealthier citizens have sepulchral chambers, with fanlights. Outside, by the door, are couches for funeral feasts.

Some of the tombs are like old-fashioned round-topped travelling trunks, and recall similar examples in North Africa. The poorest citizens, who could not afford the cost of a monument, buried their dead in the ground and marked the place with amphorae through which they poured libations; or they set up large tiles to form a peaked roof over the remains. The Isola Sacra, once a flourishing horticultural centre, was abandoned after the fall of the Western Empire, and became an uninhabited malarial marsh. It was reclaimed in 1920 when the swamps were drained, roads ballasted, and canals dug.

The road through the cemetery, the Via Flavia, is a section of the ancient road from Ostia to Porto. The tombs are numbered with small marble plaques. Of particular interest are: a CHAMBER TOMB (11), with a marble sarcophagus with a scene of a funeral feast, and two other sarcophagi; the TOMB OF THE CHILDREN (16), with an entrance mosaic of the Nile; the TOMB OF THE SMITH (29), with a façade divided by three pilasters and terracotta reliefs indicating the man's trade; the TOMB OF TELESPHORUS AND JULIA EUNIA (39), with the Christian symbols of the lamb, dove, and anchor, apparently unique in this cemetery; a two-storeyed tomb (41); a tomb with a ship mosaic with the Pharos of Porto (43). In the row behind are two tombs (55 and 56), the first pedimental, the second with a square-corniced façade, both preserving their inscriptions. Close by are a series of FOUR CHAMBER TOMBS (77–80), with pedimental façades with reliefs.

Near the necropolis is the church of **Sant'Ippolito** where excavations, still in progress, have revealed interesting palaeochristian remains and a large medieval basilica (not yet open to the public).

The main road continues towards the airport of Fiumicino (leaving on the right a road signposted 'Fiumicino' and 'Isola Sacra'). Beyond a viaduct, and a road left for Fiumicino and Fregene, the road crosses a railway and a canal before entering the **Airport of Fiumicino** (sign across the road). The airport, officially called 'Leonardo da Vinci', takes its other name from the nearby ugly seaside town, which was heavily bombed in the Second World War. With graceful cantilevered buildings, it was opened in 1961. At the roundabout this road keeps right, and on the left of the road, just before a war memorial and the main airport buildings, is the ***Museo delle Navi Romane** (open every day 9.00–13.00; Tuesday and Thursday, also 14.00–17.00 or 18.00). This fine purpose-built museum, opened in 1979, houses remains of five Roman boats found here at the entrance to the Port of Claudius. They include four flat-bottomed cargo ships or barges used to carry goods upstream to Rome, dating from AD 300–400, and a fishing boat (1C AD). Various objects found in the excavations, including lead seals and anchors, are also displayed here, and explanatory diagrams explain the history of the ports. There is a good view of the boats from the balcony.

The Museum stands in the area once occupied by the **Port of Claudius**. When the harbour of Ostia, already inadequate for its trade, began to silt up with the action of the Tiber, Augustus planned this larger sea port. In AD 42 Claudius began operations. It was connected to the Tiber by a canal. The work was completed in 54 by Nero, who issued commemorative coins stamped *Portus Augusti*. With an area of some 80 ha, and a wharf frontage of 800m, it was the most important commercial port in the Mediterranean. Part of the site is now covered by the airport buildings, and the grassy fields near the museum, in which fragments of the quays and buildings can be seen. Part of the quay survives which incorporated the form of Caligula's ship (104m x 20m) which brought the obelisk, now in Piazza San Pietro, from Egypt. The ship was sunk and used as the base of a huge four-storeyed lighthouse.

However even this harbour soon silted up, and in 103 Trajan constructed a hexagonal artificial basin, the **Port of Trajan** farther inland to the S, and better protected. It was connected to the Port of Claudius by a series of docks. This is reached from the airport by Via Portuense, an ancient road which followed the right bank of the Tiber from Rome to the Port. The remains of the port include the hexagonal *basin (650m across), perfectly preserved, constructed with travertine blocks. More than one hundred ships could be moored here at any one time, and it was surrounded by warehouses. It shows up excellently from the air when landing at Fiumicino, but it is enclosed and only visible with special permission or on guided tours organised by the Soprintendenza Archeologica di Ostia (information at the Museo delle Navi). This area, for years private property owned by the Torlonia and occupied by a safari park, is to be expropriated to save it from further destruction and the 'Parco del Litorale Romano', a coastal archaeolgical park and nature reserve may one day be opened here. Excavations have unearthed the remains of granaries, a wall, a high arch in red brick, an underground passageway, etc. To the W are more ruins, including a monumental portico, at present still overgrown and abandoned. Trajan as well as Claudius dug canals in connection with the seaport. The FOSSA TRAIANA (now the Canale di Fiumicino) survives as a navigable canal between the Tiber and the sea. Numerous marble columns and coloured marbles, imported from all over the Empire destined for ancient Rome, have been found in the area.

The village of **Porto**, 2km from the airport, on the Via Portuensis, takes its name from the ancient city of PORTUS, which grew up around the ports of Claudius and Trajan. It was favoured as a seaport by Constantine at the expense of Ostia; in 314 it had its own bishop and became known as *Civitas Constantina*. In the village are the church of SANTA RUFINA (10C, rebuilt), an old episcopal palace, and the Villa Torlonia. The suburbicarian see of Porto and Santa Rufina is one of the six held by the cardinal bishops.

A motorway (26km) leads directly back to Rome from the airport, which is also connected to the Stazione Ostiense and Stazione Tiburtina in Rome by a railway line opened in 1990.

29

Anzio and Nettuno

ROAD (Via Pontina), 60km. Buses from Rome (EUR 'Fermi' station on the underground) to Anzio and Nettuno.

RAILWAY. From Rome (Termini) to Anzio (57km) in c 1 hr; to Nettuno (60km) in 3 minutes more.

Both road and railway cross the **Agro Pontino**, a plain extending SW to the coast of Lazio from the Via Appia (N 7) between Cisterna di Latina and Terracina. Formerly known as the *Pontine Marshes* or *Pomptine Marshes* it is regarded as a part of the Roman Campagna in the widest sense of the term. Since Roman times the plain has been marshy, though when the Appian Way was built in 213 BC, the marshes must have covered a relatively small area since it seems there were 23 towns here. One of these towns was *Pontia*, which gave its name to the district. The marshes, formed by numerous small streams which could not find their way to the sea and therefore stagnated, steadily increased, and, with the spread of malaria, the population dwindled, and the area was left with a sinister reputation.

Julius Caesar planned to drain the marshes but his assassination wrecked the project. In the time of Augustus a navigable canal, which partly drained off the waters, ran alongside the Appian Way. Horace used this canal in the course of his journey from Rome to Brundusium in 37 BC (*Satires*, I, 5); he embarked on the canal barge at Appii Forum (at the 43rd milestone on the Appian Way) and left it at Anxur (Terracina). No further work of importance was undertaken until the 16C, when Leo X (1513–21) cut the *Canale Portatore* to run from the Appian Way into the sea at Porto Badino, W of Terracina. Sixtus V (1585–90) built a more ambitious canal, the *Fossa Sisto*, which runs parallel to the Appian Way on its SW side and reaches the sea to the W of Leo X's canal. Pius VI (1775–99) enlarged the Canale Portatore and built the *Canale Linea Pio*, which accompanies the Appian Way for 30km.

In 1928 the marshes were reclaimed, and in 1932 Littoria, now Latina (see 'Blue Guide Southern Italy'), was founded in the centre of the Agro Pontino. Sabaudia, on the coast near Monte Circeo was built in 1934, followed by Pontinia (1935), Aprilia (1937), and Pomezia (1939). The Second World War caused immense damage, due largely to the repercussions of the bridge-head landings at Anzio (see below).

Via Cristoforo Colombo leaves Rome and passes through EUR, see Rte 26. The road runs beneath the Grande Raccordo Annulare. At (16km) Osteria del Malpasso is an entrance to **Castel Porziano**, once a royal chase and now a holding of the President of the Republic. There are plans to protect the coastal forests of Castel Porziano, Castelfusano, and Capocotta as one huge nature reserve (see Rte 28). Among interesting Roman remains here are a villa of the early Imperial period at Tor Paterno and an aqueduct. The Via Severiana, built by Septimius Severus to link Fiumicino with Terracina, can still be seen in many parts of the forest. 28.5km POMEZIA, the westernmost and latest (1939) of the new towns of the Agro Pontino (see above), stands at a crossroads.

A road (right) leads to (2km) PRÁTICA DI MARE, on the site of **Lavinium**, which, according to an ancient legend, was the town founded by Aeneas, after his escape from Troy, and named after his wife. Numerous ancient Roman historians, as well as Virgil, upheld this myth, and as early as 300

BC a tradition existed at Lavinium itself which attributed its foundation to the Trojan hero. A huge sanctuary with 13 archaic altars in a line have been found here, built in the 6–2C BC, where Penates and Castor and Pollux were worshipped. A tomb sanctuary of Aeneas, in the form of a tumulus burial chamber, was restored in the 4C. An Iron Age necropolis with some 70 tombs has been identified.

To the E, across the modern road to Rome, another sanctuary, dedicated to Minerva, has been excavated. Here the votive deposit included more than 70 remarkable statues (some more than 2m high) made by local Italic craftsmen in the 5C to 2C BC. The terracotta sculptures, many of which have been carefully restored, include some beautiful female portraits, and striking representations of Minerva as the warrior goddess with unusual attributes. The excavation of the city on the hill occupied by the village and Borghese castle continues: so far fragments of 6C walls and the E gate, and baths from the time of Constantine have been found.

Farther along N 148, to the right, is a German military cemetery (with 15,000 graves), and beyond (33.5km) Santa Procula Maggiore, a crossroads where Via Laurentina comes in. **Ardea**, 4.5km to the right, the capital of Turnus, king of the Rutuli, is now a village with some antique remains (temples, a basilica, and fortifications). It was the birthplace of the Italian sculptor Giacomo Manzù (1908–91), and there is a museum (open 9.00–18.00; Saturday and Sunday 9.00–13.30; closed Monday) of his work just outside the village. The road now enters the province of Latina, and Via Pontina runs through the middle of the area of land reclamation (see above).

44km **Aprília** (25,000 inhab.), the fourth of the new towns of the Agro Pontino, was founded in 1937. It lies to the left of the road on a spur of the Alban Hills, 80m above sea-level. After the Allied landings at Anzio and Nettuno on 22 January 1944, Aprília was destroyed in four months of fighting. It had to be completely rebuilt. The main buildings are grouped round Piazza Roma, with the church of San Michele Arcangelo.

Via Nettuense (N 207) leads S. Beyond (48km) Campo di Carne the road traverses an extensive oak wood called the Bosco di Padiglione. 59.5km ANZIO (BEACH HEAD) CEMETERY, with the graves of 2312 members of the British forces who lost their lives in the beach-head operations.

Farther on, the trees of the Villa Aldobrandini can be seen on the left. A few metres N of the railway, which is recrossed, is the smaller ANZIO MILITARY CEMETERY, with 1056 British graves. On rising ground near by is the Carmelite SANTUARIO DI SANTA TERESA DEL BAMBINO GESÙ (1939), in the Romanesque style. Beyond the railway the road descends.

60km **ANZIO** (21,000 inhab.), the ancient *Antium*, known since the 5C BC. It became prominent again in the landings of January 1944, and suffered great damage in the ensuing fighting. Now largely rebuilt, it is a popular seaside resort of the Romans.

History. Antium was one of the chief cities of the Volsci, who were constantly at war with Rome. The city was a centre of commerce and its ship captains were notorious pirates. When Coriolanus was banished from Rome in 491 BC he went over to the enemy against whom he had won fame in battle, and asked Antium for protection. Two years later he withdrew from the gates of Rome, in response to the entreaties of his wife and mother, and returned to Antium. In 468 BC Antium was captured by the Romans, who planted a colony here; in a subsequent revolt it established its independence, but was finally dominated by Rome in 338 BC when all its ships were seized and their beaks sent to adorn the Rostra in the Roman Forum. In the late Republic and early Empire it was a summer resort of wealthy Romans. Cicero describes his villa at

Antium in his letters to Atticus. Horace, in his 'Ode to Fortune', refers to her temple at 'loved Antium'. Caligula and Nero, both natives of the town, erected buildings here. Nero built a magnificent villa, traces of which survive, and the original harbour. The site of the ancient city was a little NE of the present town, on high ground above the Villa Aldobrandini and the Villa Borghese. In the Middle Ages it declined, and the Saracens destroyed the harbour. A new harbour was built in 1698 by Innocent XII, to the E of the old one, and round it grew the modern town.

The landings during the Second World War, far in advance of the main battle line, and timed to follow an Allied attack on it, were devised to cut the German line of communications, to link up with the main Allied forces advancing from the S, and to seize the Alban Hills. The principal objective was to draw off and contain German forces from NW Europe, with the subsidiary hope of capturing Rome. The initial surprise was not exploited, and four months of bitter fighting ensued.

The tree-lined Piazza Pia is the centre of Anzio. From the railway station it is reached by the wide Viale Mencacci, Via Claudio Paolini, Piazza Cesare Battisti, in which is the MUNICIPIO, and Via dei Fabbri. In Piazza Pia is the church of SAN PIO, with a neo-classical portico. The bus terminus for Nettuno is near by. From the square Via Venti Settembre leads to the Riviera Mallozzi, a broad thoroughfare following the coastline to the W, with villas and private beaches. It passes the ancient harbour built by Nero. At the end of the avenue, high up, are the so-called GROTTOES OF NERO, a complex of rectangular chambers.

A little farther, near the promontory of ARCO MUTO, are the ruins of an **Imperial Villa**, known as 'Nero's Villa', built of opus reticulatum. It dates from 2C BC–AD 3C. Here were found the Apollo Belvedere, now in the Vatican, during the pontificate of Julius II (1503–13), the Borghese Gladiator, now in the Louvre in Paris, and (in 1878) the Maiden of Anzio, now in the Museo Nazionale Romano. Arco Muto is the probable site of the Temple of Fortune once visited by countless pilgrims and mentioned by Horace in his 'Ode to Fortune'. A Republican villa is being excavated here. Near the lighthouse some ancient sculptures have been discovered.

On the way back along the shore, the harbour built by Innocent XII is passed on the right. On the right is the breakwater, with a splendid view towards the E: it takes in Villa Aldobrandini and part of Villa Borghese on the left of the town and the wooded coastline as far as Torre Astura, with Monte Circeo in the distance. Via Porto Innocenziano runs along the harbour. From the station Viale Mencacci to the right leads to the railway bridge. VILLA SPIGARELLI (adm on request), reached by Viale Oleandri (left), incorporates remains of a Republican Villa, and has some well-preserved ancient tombs. On the high ground above is the site of the ancient city of ANTIUM; the remains include a small theatre of the Imperial era.

From Piazza Pia, Riviera di Levante, close to the shore, or the parallel Via Gramsci lead out of the town. On the latter road is the VILLA BORGHESE (left; adm on application to the owner) with its fine *park. The coastline between Anzio and (63.5km) Nettuno is almost completely built up.

NETTUNO (24,800 inhab.), comprises a medieval walled town and a modern district in process of rapid development. The well-preserved CASTLE was built for Alexander VI by Antonio da Sangallo the Elder or Baccio Pontelli. Rectangular in plan, with corner bastions and a portcullis, it is surrounded by a moat. Piazza Mazzini is the centre of the modern town. To the right is the medieval Borgo, with its narrow winding alleys and its partly surviving walls. Near Piazza Vittorio Emanuele is the medieval PALAZZO COLONNA. Beyond Piazza Mazzini the BELVEDERE has an extensive view of the bay.

About 1km N of the town, off Via Santa Maria, is the AMERICAN MILITARY CEMETERY, the larger of the two remaining in Italy, with 7862 graves of Americans who lost their lives in the beach-head operations. For Torre Astura, 13km S, see 'Blue Guide Southern Italy'.

The return to Rome (71.5km) may be made via Ostia on the coast road, Via Severiana. This passes through an almost continuous line of unattractive resorts, and can be very crowded in summer. Beyond TOR VAIANICA (28.5km), building is restricted and the President's game reserve stretches on either side of the road. 44.5km OSTIA (Lido di Castel Fusano), and from there to Rome, see Rte 28.

30

The Alban Hills

The *ALBAN HILLS (*Colli Albani*) are an isolated volcanic group over 60km in circumference rising from the Roman Campagna, with foothills reaching to within 12km of Rome. They enclose the two attractive crater lakes of Nemi and Albano, and 13 picturesque towns known as the **Castelli Romani** (Frascati, Monte Porzio Catone, Montecompatri, Rocca Priora, Colonna, Rocca di Papa, Grottaferrata, Marino, Castel Gandolfo, Albano Laziale, Ariccia, Genzano, and Nemi), most of them founded by popes or patrician Roman families. Castel Gandolfo is famous as the Pope's summer residence. Traversed by a confusing number of roads, the hills are now an elegant residential area with numerous villas amidst the chestnut woods. Vineyards on the outer slopes produce the once famous 'Vini dei Castelli'. Some of the towns are visited in summer as cool resorts.

Information Offices. 'Azienda Autonoma dei Laghi e Castelli Romani', 1 Viale Risorgimento, Albano (Tel. 06/9324081). 'Azienda Autonoma del Tuscolo', 1 Piazza Marconi, Frascati (Tel. 06/9420331).

Approaches from Rome. Three itineraries by car from Rome are described below: **A**. VIA TUSCOLANA. 21km Frascati.—24km Grottaferrata. **B**. VIA DEI LAGHI, skirting Lake Albano and Lake Nemi, beautifully landscaped and well provided with parking places and viewpoints. 22km Marino (left).—27km Byroad left for Rocca di Papa.—31km Byroad right for Nemi (1km). **C**. VIA APPIA NUOVA. 21km Castel Gandolfo.—24km Albano Laziale.—26.5km Ariccia.—29.5km Genzano.—39km Velletri.

Railway. Routes from Rome (Termini station) diverge at Ciampino Station for Frascati, Velletri, and Albano Laziale (via Marino and Castel Gandolfo).

Buses from the 'Anagnina' station of the underground (line A) run by 'COTRAL' to Frascati, Rocca di Papa, Grottaferrata, Marino, Castel Gandolfo, Albano, Ariccia, Genzano, Nemi, and Velletri.

Hotels (mostly 3-star and 2-star) are to be found at Albano, Rocca di Papa, Nemi, Castel Gandolfo, Genzano, Ariccia, Frascati (3-star 'Villa Tuscolana'), and Grottaferrata (2-star 'Villa Fiorio').

Restaurants of all kinds in all the towns, especially good in and near Grottaferrata.

Annual Festivals. MARINO: 'Sagra dell'uva' (a wine festival) on the first Sunday in October; NEMI: festival of wild strawberries in June; GENZANO: 'Infiorata', when the main street is carpeted with flowers on the first Sunday after Corpus Domini; FRASCATI: summer prose festival in the theatre of Villa Torlonia.

The hills form the rim of a vast crater in the form of a horseshoe, with its open end on the Via Appia. The numerous summits include Monte Salomone (773m), Monte Ceraso (766m), Maschio di Lariano (891m), Monte Peschio (939m) and Maschio d'Artemisio (812m), highest peak of the Artemisio range. Near the open end of the horseshoe are smaller craters, two of them filled with the lakes of Albano and Nemi, and a third, now dry, comprising the Valle Ariccia. In the centre of the hills is a secondary crater, from which rise the peaks of Monte Cavo (949m) overshadowing Rocca di Papa, and Maschio di Faete, the highest of all (956m) as well as others, including Colle Iano (938m) and La Forcella (807m). All the towns were damaged in 1944 after the Allies landed at Anzio and before they entered Rome.

The VIA TUSCOLANA was a short branch of the Via Latina and ran to Tusculum, to the E of present-day Frascati. The VIA LATINA, which left Rome by the Porta Capena (Rte 14) passed through Ferentinum (Ferentino), Frusino (Frosinone), Aquinum (Aquino), Casinum (Cassino), and Venafrum (Venafro) to Beneventum (Benevento) where it joined the Appian Way. At Ad Bivium, c 145km ESE of Rome, it was joined by the VIA LABICANA, now Via Casilina or N 6 (see Rte 31).

A. Rome to Frascati and Grottaferrata

The direct road to Frascati (21km) is the Via Tuscolana. Rome is left by Porta San Giovanni (Pl. 10; 3); Via Appia Nuova continues for a short distance to Piazza Sulmona where (left) Via Tuscolana (N 215) begins. 7.5km Porta Furba incorporates an arch of the Acqua Felice, with a fountain built by Clement XII (1730–40); near by are remains of the Acqua Claudia. 10km CINECITTÀ, the centre of the Italian film industry, opened in 1937. It is probably the only film studio in the world which provides facilities for a complete motion picture production. It covers an area of 600,000 mq, with 14 theatres. After the War it was used by Visconti, De Sica, and Rossellini and soon attracted international film directors and stars from Hollywood. In the 1950s and early sixties 'colossals' such as 'Quo Vadis?' and 'Cleopatra', with some of the largest sets ever constructed, were made at Cinecittà. Antonioni and Pasolini worked here, but it is above all associated with the name of Federico Fellini (died 1993) who here created the grandiose sets for many of his films. It is now also often used by television companies. On the right, beyond an avenue of pine trees, are seen the scattered ruins of the Villa of the Quintilii (see Rte 17). At (11.5km) Cantoniera Via Anagnina forks to the right (see below); while this road crosses the Grande Raccordo Annulare ring road.

On the right is the medieval Torre di Mezzavia (76m), marking the half-way point between Rome and Frascati. A little farther is (left) the battlemented Torre dei Santi Quattro. 17km Osteria del Vermicino, with a fountain dating from the time of Clement XII. The road crosses over the old Rome–Naples railway and the Frascati railway (retrospective views of Rome), and soon passes on the right Villa Sora, once a residence of Gregory XIII (1572–85) and now a college of the Salesians.

21km **FRASCATI** (18,000 inhab.) in a beautiful position on the NW slopes of the Alban Hills, is perhaps the most elegant of the Castelli Romani, famous for its villas and parks. Over 80 per cent of its buildings were destroyed or damaged in 1943–44. The white wine of Frascati was once renowned.

Frascati was overshadowed by Tusculum in Roman days. A small village in the Middle Ages, it expanded in 1191, when the inhabitants of Tusculum, after the destruction of their city, moved to the area around the ancient churches of Santa Maria and San Sebastiano in Frascata. Later it was a feudal holding and at the beginning of the 16C, it was taken by the Holy See. Henry, Cardinal York, was Bishop of Frascati and died here in 1807; the body of his brother, the Young Pretender (died 1788) was buried in the Duomo of Frascati, before being moved to the Vatican Grottoes. As the army headquarters of Field-Marshal Kesselring in 1943–44, Frascati was heavily bombed by the Allies early in September 1943, just before the landings at Salerno.

The huge PIAZZA MARCONI is dominated by the Villa Aldobrandini (see below) splendidly sited on a hill above the square. Below its terraced gardens a magnificent clipped hedge descends to the entrance gate. Opposite the villa is a balustrade with a wide view of the plain (and the railway station below, reached by a long flight of steps through gardens). In the centre of the square, with a few palm trees, is a First World War Memorial by Cesare Bazzani. Opposite the yellow MUNICIPIO (admission 9.00–12.00) which escaped serious War damage (and which contains a statue of Giovanni Ceccarini by Antonio Canova), is the entrance to the disappointing public park of VILLA TORLONIA (the lower part used as a car park). The villa where Annibal Caro lived from 1563 until his death in 1566 was destroyed in the War. The gardens, above monumental terraces on the hillside, contain a fountain terrace by Carlo Maderno.

*Villa Aldobrandini is the finest of the Frascati villas. It was designed by Giacomo Della Porta and built by Carlo Maderno in 1598–1603 for Cardinal Pietro Aldobrandini. The superb *GARDEN (entrance in Via Cardinal Massaia; open 9.00–13.00 except Saturday and Sunday, with permission from the 'Azienda Autonoma del Tuscolo' in Piazza Marconi), laid out at the same time, is one of the best Baroque gardens in Italy, and was much admired by John Evelyn. It was carefully repaired after War damage. There is a magnificent view extending to Rome. Paths lead up to the gardens behind the villa. Facing the fine rear façade is the *TEATRO DELL'ACQUA, a large semicircular nymphaeum with statuary and fountains designed by Giacomo della Porta and completed by Giovanni Fontana and Carlo Maderno. In the central niche the figure of Atlas is supposed to represent pope Clement VIII, Pietro Aldobrandini's uncle. On the wooded hillside above a water-staircase bordered by tall hedges descends from two 'Columns of Hercules' decorated with mosaic. From the columns there is a view of the large park with magnificent ilexs and chestnut trees. A small formal garden survives to the right of the Teatro dell'Acqua. The villa, still owned by the Aldobrandini, is not open to the public: the rooms are decorated with paintings by the Zuccari, Cavalier d'Arpino, and the school of Domenichino.

From Piazza Roma, Via Battisti leads to Piazza San Pietro, rebuilt after its devastation in the War. The fountain by Girolamo Fontana was restored. The DUOMO, on the right, has preserved most of its façade, also by Girolamo Fontana, as well as the unattractive bell-towers of later date. The interior has an interesting plan by Mascherino (1598). It contains a Madonna of the Rosary after Domenichino (third chapel on right) and a relief by Pompeo Ferrucci over the high altar. To the left of the main door is the cenotaph of Prince Charles Edward (see above).

In Piazza del Gesù, beyond the fountain, is the church of the GESÙ, attributed to Pietro da Cortona, also restored after War damage. It contains remarkable perspective paintings by Andrea dal Pozzo. Via Cairoli, to the left of the church, leads to Piazza Paolo III, in which is the CASTLE, built with three towers; it is now the bishop's palace. Beyond it is the rebuilt church of SANTA MARIA DEL VICARIO, or San Rocco, with a fine Romanesque campanile.

FROM FRASCATI TO TUSCULUM, 4km. From Piazza Marconi (see above), to the left of the entrance gate of Villa Aldobrandini Viale Catone leads up between the 16C VILLA LANCELLOTTI, (no admission; still owned by the Lancellotti), with a graceful nymphaeum in its beautiful gardens, just above the road on the right, and the public PARCO DELL'OMBRELLINO on the left. A road (signposted) soon diverges right for Tusculum (4km). This passes a by road (also signposted) which ends at VILLA FALCONIERI ('La Rufina') built in 1545–48 for Bishop Alessandro Ruffini and enlarged for the Falconieri by Borromini. Before reaching the entrance the road passes a splendid gate-way by Borromini (with a tree growing through it). The villa (no admission) was occupied before 1914 by Wilhelm II of Germany, and presented by the State to Gabriele d'Annunzio in 1925. It is now a European Centre for Education where courses are held by the Italian Ministry of Education. The once-famous garden has been altered.

The Tusculum road continues up past the church of the CAPPUCCINI which contains a replica of an altarpiece by Giulio Romano, and paintings by Girolamo Muziano, and Paul Brill. Here also is the tomb of Cardinal Guglielmo Massaia (died 1889), with a statue by Cesare Aureli. Massaia spent 35 years as a missionary in Ethiopia and an interesting museum contains the material he collected there. The road continues, up past the entrance gate of the VILLA TUSCOLANA (now a hotel), surrounded by gardens, fountains and woods. The 16C villa, damaged by bombing, had several owners, including Lucien Bonaparte, Queen Maria Cristina of Sardinia, and Victor Emmanuel II, passing c 1874 to the princely family of Lancellotti.

Farther uphill the road joins a road from Grottaferrata and follows a fence (right), beyond which can be seen a fine stretch of ancient paved Roman road, to end at a car park by the ruins of (4km) **Tusculum** (610m), an Etruscan centre said to have been founded by Telegonus, son of Ulysses and Circe. It was the birthplace of Cato the Censor (234–149 BC). The vicinity became famous in the Imperial period as a resort for wealthy Romans who built numerous suburban villas here, no fewer than 43 of which are mentioned in classical literature. The most famous of these was Cicero's villa, the 'Tusculanum', where the Tusculan Disputations were supposed to have been held. The exact site of the villa has been disputed for centuries. In 1191 the Romans destroyed Tusculum in revenge for their defeat at Monte Porzio Catone in 1167 (see below), and the inhabitants escaped to Frascati. Excavations of the ancient city were begun by Lucien Bonaparte in 1804–20, and continued by Maria Cristina of Sardinia.

The site has been acquired by the XI Comunità Montana del Lazio but is not yet enclosed and not as well kept as it might be. From the car park it is a few minutes walk to the summit of the lower hill with a few overgrown ruins from which the splendid site can be appreciated. There is a fine view of the Alban Hills and of the sea. The so-called FORUM may have been a quadrilateral annexe to the elegant little THEATRE (probably dating from the 1C BC) which is beyond to the left. It is the best preserved of the ruins, although the cavea, hewn out of the hillside, was heavily restored and bears a large inscription commemorating pope Gregory XVI's visit here in 1839.

On the hill above is the site of the acropolis and nearby are fine stretches of Roman road, and traces of walls. In the other direction, beyond the car park, are traces of a sanctuary called, since the 16C, the 'Villa of Cicero' and, at the westernmost point of the city, beneath the hillside, the AMPHI-THEATRE, almost totally overgrown. It measured 80m by 53m, with an arena of 48m by 29m and had room for 3000 spectactors. It probably dates from the 2C AD.

On the way back to Frascati a fork right leads to the CONVENT OF CAMALDOLI, on a hill and dating from 1611, often visited by James Stuart, the Old Pretender.

About 1.5km E of Frascati is VILLA MONDRAGONE, now owned by the University of Torvergata, and being restored. It is reached by Via Matteotti, to the right of the fountain in Piazza San Pietro, and then Via di Villa Borghese to the right. This road leads to Villa Parisi (formerly Villa Borghese) and, just beyond this villa, to the gates of Villa Mondragone. This was built in 1573–75 for Cardinal Altemps mainly by Martino Longhi the Elder. In 1613 it was bought by Cardinal Scipione Borghese, who enlarged it. The so-called *portico of Vignola is by Vasanzio. The terrace commands a good view of Rome. On 24 February 1582 Gregory XIII here issued his famous bull for the reform of the calendar.

FROM FRASCATI TO MONTE PORZIO CATONE, MONTECOMPATRI, and ROCCA PRIORA, 11km. The road leaves Frascati to the NE, and at a fork bears right from the road to Colonna. It passes on the right the entrance to Villa Borghese and the monumental entrance to Villa Mondragone (see above). 3.5km **Monte Porzio Catone** (451m; 4000 inhab.), is one of the 13 Castelli. Here the inhabitants of Tusculum, helped by Frederick Barbarossa, won a victory over the Romans in 1167. 6.5km **Montecompatri** (583m), is another of the Castelli, with 5400 inhabitants. It is in a charming position on a rise. Successor to the ancient 'Labicum', it was later owned by the Annibaldi and the Colonna. Its 17C parish church was enlarged in the 19C. A short distance SW of the town is the convent of SAN SILVESTRO, with a fine view. The early 17C church contains a painting by Gherardo Honthorst.

Outside the town the road forks; the right branch leads to (11km) **Rocca Priora** (768m), also one of the Castelli, with 4400 inhabitants, situated on the N side of the great crater of the Alban Hills, overlooking the classical Valle Latina. It was once thought to have been built on the site of the ancient 'Corbio', but was probably the first town built in the neighbourhood after the destruction of Tusculum in the 12C. In the 14C it belonged to the Savelli, after which it was taken by the Holy See.

From Piazza Marconi in Frascati Viale Vittorio Veneto runs below Villa Torlonia and branches left for Grottaferrata. This road passes the 17C VILLA MUTI with a splendid formal green *garden probably laid out by Cardinal Pompeo Arrigoni in 1595, with box parterres, surrounded by a large park. The villa and its grounds were sequestered in 1987 to prevent their alteration. The once beautiful VILLA GRAZIOLI (privately owned), also on this road, is being restored as a hotel and conference centre.

24km **GROTTAFERRATA** (329m; 11,300 inhab.) is known for its important monastery, and some of the finest Castelli wines were once produced in the area. At the lower end of the Corso del Popolo is the entrance (poorly signposted) to the *Abbazia di Grottaferrata**, enclosed by massive walls and bastions erected by order of Cardinal Della Rovere in 1483–91, probably by Baccio Pontelli or Antonio da Sangallo. Cars can be parked in the castle courtyard which has a statue of St Nilus by Raffaele Zaccagnini (1904). On the left is the entrance gate to the abbey founded by St Nilus, a Greek abbot who came from Rossano Calabro, and died here in 1004. The monastery was built by his disciple St Bartholomew (also from Rossano; died c 1065), who was a composer of Greek hymns and wrote a biography of St Nilus. Some 26 Basilian monks still live here; they are Roman Catholics who celebrate according to the Byzantine Greek rite.

The interesting **Museum**, founded in 1875, is shown by a monk (ring at the gate; 9.00–12.00, 16.30–18.00; Sunday 8.30–10.00, 16.30–18.00; closed Monday). The entrance is from the second courtyard beneath a beautiful portico with Corinthian columns attributed to Giuliano da Sangallo, beneath which are archaeological fragments. ROOM I contains a beautiful classical Greek *stele dating from 430–420 BC, showing a seated male figure reading from a scroll. The relief of the burial of a warrior dates from the time of Hadrian. ROOM II has busts of Euripides and Homer, and Roman statues. Sarcophagi of the 2–4C AD are displayed in ROOM III.

ROOM IV. 13C detached frescoes from the nave of the church (see below) with Old Testament scenes (and copies of them made at the end of the 19C). The 15C chalice and paten were presented to the monastery by Cardinal Bessarion. A good painting of Saints Benedict and Nicola is attributed to Stefano d'Antonio or Neri di Bicci. Church silver and Crosses as well as 12–13C Sicilian ceramics are also displayed here. A few steps lead up to ROOM V which contains finds from excavations in the area including an Iron Age tomb of a woman discovered in 1960 at Rocca di Papa. On the other side of ROOM IV is ROOM VI with a 15C French statue of the Madonna and Child, and a bowl made in Orvieto in the 16C. The vault of this room was frescoed with grotesques illustrating the life of Fabio Massimo by Francesco di Siena in 1547. In the last room are 16C and 17C paintings and 18C copes. The monastery has an important LIBRARY with precious MSS, and there is also a restoration laboratory for books.

From the first courtyard (see above) there is access to the church of **Santa Maria**, consecrated by John XIX in 1025, redesigned internally in 1754 and restored in 1902–30. The PRONAOS was beautifully reconstructed in 1930, and the campanile well restored in 1912. A finely carved Romanesque portal surrounds the 11C wood door. Above is a *mosaic of Christ between the Virgin and St John the Baptist. The font is an antique marble urn, decorated with unusual fishing scenes. In the INTERIOR the roof of the nave dates from 1595; the Byzantine mosaic of the Apostles on the triumphal arch and the damaged fresco above date from the 13C. Frescoes from the clerestory walls have been detached and are now in the Museum. At the beginning of the S aisle is the 'crypta ferrata' (unlocked on request), two small vaulted Roman rooms (probably once a tomb) with iron grilles in the windows, transformed in medieval times into a Christian chapel. It is thought that here the name of the monastery, and later the town, originated.

Also off the S aisle opens the CAPPELLA FARNESIANA, with *frescoes (1609–10) of the lives of St Nilus and St Bartholomew, by Domenichino, considered by many to be his finest works. They were commissioned by Odoardo Farnese and greatly admired by artists and travellers over the centuries. They were restored by Camuccini in 1819, and again in 1990. To the right of the entrance, St Nilus before the Crucifix, and averting a tempest by his prayers. Inside the chapel, to the left: St Nilus and the

Emperor Otho III (the page holding the emperor's horse is Domenichino, and the figures on the right of the horse are Guido Reni and Guercino). On the right, St Bartholomew averting the fall of a pillar during the building of the convent; on the end wall (left of the altar), Exorcism of a devil and (right) the Virgin presenting a golden apple to Saints Nilus and Bartholomew; in the lunette, Death of St Nilus; in the triumphal arch, Annunciation. The altarpiece of the Madonna and Child with the two founders is by Annibale Carracci. The monastery was built on the site of a large Roman villa, and near the church, is a splendid Roman cryptoporticus.

The return to Rome may be made by Via Anagnina (21km). The road partly follows the line of the ancient Via Latina. 3km The BORGHETTO, or Castello Savelli (325m), a ruined 13C castle with 13 towers, built on Roman foundations, passed from the counts of Tusculum to the Savelli, and later to Julius II, who converted it into an outwork of the Abbey of Grottaferrata. The road passes over the old Rome–Naples railway, near (5km) Villa Senni with the entrance gate to the CATACOMBS OF AD DECIMUM (open Saturday afternoon and on Sunday), probably in use from the 3C to the 5C, and so called because they are at the tenth Roman mile from Rome on the Via Latina. They have been owned by the monastery of Grottaferrata since 1910. The well preserved tombs have traces of frescoes and numerous inscriptions. Nearby is a stretch of the ancient Roman paving of Via Latina. At (11km) Cantoniera, this route rejoins Via Tuscolana to return to (21km) Rome.

B. Via dei Laghi

VIA APPIA NUOVA (N 7) starts from Porta San Giovanni (Pl. 10; 3, 6). 7.5km Intersection with Via Latina, which is no longer a continuous road. Just to the left, on Via Arco di Travertino, is the entrance to the **Parco delle Tombe Latine**, which includes a group of *tombs dating from the 1C and 2C. Most of them are square and brick-built, with recesses on the outside and interior chambers with interesting stucco ornamentation. Two of the best-preserved may sometimes be visited. On the right is the so-called TOMB OF THE VALERI (AD 160), a subterranean chamber decorated with fine reliefs, in stucco on a white ground, of nymphs, sea-monsters, and nereids. On the left is the 2C TOMB OF THE PANCRAZI, with landscape paintings, coloured stuccoes, and four bas-reliefs: Judgment of Paris, Admetus and Alcestis, Priam and Achilles, and Hercules playing a lyre with Bacchus and Minerva. Behind the tomb are the ruins of the 5C BASILICA OF ST STEPHEN. Nearer Rome, off Via Latina, about 500m before the Pisa railway line, are two hypogeum, important for their 4C paintings: the IPOGEO DI TREBIO GIUSTO, and the *IPOGEO DI VIA DINO COMPAGNI.

Via Appia Nuova continues, and the ancient Appian Way, with its tombs and other buildings, soon becomes conspicuous on the right. On the left is the long line of arches of the Acqua Claudia. The road crosses the Rome–Naples railway near (11.5km) Capannelle, with a racecourse. On the right can be seen the road to the Casal Rotondo on the Appian Way. The road passes under the Grande Raccordo Annulare near (13.5km) Barbula, and soon passes (15km) the entrance (left) to CIAMPINO AIRPORT, just beyond which, **Via dei Laghi** (N 217) diverges to the left. The road leads E and SE towards the Alban Hills climbing steadily.

22km **MARINO**, at the N end of Lake Albano, can be seen from the road which by-passes it to the S. The town, with 23,800 inhab., is less of a tourist centre than some of the other Castelli, and is celebrated for its wines. It suffered much damage during the Second World War. A colourful market is held here on Sunday mornings.

Marino was built near the ancient 'Castrimoenium', colonised under Sulla of which no traces remain. The modern name first appears in the 11C. In the 13C Marino was a stronghold of the Orsini; in 1347 Giordano Orsini, who had been driven out of Rome by the tribune Cola di Rienzo, was here besieged unsuccessfully by him. In 1419 the town passed to the Colonna. Many of its inhabitants took part in the battle of Lepanto (1571). Vittoria Colonna (1490–1548) and the musician Giacomo Carissimi (1604–74) were born at Marino.

In Piazza San Barnaba is the restored 17C church of SAN BARNABA. It contains a Martyrdom of St Barnabas by Benedetto Gennari, and a Turkish shield taken at the battle of Lepanto. In the neighbouring Piazza Lepanto is the bomb-damaged FOUNTAIN OF THE FOUR MOORS, by the local sculptor Pompeo Castiglia (1642), commemorating the battle of Lepanto. The 16C PALAZZO COLONNA is now the Town Hall, and contains an antiquarium. In the church of the TRINITÀ is a painting attributed to Guido Reni, and in the church of SANTA MARIA DELLE GRAZIE a St Roch, of the Emilian school. Attached to the Dominican convent is the church of MADONNA DEL ROSARIO, with an elegant Rococo interior. Near the station is a MITHRAEUM, with interesting frescoes discovered in 1963.

Via dei Laghi continues to climb, with magnificent views, skirting *LAGO DI ALBANO*, a small crater lake, 10km round and 170m deep. It is fed by underground sources and by the drainage of the surrounding crater, and its waters are full of fish. The 'Lacus Albanus' was surrounded by villas in the Imperial Roman era and naumachiae were held here. In 1985 Middle Bronze Age finds were made in the lake. It is possible to walk round the lake in 2 hrs by a track.

27km Ponte di Nemi. Road left for Rocca di Papa (3km), with good views of the landscape from Lake Albano to Grottaferrata. **ROCCA DI PAPA** (681m; 7800 inhab.), built up in picturesque terraces on the side of Monte Cavo, is the highest of the Castelli Romani. Surrounded by chestnut woods, it is a summer resort. The lower part of the town is modern, the upper part medieval. Originally called 'Rocca di Monte Cavo' it had adopted its present name, derived from a papal castle here, by the 12C. It was later owned by the Annibaldi and the Colonna. From Piazza della Repubblica there is an excellent view of the medieval town, with the observatory at its top, and of Monte Cavo. Relics of the CASTLE can still be seen at the highest point of the town, from which there are views of the Campagna and of the lakes of Albano and Nemi.

ASCENT OF MONTE CAVO, 5.5km. The road runs S from Rocca di Papa (leading back to Via dei Laghi), past (1km) the Sanctuary of the Madonna del Tufo, built over a block of tufa whose fall on to a passer-by was miraculously arrested by the Virgin. Just beyond, a good private road diverges left to wind up to the summit. A short way up, a sign indicates the ancient *VIA SACRA, called 'Via Triumphalis', which climbs up the hill-side to the left. Perfectly preserved, it can be followed on foot for a considerable way, through beautiful woods. It was built to reach the Temple of Jupiter Latiaris on the summit of Monte Cavo (see below), and for the triumphal processions of generals whose feats of arms were not considered important enough for a triumphal procession along the Via Sacra in Rome.

The ascent may be made on foot by following the steep and narrow streets up through the town, past the remains of its castle at the top, to the edge of the Monte Cavo crater, where a path leads to the right. On the left, in the crater, is a flat floor called the 'Campi d'Annibale', traditionally thought to be the site of the halting-place of Hannibal in his march on Tusculum and Rome in 211 BC. In fact this was probably a Roman military station protecting the Via Appia and Via Latina. The path, with splendid views, follows for some time the Via Triumphalis (see above).

Monte Cavo (949m), the second highest summit of the Alban Hills, is the sacred 'Mons Albanus' of the Latins. On its summit stood the TEMPLE OF JUPITER LATIARIS, the sanctuary of the Latin League, whose religious festivals, the 'Feriae Latinae', were celebrated in spring and autumn by the 47 towns of the confederation. Excavations have failed to find any trace of the temple. On the presumed site of the temple Henry, Cardinal York, built a Passionist Convent in 1783; this later became an observatory, founded by Father Angelo Secchi in 1876. The walls of the convent garden are built partly with blocks from ancient buildings. There is also a television station here. The splendid *view extends along the coast from Monte Circeo to Civitavecchia, and takes in the Tolfa and Cimini ranges, the Sabine, Tiburtine and Praenestine Hills, and the Monte Lepini. The descent may be made through the woods to Nemi (about 4km) and the walk continued from there to Genzano (Rte 30C).

Via dei Laghi continues to (31km) the turning (right) for Nemi and its lake. The road skirts the E and S sides of the lake, while a turning to the right after 1km leads to the attractive little quiet resort of **NEMI** (521m; 1300 inhab.) in a picturesque position above the NE side of the lake. The impressive PALAZZO BARONIALE belonged in the 9C to the counts of Tusculum, then to Cistercian monks, and in 1428 to the Colonna. It was subsequently owned by the Orsini, and the Ruspoli. The narrow old cobbled road (signposted) for the lakeside (better reached from the other side of the lake, see below) passes under its entrance bridge. On the hillside to the right of the road are the scant ruins of the TEMPLE OF DIANA NEMORENSIS (see below), first excavated in the 17C; some of the finds are in the Museo di Villa Giulia in Rome. Further excavations in 1924–28 revealed a theatre. The road continues to wind down through woods and then runs through orchards and vineyards and becomes single track just before emerging beside the Museo delle Navi Romane (see below).

The lake road continues above the E and S side through delightful stretches of ilex and manna-ash woods (branch roads lead down to the lake-side). The beautiful and well preserved *LAGO DI NEMI (316m) is another of the crater lakes in the Alban Hills. Almost circular in shape, it is 5.5km round, with a maximum depth of 34m. It is surrounded by wooded hills, with no ugly buildings. There is a well-known painting by Turner of the lake. This is the ancient 'Lacus Nemorensis', called also the Mirror of Diana, to whom were consecrated the grove and the temple on its NE side (see above). It was one of the most celebrated sanctuaries in central Italy. Diana was worshipped here with savage rites: only a run-away slave who succeeded in breaking off a branch ('the golden bough') from a certain tree in the grove could become her priest, called 'Rex Nemorensis'. He had to fight the reigning priest in single combat; if he killed him he became the next Rex Nemorensis. The new priest-king, in his turn, was liable at any time to be challenged by a further aspirant. This sinister rule of succession to the priesthood of Diana was described by Sir James Frazer in 'The Golden Bough', first published in 1890. The first temple was probably built in the late 4C BC.

Before the approach to Genzano (see below), the road bears right round the lake-side to reach the **Museo delle Navi Romane** (open daily 9.00–

14.00). The vast double pavilion erected in 1936 is an interesting building of its period. From 1936 to 1944 it housed two ancient ships built by Caligula (AD 37–41) to convey visitors across the lake for the festival of Diana. The ships were sunk at the time of Claudius, and they were located at the bottom of the lake in 1446 by Leon Battista Alberti, but only when the lake was partly drained in 1927–32 were the huge ships salvaged. The smaller was 71m long and had a beam of 20m; the other was 73m by 24m. On 1 June 1944 they were burned in the museum by German soldiers. The huge building is now almost empty: it contains models of the ships, on a scale of one-fifth, and beneath the floor are stretches of Roman road which led to the Sanctuary of Diana. Fragments of small mosaics, bronze and iron nails, ceramics, anchors and other fittings from the boats are preserved here, but the splendid *bronzes which survived the fire are still in Rome. On the upper floor are diagrams, etc. illustrating how the boats were salvaged, and explanations of the Roman edifices excavated in the vicinity including the Sanctuary of Diana.

From here it is possible to return to Via dei Laghi (turning right for Velletri, 7.5km, described in Rte 30C, or left to return to Rome) or take the road which climbs the hillside to Genzano, passing a path (left) which leads to the EMISSARIUM of the lake, comprising two superimposed tunnels 1650m long, used when necessary to drain the lake. Genzano (Rte 30C) is entered at Piazza Dante; from the centre Via Appia Nuova leads back to Rome (29km).

C.   Rome to Castel Gandolfo, Albano, Genzano, and Velletri

Via Appia Nuova leads out of Rome. To (15.5km) the junction with Via dei Laghi, see Rte 30B. The road crosses the Terracina railway 1km before (20km) Frattocchie, where this route is joined by Via Appia Antica. Here was the 12th (Roman) milestone. N 7 is now known simply as Via Appia. Via Nettunense branches off to the right for Anzio and Nettuno (Rte 29); on the left is the Palazzetto della Sirene, built by Cardinal Girolamo Colonna and now a Trappist monastery. The road passes the ruins of tombs and other buildings which lined the Appian Way. There are four imposing stumps of Roman towers, the first of them cylindrical and called the Torraccio (left), the others square. A track to the right leads to the ruins of the small Latin town of BOVILLAE, a colony of Alba Longa. Here can be seen traces of a circus excavated in the 19C, a cistern, and numerous tombs.

21km. Turning left for **CASTEL GANDOLFO**, often called just 'Castello'. A good road climbs to this lively little town in 3km. With 4700 inhab. it is built on the lip of the Lake Albano crater at a height of 426m above the sea. Here the Pope spends the summer.

The town occupies the site of the citadel of ALBA LONGA, founded, according to legend, by Ascanius, son of Aeneas. It was so called because it extended in a long line up the slopes of Mons Albanus. Head of the Latin League, Alba was the mother city of many of the Latin towns, and of Rome itself. Its war with Rome at the time of Tullus Hostilius, decided by the single combats of the three Roman Horatii and the three Latin Curiatii, the treachery of its dictator Mettius Fufetius, and its destruction around the middle of the 7C BC, are famous episodes in the legendary history of Rome. The town was never rebuilt though its temples were respected and were still standing in the days of Augustus. Domitian built a villa here, ruins of which are visible (see below). There is no trace of the ancient town, but to the W of Castel Gandolfo there is an extensive necropolis of the early Iron Age (9–7C BC), discoveries from which are in the Museo Preistorico in Rome.

Castel Gandolfo derives its name from a castle of the Gandolfi, a Genoese family of the 12C. The castle passed to the Savelli and, in 1596, to the Camera Apostolica. In 1604 it was declared an inalienable domain of the Holy See. After the papal palace was built (see below), it became the summer residence of the popes and it has been used as such ever since, except for the period from 1870 to 1929. Many distinguished people have lived at Castel Gandolfo, among them Goethe, Winckelmann, Angelica Kauffmann, and Massimo d'Azeglio.

At the N entrance of the town, 133m above the lake, extends the vast **Papal Palace**, built on the ruins of the castle and retaining some of its towers and walls. It was erected in 1624 by Carlo Maderno for Urban VIII and enlarged by Alexander VII, Clement XIII, and Pius IX. The palace, with its gardens and the former Villa Barberini (see below), enjoys the privilege of extraterritoriality.

A special permit is necessary from the Director to visit the palace. The chapel has frescoes of the school of the Zuccari. Since 1936 the villa has housed the **Vatican Observatory**, one of the most important in Europe. It was founded by Gregory XIII and from 1908 to 1936 occupied the Casina of Leo XIII in the Vatican Gardens. The observatory specialises in the study of variable stars; it contains a laboratory of astrophysics.

A short alley to the right of the palace leads to a terrace with a fine view. In the piazza are an elegant fountain and the church of SAN TOMASO DA VILLANOVA (1661, with a good cupola), both by Bernini. Inside are a painting of St Thomas of Villanova, by Pietro da Cortona, and an Assumption by Maratta.

At the S end of the town is the VILLA BARBERINI (now Vatican property; no admission). The splendid gardens were laid out in the 1930s by Emilio Bonomelli. This site was once occupied by the Villa of Domitian. Traces of nymphaea, cisterns, and of a small theatre, are still visible. The sculpture and architectural fragments found during excavations in 1841 and the 1930s are displayed in an Antiquarium, opened here in 1989 (admission only with special permission). At the beginning of the road to Ercolano is the VILLA TORLONIA, with sculptures by Thorvaldsen and a fine park.

Below Castel Gandolfo, on the W shores of Lake Albano, are two nymphaeum, the so-called NINFEO DORICO, dating from the 1C BC, and possibly part of the Villa of Claudius, and the NINFEO BERGANTINO, which was part of the Villa of Domitian. Nearby is the EMISSARIUM or outlet of Lake Albano, which maintains the water of the lake at a constant level. It is a tunnel (similar to the outlet of Lake Nemi) cut through the solid rock 1425m long, 1m wide, and 1.5m high; it pierces the rim of the crater and emerges at Le Mole, to the SW. This is a very early Roman work, traditionally dated before 396 BC and said to have been constructed after the oracle at Delphi had declared that Veio would not fall until the lake was drained.

The two famous ilex-bordered roads which lead from Castel Gandolfo to Albano Laziale were both opened by Urban VIII. They are known as the 'Galleria di Sopra' and the 'Galleria di Sotto' because the branches of the trees interlace above the roadways, forming arboreal tunnels. The less attractive lower road is used by buses. The Galleria di Sopra, that to the left of the exit of Castel Gandolfo, follows the lip of the crater and provides magnificent *views of Lake Albano, the Campagna, and the neighbouring towns. Half-way along it is the summer convent of the Collegio di Propaganda Fide. Close to the Capuchin Convent, the road forks. The left fork leads to Ariccia; the right fork to Albano Laziale, past the church of San Paolo. A path to the left of the convent leads to Palazzolo. The lower road passes on the right (near the junction with the Appian Way) a Republican tower sepulchre, once some 45m high. This is thought to have been the Tomb of Pompey.

24km **ALBANO** (378m; 24,400 inhab.), officially Albano Laziale, is an important town of the Castelli. The town rises in the form of a triangle from the Via Appia towards the top of the crater of Lake Albano; the crater cuts off the view of the lake from the town. Albano was badly damaged in the Second World War, when nearly two-thirds of its buildings were destroyed or damaged.

The name of Albano is derived from Alba Longa, but the town owes its origin to Septimius Severus, who established here (c AD 195) the 'Castra Albana' for the 2nd Legion (Parthica), to protect (among other duties) the Appian Way. The camp occupied virtually the whole of what is now the town of Albano. Adjoining the camp was a small settlement which gradually developed and eventually overran the military area. Albano became a bishopric in 460; the see was held by Nicholas Breakspeare before he became the only English pope as Adrian IV (1154–59). Albano is one of the six suburbicarian sees held by cardinal bishops. Devastated by the barbarian invasions and in the struggles of the papacy and empire, the town passed in the 13C to the Savelli, whose castle survives (to the W of Albano). In 1697 it was acquired by the Camera Apostolica. The eccentric Earl of Bristol, bishop of Derry, died here in 1803.

The town centre is the spacious PIAZZA MAZZINI, a widening of the Via Appia. On the right, coming from Rome, are the Belvedere and the VILLA COMUNALE, a public park shaded by tall pines and occupying the site of a Roman villa formerly identified with a villa of Pompey, traces of which remain. There is a good view from the Belvedere, extending to Rome. From Piazza Mazzini Via Cairoli leads to Piazza Sabatini, in which is the DUOMO (San Pancrazio), built and rebuilt on a temple dating from the time of Constantine. The temple columns may be seen incorporated in the walls.

Corso Matteotti leads out of Piazza Mazzini, past the town hall in Palazzo Savelli. In the square opposite is the church of SAN PIETRO, built in the 6C over the remains of the thermae of the Roman camp. The right flank of the church incorporates masonry blocks from the baths; the jambs of a door on the left side are made up of fragments of an ancient architrave. There is an attractive Romanesque campanile. In the spacious interior an acanthus cornice supports the modern altar rails.

Via Aurelio Saffi climbs to the upper part of the town. A turning to the left, Via Don Minzoni, leads to the ruins of the PORTA PRAETORIA, revealed by bombing in February 1944. This front gate of the camp of Castra Albana, opening from its short S side and facing the Appian Way, had three openings and was flanked by two towers. It was constructed of blocks of peperino. Its frontage was 36m and its height 13m. Only the E opening survived the bombing; of the main central entrance only the lower part is extant.

Via della Rotonda leads left out of Via Saffi to SANTA MARIA DELLA ROTONDA (open 9.00–12.30; Wednesday and Thursday, also 16.00–19.00), restored in 1937. This medieval circular domed church, once a nymphaeum belonging to the Villa of Domitian, has a Cosmatesque pulpit supported on a Roman capital. In the sacristy is a small Antiquarium with fragments of sarcophagi, inscriptions, brick stamps, and a funerary stele of the 3C AD. Nearby are remains of the walls of the Roman camp. Continuing its ascent,

Via Aurelio Saffi leads into the charming Piazza San Paolo, in which is the church of SAN PAOLO, built in 1282 and remodelled in 1769. It stands at the apex of the triangle formed by the town. In the wall of the neighbouring seminary of the Preziosissimo Sangue are incorporated further remains of the camp walls. At the top of the hill, beyond the cemetery, Lake Albano can be seen far below on the other side.

At 100 Via Aurelio Saffi is the entrance to the CISTERNONE (open 9.00–12.30, Wednesday and Thursday also 16.00–19.00), a reservoir hewn out of rock for the use (probably) of the legionaries of the camp. It is a quadrangular underground construction 46m by 30m, reached by 31 steps. It is divided into five compartments, each furnished with rows of columns. The ceilings, 12m high, are perfectly preserved. The floor slopes gently towards the W corner, where there is an underground outlet. Near the civil hospital, off Via San Francesco, are a rectangular tower and remains of what was probably the 'Porta Principalis Sinistra', or E gate of the camp, now walled up.

Via San Francesco leads to the ruins of the AMPHITHEATRE (open 9.00–12.30; Wednesday and Thursday also 16.00–19.00), between the church of San Paolo and the Capuchin Convent; it dates from the second half of the 3C and could accommodate 15,000 spectators. On the hill above is the CAPUCHIN CONVENT (1619), surrounded by a turreted wall. On the hillside extends the BOSCO DEI CAPPUCCINI, a public park with fine views. The parallel street to the SE, in which are long tracts of wall, returns to the centre of the town.

The continuation of Corso Matteotti, Borgo Garibaldi, continues past the gardens of the Villa Comunale. To the left, at 3 Viale Risorgimento, is the entrance to the MUSEO CIVICO ALBANO, which is due to reopen shortly after restoration. It is arranged in 15 rooms and contains material from the Palaeolithic era up to Palaeochristian times.

Just outside Albano, on the right of the road to Ariccia, is a majestic tomb in the Etruscan style, known as the **Tomb of the Horatii and Curiatii**, perhaps modelled on the Tomb of Aruns, son of Porsenna. It has a base, 15m square, made of peperino blocks, surmounted by two (originally five) truncated cones. The tomb in fact dates from the late Republican era.

WALKS may be taken from Albano, N to (¾ hr) Castel Gandolfo by the Galleria di Sopra (reached from the church of San Paolo); NE to (1½ hr) Palazzolo; and W to (½ hr) Castel Savelli. The castle (325m) is reached by a road under the railway and by a path to the right at a road fork. This 13C stronghold of the Savelli was last restored in 1660. For the other Castel Savelli, see above.

Beyond Albano the line of the Via Appia follows a course laid out during the pontificates of Gregory XVI (1831–46) and Pius IX (1846–78); the rectification involved the building of four viaducts over the Valle Ariccia, one of the smaller craters of the Alban Hills. As the road leaves Albano, the so-called Tomb of the Horatii and Curiatii (see above) can be seen below on the right. This route bears to the left off the ancient Appian Way.

The ancient road descends to the right, passing near the church of SANTA MARIA DELLA STELLA (below which are the Catacombs of San Senatore, probably reserved for Christian soldiers of the 2nd Legion), and then crosses the valley by an imposing Roman viaduct (c AD 19) still in part original. It rejoins the modern road near the Sanctuary of Santa Maria di Galloro, then parts again soon afterwards before reuniting near Velletri.

The modern road crosses the valley higher up by the viaduct known as the PONTE DI ARICCIA, built by Ireneo Aleandri in 1847–54, partly blown up by the Germans in 1944 and rebuilt in 1947. The viaduct is 312m long, 9m wide, and 59m above the valley floor. It is made up of a series of three superimposed arches (six below, 12 in the middle, and 18 above). Just short of the viaduct, on the right in a square, is a monument to Menotti Garibaldi, by Ernesto Biondi. Beyond the bridge, on the left, extends the luxuriant park of Palazzo Chigi (see below); on the right there is an extensive view over the valley.

26.5km **ARICCIA** (412m; 10,700 inhab.) is in a charming position in wooded country, with numerous villas. It was also damaged in 1943–44.

The ancient Latin city of Ariccia, mentioned in the legends of the kings, took a leading part in the wars with Rome until the dissolution of the Latin League in 338 BC. With three other Latin towns it then lost its independence and received full Roman citizenship. In Cicero's time it was a flourishing municipium. It was the first stage in Horace's journey to Brundusium. In the Middle Ages the town was owned by the counts of Tusculum and later passed to the Savelli; in 1661 it was sold to the Chigi. Henrik Ibsen 'disillusioned with the theatre' settled at Ariccia with wife and child in 1864 and here wrote 'Brand'. In the town in 1826 Massimo d'Azeglio, statesman and artist, entertained Severn, the artist and friend of Keats.

On the N (left) side of the town is Piazza della Repubblica with two fountains and PALAZZO CHIGI, in the form of a medieval castle with four towers, restored by Bernini and later enlarged. It has a delightful and extensive *park. It has recently been acquired by the Comune and is to be opened as a Museum. On the right is the round church of *SANTA MARIA DELL'ASSUNZIONE, built by Bernini in 1664; it has a large dome and two campanili; inside is a fresco of the Assumption, by Borgognone. In the centre of the town are remains of a small Republican temple.

On leaving Ariccia the road crosses over a second viaduct; then bends round the head of the valley over a third viaduct. Here the road is lined with ilex and manna-ash trees. On the right, on the NE edge of the Valle Ariccia, is the SANCTUARY OF SANTA MARIA DI GALLORO (429m) by Bernini, with a venerated painting of the Madonna. The road ascends gradually amid woods and crosses yet a fourth viaduct. From the top of the rise there is a gentle descent.

29.5km **GENZANO**, officially Genzano di Roma (435m; 15,300 inhab.), is built in terraces on the outer slope of the crater of Lake Nemi. The town grew up round a castle built in 1235 facing the lake, rebuilt in 1621 by Prince Giuliano Cesarini to face the Via Appia.

The town centre is Piazza Tommaso Frasconi, with a terrace on the right. On the left, beyond an interesting fountain, are three streets, Via Garibaldi, Bruno Buozzi, and Italo Belardi, all going uphill fanwise from the square. The last-named street, scene of the *Infiorata*, climbs past the Municipio to the church of Santa Maria della Cima. Via Bruno Buozzi leads to the modern Palazzo Cesarini, which overlooks the lake, 90m below. Via Garibaldi leads to Piazza Dante, where there is a road down to the lake (see above).

Beyond Genzano the road passes between (left) Lake Nemi, glimpses of which may be obtained, and (right) the Monte Due Torri (415m), with its remaining squat medieval tower. 32.5km Turning (right) for LANUVIO (3km). The ancient city was famous for its sanctuary of Juno Sospita parts of which are incorporated in the seminary and the Villa Sforza. The emperors Antoninus Pius and Commodus were born at Lanuvio. The main road turns E and the scenery becomes more and more attractive. The hillsides are covered with vineyards and chestnut woods. On the left are the wooded slopes and crest of the Maschio d'Artemisio (812m). Approaching Velletri, the road curves round the head of a valley. 38.5km. At the beginning of the tree-lined Viale Roma this route is joined by Via dei Laghi from Marino (Rte 30B).

39km **VELLETRI** (332m; 37,900 inhab.) is a busy town with a largely modern appearance on a spur of the Artemisio range. It was reconstructed after serious War damage.

Velletri is the Volscian 'Velester', subjugated by Rome in 338 BC and called Velitrae. It was the home of the Gens Octavia, of which Augustus was a member. It was an independent commune from c 1000 to 1549, when it was absorbed in the States of the Church. From a window in the Palazzo Ginnetti Charles of Bourbon escaped in August 1744 from the Irish General U.M. Brown's Austrian troops, later decisively defeating the Austrians in the same battle. Velletri is one of the six suburbicarian sees; its bishop is Dean of the Sacred College of Cardinals.

VIA VITTORIO EMANUELE runs through the town from N to S following the contour of the hill from Piazza Garibaldi, site of the Porta Romana, to Porta Napoli. About one-third of the way along opens Piazza Cairoli, the town centre, almost completely rebuilt except for the TORRE DEL TRIVIO (c 50m), a striking Romanesque campanile, dating from 1353, of alternate black-and-white courses, with single and double window-arches; it was cleverly restored after bomb damage.

To the right Via del Comune leads up to the piazza of the same name, the highest part of the town. Here is Palazzo di Giustizia (1835); in front are the little church of San Michele (1837) and the octagonal oratory of Santa Maria del Sangue, by Alessandro da Parma (1523–79). To the left is the 16C Palazzo Comunale, with porticoes by Giacomo Della Porta (on a design by Vignola), reconstructed since 1945 almost from the foundations.

At the back is the entrance to the **Museo Civico Archeologico** (open 8.30–13.30; Monday 9.00–13.00; closed fest.), founded in 1893. Beyond the first room with inscriptions, the second room displays a marble tomb *relief with Old and New Testament scenes dating from the second decade of the 4C, one of the most important Christian carvings known of this period. Room III is filled with a splendid Roman *sarcophagus of Parian marble found in 1955 6km outside Velletri. Dating from AD 190–93, and complete with its lid, it is entirely decorated with numerous mythological scenes, including the Labours of Hercules. The last two rooms on this floor contain sarcophagi, funerary cippi, and a circular relief showing a Deposition scene. On the floor above are interesting terracotta panels delicately carved in bas-relief in the 6C BC (found in 1910 in Velletri).

Via Collicello leads down from the piazza to the 18C church of SAN MARTINO, with a neo-classical façade. Over the second N altar is a detached fresco of the Madonna and Child of 1308. From Piazza Mazzini a road continues S to Piazza Umberto I. In a small square to the left is the entrance to the **Cathedral** (San Clemente), a 13C church built on the remains of a Roman basilica many times altered, rebuilt in 1660, and patched up after the War. The basilican INTERIOR has a rebuilt 13C apse and a restored ceiling, with a huge painting (1954) by Angelo Canevari. The organ dates from the 16C. The baldacchino over the 17C high altar is surmounted by a Cosmatesque tabernacle (difficult to see). The carved marble candelabrum is attributed to Jacopo Sansovino. On the lower walls of the apse are 14C frescoes. Beside the Renaissance sacristy doorway is a 15C fresco of the Madonna enthroned with four saints. In the second S chapel is a detached fresco of the Crucifixion with a donor.

The MUSEO CAPITOLARE, with a particularly fine collection of works of art, is not usually open. It contains paintings of the Madonna by Gentile da Fabriano (restored) and Antoniazzo Romano; fragments of an *Exultet (school of Montecassino; 12C); Story of the Passion (late 13C; French or English); jewelled 12C Byzantine reliquary *Cross; and *ornaments from the chasuble of Benedict XI (1303–04).

Just beyond the cathedral the road leaves the town by the Porta Napoli, flanked by cylindrical towers; to the left is the railway station. Via dei Laghi (Rte 30B) leads back to Rome.

31

Palestrina

ROAD. VIA CASILINA, 38km (return by VIA PRENESTINA, 37km). Frequent buses from Piazza dei Cinquecento along Via Prenestina and along Via Casilina.

AUTOSTRADA DEL SOLE, 27km to San Cesareo, then 10.5km E to Palestrina.

Rome is left by Porta Maggiore (Pl. 6; 8; see Rte 12). The right-hand road of the two main roads beyond the gate is Via Casilina. For the first 18.5km the road passes through perhaps the most unpleasant suburbs of Rome. Just beyond (5km) Via di Torpignattara is all that remains of the MAUSOLEUM OF SANT'ELENA (no admission), somewhat hidden to the left, behind a school. St Helena, mother of Constantine, died c 330. Circular outside and octagonal, with niches, in the interior, it is called TOR PIGNATTARA from the terracotta amphorae (*pignatte*) introduced into the vaulting to diminish the load. St Helena's sarcophagus is in the Vatican. No. 643, next door, is the entrance to the CATACOMBS OF SAINTS PIETRO AND MARCELLINO (3–4C), the most pictorially decorated in Rome (adm only with special permission).

7.5km CENTOCELLE; on the right is a military airport and beyond can be seen the arches of the Acqua Claudia; on the left are the Tiburtine and Prenestine Hills; to the N the Monti Sabini and to the NW Monte Soratte. This route crosses the Grande Raccordo Annulare before (11.5km) Torrenova, adjoining an old Borghese palace. At (18.5km) Finocchio by-roads lead S to Frascati (Rte 30A) and N to the Via Prenestina (see below). Beyond (20km) Pantano Borghese station, the road ascends and becomes more attractive. It passes on the left the TENUTA DI PANTANO, with two dried-up lakes: LAGO REGILLO, drained in the 17C, and the LAGO DI CASTIGLIONE, reclaimed in the 19C. In the famous battle of Lake Regillus, in 496 BC, the Romans were victorious over the Latins who were led by the Tarquins. This ended the last attempt of the Tarquin dynasty to recover the kingship of Rome. The Romans are said to have been miraculously assisted by the Dioscuri, Castor and Pollux, and as a result a temple was built in their honour in the Roman Forum. Between the two lakes is the ancient course of the Via Prenestina, with the ruins of Gabii (see below).

26km COLONNA (1km off the road to the right), the northernmost of the Castelli Romani (see Rte 30). This little town is built on a park-like hill (343m), with numerous vineyards; a road, the Via Colonna, leads SW to Frascati. At 30km, a road from Montecompatri and Frascati comes in from the right (see Rte 30A). 31km San Cesareo. This route leaves Via Casilina 2km farther on, and Via Prenestina Nuova continues (left).

33.5km **Zagarolo** (2.5km left of the road; 303m), a town of 10,000 inhabitants, recorded in the 12C under the name of Gazzarolo and a fief of the Rospigliosi from the 17C. The wines from its vineyards are renowned. Corso Garibaldi leads into Piazza Santa Maria (car parking) with a pretty fountain. Corso Vittorio Emanuele leads on to an unusual monumental *GATEWAY forming the entrance to the medieval district of the town. This was erected by the Rospigliosi in 1670 and completed in 1722. Built of yellow sandstone and white marble it incorporates Roman columns and several fine Imperial Roman reliefs. Beyond the arch is a fountain of 1877 with a Roman sarcophagus, and on the right, two Roman granite columns against Palazzo Rospigliosi (see below). There is a view over a wooded valley.

The road continues (ahead can be seen the lantern and drum of the church of San Pietro) past the flank of Palazzo Rospigliosi (being restored) into Piazza dell'Indipendenza with a War Memorial and the front of the huge PALAZZO ROSPIGLIOSI (16C–18C). The two protruding wings of the palace (in poor repair) are decorated with colossal red granite columns with fine bases and capitals, and two sarcophagi with lions' heads and Roman altars beneath. Via Antonio Fabrini continues past the cathedral of SAN PIETRO, a fine Baroque building (1717–22), to PIAZZA MARCONI, a beautifully designed square. The church of San Lorenzo (containing a triptych in the style of Antoniazzo Romano) faces two scenographic palaces (one of them reconstructed after its destruction in the last War), fine works attributed to Carlo Maderno. The architectural details are designed in yellow and brown stone.

The Palestrina road ascends, and at 36.5km it is joined on the right by the Olmata di Palestrina a road leading to the Via Casilina. Off this road are the CASINI BARBERINI, built in the 17C, which include 'Il Triangolo' a remarkable building on a triangular plan by Gian Battista Contini. The main road continues and the hill of Palestrina suddenly comes into view, with Castel San Pietro Romano near the top.

38km **PALESTRINA** (11,500 inhab.) occupies the S slope of Monte Ginestro, a spur of the Monti Prenestini. It is famous for its huge Sanctuary of Fortune, a masterpiece of Roman architecture, which is still the dominant feature in the townscape, especially since important elements were revealed by the clearance of buildings destroyed by bombs in 1944. The fine collection in the town's archaeological museum illustrates the importance of 'Praeneste' from the 7C BC up until the Roman era.

Information Office. 'Pro-Loco', 2 Piazza Santa Maria degli Angeli (Tel. 06/9573176).

Hotel. 2-star 'Stella' (with restaurant 'Coccia'), 3 Piazza della Liberazione.

Buses ('COTRAL') to Rome from Viale Pio XII circa every half hour.

Car parking in Piazza Santa Maria degli Angeli, or at the top of the hill near the Museum.

Annual Festival. 'Sant'Agapito', 17–19 August.

History. 'Praeneste', one of the oldest towns of Latium, is said to have been founded by Telegonus, son of Ulysses and Circe. It was a thriving place as early as the 7C BC. Strongly fortified, it resisted the attacks of the Romans for many years, but in 499 BC it joined its traditional enemy. After a revolt it took a prominent part in the Latin War of 340–338, amd then became subject to Rome. Refuge of the younger Marius, it was besieged in 82 BC by the troops of Sulla, and destroyed. The influence of the famous Sanctuary of Fortune, whose oracle delivered the 'Praenestinae sortes' survived until the 4C AD. In the golden age of Rome 'cool Praeneste', as Horace calls it, became a retreat of the patricians from the heat of summer.

In the Middle Ages a town called Città Prenestina was built over the abandoned sanctuary. In 752 this town was occupied by Astaulph, king of the Lombards. Later it passed to the counts of Tusculum and in 1043 to the Colonna; in this way it became involved in the feuds of the Guelfs and Ghibellines, and was several times destroyed and rebuilt. In 1630 Francesco Colonna sold it to Carlo Barberini, brother of Urban VII. The most famous native was Giovanni Pierluigi da Palestrina (1524?–94), the father of polyphonic music. Palestrina is one of the six suburbicarian sees.

Via degli Arcioni passes a wall made with large blocks of tufa in the 2C BC which supported the first terrace of the city. Here also are remains of the PROPYLAEA, which formed a monumental entrance to the city. Beyond (on the right) is the battlemented 17C PORTA DEL SOLE. Viale Duca d'Aosta swings round to the entrance to the town (left) by Viale della Vittoria which ends in Piazzale Santa Maria degli Angeli, with a stretch of the ancient polygonal walls. From here Via Anicia continues to the central Piazza

Regina Margherita, which is now thought to occupy the site of the ancient Forum (see below) on another terrace. In the middle of the square is a monument to Palestrina, by Arnaldo Zocchi (1921); the composer was born in a little house in the neighbouring Vicolo Pierluigi.

The **Cathedral** was bult over a pagan Roman edifice in tufa in the 5C and dedicated to St Agapito, a native of Palestrina martyred outside the town in 274, whose relics were translated to the church in 898. Modified in 1100, the building was rebuilt in later centuries after its partial destruction in 1437. The unattractive FAÇADE (restored in 1957) incorporates ancient fragments (many of them Roman). The upper part of the Romanesque CAMPANILE was rebuilt in the 15C. The INTERIOR was redesigned in 1882–1917. On the first S altar, Transport of St Joseph by Achille Guerra (1888). In the SANCTUARY are late 19C frescoes by Domenico Bruschi, and two oval paintings by Giovanni Odazzi. North aisle: Martyrdom of St Agapito by Carlo Saraceni, and (second altar), with a Cosmatesque altar frontal, Crucifix with Saints and donors by Sermoneta (Girolamo Siciolante). Beyond a copy of the Pietà of Palestrina formerly attributed to Michelangelo (see below), in the baptistery, is a painting of the Saviour also by Sermoneta. In the CRYPT are remains of part of a pagan Roman edifice which may be the Iunonarium, or temple of Imperial Jupiter dating from the 4C BC. There is also a stretch of Roman road visible here, and traces of 13C frescoes.

In the piazza, on the right of the cathedral (below ground level) are further remains of the Roman road and the steps of the Iunonarium. Behind rises the high wall of the former Seminary which incorporates four Corinthian half-columns from the façade of the Apsidal Hall (see below). The public buildings throught to have been connected with the ancient **Forum** are at present closed to the public. This area was formerly called the SANTUARIO INFERIORE since it was thought to be part of the Sanctuary of Fortune. The entrance to the buildings is through the former Seminary.

The various edifices, dating from the 2C BC, were skilfully constructed on several levels, with columns one above the other, to make use of the uneven ground. The AERARIUM, or treasury, a small barrel-vaulted room with a contemporary inscription, contains busts, votive offerings, architectural fragments, and two pieces of an Egyptian granite obelisk. Beyond the courtyard, known as the AREA SACRA, carved out of the hillside, is the so-called ANTRO DELLE SORTI, a small cave sanctuary (possibly a Serapeum) with three deep niches and preceded by an arch. Remains of an extensive polychrome *mosaic depict an Egyptian seascape, possibly the port of Alexandria, a remarkable Hellenistic work by craftsmen from Alexandria. On the other side of the court is an APSIDAL HALL (formerly part of the Seminary). This is a rectangular room in opus incertum, with an apse and a frieze of metopes and triglyphs, and niches framed in half columns and a white mosaic. Here was found the Barberini mosaic now in the Museum (see below). It has recently been suggested that the hall was used as a sanctuary of Isis.

From the piazza Corso Pier Luigi da Palestrina leads to Piazza della Liberazione. Below the gardens of the PARCO BARBERINI can be seen a long stretch of the wall of the first terrace and part of a Roman road.

The Museum and the parts of the Sanctuary of Fortune open to the public are entered from the top of the hill which can be approached by car beneath the arch in Piazza Santa Maria degli Angeli up a zig-zag road, or by the easier (signposted) approach road which diverges from Viale della Vittoria before the piazza. Both roads diverge in Via Porta Santa Croce at the top of the hill and run beneath the medieval Porta Santa Croce before reaching Piazza della Cortina in front of the Museum. On foot from the Duomo, it is quite a tiring climb of c 15 minutes: the stepped Via Thomas Mann (named after the writer who spent two summers here in 1897–8, with his brother Heinrich, during which he wrote most of 'I Buddenbrook') leads up to Piazza del Borgo. Via del Borgo, with a fine view over the plain, continues left on the site of the first terrace of the Temple of Fortune which runs below the splendid polygonal wall supporting the double ramp of the sanctuary (described below). The houses here were destroyed in the War. At the end is the church of Sant'Antonio Abate, to the right of which the stepped Via dei Calderai continues up to join a road which winds up past more terrace walls to Via Barberini. Here is the charming little church of SANTA ROSALIA, built by Francesco Contini in 1660, which contained the Pietà once attributed to Michelangelo, now in the Galleria dell'Accademia in Florence. A short way to the right is the Museum.

The *Museo Archeologico Nazionale Prenestino (open every day 9.00 to one hour before sunset) occupies Palazzo Colonna Barberini, built in 1640 by Taddeo Barberini on the site of an 11C Colonna palace, which in turn had been built over the highest part of the Sanctuary of Fortuna Primigenia. The façade reflects the shape of the ancient theatre or hemicycle of the Sanctuary, destroyed in the 14C, and the palace is approached by steps which are the (restored) seats of the cavea. The modernised interior incorporates the foundations of the round (reconstructed) temple at the highest point of the Sanctuary. Although many antiquities from Praeneste are now in the Villa Giulia in Rome and other museums, the collection here offers as complete a picture as possible of local civilisation from the 8C BC to the 4C AD. The Barberini collections were first opened to the public in 1913, and the present museum founded in 1956.

GROUND FLOOR. **Room I** (with a ceiling fresco by the Zuccari brothers) contains headless statues from the Roman town, and a relief of a she-wolf suckling her young in a wood, a fine work of the Augustan period found in the area of the Forum. **Room II**. Cippus of two praetors (2C BC?); small sculpture with two representations of Fortune (the heads are missing), dating from the late 2C BC. 44–45. Marble plinths dedicated to Security and Peace by the emperor, and consecrated by the council and people of Praeneste (first half of the 1C AD). **Room III**. *27. Large fragment of a statue of Fortune in grey Oriental marble (Hellenistic Rhodian school) found at the bottom of the well in front of the E hemicycle of the sanctuary. **Room IV**. Funerary altars including (40.) votive altar to the Di Manes (Flavian period). Stairs lead up past remains of part of the semicircular portico of the Sanctuary above the cavea (see above); the roof has been reconstructed.

FIRST FLOOR. **Room VII**, 62, 63. Two painted Archaic metopes in terracotta (6C BC), with scenes of horses and chariots. **Rooms VIII and IX** contain mirrors, cistae, and other toilet articles coming from tombs of the 4C BC. Palestrina is famous for the beautiful cistae (bronze caskets, used as 'beauty cases') and bronze mirrors which were produced here by local craftsmen from the 7C BC to the 3C BC, of a type seldom found elsewhere. **Room VIII**. Case III. 64, 65. Mirrors with Silenus on horseback and Silenus and panther; Case IV, *72. Cylindrical cista, with fine graffiti; Case V. 81. Cista with battle between Hercules and the Amazon Hippolyta, and on the lid, two warriors carrying a wounded man; 82. Oval cista with battle scenes, and a female acrobat on the cover; also, 85–87. Three strigils (used by athletes).

Room IX. Case VI. 83. Cista with two figures (a third lacking) forming a circle on the cover; Case VII. 89. Bronze statuette of an ephebe (in the style of an Archaic kouros); Case VIII. Bronze mirrors decorated with mythological scenes; Case X. *Cista with Dionysos supported by Pan on the cover. **Room X**. 110. Lid of a sarcophagus in peperino, with a frieze of animals; floor mosaics. Model of the Sanctuary of Fortune. The curved wall here in opus incertum is the only part to have survived of the temple which crowned the Sanctuary. **Room XI** contains decorative fragments and votive objects from the temple. **Room XII**. Architectural fragments in terracotta.

From Room XI a staircase ascends to **Room XIV** with the celebrated *Barberini mosaic, found at the end of the 16C or beginning of the 17C in the Apsidal Hall in the area of the Forum (probably a sanctuary of Isis). Measuring 5.85 x 4.31m it is one of the largest Hellenistic mosaics to have survived. It probably dates from the 2C BC, although it has been extensively restored. It depicts Egypt during the floods of the Nile, from its source in the mountains of Ethiopia to the Delta. At the bottom is a banqueting scene on a canal shaded with vines. Here is the Canopus of Alexandria, with the Serapeum to the right, in front of which are warriors and a priestess. Higher, to the right, is a sacred precinct, with pillars, towers, and statues; to the left, near a building with obelisks, is a well, perhaps that of Aswan which helped Eratosthenes to calculate the meridian. The highest section shows regions of cataracts and deserts, inhabited by tropical animals.

The left-hand staircase descends; here can be seen the circular *Shrine (reconstructed using many original fragments), which sheltered the well beside the E hemicycle at the back of the Terrazza degli Emicicli of the Sanctuary of Fortune (see below).

The *Sanctuary of Fortuna Primigenia, mentioned by Cicero, is a colossal monumental edifice laid out in a series of terraces conforming to the slope of the hill and connected by ramps and staircases converging towards a temple on the summit. Much of the medieval town was built over it. The most grandiose Hellenistic edifice in Italy, it has an important place in the history of architecture since it is one of the earliest instances in which concrete was used by the Romans as a building material in vaulting. Its baroque concept and intricate design, perhaps derived from the smaller sanctuaries in Cos and Rhodes, did not, however, have a direct influence on later Roman buildings. The date of its construction has for long been under discussion, but it is now thought almost certainly to date from around 130–100 BC.

The plan is a quadrangle 118m square. The sanctuary was dedicated jointly to Fortuna and Juno. The cult of Fortuna was connected with an oracle which claimed to foretell the future by delivering to enquirers 'sortes' or lots, which were pieces of wood with letters carved in them. When the town was bombed in 1944 the houses on Via del Borgo were destroyed and clearance of this part of the sanctuary was carried out.

The parts of the sanctuary at present open to the public are entered from a gate across the road from the Museum (admission with the same ticket). The sanctuary was designed, instead, to be approached from below (from the level of the present Via del Borgo). The TERRAZZA DELLA CORTINA, on the highest terrace, was originally a courtyard with side porticoes in front of the cavea of the theatre (now occupied by the Museum building). This upper sanctuary was probably damaged in the siege of 82 BC and restored by Sulla. The scena of the theatre would have been a temporary construction erected for each performance. The central staircase descends to the next level, the TERRAZZA DEI FORNICI A SEMICOLONNE, with a colonnade stretching the whole width of the sanctuary. The monumental staircase continues down to the TERRAZZA DEGLI EMICICLI which is supported by a massive wall and divided into halves by a central staircase. Along the back of each half ran a Doric colonnade, the line of which was broken by a monumental hemicycle, also colonnaded. Over the hemicycles was a coffered vault carried on Ionic columns, part of which is still in place. A fragment of the high attic and some Ionic columns of the right hemicycle survive. This was the shrine of the oracle of Fortune, the most important part of the sanctuary. A colossal head of Fortune, now in the Museum, was found in the well here from which the 'sortes' (see above) were extracted.

The view from the terrace is splendid: to the W is Rome, with Soracte in the far distance; to the N the Monte Tiburtini; to the E the Monti Ernici; to the S the Monte Lepini; and to the SW the Campagna as far as the Tyrrhenian Sea. Two great ramps (formerly covered), constructed on rubble lead down to the great polygonal wall at the foot of the sanctuary (on Via del Borgo). Below are two terraces and the level of the Forum of the ancient city (beside the Duomo, described above).

Just outside the town, off the Valmontone road, an avenue leads to the remains of the 4C BASILICA DI SANT'AGAPITO (recently restored).

FROM PALESTRINA TO CAPRANICA PRENESTINA, 12km. This road, a continuation of Via Pedemontana, climbs in spirals to (3.5km) **Castel San Pietro Romano** (752m), a hamlet on the site of the citadel of Praeneste. Its church of San Pietro has an altarpiece by Pietro da Cortona. On the top of the hill is the ruined Castle of the Colonna. The *view is magnificent, reaching all the way to Rome and beyond. The road continues to climb. 12km Capranica Prenestina (914m). Beyond this point the road gradually descends in a huge curve round the E side of the Monti Prenestini and across the Monti Tiburtini to (29.5km) Tivoli (Rte 33).

FROM PALESTRINA TO TIVOLI, 41.5km. Via Prenestina leads out of Palestrina and at 8km a turn (right) leads to **Gallicano nel Lazio**, situated on a high tufa rock between two valleys, probably on the site of the Latin city of 'Pedum' conquered by Rome in 338 BC. The present village dates from the 10C, and has picturesque roads leading off the central street. 18.5km POLI, a pretty town with a 16C Conti palace (frescoes by Giulio Romano). 25.5km CASAPE, in the wooded folds of the Prenestine Hills. 28.5km **San Gregorio da Sassola**, a charming hill town with a 15C castle, later converted into a baronial palace. From here the road, clinging to the hillside, passes through olive groves with views to the plain towards Rome on the left. 41.5km Tivoli (Rte 33).

FROM PALESTRINA TO GENAZZANO, 10km. The road (N 155) follows the remains of the old disused tramway from Rome to the spa town of Fiuggi. It descends through (6km) Cave and just before (10km) the turn for Genazzano the view opens out with hills ahead and Genazzano up to the left. **Genazzano**, a rather gloomy small town (4700 inhab.) of medieval origins, is best entered from beside the huge Castello Colonna, at the far end of the town, with a concrete flying bridge from the castle to the public gardens (also reached by a flight of steps). Cars should be parked here. A road leads up past the right side of the castle to the Corso where the CASA APOLLONI (No. 41) has interesting Gothic windows. Opposite is another old house with a decorative two-light window. On the left is the entrance, across a bridge, to the courtyard of CASTELLO COLONNA (in very poor condition, but being restored). It was rebuilt in the 15C by Oddone Colonna, and enlarged by the Borgia. The door into the courtyard is usually open: here three arches support a graceful double loggia with a mosaic inscription beneath which is access to the flying bridge over to the public gardens. The courtyard also has a fountain and handsome windows in the left wing.

The Corso leads down to the SANTUARIO DELLA MADONNA DEL BUON CONSIGLIO founded in the 13C but rebuilt in the 17C and heavily restored in 1844. It contains a venerated painted image of the Madonna and Child (in a 15C tabernacle at the end of the N aisle). This is supposed to have been transported here from Scùtari in Albania in 1467, and is the prototype of images of the 'Madonna del Buon Consiglio'. In the S aisle is a font and delicately carved Renaissance tabernacle, and (second altar) a painting of St Thomas attributed to Tommaso Luini (c 1630). In the chapel to the right of the sanctuary is a ruined 15C fresco of the Crucifixion. The odd marble balustrade in front of the sanctuary is a heavy Baroque work. There is a museum in the adjoining convent with reliquaries, vestments, etc.

The Fiuggi road can be followed as far as the turn for Piglio; this road continues up to the ALTIPIANI DI ARCINAZZO (845m), an upland area spaciously laid out as a resort. N 411 descends through pretty countryside towards Subiaco (Rte 32), with good views ahead of the mountains.

The return to Rome may be made by Via Prenestina (37km). 8km Turning right for Gallicano nel Lazio, and other attractive hill towns on a road to Tivoli (see above). At (8.5km) Santa Maria di Cavamonte there is a cross-roads. To the left is Zagarolo (see above); to the right, Tivoli (18.5km). From here the narrow straight Via Prenestina leads back to Rome, through gently rolling country. The road passes a long stretch of Roman pavement on the approach (16.5km) to GABII (right), which gave the road its original name, the VIA GABINA. It passed through Gabii and Praeneste (Palestrina) and joined the Via Latina at Anagnina (Anagni). A legend relates that Romulus and Remus were sent to Gabii to study Greek, and the ancient Latin town was supposed to have been captured by Tarquinius Superbus. The ruins (conspicuous to the right of the road near a tower) include those of a Temple reconstructed in the mid 2C BC, with its altar. This is known as the Temple of Juno, but may instead have been dedicated to Fortune. In a sanctuary here a vast number of bronze statuettes were found in 1976.

To the W, at Osteria dell'Osa, recent excavations have revealed an Iron Age necropolis. In the neighbourhood are the stone quarries from which parts of Rome were built. 22km PONTE DI NONA, at the 9th (Roman) milestone, a fine Roman bridge of the Republican era, in excellent preservation; it has seven arches and is 72m long. 30km TOR DE' SCHIAVI (left) is a circular mausoleum, which, with the ruins of an octagonal hall, and a funerary basilica, formed part of the 3C VILLA DEI GIORDANI, one of the largest suburban Roman villas, surrounded by a public park. 37km. This route rejoins Via Casilina, just outside Porta Maggiore to return to the centre of Rome.

32

Subiaco

ROAD, N 5 (Via Tiburtina and Via Valeria), 74km. From Rome to (31.5km) **Tivoli**, see Rte 33—45km **Vicovaro**—46km Turn for Licenza and HORACE'S VILLA (8km)—48km Mandela—55km ANTICOLI CORRADO (2km)—58km Turn for Subiaco—74km **Subiaco**.

MOTORWAY (A 24 for Aquila), 49km to 'Vicovaro–Mandela' exit, then road, as above.

Frequent BUS SERVICES from Castro Pretorio in c 2 hrs via Castel Madama, and in c 1½ hrs via Vicovaro.

TRAINS on the Rome–Pescara line. From Rome (Termini) via Tivoli to Mandela-Sambuci, 54km in c 1 hr. Buses connect with the trains from Rome to Subiaco, 25km in 40 minutes.

From Rome to (31.5km) Tivoli, see Rte 33. Beyond Tivoli, the N 5 is called VIA VALERIA, one of the great Roman roads across the Apennines, probably built by the Censor M. Valerio Massimo around 304 BC. It passed through Carseoli (Carsoli) and Corfinium (near Sulmona) to Aternum (Pescara), on the Adriatic. From there it followed the coastline to Castrum Truentium (near San Benedetto del Tronto), where it joined the Via Salaria. Beyond Tivoli the road accompanies the Rome–Pescara railway as it winds NE between wooded hills up the Aniene valley, followed, farther on, also by a motorway (A 24; for Aquila). 36km San Polo station (SAN POLO DE' CAVA-LIERI, with a medieval Rocca, is 7km along a branch road left). 40km Castel Madama station lies 3km below CASTEL MADAMA whose Orsini castle, on top of a green hill (453m), is prominent to the right. Remains of arches of the Acqua Marcia are seen here and there. The valley widens and the landscape becomes more attractive, with numerous chestnut trees, olive groves, and vineyards.

45km **Vicovaro** (300m; 3600 inhab.) occupies the site of the citadel of 'Varia', a town of the Equi. The main road continues to the far end of the town, and, by a (signposted) turn for the Tempietto, just below the road on the left is the little church of SANT' ANTONIO with antique columns in its portico. The road on the right leads up to the pretty Piazza (car parking) with the Baroque flank of San Pietro (being restored) opposite the delightful little *TEMPIETTO DI SAN GIACOMO, an octagonal Renaissance chapel begun by Domenico da Capodistria in 1454, and thought to have been completed by Giovanni Dalmatia in 1465. Numerous sculptures decorate the unusual exterior, Gothic below, and Renaissance above. The lunette of the richly decorated portal is particularly fine. The interior, with numerous ex-votos, is in poor condition. In front of San Pietro is the large 18C Palazzo Cenci-Bolognetti which incorporates part of a 13C Orsini palace. Outside the little town the monastery of SAN COSIMATO can be seen on a rise to the right, surrounded by a pretty garden.

After several sharp bends in the road, a lovely road diverges left through the valley of the turbulent Licenza (the ancient Digentia). To the right can be seen the beautiful hill-town of Mandela (see below), and on the left ROCCAGIOVINE with remains of an Orsini castle. Before Licenza (8km), a rough road (signposted) on the left (and a footpath) lead to the ruins of a simple Roman villa. This was almost certainly **Horace's Sabine farm** (open every day 9.00–1 hr before sunset), given to the poet in 33/32 BC and described in many of his letters. It was first excavated in 1911, and its beautiful, peaceful setting has been preserved.

Beside the entrance is a plan of the site. Some of the rooms have fine mosaic pavements; the first one is the most sumptuous, with an area of different mosaic design for a bed. The rooms are raised above an oblong garden with a swimming-pool in the centre. They are grouped round an open court with a square pool; parts of the original lead piping used to channel the water from it can be seen under the floors of neighbouring rooms. On the W side of the site are baths with later Imperial extensions (used as a church in the Middle Ages). Further S is a 2C aquarium, which was later covered by the church of a medieval convent. The site is now within the 'Parco Regionale dei Monti Lucretili', a protected area of 1000 hectares, where numerous wild orchids grow.

The spring or 'Fonte di Orazio', presumed to be the Bandusian Spring apostrophised in one of Horace's odes (iii, 13), can still be seen up the rise to the SW of the site (from which its sound can be heard). A rough road continues up from the car park to a NINFEO constructed in the 15C by the Orsini, probably replacing a similar edifice of Horace's time.

The main road continues up to the little hill-town of **Licenza**. (8km). The town has been known since Roman times for its 'farro', a species of grain called spelt, which is here made into 'sagne' (annual festival in late November). At the top of the town (best reached on foot), in a charming little piazza, is an ARCHAEOLOGICAL MUSEUM (open daily 9.00–12.30, 15.00–18.00). It contains some material found during excavations of Horace's Sabine Farm, beautifully arranged, including ceramics, glass, bronzes, coins, and water pipes. Also here: a delicately carved ceiling boss, fragments of a statue, and of 4C frescoes.

The byroad continues N from Licenza, passing close to the well-preserved little hill-town of CIVITELLA and then following a deserted wooded valley. The road climbs through the village of ORVINIO (12km), with decorative flower pots. The Corso (not suitable for cars) leads through an archway on the right past the oval Baroque church of San Nicola towards the large 16C castle (privately owned; no adm). On the left of the main road is a 19C public fountain and steps up to the church of the Madonnna dei Raccomandati (if closed, key at No. 3), with 17C frescoes by the local painter Vincenzo Manenti. The deserted road, now in the province of Rieti, descends through woods and then olive groves via Poggio Maiano to join the main road (N 4) for Rieti, see Rte 34.

The main Subiaco road (N 5) continues past (48km) another turning left for the village of MANDELA which stands on the spur of a hill to the N. Its position provides magnificent views of the valleys on either side, which are glimpsed down its narrow streets. The castle belonged to the Orsini. The village of SAMBUCI lies 4km S of the main road. The valley of Subiaco, the 'Valle Santa', soon comes into view.

56km Turning right for **Anticoli Corrado**. The byroad crosses the Aniene and in 2km reaches this small town, beautifully situated on a hillside. The story is told of a group of artists who, on a journey to Subiaco in the early 19C, stopped on the way at Anticoli and fell in love with its charm and most of all its beautiful women, whom they used as models in their work. Nino Costa, Felice Carena, Arturo Martini, and Emanuele Cavalli all lived here for certain periods of their lives. In the spacious main square is a Noah's Ark fountain by Arturo Martini (1926), and the 11C church of SAN PIETRO, well-preserved, with Gothic arches. The bronze doors are by Carlo Toppi (1975). Above the W door is a 14C fresco of the Madonna and Saints and in the centre of the nave, a Cosmatesque pavement. The first S chapel has 16C frescoes and the first N chapel frescoes of Saints Cosma and Damiano. A Roman cippus is incorporated in the high altar. In the second N chapel is a bronze Madonna and Child by Attilio Selva (1946).

From the opposite corner of the piazza, a road leads through the ancient gate of the city up to the MUSEUM OF MODERN ART, housed in an old villa, used as a prison in the 16C. The small collection has been donated over the last 50 years by artists of all nationalities who have worked in Anticoli, as well as those who were born here, and the collection is particularly impressive.

At 58km this route leaves Via Valeria and turns right along the beautiful wooded Subiaco road (Via Sublacensis), following the course of the Aniene upstream, with the Monti Simbruini on the left. On the right can be seen the hill-town of Marano Equo. In this area are springs, which are the source of the Acqua Marcia, and still supply Rome with water. 64km AGOSTA (left) is a hamlet founded by the monks of Subiaco. From (68.5km) Madonna della Pace, a secondary road, the Via Empolitana, leads W to Tivoli past the conspicuous hill-top village of Rocca Canterano (747m).

74km **SUBIACO** (408m; 8400 inhab.) lies near the head of the narrow Aniene valley, on the W slopes of Monte Livata. Famous as the birthplace of western monasticism under the rule of its founder St Benedict, it is particularly interesting for its two monasteries just outside the town.

Subiaco, anciently 'Sublaqueum' ('under the lakes') is thought to owe its origin as a town to the necessity of accommodating the workmen employed by Nero to build a huge villa here. The Emperor created three small lakes, the 'Simbuina Stagna', mentioned by Tacitus, in the valley by damming the Aniene (destroyed in a flood in 1305). Tacitus relates how Nero narrowly escaped being struck by lightning in his villa here. Only scant remains survive of the villa, first excavated in 1883 (and again in 1957).

A monastery dedicated to St Clement was founded at Subiaco early in the history of the church. Towards the end of the 5C Benedetto da Norcia (St Benedict; 480–543?), a rich young man, rebelled against the dissolute life of his contemporaries, and decided to live in a cavern on the slopes of Monte Taleo. Here he stayed, in prayer and contemplation, for three years. The fame of his saintliness spread all over Italy and numerous people came to Subiaco to see him. His cavern was known as the *Sacro Speco* (Holy Grotto). His twin sister Scholastica later persuaded him to build a monastery near the ruins of Nero's villa. Having aroused the jealousy of a monk called Fiorenzio, he decided to leave, and, guided by three tame ravens, moved to Monte Cassino, where in 529 he founded a new monastery.

Some of his companions stayed behind with the abbot St Honorius, and built the convent of Saints Cosmas and Damian (now St Scholastica) and other retreats, most of which were destroyed by the Lombards. The convents which survived were of great importance in the 11–12C, but the ambitions of the monks, earthquakes, and the plague of 1348 contributed to their decline. In the 16–18C the monastery was ruled by powerful prince-abbots, from the Colonna, Borghese, and Barberini families, until, in 1753, Benedict XIV abolished the temporal power of the abbots.

Arnold Pannartz and Conrad Sweynheim, pupils of Fust, from Mainz, set up the first printing press in Italy, in the Convent of St Scholastica, in 1464. They soon quarrelled with the scribes in the monastery, and in 1467 transferred their press to Rome (see Palazzetto Massimi).

Outside the town, to the right of the road and reached by a tiny 14C hump-backed bridge (new bridge downstream), is the church of SAN FRANCESCO. Over the high altar is a triptych signed and dated 1467 by Antoniazzo Romano. A wooden altar frames a painting of St Francis receiving the stigmata, attributed (with little foundation) to Sebastiano del Piombo. In the third chapel on the left are frescoes once attributed to Sodoma, and an altarpiece of the Nativity attributed to Pinturicchio. The second chapel contains a wooden Crucifix by Fra Stefano (from Piazza Armerina; 1685).

At the entrance to the town is the conspicuous ARCH OF PIUS VI, erected in 1789 in honour of the Pope, who, as Cardinal Braschi, had been abbot of Subiaco and had done much for its inhabitants. The main street leads to the CATHEDRAL (Sant'Andrea), built by Pius VI in 1766 (reconstructed after its partial destruction in the War). In the apse is a 16C Crucifix and in the right transept a large painting of the Miracle of the Fishes by Sebastiano Conca.

The altars in the transepts incorporate antique marbles from a Roman villa. On the left a road leads up through the medieval part of the town to the ROCCA ABBAZIALE, founded in 1073. Pius VI converted the castle into a stately residence for high ecclesiastical dignitaries.

The monasteries outside the town are reached by the Ienne road, called 'Via dei Monasteri' (or on foot by a path which crosses and recrosses the road). The road passes the round chapel of San Mauro and continues to ascend. It skirts a few ruins of part of NERO'S VILLA (see above); on the right of the road was the lake (now dried-up) formed by the dam that Nero built across the river.

The road continues to climb to reach (2.5km) the **Monastero di Santa Scolastica** (500m), now a Benedictine convent with 19 monks. It is shown by a monk on a guided tour, 9.00–12.30, 16.00–19.00; Mass on Sunday 10.00–11.30. It was a powerful abbey in the Middle Ages, with feudal privileges, but was badly damaged in the last War. From the LARGE CLOISTER, dating from 1569–80 (with photocopies of the precious MSS in the library, see below) there is a good view of the campanile of the church. Also here is a fresco of James Stuart, the Old Pretender. The irregular Gothic SECOND CLOISTER has an interesting arch (1450) in the Gothic style with statuettes of German workmanship. There are also fragments from Nero's villa. Around an entrance to the church are mid-14C frescoes of the Sienese school and an inscription recording the properties of the abbey in 1052. A coarse bas-relief showing two deer drinking from a chalice bears the date 980. The *THIRD CLOISTER is a fine work with beautfiul little columns, signed by Giacomo Cosmati (1210–43). The frescoes, showing the properties of the monastery, are by the late 13C Roman school.

Beyond a 9C porch which supports the base of the campanile is the entrance to the CHURCH OF ST SCHOLASTICA, on 7C foundations (and rebuilt in 975). It was reconstructed in 1770 by Giacomo Quarenghi, his first and only work in Italy; the architect then went to live in Russia where he built much of Leningrad. Here are two columns in green cipollino from Nero's villa. Frescoes from the earlier church (1426) are preserved in the vault (visible only with special permission). Beneath the church is the Cappella degli Angeli, with an altar recomposed from Cosmatesque fragments. The LIBRARY and archives (open to scholars) contain 380 MSS and over 30,000 printed books (among them 90 incunabula), as well as papal bulls, royal and imperial edicts, and other rare documents. It also contains the first two books printed in Italy, Cicero's De Oratore and a Lactantius of 1465.

The road continues up beneath arches of the convent to the *Monastero di San Benedetto, or Sacro Speco (640m; open daily 9.00–12.30, 15.00–18.00), consisting of two superimposed churches, chapels, and grottoes, naturally formed in or artificially carved out of the mountainside. Five Benedictine monks still live here. From the car park an easy stepped path leads up beneath a Gothic archway through a venerable ilex grove. A narrow stair continues up to a terrace from which can be seen the monastery built into the hillside. A small Gothic door opens into a loggia, with a view of the wooded valley. In the last bay are 15C Umbrian frescoes of Benedictines, and above the door is a worn fresco of the Madonna and Child. Beyond is the old chapter house with frescoes of the school of Perugino.

Three steps lead down into the UPPER CHURCH (c 1350) with an aisleless nave and a chancel, and good cross-vaulting. The nave is decorated with 14C frescoes, mainly by the Sienese school. Outstanding among these are

The Kiss of Judas and the Way of the Cross (left wall), the Entry of Christ into Jerusalem (right wall), and the Crucifixion (front wall). Steps lead down to the sanctuary with more frescoes and a Cosmati altar. The frescoed transept has a stoup made from a Roman urn. The sacristy (shown on request) has a 15C fresco of the Crucifixion, two panels of the Sienese School, a painting showing the lake of Subiaco, and a fresco fragment of St Benedict by Consulus. Steps in front of the altar lead down to the LOWER CHURCH, with a series of chapels at different levels. Nearly all the frescoes here of episodes in the life of St Benedict (as told by St Gregory the Great) are by 'Magister Conxolus', a master of the Roman school of the second half of the 13C (usually called 'Consulus'), whose signature can be seen in the niche at the top of the stairs on a fresco of the Madonna and Child with two angels.

After a second flight of steps, the level of the **Sacro Speco** is reached, which gave the convent its alternative name. The Holy Grotto is a small dark natural cavern in the rock. Here is a marble statue of St Benedict, by Antonio Raggi (1657). The lower part of the walls of the grotto are lined with cipollino from Nero's villa.

From the landing a little spiral staircase leads up to the CHAPEL OF ST GREGORY (usually closed), with further frescoes by Consulus, and a *Portrait of St Francis, without halo or stigmata, painted at the time of his visit to the convent (c 1210) and claimed to be the first example in Italy of a genuine portrait. The SCALA SANTA was so-called because it is on the line of the path taken by St Benedict on his way to and from his cavern. The stairway, decorated with macabre 15C Sienese frescoes depicting Death, leads down past the 14C CHAPEL OF THE MADONNA, covered with more 15C frescoes and the GROTTO DEI PASTORI, a small cave where St Benedict is said to have preached to the local shepherds. It contains the oldest fresco in the convent, an 8C or 9C fragment representing the Madonna with St Luke and another saint.

Outside the cave is a small terrace from which can be seen the great columns and arches supporting the convent buildings. Here is another 15C fresco of the Pietà. The overgrown rose garden is on the site of a bramble where St Benedict is traditionally thought to have mortified his flesh, which centuries later was turned into a rose tree by St Francis. The REFECTORY (no adm) contains interesting 15C frescoes of the Umbrian school. From the terrace at the entrance to the monastery, paths lead through delightful woods with views.

An alternative (slower) route back to Rome is via the Altipiani di Arcinazzo and Piglio, to Palestrina (see Rte 31).

33

Tivoli and Hadrian's Villa

ROAD (VIA TIBURTINA), 31.5km. The fastest way of reaching Tivoli by public transport is now by the underground line 'B' from the Colosseum or Termini railway station to its terminus at *Rebibbia* which is connected by a bus service (every 20 minutes) to Tivoli (20km in 35 minutes). There is also a bus from Rebibbia for Hadrian's Villa (along the Via Prenestina). There is a bus service between Tivoli and Hadrian's Villa.

RAILWAY. A somewhat roundabout route from Rome (Termini) to Tivoli via Guidonia, on the Rome–Pescara line (40km in c 1 hr).

VIA TIBURTINA (N 5), on the line of the old Roman road to Tibur (Tivoli), starts from Porta San Lorenzo (Pl. 6; 5, 4). The road passes the huge Campo Verano Cemetery on the right, and then crosses the railway (Rome Tiburtina station, left). The next 10km traverse ugly suburbs, and the Aniene is crossed by (8km) the PONTE MAMMOLO, successor (1857) to the ancient PONS MAMMEUS, dating from the Republican era and rebuilt by Julia Mammaea, mother of Alexander Severus. On the left is a road leading to Via Nomentana. The river ANIENE, the classical *Anio*, rises in the Monti Simbruini, to the E of Subiaco. It flows past Subiaco and Tivoli, where it forms impressive cascades, and joins the Tiber N of Rome, near the Ponte Salario. In Roman times its waters were carried to Rome by two aqueducts, the *Anio Vetus* (70km), begun in 273 BC, and the *Anio Novus* (95km) begun in AD 36.

The Rome Circular Road is crossed just before (13km) SETTECAMINI (48m). Farther on, a road leads S to LUNGHEZZA, with a 13C castle. Here is the site of COLLATIA, where archaeological material dating from the Iron Age has come to light. 19.5km Le Tavernucole; on the left is the crenellated CASTELL' ARCIONE, probably erected in the 12C on ruins dating from the Imperial era, and restored in 1931. Beyond it are the three summits of the Monti Cornicolani with Monte Gennaro rising behind them; ahead are Tivoli and the Monti Tiburtini; to the right the Monti Prenestini and the Alban Hills. 21.5km Turning (left) for Guidonia.

22.5km **Bagni di Tivoli** (80m), a spa (hotels of all categories) which uses the water from two nearby lakes which are fed by hot springs (24°C), the Roman *Aquae Albulae*, charged with sulphuretted hydrogen which gives a strong smell to the locality. To the S are remains of Roman baths. Beyond the railway the road passes travertine quarries that provided stone for the Colosseum, St Peter's, and many other buildings in ancient and modern Rome. The stone is the 'lapis tiburtinus' which hardens after cutting. The Aniene is crossed near (26km) the five-arched PONTE LUCANO, a Roman bridge named after Lucanus Plautius and rebuilt at various times from the 15C to the 19C. Immediately beyond the bridge is (right) the tower-like *TOMB OF THE PLAUTII, dating from AD 10–14, and resembling the Tomb of Cecilia Metella on the Appian Way. Aulus Plautius commanded the army which invaded Britain in AD 43.

At (28km) *Bivio Villa Adriana* (41m) the road to (1.5km) Hadrian's Villa (described below) branches off to the right. Via Tiburtina now begins its long serpentine climb to Tivoli, passing through a beautiful olive grove. The town (31.5km) is entered by Via Nazionale.

TIVOLI, the classical *Tibur*, is now a busy noisy town (52,000 inhab.), surrounded by ugly high-rise buildings. In the centre of the town are the famous gardens of the Villa d'Este, and below the hill, protected by a beautiful park, are the magnificent ruins of Hadrian's Villa. Tivoli was built in a delightful position on the lower slopes (230m) of the Sabine Hills at the end of the valley of the Aniene, which here narrows into a gorge between Monte Catillo (348m) on the N and the Colle Ripoli (484m) on the S and forms spectacular cascades. The river makes a wide loop round the town and borders it on three sides.

Information Office, Azienda Autonoma, Largo Garibaldi.

Hotels of all categories in Via di Villa Adriana (below the town, near Hadrian's Villa).

Numerous **restaurants** all over the town. Hadrian's Villa is a superb place to **picnic**.

Transport from Rome (see above). Railway station, Viale Mazzini (a few hundred metres from the Villa Gregoriana). Bus Station in Piazza Garibaldi (Bus No. 4 from here to Hadrian's Villa).

History. *Tibur* is supposed to have been founded four centuries before the birth of Rome, by the Siculi, who were later expelled by Tiburtus and his brothers, grandsons of Amphiarus. It was captured by Camillus in 380 BC. By the end of the 1C BC numerous wealthy Romans came to live here or pass the summer here: the area was noted for its abundance of water and its cool climate. Temples were erected to Vesta, Hercules, and other deities. Marius, Cassius, Sallust, Maecenas, and Quintilius Varus all had sumptuous villas in the town or nearby. Augustus and the poets Catullus, Propertius, and Horace frequently visited the town. Trajan also favoured Tibur, but it reached its greatest fame when Hadrian chose it as his residence and built his remarkable villa on the outskirts of the town. Tibur was sacred to the cult of the Sybil Albunea. Later it was used for the confinement of state prisoners, including Syphax and Zenobia.

In the 6C Totila, the Ostrogoth, sacked the town, but then rebuilt it as his capital. By the 10C it had recovered its prosperity, and withstood a siege by Otho III. It became independent as an Imperial free city, and was occupied by the Caraffa in the 16C. It did not lose its autonomous character until 1816. Among its natives were Munatius Plancus (consul 42 BC), the founder of Lyons, Pope Simplicius (468–83) and Pope John IX (898–900).

Via Tiburtina enters the town from the SW as Via Nazionale and ends at **Largo Garibaldi**, a busy traffic centre. On the left is the Giardino Garibaldi, with a splendid *view of the open country below. To the NW can be seen the air station of Guidonia, with the Monti Cornicolani villages above it; almost due W is Rome; to the SW the Campagna extends to the sea.

Viale Nazioni Uniti leads out of the right side of the square up past the bus station to the imposing **Rocca Pia** (closed for restoration in 1994), a castle built by Pius II (1458–64) to dominate the inhabitants of Tivoli. It is rectangular in shape and has four crenellated cylindrical towers, two large and two smaller. The castle was built over the ruins of a Roman amphitheatre, best seen from Vicolo Barchetto to the N. Viale Trieste continues to Porta San Giovanni, now the entrance to a hospital. Here is the little church of SAN GIOVANNI EVANGELISTA, containing good frescoes by Antoniazzo Romano.

From the other side of Largo Garibaldi (see above) Via Boselli leads to Piazza Trento outside the Romanesque church of **Santa Maria Maggiore**, with a fine rose-window attributed to Angelo da Tivoli above a later Gothic

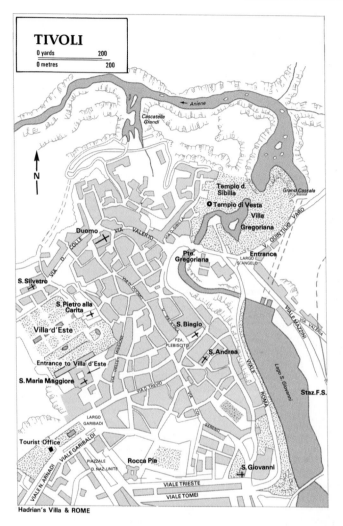

Hadrian's Villa & ROME

narthex (which contains a 13C fresco of the Madonna and Child, in a fine tabernacle). The INTERIOR contains remains of the original floor at the E end. In the presbytery are two triptychs, the one on the right dates from the 16C, and the one on the left is signed by Bartolomeo Bulgarini of Siena (14C). Above the latter, Madonna and Child, by Iacopo Torriti. Over the high altar is a Byzantine Madonna (12C?). In the right aisle, Crucifix attributed to Baccio da Montelupo.

Adjoining the church, on the right, is the present entrance to the *VILLA D'ESTE** celebrated for its remarkable gardens, decorated with spectacular fountains. These were created by Pirro Ligorio for Cardinal Ippolito II d'Este (1509–72), a rich Renaissance prince, collector and patron of the arts, who was a friend of Ariosto, Tasso, Benvenuto Cellini, and the musician Pierluigi da Palestrina. The villa and gardens are open every day 9.00 to dusk, and there is a café in the villa.

Originally a Benedictine convent, the property was confiscated as a residence for the governor of Tivoli. When Cardinal Ippolito II d'Este became governor in 1550 he commissioned Pirro Ligorio to transform the convent into a sumptuous villa. The district of the town below the convent was destroyed and the hillside was levelled to provide space for the gardens. An underground conduit was constructed from the Aniene, to increase the water supply. The use of water as the main theme of the gardens may have been inspired by Hadrian's Villa and the plan, based on a series of terraces, is similar to that of the Temple of Fortune at Palestrina. The work had not been completed by the time of the Cardinal's death in 1572, and it was continued by his successor Cardinal Luigi d'Este who employed Flaminio Ponzio after 1585.

In the 17C numerous additions and restorations were carried out for Cardinal Alessandro d'Este, and (by Gian Lorenzo Bernini) for Cardinal Rinaldo d'Este. In the 19C the villa and gardens were neglected, and all the Roman statues were sold. It passed by bequest to Austria, but after 1918 the Italian Government resumed possession and undertook a general restoration. The top floor was the Italian home of Franz Liszt (1811–86) from 1865 to the year of his death; from this base he travelled to many parts of Europe and, while here, he composed the third book of his *Années de Pélerinage*, one of the most popular pieces in which is *Les Jeux d'Eau à la Villa d'Este*. A fine Roman mosaic pavement was found beneath the villa in 1983.

The entrance (formerly the back entrance) leads into a COURTYARD designed in 1567 on the site of the cloister of the convent. The FOUNTAIN OF VENUS here incorporates a Roman statue. Off the courtyard is the APPARTAMENTO VECCHIO (closed for restoration), on the first floor. This was decorated with frescoes c 1568 by Livio Agresti and assistants. The Cardinal's bedroom has a fine carved wood ceiling, and the Chapel has frescoes by the bottega of Federico Zuccari.

A staircase descends to the **Appartamento Nobile** on the ground floor, a series of rooms off a long corridor, overlooking the gardens. The largest room is the SALONE with the FONTANA DI TIVOLI, a wall fountain in mosaic, begun by Curzio Maccarone and completed in 1568 by Paolo Calandrino. The frescoes are by the school of Gerolamo Muziano and Federico Zuccari. On the walls are views of the garden painted by Matteo Neroni in 1568. From the loggia stairs lead down to the gardens. The two rooms behind the fountain were decorated by Cesare Nebbia and assistants, and the rooms on the other side of the Salone have frescoes by Federico Zuccari and assistants. Beyond the Sala della Caccia, with 17C frescoes, a spiral staircase descends to the gardens (which can also be reached from the loggia off the Salone).

The main FAÇADE of the villa overlooking the gardens has an elegant LOGGIA (1567) in the centre on two storeys, connected to the gardens by a double flight of steps. The *Gardens are laid out on terraces which descend from the villa and are connected by steps and paths. The original vegetation (which included many plane trees and elms) was altered when evergreen trees (ilexs, pines and cypresses) were introduced in the 17C, and sequoia and cedars were planted in the 19C. The terrace along the front of the palace is called the PASSEGGIATA DEL CARDINALE with a balcony on which is a pretty fountain basin. Beneath it is a loggia with a mosaic vault, and on a lower level the FONTANA DEL BICCHIERONE, added in 1661 by Gian Lorenzo Bernini.

A path descends to a lower walk, at the far left end of which is the GROTTO OF DIANA, with Mannerist decorations (in stucco, mosaic, coloured glass, and shells) by Lola and Paolo Calandrino. Steps descend from here to the elaborate **Fontana di Roma** or **Rometta** designed by Pirro Ligorio and executed by Curzio Maccarone. This has a model of the Tiber with an islet (representing the Isola Tiberina) in the form of a boat, on which is an obelisk. Behind are a seated statue of Rome, with the wolf suckling Romulus and Remus, and miniature reproductions of the principal buildings of ancient Rome.

From the Rometta the VIALE DELLE CENTO FONTANE leads right across the garden, parallel to the villa. It is skirted by a long narrow basin lined with hundreds of jets of water, surmounted by a frieze of obelisks, models of boats, Estense eagles, and lilies of France, and below, overgrown with maidenhair fern and moss, are water-spouts in the form of animal heads. At the far end is the grandiose **Fontana di Tivoli** or *dell'Ovato*, by Pirro Ligorio, with the end of the conduit from the Aniene, one of the water supplies for the fountains, which descends in an abundant casade. In the hemicycle of the fountain are statues of nymphs, by Giovanni Battista della Porta. Above, in a laurel grove on the steep hillside, is the FONTANA DI PEGASO. On the right of the hemicycle is the GROTTA DI VENERE and the rustic FONTANA DI BACCO (very ruined).

On a lower level, still against the perimeter wall of the gardens, is the monumental **Fontana dell'Organo**, built around a water-operated organ (1568) in the centre of the niche (later protected by a little temple). This was one of the most original and famous features of the garden. The mechanism of the organ was destroyed in the 18C; only the outer structure survives. This fountain faces another scenographic terrace which runs parallel to the façade of the villa. Below the organ fountain is the FONTANA DI NETTUNO, with high jets of water (reached by Viale del Drago and the first ramp on the right), created in 1927. In front extend the three PESCHIERE or fish ponds.

In the centre of the lowest terrace is the **Rotonda dei Cipressi**, surrounded by some of the mightiest cypresses in Italy (three of them survive from the 17C). New trees have replaced some that were struck by disease and had to be felled. At the end of the gardens (left) a box and laurel hedge leads to the FONTANA DELLA MADRE NATURA, with a statue of Diana of the Ephesians. From the Rotonda dei Cipressi a central path leads back up towards the villa across the terrace with the fish ponds and up to a terrace with the FONTANA DEL DRAGO by Pirro Ligorio. This was probably intended as a homage to Gregory XIII (it reproduces the dragons in his coat of arms), who was a guest of the Cardinal in 1572.

The Viale del Drago leads right past the SCALA DEI BOLLORI an ingenious water staircase designed in 1567, to the bizarre FONTANA DELLA CIVETTA, which once used water power to produce the song of birds which was interrupted by the screech of an owl. It was begun in 1565 by Giovanni Del Duca, and finished by Raffaello Sangallo in 1569. Nearby is the FONTANA DI PROSERPINA (1570) used as an outside dining room. There is a splendid view of unspoilt countryside from this side of the gardens. Above are the Fontana di Roma and Grotta di Diana, described above.

The church of SAN PIETRO ALLA CARITÀ, outside the garden to the NE, contains ten cipollino columns, probably from a Roman villa, and an interesting crypt (open Sunday mornings; otherwise ring at the base of the campanile). From Largo Garibaldi Via Pacifici and Via Trevio lead towards Piazza del Plebiscito (see the plan), the town centre. Here is the church of **San Biagio**, founded in the 14C. Rebuilt in 1887, it is a remarkable example of the neo-Gothic style, with three impressive stained glass windows. On the second S altar is a good painting of San Vincenzo by the 15C Tuscan school. Behind the altar is a 15C detached fresco of the Crucifixion. Off the N side are interesting 15C fresco fragments of the Madonna enthroned and the Glory of St Thomas.

To the S, in Via Sant'Andrea, is the church of SANT'ANDREA, with a Romanesque campanile. From the square Via Palatina and Via Ponte Gregoriano, with interesting medieval houses, lead to Piazza Rivarola, an important traffic centre. From here Via San Valerio leads left to the **Duomo** (San Lorenzo), rebuilt in 1650 but retaining a Romanesque campanile of the 12C. In the INTERIOR, the fourth chapel in the south aisle (light on right), contains a 13C *group of five carved wooden figures representing the Descent from the Cross. The third chapel in the north aisle contains the so-called *Macchina del Salvatore*, which encloses a precious 11C or 12C triptych, painted in tempera, with silver and gilt decoration of the 15C and 16C. It is shown only on High religious festivals (copy in the adjoining chapel). Also in this aisle are two episcopal tombs (late 15C and early 16C).

From Piazza Duomo the medieval Via del Duomo (partly stepped) leads past (No. 78) the entrance to the PONDERARIUM, containing two tables with measures of capacity, used by Roman inspectors of weights and measures. In Piazza Tani, outside the side entrance to the Cathedral, is a pretty fountain made up from a medieval sarcophagus. From here the narrow Via del Colle (impracticable for cars) descends steeply past medieval houses and remains of ancient buildings through one of the most picturesque parts of the town. It passes the Romanesque church of SAN SILVESTRO (if closed ring to the right of façade at No. 2), recently restored. Inside are interesting 12C or 13C frescoes and a wooden figure of St Valerian of 1138 (right wall).

At the end of the street, outside Porta del Colle, is the **Sanctuary of Hercules Victor**, in a large area until recently occupied by a paper-mill. It is now being excavated and studied and there are long-term plans to open it to the public. This huge Hellenistic sanctuary was mentioned by numerous classical authors as being the most important in the city. There was an oracle here similar to the one in Palestrina. The buildings are thought to date from the end of the 2C BC. The most conspicuous remains are the Cyclopean substructures to the NW where the hill descends to the Aniene valley. Above the mighty foundations are arches and vaults which supported a huge Piazzale, with a portico on three sides, a temple, and a theatre. A market was connected to the sanctuary.

From Piazza Rivarola (see above) Via della Sibilla leads NE to the edge of the cliff which dominates the valley, the site of the Roman acropolis. Here is the so-called *Temple of Vesta, a circular Roman temple famous for its picturesque position. It is not known to whom the temple was dedicated; it is circular peripteral and dates from the last years of the Republic. It was converted in the Middle Ages into the church of Santa Maria della Rotonda. Ten of its 18 fluted Corinthian columns survive, and there is a frieze of bucrania, garlands, rosettes, and paterae. The doors and windows of the well- preserved cella are trapezoidal. Close by is an earlier temple, known as the **Temple of the Sibyl**, but also of uncertain attribution. It is rectangular with a tetrastyle Ionic façade. Until 1884 it was the church of San Giorgio.

From Piazza Rivarola Ponte Gregoriano leads over the Aniene to an open space by the Porta Sant'Angelo, a busy traffic centre. Here is the entrance to the ***Villa Gregoriana**, a park on a very steep hillside with the cascades of the river Aniene (adm daily 9.30–dusk). The park commemorates Gregory XVI, who took decisive steps to put an end to the periodic local floods, which in 1826 had seriously damaged the town. On his accession to the papacy in 1831, he instructed the engineer Folchi to build a double tunnel under Monte Catillo, to ease the flow of the river. From this tunnel (300m and 270m), known as the Traforo Gregoriano, the water plunges down in another waterfall, known as the Great Cascade. The park is not very well kept, and the climb down to the floor of the valley is extremely strenuous.

From the ticket office a path bears a little right, following the sign post ('Grande Cascata') to a terrace, with a view through an arch of the temples of Vesta and of the Sibyl across the valley. The path continues along the side of the hill to a parapet overlooking the crest of the GREAT CASCADE. Steps lead down to another terrace from which you can see the mouth of the tunnel. Here the Aniene makes a leap of 108m as it emerges from the Traforo Gregoriano. The tunnel (no adm) bears inscriptions recording the visits of popes and kings. From the first terrace a path marked 'Ruderi della Villa-Grotte della Sirena, di Nettuno, e Cascata Bernini' descends to another terrace planted with ilexes, at the end of which is a tunnel which passes through impressive remains of a Roman villa.

At the exit a path continues to descend with a good view of the LITTLE CASCADES and of the BERNINI CASCADE. Farther down, a little square is reached marked with two signposts, to the right of which there is a viewpoint about half the height of the Great Cascade, which gives you an idea of its volume, its noise and the rainbow colours of its spray. From the little square a path follows the signpost marked 'Grotte Nettuno e Sirena, Cascata Bernini', descending for some distance and bearing sharp left at a signpost marked 'Ingresso Grotta della Sirena' to reach the fantastic GROTTO OF THE SIREN, a limestone cavern in which the water tumbles down a narrow ravine. A path climbs the other side of the valley. From a fork marked 'Grotta di Nettuno e Tempio di Vesta', a path turns left, passing through two tunnels lit from the side. At another fork a path descends (left) to the GROTTO OF NEPTUNE, through which the Aniene originally flowed, and another one on the right leads to an exit-gate (closed on Monday) through a restaurant beside the Temple of Vesta.

From Porta Sant'Angelo Viale Mazzini leads S to the Station. Here, in a park, the tomb of the Vestal Virgin Cossinia has been set up.

From Porta Sant'Angelo the VIA DELLA CASCATELLE (3km long) is reached by Via Quintilio Varo which winds between olive plantations, and passes several times beneath the viaducts of the Rome–Tivoli railway. From the *BELVEDERE there is a fine view of the Great Cascade, and, after crossing beneath the railway for the last time, there is an excellent *view of the Great Cascade, the Cascatelle, the town of Tivoli, and the Campagna. The road passes the church of SANT'ANTONIO (left) and the ruined arches of the ACQUA MARCIA. This aqueduct, 58km long and dating from 144 BC, ran from Via Valeria to Rome. Five hundred metres further on a byroad (left; unsignposted) diverges from the main road and leads down past a group of houses to the conspicuous SANTUARIO DI SANTA MARIA DI QUINTILIOLO, near the ruins of a Roman villa, said to have been that of Quintilius Varus.

The road soon deteriorates and becomes less interesting. Farther on it crosses the PONTE DELL'ACQUORIA over the Aniene, and, going straight on, begins to climb the

Clivus Tiburtinus, partly levelled by Constantine. On the right, is the so-called TEMPIO DEL MONDO, with a large interior chamber and farther on, also on the right, is a Roman building known as the TEMPIO DELLA TOSSE. Probably dating from the 4C, this is an octagonal building with a circular exterior. Traces of Byzantine decoration suggest it may have been adapted for Christian worship. The road passes round the ruins of the Temple of Hercules Victor (see above), and re-enters Tivoli by Porta del Colle.

From Tivoli to Subiaco, see Rte 32; to Palestrina, see Rte 31.

About 5km below the town of Tivoli, reached off the main road to Rome, is ****HADRIAN'S VILLA**, the largest and richest Imperial villa in the Roman Empire. Hadrian became emperor on the death of Trajan in 117, and began the villa the following year, completing it ten years later. It is known that Hadrian prided himself on his abilities as an architect, and it is therefore presumed that the remarkably original buildings, many of them inspired by famous buildings in Greece and Egypt, were directly designed by him. They were spaciously laid out between numerous gardens. It is significant that the emperor chose to live here, and not in Rome, although the capitol was within easy reach of his residence. Of all the splendid buildings left which were erected by Hadrian throughout the Empire this is probably the most interesting. It is now one of the most evocative classical sites which survives in Italy, protected by a beautiful park.

Admission every day from 9.00 to dusk. The road for the Villa leaves the Via Tiburtina (the main road from Rome to Tivoli) at the *Bivio Villa Adriana*, 28km from Rome, and 4km from Tivoli. From the turn an ugly byroad (1.5km) continues to the entrance. For transport from Rome and from Tivoli, see the beginning of this route. The Villa is a splendid place to picnic, and there is a café near the entrance.

History. It is difficult to understand why Hadrian, with all the resources of the Empire at his disposal, should have chosen such an unprepossessing site for his magnificent estate. Though little over 5km from the scenic Roman health resort of Tivoli, the low lying surroundings of the villa have no particular attraction. In the emperor's day the flat plain was not even healthy. One reason for the choice of this site is probably the fact that its owner was the Empress Sabina; another reason may have been the emperor's desire to keep himself apart from his courtiers, many of whom owned villas on the hills around Tivoli. Parts of a smaller country house of the 1C BC, overlooking the 'Vale of Tempe', were incorporated into the emperor's villa.

Many of the buildings of the villa are derived from famous classical monuments, some of which Hadrian saw during his prolonged travels in the Empire. These were the Lyceum, the Academy, the Prytaneum, and the Stoa Poikile in Athens; the Canopus of the Egyptian Delta; and the Vale of Tempe in Thessaly. He also included a representation of Hades, as conceived by the Greek poets. An extensive system of underground passages (no adm), some corridors and others wide enough for a horse and carriage, exist beneath the villa; these were presumably service areas. Hadrian's successors enlarged the villa, but Constantine is supposed to have stolen some elements to decorate Byzantium. Barbarian invaders plundered the site, and it later became a quarry for builders and lime-burners. Until the Renaissance the ruins continued to be neglected or abused.

The first excavations were ordered by Alexander VI and Cardinal Alessandro Farnese. Soon after he took up residence at the Villa d'Este in 1550, Cardinal Ippolito II d'Este employed Pirro Ligorio to continue excavations, but he took many of the finds to decorate his villa. Further excavations were carried out in the 17–19C. Giovanni Battista Piranesi drew a plan of the site, and made engravings of the buildings and sculptures (now in the Calcografia Nazionale in Rome). In 1730 Count Fede planted cypresses and pines among the ruins. In 1870 the Italian Government acquired most of the site, and systematic excavations were begun (still far from complete). The works of art discovered in the villa (more than 260) are scattered in museums all over Europe, as well as in Rome (the Museo Nazionale Romano, the Capitoline Museum, and the Vatican Museums).

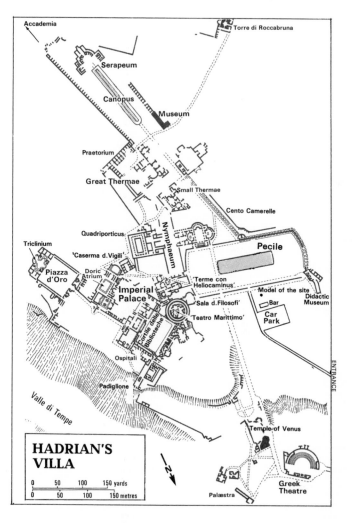

The general plan of the villa, which covers some 120ha, is capricious, although the buildings are grouped round four principal structures: the Poikile, the Canopus, the Academy, and the Imperial Palace. Excavations and restorations are in progress on the hillside overlooking the Canopus, and the Museum there is closed. Recent studies and excavations suggest that the traditional interpretation of many of the buildings is probably wrong (see the description below), and some of them were used for different purposes than those formerly ascribed to them. Numerous areas between the buildings were reserved for gardens and open courtyards. All the ruins are labelled with explanatory diagrams (also in English). It is not easy to understand the connection between all the buildings since the order of the visit does not begin at the main entrance to the villa (only recently identi-fied). A whole day is needed for a detailed visit to the vast site.

From the ticket entrance (with a car park), a short drive leads on to a second car park. There is a café here, and a building which houses a model of the villa. On the far right (not well signposted) an 18C villa is used as a **Museum** with an excellent didactic display on three floors, providing a useful introduction to the ruins. On the ground floor are models of various parts of the villa. The first floor illustrates its architecture, with fragments of friezes, capitals, and a Roman marble model of a stadium. The building techniques are illustrated, and the various brick stamps shown. The finds from the villa now in museums are recorded by photographs. On the second floor are engravings of the site (including copies of Piranesi's works) and examples of the various marbles used in the buildings. Fragments of floors, mosaics and painted intonaco are displayed.

The entrance to the ruins is now through the massive N wall of the **Pecile**, which seems to have been inspired by the *Stoa Poikile* (painted porch) in Athens, famous for its paintings by Polygnotos and Panainos, and for its association with the Stoic philosophers. Hadrian's version is a rectangular peristyle (232m x 97m) with the ends slightly curved, similar to a Greek gymnasium. The huge N wall (9m high), running almost due E and W, still exists. On the S side the wall is no longer standing, but there are remains of a pavilion with three exedrae and a fountain. This was probably a monumental atrium. On both sides of the Pecile ran roofed colonnades; here the sun or shade could be enjoyed at any hour of the day, and either warmth or coolness, depending on the season. In the middle of the rectangle the fish-pond has been restored. The free area round it was probably used for exercise. On the SW the Pecile had as a substructure a wall with three rows of small chambers, now called the CENTO CAMERELLE, which are thought to have been used as accommodation for the Praetorians.

At the NE angle of the Pecile, a few steps lead up to the so-called SALA DEI FILOSOFI (17m x 9m), with an apse, seven niches, and four side-doors. This is now thought to have been a large throne room, or *Auditorium*, where the emperor held audiences, and met in council with court dignatories. It was probably part of the complex which includes the Pecile and the so-called 'Terme con Eliocamino'. Beyond is a charming circular building, with an Ionic marble peristyle, known as the *Teatro Marittimo, almost certainly a private retreat for the emperor, where he could be totally isolated. A circular moat (3.5m broad), lined with Luni (Carrara) marble, encloses an island on which stand an atrium with fluted Ionic columns in an intricate design, and a series of living-rooms, and baths. It could be reached only by two small wooden (removable) bridges. A reconstruction of one part of the building is displayed on the S side.

On the E side stairs lead up to the first nucleus of buildings belonging to the **Imperial Palace**, which is disposed parallel to the Vale of Tempe (see below); its elements are grouped round four peristyles. The so-called CORTILE DELLE BIBLIOTECHE is now a secluded olive plantation. The 'Greek and Latin Libraries' on the NW side have recently been identified as the monumental **entrance to the villa**, with towers, on three floors. The third floor had a heating system and may have been used by the emperor before the villa had been completed. Behind, excavations have revealed part of a delightful garden.

To the N of the Cortile delle Biblioteche are the OSPITALI, rooms used by the high-ranking staff of the villa who were particularly close to the emperor. Here are ten well-preserved small rooms leading off either side of a wide corridor. Rectangular alcoves indicate space for the beds (three in each room). Lighting was provided by the high openings. The rooms are decorated with well-preserved mosaics. Steps lead down to a TRICLINIUM, a dining room with (left) some capitals with a lotus motif, and a mosaic floor. To the right is a long corridor with oblique openings in the vault, to allow the light of midday to enter. This leads to the PADIGLIONE which overlooks a landscape with a stream which is probably the VALE OF TEMPE created by Hadrian to evoke the famous valley in Thessaly.

From here steps lead up to a path (S) which leads to the GREAT PERISTYLE of the palace, with a private library and other small rooms overlooking the Cortile delle Biblioteche. Here also is the ROOM OF THREE NAVES, a delightfully proportioned room with two rows of small columns. Nearby, stairs lead underground to a CRYPTOPORTICUS, with well-lit corridors. At the other end of this nucleus of the palace is the ROOM OF THE DORIC PILASTERS, with a fine entablature, which connected the E and W parts of the villa. The so-called CASERMA DEI VIGILI, beyond the apse of the basilican hall (right), was more probably a storehouse near the kitchens. Beyond it is a QUADRIPORTICUS, with a pool and a portico of fluted composite columns. Formerly known as the *Palazzo d'Inverno*, this is now considered to be at the centre of the most important part of the Imperial palace and the residence of Hadrian. The upper floors were supplied with heating systems. Beneath it is a well preserved extensive cryptoporticus. Beyond it, on a lower level, is the large NYMPHAEUM, described below.

On the left is another nymphaeum, which had two round fountain basins, and from here a path leads to the **Piazza d'Oro**, a rectangular area at the SE end of the palace. It was so named because excavations here yielded such rich finds. It is entered through the fine octagonal VESTIBULE. The peristyle was formed of alternate columns of cipollino and granite in two rows. On the far side (SE) is an intricate series of exedrae and nymphaea; the central one seems to have been a summer TRICLINIUM. This was an open courtyard with a remarkable Greek cross plan, with alternate convex and concave sides. The plan of the portico recalls Greek gymnasiums. It was formerly thought that this was used for banquets, but a recent interpretation is that it was in fact a stoa with libraries, similar to that which Hadrian had built in Athens in this period.

A path continues W past the back of the 'Caserma dei Vigili' and of the main nucleus of the palace, and descends to a clump of mighty cypresses and the *Small Thermae and the *Great Thermae. The small baths are well-preserved, with a large rectangular hall, perhaps the frigidarium, and an octagonal hall with a domed vault. They were particularly elegant and refined and may have been reserved for the use of the emperor alone. The large baths, on a simpler design, were probably used by court dignatories, visitors, etc. They include a circular hall, with cupola and skylight. A huge SALA ABSIDATA has a superb cross-vault, mostly collapsed. Opposite is another cross-vaulted room (closed; but well seen from the SE) decorated with exquisite stucco reliefs. On the E is a swimming-pool, bounded on the NW by a CRYPTOPORTICUS on the ruined walls of which are numerous graffiti of the 16C and 17C. This gives access to the so-called PRAETORIUM, a tall edifice which was divided into three storeys by wooden floors. It may have been used as a warehouse, or as a service wing.

Beyond a row of six huge ilexes is the celebrated *****Canopus**, designed to imitate the famous sanctuary of Serapis, that stood at the 15th milestone from Alexandria. Hadrian dug a hollow (185m by 75m), in which he constructed a canal, bordered on one side by a block of 20 rooms and a portico, and on the other by a heavy buttressed wall (238m long), against which were more rooms. Around the curved N end of the canal reproductions of statues found on the site have been set up between marble columns surmounted by an epistyle arched over alternate pillars. Along the right side are reproductions of caryatids and sileni. At the S end is the so-called SERAPEUM, a monumental triclinium, in the form of an Iseum, with a semicircular banqueting table from which the diners had a scenographic view of the canopus. It is now thought this may have been intended as a symbolic representation of the Nile: a series of fountains represent its source (in the niche behind), the cataracts, and its delta (in the piscina in front). The canal would then have represented the Mediterranean, with Athens to the W (represented by the caryatids), and Ephesus to the E (represented by statues of Amazons). The canopus is thought to have been built by Hadrian in honour of Antinoos, who was represented as an Egyptian divinity in numerous statues found here. Most of the Egyptian sculptures now in the Capitoline and Vatican museums come from here (those in the Museo Gregoriano Egiziano have recently been rearranged, according to the above interpretation).

There is a fine view of most of the villa from the hill behind. On the NW side of the hollow is the **Museum** (closed for restoration), housing finds from excavations since 1950. The statues include: a bust of Caracalla; Venus, copy of a work by Praxiteles; Wounded Amazons, one a mutilated copy of a Polykleitan original, the other a fine replica of the famous original by Pheidias; portrait of Verres; Athena and Mars, both from mid 5C originals; two athletes; a crocodile; tondo with the bas-relief of a satyr; four marble caryatids, copies of the 5C originals on the Erechtheion at Athens; and two sileni.

A path leads from here W to the TORRE DI ROCCABRUNA, a belvedere or pharos, which has square outer walls and is circular inside. This is possibly an imitation of the Tower of Timon of Athens, which stood near the Academy. It stands in the Oliveto Roccabruna, which is famous for the size of its olive trees, one of them (the 'albero bello') claimed to be the largest in the Tivoli district.

To the SE, in another olive-grove, is the so-called **Accademia**, a complex of buildings which some scholars identify as a secondary palace. The group includes a round hall, known as the TEMPLE OF APOLLO, a peristyle, and the remains of three rooms with delicate stucco ornamentation. About 300m SE are the remains of an *ODEION or THEATRE (45m in diameter) with the Imperial box in the centre of the cavea. To the E of the Odeion a path descends to a hollow (150m long), hewn in the tufa and overshadowed by thick vegetation, which leads to a semi-circular vestibule (once perhaps guarded by an image of Cerberus). This was the entrance to **Hades** or the **Inferi**, represented by a quadrangle of four subterranean corridors, 5.5m wide and 91m in total length, with 79 apertures for light. Smaller tunnels connected Hades with various parts of the Villa.

A broad main path returns towards the entrance. To the right, just before the Poikile, is the large NYMPHAEUM, formerly called the *Stadio* from its elongated form. It was a decorative garden surrounded by porticoes, with three exedrae. Between it and the 'Teatro Marittimo' are remains of the first BATHS constructed in the Villa, formerly known as the TERME CON HELIO-

CAMINUS, with a large circular room with a heating system used for 'Turkish baths'. On the other side of the Nymphaeum, reached by steps which lead up past a well-preserved CRYPTOPORTICUS, is the main part of the Imperial palace (see above). A path leads back across the Poikile to the entrance.

From here a fine avenue of cypresses leads N to the Greek Theatre, passing the Casino Fede (now the excavation office), built on part of the ruins of the so-called NYMPHAEUM, a semicircular portico. This frames a small TEMPLE OF VENUS, a goddess particularly venerated by Hadrian. The temple was modelled on the Temple at Cnidos and a statue of Aphrodite of Cnidos, a copy of the famous statue by Praxiteles, discovered here has been replaced by a cast (original in the Museum, see above). Beyond, to the right, a walk leads to the modernised FONTANA DI PALAZZO, near which are a few traces of the PALAESTRA. Beyond this extends the VALLE PUSSIANA, the Emperor's reconstruction of the Vale of Tempe, with a stream representing the Peneios (see above). Descending (left) through olives and cypresses, the path passes the **Greek Theatre**, c 36m in diameter; its cavea or auditorium is carved out of the hillside.

34

The Province of Rieti

FROM ROME TO RIETI. Via Salaria (N 4), 78km.—16km Settebagni—24km By road for MONTEROTONDO and MENTANA—36km Passo Corese—(44km By road for Farfa)—54km Osteria Nuova—78km **Rieti**.

The VIA SALARIA leaves Rome at Piazza Fiume (Pl. 12; 7), on the site of the Roman Porta Salaria. It is one of the oldest Roman roads, which takes its name from its association with the salt trade between the Romans and the Sabines. Beyond Rieti it runs via Ascoli Piceno to the Adriatic, near San Benedetto del Tronto. The first part of the road, as far as the Catacombs of Priscilla is described in Rte 20. Nearly 4km from Piazza Fiume Via Salaria crosses the Aniene, near its confluence with the Tiber, by the Roman PONTE SALARIO. This was rebuilt in 565 by Narses, and then reconstructed after it was blown up by papal troops in 1867. Only the two side arches are original. Close by is the traditional spot where, in 360 BC, Titus Manlius Torquatus killed the gigantic Gaul in single combat and robbed him of his torque or collar.

Just short of the brige a byroad leads left to MONTE ANTENNE (62m; military zone) commanding a view of the confluence of the Tiber and Aniene. This was the site of the ancient Sabine town of ANTEMNAE, said to have been founded by the Siculi. It had probably already disappeared by the time of the kings. At the foot of the hill, with an approach road from the Parioli district, Rome's first MOSQUE was completed in 1993, designed by Paolo Portoghesi, Vittorio Gigliotti, and Sami Moussawi. It can hold up to 3000 people and is the largest in Europe. It was financed by some 24 Arab countries, and there is also a cultural centre and library here.

Via Salaria continues past (left) URBE AIRPORT, surrounded on three sides by the Tiber. 9km (right) VILLA SPADA is on the site of the ancient FIDENE, a Latin city contested between Rome and Veio. CASTEL GIUBILEO, a medieval fortress, stands above the bank of the Tiber. The road passes under (12km) the Grande Raccordo Annulare. 16km SETTEBAGNI and MARCIGLIANA. Near here was the Allia, a stream which was the scene of a disastrous defeat of the Romans by the Gauls in 390 BC. At (24km) Monterotondo Scalo a byroad diverges right for Monterotondo (3km), Mentana (6km), and Palombara Sabina (20km).

Monterotondo is a small town (15,800 inhab.) with ugly sprawling suburbs. One-way roads lead up to the piazza (with car parking) in front of the DUOMO. The interior contains a good vault fresco, and a handsome large Roman sarcophagus serves as high altar. In the chapel to the right of the sanctuary, Marytrdom of St Stephen by Giovanni Battista Crescenzi, and a Madonna enthroned by Antonio Gherardi. From the Duomo the Borgo (closed to traffic) leads to Piazza del Popolo with a lion fountain. Downhill is the 18C Porta Garibaldi beside which is the Teatro Francesco Ramarini built in 1920 (closed).

Outside the gate an uninteresting road leads in under ten minutes to SANTA MARIA DELLE GRAZIE (if closed, ring at the door at the E end of the left flank). It contains the well-preserved monument, attributed to Luigi Capponi, of Girolamo Orsini (died 1484), who is depicted mounted on a fine horse. Other chapels on this side have interesting painted decoration dating from the 1940s. On the N side are frescoes (Birth and Death of the Virgin) by the school of Giovanni Francesco Romanelli, and other 17C works. The town hall is in a 17C Orsini palace.

3km S of Monterotondo is **Mentana**, on the approximate site of the ancient Nomentum, also surrounded by new suburbs. On the left of the main road (signposted) is the monumental tomb of the soldiers of Garibaldi who were defeated by French and Papal forces near here in 1867 (a small museum records the battle). The old district of the town is on the right of the road near Piazza Garibaldi (limited car parking). A restaurant here incorporates two good Roman sculptures in its façade. A short distance below the piazza, on the main road, just beyond the flank and clock-tower of San Nicola is an old gateway (open to pedestrians) which leads into Piazza San Nicola, which retains its old paving stones. Here is the splendid huge 16C *Palazzo Baroniale (now the town hall) with a fine doorway (and a 15C wing). Opposite is the side of San Nicola (only open on Saturday) with an oval 16C fresco of St Sebastian above the door, and high up on the wall two fragments of Roman friezes. Near an old archway is a (headless) Roman statue of a man in a toga. The archway beside the portal of Palazzo Baroniale leads into the picturesque old borgo past Palazzo Crescenzio (now the Biblioteca Comunale) and round under two archways into a simple piazza by the back entrance of Palazzo Baroniale. The road continues to emerge beside a round tower in Piazza Garibaldi.

A byroad (16km) leads E from Monterotondo for Palombara (well signposted). Beyond the TERME DI CRETONE, a little spa, the countryside becomes prettier and there is a good view of the Sabine Hills ahead. Palombara, with its tall tower, comes into view on a small hill surrounded by olives, and just before the town a very sharp turn right is signposted for **San Giovanni in Argentella**, c 2km off the road. The bell-tower of the abbey, with its three-light windows, can be seen on the green valley (with numerous cherry trees) ahead. The church (open Saturday 16.00–18.00; fest. 10.00–13.00, 16.00–18.00; ring) belongs to an abbey founded in the 7C or 8C. Beyond a ruined gateway with a tower, a walk shaded by vines leads to the façade of the Romanesque church with a primitive Cross, symbol of the Benedictines, over the door, and, high up, a fresco of the Madonna and Child in a tabernacle. In the portico is a fragment of a Roman sarcophagus. An unusual deep vaulted atrium leads into the interior with pretty arcades with 3C Roman Ionic capitals and a beautiful ciborium, with four marble columns and lovely 7C or 8C stucco capitals, in the apse. On the right side are remains of interesting 14C frescoes including the scene of a cavalcade. An attractive garden surrounds the ruined Benedictine monastic buildings.

Palombara Sabina is in a good position with wide views. A one-way road leads up to PIAZZA VITTORIO VENETO, with the town hall, an information office, a large fountain, and some handsome pink and red palaces. A terrace, with a bust of Umberto I (1903), has a good view of the plain and rolling hills in the distance. The church of Sant'Egidio (1903) has an outside stair (and an earlier bell-tower), and at the far end is a round 15C tower (recently restored), and, beyond pine trees, there is a view of the wooded Monte Gennaro. A road continues to a War Memorial and the church of San Biagio which contains a Madonna della Neve attributed to Antonio da Viterbo. From the piazza, Via Piave (for pedestrians) leads up through the attractive little medieval borgo into the huge 13C *CASTELLO SAVELLI (no admission as work is in progress by the Comune to restore it as a congress centre).

N 636 continues N for 18km to rejoin N 4. It passes MORICONE, in a fine position with a 13C castle. The pretty undulating hills are covered with olive trees, vineyards, and woods, typical of the landscape of the Sabine Hills (see below). The well-preserved walled hill town of MONTELIBRETTI, with its onion-shaped bell-tower, is well seen across a valley.

Via Salaria continues from Monterotondo Scalo and soon passes under the A1 motorway. At (36km) PASSO CORESE a link road leads across the Tiber for the motorway exit at 'Roma Nord' near Lucus Feroniae (see Rte 35). N 4 now enters the province of Rieti and at 44km passes the by road (left) for Canneto which leads to Farfa and the Sabine Hills (described from Rieti, see below). Via Salaria, a fast road, continues up the wooded valley. At (54km) OSTERIA NUOVA a byroad leads right for Monteleone Sabino (described below), off which N 314 leads S via Orvinio and Licenza (both described in Rte 32). There is a good view up right of the unspoilt little hill town of ORNARO before reaching (78km) Rieti.

RIETI is a pleasant provincial capital (44,000 inhab.) with some fine buildings in the historical centre. It was the ancient REATE, chief town of the Sabines. The attractive province includes the Sabine Hills with the Abbey of Farfa, the ski resort of Monte Terminillo, and the plain of Rieti with its Franciscan convents.

Information Offices. 'EPT' Rieti, and 'Azienda Autonoma', 87 Via Cintia (Tel. 0746/201146). Information Office, 17 Piazza Vittorio Emanuele.

Railway Station, Piazza della Stazione, near the centre, on the line from Rome to Terni.

Buses ('COTRAL') from Piazza della Stazione for Rome (in 1 hr 30 mins), and to places of interest in the province.

Car Parking. Free car parks in Via delle Palme, Via San Pietro, and Piazza Beata Colomba.

Hotels in Rieti. 4-star: 'Quattro Stagioni', 14 Piazza Cesare Battisti; 'Miramonti', 5 Piazza Oberdan; 3-star: 'Cavour', 10 Piazza Cavour; 2-star: 'Massimo d'Azeglio', 4 Viale Canali.

Hotels in the province of Rieti. At **Amatrice**: 3-star: 'Il Castagneto' and 'Roma'; at **Cittaducale**: 2-star: 'Pace' and 'Da Baffo'; at **Labro**: 3-star 'Palazzo Crispolti'; at **Leonessa**: 4-star 'La Torre'; at **Poggio Catino**: 5-star 'Borgo Paraelios'. Hotels of all categories at the ski resort of **Terminillo**.

Agriturismo accommodation is available in various localities, especially in the Sabine Hills (information from the 'EPT'). **Camping Site** (2-star) at Terminillo. **Youth Hostel**, 'Ostello della Neve' at Campoforogna, Terminillo.

Restaurants in Rieti. LUXURY-CLASS: 'Al Calice d'Oro', 10 Via Marchetti; 'La Pecora Nera', 33 Via del Terminillo; 'Bistrot', 25 Piazza San Rufo. 1ST CLASS: 'Il Fioretto al Cavour', 19 Piazza Cavour; 'Club degli Spaghetti', 85 Via Varrone; 'La Montagnola', 36 Via San Francesco (for fish); 'La Piazzetta', 18 Via Ceccotti; 'Last Paradise', Poggio Fidoni. SIMPLE TRATTORIE: 'Da Mimmo (Cantina Centro d'Italia)', Via dei Crispolti;

'Trattoria La Favorita', 3 Piazza Cavour; 'Tito Brucchietti', 5 Via San Rufo; 'Il Grottino', 4 Piazza Cesare Battisti.

Restaurants in the province of Rieti. Numerous restaurants and trattorie at **Amatrice**, famous for its *spaghetti all'amatriciana*. At **Stipes** (above the Lago di Turano), trattoria 'Il Tartufo'. **Greccio** has five simple restaurants, including 'Nido del Corvo'. At **Labro**: 1st class restaurant 'L'Arcolaio'; simple trattorie: 'Da Santa' and 'Il Pergolato' (a club; membership subscription). Near **Leonessa** at Albaneto, trattoria 'La Tana del Lupo'. Luxury-class restaurant (booking only) at **Vaccone** 'Solo per Due'.

Theatre. Teatro Vespasiano, Via Garibaldi.

Annual Festivals. Sant'Antonio, 13 June, and summer festivals in July and August in Rieti, Amatrice, Antrodoco, and Contigliano. On 24 and 26 December at Greccio the crêche of St Francis is commemorated.

History. The ancient Sabine town was defended by Cicero in a quarrel with Terni in 54 BC. When he visited the town he compared the plain of Rieti to the Vale of Tempe in Thessaly. Here was born the historian Terentius Varro (116–27 BC), and the family of the Emperor Vespasian came from the district. Rieti was destroyed by Roger II in 1149, but was rebuilt. In 1185 the Emperor Henry VI was married here to Constance of Altavilla; in 1234 their son, Frederick II, was received here by Pope Gregory IX, then in need of help against the rebellious citizens of Rome. In the Cathedral on Whit Sunday, 1289, Pope Nicholas IV crowned Charles II of Naples with the empty title of King of Sicily, which initiated the confusion of the two Sicilies. St Francis spent much time in the surrounding plain, which still has four Franciscan sanctuaries. Rieti was the birthplace of the painters Carlo Cesi (1626–86) and Antonino Gherardi (1638–1702). The province was part of Umbria up to 1923.

The centre of the town is **Piazza Vittorio Emanuele II**, on the site of the Roman forum. The PALAZZO COMUNALE, first built in the 13C, has a façade by Filippo Brioni (1748). It contains the **Museo Civico** which has been closed for many years, and shows no signs of reopening. The collections include archaeological material, classical and medieval sculpture, and paintings by Antoniazzo Romano, Luca di Tommè, and Zannino di Pietro. The adjoining **Piazza Battista** is a pretty square. The handsome PALAZZO DEL GOVERNO has a fine loggia dating from 1596. Its little garden, with five palm trees, is open to the public and has a good view.

The end of the piazza is occupied by the beautiful exterior of the **Duomo**, with its campanile dating from 1252. The church was begun in 1109 and consecrated by Honorius III in 1225. Beneath the side PORTICO (1458) are three fragments of a classical cornice and a Roman bracket. Near the campanile is a Roman column. The main W portal of the Duomo is well decorated. INTERIOR. SOUTH SIDE, first chapel, (left wall), Madonna and Child with saints by Lorenzo Torresani (1528). Second chapel, 16C wood polychrome statue of St Roch, and paintings by Vincenzo Manenti. Third chapel, altarpiece of the Guardian Angel by Andrea Sacchi; fourth chapel, paintings by Lattanzio Niccoli. The pretty Cappella del Sacramento, in the S transept, dates from the 17C (with a ciborium of 1755). A small chapel off the N transept contains a venerated fresco of the Madonna del Popolo probably dating from the early 14C. The chapel is decorated by Emmanuele Alfani (1745).

NORTH SIDE. The fourth chapel is a fine 18C work, with a good statue of St Barbara by Giannantonio Mari (probably designed by Bernini), four other statues by Lorenzo Ottoni, and a vault frescoed by Giovanni Odazzi. The third chapel was rebuilt in 1841 on a design by Giuseppe Valadier. The second chapel has 16C tombs of the Aligeri family, and the first chapel contains a fresco by Marcantonio Aquili, son of Antoniazzo Romano. The large crypt with numerous fine columns dates from 1109–57.

Beneath the portico, beside two ancient sculpted lions, is the entrance to the **Museo del Duomo** (sometimes open Saturday and Sunday, 16.00–18.00; otherwise enquire at the Curia). It is arranged in the 14C BAPTISTERY with two 15C frescoed niches and a fine carved 15C font. The collection of processional *Crosses (the earliest dating from the 13C) is particularly fine. Works from the diocese include a beautiful Cross by a follower of Nicola Gallucci da Guardiagrele from the church of Antrodoco, and 14C silver Crosses from Borbona and Cittaducale. The contents of the treasury of the Duomo include two pyxes of 15C Hungarian workmanship; a Cross made by the local craftsman Giacomo Gallina (1418–93); a 15C Cross in rock crystal; and a reliquary bust of St Balduino by Bernardino da Foligno (1496), as well as 18C and 19C church silver. The polychrome wood statues include a female Saint, and a 14C and 15C Madonna and Child from Santa Maria di Sambuco and Collemaggiore. The 15C chasuble is probably of Flemish or German workmanship.

In the piazza on the other side of the Duomo is **Palazzo Vescovile**, restored in 1931, which preserves a fine loggia of 1288 and some Renaissance windows. A pretty wall fountain incorporates a Roman sarcophagus and a 12C griffin. On the ground floor is a remarkable vaulted hall (seen from Via Cintia), and above is the huge SALA DEI PAPI (admission sometimes on request at the Curia).

Via Cintia continues under the ARCO DEL VESCOVO erected by Boniface VIII, and then the stepped Via dell'Episcopio descends left to the church of SAN PIETRO MARTIRE, with a fine wood ceiling by the local artist Andrea Masini (1628), and works by another local artist Vincenzo Manenti. At the W end of the S side are simple frescoes of St Agnes. Via Cintia continues past Palazzo Vincentini (No. 75) and another pretty palace (No. 73). Via Sanizi (well paved) now diverges from Via Cintia and leads down past the ex Palazzo di Giustizia (just restored as a school) to SAN DOMENICO, a roofless church awaiting restoration. Via Giordano Bruno returns to Via Cintia which continues down to Piazza Marconi, a busy road junction with the avenues which skirt the imposing 13C WALLS.

Several long straight streets leads out of Via Cintia, including Via Varrone, with a nice Art Nouveau palace (1913) at Nos 12/14, towards Piazza Mazzini with a huge school building, a War Memorial, and the railway station. Here is the church of **Sant'Agostino**, a 13C church restored in the 18C. The 14C portal has a lunette fresco by the Sienese school of 1354. In the INTERIOR, on the W wall and the SOUTH SIDE are ancient fresco fragments. The fourth altarpiece is by Giovanni Giacomo Pandolfi (1599), and at the end of this side is a fine neo-classical monument to Angelo Maria Ricci with bas-reliefs and his bust above by Giuseppe Fabris. In the N transept is a huge detached fresco of the Crucifixion, an interesting work dating from the late 14C. On the first N altar is a fine 16C Crucifix. On the right side of the church Via Tancredi leads to the church of SANT'ANTONIO on a design by Vignola (being restored).

Adjoining Piazza Mazzini is Piazza Oberdan with Palazzo Ricci (1789; restored in 1901). A ramp leads up out of the square to the **Teatro Flaminio Vespasiano**, begun in 1854 by Vincenzo Ghinelli, and inaugurated in 1893. The delightful painted decorations (1901–08) are being restored. In **Via Garibaldi** is the white Post Office by Cesare Bazzani (1934). The narrow Via Cerroni leads to PIAZZA SAN RUFFO CENTRO D'ITALIA which has a plaque known as the UMBELICUS ITALIAE which records Rieti's claim to be in the exact centre of Italy. The church of SAN RUFFO, founded in 1141 and reconstructed in 1746 has a dark interior. Via Garibaldi continues past a bank with a good portal by Giuseppe Subleyras (1818). The church of SAN GIOVENALE (closed) contains a bas-relief by Bertel Thorvaldsen (1829). Farther downhill, the road becomes winding and there is a good view of wooded hills on the right. The little church of SAN GIUSEPPE has a bright yellow and brown Baroque façade.

From Piazza Vittorio Emanuele II (see above) Via Roma leads downhill. On the left Via Pellicceria and (right) Via Mattonato lead down to the church of SAN FRANCESCO (only open on Sunday). Founded in 1245 it was restored in 1636. It contains works by Vincenzo Manenti. Via San Francesco leads back to join Via Roma by Ponte Velino. From it can be seen a Roman bridge, up river, now almost totally submerged. The view takes in San Francesco, and the mountain of Terminillo in the distance. Via Roma continues back uphill past a fine palace at No. 47, and PALAZZO VECCHIARELLI (No. 57) by Carlo Maderno (recently restored) with a delightful courtyard. The Romanesque church of SAN PIETRO has been closed for restoration for many years.

The Province of Rieti

A. The Plain of Rieti and the Franciscan Convents

The beautiful fertile Plain of Rieti, to the N of the town, is traversed by the Velino. A few small lakes here are relics of a much larger lake surrounded by marshes which were drained in 271 BC. To the E rises a mountain range dominated by the peak of Monte Terminillo. Overlooking the plain are four Franciscan sanctuaries, testimony to the time St Francis passed here from 1209 to 1223. From Porta Romana the road for Rome leads SW, and on the avenue just outside the town a well-signposted byroad diverges right for Fonte Colombo and Greccio. 5km. Byroad (left) for the **Convent of Fonte Colombo**, with ten friars. Here in 1223 St Francis dictated the last Rules of his Order before leaving for the East; he returned two years later to cure himself of an eye disease. The church has stained glass windows designed by Duilio Cambellotti (1925). In the ilex woods are various chapels, and a Via Crucis in 18C Capodimonte majolica.

The road for Greccio continues to a road junction where it diverges left (signposted Poggio Mirteto). Beyond Contigliano (described from Farfa, at the end of this Route), well seen up on the left of the road, is Spinacceto where a winding road diverges up to Greccio (the convent can also be approached by another, signposted, road further on). The quiet little hamlet of GRECCIO has an attractive piazza with two churches. There is a view of the convent in woods below. The road continues to the **Convent of Greccio** (open 8.00–13.00, 15.00–19.00) where St Francis stayed in 1223. It is in a beautiful peaceful position on the side of a steep wooded hill (638m), and four friars still live here. A long flight of steps zig-zags up the hill out onto a little terrace overlooking the plain. Here is the GROTTA DEL PRESEPIO where St Francis is supposed to have assembled a crêche to celebrate Christmas, so beginning a tradition which survives to this day. The late 14C fresco shows a crêche and a scene of the Nativity. A corridor with two 15C frescoes leads to the tiny rooms occupied by St Francis (the room where he ate, with a primitive little fireplace and 16C fresco fragments, and the cave where he slept). Stairs lead up to the charming DORMITORY OF ST BONAVENTURA, built in 1260–70, panelled in wood. The tiny CHURCH dates from 1228 and preserves its stalls and lectern in the choir. In the church, with a pretty barrel vault, are a lunette with the Deposition by the Umbrian school, a tondo of the Madonna and Child by Biagio di Antonio da Firenze, and a carved 14C Crucifix. In a little adjoining room is a 14C copy of a contemporary portrait of St Francis wiping his eyes (he suffered from an eye disease).

A road descends from the convent to the main road which continues left for Terni (22km) in Umbria (see 'Blue Guide Umbria').

It is now necessary to return to Rieti, and take the by road N of the town for the **Convent of La Floresta**, 3km from Rieti. Here St Francis stayed in 1225, and since 1989 it has been occupied by a community founded to help young people in need called 'Mondo X' (admission on request). Along the approach road are Stations of the Cross in 18C Neapolitan majolica tiles. The beautifully kept convent is in a lovely setting, beside a vineyard. A story relates how another vineyard here was trampled on by a crowd who had come to see St Francis, but when the grapes were harvested and pressed they produced more wine than in other years. In the 13C CHURCH (right apse) is a 15C fresco of Christ blessing, and on the left wall, Madonna and Child, and Presentation in the Temple. The attractive little CLOISTER dates from the 15C. Here a room is shown where the miracle of the grapes took place, and a grotto where St Francis is supposed to have slept.

The Franciscan convent of Poggio Bustone is c 19km N of Rieti, reached by N 19. Beyond the village of **Poggio Bustone** a road leads up to the **Convent of San Giacomo** in a pretty setting (818m) above the plain. The 15C church has a small 15C painting of the Holy Family. A path leads further up the hillside (in c 20 minutes) to a hermitge where St Francis stayed.

Labro, 13km NW of Poggio Bustone, is an exceptionally well-preserved stone-built village with numerous medieval streets (cars are left in a car park outside), with a number of restaurants. It overlooks the Lake of Piediluco in Umbria. In recent years a number of houses here have been bought by Belgians. The CASTELLO NOBILI-VITELLESCHI is shown on a guided tour by the proprietor every day on request (10.00–13.00, 14.30–20.00). The castle used to be much larger and incorporated the buildings at the top of the hill (the church was the armoury). The walkways on the roof and the tower can be visited. The house is now interesting for its contents: a painting by Simon Vouet, 16C and 17C furniture, an 18C Neapolitan presepio, 18C Pesaro ceramics, 19C Murano glass, and two tiny octagonal paintings by Leon Bremer. Firearms and swords from the 16C up to the Second World War are kept in a room with a little 12C fireplace decorated with two carved swords. The last room has a piano of 1835, and the family archives dating from 1068.

A road (24km) leads E from Labro for **Leonessa** a pretty small town with numerous fine palaces. The Corso is entered by Porta Spoletina. On the left is the church of SANTA MARIA DEL POPOLO, with a lovely high relief of the Madonna and Child in a lunette. Via Ciucci leads down to the 15C church of SAN FRANCESCO. It contains a large presepio in terracotta dating from the early 16C. On the Corso, beyond the ex church of San Nicola (now a bank) is the elaborate sanctuary of SAN GIUSEPPE DA LEONESSA (1746), with the body and relics of this local saint (1556–1612) who was a Capuchin monk and missionary in Turkey.

Piazza del Municipio (dedicated to 51 victims of 'Nazifascism' who were killed here in 1944) has an attractive shape and a pretty fountain. Some of the houses have porticoes, and above a flight of steps is the church of SAN PIETRO (closed for restoration), with a fine campanile. Behind can be seen a green wooded hillside. The portal of 1467 is in very bad condition. A road (18km) leads down a wooded valley to Posta on the main road from Rieti to Amatrice, see below. The mountain road from Leonessa to Terminillo (see below), is at present closed.

B. Terminillo

Terminillo, 21km NE of Rieti, is a summer and winter resort (1575–1675m), developed from 1937 to 1950. It has two 4-star, five 3-star, and three 2-star hotels (some of them closed out of season). It also has a camping site, and a youth hostel (EPT information office at Pian de' Valli, Tel. 0746/261121). It is reached by a mountain road which diverges left from the N 4 a little E of Rieti. It passes Vazia and beyond Lisciano continues the ascent in sharp curves. A funicular railway ascends to **Monte Terminillo** (2216m). Facilities for skiing include chair-lifts and ski-lifts.

C. From Rieti to Amatrice

N 4, 63km (the road has recently been improved). 10km **Cittaducale** (5440 inhab.), founded in 1309 by Charles II of Anjou, and named after his son Robert the Wise, Duke of Calabria, afterwards King of Naples. It is laid out on a regular grid plan, and has suffered from earthquakes. The main road leads through Piazza del Popolo, where a medley of buildings surround a fountain and gardens.

On the right is SANTA MARIA DEL POPOLO with a late Romanesque façade. The entrance is by the door on the left. It contains several 16C polychrome wood statues including (first altar on the left), St Roch. At the W end of the S aisle is a 15C font with a statue of St John. The pretty second S altar, flanked by two Baroque angels, encloses a Madonna and Child with two saints by Girolamo Troppa. On the right wall of the sanctuary is a quaint 14C bas relief of the Annunciation, and unusual 18C painted tapestries. At the W end is a Baroque organ and cantoria. The church of SANT'AGOSTINO, with a portal of 1450, is usually closed. The Corso continues uphill and leaves the town beside a tall 14C tower which is square on its inner face and round on its outer face.

The main road continues through the TERME DI COTILIA, a spa which uses the sulphur springs of *Cutilia*, where Vespasian died in AD 79. The PESCHERIA, nearby, is the most copious spring in the Apennines. From Canetra there is a view of the well-preserved medieval hamlet of CASTEL SANT'ANGELO up to the left. The road continues through green wooded hills and crosses the Velino river; it straightens out as it approaches the imposing face of Monte Giano (1820m) ahead.

24km **Antrodoco**, the ancient *Interocrea* is in an enclosed position at the junction of three gorges. Just before the town, below the main road, on the left, can be seen the Romanesque church of SANTA MARIA EXTRA MOENIA and the BAPTISTERY OF SAN GIOVANNI surrounded by a lawn (reached across the railway, but usually closed). Of ancient foundation, the present church was probably consecrated in 1051. The attractive campanile dates from the 12C. The church contains frescoes of the 13C and 15C, and a 15C polychrome terracotta group of the Pietà. The hexagonal baptistery has 15C frescoes.

The Via Salaria now enters the **Gole del Velino**, a narrow winding ravine about 10km long, between Monte Terminillo (2216m) on the left, and Monte Giano (1820m) on the right. The road follows a single-track railway line along the green floor of the valley with vineyards past the picturesque ruins, overgrown with ivy, of the medieval abbey of San Quirico e Giulitta, abandoned since the 17C. Just before the turn for Micigliano the road has been 'improved' and, raised on stilts. It now traverses long tunnels before emerging beyond Posta from the valley. From (38km) POSTA (721m; founded in 1301), which is seen with its tower above the road, a pretty road ascends to Leonessa (described above). The wooded valley, with poplars, opens out with a view of the hills ahead. Beyond the turning for CITTAREALE (founded by Charles I of Anjou in 1261) the road rises to a summit level of 1018m; near here is the source of the Velino. Ahead can be seen the little village of TORRITA in a wide open landscape. 59km Turning for Amatrice; the road (4km) descends past the artificial LAGO DI SCANDARELLO with pretty wooded shores.

Amatrice is a pleasant little town (1117 inhab.) founded in the Middle Ages. It was taken by Charles of Anjou in 1274, and in the 15C was often in conflict with L'Aquila. It was conquered by Charles V of Spain in 1529, after which it was reconstructed on a new plan traditionally attributed to Cola dell'Amatrice. In a fine position (950m) close to Abruzzi, Umbria, and the Marches, it is overlooked by the mountain range, with numerous springs and luxuriant vegetation, called Monti della Laga, which includes Monte Gorzano (2458m), the highest peak in Lazio. Amatrice suffered from a number of earthquakes in the 17C and 18C (and another in 1979). It was the birthplace of the painter and architect Nicola Filotesio, known as Cola dell'Amatrice (c 1480–after 1547). It has also given its name to a well-known pasta dish, 'spaghetti all'amatriciana' (a spicy sauce made with bacon, onion, and tomatoes served with grated pecorino cheese): a festival in its honour is held here on the last Sunday in August.

The pretty Corso Umberto slopes uphill through the town. At its lower end is the Baroque church of SAN GIUSEPPE (or 'dei Paolini'), at present closed, opposite the Casa dei Paolini (No. 130; now a restaurant). The 'Banca della Cassa Rurale e Artigiana' here owns two fine paintings by Cola dell'Amatrice (Mary Magdalen and St John the Evangelist, and Saints Peter and Paul). Half-way up the Corso is the tall thin isolated bell-tower of the Comune, and on the other side of the Corso is the COMUNE with a portico. In the Sala Consiliare are three fresco fragments from the church of Sant'Apollonia near Amatrice, a painting of the Holy Family by Cola (1527), and an interesting *Madonna and Child from the church of Cossito. Dating from c 1280, it shows the influence of the school of Spoleto and of the Marches. After its theft in 1964 it was recovered in Switzerland in 1967.

A road to the right of the town hall leads to the church of SAN FRANCESCO (key at the town hall), a fine 14C church with a beautiful exterior. The portal has a polychrome sculpture of the Madonna and Child with two angels. In the interior, at the W end, is a pretty little Renaissance narthex. The walls of the church are covered with numerous (fragmentary) frescoes dating from the 14C and 15C: on the N wall, in a niche, St Anne greeting St Joachim at the Golden Gate, and a Nativity scene, and on the S wall, also in a niche, another delightful scene (Visitation?). The marble bust of Camillo Orsini is by Alessandro Leopardi. The elaborate gilded wood altar (1641–1739) is dedicated to the Madonna 'di Filetta' and encloses a precious reliquary, attributed to Pietro Vannini. On the wall around it is a fragment of a fresco of the Last Judgment. In the fine apse, with a fan vault, are more fresco fragments, including a Tree of Jesse. The delightful wood pulpit is a very unusual work.

Off the other side of the Corso is the church of SANT'EMIDIO (or 'Santa Maria delle Laudi'; key at the town hall), used by a cultural society. The interior is divided in two: in the first part are interesting frescoes (partly ruined) on the vault and on the walls (Crucifixion, Birth of St John with scenes from his life, St George and the dragon, St Sebastian, attributed to Dionisio Cappelli). The two altars, one in gilded wood, are in poor condition.

At the top end of the Corso is the church of SANT'AGOSTINO with a fine exterior and a Gothic arch beneath the campanile. The beautiful portal dates from 1428 (the statues of the Annunciation have been removed). Inside are fresco fragments including an Annunciation. Near the church are public gardens with a monument (1915) to Cola dell'Amatrice.

The N 4 continues N, passing ACCUMOLI, with some fine palaces in Via Tommasi. The road soon leaves Lazio and enters the Marches on its way to Ascoli Piceno.

D. From Rieti to Rocca Sinibalda

From the avenue S of Rieti a good byroad (16km) diverges left (signposted 'Terme di Cottorella'). Beyond the mineral spring of TERME DI COTTORELLA (where the water is bottled), the peaceful road leads up the pretty wooded valley of the Turano. There is a *view of **Rocca Sinibalda** at the head of the valley on a wooded spur with a hill behind. The unspoilt hamlet which probably takes its name from a certain Sinibaldo who was proprietor of the castle in 1050–65, lies below the castle with its garden.

The lower road in the village leads to Piazza del Plebiscito (car parking), and Via di Castello leads up to the *CASTLE (ring; shown at weekends at 10.30, 11.30, 12.30 and 16.00, 17.00, and 18.00, but up for sale in 1994), which dominates the valley. It was begun for Cardinal Alessandro Cesarini c 1530 by Baldassarre Peruzzi, and finished by Giovanni Sallustio Peruzzi. Off the courtyard is the beautifully kept hanging garden from which the interesting architecture of the castle can be seen. On the ground floor is a chapel and a winding staircase leads up to the first floor where the Salone has three good frescoes of Rocca Sinibalda and other hamlets nearby dating from 1730. A room contains armour (and an interesting painting of an armoury). There is also a music room, a gaming room, library, a charming terrace, cellars and storerooms, and the battlements.

15km SW of Rocca Sinibalda is **Monteleone Sabino**, a medieval village near the site of the ancient Sabine town of TREBULA MUTUESCA, birthplace of Mummius, the Roman general who sacked Corinth in 146 BC. A number of stone lions survive here. Outside is SANTA VITTORIA (key in the village), an 11C church. It is surrounded by a lawn with cypresses, and has Roman fragments incorporated in its interesting façade. Inside is a Roman sarcophagus, and relics of a much earlier building.

10km S of Rocca Sinibalda is the **Lago di Turano**, formed by a dam built in 1938. A road for Stipes and Longone runs across the dam, and a windy road descends with a view of the lake. Opposite Colle di Tora, on a promontory, can be seen CASTEL DI TORA, with the conspicuous tower of its castle, on the other side of the lake, approached by a bridge supported on wooden piles. A road continues S along the lake through Ascrea towards Arsoli on the Via Tiburtina (see Rte 32). It passes a turn for the pretty little village of **Collalto Sabina**, surrounded by woods, with a fine castle rebuilt in the 15C and restored in 1895 (now used for meetings).

25km SE of Rieti (reached by N 578, recently improved) is the **Cicolano**, the remote wooded valley of the Salto, suffering from depopulation. There are fine mountain walks in the area (information form the 'VII Comunità Montana Salto-Cicolano', Fiumata di Petrella Salto, Tel. 0746/558191). The LAGO DI SALTO created in 1940 is the largest artificial lake in Lazio. Above it are the medieval villages of PETRELLA SALTO and FIAMIGNANO. Above Petrella is the ROCCA CENCI where the tyrant Francesco Cenci was murdered in 1598 at the instigation of his family, including his daughter Beatrice, who was herself beheaded a year later in Rome (see Shelley's tragedy 'The Cenci', published in 1819).

E. From Rieti to the Abbey of Farfa and the Sabine Hills

The Via Salaria (N 4; described at the beginning of this Route) leads S from Rieti and at 23km a byroad diverges right for (33km) FARA IN SABINA, a village with fine views, and a 15C church. Outside the village on a bare stony hillside can be seen the conspicuous ruins of a basilica begun by Abbot Berardo II in the 11C and never completed. **Farfa**, 3.5km NW, is a charming, well-preserved little *borgo with two gates across the road, in a delightful setting on a wooded hillside. The houses have characteristic shops on the ground floor which were let to the monks of the abbey during fairs.

On the right of the road is the ***Abbey of Farfa**, one of the most important monastic centres in Italy in the Middle Ages. It is shown on the hour every hour from 9.00–dusk (the tour takes c 30 minutes; tickets at the Erboristeria). It is thought to have been founded in 554 by St Lawrence the Illuminator, a Syrian who had been Bishop of Spoleto. He was a peacemaker and is said to have had a gift of healing blindness. The monastery was rebuilt in 705 by St Thomas of Farfa, from Maurienne in Savoy, with the help of the Duke of Spoleto. It was granted important privileges by Charlemagne in 775, and from then on flourished as an important monastic centre. After a period of decline in the 9C, it recovered importance under Abbot Ugo (997–1038) who introduced Cluniac reforms. The chronicler Gregorio da Catino (1062–1133) worked at the abbey. Five Benedictine monks still live here. Remains of a Roman building have recently been found, dating from the 2C AD.

The entrance is through a courtyard, on the left of which is the Erboristeria and ticket office. Another door off the courtyard leads into the 14C SMALL CLOISTER with a good view of the CAMPANILE which preserves its 9C base, above which is a three-light window added in the 11C; the three upper storeys date from the 12–13C. The LARGE CLOISTER dates from 1580. In the CRYPT is a 2C pagan *sarcophagus carved with very well-preserved battle scenes, found in an orchard of the abbey in the 1960s. The apse of the crypt is part of the original 8C church, with fragments of frescoes. The LIBRARY (40,000 vols), approached by an interesting little doorway, displays some of its most precious contents including choir books, a Papal bull of 1286, an 11C breviary with illuminated letters in the unique style of Farfa, the third book printed in Italy by Sweynheim and Pannartz at Subiaco in 1467, and 16C printed books.

The CHURCH is entered from behind the altar. The choir has 17C frescoes by the school of Zuccari. Beneath the ciborium is a 9C stone with fresco fragments and in front of it is the original antique altar. The ancient marble pavement is surrounded by a Cosmati floor. The nave has re-used Roman columns, a 15C wood ceiling and 16C frescoes. On the W wall is an interesting painting of the Last Judgment of 1561 by a Flemish painter. A 9C bas-relief has the four symbols of the Evangelists. The three chapels off the N side have altarpieces attributed to Orazio Gentileschi. On the second S altar is a venerated painting of the Madonna 'of Farfa', dating from the 13C. The church has a good façade preceded by a courtyard paved with pebbles. The doorway has a lunette fresco of the Madonna and Child and two Benedictine saints and donors (c 1494) attributed to Cola dell'Amatrice. Near the rose window and in the tympanum are Roman fragments. A large square tower is being restored.

Farfa is in the centre of the district known as the **Sabina**. The name is derived from the ancient *Sabini* an Italic tribe who occupied the hills between the Tiber and the Aniene and who came into conflict with the Latini and later the Romans. In 290 BC they were finally subjected to Rome. They are now mostly remembered for the famous legend of the Rape of the Sabine Women, depicted in numerous Roman sculptures. The Sabina is now taken to refer to the pretty area of the Sabine Hills in the province of Rieti. The beautiful landscape here is characterised by olive groves, and oak and chestnut woods between numerous little remote hill towns, many of which still have 'Sabina' or 'Sabino' attached to their names.

FROM FARFA TO CONTIGLIANO, 52km. This is a pretty route which traverses the Sabine Hills. 9km MONTOPOLI DI SABINA. The 17C church of Santa Maria delle Grazie has frescoes attributed to Vincenzo Manenti. 12km **Poggio Mirteto** is divided into a medieval district and an 18C district around the cathedral. On the outskirts of the town is the 13C church of San Paolo, with 12C and 14C votive frescoes, and the apse and triumphal arch decorated with frescoes by Lorenzo Torresani (1521). Beyond (16km) Poggio Catino is (22km) **Roccantica** in a fine position surrounded by olives. The church of Santa Maria Assunta has a high altarpiece by Bartolomeo Torresani, and on the right is a Madonna with Saints Dominic and Catherine by Sebastiano Conca. The little church of Santa Caterina has late Gothic frescoes (1430) by Pietro Coleberti.

25km **Casperia** where the fine Romanesque campanile of San Giovanni Battista survives. Outside the village is the church of the Annunziata which contains an Annunciation by Sassoferrato. Another church on the outskirts, Santa Maria di Legarano, contains 16C frescoes by the Torresani and a wood statue of the Madonna and Child signed by a certain Carlo Aquilano (1489). 6km S of Casperia is CANTALUPO IN SABINA, with the fine Palazzo Camuccini with double porticoes by Giandomenico Bianchi (16C). 35km **Cottanello**, in a beautiful position, which preserves its medieval walls. Outside, built into a rock face, is the little church of San Cataldo which contains an interesting late 12C fresco of the Redeemer with the Apostles, and praying figures below. The locality used to be famous for its red marble quarries.

17km SW of Cottanello is **Santa Maria in Vescovio**, a church built on a site already occupied in Roman times. It contains an important fresco cycle of the early 14C by Roman artists in the circle of Pietro Cavallini, a 9C pulpit, and a 14C wood Crucifix. 20km further W, close to the border with Umbria, is **Magliano Sabina** overlooking the Tiber valley, and just above the A 1 motorway. The cathedral of 1498 was restored in 1735 and contains an altarpiece by Rinaldo da Calvi (1521). The Museo Civico contains archaeological finds from the area.

52km **Contigliano** (2700 inhab.) has expanded at the foot of its hill, but the old part of the town is still dominated by the fine Collegiata of San Michele Arcangelo with a fine exterior begun by Michele Chiesa in 1693 and completed in 1747. It contains good 17C and 18C works including an organ of 1748. Two kilometres outside the town is the ruined 13C abbey of San Pastore. Contigliano overlooks the plain of Rieti: from here the road from Greccio (described above) to Rieti leads back to Rieti (10km from Contigliano).

35

The Via Flaminia and the Tiber Valley

ROAD, N 3 (Via Flaminia). 12km Prima Porta—30.5km Morlupo Station (for LUCUS FERONIAE, 14km E)—52.5km **Civita Castellana** (for FALERII NOVI, CASTEL SANT'ELIA, and NEPI)—60.5km Station of Civita Castellana. N 113—77km **Orte**. N 204—93km **Bomarzo**.

RAILWAY from Rome (Tiburtina), following the Via Flaminia, stopping at nearly all stations 3 times a day to Civita Castellana (71km) in 1¼ hr. The stations of Orte and Attigliano (for Bomarzo) are on the main line from Rome to Florence (slow trains only).

Via Flaminia runs almost due N from Piazzale Flaminio (Pl. 11; 7), which adjoins Piazza del Popolo. The Roman road to the N, it traverses Umbria and reaches the Adriatic at Fano (from where it continues as N 16 to Rimini). Begun in 220 BC it was named after Gaius Flaminius, censor and afterwards consul, who was killed at the battle of Lake Trasimene in 217 BC. Its initial section is described in Rte 24. At 7.5km the road passes the so-called TOMB OF THE NASONI (left), discovered in the 17C and now virtually destroyed. At GROTTAROSSA, with pozzolana quarries, a Republican villa was discovered in 1944, and there are several tombs in the vicinity. The road passes under the Grande Raccordo Annulare which crosses the Tiber and Via Salaria beyond. Here also is the Fosso di Valchetta, which flows past Veio.

At (12km) **Prima Porta** this route leaves the Tiber, and the Via Tiberina branches right. At the road fork an inscription (1912) commemorates the battle of Saxa Rubra where Constantine defeated Maxentius in 312, after being converted to Christianity by a vision of the flaming Cross with the words 'conquer by this'. On the hill between the roads are the ruins (no admission) of the Imperial **Villa of Livia** (*ad Gallinas Albas*), the residence of the wife of Augustus and mother of Tiberius. The fine statue of Augustus ('of Prima Porta'), now in the Vatican, was found here in 1863, as well as splendid wall-paintings, removed to the Museo Nazionale Romano. Beyond the fork, the huge Cemetery of Prima Porta extends on the right as far as Via Tiberina. 19.5km SACROFANO STATION. On the right, in pine trees, is the CASALE MAL BORGHETTO, a farmhouse which incorporates a Roman arch almost certainly erected by Constantine on the spot where he camped the night before the battle of Saxa Rubra (see above).

7.5km NW is SACROFANO, a picturesque medieval town at the foot of the prominent Monte Musino. 8km farther W is the larger medieval town of CAMPAGNANO DI ROMA (with an interesting parish church), from which a road through beautiful countryside leads E to rejoin the Via Flaminia 1.5km N of Morlupo Station (see below).

Via Flaminia continues from Sacrofano Station past (25.5km) a turning right to RIANO (2km), with a Ruspoli castle (now the town hall). At (28km) CASTELNUOVO DI PORTO (right), an ancient fortress remodelled into a palace in the 17C (in urgent need of restoration) dominates the town, which has been spoilt by modern buildings. 30.5km MORLUPO STATION.

From Morlupo Station a byroad leads right via **Morlupo** (2.5km), of ancient origins, to **Capena** (5km) near the site of an Etruscan city thought to have been the chief town of the Capenates, an Italic tribe subject to Veio. The road leads on to **Lucas Feroniae** (10km) where excavations were begun in 1962 of the ancient town, famous for its Temple of Feronia, who was venerated here from the 3C BC or earlier. The city was founded in the 6C or 5C BC, and sacked by Hannibal in 211 BC. A Museum is being arranged near the entrance to the site. So far the forum, baths, and a small amphitheatre have been unearthed. From the A 1 motorway the site can only be reached by taking the *Roma Nord* exit and then the road immediately on the left signposted 'Fiano Romano'. FIANO ROMANO, 5km N, is an old town, overlooking the Tiber valley, which used to have its own river-port and ferry boat in Roman times.

The **Villa of Gens Volusia** was built in the suburbs of Lucus Feroniae, but is now right beside the A 1 motorway in the service area of *Feronia Ovest*. This is reached just past the toll gates of the *Roma Nord* exit; it is usually closed, but part of it can be seen through the gate. It is one of the most important private villas near Rome, discovered in 1961, and dating from the 1C BC. On the left in front of a pretty little two-storeyed medieval tower (which contains an antiquarium) is the atrium and garden (partly under the motorway), and on the right a peristyle with a few columns still standing. Some of the rooms have fine mosaics. It is not possible to visit Lucus Feroniae (see above) by road from here; from the service station it is necessary to proceed towards Rome on the motorway (next exit *Settebagni*).

The Via Flaminia continues N through (39km) RIGNANO FLAMINIO, which preserves the ruins of a Savelli stronghold. The church of Santi Vincenzo e Anastasio has an altarpiece by Anastasio Fontebuoni. The ancient church of Sant'Abbondio, outside the village to the E, has a campanile and other relics of the 11C. 42km Turning for **Sant'Oreste**, 5km E, in a fine position at the foot of **Monte Soratte** (691m), the *Soracte* of Horace and Virgil. This long isolated ridge is conspicuous from miles around, and the view from the summit takes in southern Etruria and the fertile Sabine Hills, with the Apennines behind them across the Tiber valley. A rough road (11km) leads E from Sant'Oreste to PONZANO ROMANO between the Tiber and the A 1 motorway. Just outside, and very close to the motorway, is the abbey of SANT'ANDREA IN FLUMINE (being restored). First mentioned in 762 it has a fine fresco in the apse of the Resurrection.

The Via Flaminia continues to (53km) **CIVITA CASTELLANA** (148m) which stands on a tufa hill surrounded by picturesque and precipitous ravines spanned by high bridges. The town (15,900 inhab.) is on the site of the ancient *Falerii*, capital of the Falisci, a tribe belonging to the Etruscan Confederation but otherwise distinct and speaking its own language. It was taken by Camillus in 394 BC. In 241 BC it was destroyed by the Romans who built *Falerii Novi*, 6km W. The new town prospered, but in the 8C and 9C the population returned to the ancient site, which acquired its present name.

The **Duomo** has a magnificent *PORTICO and W door by the Cosmati family (1210), of unique design and particularly delicate workmanship, considered the masterpiece of this Roman family of marble sculptors. Beneath the portico are interesting architectural fragments, including Roman and medieval pieces, and a rare 8C relief showing a wild-boar hunt. In the 18C INTERIOR is an extensive and well-preserved Cosmatesque pavement. The modern pulpit and altar incorporate palaeochristian fragments. The interesting CRYPT has good antique columns and capitals. In the SACRISTY are preserved two *plutei from the Cosmatesque choir-screen (1237). A Diocesan museum is being arranged at No. 4 in the piazza.

Nearby in Via Roma is the entrance to the ***Rocca** a remarkable pentagonal fortress with two fine courtyards begun by Alexander VI and completed for Julius II by Antonio Sangallo the Elder. Used until recently as a prison, it has been well restored. Cells open off the courtyard which has some frescoes in the vault attributed to the Zuccari. The **Museo Archeologico dell'Agro Falisco** (open Tuesday–Friday at 14.00, 15.00, 16.00 and 17.00; Saturday and Sunday, 9.00, 10.00, 11.00, and 12.00) was beautifully arranged here in 1977. The collection includes material excavated in the Agro Falisco (Falerii Veteres, Narce, Vignanello, Corchiano, and Nepi) at the end of the 19C and the beginning of the 20C. Rooms 1–5 and 7 display finds from Falerii Veteres, including interesting tomb furniture (8–7C BC), imported Attic vases, and local 4C red-figure pottery. Finds from local sanctuaries include architectural terracottas, antefixes, and an Archaic head in tufa (with a bronze crown). Room 6 has Roman objects.

At **Falerii Veteres**, 1km W on the road to Fabrica di Roma, the most interesting relics are an aqueduct, the nucleus of the necropolis, in which the tombs, cut in the tufa, take the form of an antechamber with a vertical shaft (apparently for the escape of the gases of decomposition) and a sepulchral chamber. Beyond the medieval bridge over the Fosso Maggiore are the ruins of the so-called Temple of Juno Curitis, with a triple cella. The same road leads on to (6km) the romantic site of **Falerii Novi**, its remarkable *walls marked by a line of vegetation conspicuous in the open countryside. Triangular in plan and c 2100m round, they retain 50 of the original 80 towers and two of the nine gates. No other ruins give so complete an idea of a Roman walled town. The Porta di Giove gives access to a pine aveune which ends at the old abbey, now a farmhouse, with fine windows and ancient masonry. Here is the large roofless church of SANTA MARIA DI FALLERI built in the 12C (opened in the morning by a custodian), and nearby the area of the forum and theatre can be seen. The view embraces the line of walls and Monte Soratte in the distance. A track follows the walls from the gate; the Porta del Bove ('Ox Gate') is also well preserved.

Nepi, 13km SW is another ancient place known for its mineral water. At the entrance to the town an 18C aqueduct stands beside the huge ruined Rocca and the medieval walls on Etruscan foundations. In the main square is the town hall begun by Antonio da Sangallo and completed in the Baroque period. It contains an antiquarium. The Duomo, nearby, has an ancient crypt.

3km E of Nepi is **Castel Sant'Elia**. The approach road passes the Franciscan convent of Santa Croce in Sassonia; at the other end of the town a road descends (left) to the cemetery with its old cypresses beside the *BASILICA DI SANT'ELIA, an 11C Benedictine foundation on the site of an ancient temple, in a splendid position below a tufa cliff in a wooded valley. The simple façade incorporates ancient sculptural fragments. The interior (if closed, the entrance is through the crypt from the cemetery) has Roman columns and capitals and fragments of a Cosmatesque pavement, as well as a pergamum made up from ancient fragments, and a pretty ciborium. The interesting primitive *frescoes at the E end are signed by two brothers 'Giovanni' and 'Stefano' (late 11C or early 12C). The bright colours and delightful costumes show Byzantine influence.

60.5km. Station of Civita Castellana. The Flaminia now leaves this route, and crosses the Tiber near Magliano Sabina (described in Rte 34) to enter Umbria on its way to Narni (see 'Blue Guide Umbria'). N 315 continue N on the right bank of the Tiber to (77km) **Orte** ('Trattoria da Saviglia', 12 Via Cavour) a pretty little town perched on a tufa rock overlooking the Tiber. It has numerous handsome small palaces and has been well preserved. It occupies the site of the Etrusco-Roman *Horta*. The main road leads up past the Museo Diocesano into the piazza by the Duomo (limited car parking).

The MUSEO DIOCESANO is displayed in the fine Romanesque deconsecrated church of San Silvestro, beside a little garden with its ancient campanile. It is unlocked on request at the Curia (or Tel. 0761/494062). The collection includes a Madonna in mosaic (8C; restored) from the old basilica of St Peter's in Rome; a Madonna by Taddeo di Bartolo; a 13C panel of St Francis; four 15C panels depicting the life of Sant'Egidio; a late 15C painting of the 'Madonna dei Raccomandati' (being restored); and an interesting large painting of the Madonna in Glory with Saints by a Flemish painter known as Francesco da Castello (1595). Among the church silver is a reliquary Cross by Vannuccio di Viva da Siena (1352). A local archaeological collection is also displayed here with bronzes and terracottas of 5–4C BC; there are long-term plans to open a Museo Civico in the deconsecrated church of Sant'Antonio.

The CATHEDRAL has an attractive façade of 1901. The one-way road out of the town passes a terrace with a delightful view of the Tiber in the valley and then passes three arches of an aqueduct and crosses a narrow bridge before descending into the valley.

From Orte a 'superstrada' runs W to Viterbo (see Rte 37), and E to Narni (see 'Blue Guide Umbria'). N 204 now runs NW to (93km) **BOMARZO**, an interesting little town on a precipitous hill, built of dark grey stone which gives it rather a grim aspect, and recalls its Etruscan origins. It is particularly well preserved around the castle, but is usually visited for its famous park at the foot of the hill. There is a car park below the huge CASTLE (being restored) built by the Orsini in 1523–83, and now partly occupied by the town hall. Beside the statue of St Anselmo can be seen its massive walls; a narrow road leads up (right) under several arches (with a view of the little town) to a secondary wing of the castle with good windows (and the entrance to the town hall). Beyond is an attractive secluded piazza in front of the 16C DUOMO approached by a pretty flight of steps. Inside are grey stone altars, and, in the right aisle, a sarcophagus (with a lid in two parts). A few frescoes have been restored. The campanile has a Roman base, with a Roman funerary monument with three busts incorporated into the masonry. The tiny Via Regina Elena leads through the attractive, well-kept, old town with numerous outside stairs decorated with plants.

The •'**Parco dei Mostri**' (open every day 8.00–18.00) in the valley below the town is well signposted. This was the park, called the **Sacro Bosco** of the Orsini castle created by Vicino Orsini in the mid 16C. Gigantic fantastic creatures and bizarre monsters were carved in the natural rocky outcrops and surrounded by a wood, producing one of the strangest sights in Italy. It is thought that Pirro Ligorio or Vignola might have been employed by Orsini. Outside the entrance a shop and bar, a picnic area, children's playground, and small zoo, have recently been installed. However, beyond the castellated entrance gateway, the park retains, to a certain extent, its original character, although the vegetation (formerly thick woods of oak, pine, and chestnuts) has been altered and the stone inscriptions filled in with red paint.

Wooden arrows indicate the various paths which lead past the bizarre statues which include a monster with a wide open mouth near the entrance. To the right steps lead down past two giants wrestling. By a stream below is a gigantic tortoise with a female statue of Fame on his back. Nearby is a lop-sided house on two floors. On a terrace above, with monumental vases and statues of Neptune and Ceres, is a life-size Carthaginian elephant killing a Roman soldier, and a dragon. Behind the elephant a terrace surrounded by stone acorns, pine-cones, and bears (from the Orsini coat of arms) has statues of exotic sea monsters. Steps lead up from this terrace past the three-headed Cerberus to a miniature temple, intended as a mausoleum to Giulia Farnese, wife of Vicino Orsini, with a pronaos derived from the Pantheon. Nearby is an ogre with a stone table in its open mouth. Across a lawn above the temple can be seen another former entrance to the park, on a bizarre design.

From Bomarzo a road (6km) leads E to Attigliano (see 'Blue Guide Umbria'), where the A 1 motorway can be taken back to Rome. Viterbo, c 20km W of Bomarzo, is described in Rte 37.

36

Veio and Lake Bracciano

ROAD (VIA CASSIA), N 2. 18km Veio—40km Bracciano.

BUSES from Via Lepanto (corner of Viale Giulio Cesare) for Bracciano. Bus No. 201 from Piazzale Ponte Milvio for Isola Farnese (Veio).

RAILWAY from Rome (Termini), Viterbo line. To La Storta-Formello, for Veio (slow trains only), 27km in c 1 hr; to Bracciano, 52km in 1–2 hrs.

From Porta del Popolo (Pl. 11; 7) Via Flaminia and Viale Tiziano lead to Piazza Apollodoro, from where Corso di Francia turns off to the right to cross the Tiber by Ponte Flaminio. At the end of Corso di Francia this route branches left into Via Cassia Nuova. The VIA CASSIA, originally a rough road connecting Rome with Etruria, was paved by C. Cassius Longinus, consul in 107 BC, and was named after him. Now the N 2, it is a beautiful road which runs through Viterbo, Siena, and Poggibonsi to Florence.

The road undulates between gardens and parks, with tall pines and oak trees, and almost continuous ribbon development. To the left, soon after the junction with the old Via Cassia, is the SCOTS COLLEGE (1962). 9.5km On the left, half-hidden in a clump of cypresses, is the tomb of P. Vibius Maranius (2C AD), called, since the Middle Ages, the TOMB OF NERO.

Beyond (13km) La Giustiniana the Viterbo railway approaches on the left. 17km LA STORTA is a former posting stage, dominated by its large modern church. Near by, a chapel commemorates St Ignatius' vision of Christ here in 1537. 17.5km Madonna di Bracciano is a chapel at a road fork.

The left-hand road, the Via Claudia, leads to Bracciano (see below). To see Veio it is necessary to continue for another 500m on the Via Cassia. A byroad here leads E (signposted 'Isola Farnese e Veio') to ISOLA FARNESE (2km), a tiny hamlet beneath a medieval castle in a pretty position (the church contains interesting 16C frescoes). Veio can also be approached directly from the Via Cassia, 1.5km farther on.

VEIO, one of the most famous of the Etruscan cities, was built on a triangular tufa plateau (124m) bounded by two streams, the Fosso di

Formello-Valca and the Fosso di Valchetta, the ancient Cremera. At the confluence the sides are precipitous; on the promontory above it was the citadel, now called the PIAZZA D'ARMI. The city was directly accessible only from the NW angle.

Veio was one of the 12 cities of the Etruscan Confederation and apparently the largest of them all. Its walls had a circuit of 11km and its territory (*Ager Veiens*) was extensive, reaching to the Tiber on the S, E, and SW. It controlled the salt-works at the mouth of the Tiber. On the W its neighbour was Caere. Veio reached the zenith of its power between the 8C and the 6C BC and its position brought it into frequent conflict with Rome during the period of the kings and the early days of the Republic. It took the side of the deposed Tarquins in their attempt to return to Rome.

In the year of his third consulship (479 BC) the patrician L. Fabius Vibulanus, after a disagreement over the treatment of the plebeians, left Rome, and, at the head of 306 members of his gens, marched towards Veio. The Fabii established themselves on a hill to the right of the Formello-Valca, and harassed the Veientines for two years. In 477 they were trapped in an ambush near the Cremera and all were killed, except one, from whom all the later Fabii were descended. In 396, after a historic siege of ten years, M. Furius Camillus tunnelled through the rock and captured the city. It was destroyed and remained in ruins until Julius Caesar established a colony here, which Augustus elevated into a municipium. But the new city did not prosper; it was in decline by the time of Hadrian and soon disappeared from history. Excavations on the site began in the 18C. Many of the finds are in the Villa Giulia in Rome, among them the celebrated Apollo of Veio. The splendid bronze coffin of an Etruscan prince was found here in 1983.

Below Isola Farnese a steep narrow road descends right; it deteriorates as it approaches a barn near the Mola torrent. This can be forded on foot above the waterfall. A path leads up (right) to the PORTONACCIO gate and the ticket entrance (adm officially 9.00–dusk except Monday, winter 10.00–14.00; but the site is often closed). Beyond, on a terrace, are remains of the TEMPLE OF APOLLO, a cistern, and a rock-hewn tunnel. Outside the enclosure, and above it to the east, is the WEST GATE of Veio. Here, besides remains of walls, are a large cistern and the foundations of a rectangular building (possibly a temple).

Other remains are widely dispersed over the site; a whole day is needed for a complete tour. Since the area is now under cultivation it is difficult to explore without a guide. Beyond the ruins of the Roman city (on the S) stands (2.5km) the CITADEL, which is separated from the rest by a slight depression. Here the sides of the plateau are sheer and rise 60m above the torrents, and from the promontory can be seen Rome and the semicircle of the Alban, Tiburtine, and Sabine Hills beyond. Then, descending the E into the Cremera valley, a path leads left and comes first to the ruins of Roman baths, and then (on the right) the GROTTA DEGLI INGLESI or TOMBA CAMPANA (shown by the custodian). This (discovered in 1843) is a chamber-tomb of the late 7C cut in the rock, and one of the earliest painted tombs in existence. It consists of a deep-cut approach flanked by lions (two of which remain) and two quadrilateral chambers. The arch is of a transitional type between the beehive and the keystone systems, and on the walls are archaic paintings representing Mercury conducting the dead, and fantastic animals. A path continues W up the valley with the city to the left, to reach the PONTE SODO, a broad gallery cut by the Etruscans to open a passage for the torrent (one of the most romantic spots in the Campagna). From there a path continues up to the level of the city and on to Isola; or (easier but longer) the valley may be followed to the Ponte di Formello, where it is necessary to cross the torrent and bear left to reach the Fosso di Valca at Ponte di Isola, 1km NW of Isola Farnese, and so continue back to the main road.

It is necessary to return to the crossroads (see above), and take Via Claudia (right) for Lake Bracciano. By a tavern, just beyond (24km) the prominent

Vatican radio station (opened in 1957), a by-road (left) leads to SANTA MARIA DI GALERIA, a tiny hamlet with a delightful piazza approached by a fine gateway. The 15C church of Santa Maria in Celsano, with a good portal, has an interior divided by wide low arches supported by four columns; the two on the left have fine Corinthian capitals. It has a painted ceiling, and frescoes on the right wall (probably 16C; restored), and in the two side apses (much damaged). Just before the ascent to the piazza, a road forks below to the right. The first rough road to the right leads to the ruins of GALERIA. Situated above a beautiful wooded river valley, the castle, with a long history from before the 9C to the 19C, is a magnificent ruin. It stands on the site of the Etruscan *Careiae*; more remains can be seen across the river Galera.

Via Claudia continues to (40km) **BRACCIANO** (280m; 10,700 inhab.), a small town on the SW shore of the Lago di Bracciano. Information office, 58 Via Claudia (2-star hotels and a camping site open in summer). It was associated with the Orsini family from the 14C until 1696. The *Castello **Orsini** (1470–85) is a magnificent and perfectly preserved example of a Renaissance baronial castle, now belonging to the Odescalchi family. It was begun c 1470 by Napoleone Orsini, and finished by his son c 1485. Charles VIII stayed here in 1494. It has five crenellated round towers supporting the superb pentagonal structure. It was the first place that Sir Walter Scott wanted to visit on his arrival in Rome.

Visitors are conducted every hour, 9.00–12.30, and 15.00–17.00, except Monday. A steep ramp leads up to the entrance; on the wall to the right are frescoes by Antoniazzo Romano (1491). The vaulted kitchen off an imposing triangular interior courtyard, has huge fireplaces. FIRST FLOOR. The LIBRARY is decorated with frescoes by the Zuccari. Room III has a wooden ceiling painted by Antoniazzo Romano and pupils and a 15C bed. In the SALA DEL TRITTICO are the panels of a large triptych (late 15C), with a Crucifixion in the manner of Giotto and an Annunciation. Room V is frescoed with scenes from the Renaissance legend of the Fountain of Youth. Room VI has a large fresco by Antoniazzo Romano showing episodes in the life of the Orsini. The SALA DEGLI ORSINI contains busts (by Gian Lorenzo Bernini) and portraits of the Orsini and Medici families. The paintings in the SALA DEL LEONE date from the 15C. The CAMERA ROSSA has another ceiling painted by Antoniazzo Romano.

SECOND FLOOR. Beyond Room XI, with a 15C water-clock, Room XII has a frieze of the Labours of Hercules (15C) and a collection of arms. In the SALA D'ARMI are three suits of tournament armour: one Milanese (15C), and two German (16C). Room XVI contains a collection of finds from the cemeteries at Cerveteri and Palo. Beyond Room XVII is a loggia with a splendid view of the lake. The CAMMINO DI RONDA follows the ramparts.

In the town the **Collegiata** (Santo Stefano) has a Baroque façade and a campanile of 1500. Inside are paintings by Francesco Trevisani and Domenichino, and a gilded wooden triptych of 1315 by Gregorio and Donato d'Arezzo.

The **LAGO DI BRACCIANO** (164m) is the classical *Lacus Sabatinus*, named after the Etruscan town of *Sabate*. A prehistoric village was found here in 1977. It occupies an almost circular crater in the volcanic Monti Sabatini, with a diameter of 9.5km an area of 58sq km and a maximum depth of 160m. Its outlet, the Arrone is on the SE side, near Anguillara Sabazia. The *Acqua Traiana*, built by Trajan c 110, from the Lacus Sabatinus to Rome, was restored by Paul V in 1615 to supply some of the fountains in Rome (including the Fontana di Acqua Paola, on the Janiculum).

The waters of the lake (known for its trout, tench, and eels), as well as those of the Lago di Vico and the Lago di Bolsena, are harnessed to a great hydro-electric scheme. To the E of Lake Bracciano is the much smaller LAGO DI MARTIGNANO (Alsietinus Lacus), another crater-lake (207m).

The upper road out of Bracciano (the lower one leads only to the lake-side) skirts the entire lake. The scenery is particularly beautiful near **Vicarello** which has extensive olive plantations and a 17C farmhouse built above a Roman villa. The TERME APOLLINARI, a little spa in a 16C palace, closed since 1981, are near remains of Roman baths. This side of the lake has recently been threatened with 'development'. The beautiful road continues to (52km) **Trevignano Romano**, a picturesque village approached through its old town gate (car parking outside the gate or on the lake-side). A narrow road leads up to the church of the ASSUNTA, just below the ruined Orsini castle. Here there is a magnificent view of the lake over the roofs of the village. The interior has a striking fresco (1517) of the Death and Coronation of the Virgin, by the school of Raphael, beautifully designed to fit the curved apse. On the entrance wall is a stoup of 1541, and over the first altar (left), a copy of a precious 13C triptych of Christ enthroned with the Madonna and St John, which belongs to the church. Over the second altar, a fine 16C fresco of the Madonna with Saints, and on the altar, a marble 16C Pietà.

The road now skirts a small crater-lake with a good retrospective view of the village, and passes Grotta del Pianoro. 57km Road fork left to join the Via Cassia (see above; an alternative route back to Rome). The lower road to the right leads on to (63.5km) **Anguillara Sabazia** on high ground above the lake. The church of the ASSUNTA, with an interesting 18C façade, has a magnificent position above the lake. At SANTO STEFANO a medieval fortified farm occupies the site of a Roman villa. The town can be well seen from the road which continues to Bracciano, now passing through more hilly and wooded country. At **Vigna di Valle** a MUSEUM OF MILITARY AEROPLANES (open 9.00–18.00; winter 9.00–16.00; closed Monday) was opened in 1977 in three huge hangars. The collection includes some of the earliest planes used in the First World War, as well as modern aircraft. The road recrosses the railway to rejoin (70km) Via Claudia.

The Via Claudia or the Via Cassia return to Rome. Cerveteri (described in Rte 39) is 18km SW of Bracciano.

37

Viterbo and environs

From Rome to Viterbo, Via Cassia (N 2). From Rome to (20km) Veio, see Rte 36. N 2 continues N through (48.5km) **Sutri** and (67.5km) **Vetralla** (both described at the end of this Rte) for (80km) Viterbo. Viterbo can also be approached by the motorway (A 1) from Rome as far as (73.5km) Orte, where a 'superstrada' diverges left for (104km) Viterbo.

VITERBO (325m), once a rival of Rome as the residence of the popes, is a town (58,000 inhab.) of great interest, which preserves its old walls as well as numerous medieval buildings, built in the local grey stone called *peperino*, and beautiful fountains. The lion, the ancient symbol of the town, recurs frequently as a sculptural motif. It is the capital of a province which covers the whole of northern Lazio, and outside the walls the city has expanded in a disorderly way and it has particularly unattractive suburbs. It is the seat of the University of Tuscia.

Information Office. 'EPT', 14–16 Piazza dei Caduti (Tel. 0761/346363). Information office (open in summer), Piazza della Morte.

Railway Stations. PORTA FIORENTINA at the N end of the town, for Orte, and for Rome via Capranica–Sutri; PORTA ROMANA, an intermediate stop on the Capranica–Sutri line.

Buses run by 'COTRAL' from Viale Trento for Rome (Saxa Rubra) via the Cassia bis in 1hr 30 mins. Also to places of interest in the province, including Bolsena, Bomarzo, Caprarola, Tarquinia, Tuscania, and Civita di Bagnoregio.

Car Parking in or near Piazza della Rocca.

Hotels. 3-star: 'Tuscia', 41 Via Cairoli and 'Leon d'Oro', 36 Via della Cava. 2-star: 'Roma', 26 Via della Cava.
  Numerous first-class **restaurants** all over the town.

Theatres. Teatro Unione, Piazza Verdi (winter theatre season). Baroque Music festival (June–July) in the church of Santa Maria della Verità. In summer performances are held at the Roman theatre of Ferento.

Annual Festival of Santa Rosa on 3 September, celebrated by a grand procession (traditional since 1663), when a great *macchina* is carried through the streets by some 80 men. Its design is changed every five years (earlier designs are kept in the Museo Civico).

History. Viterbo, a minor castle in the 8C, was for centuries disputed between the papacy and the empire. For a short time, in 1095, it was a free commune; in 1145 Eugenius III took refuge here, and in 1167 it was raised to the dignity of a city. In 1243 the emperor Frederick II unsuccessfully besieged the city. In 1257 Alexander IV chose Viterbo as his residence. Five popes were elected here (the last of whom was Martin IV, 1281–85), and four died here. During this short period Viterbo rivalled Rome in importance, and the struggle between the two cities lasted some three centuries. After the popes moved to Avignon in 1309, Viterbo was disputed between various factions, and came under the rule of the tyrannical Di Vico family, before it ultimately declined in importance. The town was heavily bombarded during the Second World War.

Via Cassia runs past the public gardens, first laid out in 1865 by Virginio Vespignani, to PORTA FIORENTINA, restored in 1768. Inside the gate opens the large PIAZZA DELLA ROCCA, with a fountain by Raffaello da Montelupo, altered by Vignola. The **Rocca** was built by Cardinal Albornoz in 1354, but many times altered and enlarged. It has an attractive courtyard. It is being restored to house the **Museo Archeologico**: so far only the ground floor is open (admission 9.00–19.00; in winter 9.00–18.00; closed Monday). Here are displayed finds made during excavations in 1956–78 by the Swedish Institute of Classical Studies in Rome at Acquarossa and San Giovenale. The material is particularly interesting for the light it throws on Etruscan domestic architecture in southern Etruria, and includes painted tiles, antefixes, panels with reliefs (6C BC), and bronzes. Some of the houses have been partially reconstructed. On the upper floor will be displayed nine

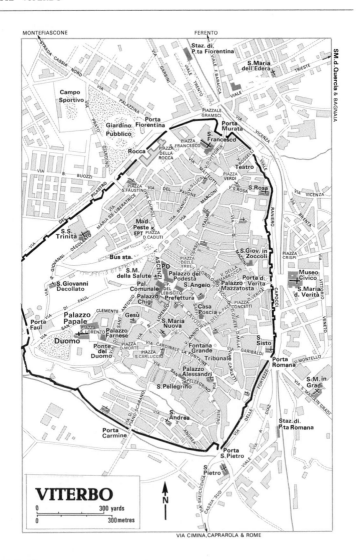

VITERBO

0   300 yards
0   300 metres

N

VIA CIMINA, CAPRAROLA & ROME

colossal statues of the 1C AD of the Muses from Pothos from originals by Skopas. They were found in 1902 in the Roman theatre of Ferento, where they formerly decorated niches in the scena.

Via Santa Faustina leads to Piazza San Faustina with its church (closed) and Via Carioli leads downhill to the busy PIAZZA DEI CADUTI. Here, surrounded by a little garden, is the church of SANTA MARIA DELLA PESTE, a small octagonal oratory built in 1494. By the large deconsecrated church of SAN GIOVANNI BATTISTA (1515), with an earlier campanile, Via Ascenzi mounts past the Post Office, a typical example of Fascist architecture, opposite SANTA MARIA DELLA SALUTE, a small 14C church built on a centralised plan with a delicately carved *portal (recently restored).

An archway leads into **Piazza del Plebiscito**, the centre of the town, and the junction of numerous roads. **Palazzo Comunale**, begun in 1460, has a portico, beyond which is a picturesque garden courtyard with a 17C fountain. Stairs lead up past Etruscan fragments to a 17C CHAPEL (open weekdays 8.00–19.00; fest. 8.00–13.00) with stuccoes and a good carved wood ceiling. The altarpiece of the Visitation is by Bartolomeo Cavarozzi.

Here are temporarily displayed four works from the Museo Civico which has been closed for years for restoration (see below). The *Flagellation (1525) and *Pietà (c 1515) are two masterpieces by Sebastiano del Piombo. They were commissioned by Monsignor Giovanni Botonti for churches in Viterbo. The Flagellation is derived from Sebastiano's fresco in San Pietro in Montorio in Rome (see Rte 22). Some critics think it possible that Michelangelo had a hand in the Pietà. Both paintings have charcoal studies on the back, also by Sebastiano. The Nativity with Saints John the Baptist and Bartholomew (1488) is by Pastura, who was born in Viterbo. The *Madonna and Child enthroned is a work of the 13C Roman school (removed from Santa Maria della Verità in 1953). Other frescoed rooms in the Palazzo Comunale are also shown on request. The Sala della Madonna, with a barrel vault, has a pretty lunette over the door of the Madonna attributed to Giovan Francesco d'Avanzarano (1488). The Sala Magna has frescoes by Baldassarre Croce, and landscapes on the ceiling dating from 1592. The Sala del Consiglio has painted statues in chiaroscuro (1558).

PALAZZO DEL PODESTÀ first built in 1264 has been restored. It has a good central window with a balcony. The slender tower dates from 1487. On the corner is a column with a carved lion and a palm tree. The Romanesque church of SANT'ANGELO was altered in 1746. Embedded in the façade was a Roman sarcophagus (at present replaced by a photograph) said to contain the body of Galiana, a girl whose beauty caused a war between Viterbo and Rome in the Middle Ages.

Off Via San Lorenzo, which runs S from Piazza del Plebiscito, Via Chigi leads right to the rambling PALAZZO CHIGI, a fine Renaissance building of the 15C, and then Via del Gesù leads up left to an attractive old market square with a medieval tower and pretty 17C fountain. The church of the GESÙ (formerly called San Silvestro) dates from the 11C. In this church, in March 1272, Prince Henry of Cornwall, nephew of Henry III of England and son of Richard Plantagenet, King of the Romans, was murdered at the altar by Simon and Guy de Montfort in revenge for the death of their father Simon at the battle of Evesham in 1265 (see Dante 'Inferno', Canto xii, 118–20). At the end of Via San Lorenzo is the shaded Piazza della Morte, with another fountain and three bays of a 12C loggia (now used as a Tourist Office). The old PONTE DEL DUOMO has visible remains of its Etruscan origins beneath it. Beyond the bridge, hospital administration offices occupy the restored 15C PALAZZO FARNESE, the supposed birthplace of Paul III (Alessandro Farnese).

The secluded *Piazza San Lorenzo is a charming survival from the Middle Ages. The CASA DI VALENTINO DELLA PAGNOTTA, with two arches, dates from the 15C (it was reconstructed after war damage). The *Palazzo Papale (c 1266) has been used as the episcopal palace since the 15C. The elegant Gothic loggia frames the sky. It was restored in 1887–1919. Beneath the arch can be seen Etruscan remains. The large hall (usually open), at the top of the steps (1267), witnessed the elections of Popes Gregory X (1271), who made the rules under which conclaves are still held, John XXI (1276), who died a year later of injuries when the ceiling of the new wing collapsed on his head, and Martin IV (1281). Intrigues protracted the first of these elections for two years, until Rainero Gatti, Captain of Viterbo, forced a decision (on the advice of St Bonaventura) by shutting the electors in the palace, then removing the roof of the hall, and finally reducing the food supply. The holes made in the floor for the cardinals' tent-pegs are still visible. In two rooms beyond the hall, the MUSEO DIOCESANO contains 16C paintings and sculptures (for admission, ask at the Curia).

The Romanesque **Cathedral** (San Lorenzo) was built in 1192, and the façade (covered for restoration) erected after 1560. The fine campanile dates from the late 14C. The nave arcades have good capitals. On the W wall is a tomb effigy of John XXI. The panel showing Christ blessing, in the left aisle, is by Gerolamo da Cremona. To the left of the high altar a panel representing the Madonna 'della Carbonara' is a good 12C work. The floor retains some 12C mosaic. The font in the right aisle has a basin by Francesco da Ancona (1470). From the sacristy (if closed apply at the Curia) is the entrance to the chapter house library with the 'Pantheon' of Gottifredo Tignosi, which has extremely interesting 14C miniatures.

In a small square off Via Cardinale La Fontaine (which runs parallel to Via San Pellegrino, see below) stands the church of **Santa Maria Nuova**, one of the finest in the city. It dates from the 12C, and was restored after war damage. The central portal is surmounted by a head of Jupiter, and on the left angle of the façade is a tiny outdoor pulpit from which St Thomas Aquinas preached. The most notable features of the basilican interior are the excellent capitals and a fine *triptych of Christ with saints, dating from the 13C. The miniature CLOISTER probably dates from the Lombard period.

The *medieval district** traversed by Via San Pellegrino, to the E of Piazza della Morte, provides an almost unspoiled picture of a 13C town. In **Piazza San Pellegrino** are the church of SAN PELLEGRINO and PALAZZO DEGLI ALESSANDRI, a severe 13C building. Via San Pietro continues SE to the medieval Porta San Pietro, outside which Via delle Fortezze skirts the fine city walls. Inside the walls (see the Plan) is the 12C church of SANT'ANDREA (restored) with interesting frescoes. The PORTA ROMANA, a busy entrance to the city, was rebuilt in 1653. Just beyond it rises the massive campanile, in part 9C, of the church of **San Sisto** (restored). Its fine basilican interior has a splendid raised choir with massive pillars. It contains a high altar composed of 4–5C architectural fragments, to the right of which is a painting by Neri di Bicci. The last column in the N aisle is interesting.

Outside Porta Romana Via Romana leads to a prison (there are plans to transfer it to a new building under construction), in the ground of which (admission at present only with special permission) stand the remains of the church of SANTA MARIA IN GRADI, destroyed in the war, with the exception of its façade, but still retaining its splendid 13C cloister, built in the Gothic style by Roman marble workers. A second Renaissance cloister has at its centre a fountain of 1480.

Inside the walls Via Garibaldi runs to PIAZZA DELLA FONTANA GRANDE where the *fountain, the finest and oldest in the city, was begun in 1206 by Bertoldo and Pietro di Giovanni, finished in 1279, and restored by Benedetto da Perugia in 1424. To the right of Via Cavour (which leads directly to the centre) is the narrow Via Saffi, in which stands the CASA POSCIA, a picturesque 14C house. Via della Pace and its continuation lead

NE to the PORTA DELLA VERITÀ. Just outside this gate is **Santa Maria della Verità**, a 12C church altered and decorated at later dates. On the W wall is a damaged detached fresco of the Annunciation (copy of a fresco by Melozzo da Forlì in the Pantheon in Rome), and Saints attributed to Lorenzo da Viterbo. The Cappella Mazzatosta is decorated with *frescoes by Lorenzo da Viterbo (1469; restored). The convent on the N side houses the **Museo Civico**, which is closed for restoration. When it reopens the arrangement described below may be changed. The four most important works, including two masterpieces by Sebastiano del Piombo, are at present exhibited in Palazzo Comunale (see above).

Rooms leading off the NE corner of the *CLOISTER (of which three walks date from the 13C and the fourth from the 14C) contain Etruscan antiquities. ROOM I. Cases of finds from Bisenzio (end of 7C BC); pottery; small bronzes; vases, including Bucchero ware; terracotta votive statues from Bomarzo; finds from Norcia and Ferento. ROOM II. Terracotta tombs; case of bronze ware and gold jewellery. FIRST FLOOR. The first rooms contain a marble sphinx by Pasquale Romano (signed and dated 1268) and a lion, both from Santa Maria in Gradi; St Bernard, by Sano di Pietro, an unglazed terracotta bust of Giovanni Battista Almadiani by Andrea Della Robbia (and a glazed lunette by his school); also a fine bronze ewer in the shape of a lion, an early 13C Sassanian work. The paintings include works by Antoniazzo Romano, Giovanni Francesco Romanelli, Salvator Rosa (Incredulity of St Thomas), and local 15–16C artists.

Viale Raniero Capocci follows the best preserved sector of the medieval WALLS, here battlemented and strengthened by towers. Via Mazzini, on the right inside Porta della Verità, leads N to SAN GIOVANNI IN ZOCCOLI, a much restored 11C church with a rose window and handsome interior with an unusual variety of capitals. It contains a primitive episcopal throne and a polyptych by Balletta (1441). The confined Via della Marrocca and Via dell'Orologio Vecchio descend to Piazza delle Erbe (fountain of 1621) at the S end of the long **Corso d'Italia**, venue of the evening *passeggiata*. The CAFFÈ SCHENARDI here was decorated by Virginio Vespignani in 1818.

From the N end of the Corso, Via di Santa Rosa leads to the right (E) to the sanctuary of SANTA ROSA (1850), in which is preserved the body of St Rosa (died 1252), who helped the town and inspired its inhabitants to defend themselves against Frederick II. The festival of her translation is celebrated on 3 September (see above). The church contains a polyptych by Balletta (1441).

At the N end of the town stands SAN FRANCESCO, a Gothic church of 1237, restored after war damage. A 15C pulpit built into the façade records the preaching in 1426 of St Bernardine of Siena. Inside is the *tomb of Adrian V (died 1276), thought to be the first work of Arnolfo di Cambio. The tomb of Clement IV (died 1268) is by Pietro di Oderisio.

The environs of Viterbo

A. Ferento, Santa Maria della Quercia, Bagnaia, and Soriano nel Cimino

To the E of Porta Fiorentina and Piazzale Gramsci, and just beyond the railway, Viale Baracca (signposted for Bagnoregio) diverges left for Acquarossa and Ferento. At ACQUAROSSA (7km; byroad right) excavations carried out by the Swedish Institute of Classical Studies in Rome in 1966–78 revealed remains of an Etruscan city including interesting houses of the 7–6C BC (finds in the Museo Archeologico in Viterbo). The ruins of **Ferento** (8km; byroad 1.5km right) are not open regularly to the public (for admission enquire at the Museo Archeologico in Viterbo). Founded by the Etruscans in the 4C, this was a flourishing town in Roman times and the birthplace of the Emperor Otho (AD 69). It was destroyed by Viterbo in 1172 for heretically representing Christ on the Cross with open eyes. The most interesting ruins are those of a *THEATRE (restored and used in summer). Recent excavations have revealed remains of the baths and other buildings. A church lower down the hillside dates from the 9–10C.

Viale Trieste leads straight from Viterbo to (3km) LA QUERCIA, where the church of *Santa Maria della Quercia** (closed 12.00–16.00), built in 1470–1525, is one of the finest buildings of the Renaissance. The simple façade is by Carlo di Mariotto and Domenico di Jacopo da Firenzuola (1509) and the graceful main portal by Giovanni di Bernardino da Viterbo. The terracotta lunettes above the three doors are by Andrea della Robbia. The massive campanile is the work of Ambrogio da Milano.

The *INTERIOR has a ceiling by Giovanni di Pietro on a design by Antonio da Sangallo the Younger (1518–25). The splendid *tabernacle, by Andrea Bregno (1490), behind the high altar, encloses a tile with a miraculous image of the Madonna. In the apse are fine inlaid stalls (1514) and an altarpiece by Fra Bartolomeo, Mariotto Albertinelli, and Fra Paolino da Pistoia. In the S aisle is a Madonna and Child with St Anthony Abbot, by Monaldo da Viterbo (1519). A door in the N aisle leads to a small museum with a collection of ex votos (15–18C). From the right of the high altar a door leads to a cloister in two orders: the lower by Daniele da Viterbo (1487) was inspired by that of Santa Maria in Gradi, the upper part was added in the 16C. The other conventual buildings, including a second (17C) cloister, and the refectory, constructed by Giovanni Battista di Giuliano da Cortona (1519–39) to a design of Antonio da Sangallo the Younger, are now closed.

N 204 continues to the pretty little town of (5km) **Bagnaia** (3800 inhab.), famous for the gardens of Villa Lante. It can be reached by bus No. 6 (every 20 minutes) from Piazza Caduti, Viterbo. The park of the Villa Lante is a lovely place to picnic. Just before the town, the road passes a little octagonal church of 1569 and crosses a bridge with a good view of Palazzo Vescovile (see below), and then runs through the middle of PIAZZA XX SETTEMBRE (car parking here or just below the bridge). The medieval district is to the left and the Villa Lante, preceded by 16C streets, to the right. Behind a 16C fountain and a round tower, an arch leads into the medieval borgo where the PIAZZA DEL CASTELLO has another pretty round fountain (perhaps designed by Vignola) and the Palazzo Vescovile.

On the other side of the main road three attractive small 16C roads lead up to the *VILLA LANTE**, with perhaps the most beautiful and best preserved formal gardens in Italy. The entrance is at the end of the road on the right (the park is open daily to the public 9.00–dusk; the gardens can be visited every half hour from 9.00–dusk; the upper floors of the two 'Palazzine' are open only by previous appointment, Tel. 0761/288008).

The PARK extends beyond the monumental Pegasus fountain attributed to Giambologna, which has a hemicycle decorated with busts of Muses. The CASINO DI CACCIA was built in the early 16C by Cardinal Ottaviano Riario. The fountains in the park were added by Cardinal Montalto. Steps on the left lead up to the gate into the *Gardens**. They were created by Cardinal

Giovanni Francesco Gambara after 1566; he almost certainly employed Vignola to lay them out. He also planned the two symmetrical little garden pavilions or 'Palazzine'; he used one as his summer residence, but the second one was not built until 1590 when Cardinal Alessandro Montalto continued work on the gardens (not finished until 1612). The gardens, designed around a series of delightful fountains, were greatly admired by Montaigne and John Evelyn.

The villa was the property of the Lante family from 1656 until 1973 when it was bought by the Italian State. The ground floor vaulted logge of the two little garden PAVILIONS are open. The one on the right, built by Cardinal Gambara, has frescoes of four villas in Lazio with their gardens (including Villa Lante) and grotteschi by Raffaellino da Reggio, and the one on the left added by Cardinal Montalto has frescoes by Agostino Tassi and birds in the vault by Marzio Ganassini. The upper floors can only be visited by previous appointment; they contain frescoes by Antonio Tempesta, Raffaellino da Reggio, Giovanni Battista Lombardelli, and Cavalier d'Arpino.

The water parterre 'all'italiano' here has box and yew hedges planted in intricate designs around square ponds and a large central fountain with four elegant statues (known as 'moors' since the peperino stone has darkened) holding up the Montalto arms. They are attributed to Taddeo Landini or Ambrogio Buonvicino. The houses of Bagnaia can be seen above the wall at the end of the garden in which was the former entrance. Steps lead up through the beautifully kept gardens (planted with hydrangeas, camellias, and rhododendrons), laid out on the little hillside on five terraces connected by a central walk with a series of fountains, possibly by Ammannati and Jacopo del Duca. The vegetation is dominated by splendid old plane trees and ilexes.

The first fountain is decorated with numerous jets of water from little stone lamps. On either side are grottoes with statues of Venus and Neptune. Above is a terrace with a long stone dining table kept fresh by rivulets of running water and a semicircular fountain with two reclining statues of river gods. Behind them is a water staircase in the form of a huge chain which descends from an octagonal fountain decorated with dolphins. At the top of the garden is a grotto overgrown with mosses and maidenhair fern where the spring water which supplies all the fountains in the garden issues from a monster's mouth. On either side are little logge, with the name and coat of arms of Cardinal Gambara, and two gigantic herms. In one of the logge are fresco fragments of the Muses and birds. On the left, columns surround a rose garden laid out between box hedges near a venerable ilex grove.

The main road continues past peperino quarries and winds along the side of Monte Cimino (see below) and crosses a single-gauge railway before reaching (17km) **Soriano nel Cimino** (7500 inhab.), with unattractive buildings in the valley. The area is known for its chestnuts and a festival is held here on the second Sunday in October. On the way up to the main piazza, a narrow road (right; yellow signpost) leads to PALAZZO CHIGI built by Vignola in 1562, with an unusual exterior. Beyond a gate (usually open) are two terraces; at the end of the second is a remarkable Mannerist fountain with Moses on one side and, on the end wall, the fantastic 'Fontana Papacqua' with extraordinary monsters. The water ends in a waterfall below the terrace and drops to a pool far below. The palace is privately owned (no admission).

The road continues up to Piazza Vittorio Emanuele II in front of the DUOMO with a neo-classical interior. It contains an interesting 15C marble high relief with the seated figure of St Nicholas, with a porcupine at his feet. By the side door at the W end is a large font. An archway leads into the medieval borgo, with a fountain in the pretty piazza. Above the church of Sant'Eutizio, which contains a little tabernacle attributed to Andrea Bregno at the W end, is the imposing 13C Orsini CASTLE (no admission), used until recently as a prison.

The extinct volcano of MONTE CIMINO (1053m) is reached by a road (8km) from Soriano. It is now covered with woods of chestnut and beech. Some 45m below the summit is the *Sasso Menicante*, mentioned by the Elder Pliny, a trachyte block 8.5m long which was thrown up in an eruption and was caught by a projecting crag so that it became a rocking stone. 11km SE of Soriano is the interesting town of VIGNANELLO with the moated Castello Ruspoli, reconstructed in the 16C, and well preserved (privately owned). The church of Santa Maria was built in 1723 by Giovanni Battista Contini. VALLERANO, nearby, has a fine church of 1609. A byroad (9km) leads N from Soriano to Bomarzo (described in Rte 36). There is a good view back of the castle of Soriano as the road descends through farming country and crosses the 'superstrada' between Orte and Viterbo. The pretty road continues through woods (with Monte Soriano prominent to the S).

B. The Via Cimina, San Martino al Cimino, Caprarola, and Ronciglione

The Via Cimina (signposted 'Roma, Via Cimina') leaves Viterbo outside Porta Romana and climbs steeply uphill though woods. At 10km a byroad leads right for SAN MARTINO AL CIMINO (8km), a medieval town which was rebuilt in the 17C, and retains its interesting plan from that time. It has a splendid 13C Cistercian abbey *church (open all day). The main road continues above the *LAGO DI VICO, surrounded by a beautiful wooded nature reserve on the edge of the crater of MONTE VENERE whose cone (838m) rises above the lake. This was the ancient *Lacus Ciminus* a crater-lake 17.5km round with a surface at 507m. The road follows the rim and just below (15km) the turning for Caprarola there is a good view right of the lake.

A byroad (3.5km) leads down to **Caprarola** (510m), a little town (4600 inhab.) famous for its Palazzo Farnese. Buses ('COTRAL') from Rome (Saxa-Rubra and Via Lepanto) and from Viterbo (the nearest railway station is 3km outside the town on the line between Orte and Capranica). The approach road leads past the huge stable block built by the Farnese (being restored to house a school of architecture), and there is a good view right of the convent and church of Santa Teresa (see below). The road skirts the wall of the Palazzo Farnese, and it is best to park by the little side entrance to the palace.

The *PALAZZO FARNESE is perhaps the most magnificent Mannerist villa in Italy, in a splendid position dominating the little town of Caprarola. Guided tours of the piano nobile of the palace and of the winter garden are given 9.00–17.00; summer 9.00–19.00, but the park, with the most interesting part of the gardens, is only shown Monday–Saturday at 10.00, 11.30, and 15.00.

The palace, designed by Vignola (1559–73) for Cardinal Alessandro Farnese, was built on the foundations of a pentagonal fortress begun c 1515 by Antonio da Sangallo the Younger for his uncle, Alessandro Farnese (later Paul III). The piano nobile has empty apartments richly decorated with stuccoes and frescoes in 1560–83 by Taddeo and Federico Zuccari, Giacomo Bertoia, Giovanni de' Vecchi, Raffaellino da Reggio, and Antonio Tempesta, on a scheme worked out by Annibal Caro illustrating the glorious history of the Farnese family since the time of Pope Paul III.

The very fine exterior, approached by a series of monumental steps, ramps, and terraces (the grey door was the entrance for carriages), has recently been over restored, so that the local grey peperino stone now looks like white travertine. The gardens are divided into two parts: two symmetrical rectangular formal gardens are approached directly across bridges from the piano nobile, and, a long way uphill beyond a wood (not visible from the palace) is a second garden with fountains and parterres around an elegant garden 'casinò'.

The entrance to the palace is through the SALONE DELLE GUARDIE which has a frescoed vault by Federico Zuccari and assistants. A splendid spiral *STAIRCASE, with a dome, designed by Vignola, has grottesques and landscapes frescoed by Antonio Tempesta. It leads up to the **piano nobile** where a circular loggia overlooks the beautiful circular *COURTYARD. The SALA DELLE FATICHE D'ERCOLE is named after the vault fresco by Federico Zuccari. It has a rustic wall fountain with mosaics and stuccoes. The fine view takes in the plain and Monte Soratte beyond the town's long main street. On the walls are frescoes showing the Farnese possessions including the duchies of Parma and Piacenza. The CHAPEL has a lovely vault decorated by Federico Zuccari and a pavement by Vignola. The figure of St James the Greater is supposed to be a portrait of Vignola. The *SALA DEI FASTI FARNESIANI has splendid frescoes by Federico and Taddeo Zuccari celebrating the life of the Farnese family (the scene of Francis I incorporates self-portraits of the Zuccari brothers). The ANTICAMERA DEL CONCILIO has frescoes by Taddeo Zuccari illustrating the life of Paul III. The four corner columns are trompe l'oeil frescoes by Vignola. There follows the SUMMER APARTMENTS, a series of four smaller rooms facing north and overlooking the gardens (approached from here through a door). These were the last to be frescoed by the Zuccari: the CAMERA DELL'AURORA, STANZA DEI LANIFICI and STANZA DELLA SOLITUDINE are all frescoed by Taddeo, and the GABINETTO DELL'ERMATENA has frescoes by Federico. The CAMERA DEL TORRIONE is the only room with a wood ceiling.

A corridor decorated with vines leads into the WINTER APARTMENTS, with a door into the winter gardens. The CAMERA DELLA PENITENZA and the CAMERA DEI GIUDIZI are frescoed by Jacopo Bertoia. The STANZA DEI SOGNI has a fresco of Jacob's dream, also by Bertoia. The beautiful *SALA DEGLI ANGELI has frescoes on the walls by Raffaellino da Reggio, and the vault fresco of the Fall of the Rebel Angels is attributed to Giovanni de' Vecchi (1574–75). The SALA DEL MAPPAMONDO has extremely interesting and accurate maps of the world dating from 1574 by Giovanni Antonio da Varese. Raffaellino da Reggio and Giovanni de' Vecchi also worked here but it is not known who painted the delightful vault with the constellations.

A modern bridge leads out high above the moat to the small WINTER GARDEN with box hedges, at the back of which is an elaborate grotto once used as a theatre. The *Park (for admission, see above) extends for 18.5ha on the hillside behind the palace, and has extensive chestnut woods. A walk of about 20 minutes leads up through woods and a grove of silver firs to a circular fountain. This is set beside two grottoes and in front of a delightful water staircase, decorated with dolphins, which descends from a fountain with two river-gods in a hemicycle. It provides a splendid approach to the CASINÒ DI CACCIA, a hunting lodge with a double loggia, designed by Vignola and completed by Jacopo del Duca. It is surrounded by a garden on a terrace with huge herms on the balustrade. Pretty stairways lined with more dolphins lead up to yet another garden which slopes gently down towards the lodge and has pebble mosaic paving. This was used for outdoor entertainments, and here is the aqueduct which supplies all the fountains in the garden. Thick woods of chestnuts, cypresses, and pines extend over the hillside beyond.

The little town of Caprarola is laid out on either side of its long straight main street, designed by Vignola, which leads downhill from the palace. Opposite Palazzo Riario is the 16C Duomo, rebuilt after a fire in 1817. Farther downhill on the left is the 16C church of SANTA MARIA DELLA CONSOLAZIONE with a fine carved wood ceiling. Outside the town, across the valley from Palazzo Farnese in a scenographic position, is the huge church and convent of SANTA TERESA, a very fine building by Girolamo Rainaldi (1623). The high altarpiece is attributed to Guido Reni.

Via Cimina (see above) continues from the turning for Caprarola to (21km) **Ronciglione** (441m), once perhaps an Etruscan settlement, and later a duchy of the Farnese family. In Piazza Duomo is a 16C fountain with unicorns' heads, and the sombre 16C town hall. The DUOMO was rebuilt by Carlo Rainaldi in 1671–95. It contains a triptych by a local 15C painter and a Madonna and saints by the school of Giulio Romano. The abandoned CASTLE is in need of repair. Via di Castello on the right follows the walls round to BORGO DI SOPRA, a pretty medieval street which leads downhill past a series of alleyways. The impressive 15C campanile of SANT'ANDREA, by Galasto da Como, in dark grey peperino, stands in front of a few remains of the church. At the end of Borgo di Sopra steps wind down to the left to emerge on a charming little terrace with a fountain and a loggia overlooking a gorge. Here is the church of SANTA MARIA DI PROVVIDENZA with a 13–14C bell-tower. In another part of the town is the church of SANTA MARIA DELLA PACE attributed to Vignola or Rainaldi, with an interesting interior.

C. Vetralla and Sutri

BAGNI DI VITERBO, 5km W of the town, is a little spa. Nearby is the *Bullicame* spring, a hot sulphur pool mentioned by Dante ('Inferno', XIV, 79). About 5km farther SW (8km from Porta Faul in Viterbo) are the 15C ruins of CASTEL D'ASSO, which preserves the name of Castellum Axia, an Etruscan town. Below the castle are a few remains of the town and an extensive (unenclosed) necropolis, with the two-storeyed Tomba Orioli, and the Tomba Grande, which contained 40 sarcophagi.

The Via Cassia (N 2) runs S from Viterbo to (13km) **Vetralla** (300m; 9000 inhab.) which has a Vignolesque Palazzo Comunale, and a cathedral begun in 1711 by Giovanni Battista Contini. On the main road is the Romanesque church of SAN FRANCESCO, with good capitals, a restored Cosmatesque pavement, an interesting crypt, the sepulchral monument of Briobris by Paolo Romano (early 15C), and restored 15C frescoes. The church of SANTA MARIA FURCASSI, 3km NE, preserves the name of the ancient *Forum Casii*.

A good byroad (signposted) leads W through fertile farming country with numerous eucalyptus trees to (6km) the unenclosed site of the Etruscan necropolis of **Norchia** (a rough track continues for 500m from the end of the surfaced road to the edge of the ravine). In this romantic isolated spot there is a view across the valley of two ruined medieval buildings (a castle wall and the apse of San Pietro). Steep paths lead down the side of the cliff face; the path on the left soon emerges beside rock-cut *tombs of the 4–2C BC, some with the appearance of temples with figured pediments (a torch is necessary to see the interiors).

On the main road (N 1 bis) from Vetralla to Tarquinia (see Rte 40) is MONTEROMANO (16km) founded in 1644 as an agricultral colony. Its 17–19C buildings give it a specious appearance, and it has an antiquarium (enquire at the Comune).

To the S of Vetralla (reached via Cura, see below) is an area where, from 1956–65, the Swedish Institute for Classical Studies in Rome carried out important excavations which revealed much about the origins of the Etruscans. Work was continued in 1966–75 by the Italian State. At (12km) BLERA, the *Phleva* of the Etruscans, the remains of the ancient town include two large necropoli (unenclosed), two bridges, and a sarcophagus (in the church of Santa Maria). 4km NW is the Grotta Porcina, a conical tomb 28m in diameter dating from the early 6C BC. About 11km S, reached by a minor road, is CIVITELLA CESI, c 3km W of which is the ancient citadel of SAN GIOVENALE, crowned by the ruins of a medieval castle. Here the Swedes excavated the oldest Etruscan houses known (unenclosed, two of them protected by iron roofs), and abutments of bridges dating from the 6C BC. Finds and models of the excavations are exhibited in the Museo Archeologico in Viterbo.

18km BARBARANO ROMANO, a picturesque hill village, is built near the site of an Etruscan township; an obelisk, a form of monument not previously associated with the Etruscans, was unearthed here in 1963. In the 18C town hall is a small local archaeological museum (usually open in the mornings). In the locality known as SAN GIULIANO, 2km NE, more excavations bought to light an interesting necropolis (6–5C BC). This is now in the protected area of the PARCO NATURALE MARTURANUM.

The Via Cassia passes the Blera turning (see above) at (16km) CURA. At (21.5km) QUERCIE D'ORLANDO the Via Claudia (N 493) starts its winding course towards Rome to the W of Lake Bracciano; it passes ORIOLO ROMANO (16km) where the late 16C Palazzo Altieri is open from 9.00–13.30. Recently purchased by the State, it contains frescoes by the Roman Mannerists. The main road continues towards (27km) **Capranica** (373m; 3700 inhab.) passing the church of the Madonna del Piano, with frescoes attributed to Francesco Cozza or Antonio Carracci. The church of San Francesco contains a Gothic tomb of two Counts Anguillara (died 1406 and 1408). The Ospedale has a fine Romanesque portal.

32km **SUTRI** (291m) is the ancient *Sutrium*, called the 'Gate of Etruria', which was captured by Camillus in 389 BC. Its cession by the Lombard king Liutprand to Pope Gregory II in 728 is traditionally seen as marking the beginning of the temporal power of the popes. The rival Popes Gregory VI and Sylvester III were deposed for simony by a synod held here in 1046. The pleasant central PIAZZA DEL COMUNE is entered by a Roman arch built of peperino blocks (2C BC) beneath a clock-tower, which was probably the former entrance to the Roman Forum. The pretty fountain dates from 1722. In the courtyard of the PALAZZO DEL COMUNE are Roman and medieval sculputral fragments including a a sarcophagus of the 3C AD. Via Vittorio

Veneto leads down to the DUOMO, with a campanile of 1207 and a portico of 1745–52. The interior was redesigned in 1745 and the frescoes in the vault are by Luigi Fontana (1889–91). The Cosmatesque pavement and *crypt survive from the medieval church. On the second N altar is an unusual 13C *icon of Christ blessing in the Byzantine style. Numerous other parts of the little town are worth exploring.

Just outside the town, off the main road, surrounded by trees, is an *Amphitheatre carved out of the tufa rock (usually kept locked, but visible through the gate). A remarkable building, it is thought to date from the 1C BC–1C AD. It was discovered in 1835–38. Nearby, also off the main drive (in the direction of Viterbo), approached through an open gate along a road lined with hedges, is (left) the MADONNA DEL PARTO, a 13–14C church in a tufa cave which may once have been used as a mithreum. Carved out of the rock face, it has no façade, and contains fragmentary 14–15C frescoes (but is usually locked). The avenue continues uphill to the VILLA SAVORELLI (recently acquired by Comune of Sutri), built c 1730, with a fine garden, and the church of Santa Maria del Monte of the same date. At the top of the hill are remains of a 13–14C castle. From the belvedere in the park there is a splendid view of the amphitheatre (see above). Also off the Via Cassia, on the other side of the amphitheatre (in the direction of Rome), a picturesque country lane is lined with some 64 interesting rock tombs which formed part of the ROMAN NECROPOLIS of Sutri.

5km SW is BASSANO ROMANO, where the fine Palazzo Giustianiani, bought in 1595 from the Anguillara, and restored in the 16–17C, has frescoes by Domenichino and Francesco Albani. It is now owned by the Odescalchi (admission only with special permisssion from Palazzo Odescalchi, 81 Piazza Santissimi Apostoli in Rome). It is surrounded by a garden and park.

The Via Cassia continues S towards Rome passing close to Nepi (described in Rte 35), and Lake Bracciano and Veio (described in Rte 36).

38

Bolsena and Montefiascone

From Rome to Bolsena and Montefiascone, N 2 (Via Cassia). From Rome to (80km) Viterbo, see Rte 37. The Via Cassia continues N from Viterbo to (96km) Montefiascone and (111km) Bolsena on the E shores of the Lago di Bolsena. Bolsena can also be reached by taking the A I motorway from Rome to (114km) Orvieto, and from there the N 71 leads SW to (135km) Bolsena.

BOLSENA is a pretty little town (4000 inhab.) on the shores of the Lake of Bolsena, the successor to the Etruscan and Roman city of *Volsinii*. It preserves a medieval district around its castle (recently restored and opened as an interesting local museum). The important church and catacombs of Santa Cristina are also in the town.

Information Office, Piazza Matteotti.

Bus services run by 'COTRAL' to Viterbo, Acquapendente, and Montefiascone. Services from Viterbo to Rome, Bagnoregio, Tarquinia, Tuscania, and Orvieto.

The nearest **Railway Station** is at Orvieto, 23km E, on the main line from Rome to Florence.

Hotels (3-star) and **Trattorie** on the lakeside (which serve fish, including eels, from the lake).

Annual Festivals. 23 and 24 July, Festival of Santa Cristina, with the performance of 'tableaux' illustrating the Passion of Santa Cristina. On Corpus Domini there is a procession and an 'infiorata' when the streets are carpeted with flowers.

History. The Etruscan city of *Volsinii* seems to have been founded by the inhabitants of *Volsinii Veteres* (usually identified with Orvieto), after their city was destroyed in 265 BC. It became an important Roman town, especially after the opening of the Via Cassia here in 170–150 BC, and thrived up until the 3C AD. It was destroyed in the late 6C by the Lombards. The town is famous for a miracle which took place here in 1263, when a Bohemian priest who had doubts about the doctrine of Transubstantiation, was convinced when he saw blood drop from the Host onto the altar cloth during a Mass. It was in commemoration of this miracle that Urban IV (1261–64) instituted the festival of Corpus Domini and built the cathedral of Orvieto (where the stained corporal is preserved in a reliquary).

From Piazza Matteotti (car parking) Corso della Repubblica leads to the 11C church of **Santa Cristina** (open 7.00–12.30, 15.00–17.30; summer 7.00–12.30, 15.30–19.30), with good 15C terracotta sculptures by Francesco and Bendetto Buglioni. Here the miracle of Bolsena (see above) is supposed to have taken place. The elegant Renaissance FAÇADE (1492–94) is attributed to Francesco and Benedetto Buglioni (with an enamelled terracotta lunette). On the right is the façade of the 15C Oratorio di San Leonardo with another lunette attributed to Benedetto, and on the left the neo-classical façade by Virginio Vespignani of the domed Cappella del Miracolo.

The INTERIOR has interesting columns. On the W wall is a painting of the Martyrdom of St Andrew by Francesco Bertosi (on a design by Francesco Trevisani). In the S aisle, Sebastiano Conca, St Andrew (with a Pietà above), and a 16C wood Crucifix beneath an arch decorated with enamelled terracotta heads of angels, attributed to the Buglioni. In the CHAPEL OF THE ROSARY are 15C frescoes by the school of Pastura, an altarpiece of the Birth of the Virgin by Francesco Trevisani, and a beautiful polychrome terracotta *ancona of Santa Cristina with scenes of her martyrdom, formerly attributed to Giovanni Della Robbia, but now thought to be by Benedetto Buglioni. In the chapel to the right of the sanctuary, with 14–16C frescoes, is a polychrome terracotta bust of Santa Cristina also attributed to Benedetto. In the SANCTUARY is a polyptych by Sano di Pietro. In the chapel to the left of the sanctuary, altarpiece of the Martyrdom of Santa Cristina by Andrea Casali. From the N aisle a Romanesque portal admits to the CAPPELLA DEL MIRA-COLO built in 1693 with a circular interior, attributed to Tommaso Mattei, decorated with stuccoes. The altarpiece of the Miracle of Bolsena is by Francesco Trevisani. Beyond is the CAPPELLA DI SAN MICHELE ARCANGELO (closed for restoration).

The entrance to the **Catacombs of Santa Cristina** (open 9.00–12.00, 15.00–16.00; summer 9.00–12.30, 16.00–18.00) is beside the ALTARE DEL MIRACOLO or DELLE QUATTRO COLONNE, where the famous miracle took place (see above). It has four pink marble Corinthian columns supporting a lovely little ciborium of the 9C. The polychrome terracotta altarpiece is attributed to Benedetto Buglioni. Beneath the altar is a sacred stone supposed to have saved Santa Cristina from drowning, and which is said to bear the marks of her footprints. Beyond a gate (above which is a very worn 13C fresco) is the ancient GROTTA DI SANTA CRISTINA, a primitive little church. Here in 1880 a Roman sarcophagus supposed to be that of Santa Cristina was found: the balustrade, stairs, and monument to the saint date from 1892. On top of the sarcophagus was placed a beautiful late 15C terracotta *effigy of the saint by Benedetto Baglioni. Below is the Roman sarcophagus and antique urn.

The extensive CATACOMBS were probably in use from the end of the 3C to the beginning of the 5C (the later tombs are on the lower levels). Inscriptions and frescoes dating from the 5C have been found here. The oldest part of the cemetery is in the smaller LOMBARD CATACOMBS, which were reused in the 6–8C. Two little rooms nearby contain sculptural fragments, an inscription dating from 376, and a 15C bas-relief of St Roch.

In Piazza Matteotti (see above), with the large 13C church of SAN FRANCESCO a gateway of 1548 leads into the medieval borgo. From the piazza the Orvieto road leads uphill behind San Francesco and past (right) some Roman and Etruscan remains to the 12C *Castle, restored by the Monaldeschi in 1295. It dominates the pretty medieval district and has picturesque houses clustered around its walls. Here the **Museo Territoriale del Lago di Bolsena** was opened in 1991 (admission Wednesday, Thursday, and Friday 10.00–13.00; Saturday and Sunday, 9.00–13.00, 14.30–18.30; closed Monday and Tuesday; in summer daily except Monday and Tuesday 9.30–13.30, 16.00–20.00). It contains an extremely interesting archaeological collection illustrating the history of Volsinii and its territory from the Bronze Age onwards, beautifully displayed.

In the COURTYARD is a small lapidarium, and stairs in a tower here lead up to the RAMPARTS. In the ticket office is a Roman sarcophagus with Bacchic scenes found in the necropolis of Volsinii (late 2C or early 3C AD). GROUND FLOOR. Case I displays finds from the lake including fossils and minerals. Case 2 has Bronze Age material, much of it from the small volcanic lake of Mezzano. In Case 3 are finds from Bisenzio (or Visentium) dating from the mid 8C BC. Cases 4–9 display interesting material from the Villanovan hut village called 'GRAN CARRO' found at the bottom of the lake in 1959, including impasto ceramics (9C BC). Cases 10–11 display ceramics and bronzes from the necropolis of Capriola (8–7C BC). In Case 12 and in the last part of the room are finds from the ETRUSCAN VOLSINII outside Bolsena including (Case 13) ceramics from the locality of Melona (3–2C BC), and altars from the sanctuary of Poggetto, including one dedicated to the Etruscan god Tinia, and conical cippi in volcanic stone with inscriptions from the sanctuary of Pozzarello.

A wooden staircase leads to the UPPER FLOOR, which displays finds from ROMAN VOLSINII, mostly from the area of POGGIO MOSCINI (see the plan on the landing). In Cases 14 and 16 are ceramics in black varnish (3–2C BC), and red varnish (1C BC); Case 18 displays 'Arretine' pottery, with its characteristic bright red glossy finish (1C AD). Case 19 contains ceramics imported from Africa, Case 21 has a display of terracotta oil lamps, and Case 22 has brick stamps, and fragments with potters' names and their provenance. Hellenistic terracottas used as roof decorations are displayed in Cases 23 and 24. In front is the terracotta *'panther throne' (2C BC; restored), a remarkable work probably used for Bacchic rites. The arms are in the form of elegant seated panthers, with putti on their backs. In Case

25 are terracottas from a small temple of Venus (2C BC). From the little window there is a good view over the old roofs of the town to the lake. Case 26 has architectural terracottas. At the end of the room are displayed fragments of Roman frescoes, many of them bright red in colour (2C BC–1C AD).

Stairs lead down to the LOWER FLOOR, with remains of the 12C castle walls and several stretches of medieval road. Here are displayed MEDIEVAL FINDS from the Rocca Monaldeschi including (Cases 30–34) ceramics found in a dump at the bottom of one of the castle towers in use from the 14–18C. The last part of the room has a charming display illustrating the history of fishing in the Lago di Bolsena, with models of boats, nets, etc. At the end of the room is the mechanism of the clock-tower (1750).

Below the castle is PALAZZO DEL DRAGO (privately owned) built in the 16C by Raffaello da Montelupo and Simone Mosca, which contains frescoes by the school of Perin del Vaga and Pellegrino Tibaldi. Just beyond the castle, off the Orvieto road (left), are the excavations of **Volsinii** (open 8.00–13.30 except Monday), including Etruscan walls in opus quadratum. The city was built in terraces on the hillside with magnificent views of the lake. Remains of the Roman amphitheatre, baths, and basilica, and a funerary monument of the 1C AD have also been found.

Several roads (one with a fine avenue of plane trees) lead down to the lakeside. The beautiful **Lago di Bolsena** is the classical *Volsiniensis Lacus*, named after the inhabitants of Volsinii Veteres. The northernmost and the largest of the three volcanic lakes in northern Lazio, it occupies a large crater in the Monti Volsini, 13.5km long from N to S and 12km across, with a circumference of 45km and a maximum depth of 146m. The lake abounds in eel and other fish. Dante ('Purgatorio', xxiv) mentions Pope Martin IV, who is believed to have died of a surfeit of eels. Its wooded shores are exceptionally well preserved. There are two beautiful islands, the Isola Martana, and the Isola Bizantina (approached from Capodimonte, described below).

The N 2 continues N from Bolsena through San Lorenzo Nuovo in the Monti Volsini to (19km) **Acquapendente**, in the northernmost corner of Lazio. It is an attractive little town (5800 inhab.), named after its cascades. Hieronymus Fabricius (1533–1619), the master of William Harvey at Padua, was born here. The 18C CATHEDRAL covers an early Romanesque crypt and contains two reliefs by the school of Agostino di Duccio.

FROM BOLSENA TO CIVITA DI BAGNOREGIO, 18km. A hilly road, climbing 229m in 7km, runs ENE out of Bolsena through lovely wooded country into Umbria, joining N 71 just S of (9km) Poggio di Biagio. The spectacular road continues with magnificent *views of (22km) Orvieto (see 'Blue Guide Umbria'), while N 71 leads S for (18km) **Bagnoregio**. Once *Balneum Regis*, this was the birthplace of St Bonaventura (1221–74), the 'doctor seraphicus'. He was a friend of St Francis, and wrote a life of the saint, and was minister-general of the order. He was canonised in 1482. The long main street passes Sant'Agostino, an 11–14C church which contains frescoes and a 15C wood Crucifix. Outside is a statue of St Bonaventura by Cesare Aureli (1897). The road (signposted for Civita) ends at a belvedere with a beautiful view of Civita (which can be approached from here by a path); alternatively a sharp turn right before the Belvedere leads down below the tufa rock face to the hamlet of Mercatello (1st-class Restaurant 'Del Ponte'), which was once the seat of the Comune of Bagnoregio.

Here begins the viaduct, some 250m long (pedestrians only) which crosses the valley to *Civita (Trattoria 'Al Forno'), the oldest district of Bagnoregio and once connected to it by a saddle of rock which has since been eroded. The beautiful peaceful little village (which can only be approached by foot) survives on a tufa rock (443m) which is being undermined by erosion, and only about ten families have remained here (although a number of houses are used as summer holiday homes). There was probably an Etruscan and Roman settlement here, and it was occupied by the Lombards. It has suffered from earthquakes.

Its remarkable position can be appreciated on the approach across the long viaduct (built in 1965 to replace a wooden bridge; the road was destroyed by earthquake in 1764). At the other end steps lead up to the delightful PORTA SANTA MARIA, the medieval entrance gate with two lions in dark grey stone on either side of the arch, surmounted by an eagle. An arched road (with evidence of the Etruscan gate) leads into the piazza with SAN DONATO, the cathedral of Bagonoregio up to 1699 (custodian at 8 Via della Maestà). Inside at the W end is a Renaissance font and tabernacle, and a stoup made up from two old capitals. At the end of the S aisle is a revered wood Crucifix by the school of Donatello, and in the altar beneath the body of St Hildebrand, bishop of the city in the 9C, was placed in 1863. At the end of the N aisle is a fragment of a fresco of the Deposition behind the altar. In the N aisle is a painting of the Birth of St John the Baptist by Cesare Nebbia, and over the N altar a fresco fragment of the Madonna and Child enthroned.

Also in the piazza is PALAZZO ALEMANNI, begun in 1550, recently restored as the seat of a summer school of the University of Washington, and as a study centre of Italian hill-towns. The pretty Via della Maestà leads downhill past the MULINO, an interesting old oil press (shown by the owner). From his barn, on the other side of the road, there is a good view across the valley to the *ponticelli* or *calanchi*, remarkable eroded rock formations, along the ridge of which there used to be a mule path. The friable tufa has produced frequent land falls here. The road continues to the edge of the hill and then steps descend between tufa walls with fine views over the deserted valley.

The N 2 leads S from Bolsena along the E shore of the Lago di Bolsena towards Montefiascone. It passes (7km) the BOLSENA BRITISH MILITARY CEMETERY, on the right between the road and the lake, with 600 graves of those who were killed in action in June 1944 between the Lago di Bolsena and Orvieto. The woods near the cemetery later became the Advanced Headquarters of the Allied Armies in Italy. The road climbs with fine views back of the lake and its islands and wooded shore.

15km **MONTEFIASCONE**, with its Duomo conspicuous on a hill (560m) overlooking the SE edge of the lake. The town (7000 inhab.), probably on the site of an Etruscan settlement, was involved, as a medieval commune, in the struggles between the papacy and the empire. The area is noted for its wines. On the outskirts of the town (on the Orvieto road) is the large Romanesque church of *San Flaviano (open 8.00–12.00, 15.00–17.00) with a remarkable plan, on two levels. The interesting FAÇADE (1262) has a Gothic portal and an unusual 16C balconied loggia above. The LOWER CHURCH probably dates from 1032, and has splendid *capitals (the third on the right has a caricature of the sculptor and a humorous inscription). The two stoups have ancient carved decoration. The 14–15C frescoes are particularly well preserved at the W end (on the W wall and in the first two bays of the S aisle). On the N side the first chapel has a damaged fresco by Pastura of the Massacre of the Innocents.

In the third N chapel has been placed the tombstone of Bishop Fugger of Augsburg (died 1114), with its famous epitaph: 'Est, est est pr(opter) nim(ium) est hic Jo(annes) de Fourcris do(minus) meus mortuus est' ('Est, est, est' on account of too much 'Est' here my lord Bishop Fugger died). The story relates that, when travelling, the prelate used to send his servant in advance to mark with the word 'est' ('here it is') the inns where good wine was to be found; at Montefiascone the servant found such exquisite wine that he wrote 'est, est, est', with the result that his master overdrank and died. The white wine of the district is now called 'Est, est, est'.

The architecture of the church is particularly interesting at the E end where a fine twisted column is decorated with birds in its upper part. In the apse is a 16C fresco. The other column in the apse has a similar capital decorated with birds. In the sanctuary is a large 13C font resting on three lions. The restoration of the UPPER CHURCH, with a most unusual plan, has been completed, but it is usually kept locked.

At the top of the town in Piazza Santa Margherita is the **Duomo**, with a huge dome conspicuous from miles around. It was begun in 1519 probably by Michele Sanmicheli and work was continued by Carlo Fontana, who added the dome, in the 17C. James Stuart and Clementina Sobieska were married here in 1719 before taking up residence in Rome. The octagonal INTERIOR was heavily decorated in the 19C. On the second N altar is a Della Robbia Madonna and Child with Saints. Over the Baroque high altar is an 18C statue of St Margaret and the dragon. Very steep steps lead down to the crypt (1962). In a chapel (opened by the sacristan) is a fine statue of St Margaret and the dragon attributed to Arnolfo di Cambio or Niccolò Pisano. A one-way road leads downhill past some fine palaces and the small Romanesque church of SANT'ANDREA with four capitals decorated with animal carvings inside. A sharp right turn leads into Piazza Vittorio Emanuele with a pretty fountain. At the top of the town are the ruins of the ROCCA PAPALE, with good views of the lake.

A pretty road leads W from Montefiascone towards Capodimonte. It passes SANTA MARIA IN MONTE D'ORO, an hexagonal church by Antonio da Sangallo the Younger (being restored), conspicuous on the left of the road, and descends to the village of MARTA (11km), which has a medieval district, on the Lago di Bolsena. An interesting festival called 'Barabbata' is held here on 14 May. On the lakeside boats can be hired to visit the uninhabited island of MARTANA. Amalaswintha, Queen of the Ostrogoths, was strangled here in 532 by her cousin Theodahad, whom she had chosen to share her throne. Amidst olive, ilex, and laurel groves are remains of a castle and a 9C church.

Capodimonte (13km), on the S shore of the lake, is a remote, rather run down little place, with the Duomo and town hall at the top of the hill in the attractive Piazza della Rocca. A bridge leads over to the interesting CASTLE (privately owned), built by Pier Luigi Farnese on a design by Antonio da Sangallo the Younger. It is surrounded by a garden with palm trees. There is a view of the lake with the Isola Martana and, on the other side of the promontory, of the little port. Below the castle walls steps lead down through a garden to the lake.

From the lakeside a ferry runs frequently from mid June–mid September to the *Isola Bizantina, owned by the Principi del Drago of Bolsena. This beautiful little island (700m x 500m) has lovely vegetation and three buildings attributed to Antonio da Sangallo the Younger: the Palazzo Farnese, the church of Santi Giacomo e Cristoforo, with a cupola by Vignola, and a little garden 'temple'. Some of the Calvary chapels built in 1450 on the hillside contain remains of frescoes by a follower of Benozzo Gozzoli.

The pretty road continues round the lake passing the site of BISENZIO or VISENTIUM, where excavations produced Iron Age material and Etruscan remains. A road (N 312) diverges left for VALENTANO with a small local museum in the Farnese castle (open 15.30–19.00; Saturday 10.00–13.00; closed Sunday). The road from Valentano via Canino to Montalto di Castro is described in Rte 40. 8km S of Valentano is ISCHIA DI CASTRO, with a Palazzo Ducale probably designed by Antonio da Sangallo the Younger. A Museo Civico (open daily except Monday) contains prehistoric finds from the valley of the Fiora (including objects from the Rinaldone culture); a carriage dating from the 6C BC; and Etruscan sculptures, including the mask of a demon, the head of a lion and of a ram (6C BC), a winged lion and a winged horse in 'nenfro' stone; and ceramics and bronzes.

The tour of the lake can be completed by taking the road which skirts the shore from Visentium and rejoins N 2 to the N, or by continuing N from Valentano via Latera to GRADOLI, which has a medieval district and a Farnese palace built by Antonio da Sangallo the Younger.

39

The Via Aurelia and Cerveteri

ROAD. From Rome to Tarquinia, Via Aurelia (N 1), 92km.—45km **Cerveteri**—58km **Castello di Santa Severa (Pyrgi)**—77km **Civitavecchia**—92km **Tarquinia**. The coastal motorway (A 12), which diverges from the Fiumicino motorway, follows roughly the same route as the Aurelia (86km to Civitavecchia), with convenient exits for Cerveteri and Pyrgi.

The RAILWAY (part of the main line from Rome to Pisa and Genova) also follows the Aurelia (with stations at Cerveteri, Santa Severa, and Civitavecchia).

The **Via Aurelia Antica** leaves Rome by the Porta San Pancrazio (Pl. 7; 3), see Rte 22. It follows the line of a still older road which linked Rome with the Etruscan towns on the Tyrrhenian coast. It reached the shore at Alsium (Palo Laziale), a port of the Etruscan city of Caere (Cerveteri) and then followed the coastline to Pisa and Genoa. It ended in Gaul at *Forum Julii* (Fréjus, on the French Riviera). One of the most important ancient Roman roads, named after the Aurelia family, it may have been built in 241 BC. It branches to the right just W of Porta San Pancrazio, and skirts the N side of the Villa Doria Pamphilj. About 8km W of Rome it joins the modern Via Aurelia, which starts from Largo di Porta Cavalleggeri, to the S of St Peter's (Pl. 1; 6).

The road, fringed with pines, planes, oleanders, and cypresses, undulates towards the W crossing the Grande Raccordo Annulare. Before (14.5km)

MALAGROTTA it crosses the Fosso la Galeria, where the Anguillara are said to have killed a dragon that once ravaged the countryside. 20.5km CASTEL DI GUIDO is on the site of *Lorium*, where Antoninus Pius built a magnificent villa, in which he lived and died (in 161); his successor Marcus Aurelius also spent much time here. Interesting prehistoric finds were made in the area in 1981. Farther on the Arrone is crossed, flowing from Lake Bracciano to the Tiber. Here a road (left) leads to the elegant seaside resort of **Fregene** (10km), backed by a huge pine wood, planted in the 17C. It occupies the site of the Etruscan *Fregenae*, colonised by the Romans in 245 BC.

Via Aurelia ascends to CASALE BRUCIATO, with fine views of the mountains and the sea. On the right is the isolated TORRIMPIETRA. The road descends, crossing to seaward of the motorway, before reaching (25km) PONTE TRE DENARI. 30km PALIDORO, on the site of the ancient *Baebiana*. Near (32.5km) CASALE DI STATUA, a ruined 13C castle, are remains of a Roman bridge. A little farther, on the right, a byroad leads N to **Ceri** (8km), a delightful well-preserved little medieval village on a tufa hill (105m), formerly *Caere Novum*, founded in the 13C after the exodus of the inhabitants of Caere Vetus (see below). In a beautiful setting, it has an old castle of the Anguillara built c 1470, now Palazzo Torlonia. In the church interesting medieval frescoes with scenes from the life of St Sylvester were discovered in 1971 and restored in 1989. Beneath the houses are numerous tunnels, passageways, and grottoes which may date from the Etruscan era.

37km PALO LAZIALE STATION. On the left is **Palo**, a tiny fishing village on the site of *Alsium*, colonised by the Romans in 247 BC. In the neighbourhood are several chambered tumuli. Remains of a large Roman villa (3–4C AD), with good polychrome mosaics were discovered here in 1974, and a museum is being arranged. The garden of the picturesque 15C ODESCALCHI CASTLE on the sea is now part of the **Oasi Naturale di Palo Laziale**, a nature reserve owned by the World Wildlife Fund (admission twice a week from September to June on guided tours; information from WWF Lazio, 10 Via Mercadante, Rome, Tel. 06/8440108). The garden was created in the 19C by Prince Ladislao Odescalchi, and the vegetation includes turkey oaks, dwarf palms, cypresses, pine trees, and ilexes. Part of the area is covered with the typical Mediterranean *macchia*, with myrtle and laurel bushes, and cyclamens, violets, and wild orchids abound. It is a sanctuary for numerous marine birds, and has a large colony of great tits.

A road leads (left) to **Ladispoli** (2km), a popular seaside resort founded by Prince Ladislao Odescalchi in the 19C, and greatly expanded in recent years. The coast to the N, suffocated by new buildings, is dotted with old defence-towers. Beyond Borgo Vaccina the road crosses (41km) the Fosso di Vaccina, the Amnis Caeritis mentioned by Virgil. A second road leads left for Ladispoli (3km), but this route turns right for Cerveteri (3.5km).

CERVETERI (8400 inhab.), a medieval stronghold on a round tufa hill (81m), derives its name from *Caere Vetus*. The immediate neighbourhood is renowned for its Etruscan tombs.

Information Office, 'Pro-Loco', Via delle Mura Castellane.

Buses ('COTRAL') from Rome c every half hour from Via Lepanto (corner of Viale Giulio Cesare) to the centre of Cerveteri (Piazza Aldo Moro).

Railway Station at *Cerveteri–Ladispoli*, on the main line between Rome and Pisa. Services from Rome in c 1hr ('COTRAL' buses connect the station with Cerveteri).

Numerous **restaurants** near the castle.

History. **Caere**, called by the Greeks *Agylla*, was one of the most important members of the Etruscan Confederation, and one of the largest cities in the Mediterranean. It probably had a number of seaports, but the most important was Pyrgi, see below. Early in its history it was closely allied with Rome. When Rome was taken by the Gauls in 390 BC, the vestal virgins took refuge in Caere. The city became a dependency of Rome in 351 BC, but without full rights of citizenship. From then onwards it declined. In the early Middle Ages Caere was the seat of a bishop and a redoubtable fortress. In the 13C its inhabitants abandoned it because of malaria and founded *Caere Novum* (Ceri, see above). In the later Middle Ages the town became populated again. It was surrounded with walls, still partly existing, and provided with a castle by the Orsini.

Passing a turn for the necropolis on the left, the main road continues to the medieval city, with appreciable remains, including walls and towers. From the pleasant Piazza Risorgimento (car parking), with the town hall, Via Roma and Via Santa Maria (right) lead to the **Castle** in a piazza which has recently been excessively tidied up. The old Orsini (later Ruspoli) castle dating from the 16C was donated in 1967 as the **Museo Nazionale Cerite** (adm 9.00–14.00; 9.00–16.00 in summer; closed Monday).

The archaeological collection is excellently displayed in two halls. It illustrates the history of Caere chronologically through finds from tombs in the area dating from the 10C BC to the Roman period. On the ground floor are pots and objects from burials of the 8–6C BC, including protocorinthian ware. Upstairs are sarcophagi, sculpture, wall-paintings, terracottas, and two superb groups of black-figured and red-figured *vases.

Also in the piazza is the modern church of SANTA MARIA, which incorporates a Romanesque church at its E end, orientated N–S. Above the arch leading into the old church is a restored 16C painting of the Redeemer. In the S apse is an unusual Renaissance altar with the figure of Christ blessing in relief and a fresco of the Pietà. The altarpiece of the Madonna and Child with Saints signed by Lorenzo da Viterbo has been removed for many years for restoration. Against the far wall are fragments of Cosmati pavement and a detached fresco of the Madonna and Child.

From the main square below the castle a road (signposted to the necropolis) leads right; a minor road soon branches right to ascend the tufa hill NW of the town known as BANDITACCIA. Lined with pine trees the road (2km) passes numerous overgrown tombs before reaching the entrance to the *Necropolis of Cerveteri (open daily except Monday, 9 to one hour before sunset). This vast cemetery occupies an area of 270ha, not counting isolated groups of tombs. Excavations were begun in 1834 and have continued during this century. The most important finds are in the Villa Giulia in Rome and in the Etruscan Museum of the Vatican. All types of interment are represented: from the earliest *pozzetto* or *fossa* graves to the later tumuli, some of them colossal, with diameters exceeding 40m. These contain several hypogea, with chambers modelled in the rock in the form of Etruscan dwellings (which were built in wood). The tombs are especially interesting for their architectural design. From the tombs (dating from the 7C to the 1C BC), and their contents, it has been possible to obtain the fullest picture yet available of Etruscan civilisation.

The site, which contains hundreds of tombs, is beautifully planted. Only some of the tombs are fully excavated and lit; those which may be entered are described below (and numbered according to the plan). On the right of the ticket office **Via Sepolcrale Principale** (right) leads SE between various tombs. The first tomb on the left which is open (and lit) is the TOMB OF THE CAPITALS (1), dating from the mid 6C BC, with carved capitals and a roof

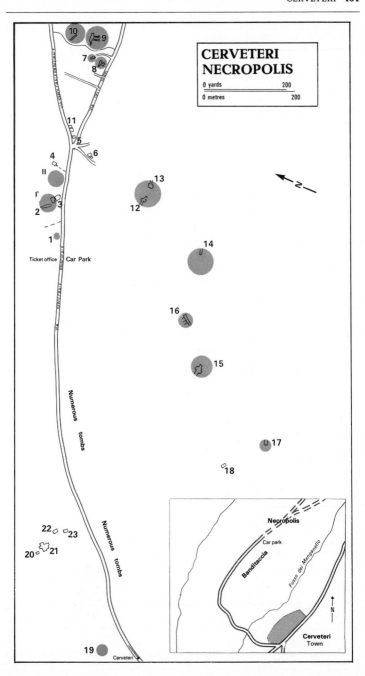

CERVETERI NECROPOLIS

0 yards 200
0 metres 200

Ticket office   Car Park

Numerous tombs

Numerous tombs

Necropolis

Car park

Banditaccia

Fosso de Manganello

Cerveteri Town

Cerveteri

imitating the wooden roof of a house. Beyond a path which diverges left there follow two huge tumuli (II and I). The first contains four tombs probably all belonging to the same family and constructed over a period of nearly two centuries. Two of these may be visited: the TOMB OF THE THATCHED ROOF (2; approached by iron steps on the far side of the tumulus) excavated in the tufa to imitate a hut (mid 7C BC), and the TOMB OF THE GREEK VASES (3; entered from the side nearest Via Sepolcrale). Beyond the second tumulus, in an opening, steps (guarded by a wood fence) lead down to the **Tomb of the Stuccoes** (4), or 'of the Bas-Reliefs' (seen through a glass door), a single chamber with numerous loculi or niches hewn out of the walls; the ceiling is supported by two columns; the walls are decorated with stuccoes and reliefs of arms, utensils, domestic animals, and mythological subjects (end of 4C BC), an important revelation of Etruscan civilisation of the period.

Via Sepolcrale continues to a crossroads where several minor roads meet. In front is the TOMB OF THE LITTLE HOUSE (5; no adm); the road on the extreme right (Via della Cornice) leads in a short way to (left) the TOMB OF THE CORNICE (6; approached up a short flight of iron steps) so-called because of a heavy cornice which decorates the rooms. From the Tomb of the Little House, Via Sepolcrale (here with conspicuous cart tracks cut in the tufa rock) diverges left (see below) while **Via delle Serpe** continues (right) to the **new area of excavations** opened in 1977.

Beyond a short flight of steps the road passes blocks of tombs constructed *a dado* or in cubes, a form of burial which was begun at the end of the 6C BC. The area to the left, traversed by Via dei Monti della Tolfa and the parallel Via dei Monti Ceriti, is interesting as an example of 'urban' planning and the symmetrical tombs have fine entrances. The tombs are unlit but may be entered; they have regular plans with small chairs on either side of the entrance. At the end of a long tufa wall a path leads left between a tumulus (left) and a series of cubicle tombs (right) and curves round to end at a flight of tufa steps which lead up to the POLYCHROME TUMULUS (7), built of various materials including peperino and tufa. Adjacent is the larger MAROI TUMULUS (8) which can also be visited.

Via delle Serpi continues to the fence which marks the end of the enclosure; some metres before the fence five iron steps lead up past two small tumuli to a path which leads round to the left towards the two largest tumuli in this enclosure (near a group of three cypresses) known as the MENGARELLI TUMULUS (9; approached by a steep flight of steps) and the COLONEL'S TUMULUS (10; the path passes beneath an iron bridge which leads into the entrance). Opposite this tumulus a short flight of steps leads up to a path which continues (via another flight of steps) to the Via Sepolcrale (see above). This may now be followed (left) back towards the entrance past the TOMB OF MARCE URSUS (11; with its two entrances facing on to the road) just before the crossroads (see above) where Via Sepolcrale forms a fork with Via delle Serpe.

Outside the enclosure an unsurfaced road continues for c 500m to an unenclosed area known as BUFOLARECCIA, excavated in the 1960s by the Fondazione Lerici. Here the tufa rock has been uncovered and the tombs left unrestored; the oldest (and simplest) tombs can be seen on the surface (round or oblong sepulchres), while the later tumuli appear on a lower level since they were excavated in the rock when no more surface space was available. The conspicuous track marks are from ploughs which have worked the surface of the earth over the centuries. An impressive tufa rock face can be seen across the valley, and along to the right, the present town of Cerveteri.

Just beyond, the road ends on an open hill-side from which you can get a good idea of the site of the necropolis surrounded by low hills. Here **Via degli Inferi** curves down to the right between the rocks. This was the first part of the Via Sepolcrale which led from the city to the necropolis. It is practicable on foot for several hundred metres and has conspicuous cart ruts. On the right, at the beginning, is the TOMB OF THE DORIC COLUMNS (unlit) with two Doric columns (4C BC).

The other tombs, widely scattered over the necropolis, can be seen only with a guide (sometimes available at the ticket office), since they are kept locked (most of them are unlit and a torch is needed). Some of these tombs are more or less permanently flooded. In a tumulus E of the monumental enclosure are the TOMB OF THE PAINTED LIONS (12) and the TOMB OF THE CHAIRS AND SHIELDS (13). The former has a fine ceiling decoration and traces of colour on the walls; in the latter the walls are decorated with reliefs of shields and the vestibule has two rock-hewn chairs. Other large tumuli to the SW contain the TOMB OF THE PAINTED ANIMALS (14; closed for restoration), the TOMB OF THE SHIPS (15), and the TOMB OF GIUSEPPE MORETTI (16). This is the largest tomb yet known with an atrium with Doric columns and ten rooms (difficult to see as it is normally flooded).

The tombs farther S are not normally accessible. These include the TOMB OF THE TABLINO (17), and the TOMB OF THE WAVES (18), with traces of painted decoration. Another important group of tombs (all unlit) lies to the NW of the road which leads up to the monumental enclosure (see the plan). These include the TOMB OF THE FIVE CHAIRS (19); the TOMB OF THE ALCOVE (20), with a pillared vestibule and a flight of steps leading up to a rock-hewn alcove with a nuptial bed; the TOMB OF THE TARQUINS (21), so-called because of the names inscribed in it; the TOMB OF THE SARCOPHAGI (22); and the TOMB OF THE TRICLINIUM (23), with traces of paintings of a funeral banquet.

On a hill c 2.5km S of Cerveteri is the famous **Regolini-Galassi Tomb** (unlit; sometimes opened by a custodian on request) the oldest of all (late 7C BC) discovered in 1836. Named after its discoverers, it is a circular tumulus 48m in diameter, surrounded by a double wall and surmounted by the typical conical grass-grown top. Its hypogeum, of two compartments, is divided by a wide corridor with a ceiling of overlapping stone blocks. Its most valuable contents are exhibited in the Etruscan Museum of the Vatican. In the same area (Ripe Sant'Angelo) rock tombs of the 4C BC have recently been discovered on private property. These can be seen carved in the rock face with 'mock' doors.

About 1.5km NE, on Monte Abetone, is the CAMPANA TOMB (unlit) with remarkable carvings imitating household furnishings; 1.5km farther on is the TOMB OF THE ROUND VESTIBULE, with a noteworthy fan vault. To the SE of Monte Padula is another tomb, covered by a kind of pyramid, containing a vestibule, two side chambers, and a central room with two biers and a throne carved in the rock. Close by is the TORLONIA TOMB (more or less permanently flooded), with a vestibule having columns in the Greek style, and two chambers, of which the first contains 54 loculi. From this point the Monte Cucco track leads direct to (6.5km) Cerveteri.

Via Aurelia and the motorway continue N. At (50km) Stazione di Furbara a byroad diverges right for SASSO (6km) near which (Località Pian della Carlotta) excavations in 1988/89 identified the site of the ACQUAE CAERE-TANAE. These Roman baths, dating from the Imperial era and on a monumental scale, were famous for their curative qualities, mentioned by Livy and Strabo. So far the marble-lined calidarium surrounded by a portico, and another basin, probably a tepidarium, have been unearthed.

58km SANTA SEVERA, a seaside resort, just before which a signposted road (500m) leads left along a splendid avenue of palm trees and umbrella pines to the **Castle of Santa Severa**, on the sea, beside the site of **Pyrgi**, the most important port of the Etruscan city of Caere (Cerveteri). Evidence of a Bronze Age settlement has been found here, but it was famous in Etruscan times for its sanctuary, one of the largest known in Etruria, with two temples built c 500–460 BC (mentioned by the Greeks and Romans). It was sacked by the elder Dionysius of Syracuse in 384 BC. The port was taken over by the Romans in the early 3C BC and remains of the Roman castrum survive. The site was abandoned in the 5C or 6C AD but in the 7–9C a castle was erected here which became the property of the monastery of Farfa and was enlarged in succeeding centuries, and is now being restored.

On the left in front of the castle gate are remains of a Roman gate and road. Also on the left is the small ANTIQUARIUM (open Tuesday, Thursday, Saturday, and the last Sunday of the month, 9.00–12.00; ring), opened in 1972. It has explanatory models and plans of the site. The finds from excavations since 1956 include part of the sculpted terracotta decorations from the two sanctuary temples.

The SANCTUARY can be visited on request at the museum. It is approached by a lane (signposted 'Area Sacra di Pyrgi') on the left of the museum building, which ends by a fine stretch of polygonal Roman walls. Outside the gate into the enclosure is a plan of the site and explanatory panels. The SE and NE perimeter walls have been exposed as well as the foundations of the two temples. The larger (Temple A), dating from c 460 BC, had a large colonnaded pronaos and three cellae; the second (Temple B), smaller, with a single elongated cella, was the first to be built (c 500 BC). The entrance to the Sanctuary was at the NE side where a road from Caere, built in the early 6C BC, terminated, and along which the red tufa used in the construction of the temples was transported. The temples were demolished after 270 BC. A remarkable high relief which decorated a tympanum of Temple A, illustrating the Seven against Thebes (showing marked Greek influence), was found here.

In a sacred area between the temples three folded sheets of gold leaf were found, with extremely interesting inscriptions in Phoenician and Etruscan recording the dedication of the Sanctuary to Astarte, the Phoenician goddess (called Uni by the Etruscans) by Thefarie Velianas, tyrant of Caere (these are now kept in the Villa Giulia in Rome, where copies of them are exhibited). A hoard of Athenian 'owls' and Syracusan coins (5C BC) was also found here, thought to be part of the rich sanctuary treasury and overlooked by Dionysius when he looted the rest of it. Another sacred area to the S has been in the process of excavation since 1984.

On the right of the approach road to the castle is a car park beside a large fountain of 1791, surrounded by a grove of fine palm trees. Outside the right wall of the castle can be seen remains of the Roman wall. The gate leads through 18C walls which enclose a picturesque little village inhabited in summer by holiday-makers. Between the second and third wards is the 16C church of the Assunta, and by the outer ward of the 14C is a little chapel with restored 15C frescoes. Right on the sea is the concentric CASTLE itself (now owned by the Comune of Marinella), which dates in its present form from the 16C. On its seaward side, and connected with it by a wooden bridge, is an imposing cylindrical tower built over the foundations of a Norman fort. Remains of the polygonal wall of the Roman castrum are visible. Excavations are in progress, and the Roman port has been identified beneath the sea, just offshore. The coastline is particularly attractive here.

The Via Aurelia continues past (67km) **Santa Marinella**, another attractive seaside resort. It occupies the site of the Roman station of *Ad Punicum* at the end of Cape Linaro. On the promontory E of the town in 1966 a lead plaque bearing one of the longest known Etruscan inscriptions was unearthed. This came from a sanctuary (6C BC) of Minerva. Here also is a 15C castle of the Odescalchi. On the right the summits of the Tolfa range are still visible; prominent, as the road passes the 'Boys' Town' (Repubblica dei Ragazzi) founded in 1945, is Monte Paradiso (327m).

77km **CIVITAVECCHIA**, a town of 48,300 inhabitants, is the modern port of Rome and a base of sea communications with Sardinia. It has been largely rebuilt since the war.

Information Office of the 'EPT', 42 Viale Garibaldi.

Railway Station at the end of Viale Garibaldi; some trains from Rome continue to the dockside for connections with boats.

Buses to Rome, Tarquinia, Tuscania, Viterbo, Santa Marinella, Santa Severa, etc.

Car Ferries run by 'Tirrenia' and the Italian State Railways daily to Sardinia (overnight to Cagliari, in c 11 hrs; Olbia, in c 7 hrs, and Golfo Aranci, in c 8.5 hrs), with sleeping berths. Some services also run during the day. It is essential to book well in advance in summer.

Hotels (4-star and 3-star) and numerous good fish **restaurants**.

History. After the silting up of Ostia and to supplement his new harbour at Porto, Trajan built a new port here in c 107, perhaps with the help of the great architect Apollodorus, called *Centum Cellae*. Among its buldings was a splendid Imperial villa, described by the younger Pliny (see below). In 828 the port was destroyed by the Saracens and the inhabitants fled inland. In 855 Pope Leo IV established for them the village of Leopoli or Centocelle, which still exists, 14.5km N of the port. Soon the population returned to their original home, which they now called *Civitas Vetula*, Italianised into 'Civitavecchia'. From then on until modern times the city was included in the Papal States. Under the Renaissance popes Civitavecchia became one of the most important of the Mediterranean seaports. Gregory XII kept the pontifical fleet here; Sixtus V built the lighthouse; and Alexander VII commissioned Bernini to build the dock basin (both of them destroyed in the War). Stendhal was consul here (after 1831) and wrote his autobiography 'The Life of Henri Brulard'.

The **Forte Michelangelo** (no admission) on the harbour, begun by Bramante in 1508 and continued by Antonio da Sangallo the Younger, was completed by Michelangelo. The central basin of Trajan's harbour and the docks are still of interest. The MUSEO ARCHEOLOGICO NAZIONALE (open 9.00–14.00, except Monday) in Largo Plebiscito, contains a good collection of local archaeological finds. Frescoes in the Franciscan Church by the Japanese artist Hasegawa (1950–54) commemorate the Franciscan missionaries to Japan, who sailed from Civitavecchia and were martyred with many converts at Nagasaki in 1597.

About 4.5km E, beyond the motorway entrance, are the ruins of the so-called TERME TAURINE, now identified as part of the large Imperial villa mentioned by the younger Pliny, and used by Trajan, Marcus Aurelius, and Commodus. The baths were fed by the warm sulphur-impregnated waters, which are still effective in the treatment of rheumatism.

From Civitavecchia a hilly road winds inland towards the Lago di Bracciano. It passes ALLUMIERE (16km), on Monte Rovello, where remains of a proto-Villanovan settlement have been found. Local archaeological finds are exhibited in a museum (open 9.00–13.00, except Monday), which also has a natural history section. TOLFA (22km) was built on the ruins of an Etruscan town (finds are displayed in the small Museo Civico). The road continues past the ferruginous BAGNI DI STIGLIANO (36km) to the Lago di Bracciano (see Rte 36).

Beyond Tarquinia the Via Aurelia has recently been realigned and a new fast road continues to cross the Mignone river which flows down from the volcanic Tolfa range. At its mouth is TORRE DI SANT'AGOSTINO or DI BERTOLDA, supposed to be the spot where St Augustine found the child pouring the water of the sea into a hole in the sand, which he saw as the image of a finite conception of infinity. N 1 bis diverges right for Viterbo (see Rte 37), while the Via Aurelia continues to (92km) **Tarquinia**, described in Rte 40.

40

Tarquinia and Southern Etruria

From Rome to Tarquinia, see Rte 39.

TARQUINIA stands on a hill (145m) E of the Via Aurelia, 5km from the sea. This pleasant, peaceful town (14,000 inhab.) has a medieval district, which preserves numerous towers. It is famous for the remarkable painted tombs in the Etruscan necropolis on the outskirts of the town. Remains of the Etruscan city of *Tarxuna* or *Tarxna* can be seen on the hill to the E, and the finds from excavations, which include some of the most important Etruscan antiquities yet discovered, are housed in a splendid museum here.

Information Office. 'Azienda Autonoma di Soggiorno e Turismo dell'Etruria Meridionale', 14 Piazza Matteotti (Tel. 0766/842164); Information Office, 1 Piazza Cavour. Interesting tours are organised in summer by the 'Azienda Autonoma' of the medieval city and of the necropolis, as well as Tuscania, Canino, and Vulci.

Railway Station, 3km outside the town, on the line from Rome to Pisa, with services from Rome (Termini or Tiburtina stations) in 1hr 15 mins. Buses connect with the trains from the station to Tarquinia.

Buses ('COTRAL') from Barriera di San Giusto for Rome (a change is necessary at Civitavecchia); and for the railway station, Tuscania, Viterbo, Canino, and Civitavecchia. Urban buses from Tarquinia (Barriera di San Giusto) to the necropolis (four times a day), and to Lido di Tarquinia, on the sea.

Car Parking, Barriera di San Giusto, or outside Porta Garibaldi (the town is closed to traffic in the middle of the day).

Hotels. 3-star: 'Tarconte', Via Tuscia. The Hotel 'San Marco' in Piazza Cavour is to be restored. At LIDO DI TARQUINIA, 6km SW: 3-star 'La Toraccia' and 'Velca Mare' (with a swimming pool); 1-star 'Miramare'.

Camping Sites open in summer on the sea at Lido di Tarquinia and Riva dei Tarquini.

Restaurants. 1st-class restaurants: 'Da Prassede', Via Cavallotti; 'Le due Orfanelle', near Piazza Trento e Trieste; 'Scacciapensieri', Via dello Statuto. Trattoria 'Arcadia',

Via Mazzini. The fish restaurants at Lido di Tarquinia open in summer are mostly 'luxury-class'.

Picnic Places in the little gardens above Via della Ripa (near Santa Maria in Castello), in the necropolis, and on the acropolis outside the town.

Theatre performances are held in summer in the ARENA DI SAN MARCO, Via Umberto I. The auditorium in the church of San Pancrazio is not at present in use.

Annual Festivals. Procession of the Risen Christ on Easter Sunday by the local confraternities. On the first Sunday in April outside the town (località La Roccaccia), cattle are branded at the 'Festa della Merca', and there is a local rodeo.

History. *Tarxuna* (or *Tarxna*), cradle of the 'great house of Tarquin', was one of the 12 Etruscan cities and probably the head of the Etruscan Confederation. It is said to have been founded by Tarchon, son or brother of the Lydian prince Tyrrhenus, who is mentioned by Virgil as the person who helped Aeneas against Turnus. According to a legend, Demaratus of Corinth settled here in c 700 BC; his son, Lucius Tarquinius Priscus, became the fifth king of Rome. After the 3C BC it became a Roman colony and municipium and its power declined. In 181 the Roman colony of Gravisca was founded on the coast. After invasions by the Lombards and Saracens, in the 7C it was deserted and the inhabitants founded *Corneto* on the opposite hill. In 1489 the first recorded archaeological 'dig' in modern times took place here.

The BARRIERA DI SAN GIUSTO, laid out in the 19C, provides a monumental entrance to the town. Here can be seen a stretch of the walls which still surround part of Tarquinia. Above is PIAZZA CAVOUR, with the tourist information office. Here is the very fine *Palazzo Vitelleschi (1436–39), with Gothic and Renaissance windows, built by Cardinal Giovanni Vitelleschi (restored after War damage). It contains the *Museo Nazionale Tarquiniese (admission 9.00–14.00, except Monday), one of the most important Etruscan museums in existence. It was founded in 1916 with material from the Bruschi collection and with finds from excavations owned by the Comune.

In the beautiful **courtyard** are a collection of sarcophagi, the most important of which are displayed in the two rooms off the courtyard. In ROOM I are sarcophagi found in 1876 in the Partunu family tomb, most of them in the local grey-coloured stone called *nenfro*, except for the three most important ones which are in white marble: the so-called 'Sarcofago del Sacerdote' is in fact that of Laris Partunu, head of the family. His fine *effigy in relief may be the work of a Greek sculptor (4C BC); on the sides of the sarcophagus are polychrome mythological scenes by a local painter. The tomb of the 'Magnate' is thought to be that of the son of Laris; it has a carved lid with lions and sphynxes. The so-called *'Obesus' sarcophagus, against the left wall, dating from the early 3C BC is surmounted by a splendid figure of the defunct, who may be the grandson of Laris. In the second part of the room are sarcophagi found on Poggio del Cavalluccio in 1950. All in nenfro, they have reclining figures and carved reliefs with scenes depicting the journey of the defunct. In the smaller ROOM II are three sarcophagi of the Pulena family. The one known as the *'Sarcophagus of the Magistrate' is in fact that of Laris, who is portrayed holding a long Etruscan inscription on a scroll. The other three sarcophagi of the Camna family are part of the Bruschi collection.

First floor. In the loggia are five terracotta sarcophagi. In the room at the top of the stairs (left) is the beautifully displayed polychrome *group of two winged horses (4–3C BC) found on the Acropolis. In rooms off the loggia are displayed vases in chronological order. ROOM I (at the far end). Villanovan material (9–8C BC) from the necropolis of Monterozzi, including a cinerary urn in the shape of a hut, and an incense burner in the form of a carriage with a deer's head. ROOM II. Material from the tomb of Bocchoris (7C BC) including a glass Egyptian vase. ROOM III. Objects imported from Egypt and the East; series of small bronze griffins' heads (7C BC). ROOM IV contains Corinthian ware, bucchero vases, some with decoration in relief (6C BC), and black-figure amphorae. ROOM V. Fine black-figure vases of the 6C BC by various artists identified by their individual styles. ROOM VI. Red-figure Attic kylixes and kraters (500–480 BC) and two oinochoe by the Berlin painter.

The beautiful GREAT HALL, interesting for its architecture and fresco fragments, contains the most precious red-figure Attic vases: *stamnos by the Berlin painter (480–470 BC); *amphora signed by Phintias (510–500 BC) with Apollo and Heracles fighting for the tripod and Dionysus between satyrs and maenads; *kylix attributed to Oltos and Euxitheos, with a meeting of the gods, and Dionysus in a quadriga between satyrs and maenads; a very well-preserved *rhyton shaped like a woman's head by Charinos (510–500 BC); a kylix by Douris (500–490 BC), and a krater by the Kleophrades painter (500–490 BC). In two connecting rooms off the great hall: votive terracottas from the Ara della Regina (3–2C BC); anatomical ex votos; red-figure vases (end of the 4C BC) including three askoi in the form of birds. Also displayed here are Roman glass and coins; Etruscan jewellery and bronze mirrors, candlesticks, utensils, ceramics with relief decoration, black-varnished ceramics, etc.

On the **second floor** only the enclosed LOGGIA is open (with a splendid view), used as a bookshop. Beneath the loggia is the tomb of Aurelio Mezzopane (1500). The rooms here have been closed for many years. They contain early 15C frescoes attributed to Jacopo Salimbene from the Marches, and a small collection of paintings (portraits of Count Nicolò Soderini and Pius VII by Batoni and Camuccini). The Salone d'Armi houses frescoes removed from Etruscan tombs, including the famous *Tomba del Triclinio.

Via Mazzini leads along the side of the palace to the **Duomo**, rebuilt in 1656 and restored in the 19C. In the sanctuary are good *frescoes (1508) by Antonio da Viterbo (Pastura), showing the influence of Signorelli. Most of the altarpieces date from the 19C (many by the local painter Luigi Boccanera), but the second N chapel houses a Byzantine Madonna removed from the church of Santa Maria di Valverde, and the last chapel on the S side has two paintings by Giacinto Brandi (1653).

Via di Porta Castello continues (in 5 minutes) to a fine double GATEWAY in the walls. Beyond it is a splendid view of the tallest and best preserved tower in the city standing beside the Romanesque church of *Santa Maria di Castello** in a peaceful corner of the town. The church was begun in 1121 and consecrated in 1208 (and restored in 1988). The FAÇADE contains Cosmatesque work (very ruined) signed by Pietro di Ranuccio (1143). The N flank has pretty arcading decorated with carving. The fine INTERIOR (unlocked by the custodian who lives in the house with steps beside the tower) has an interesting plan with a rose window and pretty dome in the nave. It contains remains of a Cosmatesque pergamum by Giovanni di Guittone (1208; some of the sculptures were stolen in 1969), two plutei and a ciborium by Giovanni and Guittone, sons of Nicolò di Ranuccio (1168), a font for total immersion, and parts of the Cosmatesque pavement. Porta Castello, on right of the façade, leads out into the open countryside. About 1km from the gate are the remains of the 12C FONTANA NOVA, a public fountain with six massive Romanesque columns.

Inside the double gateway is a little garden by the walls, with a view of the countryside. Via della Ripa leads towards the medieval district of the town past a tall tower in a field and a medieval building (being rebuilt). SAN MARTINO, a small Romanesque church, with an interesting exterior, stands beside another tower. Via del Orfanatrofio leads uphill and Via Marcantonio Barbarigo (left) ends at the church of the SANTISSIMA ANNUNZIATA (closed), with a good rose window and portal. From here Via San Giacomo leads under an arch to the tiny disused church of SAN SALVATORE and the abandoned church of SAN GIACOMO on a promontory on the edge of the cliff. From here there is a view of the valley, and of Santa Maria di Castello and the towers of the old city

Downhill, in the centre of the town, is the 13C church of SAN PANCRAZIO (now an auditorium), with an interesting exterior, a rose window, and a campanile, near the PALAZZO DEI PRIORI, with a fine arch and four towers. Via delle Torri here is a characteristic medieval street. Nearby is the large **Piazza Matteotti**, scene of a weekly market, with an 18C fountain. Here the exuberant façade in the Baroque style of the church of the SUFFRAGIO (1761) stands next to the large MUNICIPIO, built in a medley of styles (Romanesque material is incorporated into the fabric of the building behind). Via Porta Tarquinia leads to the 13C church and convent of SAN FRANCESCO, with a handsome interior with high Gothic arches in the transept. The chapel to the right of the sanctuary is decorated with good stuccoes.

The Corso leads downhill from Piazza Matteotti to Piazza Cavour past a bronze female statue by Emilio Greco given by him to the city in 1990. Below the piazza Via di Valverde leads from the Barriera di San Giusto to the Romanesque church of SANTA MARIA DI VALVERDE. Via Roma leads out of the piazza to the church of SAN GIOVANNI, with a Roman sarcophagus over the left door. In the interior, around the W door is a fine Renaissance portal. At the end of the N aisle is a lovely little Gothic chapel, and a fresco fragment of the *Deposition attributed to Pastura. The main apse has a good fan vault. In the parallel Via Umberto I is the church of SANTA LUCIA with a high altarpiece by Giovanni Francesco Romanelli. Outside Porta Romana can be seen a good stretch of walls.

Via Porta Tarquinia and its continuation Via Ripagretta (see the plan) lead in c 2km (bus, see above) to the cemetery on the outskirts of the town beside the vast ***Necropolis of Tarquinia** (known as MONTEROZZI), open 9.00–14.00, except Monday. The tombs are of immense interest and value for their painted interiors. The paintings range from the first half of the 6C BC to the 2C BC, and the styles of the various phases show the Ionic influence of the 6C, the Attic influence of the 5C and, after a static period, a revival in the 4C, followed by a decline. Excavations here date back to the 15C, but the greatest number of tombs have been discovered in the 19C and 20C. Unfortunately the opening of the tombs has in many cases caused the deterioration of the paintings. When one tomb was opened in 1823 the excavators found a warrior stretched on a bier who crumbled away on the admission of fresh air. So far 5735 tombs have been found, of which 62 are painted. In 1986 an important painted tomb was discovered known as the TOMBA DEI DEMONI BLU. The tombs are now protected with modern huts and only some of them can be seen (others are kept closed for conservation reasons or if they are being restored).

The six tombs at present visible (through glass panels) are: the TOMBA DELLE LEONESSE (6C) with paintings of lionesses or panthers, dolphins in the sea, and banqueting scenes; the TOMBA DEL FIORE DI LOTO (mid 6C), with colourful paintings including a lotus flower; the TOMBA CARDARELLI (end of 6C) with four groups of figures, probably depicted just after the funeral banquet; the TOMBA DELLA FUSTIGAZIONE (late 6C BC), with dancers, boxers, and erotic groups; the TOMBA DEL GORGONEION (early 4C BC), with decorations in brown and red including two male figures in tunics; and the TOMBA BARTOCCINI (6C BC), with four chambers, and paintings of a banqueting scene and sea-horses.

Other tombs of the greatest interest not at present open include: the TOMBA DEI GIOCOLIERI (end of 6C, early 5C), with the standing figure of the defunct, and old man and boy, and the portrait of a dancing girl; the TOMBA DELLA PADIGLIONE DELLA CACCIA (early 4C), with painted hangings with hunting trophies, and a colourful frieze and ceiling; the TOMBA DELLA CACCIA E PESCA (mid 6C), a large tomb, with two rooms with scenes of the chase and fishing.

Other tombs, some of them near the modern cemetery, and others further from the town gate, include: the PULZELLA or 'young girl' (mid 5C), with a banqueting scene (damaged in the War); the LEOPARDI (5C) with more banqueting scenes and musicians; the BACCANTI (end of the 6C) with a Bacchic scene; the TIFONE (2C), a large tomb with a central column, preceded by an altar on which is a painted figure of a demon; the SCUDI (3C), with painted shields and banqueting scenes; the CARDINALE (probably late 2C), restored in 1799 by Cardinal Garampi, the largest of all with four columns supporting a coffered ceiling; the *ORCO ('ogre'; first half of the 4C), with scenes of the inferno and the beautiful protrait head of a girl of the Velcha family; the *BARONE (end of the 6C), with figures of men and women standing and of youths on horseback; the

DUE BIGHE ('chariots'; 5C); the AUGURI or 'augurs' (mid 6C) with a cruel scene of a blindfolded man tortured by the attacks of a fierce dog; the *TORI (early 6C), well preserved, with a painting of Achilles lying in wait for Troilus.

FROM TARQUINIA TO THE ETRUSCAN ACROPOLIS, 8km. Tarquinia is left by Via Porta Tarquinia and Via Ripagretta. Beyond the cemetery and the Necropolis (see above) the pretty, narrow road continues to the junction with the Viterbo road (N 1 bis). This should be followed left past long streches of aqueduct (first built by the Romans, adapted in the medieval period, and still in use) for c 3km. A yellow signpost indicates the rough road left for the **Etruscan Acropolis** on the hill called PIAN DI CIVITA (locally famous for its *ferlenghi* mushrooms). At the end of the road a path (left) leads uphill in c 100m to the so-called ARA DELLA REGINA, the impressive basement of a large temple or sacred area (77m x 35m). Here was found the beautiful sculpture of the winged horses now in the Museum. Skirting the hill are tracts of the old town walls with several gates, and the views are particularly good. Excavations, still in progress, have revealed remains of Etruscan and Roman buildings.

Lido di Tarquinia, 6km SW of Tarquinia, is a resort with a long sandy beach (for hotels and restaurants, see above). To the S are remains of Porto Clementino, the port of the Roman GRAVISCA, destroyed in 1449 (excavated in 1969). The extensive salt-flats nearby were declared a bird sanctuary in 1980.

From Tarquinia to Tuscania

A secondary (signposted) road (24km) runs NE. There is a good view across fields in an unspoilt landscape of Santa Maria di Castello and the towers of Tarquinia. The road follows the pretty valley of the Marta river and then climbs to a plateau with wide open views (Monte Canino can be seen in the distance on the left). For several kilometres before Tuscania the road is lined with a fine avenue of trees (mostly cypresses), many of which have had to be felled recently because of disease.

*TUSCANIA is a charming well-preserved little town (7000 inhab.), in beautiful countryside. Numerous traces of the town's Etruscan origins have been found in the area in the last few decades, and its importance in the Middle Ages is testified by the two splendid Romanesque churches of Santa Maria Maggiore and San Pietro, which were left outside the town walls when the city expanded to the NW. Careful restoration has been completed since an earthquake hit the town in 1971.

Information Office, Piazza Basile.

Buses ('COTRAL') from Tarquinia (weekdays only), which continue twice a day to Viterbo. The nearest **Railway Station** is at Tarquinia, see above.

Car Parking, Largo della Pace.

Hotels. 3-star: 'Al Gallo' (with a restaurant), 24 Via del Gallo.

Restaurants. 1st-class: 'Il Tartaglia', Largo Torre di Lavello. Simple restaurants: 'Al Gallo', Via del Gallo; 'Osteria Da Alfreda', Largo Torre di Lavello; and 'Tomba della Regina'.

Picnic places in the Parco Torre di Lavello, and near the church of San Pietro.

Annual Festivals. Procession on Good Friday, and celebrations in honour of the local Saints Marcelliano, Veriano, and Secondiano in August.

History. Evidence of an early Etruscan settlement has been found on the hill of San Pietro, and there are numerous Etruscan tombs just outside the town. This was the Roman town of *Tuscana*, and a bishopric was established here by the 6C. It became a free comune in the 13C, and as a punishment imposed by Pope Boniface VIII its name was changed to *Toscanella*. It was sacked by Charles VIII in 1495, and changed its name back to *Tuscania* in 1911. Little sign remains of the earthquake here in 1971 which left 30 dead.

The road from Tarquinia reaches the town at Piazzale Trieste. It is best to follow Via Fabio Filzi around to the right which skirts the impressive walls to first visit the two most important churches just outside the town. Strada Maria diverges left beside *Santa Maria Maggiore (opened by a custodian; if closed ask at San Pietro, see below). This is the oldest church of Tuscania, and was the seat of the bishopric before it was transferred to San Pietro in the 8C. Roman remains have been found beneath the church. The building was enlarged in the 12C when the fine CAMPANILE was built and the sculptural decoration was added (some earlier fragments were re-used at this time). The *FAÇADE, partly rebuilt in the mid 13C, has numerous interesting sculptures: above the central portal with marble columns and capitals, the figures of Saints Peter and Paul, and an irregular group of sculptures in the lunette, is a loggia with small columns flanked by two griffins. The beautiful *rose window, with two circles of columns is surrounded by symbols of the Evangelists. The side portals are also richly decorated.

It has a beautiful Romanesque *INTERIOR. The octagonal font for total immersion dates from the 9C, and the pulpit is composed of 8C and 9C panels, with primitive carvings. A fine Gothic ciborium, with frescoes, surmounts the high altar. Above the apse arch is a 14C fresco of the Last Judgment attributed to Gregorio and Donato of Arezzo, which includes the humorous figure of the devil having difficulty in digesting the wicked. In the apse are late 13C figures of Apostles in the Byzantine style, and in the N aisle a beautiful fresco of the *Madonna holding the Christ Child (detached from the chapel to the right of the high altar).

The road continues uphill past remains of Roman baths, and another road diverges right for San Pietro on a little fortified hill, almost certainly the acropolis of ancient Tuscania, with excavations of Etruscan, Roman, and medieval buildings beside the splendid 8C apse of the church. In the 16C the hill was left outside the main part of the town. Around a green are two medieval towers, the ruined remains of the 13C Bishop's Palace, and the façade of the church of *San Pietro (opened by a custodian). Founded in the early 8C, it is one of the most important churches of its date in Italy. The *FAÇADE, similar to that of Santa Maria Maggiore, is made up of two wings in the Lombard style of the 12C, built in tufo and peperino (with two Roman marble lions' heads), and a projecting central portion built in nenfro with decorations in marble. The main *portal has refined geometrical decoration in polychrome marbles by Roman sculptors. Above is a loggia, similar to that on Santa Maria Maggiore, with little Ionic columns, flanked by two winged griffins. The splendid *rose window is surrounded by symbols of the Evangelists and carved marble decorations, which include two extraordinary three-faced devils on the right, and a strange relief of a man (perhaps Etruscan) on the left.

The beautiful *INTERIOR has low columns with massive capitals supporting arches decorated with an unusual toothed decoration. Beneath the arcades are benches. The fine Cosmatesque pavement survives. In the S aisle is a little ciborium (1093) with a fresco fragment of St John the Baptist. On the right of the triumphal arch are three primitive little frescoes in black, white, green, and yellow. At the top of steps, 8–9C carved panels divide the nave from the sanctuary. In the right apse is a worn fresco of Christ between two bishop saints, and St Peter. The two wide arches in the sanctuary have more remains of frescoes. In the left apse is a worn fresco of the Baptism of Christ and two angels. In the N aisle are seven Etruscan sarcophagi. The 11C *CRYPT, approached from the S aisle past columns with 11C capitals, has Roman columns and a lovly old fresco of the Madonna enthroned above the altar. On the wall is a 14C fresco of the three patron saints of Tuscania, in their red robes.

At the bottom of the hill a road continues straight into the town below which remains of the Roman Via Clodia have been revealed. Opposite the façade of the ex-Romanesque church of SAN LEONARDO (with Gothic elements) with a lion above the door, is the new brick-built TEATRO COMUNALE. On the right a short road leads to the ruined roofless church of **San Francesco**, dating from the 13C. It was turned into a slaughter-house in the 19C, but a beautiful frescoed chapel has survived (kept locked; enquire at the Comune). Excellently preserved in parts it was painted by Giovanni and Antonio Sparapane from Norcia (1466). Nearby is a locked gate in front of the 14C church of the MADONNA DELLA PACE.

From San Leonardo a street leads into the attractive **Piazza Basile**, laid out in the early 19C. The neo-classical PALAZZO COMUNALE, decorated with two 17C statues, has an outside stair and two protruding wings. Beyond the gate at No. 6 steps lead up to the ex-12C church of SANTA CROCE, now the municipal library, surrounded by a small raised garden with cypresses and lids of Etruscan sarcophagi on the wall. The church of the SANTI MARTIRI with a lantern (1829) is closed. A balustrade (decorated with more, damaged, sarcophagus covers) overlooks the valley with a good view of the Palazzo Baronale (with its large arch and two-light windows) and the Torre di Lavello (see below). Immediately below the terrace is the delightful FONTANA DELLE SETTE CANNELLE, opened in 1309.

From the piazza Via di Rivellino leads up past the charming 14C PALAZZO SPAGNOLI, with an outside stair, balcony and portico, near the picturesque Via degli Archi. Piazza Matteotti has a well-sited red building with a high arch (and an old shop front beneath it). On the left is the church of SAN GIOVANNI DECOLLATO, a medieval church rebuilt in the 18C. Via Cavour leads through Largo Cavour with the 17C church of SAN GIUSEPPE. Uphill on the right, above a wall, is a good view of the PALAZZO VESCOVILE (being restored; see below). The road continues up to Piazza Mazzini on a little hill, just out of which is SAN MARCO with an attractive portal with twisted columns, and which contains 14C and 15C frescoes. In the piazza is a wall fountain of 1624. From here Via Marconi can be seen leading downhill to a 15C gate in the walls.

From San Marco Via XII Settembre leads right to the church of SANTA MARIA DELLA ROSA, below the level of the road. It has a wide and low façade and a squat campanile. It contains 13C and 14C frescoes, but a polyptych by Giulio d'Amelia was stolen from here in 1990. The road continues to the church of SAN SILVESTRO, with another characteristic portal. It is deconsecrated and used for exhibitions (inside is a 14C fresco of the Tree of Jesse attributed to Gregorio and Donato of Arezzo). From here a road leads past its well-sited campanile along the fine wall of the convent garden to the 16C convent of SAN PAOLO. From San Silvestro Via dell'Annessione (with a view of the open countryside ahead) leads down to Largo Belvedere, with a fountain, beside the PALAZZO VESCOVILE, built in 1653 (being restored). It has good windows and nice chimney pots, and a little round slender tower with a dome on top. A double flight of steps leads down to Piazza Matteotti (see above). The short Via della Salute, on the left of San Giovanni, leads to Via Oberdan, off which Via Garibaldi leads uphill past an old cinema (1928), with attractive views down the side streets. At the top is Largo Indipendenza with the flank of the Duomo, and a pretty little wall fountain of 1628. At No. 2 is a red palace with handsome windows.

Adjoining is Piazza Bastianini with the splendid *FONTANA GRANDE (1621) and the façade of the **Duomo**, rebuilt in 1566–72, with a recently restored white interior. At the end of the N aisle is a marble tabernacle with angels and a Crucifix possibly by the school of Sansovino (also attributed to Isaia da Pisa). This was part of a large monument which has been dismantled: it included the six carved *reliefs of saints at the end of the S aisle. Here is a little chapel (unlocked on request) with a fine collection of paintings and frescoes: on the end wall is a *polyptych of the Madonna and Child with four saints by Taddeo di Bartolo (also attributed to Andrea) with seven scenes of the Passion below. The triptych painted on both sides, with folding doors, of the Redeeemer is by Francesco d'Antonio (called Il Balletta) who also painted the fresco of the Madonna and Child on the left wall. Also on the left wall are frescoes of the Crucifixion and Assumption by Domenico Velandi. The 15C fresco of the Madonna and Child enthroned is from the Madonna della Pace, and the Madonna of the Misericordia is from Sant'Agostino.

Via Torre di Lavello leads up to another picturesque corner of the town with a handsome palace, a tree, and the Palazzo della Dogana next to the fine TORRE DI LAVELLO named after Captain Angelo Broglio da Lavello, called 'Il Tartaglia' who built it when he occupied the town in 1400. From the attractive little piazza is the entrance to a delightful public park above the walls. The view over lovely countryside takes in San Pietro next to a medieval tower on the skyline, and below, hidden in trees, Santa Maria Maggiore. On the left can be seen a stretch of walls and the old Palazzo Comunale. The lovely old Via della Lupa leads downhill between high walls (with a view up left of the medieval Palazzo Baronale) past an attractive public fountain back to the Fontana delle Sette Cannelle below Piazza Basile (described above).

Outside the walls, reached from Piazza Trieste (see above) is **Santa Maria del Riposo** (custodian at No. 32, or unlocked on request at the Museum next door), on the site of a cemetery. The church was rebuilt in 1495. In the INTERIOR the Romanesque font is built of 'nenfro' stone. SOUTH AISLE. First altar, Scalabrino of Pistoia, Adoration of the Shepherds; a niche contains two fresco fragments of 1536 and 1615; another fresco fragment found in 1971 of the Madonna and Child (1501) has been attributed to Andrea del Sarto who apparently stayed at the convent when 15 years old. The Deposition on the third altar is also by Scalabrino. On the grandiose HIGH ALTAR is a small painting of the Madonna and Child by Pastura (1490) in the centre of a tabernacle which is surrounded by a polyptych by Perin del Vaga (with three little lunettes and an exquisite predella). The walnut choir stalls are dated 1534. In the chapel to the left of the santuary (restored in 1983) are delightful frescoes with scenes from the life of the Virgin, by Perin del Vaga and his school. The fine altarpiece of the Presentation in the Temple is by Girolamo Siciolante (Sermoneta). NORTH AISLE. The Nativity in a niche is by Lazzaro Vasari, and the first altarpiece (very ruined) of the Adoration of the Magi is by Scalabrino.

The **Museo Nazionale Etrusco** (admission 9.00–17.00 or 18.00, except Monday morning) was opened in 1988 in the adjoining convent, in rooms off the beautiful Renaissance cloister with 17C frescoed lunettes. So far four rooms are open which display the sarcophagi and finds from the tombs of the Curunas and Vipinana families, found near Tuscania. The first two rooms contain the tombs of the Curunas family, with sarcophagi dating from 340–330 BC, and a central case of finds (4–2C BC) with bronzes and red-figure ceramics. The third room has a sarcophagus (without a lid) with reliefs of the Amazons and animals (330–320 BC). The fourth room has 12 sarcophagi belonging to the Vipinana family, discovered in 1839. On the upper floor more rooms are to be opened to display architectural terracottas found at the Ara del Tufo in 1979–83, and finds from Pian di Mola (see below).

On the outskirts of the Tuscania are a number of Etruscan tombs, most of them discovered since 1967. The only ones usually open (enquire at the Museum) are near the MADONNA DELL'OLIVO, 1km S of the town reached by Via dell'Olivo. These are the tombs of the Curunas family (5–2C BC), and include the so-called 'Tomba della Regina' with an intricate plan (the finds are in the Museum, see above). The NECRO-POLI DI PESCHIERA, to the N of the town (reached off the road to Bolsena) dates from the 6C BC, and has one tomb imitating the exterior of an Etruscan house, with its roof intact. The rock tombs of PIAN DI MOLA (on private property and difficult of access) were in use from the 8–1C BC, and they include one in the form of a temple with a colonnaded portico and three rooms (6C), one of the most interesting tombs for its architecture yet found in southern Etruria.

From Tarquinia to Vulci

31km. (Bus service to Montalto di Castro, but no public transport from there to Vulci). The Via Aurelia (here double carriageway) leads N from Tarquinia to (17.5km) MONTALTO DI CASTRO which has a medieval castle which belonged to the Guglielmi and two fine 18C fountains (recently restored). On the outskirts of the town the construction of a nulcear power station (halted in 1988) has caused much controversy in recent years (a visitors centre is open to the public). The plant was sequestered in 1994, for security reasons. A pretty byroad (well signposted) diverges right from the Aurelia just beyond the river Fiora. It traverses fertile open country with 'hedges' of olive trees and vineyards and passes a little lake on the Fiora which is now an oasis administered by the World Wildlife Fund. The isolated castle of Vulci soon comes into view ahead. 31km A road diverges right for the remains of the ancient city (see below) and the next turn right leads across the river with a good view of the Ponte dell'Abbadia on the right, high above the ravine.

The site of the Etruscan *VULCI (simple hotel 'Il Giardino' in Località Roggi, in Comune di Canino, with a restaurant; and Restaurant 'Casale dell'Osteria' on the site), is now in a totally deserted, beautiful landscape. Although unmentioned in ancient literary sources (except for its conquest by the Romans in 280 BC), it must have been one of the most important Etruscan cities of southern Etruria during the 7–4C BC. Some 30,000 tombs have been discovered since the 18C in its necropoli; their incredibly rich finds, including bronzes of the 9–8C, stone sculptures, and vases, are now dispersed in museums all over the world (the Vatican, the Louvre, the British Museum, the Hermitage, etc.). The walls seems to have enclosed c

17ha, although only very few monuments of the ancient city have been unearthed. Important excavations of the necropolis were carried out here by Luciano Bonaparte, Prince of Canino (see below) in 1828; the Torlonia continued this work when they became proprietors of the site, employing Alessandro François to explore the tombs. The area was visited and studied by George Dennis (1814–98; see his 'Cities and Cemeteries of Etruria', 1883). Clandestine excavations continue.

The city (described below), which had disappeared by the 9C, was situated on the W side of the river, and the most important necropoli have been found on the E side. Now the most conspicuous monument in this remote site, surrounded by beautiful farming country, is the *Ponte dell'Abbadia, one of the most remarkable ancient survivals in Italy. The foundations of this steeply hump-backed bridge which spans the ravine of the river Fiora are probably Roman, built with Etruscan material. The splendid central arch, 30m high, also served as an aqueduct, and the medieval footpath across it survives.

Beside it is the so-called **Abbadia**, a picturesque medieval castle, built of black trachite, surrounded by a moat full of water. It was restored in 1975 to house a **Museo Archeologico** (open 9.00–13.00, 16.00–19.00; winter 9.00–16.00; Monday, 14.30–16.00), which illustrates the history of Vulci. The lovely courtyard has architectural fragments in 'nenfro' stone. The room on the GROUND FLOOR contains two cases of proto-Villanovan ware from Ischia di Castro (10C BC) and Poggio Mengarelli, and material of the Rinaldone culture. The exhibits from Vulci include an urn in the form of a hut (9C BC), and sculpture from the necropolis.

FIRST FLOOR. ROOM I. Finds from the necropolis (8C and 7C BC); bronze amphora; bucchero ware (6C); an attic red-figure kylix (510–500 BC); an Attic black-figure amphora with the birth of Athena (540–530 BC); and interesting material from the Pantenaica tomb (630–510 BC), including a red-figure Attic cup. A group of vases are attributed to the 'Painter of Micali' (510–480 BC). ROOM II contains finds from the city including Roman terracotta heads from the N gate; and Etruscan and Roman small bronzes. ROOM III. Material from the necropolis, including a fine black-figure amphora and vases (500 BC), and bucchero ware. The small ROOM IV displays terracotta ex votos and statues, a bronze seated statue of Hercules (2–1C BC), and terracotta heads including a beautiful female *head showing the influence of Praxiteles.

A few remains of the **ancient city of Vulci** (open at the same time as the Museum, see above), can be seen on the W bank of the river. They are approached by a rough road (signposted for 'La Civita') before the turning for the museum, which leads past a trattoria and continues for c 1km (the road deteriorates suddenly and it is advisable to walk for the last few hundred metres). The custodian's hut is near the site of the W gate; from here the left-hand path leads to the overgrown excavations (1957–61) which include the brown stone base of a large TEMPLE beside a few marble columns and a fragmentary inscription. The paved Roman road (the *Decumanus Maximus*) continues past a VILLA of the late Republican era with some black-and-white mosaics, and a small thermal complex, and then leads downhill to the site of the E gate.

The immense unenclosed **Necropolis of Vulci** (usually only open on Saturday and Sunday 10.00–13.00; enquire at the museum) extends for many kilometres on both sides of the river. The only tomb which is usually shown is the *TOMBA FRANÇOIS, on the E side of the river, dating from the

4C BC, with numerous funeral chambers. Its extremely interesting painted decoration was removed to Rome by the Torlonia shortly after its discovery by Alessandro François in 1857. The *CUCCUMELLA, also on the E side of the river, is a gigantic hypogeum surrounded by a wall which contains a maze of passages, walls, and staircases. The smaller 'Tumulo della Cuccumelletta' was partially restored in 1985.

A lonely minor road leads from Vulci across hills to Manciano (25km) in Tuscany (see the 'Blue Guide Tuscany').

18km NE of Vulci, approached by a road through olive groves with a good view ahead of Monte Canino, is the little town of **Canino** (5000 inhab.), in an area noted for its olive oil (festival on 8 December). It is laid out parallel to and left of the main road. Beyond a little park with pine trees Via Cavour leads past the church of SANTA CROCE, the oldest in the town with an 11C portal, and continues uphill to Piazza Costantino De Andreis with a fine FOUNTAIN attributed to Vignola and the COLLEGIATA, begun in 1788. It contains paintings by Domenico Corvi, Monaldo Monaldi, Marcello Leopardi, and Mariotto Albertinelli. In a neo-classical chapel is the funerary monument, by Luigi Pampaloni, of Luciano Bonaparte, Prince of Canino, who lived here in the early 19C. The tomb of his son has a bas-relief attributed to Canova. The church also contains a fine wood Crucifix, and 18C stalls. In the piazza, with ancient cedars of Lebanon, is the bright orange TEATRO COMUNALE, inaugurated in 1891 (being restored). At the top end of the town is the church of SAN FRANCESCO (for admission, ask at the Comune), with the old Cappella dell'Annunziata, a large 15C convent with two cloisters, and a church with 15C paintings.

The N 312 continues N from Canino to Valentano (15km) above the Lago di Bolsena, described together with ISCHIA DI CASTRO in Rte 38.

13km N of Montalto di Castro the Via Aurelia leaves Lazio to enter Tuscany (see the 'Blue Guide Tuscany').

GLOSSARY

AEDICULE, small opening framed by two columns and a pediment originally used in classical architecture

AMBO (pl. *ambones*), pulpit in a Christian basilica; two pulpits on opposite sides of a church from which the gospel and epistle were read

AMPHORA, antique vase, usually of large dimensions, for oil and other liquids

ANTEFIX, ornament placed at the lower corners of the tiled roof of a temple to conceal the space between the tiles and the cornice

ANTIPHONAL, choir-book containing a collection of *antiphonae*—verses sung in response by two choirs

ANTIS, *in antis* describes the portico of a temple when the side-walls are prolonged to end in a pilaster flush with the columns of the portico

APODYTERIUM, dressing-room in a Roman bath

ARCA, wooden chest with a lid, for sacred or secular use. Also, monumental sarcophagus in stone, used by Christians and pagans

ARCHITRAVE, the lowest part of an entablature, the horizontal frame above a door

ARCHIVOLT, moulded architrave carried round an arch

ATLANTES (or *Telamones*), male figures used as supporting columns

ATRIUM, forecourt, usually of a Byzantine church or a classical Roman house

ATTIC, topmost story of a classical building, hiding the spring of the roof

BADIA, *abbazia*; abbey

BALDACCHINO, canopy supported by columns, usually over an altar

BASILICA, originally a Roman hall used for public administration; in Christian architecture, an aisled church with a clerestory and apse, and no transepts

BORGO, a suburb; a street leading away from the centre of a town

BOTTEGA, the studio of an artist: the pupils who worked under his direction

BOZZETTO, sketch, often used to describe a small model for a piece of sculpture

BUCCHERO, Etruscan black terracotta ware

BUCRANIA, a form of classical decoration—heads of oxen garlanded with flowers

CALDARIUM or CALIDARIUM, room for hot or vapour baths in a Roman bath

CAMPANILE, bell-tower, often detached from the building to which it belongs

CAMPOSANTO, cemetery

CANEPHORA, figure bearing a basket, often used as a caryatid

CANOPIC VASE, Egyptian or Etruscan vase enclosing the entrails of the dead

CARCERES, openings in the barriers through which the competing chariots entered the circus

CARDO, the main street of a Roman town, at right angles to the Decumanus

CARTOON, from *cartone*, meaning large sheet of paper. A full-size preparatory drawing for a painting or fresco

CARYATID, female figure used as a supporting column

CAVEA, the part of a theatre or amphitheatre occupied by the row of seats

CELLA, sanctuary of a temple, usually in the centre of the building

CHIAROSCURO, distribution of light and shade, apart from colour in a painting

CIBORIUM, casket or tabernacle containing the Host

CIPOLLINO, a greyish marble with streaks of white or green

CIPPUS, sepulchral monument in the form of an altar

CISTA, casket, usually of bronze and cylindrical in shape, to hold jewels, toilet articles, etc., and decorated with mythological subjects

COLUMBARIUM, a building (usually subterranean) with niches to hold urns containing the ashes of the dead

CONFESSIO, crypt beneath the high altar and raised choir of a church, usually containing the relics of a saint

CORBEL, a projecting block, usually of stone

CRYPTOPORTICUS, vaulted subterranean corridor

CUNEUS, wedge-shaped block of seats in an antique theatre

CYCLOPEAN, the term applied to walls of unmortared masonry, older than the Etruscan civilization, and attributed by the ancients to the giant Cyclopes

DECUMANUS, the main street of a Roman town running parallel to its longer axis

DIACONIA, early Christian welfare centre

DIPTERAL, temple surrounded by a double peristyle

DIPTYCH, painting or ivory tablet in two sections

EXEDRA, semicircular recess

EX-VOTO, tablet or small painting expressing gratitude to a saint

FORUM, open space in a town serving as a market or meeting-place

FRESCO, (in Italian, *affresco*), painting executed on wet plaster. On the wall beneath is sketched the *sinopia*, and the *cartone* is transferred onto the fresh plaster (*intonaco*) before the fresco is begun either by pricking the outline with small holes over which a powder is dusted, or by means of a stylus which leaves an incised line on the wet plaster. In recent years many frescoes have been detached from the walls on which they were executed

FRIGIDARIUM, room for cold baths in a Roman bath

GIALLO ANTICO, red-veined yellow marble from Numidia

GONFALONE, banner of a medieval guild or commune

GRAFFITI, design on a wall made with an iron tool on a prepared surface, the design showing in white. Also used loosely to describe scratched designs or words on walls

GREEK-CROSS, cross with the arms of equal length

GRISAILLE, painting in various tones of grey

GROTESQUE, painting or stucco decoration in the style of the ancient Romans (found during the Renaissance in the Domus Aurea in Rome, then underground, hence the name, from 'grotto'). The delicate ornamental decoration usually includes patterns of flowers, sphinxes, birds, human figures, etc. against a light ground

HERM (pl. *hermae*), quadrangular pillar decreasing in girth towards the ground, surmounted by a bust

HEXASTYLE, temple with a portico of six columns at the end

HYPOGEUM, subterranean excavation for the interment of the dead (usually Etruscan)

IMPASTO, early Etruscan ware made of inferior clay

INSULA (pl. *insulae*), tenement house

INTARSIA (or *Tarsia*), inlay of wood, marble or metal

KRATER, antique mixing-bowl, conical in shape with rounded base

KYLIX, wide shallow vase with two handles and short stem

LACONICUM, room for vapour baths in a Roman bath

LATIN-CROSS, cross with a long vertical arm

LOGGIA, covered gallery or balcony, usually preceding a larger building

LUNETTE, semicircular space in a vault or ceiling often decorated with a painting or relief

MATRONEUM, gallery reserved for women in early Christian churches

METOPE, panel between two triglyphs on the frieze of a Doric temple

MITHRAEUM, temple of the god Mithras

MONOLITH, single stone (usually a column)

NARTHEX, vestibule of a Christian basilica

NAUMACHIA, mock naval combat for which the arena of an amphitheatre was flooded

NIELLO, black substance used in an engraved design

NIMBUS, luminous ring surrounding the heads of saints in paintings; a square nimbus denoted that the person was living at that time

NYMPHAEUM, a sort of summer-house in the gardens of baths, palaces, etc., originally a temple of the Nymphs, and decorated with statues of those goddesses

OCTASTYLE, a portico with 8 columns

OINOCHOE, wine-jug usually of elongated shape for dipping wine out of a krater

OPUS ALEXANDRINUM, mosaic design of black and red geometric figures on a white ground

OPUS INCERTUM, masonry of small irregular stones set in mortar (a type of concrete)

OPUS QUADRATUM, masonry of large rectangular blocks without mortar; in *Opus Etruscum* the blocks are placed alternately lengthwise and endwise

OPUS RETICULATUM, masonry arranged in squares or diamonds so that the mortar joints make a network pattern

OPUS SECTILE, mosaic or paving of thin slabs of coloured marble cut in geometrical shapes

OPUS SPICATUM, masonry or paving of small bricks arranged in a herring-bone pattern

OPUS TESSELLATUM, mosaic formed entirely of square tesserae

OPUS VERMICULATUM, mosaic with tesserae arranged in lines following the design contours

PALAZZO, any dignified and impor-tant building

PALOMBINO, fine-grained white marble

PAVONAZZETTO, yellow marble blotched with blue

PAX, sacred object used by a priest for the blessing of peace, and offered for the kiss of the faithful, usually circular, engraved, enamelled or painted in a rich gold or silver frame

PENDENTIVE, concave spandrel beneath a dome

PEPERINO, earthy granulated tufa, much used in Rome

PERIPTERAL, temple surrounded by a colonnade

PERISTYLE, court or garden surrounded by a columned portico

PIETÀ, group of the Virgin mourning the dead Christ

PISCINA, Roman tank; a basin for an officiating priest to wash his hands before mass

PLUTEUS, (pl. *plutei*), marble panel, usually decorated; a series of them used to form a parapet to precede the altar of a church

PODIUM, a continuous base or plinth supporting columns, and the lowest row of seats in the cavea of a theatre or amphitheatre

POLYPTYCH, painting or tablet in more than three sections

POZZOLANA, reddish volcanic earth (mostly from Pozzuoli, near Naples) largely used for cement

PREDELLA, small painting or panel, usually in sections, attached below a large altarpiece

PRESEPIO, literally, crib or manger. A group of statuary of which the central subject is the Infant Jesus in the manger

PRONAOS, porch in front of the cella of a temple

PROPYLAEA, columned vestibule approaching a temple

PROSTYLE, temple with columns on the front only

PULVIN, cushion stone between the capital and the impost block

PULVINAR, Imperial couch and balcony on the podium of a theatre

PULVINATED, convex in profile; a term usually applied to a freize

PUTTO, (pl. *putti*) figure sculpted or painted usually nude, of a child

ROSSO ANTICO red marble from the Peloponnese

RHYTON, drinking-horn usually ending in an animal's head

SCHOLA CANTORUM, enclosure for the choristers in the nave of an early Christian church, adjoining the sanctuary

SINOPIA, large sketch for a fresco made on the rough wall in a red earth pigment called *sinopia* (because it originally came from Sinope, a town on the Black Sea). By detaching a fresco it is now possible to see the sinopia beneath and detach it also

SITULA, water-bucket

SOLOMONIC COLUMN, barley-sugar or twisted column, so called from its supposed use in the Temple of Solomon

SPANDREL, surface between two arches in an arcade or the triangular space on either side of an arch

SPINA, low stone wall connecting the turning-posts (metoe) at either end of a circus

STAMNOS, big-bellied vase with two small handles at the sides, closed by a lid

STELE, upright stone bearing a monumental inscription

STEREOBATE, basement of a temple or other building

STOA, a porch or portico not attached to a larger building

STRIGIL, bronze scraper used by the Romans to remove the oil with which they had anointed themselves

STYLOBATE, basement of a columned temple or other building

TELAMONES, see *Atlantes*

TEMENOS, a sacred enclosure

TEPIDARIUM, room for warm baths in a Roman bath

TESSERA, a small cube of marble, glass, etc., used in mosaic work

TETRASTYLE, having four columns at the end

THERMAE, originally simply baths, later elaborate buildings fitted with libraries, assembly rooms, gymnasia, circuses, etc.

THOLOS, a circular building (Greek)

TONDO, round painting or bas-relief

TRANSENNA, open grille or screen, usually of marble, in an early Christian church

TRAVERTINE, tufa quarried near Tivoli; the commonest of Roman building materials

TRICLINIUM, dining-room and reception-room of a Roman house

TRIGLYPH, small panel of a Doric frieze raised slightly and carved with three vertical channels

TRIPTYCH, painting or tablet in three sections

TROMPE L'OEIL, literally a deception of the eye. Used to describe illusionist decoration, painted architectural perspectives, etc.

TROPAEUM, (or Trophy), victory monument

TUMULUS, a burial mound

VELARIUM, canvas sheet supported by masts to protect the spectators in an open theatre from the sun

VERDE ANTICO, green marble from Tessaglia

ZOÖPHORUS, frieze of a Doric temple, so-called because the metopes were often decorated with figures of animals

INDEX TO ARTISTS

INDEX

Topographical names are printed in **bold type**, names of people in *italics*, and other entries in Roman type. The tombs of popes (given in the list of Popes, p. 23), and the building activites of popes and emperors have generally been ignored.

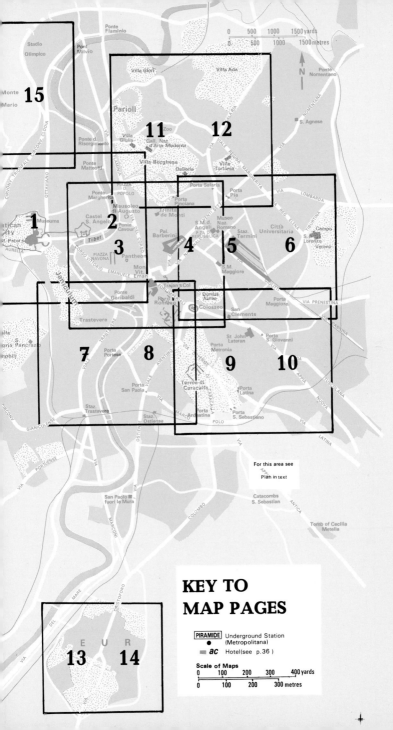

Ponte Flaminio
Stadio Olimpico
Monte Mario

15

Pont Milvio

Villa Glori
Villa Ada
Parioli

S. Agnese

Ponte Nomentano

11 Zoo
Gall. Naz. d'Arte Moderna

12

Villa Giulia
Ponte d. Risorgimento

Villa Borghese
Ponte Matteotti

Villa Torlonia

Galleria

Porta Salaria

Porta Pia

Vatican City
St-Peter's

1

Musaums

Castel S. Angelo

PIAZZA POPOLO
Ponte Margherita

Mausoleo di Augusto

2

Ponte Cavour

Tiber

3

Pantheon

PIAZZA NAVONA

Trinità de Monti

Pal. Barberini

S.M.d. Angeli
S.M. DELLA REPUBBLICA

4

Museo Naz. Romano
Staz. Termini

5

Cittá Universitaria

6

S. Lorenzo Verano

Campo Verano

Ponte V. Emanuele
Mon. Vit. Eman.

S.M. Maggiore

Ponte Garibaldi

Trajan's Col.
Domus Aurea
Foro Romano
Colosseo

San Clemente

Porta Maggiore

VIA PRENESTINA

Trastevere

7

Porta Portese

8

Porta Metronia

St John Lateran
Porta S. Giovanni

9

10

Porta Portese

S. Pancrazio

Staz. Trastevere
Staz. Ostiense

Terme di Caracalla

Porta San Paola

Porta Ardeatina

Porta Latina

Porta S. Sebastiano

For this area see Plan in text

San Paolo fuori le Mura

Catacombs S. Sebastian

Temb of Cecilia Metella

**KEY TO
MAP PAGES**

E U R

13   **14**

PIRAMIDE Underground Station (Metropolitana)
•
ac Hotel(see p.36)

Scale of Maps
0   100   200   300   400 yards
0   100   200   300 metres

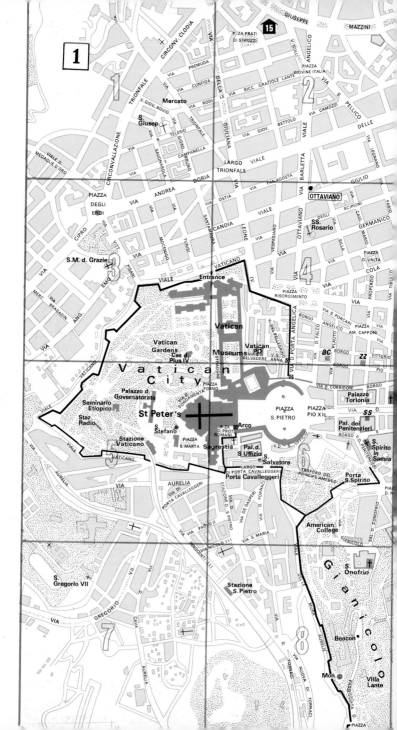

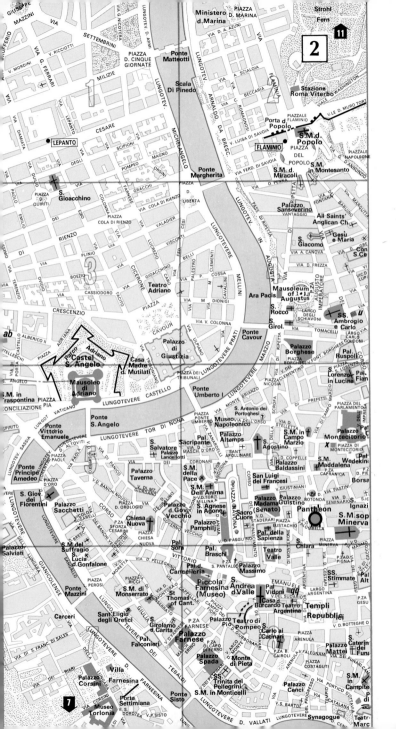

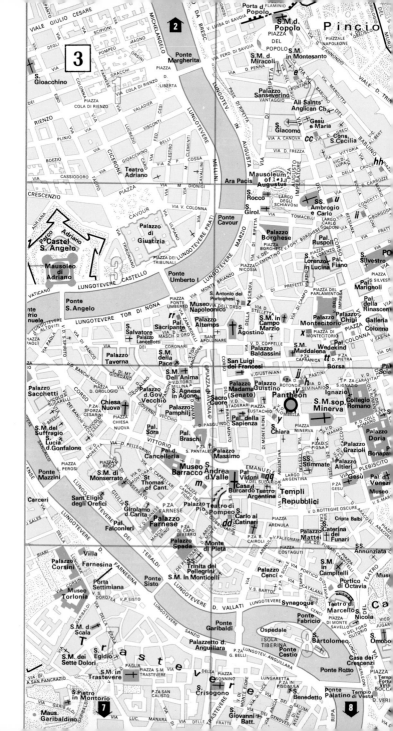

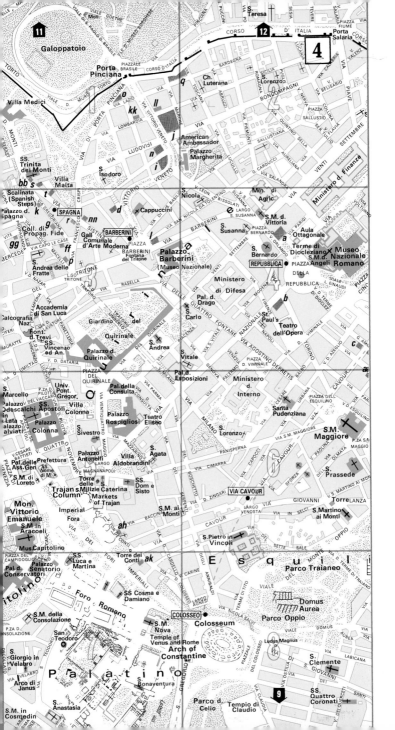

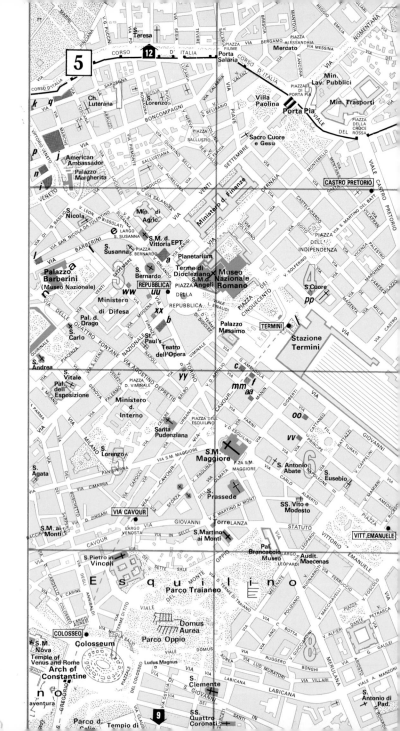

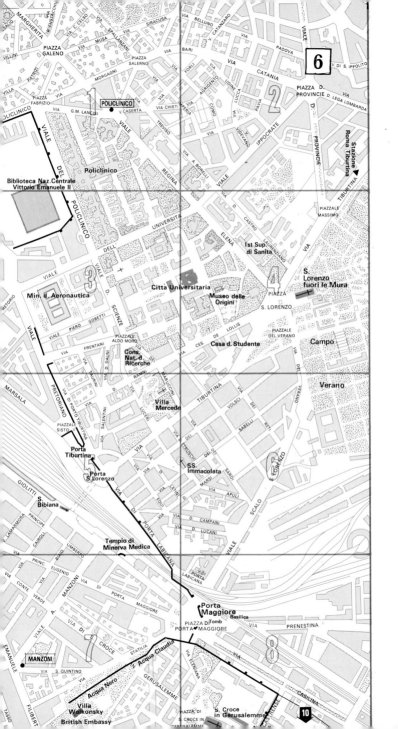

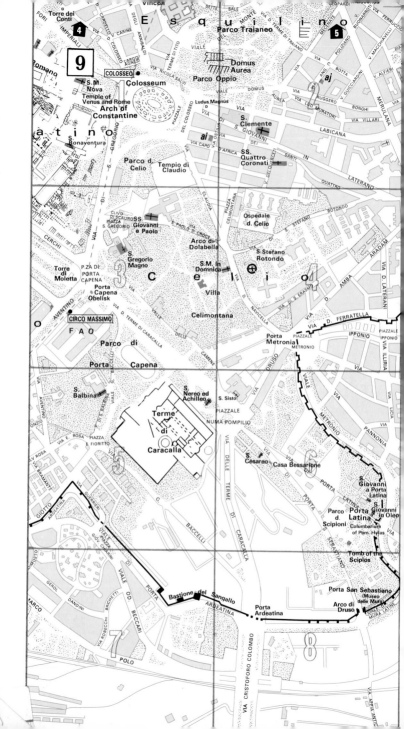

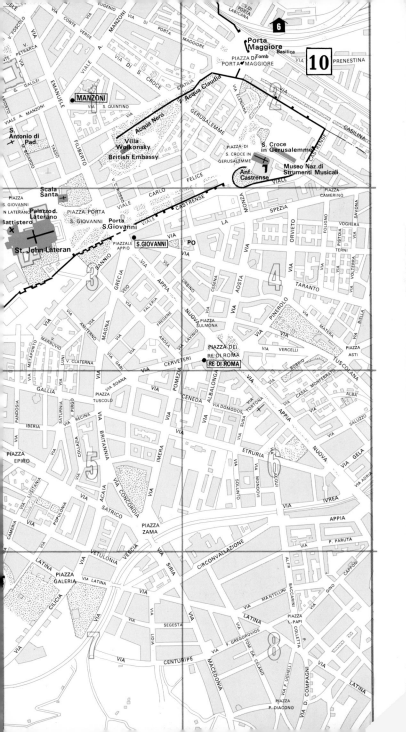

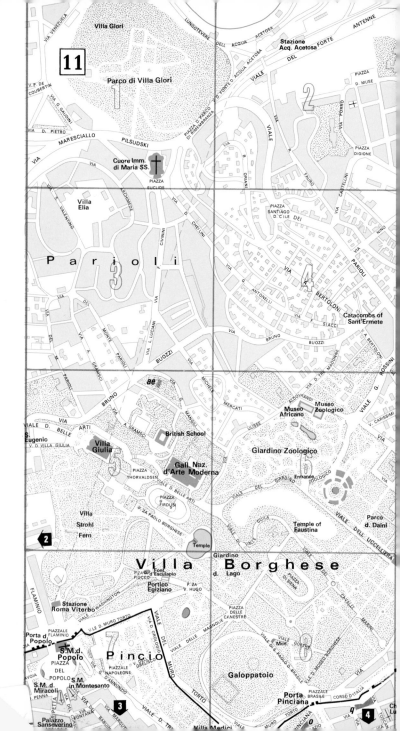

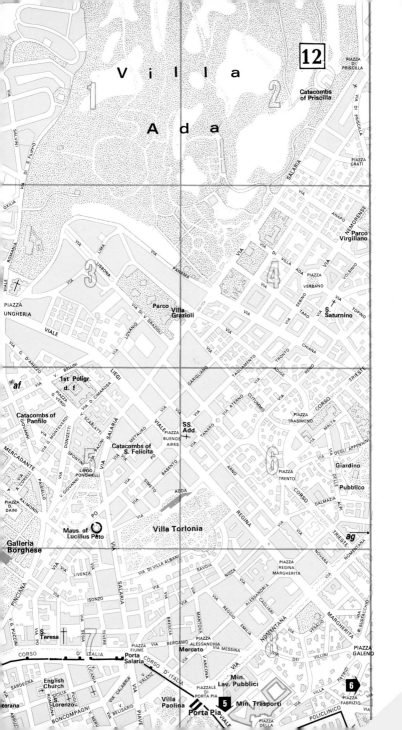

Villa Ada

Catacombs
of Priscilla

PIAZZA
DI
PRISCILLA

PIAZZA
CRATI

1

2

SALARIA

VIA

ANAPO

NEMORENSE

Parco
Virgiliano

VIA

LIMA

VIA

LISBONA

VIA

PANAMA

VIA DI VILLA

ADA

PIAZZA
VERBANO

VOLSINO

3

VIA

VIALE

VIA

ROMANIA

GALILEA

VIA DI S. FILIPPO

SALVINI

Parco Villa
Grazioli

VIA DI V. GRAZIOLI

LOVANO

VIA

SEBINO

TARO

S.
Saturnino

TOPINO

PIAZZA
UNGHERIA

VIALE

VIA G. D'AREZZO

4

CHIANA

VIA

TRONTO

ADIGE

RENO

TRIESTE

af

GARIGLIANO

TAGLIAMENTO

VIA

CORSO

1st Poligr.
d. f.

PIAZZA
G. VERDI

V. BELLINI

VIA D. CIMAROSA

LEGI

SALARIA

ATERNO

CLITUNNO

PIAZZA
TRASIMENO

MALTA

VIA DEGLI APPENNINI

Catacombs of
Panfilo

V. GIOVANNI

V. SCARLATTI

VIA G. MONTEVERDI

DONIZETTI

METAURO

VIALE

SS.
Add.

PIAZZA
BUENOS
AIRES

TANARO

VIA

ARNO

6

Giardino

Pubblico

MERCADANTE

V. A. CORELLI

PAISIELLO

SPONTINI

A. PUCINI

Catacombs of
S. Felicita

PO

BASENTO

SIDETO

PIAZZA
TRENTO

CORSO

DALMAZIA

VIA DELLE ALPI

PIAZZA
RAIMONDI

DAINI

LARGO
PONCHIELLI

V. GIOVANNI

VIA

ADDA

REGINA

VIA

ag

TRIESTE

NOMENTANA

Galleria
Borghese

Maus. of
Lucilius Peto

PO

Villa Torlonia

VIA DI VILLA ALBANI

SAVOIA

NIZZA

PIAZZA
REGINA
MARGHERITA

NOVARA

PINCIANA

VIA

LIVENZA

SALARIA

ISONZO

ALESSANDRIA

CAGLIARI

NOMENTANA

MARGHERITA

VIA DI EUSTACCHIO

S.
Teresa

V. G. PUCCINI

PO

SESIA

TEVERE

PIAZZA
FIUME

BERGAMO

MANTOVA

BRESCIA

REGGIO

EMILIA

VIA MESSINA

VIA

DEI

VILLINI

VESALIO

PIAZZA
GALENO

7

CORSO

D'ITALIA

Porta
Salaria

CORSO

D'ITALIA

Mercato

PIAZZA
ALESSANDRIA

ANCONA

VANCONA

VALENT

Min.
Lav. Pubblici

6

PIAZZA
FABRIZIO

SARDEGNA

English
Church

S. Lorenzo

VIA CALABRIA

PUGLIA

SICILIA

ROMAGNA

VIA

VELASRIO

PIAVE

Villa
Paolina

Porta Pia

PIAZZALE
DI PORTA PIA

5

Min. Trasporti

PIAZZA
DELLA

POLICLINICO

ABRUZ

BONCOMPAGNI

LUCANIA

V. NIE

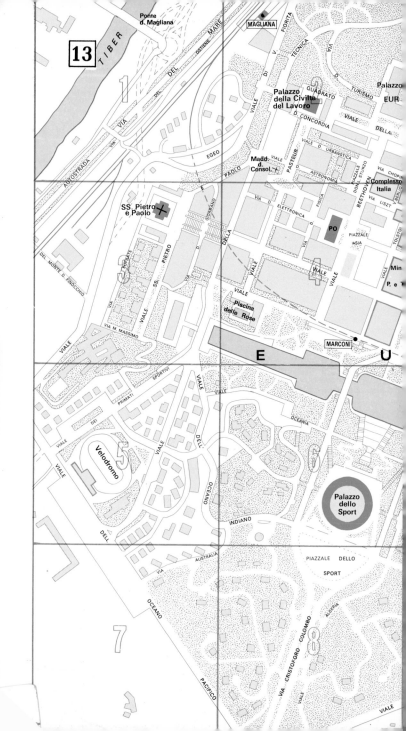

13

T I B E R

Ponte d. Magliana

MAGLIANA

V. FIORITA

VIA TECNICA

VIA D. TURISMO

Palazzo EUR

VIALE DEL MARE

VIA DEL OSTIENSE

VIA DI QUADRATO

Palazzo della Civiltà del Lavoro

D. CONCORDIA

VIALE

VIALE DELLA

VIA CHOPIN

VIA DI URBANISTICA

VIALE D. ASTRONOMIA

Complesso Italia

VIA BERLIOZ

PIAZZALE DON STURZO

VIA BEETHOVEN

VIA LISZT

Madd. d. Consol.

VIALE PASTEUR

VIALE PAOLO

VIA EGEO

AUTOSTRADA

VIA DEL

VIA DEL MONTE D. FINOCCHIO

SS. Pietro e Paolo

VIALE SS. PIETRO

VIA DI O.

VIALE

VIALE DELLA GIORDANO O.

VIA D. ELETTRONICA

VIA D. FISICA

PO

PIAZZALE ASIA

VIALE

VIA TOLSTOI

Min
P. e T

VIALE

VIA M. MASSIMO

Piscina delle Rose

WALE

VIALE

E

MARCONI

U

VIALE DEI PRIMATI SPORTIVI

VIALE

VIALE

VIALE DELL' OCEANIA

VIALE

VIALE DELL' OCEANO

Velodromo

5

6

Palazzo dello Sport

VIALE DELL'

VIALE

VIALE INDIANO

7

VIA AUSTRALIA

PIAZZALE DELLO

SPORT

VIA OCEANO

VIALE ALGERIA

VIA CRISTOFORO COLOMBO

8

VIALE

VIA PACIFICO

VIALE

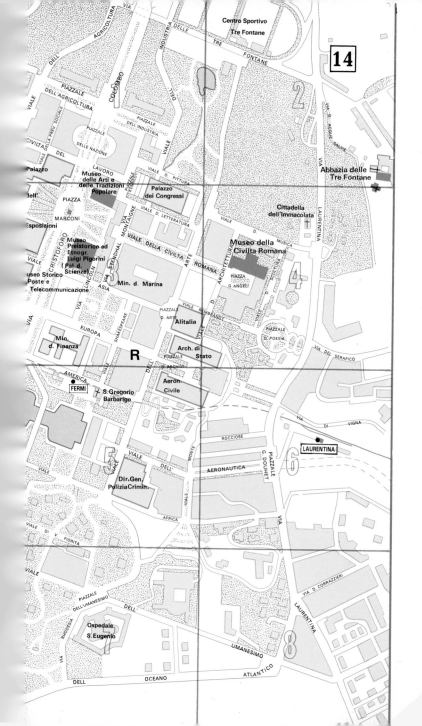

14

Centro Sportivo
Tre Fontane

VIA DELL' AGRICOLTURA

VIA INDUSTRIA DELLE

VIA TRE FONTANE

PIAZZALE
DELL'AGRICOLTURA

VIALE DELLA COLOMBO

VIA D. ACQUE SALVIE

PIAZZALE
DELL'INDUSTRIA

PIAZZALE
DELLE NAZIONE

VIALE DELL'INDUSTRIA

2

CIVILTA DEL VIALE DELLA PREV. SOCIALE

Palazzo

Museo
delle Arti e
delle Tradizioni
Popolare

LAVORO

VIA PITTURA

Palazzo
dei Congressi

Abbazia delle
Tre Fontane

dell'

PIAZZA
MARCONI

VIA MONTAIGNE

VIALE D. LETTERATURA

Cittadella
dell'Immacolata

VIA LAURENTINA

sposizione

Museo
Preistorico ed
Etnogr.
Luigi Pigorini
(Pal.d.
Scienze)

VIA STENDHAL

VIALE DELLA CIVILTA

ROMANA

VIALE ARTE

Museo della
Civilta Romana

VIA ARCHITETTURA

VIA MUSICA

4

VIALE

VIA CRISTOFORO

VIA LINCOLN

VIA ASIA

PIAZZA
G. ANGELI

useo Storico
Poste e
Telecommunicazione

Min. d. Marina

VIALE REMBRANDT

PIAZZALE
D. ARTE

Alitalia

VIALE D.

PIAZZALE
D. POESIA

EUROPA

VIA SHAKESPEARE

Min.
d. Finanza

R

VIA DELL

VIA DEL SERAFICO

Arch. di
Stato

PIAZZALE
D. ARCHIVI

AMERICA

FERMI

S. Gregorio
Barbarigo

Aeron.
Civile

VIALE

VIA DI VIGNA

ROCCIOSE

VIALE DELL'

VIA MONTE

AERONAUTICA

PIAZZALE
G. DOUHET

LAURENTINA

6

Dir.Gen.
PoliziaCrimin.

VIALE

AFRICA

VIA

VIALE DI V. FIORITA

VIA DELL'UMANESIMO

VIA D. CORRAZZIERI

VIALE

PIAZZALE
DELL'UMANESIMO

VIA RODOSSA

Ospedale
S. Eugenio

UMANESIMO

LAURENTINA

8

DELL

OCEANO

ATLANTICO

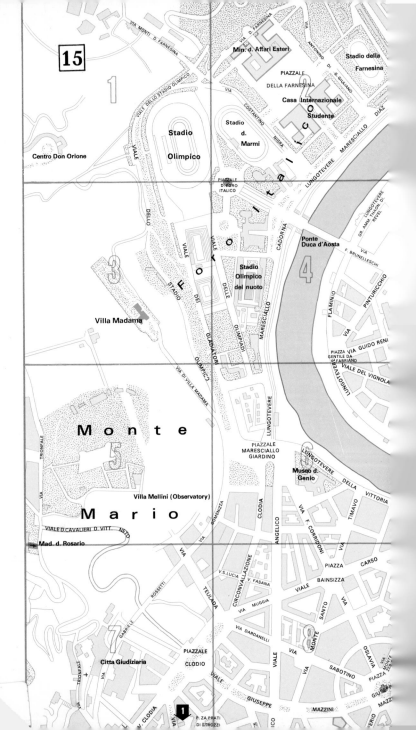